CONCEPTS OF BUSINESS
an introduction to the business system

Contributing Editors

David P. Adams
Oakland Community College
Farmington, Michigan

Earl Baer
Highline Community College
Midway, Washington

Sonya Brett
Macomb Community College
Warren, Michigan

Harvey S. Bronstein
Oakland Community College
Farmington, Michigan

Joseph Crowley
Philadelphia Community College
Philadelphia, Pennsylvania

Denver L. Ellison
Miami-Dade Junior College
Miami, Florida

Donald Jarrard
Flint Community College
Flint, Michigan

Craig Kuhns
San Francisco City College
San Francisco, California

Thomas L. Laird
Miami-Dade Junior College
Miami, Florida

Gene Logan
Diablo Valley College
Pleasant Hill, California

Andrew Lonyo
Macomb Community College
Warren, Michigan

Milton Vail
Contra Costa Junior College
San Pablo, California

Richard H. Buskirk
California State College
Fullerton, California

Donald J. Green
Chabot College
Hayward, California

William C. Rodgers
Moorpark College
Moorpark, California

CONCEPTS OF BUSINESS
an introduction to the business system

RINEHART PRESS
SAN FRANCISCO

Copyright © 1972 by Rinehart Press
5643 Paradise Drive
Corte Madera, California 94925

A division of Holt, Rinehart and Winston, Inc.

Library of Congress Catalog Card Number: 78-177981
ISBN: 0-03-085002-9

PRINTED IN THE UNITED STATES OF AMERICA

2 3 4 5   071   9 8 7 6 5 4 3 2 1

Preface

After teaching the Introduction to Business course in both two-year and four-year colleges for quite some time, we felt the need to develop a somewhat different approach for today's student.

First, we wanted to expose our students to the "systems" approach. We have tried to do this at every opportunity without getting into all the quantitative manipulations that usually accompany "systems" discussions. Ours might be called a behavioral systems approach.

Second, we wanted to stress the basic principles underlying business behavior rather than giving only the usual descriptions fortified with relatively meaningless statistics. Thus evolved the name of the book—Concepts of Business—for we want our students to learn concepts.

Finally, we wanted to do these things within the course's traditional framework, for we think the traditional topics are sound and well proven.

Some features of the book may need explanation. A disproportionately large amount of material on marketing is included, and we go into it more thoroughly than some of the other topics, because we have found that many students go directly into marketing jobs—selling and retailing.

About the profit chapter: we simply felt that it was time to bring out fully the role of profit in our system, not bury it within some other chapter.

To avoid distracting the reader with definitions of terms and laws as he reads, we have collected such information in Appendixes A and B.

The questions in the margins are a bit different, not the usual end-of-the-chapter ones. We have designed them to expand the student's thinking on the point under discussion at that moment. We want him to have to think beyond our coverage, to make him grow by extension.

Considerable material on personal finance—investments, securities markets, and insurance—has been included for the reader's personal benefit. Such matters are so important to one's welfare that whatever we can do to further skills in managing personal finances seems worthwhile.

We've tried to make the book easy to read, fun to read, informative. We hope you find it so.

We owe much to our secretaries, Sylvia Arnot of Boulder, Colorado, and Neva Mosher of Newport Beach, California, for their fine stenographic skills and patient understanding.

We particularly want to thank all the professors who have played various roles in the preparation of the book, the contributing editors who have supplied many valuable suggestions, and David Bowen and Henry Kester of the University of Colorado for their encouragement.

Newport Beach, California   Richard H. Buskirk
Hayward, California   Donald J. Green
Moorpark, California   William C. Rodgers

Contents

8

9

10

11

12

13

14

15

16

26

27

Prologue

This is an adventure story. It is about men—men who assemble resources to make things, to make money, and to build empires. It is about men who manage other men: how they do it, the problems they encounter, and the satisfactions they enjoy. We would like to start by telling you of the many young men who have plunged into the business world and encountered varying degrees of success while pursuing fascinating and challenging tasks. We would like to tell you the story of Tom Wilscom, who parlayed a job tending bar while going to college into a highly successful chain of luxurious restaurants within a decade. We would like to tell you of the adventures of Ben Howe as he deals from minute to minute in the stock market as option specialist for Dean Witter, a brokerage firm; after only two years he is already one of the firm's top producers, well on his way to a most successful career.

These stories are not exceptions, for we know far too many of them. We will not claim that they are the rule either, for business careers vary so widely that it is difficult to generalize upon them. Truly, the potential scope of activity for the business administration student is as broad as our entire society, for he can work for all types of institutions, both profit seeking and nonprofit seeking, throughout the system.

To tell you the stories of these men now, however, would be to eat dessert first. What we must do first is study some fundamentals. There is a great deal of factual and theoretical material to assimilate before one can understand business operations.

Business can be studied in many ways. Originally men were trained on the job; they were apprenticed to a businessman considered adept and wise, and by serving him they learned the trade. This can be a good way to learn the workings of a business, but it does have disadvantages. It can be horribly inefficient, taking many more years than are really warranted. Too, the apprentice usually learns only the peculiarities of the business in which he is engaged and fails to grasp the fundamentals that apply to all businesses. In training the business student we must constantly keep two things in mind: we must endeavor to equip you to be a more effective producer in a wide range of businesses and we must do so in a relatively short time. Do not be deluded into thinking you can emerge from college a finished product. If you intend to be a successful businessman, you will be learning about business for the rest of your life. The business school simply hopes to equip you to learn more aptly from your experiences. Moreover, it tries to start you off on the right foot in such matters as terminology, basic principles, and general orientation. If you intend to be an accomplished, skilled businessman, only one person can make you one, and that is you. Teachers, classes, books, services, and all of the current educational paraphernalia are tools that you may use to accomplish this job of training yourself. But only you can do it!

Another approach to the study of business is through the use of case histories. The Harvard Graduate School of Business Administration has extended the use of case histories as a major vehicle for business education throughout the world. Indeed, it is difficult to find a business curriculum anywhere in the world that to some degree does not employ case histories in its academic program. Certainly case histories add a much-needed specific flavoring, particularly in the more advanced stages of learning. Unfortunately, case histories seldom provide much of the basic information the beginning business student needs; thus, we cannot use many cases in most beginning business courses.

Yes, there is a laboratory for the study of business. It's all around you. Every store you go into, every business enterprise you observe, the whole surrounding world is your laboratory; so be observant, learn from it. Talk to businessmen you meet and learn what you can of their operations. Learn to probe for the truth, because seldom are things truly the way they seem on the surface. Learn to ask the right questions of people who know. Through the Study Guide to Concepts of Business and some of the exercises in this text we endeavor to direct your "laboratory" work along lines that should prove rewarding, but you should never feel limited by these laboratory exercises;

you can learn something from just about any real-world experience. You cry for relevance in your education; well, here it is!

Finally, throughout your study of the materials in this course, you should be screening everything for ideas concerning your career, for little is more important to your ultimate success than the early selection of a career that is of great interest to you. Find something that you really like; life is too short to spend it doing something you dislike.

PART

THE
ENVIRONMENT

OUR environment—all encompassing, all important—is the basic force shaping our activities, our institutions, what we do and must do. A man ignorant of his environment is a cripple incapable of making wise decisions, for inevitably environmental forces play a critical role in all affairs. So it is only logical that we begin our study of business by examining its environment.

An early introduction of the systems concept will be helpful as we delve into business operations. The relatively recent development of the systems concept in the management of economic affairs has so deeply affected business thinking that you should begin to understand it at the outset. Then we will examine some of the more salient characteristics of socioeconomic systems in general. Chapter 2 focuses on the American socioeconomic system and its basic concepts; we try to show what we have now, how we got it, and what is happening to it. We happen to be unabashedly proud of our system and believe that there is a great deal of misinformation circulating about it. We try to correct that grievous situation.

From the large picture of things we move in to examine the nature of society's smallest working unit—man. We see that we must understand man and his behavior if we are to deal with him successfully. Then we briefly introduce man's creations—institutions—before undertaking a most complete examination of the role of profit in our system. It seems that in recent years we have lost sight of profit's role in our society and have a need to rediscover it.

You now have the right to ask, "Why all this material about everything but business? Let's get down to business!" But that is precisely the point: this is all business. Most observers have traditionally accused businessmen of being narrow-minded specialists and a business education of being a narrow field of study. But in fact business is the broadest discipline one can study—in one way or another it encompasses everything. An appreciation of this broad aspect of business should help you plan your educational program.

1 **Socioeconomic systems**

There is no more demoralizing theory than that which imputes all human evils to Capitalism or any other single agency.
SAMUEL GOMPERS

First there were people—people who quickly formed groups, for man is a most social animal. There were compelling reasons for forming groups: protection, survival, and companionship. The people in these groups needed a few things: food and the elemental protection of clothing and shelter. As groups became proficient at producing for their needs, a few of the more adept created a surplus. Perhaps they made more stone axes than they had men to use them. So the first element of trade was created—*a surplus*. Another group had a surplus of skins. If one group has a surplus of something another group wants, a basis for a *transaction* exists. In this case it would be called a *barter*, for money would not be involved, but rather the goods would be exchanged on some mutually agreeable basis.

The *transaction* is the fundamental building block of our system. Business is a summation of billions of transactions every day. Any time anything is bought or sold there is a transaction. Admittedly, we have greatly systematized our transactions for greater efficiency, but we should never lose sight of the fact that it is the transaction that forms the basis of business.

How many transactions were you a party to yesterday?

WHAT IS BUSINESS?

Business is a system of transactions. Business is the creation of things that people want. Business is work. Business is the main street of our socioeconomic system. Business is the system we have developed for satisfying our desires. Business is how we make a living. What is business? Take your choice or define it in your own way, for the word has been applied to so many diverse activities and concepts that it defies precise definition. However, we shall define business as *a system created to satisfy society's needs and desires.* We like the systems approach to the study of business, for it leads one to a greater appreciation of the complicated interlocking network of institutions that turn out the goods and services we enjoy. Note that a system is goal directed; it has objectives it seeks to reach.

What are the goals of our socioeconomic system?

SYSTEMS AND SUBSYSTEMS

Business is only one of many subsystems that comprise our total socioeconomic system. The major subsystems of our order are: the several political systems that govern us, all of which interlock in varying ways; our educational systems, which tie together with each other and with the government in various relationships; our religious systems; our philanthropic systems such as Red Cross, the Ford Foundation, or the Salvation Army; and business, which accounts for about 85 percent of our total economic activity as measured by the *Gross National Product.*

Concept of the Gross National Product

The Gross National Product (GNP) is the total money value of all goods and services produced in a nation in some specified period of time, usually one year. It is widely used as an indicator of the material well-being of that society. We use it largely for measuring our prosperity and diagnosing economic ills.

But business itself can be viewed as a total system comprised of uncountable interlocking subsystems that we call industries. Moreover, each industry is comprised of many subsystems such as manufacturing companies, trade associations, and distributive organizations; and management assistance services such as consulting firms, advertising agencies, credit rating bureaus, accounting firms, placement agencies, consulting engineers, or janitorial services; and financial institutions such as banks, investment bankers, factors, etc. Figure 1-1 diagrams one industrial system, the airline industry.

FIGURE 1-1: A Network Depicting the Commercial Aviation Industrial System

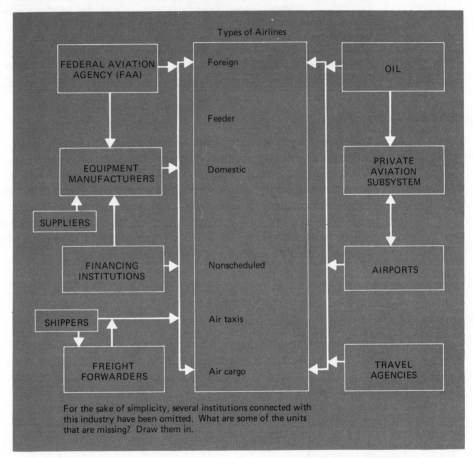

While the airline industry is unique rather than typical, one is hard pressed to find any industry that is not. Each has its own unique institutions, subsystems, and networks. One can see how the airline system is linked with other industrial systems such as the oil, aircraft manufacturing, travel, freight, and finance industries. No industry or company stands alone; each is interconnected with a great many other systems on which it depends and which in turn depend upon it.

Furthermore, each company is comprised of many subsystems—production, marketing, or financial. Each activity in a firm can be broken into its subsystems; production may be comprised of such subsystems as purchasing, materials management, plant management, personnel, and engineering. And each of these may be further divided. . . .

Definition of System

One dictionary defines the word "system" sixteen different ways. Some of the more meaningful definitions are: an assemblage or combination of things or parts forming a complex or unitary whole; any assemblage or set of correlated members; a coordinated body of methods or a complex scheme or plan of procedure.

It is enlightening to note how often the words *plan, procedure, complex, assemblage, combination, methods, orderly,* and *structure* appear in all of these sixteen definitions, for it gives an insight into the true nature of the systems concept. Our definition is a bit simpler: *a system is an arrangement of activities designed to get something done.* The systems concept studies the entire arrangement rather than just one part at a time.

Usefulness of the Systems Approach

You should begin to see that our society is a most complex order of people working within numerous systems. But do not conclude that this is merely an exercise in conceptual thinking; it is not. You are being introduced to this way of thinking because modern management has discovered that the systems approach has yielded truly significant advancements and economies in business operations. We have discovered that when something is not working as management expects it to, then the system within which the trouble seems to lie should be examined to determine the fault and the changes needed to make it work as desired.

List all the systems in which you operate.

Purpose of Systems

Man designs and develops systems over a period of time not only to serve his needs but also to do so for a reasonable cost. Without a system costs would soar, as a great deal of unproductive work would result from the random behavior of unorganized individuals.

Random, sporadic actions by individuals are not necessarily part of the actions of any system. The entire systems concept is based on the proven premise that the organization and routinization of man's actions leads to more efficient use of his time and resources.

Routinization of activities results in more efficient utilization of resources. Why?

By routinization we mean that we set up a system to handle certain inputs or events in a certain way, predetermined to be the most efficient way of handling those events to achieve the desired output or outcome. We reduce our behavior to a routine so that we need not think about it each time and so that we may learn to go through that routine more efficiently each time—the basis of the *learning-curve concept* (see p. 238). So the real purpose of devising systems is to achieve wiser and better utilization of our resources—men and materials. But the routines should not remain the same! Adapt they must!

ADAPTIVE BEHAVIOR

Healthy systems are constantly evolving, for they must continually adapt to a changing environment. The Post Office is a prime example—a huge governmental system whose mission is to perform communications services among various elements in our society. We know little about its efficiency and effectiveness during its early development; we most certainly know now that this bureaucratic system is failing to meet the usual tests of efficiency—and we have known this for years.

What are the "usual" tests of efficiency?

Why has the matter recently come to fore? Largely because until now the Post Office still accomplished its basic mission; it delivered the mail promptly. Its output was satisfactory and met whatever tests were being applied to it. This is no longer true. The postal system is now beginning to falter in its mission and is being revised so that it can once again promptly deliver the mail at a reasonable cost.

Could deliveries to the individual patron's address be eliminated from the postal system? Evaluate this possibility.

The fundamental reason that systems must change constantly is that the environment in which they operate, and the demands placed upon them by environmental forces, are changing constantly. The environmental changes that affected the Post Office were a huge growth in the work load, a decline in the number of people wanting to work for the Post Office (reducing its labor pool in both quantity and quality), and wage demands resulting from the payment of higher wages in other systems. These environmental forces require that the postal system make huge capital expenditures in mechanical equipment and overhaul its obsolete operating system. Business systems are always subject to the forces at work in their environment and will change as the environment changes. Look at the results of one such change!

The Impact of an Innovation

Let's take as an example one technological invention: the automobile. It would be impossible to trace the total impact of the automobile upon all of the various systems in our society, but a bit of thinking should quickly impress you that, along with television, the atomic bomb, and the disappearance of the nickel ice cream cone, the car has had a profound effect. Witness the highway construction, the relocation of living communities, and mode of life these highways have caused. Witness the avalanche of drive-in retail establishments such as banks, theaters, supermarkets, and restaurants. Huge regional shopping centers would be impossible without the automobile. And what about tourism? How many industries serve the automobile? Tires, auto insurance, oil, service stations, automotive suppliers of various descriptions are but a few of its dependents.

Now visualize, if you will, the changes that would be forced on all these systems if society outlawed the internal combustion engine and converted to electrical energy. It would be frightening to an oil company executive, wouldn't it?

Outline the impact of widespread use of electrical automobiles upon our various social and economic systems.

INSTITUTIONAL FRAMEWORK OF SYSTEMS

Most systems are best described in terms of the institutions that operate within them. An industrial system can be described by listing and relating the different institutions that comprise it, such as manufacturers, suppliers, retail dealers, wholesalers, freight companies, credit agencies, advertising agencies, public warehouses, banks, investment bankers, trade unions, and whatever others there may be. So by necessity when we deal with systems we are dealing with institutions. Although an institution is a subsystem, it is a separate legal entity under separate managerial guidance from the other subsystems in the industry.

Institutional Changes

Since institutions are systems in themselves, they are continually changing in line with the demands placed upon them by the system within which they operate. An example that bears close watching is the security business, which is having problems in handling its paperwork, financing its operations, and pricing its services. It is being forced to alter its ways.

What are some of the factors that have caused stock brokerage firms to alter their operating policies and methods?

Connecting Network

We can describe systems by connecting their institutions, subsystems, or operating units with lines to form what is known as a network. Figure 1-1, showing the commercial aviation industrial system, was such a network. Figure 1-2 shows the network of a department store's credit system. One of the problems in drawing such networks is distinguishing the types of relationships between the units. Some deal with each other physically—shipping goods to one another, working for each other, or sending each other money. Other relationships are less direct. Some are only a matter of communications: the people talk to one another but nothing moves between them. For example, the Federal Reserve Board plays an important part in most of our society's economic systems, but few companies have any direct contact with it.

Some relationships in a network are continuous; others are sporadic. A manufacturer has continuous relationships with his wholesalers, but he might have only occasional contact with a management consulting firm or an investment banking house.

BASIC REQUIREMENTS OF A SYSTEM

Institutions form the skeleton of a system. Its life and vitality are provided by its (1) skills, (2) knowledge, (3) resources, (4) organization, (5) administration, and (6) cultural attributes. Without these, institutions are meaningless, empty shells.

FIGURE 1-2: A Department Store's Credit System

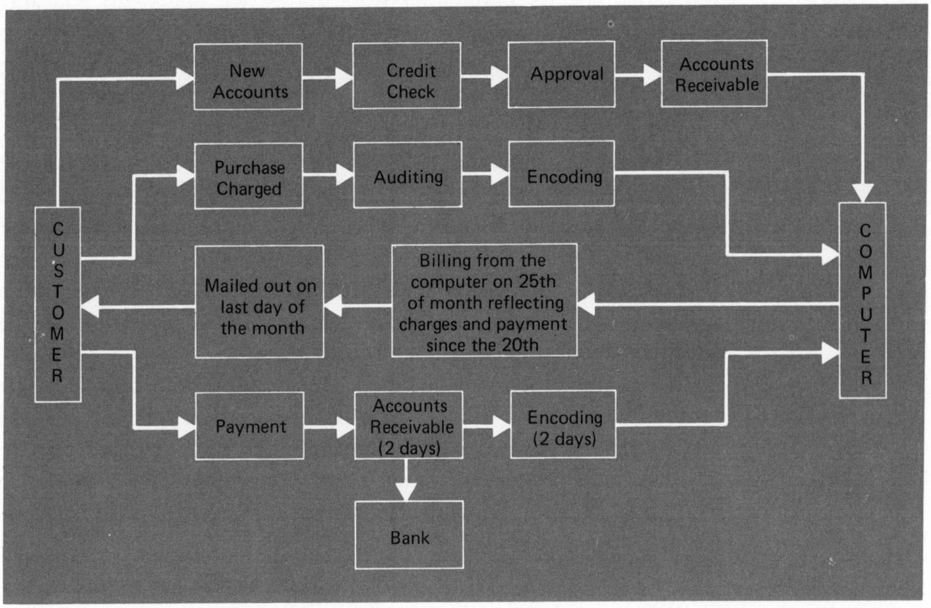

System for Handling Payments:

1. Pick up mail at the Post Office.
2. Open mail.
3. Compare payments with bill.
4. Inspect documents for regularity and clarity and to find mistakes on checks, if any.
5. Write amount received on the enclosed bill and log name and amount in ledger.
6. Send money to deposit department.
7. Send bill to encoding room.
8. Punch information into computer.

Skills

Far too little appreciation is given to the vast accumulation of skills we possess. We are able to do fantastic things. Even such a seemingly basic skill as the ability to weld aluminum is truly a great contribution. And our system contains millions of such skills; this is one of the sources of our power. Never belittle the skill of the finish carpenter, the journeyman plumber, the electrician, the garbage man, or the secretary, for the sum total of their skills has made possible what you have. Without skills, knowledge is academic. For decades we have prided ourselves on our "know-how," which is another way of saying skills. We are a most skillful people. We emphasize this point in the face of distressing evidence that today we are belittling our skills and thereby downgrading them, a most tragic development.

Knowledge

Certainly knowledge must rank as a basic requirement of all systems. Some systems have been built on only one bit of knowledge. An ancient middle eastern culture built its empire largely on its knowledge of iron. Our society worships knowledge and relies heavily upon it. The resources we devote to education are testimony to our regard for knowledge as well as its importance to the continued good health of our system. The intelligent use of skills depends upon a foundation of knowledge.

Resources—Men, Materials, and Money

While there are fundamentally only two basic resources available to a society—men and materials—in our sophisticated economic system we have added a third: money. Money is really little more than value created and stored previously by men and materials, but it is sufficiently important today as an economic lubricant that it must be raised to equal status with men and materials. And so we have three resource requisites for a successful system—men who want to work, materials for them to work with, and money to get things rolling.

Some systems have failed because their men did not want to work. Similarly, some cultures suffer simply because they lack materials with which to work. Many world systems today are faltering for lack of money, but one must hasten to point out that money is lacking in such situations because of a lack of the other two basics, men and materials. Money is available to systems that indicate their ability and willingness to use it properly.

Organization

Skills, knowledge, and resources, in order to become productive, must be organized in meaningful ways. Without organization, chaos reigns. A basic tenet of political science theory is that the fundamental purpose of government is to give organization to the system. It is that important; where organization is absent, so is productivity. We must have organization to accomplish desired goals.

Administration

Administration is considered to be distinct and separate from organization, for modern experience indicates that it is different. The best case in point seems to be Soviet Russia. Certainly Soviet Russia is a highly organized system, but all available evidence indicates that its output is being severely curtailed because of inept administration of that organization. Clearly, a highly organized system can have unsatisfactory output because of poor administration.

Figure 1-3 is presented to assist in the visualization of the requirements of a system.

Cultural Attributes of Systems

In describing a large socioeconomic system we usually describe certain characteristics that affect the well-being of its people. Some of the more important cultural attributes are detailed below.

Physical Characteristics and Vigor Unquestionably, certain cultures have prospered because of the industriousness and physical abilities of their people. The current pros-

FIGURE 1-3: Basic Requirements of Systems

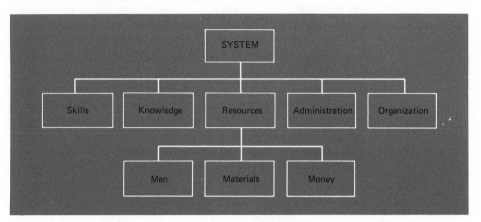

perity of West Germany and Japan are in part a result of such vigor. It would have been difficult for the pygmies of Africa to have developed an aggressive culture and overcome the territory of the Watusi tribe; they simply were not up to the job physically. But experience indicates that perhaps the physical characteristics of a people are less important than other attributes.

Religion and Philosophy   The philosophical beliefs of various cultures in history have been studied most carefully, and such investigations leave the observer profoundly impressed by the role played by one's philosophy in determining the nature of his systems. Indeed, entire cultures have perished because of their beliefs. Certain ancient cultures sacrificed such a large percentage of their output to the gods that the people starved to death. Certain philosophies have stifled productivity and activity while others have glorified it.

A widely accepted school of thought traces the present prosperity of the Western civilizations in general, and the United States in particular, to the philosophies of John Calvin. Calvinism, for the first time in history, preached that work was a virtue and that a rich man could get into Heaven just as easily as a poor one. According to Calvinistic philosophy, in fact, it was almost a sin to be lazy and poor. If the people you regard as your primary reference group believe that working hard and saving money is virtuous and that laziness and extravagance are sins, you are apt to work hard and save your money to gain the esteem of your peers. Social pressure from peer groups is an extremely forceful motivator. This is not to deny that one's philosophies create internal psychological forces that determine one's behavior, for they most certainly do. You are what you believe.

Many critics ascribe much of the economic troubles of India to some religious beliefs that result in high population, restrict its food supply, and give little status to work as an instrument of social mobility. Unquestionably, the philosophies of a people are a determiner of the end results and outputs of their culture.

Knowledge System   The importance of language cannot be underestimated. In the scheme of history, relatively few cultures have had a written language, yet we clearly see the importance of written language in communications today. Cultures without a written language could not reliably communicate with each other or pass knowledge to succeeding generations, because the spoken word was very inaccurate—as any perceptive individual has already discovered. The cultures that have survived are the ones that developed a written language. Moreover, the written language must have certain characteristics. The Japanese and Chinese have long had difficulty in using their written languages which are cumbersome and inflexible. In contrast, the Latin-based languages, particularly German and English, have demonstrated great flexibility. Whenever an American needs a new symbol he simply creates a new word or joins old words together. Our language is a living, viable instrument of our system and we use it well.

Educational System   Every successful culture that has managed to exist for a period of time has had some type of educational system. Indeed, the importance of education is so widely recognized that cultural systems not having educational subsystems usually send their leaders to other cultures to be educated. Clearly, some type of educational system is a common attribute of successful socioeconomic systems.

Technology   While our technology is so vast and complicated that it can be described only in the most general terms (such as a "chemical-electrical-mechanical" society), some cultures are described as raw-material societies; others as agrarian societies. Some cultures live off the sea almost exclusively. The Swiss system is predicated upon technology in precision manufacturing, exemplified largely by watchmaking. The technology of many cultures around the world today is rather elementary; to meet their needs they depend upon the technology of others. Unquestionably, technology is necessary if one is to have a productive system.

Political System   All cultures have governmental systems. Anarchy exists nowhere. But it is interesting to note that no two governmental systems are identical. Take the United States and Canada, whose situations in many ways are parallel. One might assume that their political systems would be quite similar, but note how different they really are. It would take many pages to list all the points of difference between the two governmental forms. The reasons for these variations in governmental systems are many, including happenstance, but the important thing is to recognize that each culture has a government that is unique in some way.

Rituals   Every culture has its rituals. A ritual is a socially prescribed activity that is triggered by some event. For example, birthday parties are rituals, as are weddings, the Fourth of July, graduation exercises, Christmas, Thanksgiving, the World Series, elections, conventions, vacations, the company Christmas party, and thousands of other similar events that have become socially habitual. Rituals can vary from highly formal ceremonies, such as the inauguration of a president, to informal social habits, such as having the neighbors over for bridge on Friday night.

Rituals are important to people and take up a great deal of time and energy. Considerable activity within every system is devoted to observing its rituals. Rituals usually evolve to serve some purpose, but they can become habitual anachronisms as times change. Rituals are continually changing in importance and characteristics; new ones are created and old ones fade. Whatever happened to the band concert in the small town park? New rituals? How about the collegiate spring break migrations to the beach areas, for a start?

Of what use to the businessman is this information about rituals?

Taboos   All cultures have taboos—behavior that is forbidden, the no-no's. There are many more taboos in a culture than casually come to mind, for many are so deeply ingrained in one's behavior patterns that he does not recognize them as taboos. Some taboos are legally inspired, while others are socially enforced. A classic mistake too many American firms made in foreign countries was to remain ignorant of the culture's taboos and consequently to violate them, to their eventual sorrow.

List the taboos that you perceive in our society.

Certainly taboos are in a state of continual evolution in a viable system. Many practices in the movie industry that were once considered taboo are acceptable today. At one time it was unthinkable for women to smoke, let alone smoke in public. Today that taboo has vanished. Divorce was once a taboo.

Personal Relationships   Some cultures are closely knit; the people have close, lasting relationships with each other, frequently based on family ties. This situation often exists in smaller cultures. One of the characteristics of our society has been the changing nature of personal relationships. Families are not as close as they once were. The mobility of population has uprooted people and placed them in new environments in which they have had to create new relationships with other people. These developments have had a profound impact upon our socioeconomic system.

Businesses frequently move executives around the country. How does this affect them? Does this practice eliminate certain types of people from corporate administrative positions?

Conclusion

The cynic might ask, "What has all of this to do with business?" The modern administrator, however, realizes that because business exists to serve society's needs, its managers must be aware of the workings of the social system and the forces with which his enterprise must contend.

You have been introduced here to the systems concept and some important aspects of socioeconomic systems to help you gain an overall view of the environment in which you and business must operate. You will better understand the specifics of business if you have an understanding of the whole system.

2 Evolution of the present U.S. socioeconomic system

Call it what you will, incentives are what get people to work harder.
NIKITA KHRUSHCHEV

One of the purposes in studying history is to illuminate our present situation and how it developed. We can understand and appreciate our present system if we examine the key concepts upon which it is founded. The system in which we now live is the result of all the historical environmental forces that have forged its present configurations. History is both the study of past events and the study of past environments.

CAPITALISM

Most people describe our present society as "capitalistic"—founded on the precepts of capitalism. Capitalism gets its name from the practice in the early stages of our system of bestowing the profits of an enterprise upon the owners of the capital that financed it. Capitalism requires the existence of several related conditions. First, there has to be the concept of private property. Second, men must be allowed to enter whatever enterprises they desire (free enterprise). Finally, individuals must have the right to make contracts and have them enforced by a judicial system. Some people lump all these concepts together as capitalism, but doing so does them great violence, for each stands independently. For example, under the Swedish form of socialism, the concept of private property, the right to make contracts, and a substantial amount of free enterprise still exist. Each of these concepts should be studied and appreciated separately, for each plays its own important role in our system.

Why must there be private property in a capitalistic system?
Why must there be free enterprise in a capitalistic system?
Why is the right to enter into a contract and have it enforced important?

In fact, if Adam Smith, one of the early classical economists, were to return to the American business scene today, it is doubtful that he would label it "capitalistic." When the various governments take about 40 percent of the national product and labor gets about 50 percent, it is not too appropriate to call such a system capitalistic; it just does not help one understand the nature of the system. As an illustration, Table 2-1 shows the distribution of the revenue of the steel industry.

Table 2–1

DISTRIBUTION OF THE STEEL INDUSTRY'S REVENUE IN 1967

Percent	Total in Millions		Dollars per Employee
100.0%	$17,241.3	Revenues from the public	$24,731
		DISPOSED OF AS FOLLOWS:	
41.1%	7,595.0	Products and services bought* (provide employment for suppliers and for their suppliers in turn)	10,894
38.6%	6,659.5	Direct employment costs* (paid to and for employees)	9,553
7.0%	1,216.6	For wear and exhaustion* (provide employment for suppliers of new plant and equipment and for their suppliers in turn)	1,745
4.2%	732.7	Taxes (provide revenues for governments)	1,051
2.1%	356.5	Income reinvested in business	511
2.9%	492.1	Dividends* (compensation for savings invested)	706
1.1%	118.9	Interest* (compensation for savings loaned)	271

* The governments get their share of this amount by taxing the recipients.

It is wise to avoid using labels such as capitalism, socialism, or any other "ism" when describing economic orders. Rather, one should carefully describe systems in detail for what they actually are. In our system the government exerts varying degrees of control in varying areas, a substantial element of free enterprise exists, and people generally have the right to own property and enter into a wide range of contractual relationships. But there are limitations on all of these concepts. As an American citizen, you have no right to make atomic bombs. You are prohibited from going into many types of businesses; do not try to operate a still. Society places such restrictions for good reasons, largely focused around people's health and welfare and its own preservation.

Perhaps the sooner businessmen shed the capitalistic label the better off they will be, for it conjures up too many antagonistic images in the minds of their many critics. Probably the sooner we admit that we have our own form of socialism and deal with it in those terms, trying to make it a flexible, workable, and highly productive system, the better off we will be.

> For our purposes here, socialism is defined as a socioeconomic system in which government appropriates a significant share of the national product and uses it for what the government in power conceives to be the public good. Also implicit in socialism is considerable control of economic activities by governmental authorities; usually key industries are owned by the government.

The Concept of Private Property

At one campus rally a self-styled radical was railing away at "the establishment," focusing his tirade on private property. He claimed that the concept of private property was at the root of all our social troubles, that it should be abolished. A young lady of seemingly similar bent bounced up on the stage and encouraged the young man to continue, vociferously agreeing with him. As she approached him, she pointed to a colorful neckband he was wearing and said, "Oh, what a pretty scarf! Give it to me. I want it."

The speaker recoiled, protesting, "No, it's mine!"

The young lady replied, "But I thought we agreed that private property was to be abolished, so that makes the scarf just as much mine as yours. You have been wearing it for a while, now it's my turn."

The crowd roared as the young man stammered and stuttered as he tried to cope with this sudden dilemma. The young woman went on to point out the hypocrisy of those people who want to abolish private property for others. Interestingly, the radical drove away from the rally in a new Corvette.

Most old-line communists now admit that they failed to realize how deeply ingrained the concept of private property is in the attitudes of men. Just try telling a farmer who raises a crop of potatoes that they are not his but rather belong to the state. Try telling a lad who has raised a small lamb that it does not belong to him, but to the community. People have an instinctive feeling about what is theirs, what they own, and they develop very strong proprietary drives to protect what they consider to be their property. The discounting of this deep-seated feeling of ownership of one's possessions, a basic feeling that one should be able to dictate the use of his possessions, has been a fundamental flaw in communistic theory. Even the most hardened communistic societies have had to give ground and allow the individual the right to own certain personal property. Never underestimate the extent to which a man will go in protecting what he believes to be his own property.

Experience indicates that the hope of acquiring property is a vital force that motivates people to work. Casual observation strongly suggests that the preservation of property is best attended to by its owner. Hence, property plays a key role in the workings of our system. Without it, one would not accumulate capital; it would be pointless to save money if you could not invest it in property.

If you developed a system in which private property did not exist, what behavior might you expect from the people in that system toward property?

Property

The concept of private property embodies the right or ability of the individual to control the use and disposition of either material objects or a legal creation, either real or personal. When property has been acquired through the procedures prescribed by the legal system, the individual is said to own such property. Real property is land and all structures or things attached to it. Personal property is everything that is not real property. In reality, what one owns is the right to do certain things with that property, but one's rights to property are not unlimited. For example, you may own your home but that does not give you the right to set fire to it.

What is a legal creation? Name some.
Why don't you have the right to set fire to your home? It's your house, isn't it?

The Concept of the Right to Contract

You are free to determine your destiny through the assumption of contractual obligations; it is your right to make contracts and have them enforced by the courts. Without this concept, business would be impossible, for transactions would be nearly eliminated. If transactions are to be consummated, one must be able to have faith that promises made will be kept. You cannot do business with someone who does not keep his word. Good businessmen carefully protect their reputation for keeping their promises, fulfilling their contractual obligations, because the willingness of others to do business with them depends upon it. Actually, a case could be made that business is little more than a continuing series of numerous contracts. The right to contract is essential to business.

A contract is a promise or a set of promises for the breach of which the law gives a remedy or the performance of which the law in some way recognizes as a duty.—AMERICAN LAW INSTITUTE

The Concept of Free Enterprise

Free enterprise embodies the right of the individual to select whatever means he desires for making his livelihood. It is a fundamental freedom to be able to enter into the social or economic enterprise one desires. Although our system allows much more freedom of enterprise than any other in the world, still many restrictions are placed upon what businesses you may enter, and you must meet certain qualifications to enter almost any business. You must obtain the proper licenses and abide by local zoning codes if you want to establish a company. You must meet certain standards of education, experience, and skill to be a physician, lawyer, or CPA. You must be a union member to practice certain trades in many areas.

In spite of such restrictions, you still have far more freedom to select the enterprise in which you will engage than has existed in any other known system in the history of man. This freedom should be most jealously guarded, for it is one of the most valuable freedoms you have. Visualize a system in which someone else tells you what you are to do with your time, your life.

Is it possible to have a highly socialistic government and yet maintain a very strong free-enterprise system? Are the two mutually exclusive?

The Concept of Freedom of Choice

Although closely allied conceptually with free enterprise, the concept of freedom of choice deserves separate mention. Whereas free enterprise refers to your freedom to select your means of making your livelihood, freedom of choice refers to your freedom to buy what you wish. In some systems, consumers have little or no choice as to what they can buy. A Russian who wants an automobile is severely restricted in his choice. Our system is predicated on the belief that the consumer should be free to buy what he wants. This freedom of choice is the basis of competition as firms strive to win the consumer's affection.

The Concept of Competitive Markets

A most important part of the conceptual basis of our system is the idea of competitive markets. Wherever feasible, we believe that it is to the best interests and welfare of the people in our system that businessmen should compete with each other for the consumers' dollars in open competitive marketplaces. While there are many imperfections in our competitive system, still ours is one of the few socioeconomic systems in the world that utilizes competition as a way of business life. We believe, and we have ample evidence to prove, that we enjoy lower prices, better products, and more innovation when doing business in a competitive setting than in monopolistic environments. A monopolist is usually assured of a suitable profit without troubling himself to improve his products and service or to lower his price; with competition this same man must at least meet, if not better, the efforts of the competition to give the market what it wants or else he will realize no profit, as his his trade will go elsewhere. We believe that competition increases productivity, thereby lowering costs.

Why do we deliberately induce monopolies into our system?

The Concept of Productivity

Productivity has various meanings. It can refer to the total output of goods and services of a system. More accurately, it refers to the relationship between the output of a system and its input; it is the ratio of output to input. Usually inputs are measured in terms of man-hours of effort and materials used; output is measured in terms of useful products and services. Naturally, it follows that the well being of a system depends upon the amount of output it can procure per unit of input. Wealthy systems obtain a great deal of output per man-hour input, whereas underdeveloped or poverty cultures realize much less. Truly, productivity is the key to plenty. It is the name of the game.

As an illustration, Table 2-2 presents the productivity of the steel industry.

Table 2–2

COMPUTATION OF PRODUCTIVITY FOR THE STEEL INDUSTRY, 1958–1967

		1958	1967
OUTPUTS =	Tons of raw steel (millions)	85.3	127.2
INPUTS =	Man-hours of hourly workers (millions)	753.0	816.0
	or		
	Wage cost ($ millions)	$2,644	$3,876
PRODUCTIVITY =	85.3 / 753.0 =	.11 ton/man-hour	
	127.2 / 816.0 =		.16 ton/man-hour
	or		
	85.3 / 2,644.0 =	.0323 ton/$	
	127.2 / 3,876.0 =		.0328 ton/$

Interpretation Productivity increased from .11 tons/man-hour in 1958 to .16 tons/man-hour in 1968. But when the increased wage paid for a man-hour is brought into the picture, productivity increased only an insignificant amount, from .0323 tons per wage dollar to .0328 tons per wage dollar. Clearly the increased productivity in the steel industry during this period went to the workers.

How can output be measured? Why are man-hours used to measure input? Should one use dollars or units in measuring productivity?

Our true source of power in the world has not been our armies and certainly not our diplomacy but rather our high productivity, productivity that for a time supplied most of the world. Later we will see that the true value of the dollar and its real attraction to foreign businessmen is all the things that it will buy in this country—our productivity.

THE PHILOSOPHICAL BASE

Puritanism

The previous chapter emphasized the importance of a culture's philosophy and outlined the role, in our system, of Calvinistic philosophies. These manifested themselves in our early formative years as Puritanism, in which people were urged to work hard, save their money, and sin not. Consumption beyond one's needs was one of the sins. Such attitudes created large savings, since consumption was minimized while productivity was maximized. These savings financed the building of our early industrial empire in New England. The tradition of Yankee stinginess has its beginning in this Puritan philosophy, which still plays a significant, though declining, role in our thinking.

Pragmatism

Combined with Puritanism was a philosophy of pragmatism—the prizing of things that work. Americans have always stressed the pragmatic, the action that delivers results. Anything that worked was good; whatever did not work was discarded. This pragmatism encouraged early inventors to find new ways of whipping the problems confronting them. If some productive technique was not delivering results, a better way was developed. Though to you this seems to be a matter of common sense, almost to the point where any other philosophy is unthinkable, the fact is that in many cultures people follow the same practices century after century even though they have been proven ineffective. Because of cultural habit, religion, or superstition, some people refuse to rid themselves of inefficient methods that simply do not work. People are starving in many countries because the farmers refuse to use better ways to raise more food and resist all efforts to show them how to do so. Many societies brag that they are still making things the same ways their ancestors made them centuries ago. While this is picturesque to the romanticist, it is insanity to the economist. Certainly pragmatism must rank as one of our more important philosophical bases.

Materialism

Another aspect of our socioeconomic philosophy is often called materialism. A large segment of our people prize the material things in life over the spiritual. We like our goods and services. We continually want to improve our material well-being. This drive has been most powerful in motivating our people toward higher productivity, for if people really do not care about the material things in life, they have little incentive to produce them. If you are satisfied to get your rewards in the hereafter, you have little motivation to do much here. Societies that are not materialistic are often not productive. This is not to pass value judgments on them, but merely to describe reality. But one becomes rather bored with complaints from societies that continually put down the material things in life and simultaneously complain about a low standard of living. You cannot have it both ways; they go together.

Idealism

These observations do not deny, as so many of our critics are wont to do, that idealism has also been a philosophical handmaiden of our people. Who but an idealist could build canals and bridge the continent with rails? Who but an idealist could make huge investments in new and unproven industries? Would a cold-blooded, materialist pragmatist found the Ford Motor Company? Idealistic outcroppings are frequent throughout the entire business community, if one is but willing to see them. Idealism has certainly been a philosophical building block of our system.

Hedonism

Some critics claim that our people are too hedonistic. Hedonism is the seeking of pleasure and the avoidance of pain. In the judgment of these critics we are too vigorous in our pursuit of pleasure. The hedonist would reply, "So who wants pain? Only a masochist." Unquestionably, the search for pleasure has led to improvement of our living standards, from which many of our pleasures are derived.

THE AGRARIAN BEGINNING

In the beginning there was lots and lots of land and very little labor. This environmental setting explains a great deal about our development. First, because labor was scarce, farmers had to innovate, seeking ways to make their existing labor more productive. Pursuing this search, we became leaders in the industrialization of agriculture. It is ironic that in the world's oldest industry, at which mankind had been working for about fifty centuries, we have in a speck of time developed revolutionary agricultural innovations in equipment, methodology, and product.

Lots of land also meant lots of opportunity, for a man in our early years was never fenced in. He could always go to the frontier and stake out as much land as he could handle. This provided an immensely important social safety valve, for the impoverished were never completely locked into their situation.

Because of the vast distances involved on this new continent, we quickly sensed the need for an excellent transportation system. Historically our society has always sought the best transportation system devisable. Transportation is so important to the prosperity of our system that we have subsidized it continually and heavily by direct and indirect governmental support. The government gave land to encourage the building of railroads in the nineteenth century and it continues such subsidies in many ways. Transportation today accounts for about 11 percent of our national product. Consider the importance of the automobile and all of its auxiliary systems put together!

In what ways does society now subsidize the transportation industry?

Self-sufficiency

With an agrarian society based on a huge land mass removed from the supporting industrial centers in Europe, our system had to become self-sufficient. The people could not rely upon others to supply their needs, for others were far removed in both time and distance. Hence, we had a powerful motive to develop a complete spectrum of industry to supply our own needs. The result was our present broad-based industrial complex.

One should understand that our present-day socioeconomic system grew from an agrarian society that was largely self-sufficient and highly decentralized, with the people spread over vast areas of land.

INDUSTRIALIZATION

The advent of the industrial revolution in eighteenth-century England is well explained in most high-school history courses, and we need not repeat all that here. Instead, we will try to trace some of the impacts of industrialization upon our present system. This transition from an agrarian society to an industrial one is involved in most of the economic and social problems we now face, for the process of industrialization is not completed. The agrarian age lingers with us, and its children are in difficulty. How can a man raised on a small southern farm compete successfully when thrust suddenly into a highly complex industrial society for which he has had no preparation? What can a sixty-year-old farmer do when his produce can no longer compete in the marketplace with that of the large corporate farms? How do cities handle bulging populations converging on the metropolis from the agricultural hinterland? How can the small farming communities from whence they came survive? And what psychological and social adjustments are demanded of the transplanted farmer?

The family farm and all of its virtues are part of American folklore. What has industrialization done to the family farm?

Urbanization

Industrialization has meant urbanization. Transportation factors dictate that manufacturers locate near their markets, which means that the big get bigger. Big metropolitan areas such as Los Angeles, Chicago, and New York, by sheer size, become increasingly attractive to manufacturers wanting to locate near their markets. We have not yet worked out a means for offsetting this strong centralizing force. While many writers have urged the decentralizing of business from the urban centers, we have yet to devise a workable scheme for doing it. We are rapidly becoming almost completely urbanized. Forecasters foresee in the not-too-distant future a nation comprised of a few huge megalopolises (large urban areas consisting of several large cities and suburbs which adjoin each other) as shown in Figure 2-1.

All of the economic and social problems inherent in urbanization are now being loaded upon our system and we are trying to solve them; but this is not the place to delve into these problems.

Devise a program for reversing the trend toward urbanization. How could it be done if we really wanted to do it?

Wage Society

A family living on a self-sufficient farm was somewhat independent of the economic well-being of the system. When times got tough they did not starve to death or lack

FIGURE 2-1: Probable Future Megalopolises in the U.S.

 1. Atlantic Seaboard
 2. Southern California
 3. Chicagoland
 4. Allegheny–Ohio–Lake Erie
 5. Southern Michigan
 6. Bay Area–Central California
 7. Erie–Niagara Frontier–Rochester
 8. Florida East Coast
 9. Miami Valley
10. North Central Texas
11. St. Louis
12. Texas–Louisiana–Gulf Coast
13. Onondaga–Mohawk Valley
14. Twin Cities
15. North Carolina Piedmont
16. Puget Sound
17. Missouri–Kaw Valley
18. Colorado Piedmont
19. Central Indiana
20. Florida West Coast
21. North Central Georgia

a roof over their heads. They still had their job to do and their self-respect. Constant cash income was not critical.

Take the family from the farm and thrust it into a large city where the breadwinners must work for a wage, and the situation reverses. Living now depends upon a continual flow of money into the family unit. The family must now pay for their food and pay the rent. They need money continuously even though they cannot continue to work past a retirement age, whereas the farmer, who needed less money, was not faced with mandatory retirement. The family is now dependent upon the economy for its survival. All of this places people in a completely different psychological setting. These factors help explain the pressures for unemployment compensation, social security, and other measures to assure a family with no breadwinner sufficient income to survive. The job and its security become extremely important in a wage society. The demands for security must be met, for the security of the farm has been lost.

Educational Requirements

Education was not necessary for survival in an agrarian society. One could learn to farm from his peers and family. But the man without an education is lost in a highly industrial society. Industrialization relies on knowledge and skills that usually cannot be acquired from one's family or friends. Industrialization demands education. But education is largely confined to the young. How do you reeducate a sixty-year-old man displaced from an agrarian society to compete in an industrial one?

Why is having a job important, other than for its monetary rewards?

Loss of Identity

Agrarian social systems are usually small, finite ones in which the status of each member is established and honored. The individual is recognized. People know him from the time he is born until they lower him into the ground. Everyone knows him by name, and everyone knows when he does something, either good or bad. This puts great pressure on the individual to behave as the group desires, but it also gives him much-needed social recognition. His identity is clearly established. He exists.

Place this man in a large city, working for a large company, and the situation is reversed. Who is he? No one knows him outside of his immediate family and a few co-workers. His next door neighbor may not know him. The man tends to lose his identity. The pressures of the group are lessened, for if he does evil, who is to know it? If he does good, who is to care? The social mechanisms of the agrarian system do not work so well in an industrial society. We are trying to develop new mechanisms, but the process is painful.

What are some ways in which people in industrial societies gain identity? How can business use such knowledge?

Money and Banking System

In true agrarian societies an excellent money and banking system is not too important. Early farmers had little money; they bartered produce for their needs. A pure agrarian society is largely a barter economy. Our money and banking system was slow to develop in the nineteenth century for many reasons. Only with the rapid industrial expansion of the twentieth century was the pressing need for a sound money and banking system realized. We solved the problem through a series of governmental acts, largely focusing around the Federal Reserve System and all of its mechanisms. Today, our industrial society has gone past the money stage toward a credit economy in which relatively little money is required; rather, most transactions are financed through the use of some sort of credit instrument. Some business seers foresee the day when money will be obsolete; transactions will be a matter of bookkeeping entries in a most complex computer system.

Visualize how a cashless society would operate. Suppose there were no money whatsoever in circulation. How would the system function? Why does money still exist?

Capital Requirements

Industrialization requires capital. In the early stages of our system it took little capital to establish a small farm; all one needed was enough courage to go to the frontier and stake out his own spread. But it takes capital to industrialize. The more industrialized we become, the higher the capital requirements will be.

Technology

With industrialization comes a dependence upon technology. Technology made industrialization possible and continues to sustain its development, but this dependence upon technology means that we must spend money on research to advance that technology. A highly industrial society is also a research oriented one, for in research rests our hopes for improving our industrial processes and systems. Hence, an industrial society puts research on a pedestal, for in it lie its hopes for survival.

During the nineteenth century research was almost unheard of. Inventors doing what today could be called research were laughed at. Indeed, the agricultural schools of the nation had a most difficult time selling the idea of agricultural research to the farm community. Only after decades of conclusively proving that research pays off in higher productivity could they gain the respect of the people they were trying to serve. Yet probably nowhere in our entire industrial picture has research paid off so obviously as in the field of agri-business. The agrarian thinker sees no need for research because he feels no reliance on technology. On the other hand, the president of a du Pont or IBM understands that his survival depends upon technical leadership in his area, so he is willing to invest in research to secure that end.

WHERE ARE WE NOW, AND WHAT HAVE WE?

One could describe our present system as a sociotechnical bureaucracy with capitalistic fringes. Our society is becoming almost completely industrialized. Even agricultural goods can no longer be considered products of an agrarian society, because the bulk of our food is being raised by large corporate agri-businesses that have little in common with the agrarian societies we have described. We use the word "bureaucracy" to describe our system, for increasingly our institutions are being managed by hired administrators, not owners of the enterprises. This makes a big difference, as we shall see. Our dependence upon technology is clear. Also becoming increasingly clear is the social orientation of our efforts: the system is concerning itself more and more with people and how they live.

Despite the cries of the critics over such contemporary issues as pollution and quality of products, our system is a changeable one; in a mere speck of time we have recognized the pollution problem and are doing something about it. We have only been concerned about air pollution since the mid-1960s, and we are acting to solve the problem. Similarly, most of our other pressing social and economic problems are of relatively recent perception, but we are in motion to meet them. Our system has survived all these years largely because it has been adaptable to meet the needs of the people.

Responsibilities of Business

The responsibilities of the businessman in this system have been greatly debated for the past two decades. Many people would have the businessman provide the primary leadership to initiate the changes they see necessary. They propose that business should be an aggressive, positive force for social change. There is much face validity to these views, and certainly there is considerable room for the businessman to play an important role in changing the system.

On the other hand, some philosophers see grave dangers in this progressive stance of the businessman. They do not want the businessman to lead the change, for they are not at all certain they will be happy about where he will lead them. This school of thought maintains that business's function is to serve the people, not lead them.

Who does lead in our society?

Conclusion

You will gain a slightly different view of our dynamic business system by casting aside the cliches usually applied to it and examining carefully what we really have and why it works so well. You should now understand the basic concepts underlying our socioeconomic system and why they are so important to our welfare. The concepts of free enterprise, private property, and freedom to contract are vital to our system, and to any free productive society.

To understand many of the present-day problems we face we must also understand the complexities of changing from an agrarian society to an industrial one. It can not be done overnight, and we are still in the later stages of the transition.

3 Men—their needs and behavior

Man is astonishingly good at dealing with the physical world, but he is just as astonishingly bad at dealing with human nature; therefore, an inch gain in the understanding of and command over human nature is worth a mile gain in the understanding of and command over physical nature.

ARNOLD J. TOYNBEE

Why do people act as they do? If you can ever develop your understanding of people to the point where you *know* people—know what they want, why they do the things they do, and how to get them to do the things you want them to do—then you will be a most successful administrator or businessman, because human behavior is the common denominator throughout all systems. You will be working constantly with people to get other people to do things. If you are inept in the behavioral skills, your future as an administrator is in jeopardy. So it will pay you great dividends to study carefully the areas we call the behavioral sciences, for in them lie many of the keys you are seeking to unlock the doors of advancement.

THE BEHAVIORAL SCIENCES

The social sciences are generally understood to cover the six fields of anthropology, economics, history, political science, psychology, and sociology. Among these the behavioral sciences—anthropology, psychology, and sociology—are those that deal directly with human behavior (although admittedly some aspects of political science and economics also deal directly with human behavior).

The history of the behavioral sciences is a short one, for most of the work in them has been done in the past four decades. These fields are not without substantial controversy, for in theorizing about anything as immensely complex as human behavior, solid agreement on theories is not to be expected. Several theories usually exist to explain any one bit of human behavior. Take something as fundamental as learning, which has been studied more than any other single area in psychology; one finds disagreement on how we learn.

Why is there such disagreement in the behavioral science fields?

Some authorities criticize the behavioral sciences at this stage for attending too much to trivial problems, paying too little respect to crucial facts as against grand theories, showing too much respect to insights that are commonplace, giving too much indication and too little proof, showing too little regard for the learning of the past, and using far too much jargon.

Why do special fields of knowledge seem to develop exotic jargon of their own? Of what use is such jargon? What harm is done with it?

During the past decade a great deal was written about the role of the behavioral sciences in business and, more specifically, about their role in management and marketing, for in these two fields of business the study of human behavior is most applicable. Administrators should be skillful in the behavioral sciences, for their jobs are based largely on the ability to understand and control the behavior of other people. The job of managing men is really a matter of managing their behavior. The marketing man's interest in human behavior focuses on consumer buying: why do people buy the things they buy?

Business as a Behavioral Science

Many businessmen take exception to the idea that business is based upon the other behavioral disciplines; they maintain that business is just as much a behavioral science in its own right as any of the others. They hasten to point out that business is concerned with a sizable segment of human behavior—the production and acquisition of one's standard of living. A good case can be made that business studies more of individual behavior than some of the other behavioral sciences; the criminologist studies a relatively small segment of human behavior in contrast to marketing's study of consumer buying.

Although business is a behavioral science in its own right with its own separate body of knowledge, nevertheless it can further its interests by drawing from what has been learned by its fellow behavioral sciences. By the same token, the other behavioral sciences could probably learn by studying some of the findings of management and marketing.

SOCIOLOGY AND BUSINESS

Sociology studies human behavior in groups and social settings in the hope of formulating principles of human nature, social interaction, social organization, and culture. It has a definite place in the study of business, for business is concerned with the behavior of groups of people—buyers, sellers, workers, middlemen, stockholders, and various groups in society who are motivated more by group pressures than by their own individual drives.

Sociology is concerned with the individual, the group, and total society. Naturally, it is interested in the individual as a social unit within groups, but mainly it studies his reactions to and influences upon his social setting. Its specific contributions to business lie in the areas of population studies, consumer motivation, human ecology, research methodology, status systems, collective behavior, communication theory, and the family.

Population and Its Stratification

A platitude frequently heard is that markets are people with money to spend. This points up the impact of population and its various components upon business. A perusal of business literature usually turns up many articles dealing with such topics as the teen-age market, the senior-citizen market, the young marrieds, the population explosion, the relocation of population, and the suburban movement.

What is the main source of information on population characteristics and trends?

Unquestionably, population studies are extremely vital information upon which the businessman depends for indications of the size, location, and probable behavior of future markets.

The present increase in the number of "senior citizens" was publicized far enough in advance that the business community had time to accommodate it—by providing, for example, more retirement communities and medical facilities.

Consumer Motivation

Buying motives are extremely critical to marketing plans. Although a lot of money is spent studying them, still little is known about the basic motives underlying much buying behavior.

Some of the most significant breakthroughs have come from sociology. Previously, motivation was discussed largely in terms of instinct, physiological needs, and some vague, inner drives that emphasized the individual and largely ignored the role of society, culture, and its significant reference groups. Today businessmen are fairly well aware that buying motives are the result not of instinct but largely of group pressures. This evolution of thought owes much to sociology, which focuses attention upon the role of class and status in the motivational patterns and life styles of different persons.

Why is it difficult to determine the motivation of people?

Human Ecology

Human ecology is the study of how man adapts to a changing environment to fill social voids and how people and institutions alter their behavior in a changing environment. Ecology has studied closely the demise and evolution of institutions that served our nation while it was an agrarian society, and how some adapted and others were created to meet the new needs of our present highly urbanized industrial order. This change has caused much economic and social dislocation. Markets have moved, desires have changed, and spending patterns have greatly altered.

ANTHROPOLOGY AND BUSINESS

Unfortunately, the potential contributions of anthropology to business have been delayed because it was overlooked in favor of sociology and psychology. This was a distinct loss, because anthropology had much to contribute to business.

Contributions

Anthropologists have participated in international business programs; because of their special sensitivity to foreign cultures, they have prevented many gross errors. They have even developed sales training procedures that involve an analysis of a salesman's correct rate of speech with different potential customers. They have also worked in many industrial situations that require the measurement of the body, as in the design of such products as chairs, clothing, and automobiles. The anthropologist is specifically trained to study national character or the differences that distinguish one nationality group from another. Hence, he can provide information pointing out the differences between a Frenchman and Spaniard or between a Swede and Norwegian. He also studies subcultures and would be able to differentiate the patterns of living in Los Angeles and New York. Of more special interest, some anthropologists are interested in nonverbal behavior cues, such as gestures, posture, and food and drink preferences. Some anthropologists are interested in the symbolic meanings of various passage rites in which persons pass from one stage of life to another, such as the marriage ceremony, the reaching of majority age, the buying of the first pair of long pants, retirement, and other similar milestones.

Weddings are one of our rituals. Itemize the buying behavior that results from them.

Many products do not sell in Quebec because to a French speaker their English names are almost unpronounceable, or else totally meaningless even when translated idiomatically. Sometimes a company is embarrassed because its brand name has unfortunate connotations in another language.

One manufacturer of women's cosmetics was uncertain whether he should continue using the fleur-de-lis emblem on his package. Anthropologists pointed out that the emblem was associated with the French kings and had definite masculine connotations. Field testing substantiated this contention, and the symbol was dropped from the package. Sellers interested in increasing their market penetration into many minority markets in the United States have become increasingly aware of the importance of understanding the special behavior of these groups; they have drawn heavily upon anthropological data to assist them.

The anthropologist is aware of the basic themes of a culture. One chain of candy shops knew that its boxed chocolates were usually bought as a gift, but it had been unable to capitalize on this knowledge. An anthropologist was able to develop merchandising and advertising formats built around gift-giving symbolism. A study of the connotations of major holidays suggested additional themes for window displays and advertising.

Develop specific promotional programs in line with the gift-giving symbolism.

It is quite easy to unwittingly violate cultural taboos, especially in selling to foreign markets. For example, blue is the color for mourning in Iran and is not likely to be looked upon with favor when used on any product. Green is the national color of Egypt and Syria; they frown upon its use commercially. Purple is generally disapproved of in most Latin American markets because it is associated with death. White is the color for mourning in Japan. Thailanders regard feet as despicable; any object or package showing feet is bound to be disfavored. On the other hand, anthropologists can indicate favorable colors, symbols, and themes in any culture that can facilitate success in that society.

PSYCHOLOGY AND BUSINESS

Among the psychological topics of interest to the businessman are perception, motivation, learning, thinking, behavioral development, personality, and experimental methodology. The psychologist is interested in the personal adjustment and emotional health of the individual. He examines attitudes, perception, and motivational systems. Happiness, or lack of it, is of interest to him.

Many topics in the field of social psychology overlap areas in sociology, for there is no clear-cut line between them. When a social psychologist studies motivational systems he must examine the role of significant reference groups and status systems— traditional fields of sociology.

Learning and Memory

One of the earliest areas of interest to psychologists was that of learning and memory. For decades they have been greatly interested in how the individual learns and how his behavior is altered by such learning. Learning and memory are directly applicable to a number of business problems such as job training, advertising, and public relations. The principles of recency, intensity, frequency, and relevance all affect the perception and retention of knowledge. Material is more likely to be learned and remembered if it has been presented recently, with a great deal of energy, with great frequency, and if it is relevant to some problem facing the individual.

What do you feel most facilitates your learning?

Perception

How people come to know and interpret their world is fundamental to the understanding of human behavior, since behavior is action that takes the environment into account. Perception is the complex process by which people select, organize, and interpret sensory stimulation into a meaningful, coherent picture of the world.

One of the more important applications of psychological findings on perception to business is Weber's law, which says that one's ability to detect differences in stimuli is a function of the initial intensity of the stimulus. This has widespread application throughout all business. In pricing, it has been discovered that usually a price must be cut by at least 10 percent before the buyer perceives the difference; a price cut of $5 on a Cadillac would not be perceived, while a $5 cut on a $10 dress would be.

Motivational Systems

An individual's behavior can seldom be explained in terms of specific reactions to specific stimuli. A woman sees a dress on a rack (the stimulus) and she immediately buys it (reaction). The stimulus of seeing the dress is seldom the real reason for the purchase. Underlying the transaction and sequence of behavior could be a number of motives. Perhaps she wishes to look particularly attractive at a coming party. Perhaps she is feeling somewhat despondent and feels the new dress will do something to improve her mental attitude. Perhaps she is mad at her husband and is seeking revenge on him through his pocketbook. Many other hypotheses are possible regarding the motives behind the purchase, but certainly the immediate stimulus was not its cause. Motivation deals with the goals and nature of human endeavor: the things one needs, wants, fears, and how he seeks to obtain or avoid them.

Personality

Some psychologists specialize in studying personality with particular emphasis on its role in the behavioral development of the individual. Naturally, this topic is of considerable interest to the businessman, for it has been well established that not only are marketing efforts attuned to the personalities of consumers, but also that managerial activities revolve around personalities.

THE BUSINESSMAN'S MAIN AREAS OF INTEREST

The administrator is largely interested in behavioral science findings as they relate to five major areas: (1) needs, (2) motivation, (3) interpersonal relationships, (4) group dynamics, and (5) personality and personal behavior development.

Needs

Business exists to serve the needs of the people. While many cynics decry this philosophy, still it is the fundamental truth of all business behavior. The businessman sees some need within the system and moves to satisfy it in the hope that by so doing he will be rewarded. Not only are needs the driving forces of businessmen, but also they are the driving forces of individuals, whose needs motivate their behavior as they act to satisfy them.

Type of Need One is apt to think of a need in simplistic terms, such as the need for food, shelter, or clothing—physical needs, what one needs for survival. In socio-economic systems in which the standard of living is at a bare subsistence level, such needs are the ones people are concerned with, for it is a monumental task for such systems to furnish these basic needs. These are called physiological needs—what one needs to survive physically. Unquestionably, these needs are extremely compelling under conditions of bare subsistence. But in an affluent society they are subordinate to psychological and social needs.

Today you read a great deal about how individuals in our society need recognition, self-esteem, an identity, a sense of self-fulfillment, social contact, personal relationships with other people, and other such experiences. These are all psychological or social needs; they are learned needs, in contrast to the physiological needs, which are biological.

Is one's standard of living solely a matter of his material possessions?

Standard-of-Living Concept

Our system has developed the standard-of-living concept, in which we have a relatively good idea of what constitutes a minimum standard of living and what we aspire to do. We have woven this concept into our political goals, in that our governmental systems are committed to providing a certain standard of living to everyone. Moreover, we are committed to the thought of an ever-increasing standard of living. We have made the seeking of this standard one of our national and personal goals. These standards of living require goods and services, for we tend to describe them in terms of material things rather than spiritual values.

Business' Concern With Needs The needs of the people are not readily apparent in our complex system. It does the businessman little good just to tell him that people need food, homes, clothing, transportation, and so on. He must know specifically what food the people need, what type of shelter they want, what type of clothing they demand, and what types of transportation they require. The businessman must deal in specifics, for generalities are of little use in directing one's machines for production.

The businessman spends considerable time and money trying to discover and delineate the needs of the market. He does considerable market research to uncover these needs, for they form the foundation for his enterprise. A great many ventures have failed dismally because they were not based upon a real need. The Hamilton Watch Company introduced an electronic wristwatch on which it lost a great deal of money, largely because the wristwatch buying public simply felt no need for the innovation at that time. It will be interesting to see what the market success will be for the highly sophisticated timepieces now coming on the market, which include computer circuitry and other exotic gadgetry. Does the market really need these innovations?

In studying needs, the businessman quickly encounters a need for quantification, for he must put numerals to these needs. He must come up with some estimate of the market potential for his need.

This brings him into a study of demographics. How many people in the segment of the market that needs his particular idea would be likely buyers for it? So the businessman is thoroughly committed to an understanding of population, its movements and changing composition, for all demands start with population.

What impact will an ever-aging population have upon the demand for products?
Would businessmen be interested in the number of marriages anticipated for the coming year? If so, how could they predict them?
What role does the birthrate play in business? What causes the birthrate to vary between a high of about 25 per thousand and a low of about 17 per thousand?

Motivation

Motivation is concerned with why people behave as they do, which is important to administrators because they are continually trying to motivate people to do something: work for them, buy their products, lend them money, sell them goods, and let them operate their enterprises as they desire. If an administrator is to be successful, he must have a workable understanding of why people behave as they do. Why does a man prefer to work for one employer rather than another? Why does a housewife buy Crest toothpaste rather than Colgate? Why does a man prefer to buy an Oldsmobile rather than a Buick? Why do workers join unions? Why is your secretary willing to work overtime? Why are people willing to pay a high price for your stock? Of course, there are no simple answers to such questions, for we are dealing with possibly the least understood and most complex area of human behavior. Indeed, research in motivation is severely hampered because the people themselves seldom know the real reasons why they behave as they do. Can a man tell you why he has an Oldsmobile rather than a Buick, if he doesn't really know himself? Moreover, the study of motivation is hampered because many of the motives of men are so socially unacceptable that they are repressed in favor of socially acceptable ones; a man when questioned will usually tell you what is socially acceptable.

Self-Concept Theory For many years motivational theorists enjoyed composing long lists of various motives that they observed in man, but such lists have distressed perceptive students of behavior, for they did not have a solid, theoretical base and they left too much behavior either unexplained or superficially covered. There were many loopholes and overlappings. Some items on such lists seemed to be synonyms such as "ego," "self-esteem," and "pride." Just what is the difference between these terms? Obviously, it depends upon how you define them. When dealing with the list approach to motivation, one gets bogged down quite quickly in problems of semantics.

Fortunately, the behavioral scientists have developed the self-concept theory and several mutations of it. It will pay you dividends to master this theory, because it seems to be the best overall theoretical explanation of human behavior now available.

The self-concept theory of behavior is tied closely to the motive of ego, although it furnishes a far more definitive explanation of an individual's behavior than just the bland assertion that one does something in order to satisfy his ego. The self-concept theory seems applicable to all behavior, both economic and social, so it has universal application.

A word of warning: the self-concept theory is a most complex concept and one that you are not expected to master at this point. We are merely introducing the concept so that you can begin to build an understanding of it. It will give you a new way of looking at your own behavior and that of others. Basically, we want to introduce you to the terminology of the self-concept theory and give you some idea of how it works.

One's self-concept is not a simple, single, psychological phenomenon that can be easily explained or understood. Instead, at least four pertinent facets must be studied: the *Real Self,* the *Ideal Self,* the *Real Other,* and the *Ideal Other.*

THE REAL SELF.   The Real Self is how one really perceives himself—what he really thinks he is. It is the man's concept of his abilities, personality, and other factors that go to make up his total existence.

THE IDEAL SELF.   The Ideal Self is how one would like to think of himself. It is his personal goal. *Most of his behavior is directed toward making his Real Self coincide with his Ideal Self.* One small portion of a man's Ideal Self might be that he can be a great football player. His Real Self proclaims that he is only average. His Ideal Self would drive him to perfect his football skills and participate in the game with extreme vigor. A man whose Ideal Self is only an average player would not behave in a similar manner.

THE REAL OTHER.   The Real Other is how one perceives that other people really see him—what other people think of him, his abilities, and his personality, Notice that this has nothing to do with how other people actually do see the individual; one's Real Other may be far out of tune with reality. He may believe that other people think him to be a social lion while in reality they see him as an utter bore. The entire self-concept theory is based on how the individual perceives himself and what he *thinks* others think of him.

THE IDEAL OTHER.   The Ideal Other is what one wants other people to think of him. A woman may want others to think that she is a good wife, a kind mother, a homemaker; she will buy many things to create this impression among the members of her reference groups.

Impact upon Behavior   People express themselves to others and to themselves through the goods and services they buy as well as through nonconsumptive activities. However, there are extremely few activities in this society that do not require the consumption of something. The individual is constantly trying to bring his Real Self and Ideal Self closer together and to make the Real Other and Ideal Other coincide. One does not necessarily try to make his Ideal Self and Ideal Other coincide in all respects: a man might wish others to think of him as an honest man, but he really has as his Ideal Self a man adept at sharp practices. Much hypocrisy can separate one's Ideal Self and Ideal Other.

Think of how driving a new Continental affects one's self-concepts. What is the man trying to say to himself and others? Wouldn't he receive much satisfaction from it even if others did not perceive his ownership—as often happens in very large cities? Think of the effect upon a woman's self-concept as she lolls around a luxurious home among her fine furnishings, even though few people may be aware of her fortunate situation. All of these tangible symbols reinforce her self-concepts. Of course, when a purchase affects the Real Other also, then far more satisfaction is obtained. But the point is that many seemingly ostentatious purchases are made partly for purposes other than impressing other people. A wealthy man may buy expensive silk undergarments solely for the effect they will have on his Real Self; they will constantly remind him that he is a highly successful man.

The point is that the mind continually requires evidence of who and what it is. It is insufficient that one is in fact highly successful, if little or no evidence of it can be perceived by oneself and others.

People constantly tell the world who and what they are by the various things they buy and do. The college student shouts his status through his clothes, speech, and other less subtle forms of behavior. He clearly wants to make certain that no one confuses him with a high-school student or with a workman of his own age. Similarly, a member of the motorcycle set clearly proclaims his allegiances. This symbolic communication is not in the least foolish; it serves as a silent, but speedy, means of communication. Walk into most offices and the boss is quite apparent, made so by the symbols surrounding him.

Behavior of Self-Concepts   One's self-concepts are not fixed. They constantly change with experiences and changes in attitudes, philosophies, and goals. It is a heartwarming experience to observe a young man in the process of upgrading his Ideal Self. Perhaps through a series of unfortunate academic selections he has been forced to conclude that he is a mediocre student at best; his Ideal Self requires only that he graduate. Then he encounters a subject that appeals to him. His interest and grades soar. But at the same time the upgrading of his Ideal Self becomes perceptible. He may start thinking of graduate school. He starts making noises like a scholar instead of a playboy; he wants to alter his Real and Ideal Others. His consumption habits may also change; he may even rashly buy some books.

On the other hand, the downgrading of one's self-concepts is an extremely painful process: morale suffers, attitudes degenerate, and one resists the process vigorously. Not only do people resist the downgrading of their self-concepts, but they resist anything that might threaten it. *Products that in any way threaten one's self-concepts will be avoided.*

What are some of the products that threaten your self-concepts?

The Role of Reference Groups

Reference-group theory is extremely important to motivational analysis. The individual has certain reference groups from which he takes most of his behavior cues: he conforms to the behavior patterns dictated by these reference groups because he wants to be accepted by their members. Hence, his Ideal Self and Ideal Other are largely determined by the characteristics demanded by the reference groups. As a person changes reference groups, the effect upon his Ideals will be immediately apparent.

Barriers to Behavior   Barriers exist that prevent certain behavior. There are four main barriers: (1) incompatibility of act with self-concept, (2) risk of moving away from image, (3) guilt, and (4) lack of authority or autonomy.

INCOMPATIBILITY OF ACT WITH SELF-CONCEPT.   Many acts are simply incompatible with one's self-concepts. A successful business executive seldom will wear shoddy clothing and allow his personal appearance to deteriorate; such behavior is incompatible with the concept he has of himself as a successful businessman. A landmark motivation study on the purchase of instant coffee discovered that many women considered it incompatible with their concept of themselves as diligent housewives and good cooks; they considered the user of instant coffee lazy and wasteful. The woman who visualized herself as hard working and thrifty could not bring herself to buy instant coffee because using it was incompatible with her self-concept. A man who visualizes himself as a top-notch golfer will not purchase cheap equipment; instead, he will buy only what he considers the finest, because in his mind the cheap equipment is incompatible with the image he has of himself as a golfer.

In selling cake mixes to housewives, the mills have found that they must leave something for the woman to do or she will not buy the mix. She must feel that her role in the making of a cake is sufficient to enable her to claim it as her own and not a baker's cake. The small part she plays helps her to fulfill her role as a housewife.

RISK OF MOVING AWAY FROM IMAGE.   A person is constantly striving to make his Real and Ideal concepts coincide, and he will do things that seem to him helpful in reaching this goal. However, if something presents a risk of moving the buyer further from his Ideals, he usually will not do it, even though that risk is small. The consumer prefers the status quo to a risk of moving further away from his goals in life.

How are brand preferences of consumers related to this matter of the perceived risk of an act?

GUILT.   Not all aspects of one's self-concepts are harmonious with each other. The man who visualizes himself as a serious golfer may have some difficulty reconciling this concept with that of a good husband. Similarly, a businessman may believe himself an exceedingly shrewd person, able to extract the largest profit from a given level of sales, and at the same time he may consider himself a good man for whom to work. In many areas of business operation these two concepts might conflict. His union, for example, might propose a substantial pension plan that he felt would unduly lower profits though it would definitely provide an attractive retirement system for his employees.

The final choice between conflicting concepts depends upon which is more important to the person. Although a man might like to own a sports car, the desire may not be fulfilled because it creates guilt feelings in conflict with more dominant concepts. A sports car is a selfish purchase for a family man, he argues, because there is room for only one other rider. Since his family cannot enjoy the car, a man who prizes his relations with his family finds it difficult to buy one. Similarly, a man who wants a Cadillac may refrain from buying it because he knows that if he spends money on it he will have to penalize his family in other areas.

On the other hand, if a person can rationalize his behavior in terms of a socially accepted concept, it becomes much easier. It is easy for men to rationalize the purchase of sporting equipment on the grounds that they are maintaining their health and having fun with their families. A man may want an expensive camera and be able to rationalize its purchase on the basis that he wants to keep a pictorial history of his beloved family. Though an inexpensive camera would probably do the job just as well, if not better, he might nevertheless spend several hundred dollars for the expensive model.

LACK OF AUTHORITY OR AUTONOMY.   It is much easier to sell a person who possesses complete authority and is autonomous than to sell one having little authority. The bachelor responsible to no one buys whatever he wants without consulting anyone. The family man must usually consider his family and often must consult his wife, who frequently has a veto power over purchases, or at least is able to influence the buying decision markedly. The business executive who owns his own company and is in charge of operations will often do things with little hesitation, unlike the junior executive, who is usually worried about what his superiors will think of his behavior.

Role Playing and Buying Motives

A slight variation of the self-concept theory of buying motives is offered by the advocates of another school of thought, who claim an individual's behavior is determined by his perception of the proper behavior required of the role he is playing at that moment. One is playing some role or other at all times. Study a hypothetical forty-year-old business executive. At the office in the morning he is probably playing to the hilt the role of the dynamic businessman. He will dress, speak, and act out the role as he perceives it should be played. Of course, different people perceive the proper behavior for the same role in different ways, thereby frequently causing difficulties for all if they perceive incorrectly. Perhaps in the afternoon he ventures over to the athletic club; through his speech and actions he will now play the role of the athlete, albeit an overly ripe one. He may do all sorts of foolish things to play this role; even his membership in such a club is part of his role playing. That evening he may go home to play the role of the family man; his behavior will change to accommodate that part. Perhaps later he and his wife will go to a party; now he plays the role of the raconteur or perhaps the role of the ladies' man, or whatever he perceives should be his role in the environment in which he is moving.

Naturally, most roles require symbols for communicative purposes. The serious amateur golfer must have his alpaca sweater, his special shoes, and certain equipment to make certain that others do not confuse him with a duffer. Hence, people buy goods and services to assist them in playing the various roles in which they cast themselves.

Role playing is a part of the overall self-concept theory, for one's various self-concepts force him into many different roles as he enters different environments. The individual learns to alter his behavior to play different roles as he encounters various situations. The college student's behavior differs between classroom and fraternity or dorm, as he perceives his role differs. Should he try to behave in the classroom as he does in the dorm, he may meet with some difficulty.

Conclusion

> In the administration of all activities, business and social, it is important to understand men and their behavior. In this chapter you have been introduced to the role played by the behavioral sciences in studying man, and you have seen how you can benefit from such studies. Examples have given you some idea of how businessmen actually use behavioral findings in the operation of their enterprises. We cannot urge you too strongly to study the behavioral sciences most diligently.

4 Men — their institutions

Individualities may form communities, but it is institutions alone that can create a nation.

DISRAELI

"What is an institution?" you might well ask. Is it a prison, an insane asylum, a college? Yes, all of those are institutions, but they are only a highly specialized few of the institutions that comprise our system.

An institution is an aggregation of people and resources dedicated to accomplishing some mission, achieving some goals. What are institutions? They are companies, trade associations, banks, stock brokers, credit unions, governments, military groups, churches, schools, country clubs, fraternal organizations, service clubs, newspapers, and television stations. Institutions are organizations with a purpose. Institutions form the skeletal framework of our system, for when one diagrams a system, as we did in Chapter 1, he draws a picture of the network of the institutions in the system. A company is positioned within a framework of institutions and operates largely by communication with them.

Sometimes one hears a scholar refer to himself as an institutionalist. What he means is that he believes the most fruitful way of studying a subject is to study the institutions that exist in the subject-matter area. An institutionalist in finance studies the operations of banks, stock brokers, individual companies—all of the institutions in the field.

Need for Institutions

Institutions in various systems are often criticized for being archaic and no longer serving their purposes. Moreover, some critics censure institutions for being stodgy, slow to change, reactionary, and generally a chuckhole in the road to progress. Certainly this does describe many institutions, for at any one time there exist a number of institutions that are losing or have lost their economic or social justification. Once an institution is created it does not die easily. A prime example was the March of Dimes charity, whose purpose was to eradicate polio. When that mission was successfully accomplished, did it fold up shop and quit? No, it refused to die! It found another mission to accomplish—the elimination of birth defects. It changed and survived. Others try to go on without changing.

One of the burdensome problems in maintaining a workable society is that of dealing with institutions that no longer serve a purpose or serve it poorly. Governments are replete with agencies whose regulatory duties are no longer required but whose existence continues year after year in a most uneconomic fashion.

How can we rid ourselves of such agencies?

Although institutions die slowly, they will die if they are no longer needed, for society inevitably exacts its toll on such anachronisms. A great many institutions have slipped away into oblivion because society no longer needed them. What has happened to the "Ma and Pa" corner grocery store? What has happened to the neighborhood drug store?

What institutions are now under attack by society because they are no longer needed?

As unneeded institutions wither away, new ones rise. The demands of society are continually changing, thereby forcing institutions to change their activities or create new institutions to serve the need. Vastly increased travel by businessmen created a need for credit cards—instant money—so the large credit-card institutions were developed to serve this need. The move of the populace to suburban areas created a need for retail institutions at more convenient suburban locations. Most leading department stores were forced to alter their operating methods by establishing branch stores in various suburban shopping centers, thereby greatly altering their institutional structure.

What institutions has society created in the last decade?

TYPES OF INSTITUTIONS

Institutions can be classified in many ways, but in our system we first classify them as either profit-seeking or nonprofit institutions, and our entire legal treatment of them depends upon the category in which they fall. There is one set of laws for nonprofit institutions and another set for profit-oriented ones. Take the matter of paying taxes: that privilege is reserved exclusively for profit-seeking organizations.

Nonprofit Institutions

The major nonprofit institutions in our system are the various governments, educational units, religious organizations, charitable organizations, and social groups.

Government   One of our economic problems is created by the fact that we are burdened by a large hierarchy of government institutions, many of which overlap their functions so badly that we pay several times for the performance of essentially the same function. For example, how many different police institutions stand ready to protect you? You have the campus police, then the city police, then the county sheriff, then the state police, and finally the FBI. While they try to obtain some division of labor by focusing their activities in certain areas, still they badly overlap in many of their activities, thereby raising the cost of police protection. Some political scientists maintain that the only real hope for tax relief is a substantial revision in the number of government authorities—taxing authorities. While it is obvious that we have the federal, state, county, and local city governments all taxing us simultaneously, what is not so obvious are some of the other governmental authorities also in the picture, such as local school boards, water districts, sanitation districts, harbor authorities, and township structures.

An institutionalist would maintain that any hope for achieving economies in government must focus on dealing with the various institutions comprising the government, evaluating them, eliminating those not needed, and consolidating others whose duties badly overlap.

The present plight of the venerable Post Office serves as an excellent case in point. Its ability to fulfill its mission is in jeopardy because of the increased burden being placed on its archaic organization. Rather revolutionary moves have been made to make the Post Office once again an efficient institution. It will be interesting to see if they work.

Should the Postal Service be made into a *private profit-making* corporation? What are some of the advantages in doing so? What are some of the problems posed by such a move?

You should be aware that government institutions provide a significant amount of employment to people in our system. About four out of every ten employees work for some governmental employer. In your lifetime, you may rest assured that dealing with the problems of governmental institutions will be one of your biggest headaches. Some fundamental changes and economies must be accomplished, because history clearly tells us that a society can only afford to pay so much of its national product to perform the function of governing itself. When the government confiscates more than a certain amount of the citizens' output, many things happen, few of which are good. Most notably, incentives to produce rapidly diminish. Productivity is stifled. Flexibilities within the organizations in the system diminish, for one of the facts of life is that governmental institutions are far more inflexible than private ones. This is one of the reasons underlying our social philosophy: we believe in private enterprise in preference to governmental enterprise.

Why have governments grown so rapidly in recent decades?
Some political scientists claim that we must completely eliminate certain levels of government, thereby eliminating that taxing authority. What level of government can be eliminated? Is there any precedent for such a move?

Educational Institutions   Looking at our educational institutions, again we can see a substantial hierarchy. Not only do we have the sequential layering of the elementary, secondary, and collegiate institutions, but also many other specialized ones such as vocational-technical schools, community colleges, and correspondence schools. Again one can witness the problems created within a system by its institutional structure, for critics blame some of our social ills on the rather rigid educational philosophies of the present elementary and secondary educational system, which views its mission largely as that of training children for college. A great deal of legitimate criticism has been leveled at educational institutions for not allowing sufficiently for the person who does not want to go to college. Public institutions have been rather negligent in the matter of vocational training, but one can see the vitality of our system at work when he observes the thousands of private vocational training schools that have leaped up around the country to teach such things as computer programming, television repair, and automobile maintenance. This phenomenon illustrates the basic principle that when society has an unfilled need, some institution will be created to fill that void—the principle of institutional ecology. A healthy system creates the institutions it needs to accomplish missions that are not being met within the existing institutional structure.

What changes need to be made to meet legitimate demands of the system?
In what way is any one educational institution really a composite of several institutions?

Religious Institutions   Certainly religious organizations constitute a significant segment of our nonprofit institutions. These, too, are currently under great pressures to meet the changing needs of our system.

What are some of the pressures on present religious institutions?
What role do religious institutions play in our economic system?

Charitable Institutions   A wide variety of organizations fall within this broad category. There are obvious fund-raising charities such as the Red Cross and the Salvation Army. There are the large foundations such as the Ford and Rockefeller Foundations.

Why are charitable organizations greatly concerned over the possible elimination of the income tax deduction for charitable contributions?
Should nonprofit institutions be fully taxed in the same manner as our present profit-seeking organizations?

Social Organizations   This catch-all category includes such diverse groups as Rotary clubs, country clubs, fraternities, athletic clubs, and the Friday afternoon marching and drinking societies. To all these, our previous observations apply. All of these institutions are constantly changing, rising and falling in importance as their needs grow and wane. What has happened to the Boy Scouts? What has happened to such venerable organizations as the Eagles and the Moose?

What pressures in the system created Little League baseball?
What forces are putting pressure on country clubs to change?

Profit-Seeking Institutions

Profit-seeking institutions can be classified in many ways: by size, form of ownership, what they do, the industries they form, or the products they make. The forms of ownership are dealt with in detail in Chapter 6.

All of the different profit-oriented institutions, whether they be proprietorships, partnerships, or corporations, can also be classified according to their function in society—what they do. They can first be broken into the major functional categories of manufacturing, distributing, financial, transportation, labor, communications, utilities, and service. Then each of these categories can be further broken down into minute sectors, much as the government does in using standard industrial classification numbers to classify business (a sample is shown in Tables 4-1 and 4-2). Then each of these major functions can be broken down into even more minute classifications. For example, there are many different types of banks. In few ways does the First National Bank of Chicago resemble the First National Bank of Orlando, Florida. They serve different types of customers and do a great many different things.

One can make a theoretical case that every institution is unique in some respect; it performs some distinct function in society. Even in examining discount houses one is hard pressed to find two that are identical, for each takes a different tangent. If one carefully examines K-Mart in comparison with some local discount competitor, he will note a great many differences attributable both to strategic decisions of their managements and to their unique placement in the society they serve.

EVOLUTION OF INSTITUTIONS

The salient fact for you to learn is that institutions are continually evolving, changing to meet the changing requirements of the system in which they operate. Institutions that fail to evolve, fail. No management has the luxury of remaining static; the status quo is a sure policy for bankruptcy. Business history is replete with examples of institutions that attempted to rest on their laurels, resisting change, only to have change rise up and smite them in the bank account. The railroads, for example, tried to inhibit the growth of the trucking industry.

Table 4-1
STANDARD
INDUSTRIAL
CLASSIFICATIONS

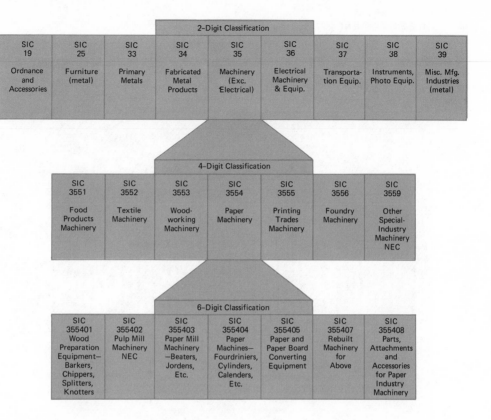

2-Digit Classification								
SIC 19	SIC 25	SIC 33	SIC 34	SIC 35	SIC 36	SIC 37	SIC 38	SIC 39
Ordnance and Accessories	Furniture (metal)	Primary Metals	Fabricated Metal Products	Machinery (Exc. Electrical)	Electrical Machinery & Equip.	Transportation Equip.	Instruments, Photo Equip.	Misc. Mfg. Industries (metal)

4-Digit Classification						
SIC 3551	SIC 3552	SIC 3553	SIC 3554	SIC 3555	SIC 3556	SIC 3559
Food Products Machinery	Textile Machinery	Wood-working Machinery	Paper Machinery	Printing Trades Machinery	Foundry Machinery	Other Special-Industry Machinery NEC

6-Digit Classification						
SIC 355401	SIC 355402	SIC 355403	SIC 355404	SIC 355405	SIC 355407	SIC 355408
Wood Preparation Equipment—Barkers, Chippers, Splitters, Knotters	Pulp Mill Machinery NEC	Paper Mill Machinery—Beaters, Jordens, Etc.	Paper Machines—Fourdriniers, Cylinders, Calenders, Etc.	Paper and Paper Board Converting Equipment	Rebuilt Machinery for Above	Parts, Attachments and Accessories for Paper Industry Machinery

What would the industry look like today if the railroads had openly embraced trucking as a much-needed transportation institution and had gone into the trucking business? How did the need for trucks arise in our system? Why has air freight been a rapidly developing transportation institution?

The commercial banks failed to perform all of the financial functions society demanded, thereby creating the need for such financial institutions as investment bankers, consumer credit companies, savings and loans, and credit unions.

Why did society create the savings and loan association?

Probably there is no area in our system so dynamic as retailing, for changes occur in this economic sector with great rapidity and severity. Witness the advent of the discount houses, drive-in self-service restaurants, and suburban shopping centers.

Explain the advent of discount merchandising.
Explain the advent of self-service gasoline stations. What has happened to the traditional appliance, drug, and hardware stores? What is happening in shoe merchandising? What role has the availability and price of labor played in the development of retail institutions?
What role has the automobile played in the development of retail institutions?

Table 4-2
FULL LIST OF SIC TWO-DIGIT CLASSIFICATIONS

DIVISION A Agriculture, forestry, and fisheries:

Major Group 01. Agricultural production
            07. Agricultural services, hunting, and trapping
            08. Forestry
            09. Fisheries

DIVISION B Mining:

Major Group 10. Metal mining
            11. Anthracite mining
            12. Bituminous coal and lignite mining
            13. Crude petroleum and natural gas
            14. Mining and quarrying of nonmetallic minerals, except fuels

DIVISION C Contract construction:

Major Group 15. Building construction—general contractors
            16. Construction other than building construction—general contractors
            17. Construction—special trade contractors

DIVISION D Manufacturing:

Major Group 19. Ordnance and accessories.
            20. Food and kindred products
            21. Tobacco manufactures
            22. Textile mill products
            23. Apparel and other finished products made from fabrics and similar materials
            24. Lumber and wood products, except furniture
            25. Furniture and fixtures
            26. Paper and allied products
            27. Printing, publishing, and allied industries
            28. Chemicals and allied products
            29. Petroleum refining and related industries
            30. Rubber and miscellaneous plastics products
            31. Leather and leather products
            32. Stone, clay, glass, and concrete products
            33. Primary metal industries
            34. Fabricated metal products, except ordnance, machinery, and transportation
                 equipment
            35. Machinery, except electrical
            36. Electrical machinery, equipment, and supplies
            37. Transportation equipment
            38. Professional, scientific, and controlling instruments; photographic and optical
                 goods; watches and clocks
            39. Miscellaneous manufacturing industries

DIVISION E Transportation, communication, electric, gas, and sanitary services:

Major Group 40. Railroad transportation
            41. Local and suburban transit and interurban passenger transportation
            42. Motor freight transportation and warehousing
            44. Water transportation
            45. Transportation by air
            46. Pipe line transportation
            47. Transportation services
            48. Communication
            49. Electric, gas, and sanitary services

DIVISION F Wholesale and retail trade:

Major Group 50. Wholesale trade
            52. Building materials, hardware, and farm equipment dealers
            53. Retail trade—general merchandise
            54. Food stores
            55. Automotive dealers and gasoline service stations
            56. Apparel and accessory stores
            57. Furniture, home furnishings, and equipment stores
            58. Eating and drinking places
            59. Miscellaneous retail stores

DIVISION G Finance, insurance, and real estate:

Major Group 60. Banking
            61. Credit agencies other than banks
            62. Security and commodity brokers, dealers, exchanges, and services
            63. Insurance carriers
            64. Insurance agents, brokers, and service
            65. Real estate
            66. Combinations of real estate, insurance, loans, law offices
            67. Holding and other investment companies

DIVISION H Services:

Major Group 70. Hotels, rooming houses, camps, and other lodging places
            72. Personal services
            73. Miscellaneous business services
            75. Automobile repair, automobile services, and garages
            76. Miscellaneous repair services
            78. Motion pictures
            79. Amusement and recreation services, except motion pictures
            80. Medical and other health services
            81. Legal services
            82. Educational services
            84. Museums, art galleries, botanical and zoological gardens
            86. Nonprofit membership organizations
            88. Private households
            89. Miscellaneous services

DIVISION I Government:

Major Group 91. Federal government
            92. State government
            93. Local government
            94. International government

DIVISION J Nonclassifiable establishments:

Major Group 99. Nonclassifiable establishments

Presently the institutions in the financial markets—the New York Stock Exchange, various brokerage houses, and investment bankers—are undergoing traumatic experiences in the management of their operations. The high level of activity in the 1960s found them woefully lacking in the ability to handle the business. Moreover, new security markets were created when the NYSE was found wanting in its ability to service the system. Mutual funds began dealing directly with one another through the so-called third market—forceful proof that our system creates new institutions when the old ones fail to fulfill their purpose. The NYSE had simply failed to alter its ways sufficiently to accommodate the changing nature of the market it served.

Recently the telephone system has been encountering difficulties in large metropolitan areas through its inability to provide the level of service it had previously maintained. What changes might be forthcoming if the telephone company is unable to provide the type and level of service demanded by the market?
Select some institution with which you are familiar and carefully examine the changes it will be called upon to make to accommodate the changing needs of the system it serves.

Conclusion

> Institutions form the skeletal framework of our system. They are the organizations through which we accomplish the work that must be done. Our institutions vary almost infinitely in characteristics, but they can be classified into two major categories—profit-seeking and nonprofit organizations. The one thing all of them have in common is a continual need to change their operating methods and strategies to accommodate the changing requirements created by the systems they are designed to serve.

PART

PROFIT-ORIENTED INSTITUTIONS

WHEN one refers to *business* he usually is talking about profit-oriented institutions, organizations that try to make a profit by selling something for more than it costs them. While a great deal has been written, and even more said, about how the businessman seeks to maximize his profits, do not be misled. He doesn't! He tries to stay alive, survive, stay solvent. Most decisions that would lead to the maximization of profit would also jeopardize the firm's existence, something the astute businessman avoids.

So we are going to be discussing concerns that seek to make a profit, but not necessarily the most profit they could make.

5 The role of profit

Society can progress only if men's labors show a profit—if they yield more than is put in. To produce at a loss must leave less for all to share.

BERNARD M. BARUCH

In some circles today profit is a dirty word. Editorialists decry the profiteer, and moralists criticize the firm whose profits seem higher than what they feel is proper. Even congressmen, in some of their statements and some of their legislation, sometimes prove how little they understand of the true social and economic role of profit. Few things are more basic and more important to comprehend than what profit is, its role in our system, and what functions it performs.

THE CONCEPT OF PROFIT

There are several ways of defining profit; unfortunately, all of them lack the preciseness we would like to have in dealing with the concept. As a way to approach this matter of profit, let us examine the transactions of an automobile dealership.

Man-in-the-Street's View of Profit

Suppose Joe Worker bought a 1972 Supersonic "8" that listed for $6000 and cost the dealer $4500. Joe paid only $5000 for it. Joe probably claimed that the dealer made a profit of $500 on the transaction, but even a beginning business student understands that this $500 is not profit at all. Sadly enough, even accountants give some credence to the idea that this difference between invoice cost and sales price is profit by calling it "gross profit," but current business usage tends to call it "gross margin" or simply "margin" on the transaction. It is not profit because none of the dealer's costs, other than that of the car itself, have been taken into account. He has to pay his salesmen, his overhead, and his direct servicing costs on the car from that $500 gross margin.

Accountant's View of Profit

The dealer's accountant presents a considerably different picture of the profit on Joe's purchase, based on the dealer's experience for the year. As shown in Table 5-1, he thinks the dealer lost money on the deal when full costs are applied to it.

Why did the dealer make the sale if he "lost" money on it?

Table 5–1
PROFIT ANALYSIS OF JOE WORKER'S CAR DEAL

	Dealer's Yearly Profit and Loss Experience in Percent	Joe's Deal	
Gross sales	100.0%	$5000	100.0%
Cost of goods sold	77.0	4500	90.0
Gross margin	23.0	500	10.0
Expenses	18.0	900	18.0
Net profit (loss) before taxes	5.0%	($400)	(8.0%)

Unquestionably, the typical businessman thinks in terms of the accounting definition of profit: what remains after all *proper* expenses have been deducted from sales revenue. The word "proper" is most critical, for much controversy arises in determining what expenses are "proper"—what expenses are connected with what sales.

In a profit and loss statement, the accountant presents what appears to be a precise measurement of an enterprise's profit for a given period. Unfortunately, this precision can be misleading, for the astute accountant and businessman realize that a great deal of latitude legally remains open in accounting for costs and revenues, thereby providing considerable leeway in setting accounting profits. Take just one simple illustration—depreciation policy. Suppose the dealer chooses to depreciate his plant and equipment over a forty-year rather than a twenty-year lifetime; his depreciation charges would be cut in half, thereby increasing his profit commensurately. While the subtleties of accounting for costs are not within the scope of this course, still the beginning student should be aware that accounting statements do not have the preciseness that one might assume, and that the measurement of profit—no matter how accurately an accountant may attempt it—is still little more than an educated estimate.

One cynic claimed that profits are what the tax man says they are. What he referred to was the incontestable fact that the Internal Revenue Code sets the rules for measuring taxable income, and so—for reasons of convenience and lack of better information—its view of income and the businessman's view of profit have tended to coincide.

Economist's View of Profit

The economist finds some grave faults with the typical business treatment of profit. His criticisms focus on certain costs that the businessman fails to take into consideration. Probably the best example is provided by the cost of imputed interest on capital employed.

The economist makes a careful distinction between profit and interest. Interest is the price paid for the use of money and all money demands interest, whether it is paid in fact or whether it must be imputed. Suppose the automobile dealer is using $300,000 of capital but he is actually paying interest ($9000) on only $100,000—the amount owed to the bank. An economist would claim that the dealer had another $18,000 imputed interest cost (9 percent of $200,000) which he failed to show as a cost of his operation. Such an economist would insist that $18,000 of the dealer's profit really was not profit at all, but rather interest on funds he employed.

The reason the economist must be quite finicky about distinctions between interest and profit is simple. The economist wants to distinguish between money earned from the operation of the enterprise itself and interest received on money, for the money tied up in the enterprise could be invested elsewhere at prevailing interest rates. For example, the dealer's $200,000 could have been invested in utility bonds at about 9 percent interest—money earned completely aside from the operations of the dealership. The economist is concerned with isolating the actual money earned as a result of the operation of an enterprise. Interest is earned by ownership of money and has nothing to do with one's managerial acumen in operating a business. So the astute businessman carefully differentiates between profits and interest.

One business observer maintains that over the past two decades American industry in total has not earned a profit. Explain his thinking. Do you agree with it?

In accounting for the profits of small enterprises, the imputed wages of management also cause the economists considerable concern. Many small businessmen fail to include the opportunity costs of their own managerial efforts in their costs of operation. The owner's opportunity cost is the amount of money he could earn if he were to work elsewhere. If he could earn $20,000 a year working for someone else, then economists would claim that figure should be his cost to his own firm. If he fails to include the $20,000 or a good portion of it as a cost in the firm's profit and loss statement he is badly overstating the enterprise's profit.

On the other hand, if he draws a salary of $30,000 a year, the economists might say that $10,000 of it is economic profit and $20,000 his true managerial cost.

> An opportunity cost is the loss of revenue one suffers by foregoing some other opportunity in favor of what he is actually doing. The imputed cost of interest previously mentioned is really an opportunity cost.

FUNCTIONS OF PROFIT

Exactly what is the profit system? Many societies seem to have outlawed the profit system as we know it today. Why are we apparently so firmly wedded to it? For several reasons: it provides our incentives; it allocates our resources; it is our yardstick for measuring efficiency and productivity; it finances our growth; and it provides society with a control over business activities.

Profit—The Incentive

The profit system is closely parallel to the concept of free enterprise, for profit is the driving force behind the free-enterprise system. Profit is the fuel that propels enterprises. Profit is the motivator that makes men seek empires. Profit is the goal of entrepreneurs. But it is far more than a mere impeller of men, a goal to be sought.

Compare the lives of a forty-hour-per-week wage earner and a small businessman. The wage earner works forty hours, draws his pay, and takes few worries home. He knows what his life is going to be like and lives in a rather secure world, so long as he does his job reasonably well. He need not put forth superhuman efforts, nor is he expected to come up with innovative ideas. If his employer gets into financial trouble, he will usually suffer little financial loss. His risks are minimal.

On the other hand, the small businessman usually works far longer hours, seldom can leave his business behind, and takes all sorts of risks from which there is no escape. If his enterprise fails, he probably will lose everything he owns. He must work hard and exhibit some imagination. Now the acid question is, "Why in the world would anybody care to lead the life of the businessman in preference to that of the employee?" For the fun of it? Admittedly, fun is a motive in the overall complex picture, but the fun can be rather short lived if the profit does not accompany it. The answer to the question is, of course, profit. Profit is what makes men build enterprises and work hard. Without it, only civil service performance can be expected. Make no mistake about it, remove profit from the picture and men's behavior and productivity are drastically altered; the history of other systems has clearly proved this fact time and again.

How does this fit in with the modern corporate executive who is also expected to work hard and exhibit most of the talents of the entrepreneur? The reality of the situation is that most corporate executives share to some extent in the profits of the corporation. High salaries are warranted only when the corporation makes large profits. Some of the profits of the large corporation filter down throughout the organization; if they fail to do so, organizational behavior will be affected. Profit's major economic function is to provide an incentive for greater productivity and efficiency.

One corporate president said, "When the company makes good money, everybody makes more money. When the company loses money, everybody suffers." Explain what he meant by this statement.

Profit—The Allocator of Resources

Every society has many resources—materials, men, money, machines, technology, skills, and land. One of the basic socioeconomic problems confronting any society is the allocation of its relatively scarce resources among activities—who gets the resources to use? In totalitarian governments the dictator allots resources on the basis of his priorities. In a free-enterprise profit system, profit is the allocator of resources. Men of talent are attracted into enterprises with good profit potentials. Similarly, money is attracted to investments that possess attractive profit potentials. With the money that is so attracted, the talented men buy other needed resources such as land, labor, materials, and whatever equipment is needed. Enterprises that fail to make a good profit are unable to command sufficient resources to sustain operations. Hence, profits are a fundamental allocator of resources.

Profit—The Measure of Efficient Productivity

The major justification for our free-enterprise system is that it is the most efficient, most productive one ever devised by man for meeting his needs. It so happens that the price for the products of many industries is determined in a fairly open market; all firms in that industry receive essentially the same price for their product. In such cases the firm's profit depends almost completely upon its efficiency. The more efficiently it produces its product, the lower its costs; hence, the more profit it realizes. Therefore, in many situations a firm's profits reflect its efficiency. An inefficient firm loses money and is eliminated from the scene, as it should be.

Many New York Stock Exchange brokerage houses lost money in 1969–1970. Explain their losses in terms of this concept of profit as a reward for efficiency.

Profit—The Basis of Growth

The growth of American industry is financed almost entirely by retained earnings. Most large corporations pay out only a small percentage (20-40 percent) of their profits as dividends. They prefer to retain most of their profits to finance their growth.

If American industry is to continue to serve the populace properly, it must grow somewhat faster than the population. Profits are the base for that industrial growth. If no profits were available to feed such growth, then industry would have to tap the money market continually for new funds on which to grow. Unfortunately, without profits money would be extremely scarce, because the funds available in the money market are supplied largely by profits somewhere in the system.

Why does industry prefer to grow on retained earnings rather than on money obtained from the money market?
Why should industry grow faster than population?

Profit—Society's Voice

In a rather direct way, society encourages or discourages certain activities by the profits it bestows upon enterprises engaging in those activities. When society wants better and more powerful wonder drugs, it pays a sufficiently high price to yield high profits, which in turn attracts additional resources into the drug industry, thereby giving society the drugs it demands. Conversely, when society no longer wants a certain enterprise, it creates a situation in which that enterprise finds it difficult to make a profit, thereby ultimately causing the enterprise to fail.

SOURCES OF PROFIT

An enterprise can make profit from one source or a combination of several. The wise executive knows the source from which his profit flows, for this enables him to see the true nature of his enterprise and avoid delusions about the reasons for his prosperity.

Innovation

One of the classical theories of profit maintains that profit is created through innovation. Management innovates something—a new product, a new process, a new way of managing things, or any other improvement on either the cost or revenue side of the business—and thereafter reaps profit from that innovation until either society tires of it or competition nullifies it.

One theory holds that the profits of a firm are being eroded continually by the onslaught of competition and that it is management's continual task to replace such eroded profits with new. This concept of profit erosion deals with innovative profits.

Unquestionably, innovative profits are important in the total profit picture of American industry, but their importance can be overestimated. In many industries innovative profits are short-lived; competition quickly reacts to innovations even though they may be protected by patents.

The profits of the Polaroid Corporation in the past two decades can be attributed to innovation. What will happen when its basic patents expire?

Managerial Acumen

The profits of some firms can be traced to a particularly adept management, one that is able to devise systems that result in profit. True, good management is also innovative, but adept managers have shown an ability to make above-average profits solely through their own skills without applying any particular innovative techniques. Some element of good management must exist in any profit picture, but some management teams are so well recognized for their skills that people invest in them on that basis alone.

Monopoly

Profits can be the result of some sort of monopoly. Indeed, although in a free-enterprise system we officially declare competition to be our goal, in actuality most businessmen constantly seek a monopolistic position. Obviously, the earnings of utility companies are monopoly profits. But monopolies can exist in other things, such as land, location, raw materials, and other cost inputs.

Locational Monopolies   Of special importance are locational monopolies, for a great many businesses derive their profits from being in choice locations. In the oil industry the key to selling gasoline in volume is building service stations in choice locations. Much money and effort are spent on obtaining choice locations.

Raw-Material Monopolies   Some fortunes have been based on the possession of raw-material monopolies. DeBeers Consolidated controls about 80 percent of the world's diamond supply; its profits result largely from this control. Alcoa's early profits were largely the result of its control of rich bauxite deposits.

Frictional Profits

Some firms profit because of marketplace inertia and frictions. Their profits are insufficient to attract competitors. Our system is so large and complex that many small to medium-size firms are able to operate almost unobserved by potential competitors.

If your profits are largely a result of inertia or friction, what might worry you? What could you do to preserve your frictional profits?

Markets are far from perfectly operating mechanisms, so frictional profits can exist for some time.

From what sources does Procter & Gamble derive its profits?

ILLUSORY PROFITS

Profits are not always what they seem to be. Many an administrator has operated for years under the illusion that his enterprise was highly profitable, only to have his final accounting of the venture disclose the bitter truth: what appeared to be profits were no more than illusions. These illusions can take four different forms: inflationary profits, paper profits, accounting profits, and windfall profits.

Inflationary Profits

Inflation covers up a great many managerial misdeeds, for it frequently allows an enterprise to show a profit when it would not have done so had prices not increased. Inflationary profits result from investing money in assets at one price level and selling those assets later at a higher price level.

The Conversion Cycle of Business Operations

The conversion cycle of business operations refers to the basic business principle that one invests money in assets (plants, inventory, and materials) and then converts those assets back into money in the hope that in the end he gets back more than he put into the enterprise. The conversion cycle is the time it takes to make the round trip from cash to cash. Some conversion cycles are extremely short; others take more than a decade. The longer the conversion cycle, the more risks inherent in the operation.

How much control does management have over its conversion cycle of assets? By what means can it shorten it?

Suppose management converts its money into assets at one price level and sells off its assets at a higher price level. The profits resulting from the price increase are not operational profits but rather are profits due solely to inflation. One might ask, "So what? It's all money that the company can spend, isn't it?" Yes and no! Yes, the company has the money now to spend. No, because sometime in the future the price behavior may reverse and cause losses due to deflation. No, because the owner's real assets have not increased.

Although our economy has had a long overall history of inflation and, in total, industry has garnered a great deal of profit from this inflation, still there are many islands of competition in which prices have dropped during certain periods. Managements operating in environments in which prices are volatile frequently find such price behavior to be a far larger determinant of their profit than the efficiency of their operation. Hence, they are forced to take many defensive actions to protect themselves from the vagaries of such price behavior. Such defensive actions include the minimization of inventory, the leasing of fixed assets, and a shortening of the enterprise's conversion cycle of assets.

One might question whether or not inflationary profits are illusory, but if he will remember that when one converts assets into cash he normally reinvests the cash into assets and this second conversion takes place at the higher price level, the answer is very clear. Hence, inflationary profits typically are simply reinvested in the business, if that enterprise is to sustain its level of operations. These profits are not available for distribution unless the enterprise is to be dissolved or cut back. But the government taxes such profits, even though they are not real.

Paper Profits

Paper profits are those one has because of an appreciation in the value of his assets that have yet to be converted into cash. Inflation or some other force increases the value of one's property, be it land, inventory, or stock, and this increased value is reflected on accounting statements even though one has not converted the asset into cash. This is an extremely dangerous situation, for experience shows that paper profits may quickly vanish when one attempts to realize them. Wall Street is replete with speculators who can attest to this phenomenon—men who thought they were millionaires—and were, on paper—until they went to collect their millions by selling out, only to find that the price of their securities had declined considerably. One of the brutal realities of the business world is that one usually tries to cash in his assets at the worst possible time—when things are not going well. Seldom do speculators bail out of a bull market at the top. Seldom does a company sell its assets when all is going well. One should learn to treat paper profits carefully lest he be misled as to his true wealth.

Accounting Profits

Closely akin to paper profits are accounting profits. The difference is that while paper profits have not been realized because the assets have not been converted into cash, the accounting profits are assets that have been converted into cash and a true economic profit realized, but the owner cannot lay his hands on the money, for it has been invested immediately in more assets. This is the typical situation of a growing business that is making a lot of money but is critically short of cash. Since the money is continually being reinvested in assets and more assets, the profits may be illusory if the entrepreneur takes a bad beating on the last conversion cycle. A great many successful conversion cycles can be completely nullified if the last one is a debacle.

Windfall Profits

Windfall profits are the result of some unusual economic event that is not part of the operational routine of the organization. A windfall profit cannot be predicted, nor is it likely to reoccur in exactly the same way. Windfall profits can take an infinite number of forms. Perhaps a company wins a large lawsuit or is able to sell off an obsolete plant or some subsidiary for a profit. Such transactions may yield handsome profits, but one cannot count on them for long-run operations. Financial analysts are very careful to separate one-time or windfall profits from the operational profits of a firm, for they use the latter in forming their forecasts of the company's future profitability. They may not be illusory if one can take the cash, but they are not operational profits.

NONPROFIT OBJECTIVES

Admittedly, in times past, economists paid far too much attention to the role of profit in economic theory and far too little to the nonprofit motives of the businessman. It was far easier to create a logical, rational field of economic theory using profit as the objective than it was to use some nonrational, erratic, nonquantifiable objective as the basis of a logical system. It is difficult to be logical in an illogical system. But there are many seemingly illogical elements in our system of which you should be aware.

Survival

One can make a very strong case that the primary objective of most institutions is survival, not profit. True, one maximizes his profits over the long run by surviving, and one cannot maximize profits if he fails to survive; but businessmen have clearly shown that they usually do not try to maximize their profits, for, in so doing, they frequently must take risks that jeopardize the very survival of the enterprise—something they dare not do. Only a rather inept administrator would make a decision that jeopardized the very existence of the firm when another decision, although not quite as profitable, would result in a respectable profit and not risk the survival of the firm. Truly, survival is one of the objectives of most enterprises, for if they fail to achieve it, little else matters.

Power

Unquestionably some men are motivated by power. They seek control over assets and people. They hold their positions and work as they do, not because they hope to gain all the profits from their activities, but rather because they enjoy the power that they hold over other people and over the course of events. Power can be a good motive or a bad one, depending upon how the individual uses it. Some men are so driven by power that the result is bad for themselves and everyone connected with them. On the other hand, power—when placed in proper perspective—can be a legitimately healthy objective. Certainly some enterprises seek power in the market to make more profit.

Employment

Many business decisions are based upon the employment factor: which decision will provide the most employment? Most modern managements are people-oriented; they are genuinely concerned about the people in the organization and feel a deep responsibility to provide them stable, continuous employment. Consequently, occasions do arise when a company might profitably buy something from an outside source but chooses to perform the service within its own company in order to provide employment for its own people. Companies in small towns often feel this pressure acutely, for if they are forced to lay off workers the results are felt painfully by everyone in the community.

Fun

Business can be fun, and many people engage in it because they enjoy it. Perhaps this is the healthiest motive. What is the wisdom of anyone's pursuing a business vocation he does not enjoy? Life is far too short to be pinned down doing something one dislikes. Many of the recent wheeling and dealing activities of business entrepreneurs can largely be traced to the fun they have in negotiating mergers and playing the role of the big, aggressive businessman.

Service to Society

Some cynics would deny that service is an objective of business concerns, but so many specific incidents of such service can be itemized that we need not spend much time refuting these contentions. Many large corporations are now promoting work-training programs for the economically disadvantaged, largely because they are genuinely interested in serving society in this manner.

> One concept of business holds that one can make a profit in our system only if he provides a service to society; that one should never make profit his objective; rather, profit will flow from service and one should concern himself solely with providing that service.

Conclusion

Do not "put down" profit as a vital motivator and lubricator, for it has provided the means by which we have developed our highly productive and efficient economic system. Do not fall into the trap of thinking that profits are tapped from our income flow by parasitic elements in our society, for such is simply not the case. Profits go to people who are productive, who in turn immediately plow them back into our system in some form, spending them either on consumption or on new productive facilities. Profits do not evaporate. Figure 5-1 is a model of the flow of profit back into the system.

FIGURE 5-1: Profit Flow

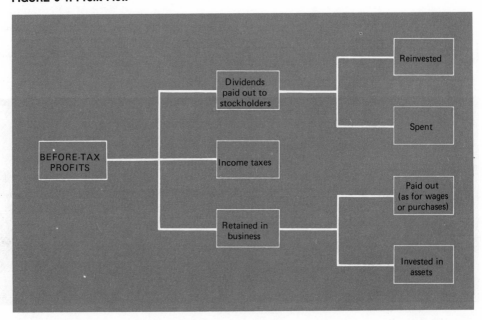

6 Profit-oriented institutions

Thrift may be the handmaid and nurse of Enterprise.
But equally she may not.... For the engine
which drives Enterprise is not Thrift, but Profit.
LORD KEYNES

In this chapter we shall examine the three major forms of business organization. The selection of the form by which one will do business has significant legal, financial, and control implications. Many businessmen have regretted not giving more thought to it at the time they started their enterprises; the price paid for correcting errors at a later date can be stiff.

SOLE PROPRIETORSHIPS

The sole proprietorship is by far the oldest form of business ownership; it has existed since the beginning of time, since each man was considered to be a business in his own right and his business and personal activities were inseparable. The farmer made no distinction between his personal activities and his economic enterprises in growing food.

Numerically, sole proprietorships are still the predominant form of business enterprise in our system, comprising (in the year 1970) 9,126,000 out of a total of 11,566,000 organizations—78 percent. However, sole proprietorships represent a much smaller portion of the total volume of economic activity—only 13 percent. Obviously, they are mostly very small enterprises. Although large operations can be and have been sole proprietorships, their number is small, for just too many practical and legal barriers confront a sole proprietor doing business on any substantial scale.

Characteristics of Sole Proprietorships

A sole proprietorship has the following characteristics: (1) it is easy to form; (2) there are no special legal formalities involved in operations; (3) financing operations can prove burdensome; (4) it may have limited salability; (5) it has no special tax status; (6) management falls upon the shoulders of the owner; (7) duration of operations varies greatly; (8) the number of transactions can vary from one to infinity; (9) business assets are inseparable from personal assets, thereby creating unlimited liability for the owner; and (10) it offers unlimited managerial flexibility.

What is meant by managerial flexibility?

Ease of Formation Whereas a partnership should create its articles of partnership, thereby coming to a mutual agreement, and a corporation must go through the legal formalities of incorporation, little is required of the sole proprietor. Perhaps he may need some licenses, but all forms of ownership need the same licenses. One can begin a sole proprietorship at an instant's whim and go out of business the same way. Legal fees may be incurred in creating other forms of business, but one need not have an attorney to create a sole proprietorship. This is a most attractive characteristic, for the vast majority of people do not know how to perform the legal formalities necessary to institute either partnerships or corporations—although an informed layman can do so if he so desires and is willing to take the risks. It is not recommended that one dispense with legal advice unless finances so dictate.

Legal Aspects The law does not create any special categories for the sole proprietor. While there is a separate body of law for partnerships and corporations, the sole proprietor is largely governed by the law of sales and contracts. He is recognized as the standard in the legal world, partnerships and corporations being the exceptions. If a sole proprietorship is involved in a lawsuit, it is the owner who is sued or does the suing. The law recognizes the man and the business as being one and the same in a sole proprietorship.

Financing   The financial resources available to the sole proprietor are his own wealth, whatever his family may be willing to contribute, and whatever he is able to borrow. Usually these funds are quite limited. Although creditors prefer to deal with a sole proprietor, since they can look to all of the owner's assets for satisfaction of any debts incurred by the business, the wealth of most sole proprietors is too limited to make this an important advantage to the enterprise. In fact, in some areas of endeavor where the law requires that a man operate as a sole proprietor, as in some professions, the wise professional reverses the normal procedure by placing his personal wealth in various corporate holding companies owned by members of his family and keeping only his business in his personal name, thereby attempting to prevent claims against the business from being applied to his personal wealth. To succeed in these tricky legal matters one needs the help of a competent lawyer.

Why are men of wealth concerned about legal liability and ways of protecting their assets from it?
By what means can a sole proprietor protect his personal assets?

Salability   An excellent merchant built up a highly enviable men's wear business under his own name—Ginsley & Company. After operating it for twenty years, he wanted to sell it. An enterprising young man desired to purchase the store, but he stipulated as a condition of sale that he would work on the floor for six weeks before making his final decision. After four weeks the potential buyer said, "No way! There's no way that I'm going to buy this business from you, for most of it hinges upon you and your name. Why should I pay $100,000 for your business when most of that value is represented by the goodwill connected with you and your name? When I own it, the goodwill naturally will follow you." So the buyer left the merchant still owning and operating his business. Sole proprietorships developed around one's personality and name have limited salability.

Taxes   While the sole proprietor is taxed only as an individual and the various governing bodies do not levy special taxes against him, still he is at a disadvantage in certain areas of income tax law. Corporations are allowed deductions for employee benefits and other personal expenditures, whereas the IRS looks unfavorably on any sole proprietor's taking such deductions. The corporation has income-tax advantages that offset the few special taxes levied against it, such as franchise fees.

At one time sole proprietorships had a theoretical advantage over corporations in that profit was taxed only once, but this is now theoretical, for an individual can incorporate and select taxation under Subchapter S as a proprietorship if he meets certain requirements.[1] Even so, if one man incorporates and does not choose Subchapter S, he can usually avoid double taxation by withdrawing profits as salary. Few proprietorships have such high profits that they cannot be legally withdrawn as salary, but there are tax dangers if the enterprise is highly profitable.

[1] Some states do not recognize Subchapter S corporations; therefore, in such states Subchapter S corporations reporting profits are subject to state income taxes, if they *choose* to show a profit.

Why did Congress create the situation in which certain corporations could avoid paying corporate income taxes?

Can you surmise what qualifications one must meet to qualify as a Subchapter S corporation?

Management   Sole proprietorships have great difficulty attracting the number and caliber of people needed to form an efficient management team. Typically, the owner is forced to actively manage the business, and he usually has difficulty in attracting employees of sufficient quality to entrust much responsibility to their shoulders. The reasons are easy to understand. What future has a man working for a sole proprietor? His chances of ever owning the business appear slight; usually a man who wants to own a business will work for someone else only until he has acquired enough skills, knowledge, and capital to establish it. Sole proprietorships tend to have a short life, so a man cannot look forward to a career with one, for at any time the owner may decide to sell or just close up shop. Moreover, few sole proprietorships offer the fringe benefits now available to employees of most large corporations, nor can they usually pay the wages obtainable elsewhere. The typical proprietorship today has a difficult time competing in the labor market.

Duration   A sole proprietorship may exist for a single transaction, or for one day, or for a short period of time. At best, the proprietorship only lasts for the lifetime of its owner, but more typically the owner decides to sell when he tires of the battle and feels he has had enough.

Unlimited Liability   Unquestionably the most important and significant characteristic of a sole proprietorship is its unlimited liability; *the owner is liable for all the debts of the business to the full extent of his assets.* If the business fails, he may be in personal bankruptcy and can be left destitute with only the minimum assets provided by law. Truly, when a man goes into business with the proprietorship form of organization he risks his entire estate. For this reason alone, men of any wealth absolutely refuse to have anything to do with sole-proprietorship forms of organization. They refuse to expose their entire estate to the high risks of business endeavors.

Present-Day Usage

Sole proprietorships are used today mostly for very small retail-type operations or for business ventures of short duration, perhaps for only a few transactions. Certainly most sophisticated businessmen today shun sole proprietorships, for this form of organization offers few substantial benefits and a great many disadvantages—largely in the areas of unlimited liability, difficulties in financing and salability, and tax practice.

PARTNERSHIPS

The Uniform Partnership Act sets forth the legal framework governing partnerships. One could make a case that a partnership is nothing more than an aggregation of sole proprietorships, with special legal provisions regulating the relationships between the partners and how they conduct business. But that would be simplifying the case somewhat, for a partnership is something more than the summation of the people comprising it.

Historically, partnerships are as old as proprietorships; very early in history men learned that by combining their talents and resources they could accomplish proportionately more than they could individually. It is a case of one + one equaling more than 2.

Types of Partnerships

In the usual type of partnership two or more people join together to operate a business, which is called a general partnership. However, special categories of partnerships deserve some consideration: limited partnerships, silent partnerships, and secret partnerships. (See Appendix B for definitions.)

How many partners can there be in a partnership?

Unique Characteristics

While partnerships have many of the characteristics of the sole proprietorship, they do have some unique characteristics of their own.

Complementary Skills   Theoretically, the soundest basis upon which people can form a partnership is their possession of complementary skills. Thus each uses his skills to complement the other's. One common combination is one partner with a sales ability and two other partners with skills in finance and production, respectively. They are able to keep out of one another's hair as each does his own job with all the motivation of a sole proprietor. The partnership is one answer to the proprietorship's problem of obtaining highly competent help. Whereas the proprietor may not be able to hire anyone with requisite skills to do certain jobs in his enterprise, he may be able to attract such talented men on the basis of a partnership. Most enduring partnerships have as a bonding cement the need of each man for the others' skills.

Liability for Others' Acts   One of the unique aspects of a general partnership is that any or all partners can be held legally liable for the actions of any one partner. Thus an essentially dangerous situation is created, in which an individual can be bankrupted through no fault of his own. This unlimited joint liability has made partnerships a most unattractive form of business operation. Indeed, many business advisors categorically deny that partnerships are a viable form of business operation, recommending instead that all businesses be incorporated.

In recent years partnerships have been restricted largely to professionals, such as lawyers, doctors, CPA's, and brokers who had previously been forced by law to operate as partnerships rather than as corporations. This legal environment is changing rapidly in most states, and professional corporations are coming to fore as the form of business operation for such professional partnerships. This is an example of how the law changes to accommodate changing situations.

Volatile Relationships   Most partnerships, sooner or later—and mostly sooner—come to an end when the partners disagree. Human nature being what it is, seldom are people able to live and work in a relationship as close as partners without having substantial disagreements. When such agonies cannot be resolved, the partnership is dissolved, frequently to the disadvantage of all, for seldom is a partnership marketable.

Taxation of Partnerships   Partnerships incur no special taxes not levied against proprietorships, and partnership income is treated as personal income, with each partner's share of the income being reported on the special partnership income tax form.

Articles of Partnership   While the agreement between partners need not be put into writing, it is highly advisable to do so for protection and clarity of agreement.

Present-Day Usage

Partnerships today are limited mostly to the professional fields of medicine, law, accounting, insurance, and stock brokerage. The major limiting factor is that the partnership really has no advantage over a corporation and does have the many disadvantages previously listed. If one can avoid forming a partnership, he should do so.

Limited partnerships are currently being used extensively in oil well drilling funds, real estate syndicates, cattle feeding and breeding enterprises, and land speculation because of the special tax shelter advantages offered to the partnership form of business organization in which certain costs incurred by the partnership are passed on directly to the partners, thus allowing them to deduct such partnership costs from their other income.

THE CORPORATION

A corporation is a fictitious legal person distinct from the actual persons connected with it. It is a creation of the state. No fiduciary relationship exists between the corporation and its stockholders, who may deal with the corporation in the same manner and to the same extent as with any other individual. A stockholder is not an agent or a representative of the corporation, and courts recognize the distinct separateness of the stockholders from the corporation, even though one man may own all of the stock of a corporation. If, however, the stockholders have used a corporate organization as a cover for questionable transactions, courts have been known to disregard the corporate entity and hold the stockholders liable for the action of the corporation.

History

Although the business corporation was recognized in Roman times and was known in England prior to 1600, it did not play an important economic role until the seventeenth century, when the colonization of America and the general increase in economic activity throughout Europe gave impetus to the creation of corporations. As a result of the industrial revolution, for the first time there were people who had money to invest, but they were extremely reluctant to assume the unlimited liability connected with partnerships. Some type of business organization was needed in which such investors could risk only the capital they invested. Although an attempt was made to accomplish this goal through the creation of the joint-stock company (a company composed of many members that attempted to acquire by contract many of the attributes of the corporation), it had little success in obtaining the desired limited liability for its investors until Parliament in 1844 passed the Joint-Stock Company Registration Act, which granted limited liability to investors in joint-stock companies.

On the American continent the same problem was developing: people in Europe had capital to invest in the New World, but they were unwilling to assume the unlimited liability connected with partnerships. Attempts were made to form organizations that would give investors their desired limited liability through the use of the joint-stock company and the Massachusetts Trust; however, the corporation proved to be the most viable form of business organization, for it gave the investor not only limited liability but also a voice in management. At first, in the United States, corporations obtained their charters from the state legislatures, which were careful to limit the powers of each corporation to the actual needs of the proposed business venture.

New York State enacted the first general corporation statute in 1811, under which any group of persons complying with the procedures set forth would be granted a corporate charter. Although other states followed the lead of New York, the business corporation as we know it today did not come into prominence until after the Civil War, when the statutes were liberalized and broadened. Corporations operating businesses of special public interest—such as insurance companies, banks, savings and loan companies, or public utilities—are incorporated under special statutes, which are far more restrictive than the general corporation law.

Forming a Corporation

In planning the organization of a corporation one should first decide in which state he wishes to incorporate. This makes a big difference in costs and restrictions, since state statutes vary considerably in their permissiveness and regulations. If one plans to do business primarily within one state, he is usually best advised to incorporate in that state unless he has strong reasons for doing otherwise.

The factors involved in selecting a state in which to incorporate are: the initial cost of incorporation, the annual tax and sundry fees imposed on corporations, transfer taxes on corporation stock, types of stock that may be issued, stockholders' rights, limitations on the powers of the directors, and provisions governing the management of the enterprise. One would want to know such things as what limitations are placed on the powers of the directors, whether or not they have the power to adopt and amend by-laws without stockholder approval, and whether or not they can mortgage the assets of the organization without stockholder action. One would also want to know the general liability of directors and management for actions performed in the course of administering the activities of the corporation. The states of Delaware and New Jersey have developed a national reputation for having permissive corporate laws that allow a corporation's management a great deal of latitude in how it can conduct the firm's affairs.

The way in which the peculiarities of a state's corporate law can sometimes play a vital role is illustrated by the case of the Irvine Company, the southern California land giant. One minority stockholder—Mrs. Joan Irvine Smith, owner of about 22 percent of the company's stock—has been able to obtain board representation and affect that company's plans in face of vigorous opposition by the company's management because it was formed under the laws of West Virginia, which provide that the owner of more than 20 percent of a corporation's stock may sue in court to have a corporation dissolved for various reasons. Not wishing to risk such a court suit, the Irvine Company has had to make concessions to Mrs. Smith. This is a rare instance, for under the laws of most states minority stockholders have few rights; they are largely at the mercy of the controlling stockholders or management.

If one plans to incorporate in one state but do business in another state, then he must register as a foreign corporation in the state in which he is not chartered. If a corporation operates in all states, it must register in all but the one in which it is incorporated.

Articles of Incorporation

The Articles of Incorporation set forth the basic structure of the corporation, as illustrated in Figure 6-1. While a lawyer is usually retained to create a corporation, and he will do so for a fixed fee of perhaps $250 to $500, it is not legally necessary.

The procedures for filing the Articles of Incorporation are set forth in detail in the state statutes. In the state of California, one must send the executed Articles of Incorporation to the Secretary of State in Sacramento with the necessary fees. Additional things must be done if the corporation's stock is to be sold to the public.

Incorporators   Usually there must be three or more incorporators, people of lawful age, a majority of whom are citizens of the United States, to execute the Articles of Incorporation.

Name and Seal   This can pose a problem, because a name currently used by another corporation in the state cannot be selected. Normally, the corporate name must include the word "corporation" or "incorporated" or some abbreviation, such as "Inc." or "Ltd.," to serve warning to creditors that the concern's management is not personally liable for the firm's debts.

Purposes of the Corporation   The purposes of a corporation usually are stated in broad, general terms to give maximum latitude in its operations. If the purposes are too narrowly defined, the company's directors may be subject to suit if their acts later prove to be outside the scope of the purposes for which the corporate charter was granted. Such acts are called *ultra vires* acts.

Financial Structure   The Articles of Incorporation set forth in specific detail the kinds of stocks to be issued, the value, preemptive rights, voting rights, and the preferences as to earnings and assets.

Management   The Articles of Incorporation set forth the general plan of the organization, such as the number of directors the corporation shall have, how the bylaws will be amended, the provision for stockholders and directors meetings, and the time and place of such meetings.

ARTICLES OF INCORPORATION

of

_____

Under the Laws of the State of California

We, the undersigned, have this day voluntarily associated ourselves together for the purpose of forming a corporation under the laws of the State of California, and we do hereby certify:

ARTICLE I

The name of the corporation is: _____

_____

ARTICLE II

The corporation's purpose is primarily to engage in the specific business of _____

_____

ARTICLE III

In addition to the foregoing primary purpose, the purposes for which said corporation is formed are as follows:

To engage in any business whatsoever, either as principal or agent or both as a partnership, which said corporation may deem convenient or proper in furtherance of any of the purposes hereinabove mentioned or otherwise; to conduct its business in this state, in other states, in the District of Columbia, in the territories and possessions of the United States, and in foreign countries; and to have and to exercise all powers authorized by the laws of the State of California under which said corporation is formed, whether expressly set forth in Article II or Article III or not, as such laws are now in effect or may at any time hereafter be amended.

The foregoing statement of purposes shall be construed both as a statement of purposes and of powers, and the statements contained in each clause shall, except where otherwise expressed, not be limited or restricted by reference to or inference from the provisions of any other clause.

ARTICLE IV

The County in the State of California where the principal office for the transaction of the business of the corporation is located is the County of _____ .

(Page 1)

ARTICLE V

The number of directors of the corporation is _____ , provided that the number of such directors may from time to time be changed by amendment of the By-Laws of this corporation; that the names and addresses of the persons who are hereby appointed to act as first directors of the corporation are:

NAMES   ADDRESSES

_____   _____
_____   _____
_____   _____
_____   _____

ARTICLE VI

The total number of shares which the corporation is authorized to issue is _____ shares. The aggregate par value of said shares is $ _____ , and the par value of each share is $ _____ . (If no par shares are to be authorized and issued, omit the foregoing sentence and in its place insert "Each share shall be without par value.") No distinction shall exist between the shares of the corporation or between the holders thereof.*

ARTICLE VII

That the directors shall have no right to assess the stock of the corporation for any purpose whatsoever, and after the original subscription therefor is paid, the stock shall be non-assessable. Any and all actions required or permitted to be taken by the Board of Directors under Division 1 of the California Corporations Code, may be taken without a meeting if all members of the Board shall individually consent in writing to such action. The stockholders shall be liable for the indebtedness of the corporation to the amount of their stock subscribed and unpaid and no more.

IN WITNESS WHEREOF, we, the undersigned, constituting the incorporators of this corporation, including all the persons named above as the first directors of this corporation, have executed these Articles of Incorporation on this _____ day of _____ , 19____ .

_____   _____
_____   _____
_____   _____

STATE OF CALIFORNIA

COUNTY OF_____

On _____ , 19____ , before me, the undersigned, a Notary Public in and for said State personally appeared _____

_____

_____

_____ and _____ known
to me to be the persons whose names are subscribed to the foregoing Articles of Incorporation, and acknowledged to me that they executed the same.

WITNESS my hand and official seal.   _____

_____

NAME (Typed or Printed)
Notary Public in and for said State.
(NOTARIAL SEAL)

*If more than one class of shares is contemplated, in place of the foregoing insert the information required by Corporations Code Section 303 or Section 304.

(Page 2)

Bylaws

The bylaws of the corporation set forth the rules by which it will be operated. Most managerial matters are included in the bylaws rather than in the Articles of Incorporation because bylaws usually are easier to amend.

Board of Directors

The top governing authority of a corporation may consist of any number of people, but most statutes require a minimum of three. While the board must meet at least annually, in most substantial corporations they meet at least quarterly. When a board of directors is a working body that participates significantly in the management of the corporation's affairs, the board may meet monthly or even more often. There is little uniformity in the duties of a board except that it is required to elect the corporation's officers and approve changes in the corporation's financial structure. Board approval is almost mandatory in such matters as changes in capital stock, flotation of new securities, borrowing funds, selling assets, or any other major transaction seriously affecting the company's financial well-being. A working board of directors is concerned with approving operating budgets, monitoring managerial performance, and establishing broad strategic policies, such as goals, businesses in which the corporation shall engage, and other such matters of critical importance.

For the most part, in most large corporations the board of directors has little real power in the management of the corporation. In many instances they are little more than rubber stamps for management, existing largely to fulfill the legal requirements that a board of directors must exist and meet occasionally.

Officers

The management of a corporation rests in the hands of its officers, who are selected by the board of directors. While the law requires that a corporation must have a president and a secretary, the creation of other managerial posts, such as vice-presidencies, is usually left to the discretion of the board of directors. Normally, the officers of a corporation are provided for in the bylaws.

Meetings

The law requires that a stockholders' meeting be held at least once a year for the purpose of electing directors. Special stockholders' meetings are called when either the law or the corporation's articles or bylaws require stockholder approval for some action. Stockholder approval is universally required for such actions as mergers, dissolution, or other such significant matters.

The method by which stockholders elect directors is set forth in the Articles of Incorporation and the company's bylaws. Normally the stockholders have either cumulative or noncumulative voting rights. If the incorporators want to protect the rights of minority stockholders, they will set up cumulative voting, so that each stockholder has as many votes for each of his shares as there are directors to be elected, but he can vote all of those votes for one man. Suppose a minority stockholder owns 10,000 shares of voting common stock and three directors are to be elected; that stockholder has 30,000 votes. He can vote them all in favor of one man for one directorship, or he can distribute them in any way he desires among the three seats to be elected. The purpose of cumulative voting is to give minority stockholders the ability to elect a proportionate number of directors to a company's board.

Under noncumulative voting the majority stockholders can elect all of the directors. Since the same stockholder is allowed only 10,000 votes for each seat to be elected, his votes are overwhelmed by those of the majority in the election held for each seat. Noncumulative voting helps majority stockholders to freeze out minority stockholders from any participation in corporation affairs.

What are the advantages to a minority stockholder of at least being on the board of directors?

There are a great many pros and cons to each of these alternatives, but usually management prefers not to have dissident minority stockholders as directors, so cumulative voting is a rarity. It usually is put into the Articles of Incorporation at the insistence of the minority stockholders at the time of organization, if such stockholders have sufficient power to do so. However, the power of a minority stockholder on a board of directors can still be almost nil, for the majority directors can persistently outvote him. About all such a minority seat on a board does is keep the minority stockholder better informed on the affairs of the corporation, thereby allowing him a little latitude in protecting his interests.

The Modern Large Corporation

Our discussion so far has presented the theoretical concept of the corporation as it exists in the eyes of the law. Reality is another matter. A strong case can be made that there are really several distinctly different types of corporations for profit. First, there is the large, publicly owned corporation with which one most frequently comes in contact, as typified by those in the nation's largest 500. Second, there is the so-called close corporation, owned by a few people, whose stock is not publicly for sale. It differs sharply from the General Motors and IBM corporate concept and deserves separate treatment, for many of the principles that apply to a large corporation simply are not applicable to the close corporation. Third, there is the one-man corporation, in which a proprietor has incorporated himself to gain various legal and tax advantages. Some of these one-man corporations are more appropriately termed "family corporations," because one's family owns the stock. Sometimes all the various assets of a family are owned by a corporation that acts merely as a holding company.

Ownership   While in corporate theory the stockholders own the company, the fact is that in large, publicly held companies a stockholder has a right to do only three things: (1) to vote his stock according to whatever provisions are made for it; (2) to receive dividends when voted by the board; and (3) to sell his stock. The provision for voting is usually an academic one, the individual stockholder's vote being quite meaningless because management has sufficient proxies to control completely the election of directors. The stockholder of a modern large corporation has no role in that company's management. This leaves him only the last two rights—those of receiving dividends and selling his stock; in recent years the latter right seems to have been more prized than the former. A great number of investors seem to be more interested in buying a stock for the profit they will receive from reselling it than for the dividends it may pay them. One could philosophize at length about this development, but that is presently the way the game is being played.

Why has the right to receive dividends become less important to many investors than the right to sell the stock?

Control   For the most part, the control of a large corporation rests in the hands of an incumbent management that is self-perpetuating. Management picks its own successors from the young men it hires for its management training programs and nurtures them up through the ranks so that eventually they can take the place of retiring officers. For the most part, managements of large corporations are closed systems in which the policy of promotion from within is followed very strictly. Control of these corporations is threatened only when management's performance has been found to be seriously wanting. Managements do manage to get into trouble, and when they do, groups of investors stand ready to challenge their control of the corporation through tender offers and proxy fights. Such battles for control are not easy or cheap; only men of great wealth can play this game. The small investor is merely a pawn in any battle for control of a large corporation.

What events are likely to lead to the unseating of a professional management team?

Board of Directors   For the most part the board of directors of a large corporation merely rubber-stamps its approval of management's actions. Usually the basic function such boards perform is the selection of the company's president. Only under extreme provocation does a board throw out incumbent management. There are several reasons for this dilution of the theoretical supremacy of the board of directors in the management of a company. First, the average director, if he is not an officer of the company, has little knowledge of what is going on in the firm other than what management tells him; he is a captive of management through the communications system. Second, the average director is not paid enough nor does he put in enough time to make himself competent to participate in management. Third, many men's motives for becoming directors lie largely in the area of prestige and connections. They really do not care to participate actively in the management of the company.

Consequently, for all but a few large companies, the board of directors is a fiction that exists mainly because the law says it must. Boards have little to do with the management of a company. Indeed, Mr. Lynn Townsend, formerly president of Avis, in his best-selling book, *Up the Organization,* thoroughly castigated directors with the statement that in all of his years as a president, he failed to hear one intelligent remark from one.

This need not be so; management could—through policy changes—create an effective, working board of directors that could provide it with some help. Few managers, however, have sufficient scope and are sufficiently secure to be interested in building up the power of their directors. Most presidents strongly prefer to run their own show and to restrain the power of the board.

Quasi-Public Fiduciary Theory

Because stockholders do not truly own and control the affairs of a corporation, an interesting theory was put forth in the 1930s that the large corporation is owned by the public. The theory is based upon the premise that a company such as General Motors, IBM, AT&T, or Standard Oil is so vital to the welfare of society that the public has acquired a quasi-ownership interest in it. This forms part of the theoretical justification for government intervention in what once were considered to be managerial prerogatives. The public interest has become so vested in the welfare of these organizations that they have acquired a public status. Indeed, some social prognosticators see our society becoming a conglomeration of a few huge corporate bureaucracies that have practically all the manifestations of government. These corporations may become little more than extensions of the government, thoroughly regulated or managed by its dictates.

What dangers are presented to our system by the concentration of economic activity under the management of fifty huge corporations?
If one wished to prevent the large concentration of economic power in the hands of a few corporate giants, what governmental policies would he advocate?
What forces in our society seem to encourage the formation of these corporate giants?

Reasons for Corporate Size

The forces creating huge corporations are well recognized. First, probably their largest advantage is their ability to attract financial resources—they can lay their hands on huge amounts of money more easily and cheaply than smaller competitors. The lower cost of abundant capital gives them tremendous competitive advantages.

Second, these large amounts of money are needed because our complex technocracy requires huge investments in plant, equipment, and research for successful operation in most key industries today; gone is the day when a man could enter most industries for a paltry million dollars. In some enterprises one must be prepared to invest hundreds of millions merely to get the venture underway. Small corporations cannot build the SST,* develop nuclear power plants, or construct entire cities. It takes huge accumulations of capital in the hands of one management to accomplish the things our system demands.

Third, large corporations find it easier to attract men because of the security and rewards it can provide talented individuals. Moreover, a talented person can accomplish things in the large company that he would be unable to do in a small corporation

*Nor evidently may big ones.

because of the resources placed at his disposal. Giants such as IBM and General Motors can attract people that the smaller company finds difficult to hire.

Fourth, unquestionably the large corporation gains disproportionate political power at all levels of government. Governments are willing to do things for large corporations that they refuse to do for smaller ones. The political power of a large firm locating a plant in a small town is awesome to behold. Its management can obtain concessions from political authorities who run roughshod over smaller entrepreneurs, harrassing them with many petty regulations and nuisances. This political advantage is not to be underestimated, for it extends to top levels; large companies have been given special tax considerations for certain problems peculiar to themselves. Firms such as General Motors and IBM are so important to our economy that the government cannot allow them to get into serious economic difficulty. When Lockheed got into trouble financially through mismanagement, the government had to bail them out to prevent a bankruptcy that would severely damage a significant sector of the economy. When a corporation becomes sufficiently large, its interests and that of the government and society *almost* coincide. Whereas the government will allow a small enterprise to fold because the impact on the economy would be negligible, it is not in a similar position when the size of the enterprise is such that the economic well-being of the system is jeopardized. The agonies of the Penn Central bankruptcy of 1970 are a case in point.

Why should the government bail out the creditors of Penn Central railroad rather than letting the courts wash them out through bankruptcy?

Fifth, modern markets are so big and the cost of distributing to them so large—because of expensive advertising media such as television—that only companies with large resources can afford to compete in many markets. Mere size influences market participation. If one cannot make enough noise in the marketplace, he will be lost in the competitive din, and it takes much money to make the appropriate noises. The cost of a new-product failure can amount to millions of dollars; a small company cannot undertake the risks of many new-product introductions.

Sixth, technology has become so complex and so expensive that large expenditures must be made on basic research, and only large corporations can afford to make such investments. The small company must live off the research of the giants. The president of one small textile mill, upon being advised that he should establish a research department, replied, "I have the best research department in the world. I call it du Pont." He was referring to the fact that du Pont spends millions of dollars a year doing research on textiles and that his small textile company could not begin to do the research needed, so he relied upon the research efforts of the big companies, knowing that they would sell the results to him in the form of, say, a finished synthetic fiber, such as Orlon or Dacron.

Problems of Corporate Bigness

While the previous discussion might lead one to believe that life in the big corporation is a bowl of cherries, the large corporation in fact suffers serious operational disadvantages—disadvantages that allow the smaller competitor to exist and prosper.

First, unquestionably the large corporation has a much higher overhead to sustain than its smaller competitor. The very nature of a large corporation's management requires a huge staff of administrative specialists, all of whom cost a great deal of money. The corporate headquarters of General Dynamics in New York requires that all division contracts contain a 6 percent overhead charge, to be forwarded to New York; that is the cost of General Dynamics' New York office. This charge is above and beyond the overhead in its various plants. If the big corporation is to prosper, in theory it must obtain lower production or marketing costs to offset its higher overhead costs, but it cannot always do so. Consequently, many large corporations find themselves with relatively high operational costs, beneath which smaller competitors prosper. Some economists claim that most of our large corporations are now operating at a level of increasing costs; that is, the larger they become, the higher their unit costs will be. Clearly, this is economically undesirable.

What evidences would indicate whether or not a company's costs are increasing with increased volume?

Second, large corporations, by their very size and multilayered organizational hierarchy, tend to become quite inflexible. It takes them a long time to react to changed conditions. Sometimes they fail to react at all—a failure that sows the seeds of destruction. Most smaller companies pride themselves on their abilities to react fast to market requirements and respond to the demands of the individual consumer, even though he may be relatively small. The large corporation inherently finds such reactive capability difficult to sustain. The railroads probably provide the classic example of this type of inflexibility in management. In their heyday, they represented the largest corporations in the nation and they wielded their power with awesome results, but they became so inflexible that they were incapable of meeting the changing transportation needs of our system.

Third, men of creative instincts frequently find life in the big corporation stifling. A great many studies testify that rather traditional, acquiescent behavior is required of one if he is to progress up through the ranks of management in the large corporation. The man who emerges at the top of such organizational pyramids is frequently called an "organization man," which has become a synonym for an intellectually sterile conformist. Men of great imagination and creativity are "turned off" by the behavior required of them in most large organizations; they frequently seek the more permissive atmosphere of the smaller corporation where they can sing their own tunes. Since experience indicates that economic well-being depends upon new ideas and creativity, without such men an organization will eventually perish. One of the dilemmas of large corporations is how to attract and keep men of creative bent.

How can large organizations hold creative people?

Fifth, controlling widespread and diverse activities is a major managerial problem. In recent years such giants as Litton Industries, General Dynamics, and LTV have encountered serious financial difficulties because they were unable to control properly the activities of their various divisions. The divisions lost a lot of money before top management was aware of it. Truly, the art of managing large companies rests largely in the art of controlling operations—keeping costs and revenues in proper relationship to each other. Control problems seem to multiply exponentially with growth in corporate size.

THE CLOSE CORPORATION

The close corporation is defined by Subchapter S in the Internal Revenue Code as a corporation with ten or fewer stockholders whose stock is not publicly traded. The IRS sets forth some other qualifications that a corporation must meet to be taxed as a partnership, but essentially the close corporation is owned by a few stockholders whose stock is not traded publicly.

The close corporation is largely confined to smaller enterprises in which large financial resources are not required. A great many local businesses are close corporations.

The reality of the close corporation is difficult to discover, for most corporate theory does not apply. First, unless one owns control (51 percent) of a close corporation, he may well own nothing. Corporation law is such that a minority stockholder in a close corporation can be completely frozen out of all earnings and dividends and may even find it difficult to get his money back. The minority stockholders in a close corporation own what the majority stockholders say they own; their rights in court are few, particularly if management carefully attends to the legal aspects of operation. A great many people who have been minority investors in close corporations have learned this reality to their sorrow, for almost inevitably the men in a close corporation fall out. Greed dictates that if a close corporation is successful, its most powerful stockholder will manage to squeeze out the others. This is so much the rule in close corporations that it has caused astute investors to refuse to invest in such situations unless they control 50 percent of the stock or have absolute veto power over all acts of the board of directors.

Second, investments in close corporations are highly nonliquid. If one wishes to sell, he has no ready market or established market price upon which he can rely. Frequently the only people to whom he can sell are fellow stockholders, and they are seldom willing to give him true value for his stock, for they know very well that they are in a favorable bargaining position. Hence, one should never put money in a close corporation if he may need it back. Liquidating an investment in a close corporation can be most difficult, particularly when one does not have control of it.

Third, financing the close corporation can be difficult, for lenders demand that the individual stockholders personally sign for all indebtedness of the corporation; they fully realize the leeway owners of a close corporation have for stripping the corporation of its assets, leaving creditors with nothing but a skeleton to sue in court.

Going Public

If a close corporation is successful and grows, sooner or later management considers "going public"—that is, selling stock to the general public. There are cogent reasons for this. First, going public is frequently the only means by which its stockholders can liquidate their investment; they must sell the stock of a successful corporation to the public in order to recognize the values inherent in it. Second, because of income and estate tax laws, it is highly advantageous to establish a market value on one's stock, rather than have the government establish it for you in case of death. Third, substantial profit frequently can be realized by going public with a highly successful close corporation, because investors may be willing to pay a premium price to be let in on a successful small corporation.

The one-man and the family corporation or holding company are forms of close corporations, but their purposes, forms, and characteristics are so diverse that we cannot cover them meaningfully here. They are almost entirely legal maneuvers performed by individuals to gain legal and tax advantages.

Conclusion

Considerable thought should be given to the form of legal organization within which one chooses to do business. Mistakes made in the beginning can prove costly in the end. The theory underlying the various legal forms of organization varies considerably from the reality of the situations, and it is reality that ultimately controls the play. The realities of the small, closely held corporation are seldom written about, and the problems of partnerships are too complex to summarize easily. The average man contemplating the beginning of business enterprise of some substance should seriously examine the advantages that can be his if he incorporates his venture.

PART

MANAGEMENT

PROFIT- seeking institutions must have someone at the controls, running things, guiding activities; we call it managing the enterprise.

The manager and his managing techniques are so vital to the ultimate success of the venture that many observers give them full credit for whatever success or failure is forthcoming.

Yes, there is a science of management—but let us not be misled into thinking that it is not also an art, a most delicate one.

7 The Administrator

*Nothing causes a prince to be so much esteemed
as great enterprises and giving proof of prowess.*
MACHIAVELLI

A salient characteristic of our system has been the rise of the professional administrator of its institutions. This is reflected in many ways, as in the proliferation of special schools teaching business administration, hospital administration, hotel and restaurant administration, public administration, and a multitude of other special skills in the administration of most significant institutions in our system.

Unquestionably the large growth in the size of all our institutions—corporations, government, and nonprofit institutions—has created a huge demand for people to administer them. This development has several sources. The professional administrator, moreover, has been called upon to be almost a trustee of the assets entrusted to his management.

Second, because of this vastly increased need for professional managers, a great deal of study has been devoted in the past three decades to the administrator and his job. Courses in management and human relations have been extremely popular. While we have learned a great deal about how the administrator does his job and what behavior seems most likely to lead to success, we still have much to learn.

Third, as a nation we have become more sensitive to how our institutions are operated. In bygone decades few people cared how the management of General Motors ran its business. Now we have become vitally interested, because we realize the impact of such management decisions on each of us personally.

Finally, students of business have broadened their scope of study to include the behavioral aspects of management, whereas at one time they were almost totally concerned with its mechanics—how to sell, how to produce, and how to keep records.

ADMINISTRATION: A DISTINCT SKILL[1]

Administration is an art, not a science. As no two artists or composers use identical methods to achieve successful results, neither do administrators find solace in a uniform set of ways in which they should behave. Administration is an art in which the administrator mixes his personality and philosophies with the personalities and philosophies of his superiors and subordinates within the context of the work situation to achieve the desired results.

The results of administrative acts are not always predictable, and predictability is one of the requirements of a science. One administrator can do a certain thing and get certain results while another man can do exactly the same thing but realize different results. It is this artistic uncertainty of administrative behavior that makes the administrator's job so challenging. Truly, administration is no place for a man who likes to work in a nice, finite, predictable world.

Technical Ability Insufficient

Although many men of outstanding technical abilities do make good administrators, the possession of technical talent does not necessarily make its owner a good manager of men. Witness the sports world, where many successful coaches (administrators) were only average players. In the sales field, it is widely recognized that the best salesman may not make the best sales manager. The very factors that allow a man to become an outstanding salesperson can be the ones that cause him to fail as an

[1] The material in this section is based on Chapter 2 of William J. Stanton and Richard H. Buskirk, *Management of the Sales Force* (Homewood, Ill.: Richard D. Irwin, Inc., 1969).

administrator. Most highly successful salesmen have in common a great liking for extensive personal contact with customers. However, the successful sales manager must attend to a considerable amount of paper work—planning, controlling, and evaluating—in the home office. Also, many successful salesmen have strongly aggressive personalities, which can be a liability to the administrator who must work closely with his superiors, equals, and subordinates. Hence, in evaluating a person for an administrative position, one must make certain that the man's proficiency at a technical skill does not overly influence his evaluation as a possible administrator; they are two separate and distinct skills.

Certainly some degree of technical proficiency is needed. The executive who lacks technical competency is continually at the mercy of his subordinates. He is unable to evaluate their technical competency and, hence, the soundness of their recommendations or methods of operation.

The individual who has acquired administrative abilities is indeed fortunate, because he will find these talents usable in the management of many organizations. The recent cross-migration of business and government administrators bears out the point.

Universality of Principles in Administering Human Activities

Most human activities such as war, business, or sports are goal-directed—their participants are seeking to achieve something. Such behavior is performed by groups of individuals who have joined together in the belief that they have the same goals and that as a group they are more likely to achieve those goals. If any semblance of efficiency and orderly progress toward the goals is to be realized, the group's activities must be managed—that is, planned, organized, and controlled. The fundamental principles underlying the guidance of these activities are basically the same.

One has but to read the memoirs of famous military leaders or coaches to recognize that the basic principles underlying their successes are no different from those supporting business statesmen. Throughout his autobiography, General Ulysses S. Grant was far more concerned about the qualities of his subordinates than he was about military strategy and tactics. Talk with a winning coach about the reasons for his success and you will hear about his subordinates, his training program, his recruiting and selection procedures, and the creation of morale. The fundamental principles underlying success in administering all types of human behavior are essentially the same.

It is this universality of management principles that allows the administrator to transfer his abilities from one job to another with relative ease. It is also the existence of these management principles that makes administration a distinct skill separate from technical abilities.

Administrative Skills Can Be Learned

Many administrators in previous years claimed that administrative talents were inherent or inborn, but this view is contradicted by the many instances of people who have acquired such skills through diligent study. Administrative skills can be learned by those who are willing to put forth the effort and who are perceptive enough to learn the lessons available from many sources, both academically and from the school of hard knocks.

Large corporations spend millions of dollars annually sending their people to schools to learn administrative skills. Do you think for one minute that cost-conscious, hardheaded managers would be willing to spend this money without being positive that such training pays off?

If you want to become an administrator, you can learn to be one if you are willing to pay the price and have sufficient intellectual and perceptive abilities to develop the needed behavior. But be not deceived: the study of administration is difficult. Often it appears to be too generalized to meet the needs of a practical, on-the-job manager. One must have some depth of understanding and considerable patience to learn to be an administrator; it is not something one learns overnight.

WHAT DOES AN ADMINISTRATOR DO?

There are several ways of looking at the job of an administrator, and we shall look at it from all those viewpoints so that you can gain a better appreciation of the job.

Keep in mind at all times that the actual work an administrator does is largely dictated by the situation in which he finds himself. No two administrators do the same things, for their immediate environments dictate their activities. Also, keep in mind that many managers do administrative work only part of the time; many managers must do nonadministrative work—sometimes plain, common labor or supersalesmanship. So clearly differentiate between a man's administrative work and the other tasks he performs. Do not be hasty in criticizing leaders who spend a good portion of their time performing production, engineering, research, or sales work, for in their situations perhaps those things are important to the overall success of operations.

Functional Analysis of Administration

Early management theory divided the administrator's job into functions: planning, organizing, assembling and protecting resources, directing, controlling, and evaluating results.

Planning   Certainly planning is one of the fundamental administrative functions. Everything starts with planning; the administrator wants his organization to achieve certain goals. Planning encompasses thinking about what activities the organization should undertake, how big it should be, what strategies it should pursue to reach its objectives, and what resources will be required to accomplish its goals. On a slightly lower level, planning includes all of the budgetary decisions that must be made and detailed planning of all aspects of operations from production scheduling to salesmen's routing, and so on.

Do you now plan?

Long-range planning has been in vogue in recent years because managements have wanted answers to such questions as: What should this company look like ten years from now? What business should we be in in 1981? How big will we be in 1981? What resources will be required to reach our goals?

Organizing   Organizing refers to grouping the activities that are needed to execute the plans. Experience clearly shows that people must be grouped into meaningful work units if work is to be accomplished efficiently. The determination of organizational grouping is one of the fundamental functions of the administrator.

Assembling and Protecting Resources   Organizations require men, money, materials, and machines to accomplish their goals. The administrator must get these resources for his people.

Some management authorities believe that assembling men—staffing the organization—is the single most important thing the administrator does, for if he fails to hire the right people, his plans are doomed. Money buys the other resources necessary for the operation, and acquiring it is no small feat.

Naturally, the administrator is also responsible for the protection of the assembled resources, for whenever wealth is accumulated in any form, the temptations are great for others to misappropriate it.

Directing   Directing refers to the day-to-day personal relationships between the executive and his subordinates. It comprises the bulk of his activity, in that people must be directed to do work. Experience teaches the neophyte manager the importance of daily supervision of his subordinates, for things can go wrong quickly without it.

Controlling   The administrator has the responsibility for seeing to it that operating results conform to the plan as nearly as possible. Controlling requires establishing such standards as budgets and quotas, developing control mechanisms that guide the workers along the desired lines, and measuring actual results against the standards.

Evaluating Results and Taking Corrective Actions   Systems that are well designed provide for a feedback mechanism so that output can be measured against standards and, if necessary, corrections can be fed back into the system so that the output is properly modified. In the typical organization, the manager must establish these feedback mechanisms by establishing means for evaluating the output and then altering the organizational behavior so that any deficiencies in output are corrected.

Policy Making

Sometimes managers are referred to as policy makers. Certainly policies play an important role in the administration of most enterprises, and many executives at all levels in the organization are vitally involved in formulating and revising policies. Their wisdom and judgment in policy making are usually the difference between a well-managed institution and the types more frequently encountered.

A policy is a premade decision; it serves several useful functions. First, policies can be applied quickly by subordinates each time a certain type of event occurs. Second, policies communicate throughout the organization the behavior that is expected of everyone concerned. Third, policies communicate to outsiders what can be expected of the company. Fourth, they give some assurance of a uniformity of decisions throughout the organization, over a span of time, so that organizational behavior is consistent in dealing with similar incidents. Finally, policies protect the administrator from the pressures of immediacy, thereby helping him resist taking the expedient route in handling the issue in front of him at the time.

How does a policy protect the administrator from the pressures of the issue in front of him?

Leadership

Another theory of management maintains that the major function of the administrator is to provide the leadership, the moral force, necessary to lead the organization to its goals. These theories of leadership place great emphasis upon various personality characteristics. While leadership does play an important role in management, it would be a mistake for you to believe that one must be an inspirational leader—a great leader of men—in order to be an executive, for the fact is that most managers provide a minimum of leadership and are far from inspiring. The true leader is a rare person.

What characteristics are commonly possessed by great leaders?

Working through and with People

Another view of the administrator's job sees him as working continually with and through people to accomplish tasks. They see his job as almost wholly people-oriented— one of motivating the workers to do the things that need doing. This view of the executive's job places great stress upon its human relations and behavioral aspects. It sees his success as depending largely upon his ability to motivate people.

The Negotiator

Another way of looking at the administrator's job is to conceive of him as continually negotiating for money, markets, men, and materials in behalf of his organization. His success naturally depends upon how good he is at negotiating. A good negotiator, of course, must be persuasive, so elements of salesmanship inevitably creep into these aspects of the manager's job.

CHARACTERISTICS OF A GOOD ADMINISTRATOR

Although a list of the characteristics of a good administrator suggests somewhat the All-American Boy, do not conclude that there is any one personality the administrator must have if he is to succeed. All of the traits described below exist in varying quantities in most people; what matters is their particular mixture.

It would be most convenient if we could discover one personality pattern that led to success in administration, but hundreds of studies have failed to disclose such a success pattern. Good administrators vary widely in their personality characteristics, and so do poor ones. Often the personality traits of the successful administrator are hardly discernible from those of the poor one. Truly, this problem of describing the personality and character of a successful administrator is a most difficult one.

It may help if we itemize a few of the traits that seem most prevalent in successful managers.

Respect The material in Table 7-1 reveals that the actions of administrators who were considered poor by their subordinates all had a bearing upon this matter of respect. It is difficult for a man to be a good manager if his men do not respect him. However, one must realize that respect is a result of a great many things—the result of the man's total behavior.

Table 7–1
CHARACTERISTICS OF "POOREST BOSSES" AS IDENTIFIED BY SUBORDINATES

	Criticism Noted	Percentage
Organizational performance		
Failure to delegate; inability to accept subordinates' ideas	27	
Reliance on rank, or fear, for compliance, bullying	13	
Over-involvement in details	11	
Failure to give support to subordinates	11	
Tendency to over-control	6	
Failure to provide needed help or guidance	6	
Improper use of organizational channels	3	
Unavailability when needed	3	
Setting of too-high standards	2	
	82	32
Decision-making skills		
Frequent reversal of self; indecisiveness	15	
Inadequate judgments or decisions	13	
Lack of self-confidence; personal insecurity	12	
Failure to take action	8	
Lack of knowledge of situation	3	
	51	20
Communicational skills		
Failure to communicate with others	18	
Inadequate oral and written communicational skills	11	
Inability to listen	3	
	32	12
Relationships with others		
Lack of respect for, or trust in, others; absence of "human relations feel"	23	
Favoritism	7	
Criticism of subordinates (in presence of others)	4	
Toadying to superiors	3	
Encouragement of divisiveness among subordinates	2	
Disloyalty to superiors	1	
Interference with personal lives of subordinates	1	
	41	16
Personal characteristics		
Emotional immaturity; extreme self-interest	19	
Bad personal habits; neuroticism; excessive use of alcohol	10	
Dishonesty; deceitfulness; unreliability	9	
Lack of adequate technical knowledge	6	
Failure to give attention to business; pursuit of outside interests	6	
Lack of foresight, imagination, or conceptual ability	5	
	55	20
Totals	261	100

SOURCE: David S. Brown, "Subordinates' Views of Ineffective Executive Behavior," *Academy of Management Journal*, December 1964, pp. 288–299.

How can a manager's behavior off the job affect the respect his subordinates have for him?

Fairness   One of the quickest ways a manager can alienate his men is to treat them in a manner they consider unfair. Most good administrators are considered by their subordinates and peers to be fair-minded. A problem often arises because some action of the manager that he believes to be completely fair is regarded otherwise by his men.

What actions might be considered unfair by one's subordinates? What do you consider to be unfair behavior by your professors? How do disagreements on what is fair come about?

Judgment   If a man desiring to be a successful executive had his choice of but one characteristic, he should choose judgment—good judgment. The manager makes judgments and is evaluated on whether they are good or bad. But again, judgment is a complicated totality of a man's wisdom, filtered through his values and his ability to perceive all the relevant factors involved in a situation. Some men of great intellect have poor judgment because they fail to perceive the critical factors pertaining to the issue at hand, or their value scales are inappropriate.

Decision Making   One aspect of management theory stresses the administrator's ability to make decisions—sound decisions. Although recent years have seen a great deal of work done on the quantitative aspects of decision making (probability theory, Bayesian theory, decision trees, and others), still most decisions are based on judgment. But there is more to it than the possession of good judgment, because some men of sound judgment are unable to make clear-cut decisions when needed; they vacillate, hesitate, and wilt under the pressure of having to commit themselves to a definite decision.

One executive said, "Many times it matters not *what* decision is made, just that one makes it." What did he mean?

Flexibility   Inflexibility is one mark of a poor executive. Most business environments are so volatile and variable that one must be flexible in his thinking toward them. "But we have always done it this way!" is the retort of an inflexible mind.

Pragmatism   A good administrator prizes what works. He is practical; he seeks workable solutions and shuns impractical or theoretical dreams. The impractical man usually does not last long in administration; he has his role in the organization, but not as its leader.

Compromise   Good administrators tend to be compromisers, for they realize that one cannot always have his own way in all affairs, that successful human relations require taking into consideration the thinking of all the key men in his organization. Men who bullheadedly demand to have their own way do not generally enjoy a very long tenure as administrators.

Mental Toughness   Mental toughness is defined as an ability to accept adversity without allowing it to affect one's determination to reach his objectives. The administrator must take defeat in stride and not allow it to affect his mental attitude or determination to do his job. He meets a great many adverse developments in his work, and if he allows them to affect his behavior significantly, he will find himself incapable of functioning effectively.

Maturity   There is no room in administration for the immature mind. Children belong on the playground, not in the executive suite. This concept of maturity has such a broad range of implications that it is impossible to delve into all of them now—nor should it be necessary.

Responsibility   There is no room in administration for an individual who cannot accept responsibility. The manager must mentally commit himself to the fact that the success of any given program depends upon him and his abilities. He assumes in advance the blame for failure or the credit for success.

Social Adeptness   Much has been made of the need for a high degree of social intelligence among administrators, for observation certainly suggests that most successful executives are socially adept. They are able to move freely in various social circles and can carry on intelligent conversations easily with a wide range of people. The social clod finds it difficult going in management.

Intelligence   Certainly it takes some intelligence to be an administrator; the number of Phi Beta Kappas among the presidents of the nation's 500 largest corporations is rather surprising. While administrators tend to be significantly more intelligent than the average man, it is a mistake to place too high a correlation between administrative abilities and intelligence. Experience indicates that many highly intelligent people have a difficult time in administrative positions, for their intellect makes them impatient with the mediocrities with whom they must deal. Their high intelligence can block their rapport and understanding of their subordinates. Many top-notch administrators are people of only average intelligence who have acquired a great many of the other characteristics that have been described.

Technical Competence   It is difficult for a man to be a good administrator if he is not technically competent in the area he is administrating. Technical competency provides the man with two critical skills. First, he gains the respect of his subordinates if he is technically competent; should he be incompetent, his subordinates lose respect for him. Second, technical competence allows the administrator to evaluate the technical competency of his subordinates. How can a sales manager properly evaluate the sales ability of a salesman if he does not know much about selling? It is a mistake to believe that a good administrator can blindly walk into any executive position.

Tolerance   The good administrator must be tolerant of a rather wide range of behavior among his workers. Anyone who expects others to do a job precisely as he would do it is bound to be disappointed, for it will seldom happen. Not all of his group will behave according to his social mores; should he try to evaluate and judge them in that light, he will create a great deal of ill feeling. People resent being judged by others' standards.

Perception—Sensitivity Perhaps one of the more critical traits a successful administrator must have is perception—the ability to detect and interpret all of the stimuli constantly bombarding him, and thereby to determine the reality of his environment. The imperceptive administrator either ignores or misses key signals by which people attempt to tell him things—to his eventual discomfort. The imperceptive man is unaware of how others feel about things and how they feel about him and his behavior. A great deal of managerial training has been focused to increase the administrator's sensitivity to the people around him. So-called "T-groups" or sensitivity training groups are presently popular in management training.

Why are some people relatively imperceptive?

Conceptual Skills The successful administrator must be able to think in terms of concepts or ideas. He must have some imagination and be able to grasp essential concepts in his environment. The individual who lacks imagination or finds it difficult to talk in terms of concepts will find his advancement in management rather slow.

LEARNING TO BE AN ADMINISTRATOR

It is rather simple for someone to tell you how to learn to be an administrator. The difficult portion of the task is your doing it. Relatively few people have sufficient mental toughness, initiative, and ambition to be willing to pay the price to become a good administrator. What must you do to learn the art?

What is the price of becoming a good administrator?

Desire

First of all, you must want to be an administrator so strongly that you are willing to pay the price of becoming one. Perhaps you do not have such a desire now; that is not at all unusual, for experience indicates that people who have not had close contact with administrative jobs seldom appreciate them. More typically, one's desire to become an executive grows as he discovers that his abilities are just as good, if not better than, those of the administrators governing him. As you gain confidence in your abilities and see what you are capable of doing, administrative positions are more apt to be attractive to you. But if you do not have sufficient desire to become an administrator, then most certainly you are not apt to become one. Few administrators happen by accident, regardless of what they may wish others to believe.

Be Observant

The best school of administration is experience. Watch the world! Carefully observe all of the administrators with whom you come in contact and observe their tactics and ways of handling situations. Try to pinpoint the characteristics that cause you to consider one administrator good and another bad. When you observe an administrative failure, try to find the reason for it. When you witness an administrative success, try to pin down the reasons underlying it.

What is an administrative failure? a success?

Self-Development Program

Over a period of time, sit down and plan a self-development program by which you intend to become a proficient administrator. Such a program can consist of several parts. First, there is your reading program. Read! Read! Read! Subscribe to such periodicals as *Business Week, Harvard Business Review, Business Horizons, Sales Management, California Management Review, Forbes,* and any other trade journal that seems pertinent to you. Money invested in such reading programs pays great dividends. Read all of the books that are pertinent to administration.

Second, attend formal training courses in the administrative arts. Organizations such as the American Management Association, American Marketing Association, and many universities continually offer short training courses on various aspects of administration. Attend ones that seem pertinent to the skills you feel you should acquire. Try to get your employer to support such training. Take advantage of all of the managerial training aids your employer can provide.

Third, undertake a deliberate program to talk to successful administrators about their skills. Engage them in conversations for the purpose of picking their brains. Learn from others.

One Ph.D. in chemistry, who had found himself promoted to a high administrative position, set as a task for one year to study and learn about administration. In addition to all of the reading and instructional programs previously mentioned, he got a job teaching management at a nearby college—for, unquestionably, one of the best ways to learn something is to teach it. So offer your services as a teacher of management or administration to the local community college or other such training center.

Get Experience

Above all, get all of the administrative experience you can in any manner whatsoever, even if it is merely heading up the local PTA or Little League. Get experience in working with and through people. Volunteer for such positions. Make it clear to your supervisors that you are willing to accept more responsibility and that you want administrative positions. It is not at all out of line to tell your employer that your ultimate goal is to become an administrator. Let people know your goal, lest your flower bloom in the desert unseen.

Conclusion

> The job of the administrator is one critical to our growing industrial society. It is one about which we are only beginning to learn. We do, however, know some things about administration and about the people who aspire to it. Let no one lead you to believe that there are set ways an administrator must behave to be successful, for it is not so. But there seem to be some things that wise administrators avoid doing, and these should be considered carefully by would-be administrators. Above all, realize that administration is something one can learn if he puts his mind to it and is willing to pay the price.

8 Concepts in management and organization

Too rigid a search for perfection can get the administrator off course and lead him into an administrative thicket of imperfections.

RAY E. BROWN

Many of the concepts introduced below are complex ones. Still, you should begin now to become familiar with the basic organizational concepts and the terminology connected with them.

ORGANIZATION STRUCTURE

A large body of management theory revolves around organizational structure—how the administrator forms his workers into meaningful groups for the purpose of increasing productivity. Connected with organizational structure theory are several separate concepts.

Division of Labor—Specialization

The basic principle underlying practically all meaningful organizational structures is that of *division of labor*, perhaps one of the most fundamental concepts in all administrative theory.

Much of the administrator's thinking on organizational structure must dwell on how to divide the tasks among the workers, for there are several ways to do so.

Concept of Division of Labor

> Division of labor involves dividing the total work among the workers in such a manner that each can specialize in doing but one task, and learn to do that one job more efficiently. Efficiencies result from eliminating unproductive time spent in changing tasks, allowing the man to perform each unit of work in less time. He learns from repetition and does not need to relearn each task as he changes back and forth between different types of work.

Functional Organization Typically, American industry has divided the work into functions, such as production, sales, engineering, accounting, personnel, and whatever other functional divisions make sense. The nature of the work done is so different from function to function that seldom would one expect to find a man who could do several functions. Could an accountant, for example, function as an engineer?

Product Organization Some managers have divided their organizational structure by products. One man is responsible for all functions relating to one product; he may be in charge of research, production, sales, and everything else pertinent to its profitability. The major advantage of the product management structural form is that it places the responsibility for the product's success on one man's shoulders.

Project Management Currently in vogue in many industries is a project management organization. Here the activities of the company are grouped by projects or missions, frequently composed of either one product or a group of similar products. This organizational development evolved largely from the defense industry, where it was found that assigning the responsibility for one weapon or system to one organizational group and giving it power to carry out everything connected with that system was the best way to get the job done.

Geographic Organization Geography usually plays a role somewhere in a firm's organizational structure. Sales operations are frequently divided by geographic regions.

International operations are usually separate. Time and costs dictate some geographic divisionalization for any large company.

Customer Organization   Recent years have witnessed a growth in the use of types of customers as a basis for divisionalizing. Xerox salesmen are so divided; one man will call only on banks, accountants, and finance companies, while another will call only on manufacturers, all within a certain geographic area.

Step-Sequence Organization   Most tasks can be broken down into steps that must be done sequentially. One or more steps can be assigned to one worker rather than having that person do the whole job. This is the traditional form of division of labor.

How does the governing board of your school divide the work to be done?
How can you use the principle of division of labor in your own work planning? How could you organize your work in each of the ways described?

Line and Staff

One of the most fundamental concepts of organization is that of the line and the staff. Figure 8-1 shows a pure line organization. Figure 8-2 shows a line and staff organization.

A line executive is a man who has a direct authority over productive workers, whether they be in the plant or in the sales force. The line executive is in the chain of command leading upward from the lowest level to the top. The staff executive does not have line authority, but rather serves in an advisory capacity to some other executive somewhere in the administrative hierarchy. The director of marketing research in Figure 8-2 reports to the vice-president of marketing and serves in a staff capacity to that executive. While it is true that the marketing research manager has line authority over the people in his department, still he is not considered a line executive because the entire department is known as a staff activity. A sharp distinction is made in industry between line experience and staff experience. As a general rule, staff people are limited in how far they can rise in the hierarchy. Seldom does the market research manager or the head of the computer center rise to the presidency. If one wishes to go to the top, he should stay in the line activities.

What is the difference between being a line executive and a staff executive?

Functional Authority

A function is a single area of activity—credit, research, legal, sales, production, or what have you. Functional authority refers to the authority an administrator has over a function, wherever it is exercised in the organization. The credit manager in the home office might have functional authority over all credit practices in the organization,

FIGURE 8-1: A Simple Line Organization

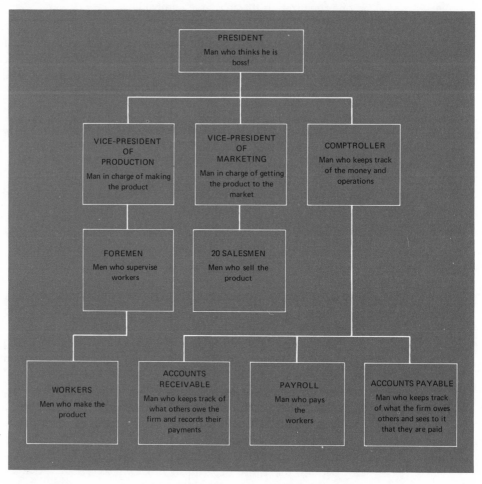

so that although a branch manager would report to his line superior in most operational affairs, insofar as his credit activities were concerned he would be governed by the credit manager.

Staff managers are sometimes given such functional authority over their areas of interest, but not always.

Why would the authority of staff people sometimes be restricted?
Why do so many college-trained people end up in staff positions? What are the attractions of staff positions?

Span of Control

Span of control refers to the number of people reporting to an administrator. In Figure 8-1 the president's span of control is three. In Figure 8-2 the marketing manager's span of control is five.

FIGURE 8-2: A Line and Staff Organization

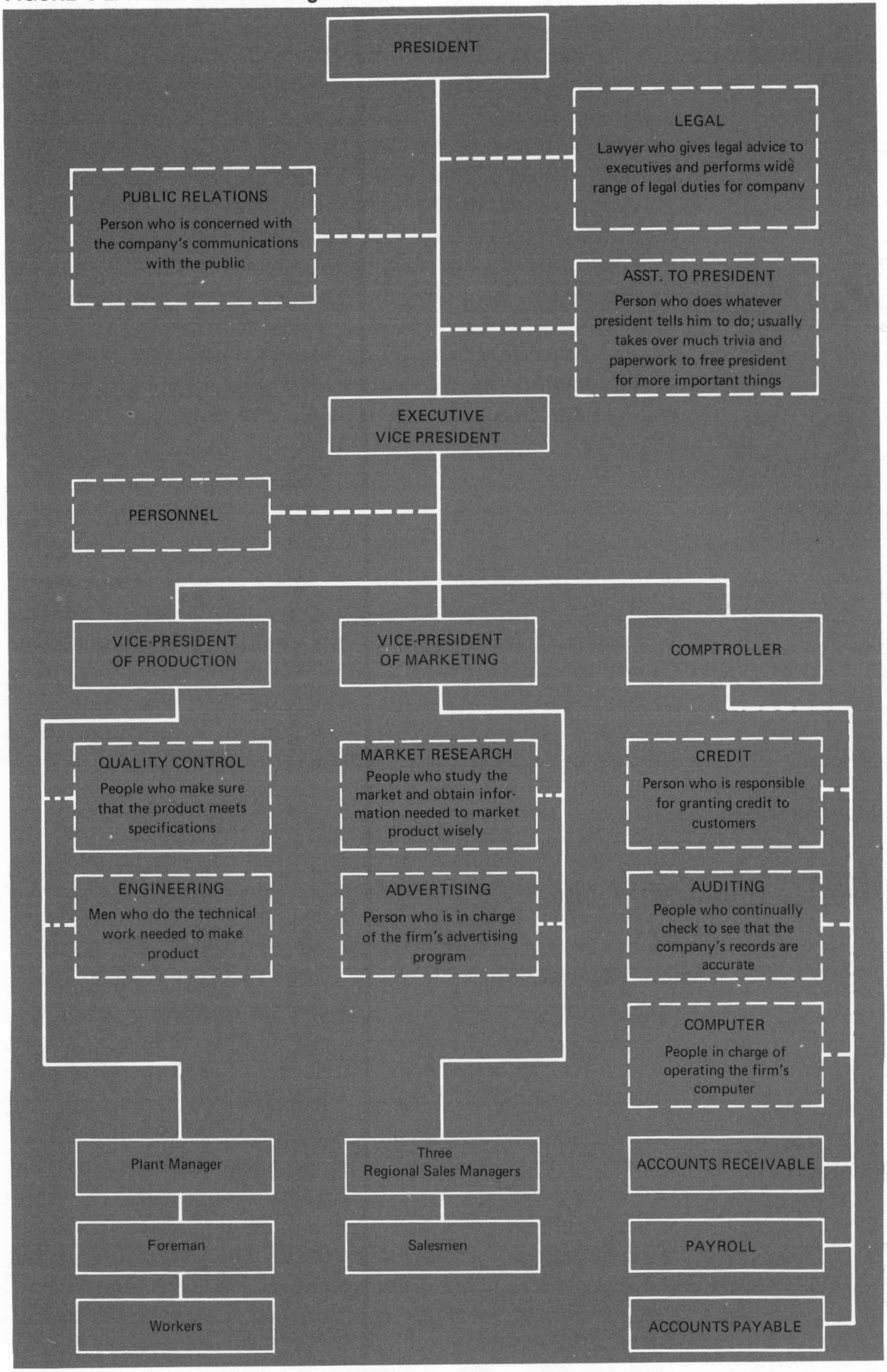

PRESIDENT

LEGAL
Lawyer who gives legal advice to executives and performs wide range of legal duties for company

PUBLIC RELATIONS
Person who is concerned with the company's communications with the public

ASST. TO PRESIDENT
Person who does whatever president tells him to do; usually takes over much trivia and paperwork to free president for more important things

EXECUTIVE VICE PRESIDENT

PERSONNEL

VICE-PRESIDENT OF PRODUCTION

VICE-PRESIDENT OF MARKETING

COMPTROLLER

QUALITY CONTROL
People who make sure that the product meets specifications

MARKET RESEARCH
People who study the market and obtain information needed to market product wisely

CREDIT
Person who is responsible for granting credit to customers

ENGINEERING
Men who do the technical work needed to make product

ADVERTISING
Person who is in charge of the firm's advertising program

AUDITING
People who continually check to see that the company's records are accurate

COMPUTER
People in charge of operating the firm's computer

Plant Manager

Three Regional Sales Managers

ACCOUNTS RECEIVABLE

Foreman

Salesmen

PAYROLL

Workers

ACCOUNTS PAYABLE

The span of control determines the number of layers of management necessary in the organization. The greater the span of control, the fewer the layers of management, as one can see in comparing Figures 8-1 and 8-2. There is much disagreement about the proper span of control, and there are no right or wrong answers. As an executive expands his span of control, he shortens his lines of communication and brings himself into closer contact with operations, reaping many benefits. But at the same time, as more men report to him, he is less able to give them time, and his own job becomes overloaded. As one's span of control narrows, he is able to give each of his subordinates more time and have more time himself, but as the layers of management increase there is a resulting increase in costs and red tape.

Factors that bear on the span of control in a given situation are: the abilities of the administrator, the nature of the jobs, the abilities of the subordinates, and the managerial philosophies of the people involved.

What might be the results of having a span of control that was too large? too small?

Coordination

Management must coordinate the efforts of all departments within the organization at all times. While production and sales appear to be separate sections in both organization charts shown, the fact is that production must be coordinated with sales and (as one can see by giving a bit of thought to it) each and every work group must be coordinated with the sales activity of the organization. The administrator must develop a way to obtain such coordination; it is achieved by developing a control system.

Delegation of Authority

Once the administrator has developed his structure, he faces the problem of deciding exactly what power should be delegated to what people in the organization. Some powers can be delegated safely down to the lowest echelon; others are reserved for the board of directors or the president. The dilemma posed for the manager is in deciding which work should be delegated to which individual. It would be just as silly for the president of a large corporation to reserve for himself the decision on how best to sweep the floors as it would be for him to delegate to the janitor the decision on whether or not bonds should be sold instead of preferred stock. The key question is: who can do the job most effectively?

Centralization-Decentralization

Delegation is the crux of the problem when we consider the degree to which an organization should be centralized or decentralized. Much has been written about the virtues of decentralization versus centralization. There are advocates and opponents of each, and again there are no definitive answers. Whether or not an administrator follows a policy of centralizing or decentralizing his operations depends entirely upon the nature of his situation and his own abilities and preferences.

Unquestionably, the present trend is toward centralization of authority. The advent of the computer alone has greatly encouraged such centralization, since decisions tend to be made at the location of the computer. The computer has allowed the accounting function to be centralized; the same thing is happening to the purchasing and inventory functions. The theory underlying centralization is that a company can run its operations best by making decisions at one central location—the home office—where it has amassed the finest brains and has the ability to see all aspects of the company's operations. The case for centralization includes such arguments as: (1) it allows better coordination of total company activities; (2) it results in uniform behavior throughout the organization; (3) it reduces the number of highly qualified people that are needed; (4) overall, better decisions are made; and (5) the bargaining power of the company is increased.

What forces, other than the computer, have encouraged the centralization of authority in American business?

The case for decentralization is that, in many situations, the man in the field, closest to the action, is in the best spot to make the decisions; an executive in a remote, centralized location cannot make decisions quickly enough and cannot be properly apprised of the market conditions in the field.

The problem really comes down to who is able to make the best decision. At times the man in the home office can do so, while at other times he cannot because he lacks knowledge of the factors in the field.

Is the pricing of General Motors' automobiles centralized or decentralized?

The Dilemma Companies have been badly burned by following either policy. During the sixties decentralization became something of a fad, and many companies prided themselves on giving their various divisions almost complete autonomy to operate as if they were independent enterprises. Litton Industries and General Dynamics were two such examples. Both were hurt when their various divisions got into financial trouble that was not perceived by top management and suddenly presented the parent operations with very unpleasant situations. Certainly one of the problems of decentralization is in knowing and controlling what is going on in the various divisions. Decentralization cannot be synonymous with divorce, for top management must still carefully control all of its divisions to make certain that they are performing adequately. Obviously, decentralization requires highly talented managers in the field.

On the other hand, some firms have become so highly centralized that they have lost contact with their markets, and they have become so inflexible and bound in red tape that they have tumbled from their top-heavy administrative burdens. It is extremely difficult to sit high in a Madison Avenue skyscraper and run an international or national business, making decisions about what is going on in Fresno, Phoenix, Omaha, Little Rock, Orlando, Columbus, or Hooterville.

Functions Amendable to Centralization   Certain functions of business are easier to centralize than others. For example, accounting, credit, research, finance, advertising, and legal functions are all relatively easy to centralize, and doing so makes considerable economic and managerial sense in most cases, though not in all.

When would it be advisable to decentralize the credit function?
Why is research normally centralized?

Normally, it is far more difficult to centralize sales operations and other activities dealing largely with local conditions. Centralized purchasing may make sense in companies buying from a few large national resources, but it would make no sense whatsoever if the organization purchased largely from many small, local suppliers. How can the purchasing agent in New York know from whom to buy in Stockton? While overall production planning and scheduling is frequently done centrally, still a great many plant production decisions must be made on the spot; the plant manager must have considerable authority to operate his plant in the most efficient manner available to him.

COMMUNICATIONS

Recent years have seen a rapidly increasing interest in communications in the administration of human affairs. It is now recognized that a great many problems exist largely because of faulty communications between people. Subordinates do not comprehend what they are told by their superiors, and the administrator does not hear clearly enough what his subordinates are trying to tell him.

The area of communications not only includes all of the face-to-face and personal relationships between people in an organization, but also includes the formal systems by which information is gathered and disseminated throughout the organization. The computer is part of a company's total communication system.

The basic theory of communications dictates that everyone in an organization should have all the information he needs to perform his job properly. If he lacks any bit of information vital to his job, his productivity is lowered. So management is greatly concerned with its information systems and how well they are working.

The methods by which it communicates are many and varied, ranging from face-to-face meetings to memos, reports, group meetings, and managerial documents and proclamations, including routine periodic managerial reports, such as budgets and cost analyses.

Do face-to-face meetings with one's subordinates guarantee communication with them?

Barriers to Communication

Communications are blocked by many barriers, such as: personal values and frames of reference, conflicts of interest, distortion in transmission of the message, distortion in receiving messages, inertia, duplicity, and a lack of desire to communicate. Attacks on the communication problem usually focus on trying to batter down these barriers.

They try to teach the administrator how to be a better communicator and show him the need for doing so.

How do each of these barriers block communications?
Why might an administrator not want to communicate with his subordinates?

Direction of Communications

Communications move vertically and horizontally. Vertical communications are messages that flow upward or downward in the organizational structure. Horizontal communications flow between people in the same level of the structure.

What constitutes the largest blockage to communications flowing upward from the field to the president of the company?

Formal versus Informal Communications

A great deal of communication in an organization is informal—the grapevine—in which one person casually talks to another, thereby passing a message. The grapevine is a most useful tool, for it frequently circumvents the red tape and inflexibilities that develop in formal organizational hierarchies. Most healthy organizations have an active grapevine, and excellent administrators use it extensively. Many times it is easier to get a message through to one's subordinates via the grapevine than it is through direct communication. Certain people in the organization become focal points in the grapevine, as experience proves that they not only know things but also are willing to disclose them. Cutting off such people from information will not dry up the grapevine, but rather will cause speculation in the organization as to what the actual information might be.

AUTHORITY AND POWER[1]

Good management balances responsibility with authority. Responsibility for each activity should be clearly assigned to some executive. Often misunderstandings occur and productivity drops, simply because someone did not know he was supposed to do a particular job.

Once the scope of the responsibility has been delineated and assigned, the necessary authority should be delegated to the same person or group. Failure to delegate adequate authority has weakened many organizations. If you are going to give a man a job, give him the tools to do it.

Matching authority and responsibility, however, is usually easier said than done. For a branch manager to produce the assigned results—his responsibility—he should be given authority to set prices, establish channels of distribution, select dealers, recruit and train salesmen, and so on. Yet it is obviously unrealistic and uneconomical to delegate authority for these tasks in such a decentralized fashion. Authority for

[1] This section is based on material in William J. Stanton and Richard H. Buskirk, *Management of the Sales Force* (Homewood, Ill.: Richard D. Irwin, Inc., 1969), Chapter 2.

several aspects of these functions may be handled more economically and effectively in some centralized manner.

No worker in a single job should have more than one boss. This point must be watched carefully in medium-sized and large companies, where the organizational structure starts to get complicated.

Why not? Don't we all have several bosses?

A salesman may be operating out of a branch where the branch manager is his immediate superior. Then a man from the home office may go straight to the salesman and ask or order him to do some added job without first clearing it through the branch manager. The salesman hesitates to object to the order and, as a result, finds that he ends up with more than one boss.

The chain of command should be followed as a matter of routine. No one in management should give orders to a subordinate without routing them through the man's immediate superior. Also, any transfers, salary adjustments, or disciplinary action should be handled, or at least approved, by the immediate superior of the worker under consideration. To do otherwise undermines the authority and control of the immediate superior.

Conclusion

Long experience has clearly proved that productivity—output—is vastly increased when work is managed according to several principles that have proven effective.

We know that work should be organized and that a structure is needed by which the workers can be purposefully arranged.

We know that efficiency depends upon a wise division of labor—people specializing in the work they do.

We have seen that administrators are continually plagued with the question of how many men they should supervise, and that answer determines the number of levels of management in the organization.

The matter of authority-responsibility cannot be taken lightly, for it has great bearing on the administrator's effectiveness.

There is also the question of where a given decision can best be made—centrally or in the field. Firms have difficulty in determining where the authority for making certain decisions should be delegated.

Finally, we have seen the critical importance of communications, both vertical and horizontal, to the administrator. He must learn to use both formal and informal channels to communicate with the various people in his organization.

PART

4

MARKETING

MARKETING, the revenue getter. Marketing, the costly process of moving goods from the end of the production line into the hands of those who need them. Marketing, the bearer of constantly rising standards of living. Marketing, the promoter, the manipulator of men and markets. Marketing, the activity that makes everything else in the organization possible. Yes, it is all of these and no doubt more. So let us learn it well, for it will stand us in good stead for our future careers.

9 Markets

Nothing happens until somebody sells something.
ANON.

Marketing is deeply interested in the ultimate consumer and the markets he creates—consumer markets—because ultimately all demand is derived from them. Ford buys a machine tool only because of the ultimate consumer demand for its output; the demand for cars creates the demand for its output; the demand for cars creates the demand for all the industrial goods that go into their creation. Similarly, the demand for motel equipment—an institutional or commercial market—is derived from basic consumer behavior. The increased desire for luxury travel by automobile has boomed demand by the "motel market." For this reason a thorough understanding of the consumer and his behavior is critical to all business.

CONSUMER MARKETS[1]

Markets are people—people with money. Without people there is no demand for the tremendous flow of goods and services pouring from the nation's businesses. And so we must study people.

Concept of the Consumer

Modern business accepts, though sometimes reluctantly, that the consumer is king—or queen, for the feminine liberationists—and that basically all activities in the system are dictated by his needs and desires. The business enterprise, indeed all institutions, are allowed to exist only because they have found some way to serve some consumers. Those who cease to serve, cease.

The Consumer Is King

Is he?

The consumer is faced with an infinite number of choices in his buying behavior. He makes a decision whether to spend his money or save it. If he chooses to spend it, he has a wide range of product choices available to him. Even within the relatively narrow field of food, an industry whose products are usually thought of as being necessities, the consumer can choose from among more than 10,000 items, most of which he can do without. The consumer has from five to ten different brands of bread from which to choose in the supermarket; obviously, no one brand is going to be sold for long if it stops giving the buyer what he wants. Hence, it is a fatal error for a marketing manager to believe that the consumer must buy his product. Truly, competition for consumer affection is vigorous.

What "price" do we pay for this freedom of choice?

The consumer bestows his favor on those who give him what he wants in products, prices, promotion, and convenience. The penalty for disobeying his mandates is almost certain failure. There are numerous illustrations of firms that refused to obey King Consumer, thereby suffering his wrath. At one time the Waltham Watch Company was held in high esteem by the watch buyers of America. As time passed, however, buyers decided that the wristwatch was preferable to the pocket watch, and they changed their buying habits. Waltham was a stubborn organization that would not make wristwatches until the market forced it to do so by refusing to buy its pocket watches. In the meantime, King Consumer decided that he wished his wristwatch to do more than tell time; he wanted a fashionably styled timepiece. The majority of firms in the industry immediately entered a competitive race on a fashion basis, but not Waltham. Its refusal to produce a properly styled watch eventually caused its failure.

Obviously, the consumer seldom directly commands a manufacturer to make a certain item. A more accurate view is to consider him a judge who passes sentence

[1] The material in the following sections is based on Richard H. Buskirk, *Principles of Marketing*, 3d. ed. (New York: Holt, Rinehart and Winston, Inc., 1970), Chapter 4.

on the life or death of a product. In any event, it is he to whom the manufacturer must look for guidance in determining what will be made and how it will be distributed.

The all-powerful position of the consumer is only logical, because the end of all marketing activities must be to satisfy the desires of the people. Any other goal would be illogical, and society would not long tolerate it. Society allows business firms their present freedom of operation in the belief that through this method of operation its desires will be best satisfied. If society ever comes to believe that another system would be better, the present one would be quickly junked. If our present economic system is to continue and prosper, the marketing managers of American industry must uniformly have as their goal the satisfying of consumer desires.

Since consumer desires are so important in determining marketing efforts, the marketing manager must comprehend them, which sometimes is difficult because the consumer does not always make his desires known. Research and insight are required to determine just exactly what the consumer wants.

Another disturbing factor is that once the executive has discovered some of the consumer's desires, he must make a constant reappraisal of them because they are forever changing. What may be true at one time may not be so at another. Many business failures have been caused by administrators who assumed a static market when they were dealing with a dynamic, ever-changing one. "Trolley cars and newsreels. Milk bottles and Mason jars. Argyle socks and blue suede shoes. Where are they now? There with shaving mugs, soap flakes, Burma-Shave signs, automobile seat covers and 78 rpm records—vanishing from the American scene."[2]

What forces dictated the demise of each of these products?

The ballpoint pen eased the skids under the fountain pen. Air conditioning makes the convertible an impractical car. Soft ice cream has pushed aside the traditional soda fountain sundaes and sodas. Who needs inner tubes? And so it goes—taste and technology constantly affecting the fortunes of even the most established institutions and products. It is not easy to serve a king so complex and ever changing; nevertheless, he must be served.

Why has soft ice cream taken over that market?

The foundation of marketing planning begins with a *consumer analysis.* Much must be learned about the consumer of a product if its marketing plans are to be sound. Market planning is easy when accurate consumer information is available, but it is hazardous without it. Wilkinson Sword, Ltd., first introduced its stainless steel razor blades through hardware stores in the United States, not realizing that the razor blade buyer does not buy his supply through that type of outlet.

Consumer analysis first studies the "who's" of marketing: who uses, who buys,

[2] "Quick Changes in Taste and Technology Hasten Demise of Americana," *Wall Street Journal,* February 6, 1968, p. 1. See also Theodore Levitt, *Innovation in Marketing* (New York: McGraw-Hill, Inc., 1962), an excellent book for a more thorough discussion of the impact of change upon our economy.

and who decides on the product. Second, buying habits and motives must be discovered: the what, when, where, how, and why of marketing. The answers to these questions provide the framework for marketing plans.

Parties Involved in a Purchase

Everyone is a consumer. Men, women, infants, small children, invalids, inmates of institutions, and all other living persons consume goods and services. Not all of these people, however, are purchasers. A large portion of all products is bought by people other than those who will ultimately use them. Similarly, the person who decides what shall be bought may be neither the consumer nor the purchaser, but a third party. The marketing manager must make a careful distinction between the *ultimate consumer* (user), the *decision maker,* and the *purchaser;* each plays a different role in the marketing process.

Select a product and make a consumer analysis of it.

User	● Product must be designed to meet users' needs and specifications.
	● Product should satisfy user and be acceptable to him.
Decision Maker or Specifier	● Promotional material must reach the decision maker to affect his decision.
	● Product must be such that decision maker believes it meets user's needs best.
	● Pricing policies must be set to motivate decision maker.
	● Channels must be acceptable to decision maker— may influence him one way or the other.
Buyer	● Product must be in channels the buyer patronizes. Point-of-purchase promotion must be aimed at buyers who have some degree of control over the buying decision.
	● Product must be packaged in accordance with the buyer's specifications.
	● Details of the transaction must suit the buyer.

The demand for a product depends on the number of persons who desire it and are able and willing to pay for it. Most quantitative market analysis therefore attempts to study the nature and number of the *ultimate consumers* for a product. On the other hand, most marketing tactics must deal directly with the decision maker and purchaser. Often the actual decision to buy a specific brand is made by the buyer and not by the person for whom the item is intended. At other times the user will dictate the actual product to be bought; the purchaser is merely a buying agent for him. In each instance the executive must know who is the consumer and who is the buyer of his product; moreover, he must understand the relationship existing between the two. In selecting channels of distribution, the manager tries to put his wares where the *buyer* wants them. In formulating promotional plans, he tries to reach the *decision maker.* However, he must design the product for the user while still making it appealing to the *buyer* and *decision maker.* Pricing decisions are usually based on the *decision maker's* motives.

These distinctions between the user, the decision maker, and the buyer apply to both consumer and industrial goods. Let's examine the sale of typewriters to a relatively large company. The users would be the typists; one might be tempted to ignore them in formulating his marketing plans, but to do so would be a serious mistake. Typists have strong feelings about the features they want in their typewriters. The machines must be designed to their specifications; a woman who does not like the way a certain typewriter "feels" usually finds a way to keep her employer from buying it. The salesman who ignores the typist can encounter difficulties in his sales presentation. In this instance, the user also plays some role in making the decision, so to a degree the two roles overlap. This is not at all uncommon; in most sales the three roles are intertwined among different people in various complex relationships.

The actual decision maker in the company might be any one or combination of the following people: the office manager, the typist, the purchasing agent, some vice-president, or even the president. This points up one of the difficult aspects of industrial marketing; the decision-making process in each firm is unique. One is rarely certain to whom he should direct his persuasive efforts. Consequently, typewriter companies use relatively widespread business advertising media, such as *Business Week, Time,* or *Fortune,* in order to reach into all levels of management. This diffusion of decision makers also makes the use of salesmen strongly advisable, for they are in a position to determine who must be persuaded and then focus efforts on him. However, it must be emphasized that more is involved than just tailoring the promotional program to the decision maker's characteristics. He is strongly influenced by the actual features of the product, its price, and its channels. In recent years business executives have been greatly influenced by development of electric typewriters with distinctive type faces. Several firms have been quite successful in introducing lower-priced electric typewriters to markets that are sensitive to price. Many firms prefer to deal with sellers that maintain local branches from which quick service can be obtained. Hence, the entire marketing program must be designed to fit the decision maker's demands.

The actual buyer would probably be the firm's purchasing agent, for he is the person who is adept at negotiating such contracts. He must be satisfied that the seller is reputable and will live up to his agreements. He can be in a position to veto a sale if something unusual is uncovered; therefore, some promotional efforts are aimed his direction so that he has a good image of the company. Often the buyer is most concerned with the seller's channels of distribution. For many items he will want quick delivery from local stocks: the seller's warehouse, a wholesaler, or air freight shipments. If so, the seller must be ready to oblige him.

Let's consider toothpaste as an example of the purchase of a consumer good. It is purchased in about every conceivable way: vending machine, mail order, retail stores, and door-to-door. Some purchases are planned, others are the result of impulse. All members of a family or household may play a role; perhaps each has his own brand or perhaps they all use the same one. Any member may be the actual buyer; however, he may not be free to act on his own, as some decision maker in the family may have given him orders. Any member may be the decision maker. Frequently all three roles are played by the same person. Many times the woman of the household, knowing the preferences of her family, acts as purchasing agent for them; if she sees the preferred brands on sale she activates implicit "buying orders." Hence, even though the actual brand decision is determined by someone else, the buyer decides where and when the transaction is to take place. Perhaps she sees some other brand on sale at such an attractive price that she overrules the at-home decision maker; point-of-purchase stimuli caused her to assume the decision-making role.

Toothpaste manufacturers take all these factors into consideration in developing their programs. They produce products of varying attributes (product differentiation) to appeal to different users and decision makers (different market segments). Stripe put a red streak in white paste to appeal to children, backing it up with advertising programs aimed directly at the children's market. (It failed!) Polident developed a product for denture wearers and supports it with TV advertising directed to that specific market. Macleans aims its product and promotion at people who are concerned mainly with the whiteness of their teeth. Crest was developed to serve people who are concerned about cavities. While Colgate seems most concerned with users who are worried about their breath, it also feels obligated to serve those who are concerned about cavities.

Each of these products is aimed at a market segment with specific buying motives; each is designed to satisfy particular motives. It is difficult to be all things to all people.

Because the market is widespread and has little focus, toothpaste must be widely advertised; everyone is exposed to its promotional activity. Because of the strong influence of impulse upon the *where, when,* and *what* of the purchase, point-of-purchase promotion and packaging are essential.

MARKET SEGMENTATION

Actually, there is no such thing as a homogeneous national market; instead, our country is a composite of many small markets. There are significant differences in market behavior among the various segments of society. Some of the market segments that will be examined here are geographical areas, age groups, sexes, nationalities, educational backgrounds, income classes, occupational groups, social classes, and special interest groups.

The marketing manager should consider the geographical incidence of the demand for his particular product; it is a mistake for him to assume that it is uniform throughout the nation. Most likely it is not. A truly national market does not exist; total U.S. sales are a result of adding together the volume of many separate markets. The vast differences in market penetration by any given brand in the various geographic regions indicates their uniqueness.

What factors cause regional differences in markets?

Age Groups People of different ages consume different things in varying quantities. Persons under two years of age use a sizable quantity of diapers; however, the demand rapidly drops off with age. In general, people between the ages of 30 and 50 are the relatively large consumers in our society. Younger persons frequently lack the income to satisfy their many desires. And there is a relatively low incidence of demand among retired persons—those over 65 years of age.

In recent years the teen-age market has attracted considerable attention in its demands for special types of goods. Although this market may not be large in total because of limited spending power, for some products—such as records and certain types of clothing—teen-age buying provides the bulk of the market.

The nature of demand is also directly affected. Young people want houses, cars, household furnishings, clothing, and the multitude of products required for a family that is growing. In contrast, a retired person may not even own an automobile, already has a house and furnishings, and his demand for clothing is greatly diminished. Older persons even eat less than younger persons. However, in certain areas of consumption, elderly individuals present a greater demand. Their need for hospitals, medical facilities, medications, and certain forms of recreation are great.

Sex

The demand for certain items is determined by how many consumers are of the appropriate sex. The sale of men's shoes depends on the number of men in the market. The purchase of women's cosmetics depends not only on the total number of women but also on the age factor.

Who buys men's shirts?

The buying habits and motives of men differ significantly from those of women. Selling to women is an almost completely different undertaking from that of selling to men. The sex of the purchaser or user affects all planning. An automobile designed for men would be a considerably different vehicle from one made for women. Men do not tend to buy in the same stores that women buy in. Promoting merchandise to housewives requires the use of media, appeals, and strategy different from those used in selling to their husbands.

Nationalities

People of different nationalities lead varying lives and thereby create demand for a wide variety of products. The consumption of beverages and food differs remarkably among nationality groups. Few statistics are available on this phenomenon, because little research has been done on it.

The field of cultural anthropology specifically studies behavioral differences among the various cultures in the world. Contrary to common thought the American market is not one homogeneous culture; within our boundaries there are many subcultures based on national heritage, such as the Spanish Americans, the Polish, the Greeks, and the Italians. These people, particularly those of the first or second generation, retain many of their traditional preferences for such things as food, clothing, home furnishings, and recreational desires.

Income Groups

Income is probably the most important factor causing variations in the demand for goods and services. The level of a family's income determines to a large extent not only the amount spent on various items of merchandise but also the nature of the wares purchased. Obviously, well-to-do persons will tend to buy higher-priced merchandise than poor families will buy. The impact of income on consumption, however, is far more complex than this. Wealthy people spend their money on many things for which the poor person has absolutely no demand, such as yachts, airplanes, trips abroad, certain forms of recreational activity, luxurious home furnishings, and jewelry.

The importance of clothing to the upper-income family was demonstrated by a study that showed clothing items to be the single most important product by which the upper-income female expresses herself. The lower-income female tended to think instead in terms of hardware (appliances, cars, and furniture).

Education

All studies have shown that educational attainment and income are highly correlated, so many of the findings with regard to income also apply to educational segments. Education in itself, however, does create certain differences of its own, irrespective of the income earned. The reading habits of college graduates differ considerably from those of persons who failed to complete high school. The goods one buys depend largely on the mores of the groups to which he belongs or hopes to join. Typically, college graduates travel in circles different from those of persons who only completed high school. Educational attributes are therefore one of the objective means of measuring the characteristics of social groupings.

Why does social mobility create inordinate demands for goods and services?

Occupational Differences

Variations in consumption patterns caused by occupation are in large part due to the different incomes earned by persons in these jobs. However, certain variances do occur because of occupational characteristics alone. A traveling salesman may be forced to purchase two cars because he requires one while on the road, whereas another person in the same income category might not feel the need of an additional automobile at all. A white-collar worker will purchase far more white shirts and suits than will a lathe operator, even though the latter may have higher earnings. Some business executives may be forced to buy homes and furnishings suitable for extensive entertaining, whereas other administrators not required to entertain are able to purchase more modest homes or furnishings.

Other Bases for Segmentation

Markets can be segmented along many diverse lines. Today marketing managers are concerned with such segmentations as the heavy user versus the light user, the brand loyalist versus the brand switcher, the replacement market versus the initial sale, the swinger versus the square, in addition to such traditional demographic segments as race, religion, size of family, and marital status. Table 9-1 visualizes how a manager might organize his analysis of the segments for a hypothetical product.

Table 9–1
MARKET SEGMENT ANALYSIS FOR PRODUCT X

Possible Segments	Best Potential Customer
Age	35–45
Sex	Male
Marital status	Married
Working wife	No
Size of family	Not a factor
Stage in life cycle	Children at home
Education	College graduate
Geographic location	Urban
Income	Over $10,000
Occupation	Professional-managerial
Race	Not a factor
Religion	Not a factor
Home ownership	Not a factor
Goods owned	Must own car
Degree of usage	Not a factor
Brand consciousness	Brand loyal
Geographic mobility	Not a factor
Social mobility	A climber
Innovation proneness	Accepts innovations
Personality	Aggressive

INDUSTRIAL MARKETS

Industrial goods and services are bought by business concerns, governmental units, and other economic or social institutions for use either in their operations or for reprocessing into other products. Goods sold to a concern that in turn intends to resell them unaltered to ultimate consumers are not industrial items; the sale is merely a wholesale transaction of consumer goods.

Because the average person seldom sees the industrial-goods manufacturer in action and he is constantly aware of the consumer items on the market, he is likely to conclude that the distribution of industrial products and services is a relatively small portion of the economy. In fact, however, about 53 percent of all wholesale volume is in industrial goods.

In addition to equipment, supplies, and services that are used to facilitate the production of consumer wares, all the materials going into the final product may have changed hands two or three times in various forms. Bales of cotton are sold to a gray-goods manufacturer who may sell the processed cotton to a converter who in turn may sell his finished yard goods to a dress manufacturer. The same cotton may be sold three times as an industrial item before it becomes a consumer product. Steel is another example of an industrial product that is sold many times in different forms before it finally ends up as a consumer product.

Characteristics of the Industrial Market

The industrial market has several distinctive characteristics of which the marketing manager should be aware. In many ways industrial marketing is different from the distribution of consumer goods; buying motives and habits, location and size of potential customers, and marketing techniques differ considerably between the two. In spite of all the differences, however, the basic principles for attacking and solving marketing problems in the two fields are quite similar. Much of the material discussing the distribution of consumer goods is therefore also applicable to industrial marketing.

High Concentration   The market for industrial goods and services is highly concentrated in the hands of relatively few corporations. Although there are close to 4.5 million business firms in the nation today, only 150,000 corporations, (those with $250,000 or more in assets) comprise about 85 percent of the industrial-goods market. That those few (3.3 per cent) corporations have tremendous purchasing power is thus to be expected. The manufacturer of carburetors, for example, has only a handful of possible buyers, each of them quite large.

This high degree of concentration permits the widespread use of direct channels of distribution. Though it would be an economic impossibility to contact hundreds of thousands of buyers, it is a relatively easy matter to contact directly a few hundred firms. The high degree of concentration also means that large sums of money can be involved in the transactions. One sale frequently will amount to several thousands of dollars and often much more. Again, this procedure encourages direct sale, since one order can easily pay for the cost of having the salesman call directly on the buyer. Another advantage of this market concentration is that the seller is able to recognize his potential customers more easily. The crude oil supplier knows precisely what firms stand ready to buy his output. The manufacturer of transistors and microcircuits can easily spot the most significant segments of his market. One small producer of rare organic chemicals sells mainly to the large industrial chemical companies: du Pont, Dow, Monsanto, Union Carbide, and Spencer.

Industrial markets are concentrated not only corporately but also geographically. Only 50 counties surrounding the 50 cities shown in Figure 9-1 account for almost 59 percent of the total manufacturing activity.

The marketing significance of this high degree of industrial concentration is that many firms need only establish distribution in a small portion of the nation to cover the majority of their potential markets. This greatly simplifies distribution and significantly lowers its costs.

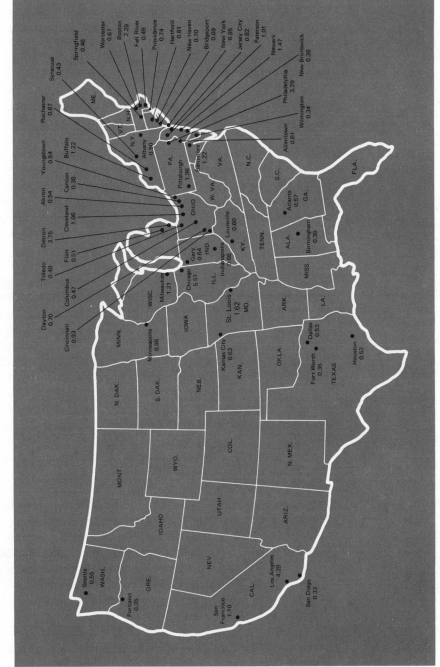

FIGURE 9-1: Location of key manufacturing market centers. Below each city is noted the percent of total United States manufacturing employment (totaling 58.64 percent). SOURCE: U.S. Bureau of the Census and U.S. Bureau of Old-age and Survivors Insurance, County Business Patterns, First Quarter 1956.

Inelastic Demand   The total demand for industrial goods and services is highly inelastic in that it is completely dependent on the level of consumer demand. If the consumer demand for a product is inadequate, its manufacturer is not going to buy additional equipment or more materials and parts, no matter how much his suppliers lower their prices. He can buy only what he can sell, and if no consumer market exists for his output, he in turn presents no market. On the other hand, if a strong primary demand exists for his output, the manufacturer will not let a price increase deter his purchasing plans. Even in such small items as operating supplies, price variation will not affect the total demand for a product. No company is going to use more paper just because a price is lowered.

Although industrial demand may be inelastic in total, it frequently is highly elastic for an individual firm marketing certain types of industrial goods. The major problem confronting an industrial-goods manufacturer who wishes to use price as a competitive weapon is that competitors are often quick to match any price reduction, thereby nullifying any advantages gained. Unless a manufacturer's cost structure allows him to undersell the market permanently, he will usually find a price differential only temporary.

On the other hand, the demand for the products of one manufacturer can be highly inelastic to price if he has developed a unique product, one that industry feels best solves some problem. IBM has been able to command a premium price for its typewriter in face of stiff competition from lower-priced units largely because a significant segment of the market (evidently a large enough segment to satisfy IBM) seems to feel that it is worth the extra price. Weyerhaeuser Company gets a $2 per 1000 feet premium in price for its plywood in a normally cutthroat industry because its customers feel the firm's quality, guarantee, and service are worth the premium. Industrial buyers will pay the price for a product if it uniquely meets some need, but at the same time they are quite price conscious if they believe that the products offered to them are essentially similar.

Reciprocity   Frequently, in the sale of operating supplies and other small purchases, some firms maintain a policy of reciprocity. They will not buy from companies that do not purchase their products. Although in theory this is a poor policy to institute, because a firm should always strive to buy from suppliers who are best able to give it what it needs, nevertheless it is frequently encountered, particularly in selling to smaller organizations, and especially in industries where the product is standardized and there is no significant difference in prices or qualities of the various brands offered.

Unfortunately, as competition increases in an industry, more and more firms officially set up a system by which each of their suppliers is surveyed to determine its potential as a customer; pressure is then applied to any supplier that appears to represent an untapped market.

Complexity of Decision Making   The industrial sales man frequently faces a situation in which it is difficult to determine upon whom he should call. Which executive will actually make the final decision on the product the company will buy? Will it be the purchasing agent, the president, the plant manager, the design engineer, or some lower employee, such as the tool-crib operator or the maintenance man? If the salesman spends his time with the wrong man while his competitor gets to the decision maker, all can be lost. With the costs of making an industrial call ranging from $20–$35 per call it becomes imperative that the salesman determine early in a sale who is the decision maker. Other promotional efforts similarly rest upon a careful analysis of industrial decision makers; it does little good to advertise to the plant manager if the president is making the decisions.

Although industry frequently employs buying committees consisting of several interested executives, experience has indicated that frequently one man greatly influences the committee's decisions. The seller must identify that man and reach him. One study conducted by a publisher determined that 64 percent of its salesmen's calls were upon the wrong men. In general, they were calling on too many lower-echelon personnel and not enough on bosses. This is not at all unusual, for most salesmen find it much easier to see the assistant to the boss rather than the boss himself. Getting through to the top man can pose problems, but in many situations it must be done if the sale is to be made.

Another situation exists in many huge organizations such as du Pont, General Motors, or the federal government. How does one go about selling to them? Whom do you see in General Motors if you want to sell them a new windshield wiper blade? How does one become a subcontractor for Hughes Aircraft? These questions are not easily answered. Each instance is different, and the only source is the organizations themselves. The seller simply must become well acquainted with each of the large organizations he wishes to sell. Sometimes this calls for "high-level" selling; the seller's president may endeavor to meet the customer's president under favorable circumstances and obtain his permission for the sales force to call upon the right men in the organization. It is amazing how a salesman's reception by a purchasing agent changes when proper introductions have been made from the top.

Selling to the government is something unto itself. First, one does not sell to the entire government at one fell swoop. Instead, each of many different agencies may have its own procurement procedures; if not, at least they have their own decision makers and influencers. Only experience and the help of someone who is well acquainted with governmental procedures can facilitate selling to it.

Central Buying   Frequently large organizations buy in one central location, usually the home office, but have the products delivered and used elsewhere. The salesman calling at a branch plant in Utah may be wasting his time if the product is purchased in the company's New York office and delivered directly to the branch. Sometimes the branch manager may have some influence in the transaction, so he cannot be completely ignored. This means that often a firm's salesmen must cooperate with each other in order to get the business of one large buyer. Perhaps all of the salesmen must be coordinated to call on all branch operations of a large firm in order to tie into the efforts of the man who is calling on the home office. This may seem an inordinate amount of effort just to close one sale, until we remember that such sales may amount to millions of dollars.

Quality Control and Vendor Reliability   Industrial buyers are quite concerned about a vendor's quality control, reliability, and ability to perform according to contract. They want to deal with responsible sellers. The Navy put out an invitation for bid (IFB) on certain electronic gear. The bid of one small electronics firm was about $800,000, while the bid of a large firm was $1,200,000. The larger firm obtained the contract by stressing the number of "reliability men" it had on its staff; the smaller firm, while going to great lengths to describe its reliability precautions, could not point to specific people. The new or small business frequently has difficulty convincing an industrial buyer that it can perform as promised. Deliveries must be made on time in the quantities and qualities desired.

Long Period of Negotiation   The sale of many industrial products requires a considerable length of time for completion of negotiations. The seller wants to make certain that the product meets his requirements in every way. One electronics firm developed an electronic holdup alarm that it wished to sell to plant protection services. The largest firm in that industry is ADT; negotiations were carried on with ADT for more than a year while it tested the product in every conceivable way. After some changes were made in the product to accommodate the buyer's particular desires, a contract was negotiated.

Value Analysis or Value Engineering   Purchasing agents are responsible for minimizing the cost of the things they buy. To that end, they have resorted to the techniques of value analysis or value engineering which were developed by the companies bidding for defense contracts to lower their bids and subsequent costs of making a given product carefully specified by a government contracting agency. Experience has clearly shown that imaginative, intelligent study of most products discloses many opportunities for cost savings.

Here are some examples of savings that were made through value analysis:

Terminal blocks, used on the control panels of some machine tools, were being mounted on strips of metal angle which cost $4.30 per foot. One value analysis team came up with a way to use standard screws and spacers. As a result, the new cost for mounting terminal blocks is only 48¢ per foot. The amount saved runs into thousands of dollars per year.

Another project, on which a purchasing member played a prominent part together with plant engineering, R&D and industrial engineering was a study of the slide for a large injection molding press. The slide was a solid casting weighing over 1,000 lbs. The study showed that the solid plate wasn't needed. Now, purchasing buys an open-frame casting that weighs only 400 lbs. Projected savings are over $5,300 annually. There are also additional savings in inbound and outbound freight.

Aggressive purchasing agents will take the product offered by a supplier, have his value engineering staff study it, and suggest to the supplier how he might lower his costs, thus his selling price.[1]

Service   Service is a word much misused and overworked in marketing. Practically all firms stoutly declare that service is a watchword with them. Be that as it may, some firms find ways of providing more and better service to their customers than others. Service is a critical component in a successful industrial marketing program. Most products and services are highly complex and technical; the buyer needs far more than the product to solve his problems—he needs assistance and advice. How could the average large concern install a computer center without considerable help from the seller? A marketing manager seeking unique packaging for a product needs technical help, for he knows little about recent packaging developments that might be of use to him.

Something goes wrong with a piece of equipment and the company wants it fixed immediately. It may be stopping an entire production line. The firm that is not able to provide such service is out of the picture.

General Automation, a small highly respected manufacturer of mini-computers for production automation, has an extremely bright future because of its emphasis on rendering outstanding service rather than just selling hardware to its customers. General Automation stresses going into the customer's plant to sell the complete service—the automated productive process in working order.

Leasing   Many industrial buyers find that leasing equipment instead of buying it offers several definite advantages. First, it minimizes the amount of capital required for fixed investment, thereby allowing the released funds to be used for working capital. Second, there may be some tax advantages, particularly if the firm has an option to buy the equipment after the "rent" has paid for it. Third, rented equipment is often serviced by the lessor, thereby relieving the user of this problem. Finally, leasing is particularly attractive to those firms whose need for equipment has wide seasonal or cyclical variations.

Previously, many sellers used leasing as a means of controlling a market; they would not sell equipment to users, only rent it. Often they would tie in the sale of supplies to the leasing of the equipment, such as by requiring the purchase of punch cards from IBM if one was renting IBM card systems. These monopolistic practices have been stopped by antitrust prosecution. Now a firm must also have its equipment available for sale in addition to any leasing plan it may have.

MARKET OPPORTUNITY

Economic endeavor begins with recognition of a market opportunity—a need that is not being satisfied among people somewhere for certain goods or services. While this theory of market opportunity has been applied almost solely to profit-seeking institu-

[1] The above material was provided by Mr. J. K. Fowlkes, President of Value Analysis, Incorporated, Newport Beach, California.

tions, an equally strong case could be made that the activity of all institutions should start with the recognition of a need among the people—the market—for some service or product. Governmental institutions have as much, if not more, need to be market-oriented than private institutions and organizations. This recognition of a market opportunity is the beginning of planning.

Recognition of Market Opportunities

While some opportunities in the marketplace are readily apparent to all, these frequently hold great dangers to management, for thousands of potential competitors can easily see the same opportunities and many are likely to react positively to them, thereby creating a future area of chaotic competition. It does not take much of a seer to see the tremendous opportunities in the areas of pollution or urban renewal; the competition in these areas will be keen in future years. It is insufficient just to say that there is an opportunity in the pollution market, for this is an inadequate basis from which to begin a business enterprise. The opportunity must be pinpointed far better than that. The pollution market is a big one, broken down into air, water, and physical pollution. In each of these categories the need for products is widespread. For instance, in the field of water pollution there is a need for instrumentation to measure the amount of pollution in rivers and lakes, plus a need for a wide range of products not only to prevent additional pollution but to rectify that which already exists. Products and services to this one area can take hundreds of different forms. Which form provides the best opportunity for a given organization? That requires research!

The need for penetrating research in discovering and pinpointing market opportunities is great, for probably there is no other single field in business in which so much money rests upon the efforts of so few. It is beyond the scope of this book to delve into the research methodology necessary to conduct such investigations, but it is important that you realize that the research efforts of the organization begin here, not with product research. Product research should be initiated only after the needs of the marketplace are recognized and defined.

Several different types of market opportunities confront the executive; each has its own characteristics and deserves separate discussion.

Market Trends

At all times in our society all forces are changing, one way or another. The demand for some things is on the increase while the demand for others is waning. The increased segment of our population over 65 years of age has boosted the demand for such things as retirement housing, geriatric medicines, travel, and shuffleboard sets. Many concerns are examining ways in which they can participate and serve the rapidly growing market among our senior citizens. Certainly a careful analysis of all trends in our society is the beginning of any trend analysis of market opportunities.

The demand for men's suits has been declining in recent years. What forces underlie this development?

What are some of the more observable of these trends? Figure 9-2 lists some of the social phenomena that dictate market opportunities.

FIGURE 9-2: Some Selected Observable Trends in the American Society of the 1970s

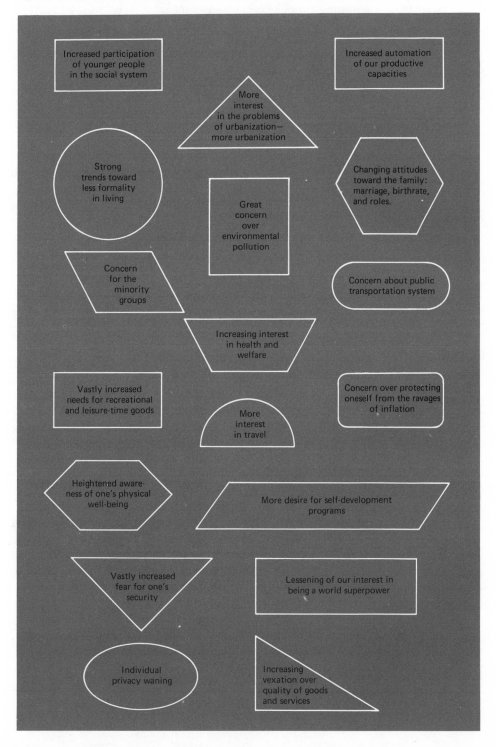

These trends and many more like them can be grouped under one or more of the following classifications of problems:

urban	age
leisure time	educational
technology	defense
environmental	psychological
service	information

Take one of the trends you observe in society and outline its potential impact upon society and the needs for products or services created by it.

Daniel Yankelovich, a marketing researcher, sees seven major trends for the seventies:

Trend Toward Physical Self-Enhancement
                Personalization
                Physical Health and Well-Being
                New Forms of Materialism
                Social and Cultural Self-Expression
                Personal Creativity
                Meaningful Work

In what ways do we evidence each of these trends in our buying? Can you add any trends to this list?

Businesses constantly appraise the markets for their wares, critically evaluating them to determine when they should be discontinued in favor of other goods. Careful market analysis has led Detroit to the threshold of deciding that the traditional introduction of new models each year is an anachronism. It will not be too long before this annual ritual will be discontinued in favor of some more rational policy of bringing out new cars when they are developed and the market demands them. The day of planned product obsolescence is coming to an end, for we are beginning to realize that we are not so rich that we can afford it.

Voids in the Market

Occasionally one is able to spot a complete void in the market in which no product or service exists to meet a clear demand. The perceptive, aggressive entrepreneur can immediately jump in to take advantage of such economic vacuums. A few enterprising financiers correctly perceived a need for creating a third market for securities in which large institutions could sell or buy large blocks of stock without going through the New York Stock Exchange and seriously disturbing the price of that stock. These men created institutions that deal solely with such large customers. The originators of the Volkswagen clearly saw the need for a small, economy car, and the company has profited handsomely from that foresight for many years.

What voids in the market do you now see? Why do they exist?

Of course, a businessman must be wary of jumping into such voids blindly, for there may be forceful economic or social reasons for their existence. One young man thought he saw a void in the market for men's clothes in a small midwest college community; there was no quality men's store. He opened one; he found out the hard way why there had been no such outlet previously: students at that school were not conscious of clothing styles.

Profitability

Much market analysis focuses around determining what economic areas are most profitable and then concentrating one's activities in that area. High profits attract many enterprises. When drug profits were high, thousands of new drug manufacturers began operations. When electronic and defense hardware profits were high, many thousands of new concerns jumped into the fray. While the profits in the computer industry were large, hundreds of new computer concerns ventured forth.

Similarly, the lack of profits drives people away. Several drug manufacturers have shifted their attention from drugs to cosmetics, because the latter's profits are more attractive than the declining profits in drugs. Much attention is devoted to determining where profits are realized and it is through this attention that society is able to direct resources into the areas it wishes to encourage.

Innovation

Certainly innovation creates many market opportunities when it makes realities of things previously considered impossible. Consider the economic impact of television alone. Look at all of the market opportunities it created and sustains.

What market opportunities might be created if someone develops a truly economic and feasible electric automobile? What values would it destroy?

Modern management carefully keeps abreast of technological developments, for each breakthrough may open tremendous opportunities for it to exploit. Suppose some solitary scientist developed a battery that was rechargeable, long-lasting, and capable of delivering a relatively large amount of power over a sustained length of time. Imagine the consequences of such an innovation! What would be the opportunities created, should someone develop a safe, small atomic reactor?

Or, in reviewing the past, look at the market opportunities created when du Pont developed nylon, Dacron, and Orlon. Clearly, management must keep an alert eye on all innovations, for one never knows what opportunities they may present or what damage they may do to markets. Innovations create new values and destroy old ones.

Competition

While the degree of competition in any market is a function of its profitability, size, ease of entry, and public attention, still management can frequently spot small niches in the market in which competition is such that the market opportunities are attractive.

At one time the laundry bleach business was largely divided between Purex and Clorox, two small companies. This lack of competition, once discovered, quickly enticed all of the major soap makers to introduce various products into that market. Hertz's success in the rental car business and its almost solitary position in that market for some time attracted many competitors. Not only did the competition appear to be minimal, but also the profits seemed to be there.

MEASURING MARKETS

So far we have dealt in qualitative terms in describing market opportunities. Certainly one can sit in an easy chair and reel off rapidly a wide range of market opportunities in qualitative terms. But qualitative market evaluations are not sufficient evidence upon which to base good, sound organizational planning. They must be quantified as numbers—numbers of things demanded by the opportunity. Markets must be measured.

Measurement is the major difficulty facing management in attempting to evaluate the opportunities presented by pollution. Not only is the precise nature of the hardware required still indeterminate, but it is difficult to assign numbers to the market, other than in terms of the total amount of money being budgeted in the area. This is a most unsatisfactory measure, for it is difficult for any one organization to pinpoint exactly how much of the total funding will be available for its product. When a new manufacturer of men's after shave lotion discovers that the market is about $200 million a year, he has something fairly tangible on which to base his planning.

A great deal of market research is devoted to the quantification of market demands—determining market potentials and sales potentials, and sales forecasting. All of these techniques form the basis for planning the activities of the entire organization.

Conclusion

Marketing requires rather precise analysis of who buys the product, for success in selling some article depends upon a good knowledge of its market, both qualitatively and quantitatively. There is considerable strategic planning in selecting the markets one wishes to solicit; it is usually a mistake to try to sell to everyone.

And one must never forget that the consumer is the key to marketing decisions. What does the consumer want? The answer does not come easily, for consumers are most complex animals. They seldom know what they really want. It takes great insights to understand consumer behavior.

10 Product development and strategy

When asked what his thoughts were during a space flight, one astronaut said, "I just kept thinking that everything in that machine was made by the lowest bidder."

Once a market has been recognized and quantified, and management deems it sufficiently attractive to invest in, the company begins to develop the right product for it. Note that in modern management theory products are designed for markets. In past years the traditional procedure was to discover or develop a product and then see if there was a demand for it. What an utter waste of resources! It is pointless to spend money on products unless there is an identifiable demand for them. A great many corporate failures have resulted from placing the cart before the horse—developing the product before identifying the market.

Examine the record of one small, engineering-oriented electronics manufacturer. In the late 1950s it developed a small ultraviolet-light water purifier that fastened onto a faucet. It invested about $200,000 in the development and production of working units, only to discover that there was little demand for them.

Subsequently, in 1960, one of the company's engineers developed an FM radio tuner that could be attached to an existing AM system in a car. After investing about $70,000 the company retained a marketing consultant to investigate the marketing opportunities for the product. The company was told that other firms, such as Motorola, were about to enter the market with superior units.

This chronology of incidents could go on for some time, as the company has never learned the basic lesson of not investing in product development until the market opportunities have been clearly identified and specifications for the product have been developed from the market's requirements.

What is a Product?

There are two rather opposite views about what a product is. The older, traditional view maintains that a product is merely a conglomeration of various attributes. A car is made up of metal, plastic, glass, and other materials, all forced into various configurations; the product is the result of the combining of all these attributes to create its performance, size, capacities, functions, and so on. This is the "physical-characteristics concept" of the product.

A more modern concept maintains that the product is what its users perceive it to be. The product exists in the mind of the user. Consequently, the same Cadillac might be two different products to two different users. This concept is especially applicable in those areas in which marketers attempt to instill additional values in a product through advertising and marketing programs. While the physical makeup of Smirnoff vodka and some off-brands are identical, the fact that Heublein, Inc. has managed—through adroit advertising—to associate certain values with Smirnoff makes that product different in the minds of its users.

NEED FOR PRODUCT DEVELOPMENT

Product development refers not only to the creation of new products, but also to the alteration or improvement of existing ones.

Unquestionably, the need for continual product development is great, for society's needs are always changing, and different products must be forthcoming to fulfill them. Apparently the internal combustion engine, as we have known it for seventy years, will no longer do for the 1970s, as it fails to meet a new market specification—too much pollution. All products have certain deficiencies, for they are the result of a great many compromises. The perfect product has yet to be made. Research makes possible the reduction of these deficiencies, resulting in improved products. But there are other reasons underlying the tremendous impetus behind product development efforts in modern industry.

Take some product and recommend improvements you feel should be made on it.

Product Life Cycle

Figure 10-1 is a visualization of the *concept of the product life cycle,* which holds that each product has a natural lifespan, varying from a very short time for certain fads to a relatively long time for certain stable products, and that it moves through its lifetime by stages.

The first portion of a product's life cycle is the pioneering stage—competition is slight or nonexistent, prices are relatively high, distribution and market are limited, and rapid improvements are being made in its technology. As the product grows in popularity it moves into the second phase of its life cycle—the growth stage, in which demand rapidly expands, prices fall, more companies enter the market, thereby making competition more intense, distribution is greatly broadened, and good profits are being made. As competition intensifies and the market grows saturated, the product moves into its maturity and saturation stages at the top of its cycle, where prices have bottomed out because of competition and technology. The product is well recognized in the market and has maximum distribution. Saturation may last for a long period, as in the case of many products with long-run demand characteristics. But sooner or later demand for the product begins declining as new products displace it. With sales declining, competition becomes ferocious. Marginal competitors fall by the wayside. Profits become almost nonexistent. And so the life of the product comes to its end, prolonged perhaps for a while by a few hard-core users.

FIGURE 10 -1: Illustration of Product Life Cycle

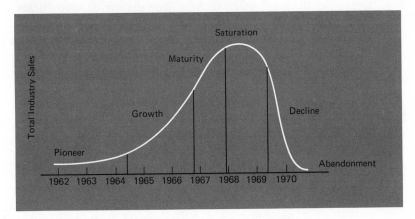

The concept of the product life cycle is extremely important, for it indicates that sooner or later all products die and that if management wishes to sustain its revenues it must replace the declining products with new ones. The product-life-cycle concept also indicates what can be expected in the marketplace for a new product at various stages of its development. Thus one learns to accept as normal the fact that a number of companies will be shaken out of an industry as a product matures and profits drop.

Why do prices drop significantly as a product emerges from the pioneering stage of its life cycle? How can you use this information personally?

Innovation

Continual innovation of new products renders existing ones obsolete. For that reason management has become accustomed to the fact that no matter how good its product is today, someone will bring out a better one tomorrow. IBM's bringing out of a copier to match Xerox's is a case in point. Xerox management realized that sooner or later some large company was bound to come after their lucrative copier market. But Xerox's management was not sitting idly by, for no sooner did IBM management announce its new copier than Xerox announced the introduction of a superior product; one could surmise that Xerox was undoubtedly aware of IBM's intentions and had been withholding announcement of its new development in order to top IBM's new-product introduction.

Continual research on new-product innovation is now viewed as a constant function of business. It is a mistake to wait until one has been defeated in the market before tooling up to meet the competitive challenge. The small electronics company described earlier pioneered the first remote-control garage door opener. For several years it had a very profitable position in this market, during the pioneering and growth stages of the product's life cycle. But the company did no research to improve its basic product. Inevitably other concerns, spotting the market opportunity, jumped in with improved door openers and quickly took the market away from the originator. Only after the market damage was done did the company begin research to counter the competitive invasion—too late, for the market had been stolen. The company never regained its position in the market, even though it has brought out several technically superior products since that time. Market position is such an important asset that few intelligent managements wish to risk it by resting on their laurels with the same old products.

Modern management operates on the theory that sooner or later—and it will probably be sooner—someone is going to make its products obsolete, so let it be us. We will be our own toughest competitor.

Growth

Many organizations have growth as one of their objectives. While some growth can be realized as a result of normal expansion in the market, and additional growth may be realized if one's products are in a segment of the market that is growing rapidly, still many concerns are not satisfied to grow only at the rate of their markets. They want faster growth. To obtain it they see the introduction of new products to be good strategy. So new-product development has become one of the cornerstones underlying the strategy of growth.

PLANNING PRODUCT DEVELOPMENT

Product development does not just happen—it must be planned. It is not uncommon to find large corporations planning their innovations for five or ten years in advance. Management likes to know where it is going.

Moreover, product development is not allowed to just happen in some haphazard or random manner. Most managements have a rather definitive idea of exactly what product developments they want and what new products they will need. In essence, a blueprint is drawn up of the organization's product research efforts for a certain coming period, giving the company's researchers fairly clear-cut guideposts for their expected performance.

ORGANIZING FOR PRODUCT DEVELOPMENT

Experience has shown that those organizations that are most successful in developing marketable products are the ones that have formally organized this function within the organizational structure. Typical management of yesteryear seldom provided for new-product development as a basic function of the enterprise. Rather, new products resulted from happenstance, usually in the engineering department, although sometimes marketing would come up with something. But new-product development was an auxiliary to the other normal functions of the business; it was a stepchild, often neglected.

Modern management creates a separate organizational niche for new-product development, frequently placing it under the guidance of a vice-president for new-product development who has his own staff. Usually such departments have the responsibility for procuring ideas, screening them, researching them, developing prototypes, market-testing, and bringing the product to the stage where it is ready for full-scale commercial exploitation. Only after a product is ready to go into regular commercial production is it given to operations. The new-product development manager makes certain that his child is fully grown and ready to take care of itself before handing it over to the organization's regular line executives.

This organizational structure has proved to be successful, because the problems of new-product development are unique and are difficult to master. They are usually outside the technical competency of the average production or sales executive. It takes a great deal of time and effort to wet-nurse a new product from its conception to its final production stage. Line executives usually do not have the time or experience necessary to do the job.

PROBLEMS ENCOUNTERED

Unquestionably the percentage of new products that fail is quite high: estimates have ranged from 50 to 95 percent. Clearly, the risks of new-product development and introduction are substantial. The reasons lie in the serious problems faced by the new product.

Problems of Time

A great deal of time elapses between conception of an idea and its introduction to the market as a product. This interval can be a matter of years, perhaps five or more, and it creates several auxiliary problems. First, time is money; all business experience clearly indicates that expenditures are a function of time. Overhead and salaries are almost solely a function of time; hence, the longer a project drags on, the higher its costs. So the relatively long time required for product development makes investments in it relatively high.

Second, time inserts additional risks into the picture. Ford Motor Company discovered this in developing the Edsel. At the time Ford conceived of the Edsel, research indicated a need for such a car, but five years later when it finally came to the dealer's floor the market had changed; it no longer wanted an Edsel. The medium-price market segment had drastically declined in the interim. Markets change rapidly and can catch many product developments in an embarrassing position.

Finally, the relatively long time required for new-product development poses psychological problems for the organization, for the excitement and emotion generated when an idea is first put forth is difficult to sustain over a period of years. When the product finally comes to market, the organization's enthusiasm may have waned, or its original sponsors may have gone elsewhere.

Financial Problems

Understandably, management is quite reluctant to invest much money in new-product development, because experience has indicated that the risks of doing so are high. It is easy to invest millions of dollars in some new product that proves to be a flop. Investments in ideas can mount rapidly in the early research stages, only to be lost when the product idea is killed off later because of some new factor in the picture.

New-product management typically operates with very spartan budgets, which hinder its activities. Clearly, the wise product development manager selects carefully the ideas he wishes to pursue, for he must marshall his limited resources behind only the most favorable ones.

Market Acceptance

The market is a fickle master. All market research may indicate that the market needs and wants a certain product, on which in fact people turn thumbs down when it is finally made available in the stores.

Business history is replete with the failures of many excellent products that did not find market acceptance. Think for a moment of the difficulty society had in getting people to take polio shots when they were first introduced, even though they were being given away free and were backed by one of the largest promotional programs ever devised. If you have trouble giving a product away—such as a polio shot—when backed by huge amounts of advertising, you can imagine the problems confronting the marketer of a mediocre new product.

Emerson said that if one builds a better mousetrap the world will beat a path to his door. That is bunk; it simply is not so. One can have the best product imaginable but still encounter tremendous problems distributing it and gaining its acceptance in the marketplace. It took the market more than twenty years to accept the electric refrigerator over the old ice box.

Why has it taken so long for color TV to gain market acceptance?
The automatic dishwasher has had a very slow market acceptance. Why?

Technical Problems

Many ideas prove to be technically infeasible. A new-product manager may observe a market opportunity and have an idea for a product to meet it. He puts the idea through the initial stages of screening and testing and then develops some prototypes, but inevitably there are technical problems connected with prototypes that must be ironed out. Sometimes these technical problems cannot be resolved.

Some managements have marketed products containing technical difficulties that only became apparent after the product was in the hands of the users. This unfortunate circumstance has ruined the reputation of many a company. Technical problems in the early Salk polio vaccine resulted in the death of some recipients; the maker has been a long time recovering from the debacle. Few things jeopardize the future of an organization so much as the marketing of a faulty product, for the market is not prone to forgive the errant businessman. A good reputation is a priceless asset.

PRODUCT STRATEGY

Much managerial strategy revolves around product decisions. Some of the more basic areas of product strategy are so important to your understanding of business that we must consider them at this point, even though they will be studied in detail in other courses you may take.

Product Differentiation

Probably the most fundamental product strategy in American business today is that of product differentiation—making one's product different in some manner from those of the competition, no matter how small the differentiation may be. No management wants to market a product that is identical in all respects to those of its competitors, for such products are known as commodities—standardized commodities—and are sold for standard market prices. When one sells a commodity he loses control over its price.

Why does the businessman want to avoid selling products for a market price?

Consequently, the basic strategy of modern management is that of product differentiation. Hopefully, management wants to introduce differences that are significant to the market—that are improvements over competitive products. Competition is strenuous along these lines, for each company vies vigorously with others to develop meaningful differentiations that will make its products more attractive.

Differentiation for Market Segmentation   A further refinement of the theory of product differentiation maintains that companies differentiate their products in line with the desire of the various market segments they wish to solicit. In essence, this strategy tailors the characteristics of each product to the desires of each market segment to which the product is to be sold.

What differentiations have the cigarette firms made in tailoring their products to the women's market segment?

While many critics of our business system are quick to point out meaningless product differentiations as a social waste, in the total scheme of things most product differentiations are demanded by the market and are meaningful. Volkswagen has certainly differentiated its product from Cadillac: a needed and meaningful differentiation. The critics ignore the bulk of differentiations in their intolerance toward the trivial differentiations that are bound to exist in any free system.

What is a trivial product differentiation? Is it always trivial?

Product Line

Most managements do not think in terms of a single product, but rather a product line—a number of related products all meeting varying needs of a certain market.

Concept of the Product Line

While we glibly speak in terms of a market, implying a certain homogeneous group of people demanding one thing, actually markets are anything but homogeneous. Each market is comprised of many buying units, each wanting a slightly different product. Economics of production force each buying unit to compromise its desires somewhat and settle for a product that meets its most critical specifications. Minor specifications must usually be ignored. One concept of the product line is an attempt by management to give each segment of the market a product more closely meeting its specifications by offering the basic product in a range of variations.

In other cases the product line may be composed of items of vastly dissimilar nature that may go either to one market or to different markets.

General Motors has a line of automobiles—a vehicle for every segment of the automotive market. Sometimes product lines are merely variations in sizes and capacities; at other times they consist of products performing varying functions. The truck performs different functions from the passenger vehicle. The computer is more than a big adding machine; it serves diverse functions.

Typically, marketing managements spend a great deal of time deciding what products need to be put together as the product line demanded by the market and the distributive organization. If one's product line is lacking in some significant respect, the market's preference may shift elsewhere. An American Motors dealership is not as attractive as a Chevrolet dealership, partly because the product line offered to each dealer is significantly different.

Costs severely limit the size of a firm's product line, as each new item adds considerably to expenses.

How are costs increased by adding items to a product line?

Price Lines

Frequently the product line is also classified into price lines. The company offers various modifications of its basic product at different prices, endeavoring to compete effectively in each price segment of the market.

Practically every market can be classified according to price—low, popular (medium), and high. The person wanting a luxury product refuses to buy the economy model, and the person who can only afford the economy model is blocked from the luxury markets. A firm wanting to do a large volume of business must have entrants in each of those races, so it brings out a product priced to the dictates of the particular market segment. You can buy approximately the same Sears Kenmore automatic washer at a price ranging from $100 to $300, depending upon how fancy a product you want. Of course, some product differentiation usually accompanies price lining.

Considerable corporate strategy comes into play in selecting price lines in which to compete, for in many instances a firm does not wish to compete across-the-board with all comers. Experience indicates that it is difficult to make a profit in the lower price lines; profits come easier in the higher prices because gross margins are more attractive—it does not cost that much more to make the luxury product.

Why do low-price competitors seem to have difficulty making a profit and staying in business over the long run?
Why can one get a larger margin on a luxury product than on a low-priced one?

Planned Obsolescence

For the past three decades the concept of planned product obsolescence has been one of the cornerstones of the consumer durable-goods industry. Planned obsolescence refers to the strategy of deliberately bringing out—periodically, usually annually—a slightly different model in order to make last year's model obsolete, thereby encouraging a certain segment of the market to purchase the new product, even though their old one may still be functional.

The goal of planned obsolescence was to sell more goods. American industry was, and is, faced with a situation in which the quality of many of the goods it makes is so high that the product's physical lifetime vastly exceeds the desired functional lifetime. So industry shortens the product's functional lifetime to the consumer by encouraging him to consider it obsolete. True, occasionally significant product improvements are included with this annual model change, but not always.

The strategy of product obsolescence is becoming less attractive to American industry for three reasons. First, the high cost of discarding dies and retooling for the annual change is making the strategy too expensive for the market to stand. Second, current concern over pollution and waste make planned obsolescence stand out as an economic waste. Third, the consumer market, in many instances, is becoming bored with the trivial changes offered each year. Consequently, the strategy is losing its effectiveness. Volkswagen has done rather well without using the strategy.

Quality Decisions

In recent years management has been plagued with complaints about the quality of its products. Indeed, the hue and cry over shoddy goods has reached the halls of Congress and resulted in legislation. Much more legislation is pending, unless American industry revises its strategies concerning the quality of its products.

Strategies pertaining to quality revolve around planning on the useful life of the products, for obviously the shorter the life of the product, the higher will be its replacement market. There is little desire in the automobile tire industry to produce a product that will last for 100,000 miles, for the resulting impact on replacement sales would be devastating.

What would happen in the tire business if a 100,000-mile tire became economically feasible?

Management plans the product life it wants. The question then rests in the marketplace as to whether the market accepts this decision, for if the product does not have sufficient quality the market may refuse to buy it. Unfortunately, faulty information sometimes disguises many inferior products. How can one know that the brand of automobile tires he bought will only last 8000 miles?

While it is quite easy to say that industry should increase the quality of its products, one must keep in mind that quality costs money, sometimes a great deal of money. A trade-off decision must be reached to determine the point at which the market will no longer pay for additional quality. This is the crux of the matter: while the market frequently cries for better products, it will not pay for them, but instead continues to subsidize cheap, shoddy merchandise by its willingness—even downright eagerness—to buy it. The easiest and most effective way we have of removing shoddy goods from the shelves of America is to refuse to buy them. But the lure of the lower price tag is so strong that most of us are unable to resist its blandishments. Hence, management is posed with a most difficult strategic decision: how much quality to put into its products.

Complementary Products

Head Ski's management was bound to consider the development of ski poles, ski clothing, and other items connected with skiing, for they are complementary products—things that are used together. Once a firm has established distribution channels and contact with a market, it is only natural that it should think of other things it can sell through those channels to that same market. If the additional products are complementary to one another, so much the better, for they can be tied together for more effective merchandising. Hence, it was only a matter of time before the makers of the Titlist golf ball went into the golf club business.

Joint Products

When one refines crude oil into gasoline, he also obtains other residual products in the process. Markets must be found for these residuals, lest the entire cost burden of the crude oil be borne by the gasoline consumer.

What has enabled the oil companies to keep the price of gasoline down relative to other prices during the past two decades?

The old saying among the meat packers, "We sell everything but the squeal!" had much validity, for competition was such that every part of the animal had to be converted into some marketable product if a profit was to be made on the beast.

Conclusion

> Product development is the lifeblood of business success. Without continual product improvements and new products the enterprise will eventually perish, as other firms bring out superior wares or the market's whims shift to another's goods. But product development is not easy. It is expensive and time-consuming. Success, at best, is most difficult to achieve. We have learned that product development is a separate function of the business enterprise and should be organized as such with its own staff of experts.

11 Distribution systems —wholesaling[1]

It is a very hard undertaking to seek to please everybody.
PUBLILIUS SYRUS

Society allocates a large share of its resources to moving goods from where they are made into the hands of the users. A huge network of institutions comprise the distribution channels through which the goods travel to their markets. The success of many companies is traced largely to management's skills in developing and maintaining good, efficient channels of distribution. Avon Products has prospered immensely because it developed and sustains a rather unique distribution channel for cosmetics: door-to-door saleswomen. Figure 11-1 is a chart of the various types of institutions comprising our distributive network.

[1] Much of this chapter is based on material from Richard H. Buskirk, *Principles of Marketing*, 3d ed. (New York: Holt, Rinehart and Winston, Inc., 1970), Chapters 12 and 14.

FIGURE 11 -1: Channels of Distribution from Raw Materials to Consumer

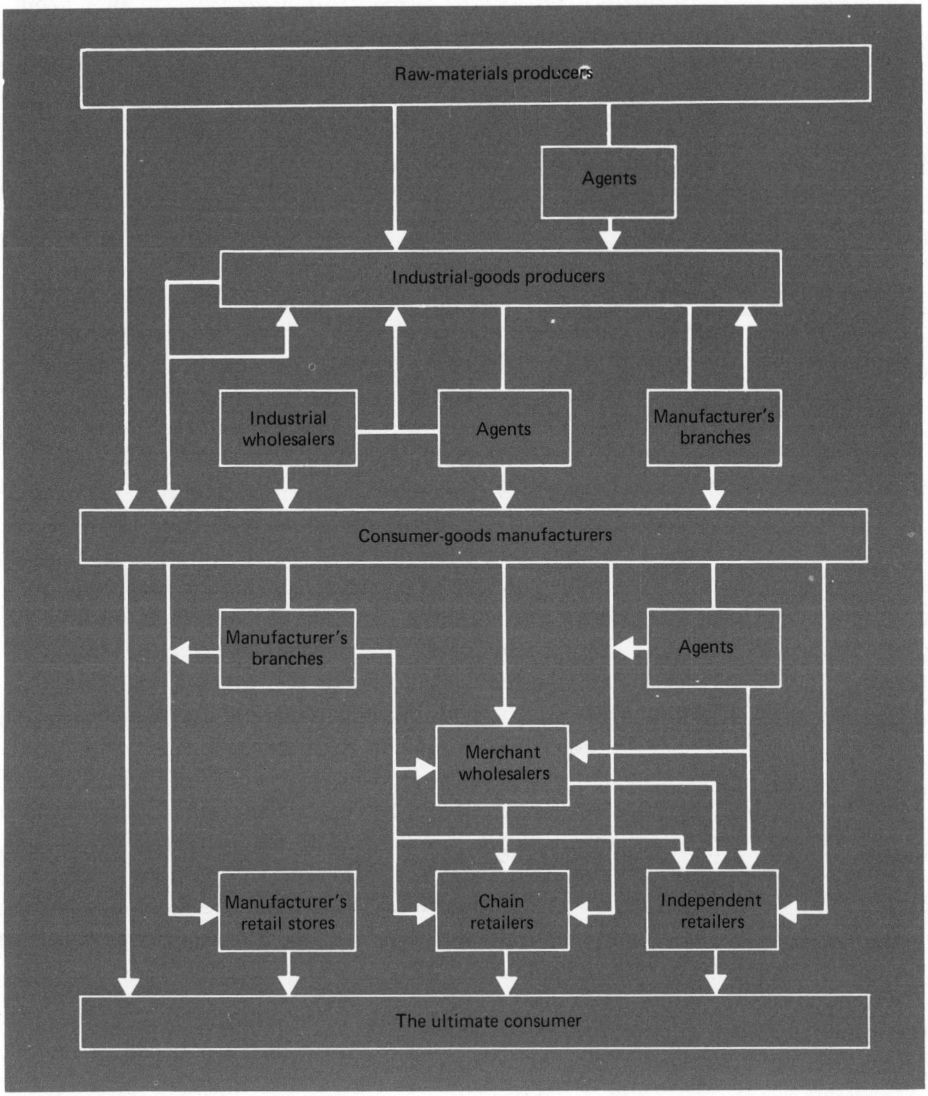

THE ROLE OF DISTRIBUTION SYSTEMS

Distribution systems are networks of economic institutions through which producers deliver goods to their users. As society shifted from producing things in the home to buying goods manufactured in centralized locations, there arose a need for some means to distribute products from the points of production to the dispersed populace. Channels of distribution furnish this bridge between the producer and the consumer.

Visualize the chaos that would result if each consumer had to search out the manufacturer of each product he wanted to buy. A tremendous amount of time and money would be expended in just acquiring the minimum amount of goods one would need for survival. Marketing channels funnel the goods demanded by the consumer to the place where he wishes to buy them, thereby creating three basic utilities: (1) place, (2) ownership, and (3) time. Sometimes middlemen alter the product in such a way that *form utility* is also created.

How?

Marketing institutions create *place utility,* because goods have no value to the buyer while they are still in the hands of the manufacturer. Marketing channels arrange for the transfer of title to the goods from the manufacturer to the buyer, creating *ownership utility.* Marketing channels arrange to have the goods available when the user wants them, creating *time utility.*

Frequently different institutions create each of these utilities. The title does not always automatically follow the actual trail of the merchandise. The ownership of automobiles passes from the manufacturer directly to the retail dealer, to the ultimate consumer; however, the actual merchandise is handled by several other institutions, such as trucking companies, railroads, storage concerns, and branch warehouses. Many persons involved in marketing channels play an important role in the distribution of merchandise they never see or own. A sales agent for a fir plywood manufacturer sells the plant's output, but the plywood never passes through his hands nor does he ever own it. Instead, he forwards the orders to the plant, which ships the panels to the buyer directly, with ownership passing directly between the two.

Another way of looking at distribution channels is to differentiate them into two classifications: psychological and physical. The physical channels are those through which the product itself travels, while the psychological channels are those used to persuade other people to take title to the merchandise. Though often the two are identical, frequently they are not. Parke Davis, a drug producer, distributes its output physically through drug wholesalers to retail drugstores and hospitals, but its psychological channel is to doctors, pharmacists, and hospital administrators by its own sales force.

THE FUNCTION OF MARKETING CHANNELS

Marketing channels fulfill several definite functions in society. First, they routinize decisions, thus lowering distribution costs. Second, they serve as a means of financing the entire process of moving goods from the producer to the consumer. Third, they are active participants in the pricing process. Fourth, they serve as an intelligence agency for the producer in his problem of communicating with the market. Fifth, they assist in the promotional aspects of marketing. Sixth, marketing channels perform an invaluable service to society by filling voids left in the economy by imperfections in our systems. Finally, the existence of middlemen minimizes the number of transactions in the system.

Routinization of Decisions

Marketing channels establish a routinization of decisions and transactions that result in lower costs. A department store buyer takes on a line of merchandise and thereafter reorders automatically whenever he is in need of additional goods; the salesman usually calls only to introduce the new styles. It would be frightfully expensive if the manufacturer were forced to solicit separately each order he obtained. Once a channel is established, goods tend to flow through it with a minimum of effort, in comparison with the work that was required to establish the channel originally.

In what ways other than costs does routinization help both the manufacturer and the middlemen?

Financing

One of the realities of business is that everything must be financed, from its inception to its consumption, and that at all times somebody has funds tied up in every item of merchandise in existence. There is a considerable amount of business strategy and tactics involved in shifting the financing function in business between various institutions. Typically, most business firms operate with insufficient funds; rare is the businessman who can truthfully say that he does not need additional working capital.

Once a manufacturer has made a product, normally he would like to get his money back as quickly as possible in order to reinvest it in other merchandise and to reduce his risks. Various institutions stand ready to provide this service to the producer. A wholesaler may buy merchandise and pay for it within a relatively short time. The wholesaler in turn resells the goods to retailers but may finance the dealer's operations for a lengthy period. In such an instance the wholesaler performs a definite financing function in society. Sometimes producers allow sales agents to sell their entire output, and the agent finances the customers by paying the producer upon shipment. At other times manufacturers shift the financing function on to various financing institutions willing to carry a good portion of the load while the merchandise is in transit to the market.

At the other end of the channel, retailers and banks must often finance the consumer. Frequently retailers have 45 to 60 days' sales tied up in accounts receivable—a financial burden that might have to be carried by the manufacturer if the retailer were not involved. The financing function performed by marketing channels is of no little importance to the producer. On many occasions a manufacturer who normally would prefer to sell directly to his market is forced to use other channels in order to avail himself of financing. Sometimes manufacturers have found that one of the most important weapons they possess in selling a product is the ability to finance the entire transaction. For example, leasing arrangements are little more than a means by which the manufacturer is financing the customer's use of the product.

Pricing

Distributive institutions usually set the retail price of a product. First, manufacturers consult with middlemen in establishing a factory price. Retailers are in closer touch with what the market will pay for an article than the producer is. Manufacturers rely heavily on middlemen's recommendations regarding retail prices and the various margins the middlemen require.

Next, the operating characteristics of the institutions through which a product is distributed determine how much must be added onto the manufacturer's price. A food item sold in a department store will carry a higher price than a similar one in a supermarket because the department store renders more services to the buyer.

Channels of Communication

Middlemen also serve as intelligence agents for the producer. One problem faced by most manufacturers is that they have lost contact with their markets. One way they keep in touch with the market is through their dealers who are in contact with customers. When retailers note a significant change in demand patterns, they pass it on to suppliers quickly.

Why are middlemen good sources of market information?

The owner-buyer of a relatively small collegiate men's apparel store, on his semiannual buying trip to New York, was viewing the fall line of one of his regular clothing sources. He was buying substantial quantities of sport coats but was not taking any slacks. When the salesman asked why, he was told that fashions had changed on the campus and that the firm's slacks were unacceptable; the buyer strongly preferred another line of slacks. The buyer went on to explain that the slacks were cut too full in the legs for the collegiate male; current fashions dictated tightly fitted pants. The salesman called the president, who immediately came down for a firsthand, detailed explanation. The buyer had such an excellent reputation among suppliers for being knowledgeable about campus fashions that the president ordered immediate changes in the slack line to accommodate the style change.

It is all too easy for management, sitting in an office in New York or Chicago, to lose contact with the market, for it is constantly changing, sometimes with unbelievable speed. By maintaining close contact with key middlemen, those who are on top of market trends, executives keep up-to-date.

Promotional Activities

Much of the promotional activity behind the final sale of a product to the consumer is performed by middlemen. The point-of-purchase display of merchandise in the store is almost completely in the hands of the retailer, who also does a great deal of the advertising, selling, and promoting of the wares he handles. Frequently his promotions are far more effective than the efforts of the producer. Many manufacturers, recognizing this, provide funds to assist him in these promotional efforts. They know that sometimes more revenue is obtained by spending a dollar at this level than by spending it on national advertising. Just as aggressive promotion by middlemen can greatly facilitate the sale of a product, inadequate promotion by them can hamper the sale of an otherwise good item.

Why is point-of-purchase promotion important?

Manufacturers undertake a multitude of activities to support their middlemen's promotional efforts. Many offer advertising allowances in which they agree to pay a portion of the middleman's cost of advertising of the manufacturer's brand under varying, specified conditions. If in-store display is important, then manufacturers usually provide display materials such as display racks, posters, and shelf strips. If the recommendations of the clerk are important or influential, then "push money" (PM's) or "spiffs" are offered him (a small tag on the article is torn off by the sales clerk upon selling the item; these are then sent in for cash). After-shave lotions, home permanents, and vitamins are among the items that frequently have push money behind them.

In what way does push money present a conflict of interest?

Many times the manufacturer must train and work with the middleman's sales force, particularly when technical knowledge is necessary. Automobile manufacturers furnish comprehensive sales aids and hold many clinics for dealers' salesmen.

Channel-Originated Behavior

It should not be assumed that marketing channels are passive institutions, moving only at the order of the manufacturers. Aggressive middlemen institute economic behavior of their own when they see a need for it in the marketplace. Sears has no fear of making a product when it sees a need that is not being met by other manufacturers. Many retailers and wholesalers have originated private brands with which they compete in the marketplace, side by side with manufacturer's brands. Thus middlemen are frequently in direct competition with the manufacturer in the sale of certain products.

It should never be assumed that distributive channels automatically follow orders of the manufacturers from whom they buy. Middlemen are independent businessmen who have thoughts of their own on the best way to conduct their businesses. They have learned through bitter experience that the interests of the manufacturer are not always identical with theirs.

Are retailers becoming more or less powerful in their dealings with manufacturers?

Minimizing Total Transactions

Suppose, for the sake of simplicity, that ten manufacturers each sold one unit of their merchandise directly to each of 100 users; 1000 separate transactions would result, with 1000 separate shipments being made on which 1000 transportation bills would have to be paid.

However, if one middleman is inserted into the picture, each manufacturer would sell 100 units of his product to the middleman (10 transactions and 10 shipments) who in turn would sell the goods to the users (100 transactions with 100 shipments). So the total number of transactions and shipments would be reduced from 1000 to 110, thereby reducing distribution costs significantly—for transactions cost money, as do separate, small shipments. It costs a manufacturer no more to take and execute an order for 100 units than it does for one unit. Similarly, the transportation costs for 100 units are proportionately much less per unit than they are for one unit; since middlemen are usually located near their customers, the longer portion of the haul from factory to users is accomplished in 100-unit quantities, leaving only a short distance for the single-unit delivery. Therefore, middlemen are economically justified by their role in reducing the transaction and transportation costs of marketing.

CHANNELS: A MANUFACTURER'S ASSET

The major asset of many firms is access to a channel through which they are able to market different products repeatedly with a minimum of effort. When Sunbeam wishes to introduce another electrical appliance, it has immediately available to it channels that will readily accept the new product. In contrast, an unknown manufacturer attempting to market the same product would be forced to incur substantial expense in order to set up channels of distribution. Because established channels result in higher profits in marketing a new product, they can be considered an earning asset.

It costs money to buy channels of distribution. One does not establish channels without considerable expenditure of funds and effort. It may take years and many thousands of dollars to establish firmly a sound system of distribution. Once established, however, the system begins returning dividends on the investment.

In some lines of endeavor channels are the most important asset that a company can possess. In marketing convenience goods, distribution is an extremely vital factor, for without it success cannot be obtained. In selling impulse items all one really needs is distribution, because volume will automatically follow distribution. One of the enigmas of marketing is the history of the Hershey Chocolate Company. Although many of Hershey's competitors are extensive advertisers, Hershey scarcely advertises, yet it outsells its competitors. The usual explanation is that Hershey obtained excellent distribution early in the industry and has maintained its channels vigorously. If a candy bar is on the counter of every convenience outlet in the nation, it cannot help being a large seller because of the strong impulse nature of its purchase. A good product helps, too.

Hershey began a small advertising campaign in 1970. Why?

Before a person can intelligently attack the problem of selecting and putting together the marketing channels he wishes to utilize, he must first have a thorough comprehension of the middlemen who are available for his use. Small businessmen often experience difficulties obtaining distribution for their products because they are unaware of the institutions ready to assist them in moving goods to the market.

Figure 11-1 is a simplified diagram of the movement of materials from producer to consumer. The major existing institutions are shown as either merchant or agent middlemen. It must be realized, however, that in generalizing on all channels one is bound to gloss over many of the small but important realities of the marketing world. For example, although furniture is normally sold directly from manufacturer to dealer, some of the major institutions facilitating these transactions are furniture shows held in various merchandise marts throughout the country. In the toy industry one of the major facilitating institutions is the annual toy fair held in New York during March of each year, in which the retail buyers meet with toy manufacturers and the sales agents representing them. In understanding the channels for a product one must therefore focus attention on the trade practices of the industry in question.

There is a common tendency to assume that all of these middlemen exist and operate in all industries. Such is simply not the situation. In many industries manufacturers' agents are nonexistent. In others, jobbers or wholesalers do not exist. The manufacturer is therefore usually forced to stay within the limitations of the institutions that service his industry. One inventor of a latch for livestock gates desired distribution through feed stores and farm-implement outlets by using manufacturers' agents. However, he discovered that he could not find one who called on these two outlets. Manufacturers' agents simply were nonexistent in this field of endeavor.

CHANNELS: THE MANUFACTURER'S ENIGMA

Middlemen are not passive links in the chain of distribution leading from producer to consumer. They are not standing around awaiting directions from the manufacturer. They do not exist for the manufacturer's convenience, nor are they all puny institutions that can be pressured to conform to the manufacturer's wishes. Many wholesale and retail institutions are more powerful than the makers of the goods they sell. Sears, Penney's, Macy's, Wards, Gimbels, Safeway, and A&P are but a few of the huge retailing concerns that are larger than most of the firms selling to them. Their suppliers find themselves on the weak side of the bargaining table, certainly incapable of exerting any undue influence upon them. Indeed, it is not at all uncommon for manufacturers selling to large retail concerns to complain bitterly about the unusual pressures applied to their selling terms by such buyers. However, in many circumstances even small retailers can exert a considerable amount of pressure upon hungry manufacturers. One small men's apparel store owner was able to obtain several valuable concessions in terms of sale from his key sources when he was building a new store because his volume was significant to the sellers and they wanted to keep him from taking on competitive lines.

One can easily be led to believe that middlemen come wrapped in neat, well-defined packages, that each middleman can be easily classified into wholesaler and retailer and further classified into specific types according to the various criteria set forth later. Such is simply not the case. Many middlemen defy classification except by meaningless arbitrary decisions. There are economic institutions that sell substantial volumes both at retail and wholesale; what are they? wholesalers or retailers? There are wholesalers who behave in every possible way; they own some goods and serve as agents for others; they stock some merchandise but drop ship others; they have permanent relationships with some suppliers but deal with others on a one-time basis.

The only principle that can be put forth is that each middleman behaves in whatever manner he feels will be most profitable, and he will initiate any type of relationship with any other institution if he feels it will be profitable. The middleman will make whatever arrangements necessary to give his customers what they want while trying to minimize his costs within those mandates. Other things being equal, he will try to minimize his investments and costs. This means he does not want to carry any more inventory than necessary, does not want to finance the transactions, and does not want to promote the goods or own them. The closer the manufacturer can come to meeting these rigorous specifications, the easier it will be for him to obtain the services of the middleman.

IDENTIFICATION OF MIDDLEMEN

Marketing channels are not static, simple behavior systems; they form, rather, a complex network of interlocking institutions that is extremely difficult to describe accurately. The task is made more difficult because few middlemen fit any clear-cut definition. Table 11-1 is an outline of the types of middlemen we will discuss.

Table 11–1

CLASSIFICATION OF MIDDLEMEN

MERCHANT MIDDLEMEN–Take title to the goods
Manufacturer-owned
Sales branches
Sales offices
Retailer-owned warehouses
Independent
Full-service wholesaler
Cash-and-carry wholesaler
Drop shipper
Truck jobber
Rack jobber
Mill supply houses
Industrial distributors
AGENT MIDDLEMEN–Do not take title to goods; act as salesmen
Sales agent
Broker
Manufacturer's agent

Care must be taken in attempting to identify various middlemen and institutions functioning as marketing channels. Although definitions for each type of middleman have been created, businessmen do not always fit nicely into them. The so-called food broker fits the definition of manufacturer's agent, not that of broker, because he has continuing relations with his manufacturers and tends not to handle competing lines. In the plywood industry, a merchant middleman who is technically defined a drop shipper is widely utilized, but he is called a direct-mill shipper. Certain middlemen act as sales agents for certain producers, manufacturers' agents for other producers, and brokers in still other transactions. One businessman in northern Ohio was normally a broker of groceries; he kept close contact with many packers and would notify his customers each week of merchandise that was available. He acted as a true broker in the transactions. Frequently, though, he would purchase in his own name a carload of distressed merchandise and sell it directly to interested wholesalers. On such occasions he acted as a drop shipper because he did not take possession of the merchandise, but did take title; the goods were shipped directly from the packing plant to the customer. Besides all these activities, he maintained a steady relationship with two brand-name canners; he continually represented them in the capacity of a manufacturer's agent. It can thus be seen that many middlemen defy clear-cut definition. About all that can be said about them is that they stand ready in a particular market to help move goods from the producer to some institution closer to the market, and that they will act in any way in which they can make money or effect lower costs.

Nevertheless, before studying the detailed operations of various middlemen, so that we can understand the basic characteristics of their various activities, we need to know their classical definitions.

WHOLESALING

The wholesaler sells to parties whose motives for buying goods are to resell them in one form or another. His market is a distinct contrast to that of the retailer, whose customers purchase goods for the purpose of consuming them.

Need for Wholesaling

Wholesalers vary widely in the services they provide, some of which are: (1) maintaining a sales force; (2) storage; (3) delivery; (4) credit to the buyer; (5) financial assistance to the manufacturer; (6) product servicing; (7) sales promotional work; and (8) market information. Since every service costs money, both manufacturers and retailers do business only with the wholesalers who offer the precise services needed, for it would be foolish to pay for unnecessary services.

Is it possible to eliminate the wholesaler? the wholesaling functions?

Wholesaling by some type of institution is mandatory if goods are to be brought to market. The question of whether or not wholesalers are necessary is a useless one. The real question is who should do the wholesaling—because somebody must perform the necessary wholesaling functions.

Types of Wholesalers

Wholesale institutions can be classified in three ways: (1) who controls them? (2) who owns the merchandise? (3) what services are performed? Many manufacturers perform wholesaling activities through their own sales offices, branches, and warehouses. Other producers utilize one or more of the many different independently owned and operated wholesale institutions. Some retailers control the wholesale operations with which the manufacturer must deal. Some wholesalers take title to the goods they handle; others do not. Those who own the goods they sell are called merchant wholesalers, and those who do not are called agent middlemen.

Manufacturer-Owned Wholesale Institutions Although merchant wholesale institutions comprise about 68 percent of all wholesaling enterprises, they account for only 44 percent of total wholesale sales volume. Manufacturer's sales branches and sales offices represent only 9 percent of all wholesaling institutions, but account for 33 percent of total volume.

What is the significance of these statistics?

Strictly speaking, all sales by manufacturers other than those made directly to the ultimate consumer are wholesale transactions. However, many manufacturers—by establishing sales offices, sales branches, or warehouses—undertake far more extensive wholesaling endeavors than others do. Some manufacturers maintaining these wholesale outlets sell to other wholesaling institutions as well, although a number of manufacturers undertake wholesale endeavors to circumvent independent wholesale channels and sell directly to retail outlets or industrial users.

The major reason manufacturers perform wholesale functions is to get more aggressive promotion of their goods and to render better service to their customers. Any lowering of distribution costs usually results from increased volume or efficiencies rather than elimination of the middlemen's profits. Sometimes wholesaling manufacturers encounter relatively high distribution costs in comparison to their competitors who use independent institutions, but the executives feel that the increased control gained over distribution more than compensates for the increased costs and efforts incurred.

Why do manufacturer-owned wholesale institutions tend to be more expensive than independent wholesalers, in view of the fact that they tend to be larger-volume operators?
What is meant by control?

Independently Owned Wholesale Institutions By number and volume alone, independently owned wholesale establishments are far more important than manufacturer-owned wholesale institutions. They are classified into two major groups: merchant wholesalers and agent middlemen. In each of these categories several different types of institutions exist, each performing different services.

MERCHANT WHOLESALERS Inasmuch as merchant wholesalers own the goods they handle, their behavior differs significantly from that of agents. When one invests his own money in goods, he feels entitled to have complete authority over its disposal and his own operations. Hence, the merchant wholesaler has a far higher degree of autonomy and freedom of action than do agent middlemen.

Because margins in wholesaling are small and profits modest, merchant wholesalers are cautious about the lines they handle. They will not take on an item unless they are convinced that their customers demand it. Many of these wholesalers carry thousands of items, making it difficult for their salesmen to push the product of any one manufacturer. If the wholesaler's salesmen only writes up the orders of his customers, he is doing a good job. A manufacturer finds it difficult to *push* his product through independent merchant wholesalers; he must *pull* it through by sales promotional activities aimed at the consumer and retailers. Once there is a proven demand for a product by retailers, wholesalers are only too eager to carry it in stock. In fact, they are forced to carry it if they are to render adequate service, because their success depends in large part on their ability to fill the needs of their customers. If a retailer learns that he cannot get a significant portion of the merchandise he wants from one wholesaler, he tends to eliminate this concern from his list of suppliers to minimize the number of houses with which he does business.

Merchant wholesalers are usually encountered in industries in which the retailers are relatively small and carry a large number of relatively inexpensive items, each of which is not stocked in any depth.

Why?

A producer of a new scenery product to be sold to HO model railroad enthusiasts through hobby shops fully expected to find hobby wholesalers the dominant channel in this industry, because the retail hobby dealers were small operators who carried only a few of each of many thousands of items. The dealer therefore had to have quick delivery to replenish what he sold. No manufacturer can economically afford to contact these dealers directly; there are too many of them, and the total order from each would be insufficient to pay the sales cost. The hobby wholesaler will do the job for 15 percent of the retail price; his usual discount from list is 50–10 percent, and he passes along 40 percent to the dealer.

How does this arithmetic work?

FULL-SERVICE MERCHANT WHOLESALERS   The regular full-service merchant wholesaler, frequently found in the hardware, drug, and industrial supplies fields, provides a great many services to both the manufacturer and the buyer. He maintains a sales force that regularly calls on the trade. He owns warehouses in which he carries adequate inventories and from which he makes deliveries. Usually he extends credit to qualified buyers. In instances where repair services are needed, sometimes he will perform these duties. Under certain circumstances, if it is attractive financially, he will do sales promotional work on behalf of a manufacturer. The wholesaler, by paying bills promptly, is rendering financial assistance to the manufacturer, who obtains his money much sooner than he would if he attempted to perform his own wholesaling functions. Since these middlemen are performing a great many services, naturally their operating expenses will be considerably more than the expenses of those performing fewer services (about 13.4 percent of their sales volume).

RACK JOBBER   The rack jobber is a full-service merchant wholesaler who developed to meet a need created when supermarkets began carrying nonfood items. Not only does the rack jobber perform all the usual services of the full-service wholesaler; he also does several other important things. First, he assumes complete responsibility for keeping each dealer fully supplied with an adequate, balanced inventory. The rack jobber derives his name from the fact that most of his customers furnish him a certain amount of shelf space or assign him floor space in which to place his rack. Thereafter he is responsible for seeing to it that the rack is kept adequately stocked with the proper goods.

Frequently the merchandise is placed in the store on consignment; that is, the retailer does not have legal title to the wares, but pays the rack jobber only for what is sold. The rack jobber assumes the risk that his merchandise will not sell. He is completely financing the transaction, because the dealer has none of his funds invested at any time. In a strictly legal sense, the rack jobber is actually a retailer; title to the goods moves directly from him to the ultimate consumer. One way of looking at the operation is that the dealer is merely leasing space in the store to the rack jobber on a percentage-of-sales basis.

Usually a rack jobber will specialize in only one line of merchandise, such as drugs, records, hardware, magazines, books, or wearing apparel. The reason for his existence is really quite simple. The managers of supermarkets realize that they are in the food business and that is the only field in which they are competent to buy goods. They realize that it would be a tremendous amount of work to purchase all the various nonfood items and that they are less competent to judge what items would or would not be good sellers. By using a rack jobber they shift the entire risk of carrying nonfood items onto the shoulders of people who are more competent to bear this risk. The rack jobber handling the drug counter knows from past experience which items sell readily in supermarkets and which do not. The jobber also performs all the physical work connected with maintaining these items on the shelves.

Naturally, the margins paid to the retailer are smaller than he would realize if he were to handle the entire business himself. As in all businesses, everything costs money; the more activities a business performs, the higher will be its costs. The rack jobber is a relatively high-cost wholesale institution. One rack jobber distributing a line of children's books passed on 25 percent of the retail price to the retailer. He kept the remainder of the 40 percent retail margin usually allowed on such products, in addition to the usual jobber's margin. On drug items, the rack jobber usually allows the retailer 20 percent of the retail price, instead of the usual 33 percent; the rack jobber also obtains the wholesaler's margin of $16\frac{2}{3}$ percent. Housewares rack jobbers sell to large chain operations at 40–10 percent off list price, even though these accounts could buy directly from manufacturers at 50–10 percent off list. This would give the jobber about a 17 percent gross margin on his sales volume. Many dealers are willing to take this reduced margin simply because, if they were to perform all these activities themselves, they would ultimately have a lower net profit on the business.

How do these percentages figure out?

CASH-AND-CARRY WHOLESALERS   In an attempt to reduce their operating expenses to become more competitive with chain operations, some wholesalers during the 1930s instituted cash-and-carry outlets. Just as the name implies, the retailer must come to the warehouse to get goods, thereby eliminating delivery costs, and he must pay cash, thereby eliminating credit expenses. Unquestionably such wholesalers succeeded in lowering their costs of operations, because their operating expense as a percentage of sales is approximately 10.9 percent. Implicit in this type of operation is the elimination of field-selling costs, which are substantial. The major functions performed by cash-and-carry wholesalers are mainly storage and the breakdown of large transportation shipments into small units. Frequently these cash-and-carry operations are offshoots or special departments connected with other full-service wholesalers.

DROP SHIPPERS   The so-called drop shipper, sometimes known as a "direct-mill shipper," "desk jobber," or a "distributor without a yard," performs most of the wholesaling functions with the exception of storage and handling. He obtains orders and forwards them to the manufacturer for shipment directly to the buyer. The drop shipper takes title to the merchandise; he pays the manufacturer for the goods shipped and frequently extends credit to the buyer. Because storage and handling costs are eliminated, the drop shipper's operating expenses are usually quite low (approximately 4.5 percent of sales).

Drop shippers usually operate in fields where the product is bulky; the customers usually purchase in carload or truckload lots. It would be senseless for a wholesaler to sell from his own inventories in carload lots, because tremendous waste would be incurred in unloading a carload shipment. Also, drop shippers are more likely to operate where producers do not make the assortment of goods demanded by the buyers. The drop shipper puts together the right assortment by representing several producers. Few coal companies mine all the types and grades of coal demanded by the customers; it is thus inefficient for a limited-line coal company to try to call on coal dealers. Instead, a drop shipper puts together a full line of coal so that the dealer can order just what he needs with a minimum of effort.

Drop shippers operate in the lumber industry. Why?

Moreover, full-service wholesalers have the manufacturers drop-ship large orders directly to the buyers. Frequently trucks are used instead of railroads, in which event the smallest economical shipment may be from 100 to 300 pounds. If a wholesaler gets a large order from a customer, he may have the supplier ship directly to the buyer rather than incur the cost of handling it through his warehouse. Not only are handling costs reduced, but total transportation costs from factory to customer are minimized; it costs substantially more to ship something twice, even though the weight and total distance are the same.

Agent Middlemen

Unlike the wholesalers described above, the agent middleman does not own (take title to) the goods in which he deals. The actual market behavior of agents varies so much that accurate classification is difficult at best and confusing at worst. This discussion will be organized along traditional lines, classifying them as brokers, sales agents, and manufacturer's agents—but keep in mind that any one agent middleman frequently acts in all three capacities. The specific arrangements between an agent and his principal will vary in each instance.

BROKER   Strictly defined, the broker does not maintain constant relations with either the buyer or seller but acts in behalf of either, depending on the situation. The broker does not take title to the goods or take possession of them. The only service he renders is that of negotiating for exchange of title. Because of this, he is an extremely low-cost operator; his expenses may run less than 2 percent of sales.

The broker is usually operative where there are many small suppliers whose market consists of many small buyers. Under such circumstances it is difficult for any one seller to know who is in need of his goods. Similarly, it is difficult for any buyer to know from what source he could best obtain a given item. The broker's function is to know both the supply and demand side of the market and bring the two together for the maximum satisfaction of both parties. Although the broker is usually paid by the seller of the merchandise, when he is under the direct control of the buyer he must be paid by him.

Why do brokers dominate the marketing of real estate?

Although the broker has ready access to a market that is attractive to a manufacturer in terms of both cost and accessibility, most manufacturers do not like to rely on brokers, because brokers have little loyalty to any one supplier. Instead, they usually act in their own best interests and those of their customers. It is to the broker's best interest to please his customers rather than to please his manufacturers; suppliers are relatively easy to obtain, but customers are not.

SALES AGENTS   Sales agents are comparable to the sales department of a firm, in that they perform several functions other than selling. Normally, a sales agent sells the entire output of one or more products of the firms he represents. He usually has the exclusive right to sell the product or products in a wide area, frequently over the entire world or at least the United States. He often has authority over prices, terms of sale, and other marketing decisions. He may finance the manufacturer to some extent. Many sales agents are responsible for the entire sales promotional program behind the product.

It would be impossible to give any meaningful average cost of a selling agent, because it varies with the field and the exact nature of the services provided.

One sales agent handling all marketing for a manufacturer of sterling silver jewelry was paid 20 percent of the manufacturer's sales price for his efforts. In addition to the usual functions performed by sales agents, this operator maintained showrooms in all the major merchandise marts. He also carried inventories from which to effect rapid delivery.

The sales agent is an attractive channel of distribution for the small, inadequately financed, production-oriented manufacturer. The producer, by obtaining the services of a good sales agent, has immediate access to the market, because the agent has established relations with the market and will be able to begin immediately soliciting orders from the customers. It may take the manufacturer many years to establish such contacts. The use of a sales agent allows a manufacturer to concentrate strictly on production and ignore distribution problems.

Unfortunately, there are several serious drawbacks to the use of sales agents. When using this method the manufacturer has little contact with his market, thus he is at the mercy of the agent. If the sales agent demands that prices be reduced, the manufacturer may have little alternative, because he has no other channel of distribution readily available through which to sell his goods. Moreover, if the sales agent finds a more attractive source for the product, the manufacturer can find himself without distribution almost overnight and be right back where he was when he entered business. There may be a basic conflict of interest between some sales agents and manufacturers—grounds for problems in their relations. Most businessmen do not wish to risk the long-run success of their company by relying on the integrity and good will of a sales agent, no matter how attractive such a marketing channel may be initially. On the other hand, there are many examples of long, profitable relations between the two. The wisdom of using this channel depends entirely on the circumstances.

MANUFACTURERS' AGENTS   Although a firm might have only one selling agent for a product, it may employ any number of manufacturers' agents. A manufacturers' agent is basically a salesman operating on a straight commission basis. Typically, he will cover a certain limited territory, and the only function he performs is that of selling. He will take neither title to nor possession of the goods. He does no financing, nor does he attempt to service what he sells. He is strictly a salesman. Sometimes he is called a manufacturers' "rep."

The economic function of the manufacturers' agent is that of representing several noncompetitive producers concurrently. Instead of having just one or a few of the products of one manufacturer to sell, he normally assembles a rather substantial line of related—but noncompetitive—products to offer his customers. His operating costs thus are not borne by just one manufacturer but are spread among all of them; so his operating expenses, as a percentage of his sales, are lowered.

One manufacturers' representative operating in the plumbing field maintained headquarters in Kansas City, Mo. With the assistance of the three salesmen he employed, he covered the states of Missouri, Nebraska, Kansas, Oklahoma, Iowa, and Arkansas. He had assembled a complete line of plumbing supplies, such as bathroom fixtures, pipe, fittings, soil pipe, and all the items that a plumbing wholesale house would carry. He and his men contacted plumbing wholesalers and large plumbing contractors throughout the area, taking orders to be forwarded to the various suppliers, who in turn shipped directly to the customers. The agent was paid 3 percent commission on the sales price.

Manufacturers' agents are a predominant channel of distribution in the apparel industries, in which there are thousands of relatively small manufacturers and thousands of relatively small buyers. One manufacturers' agent selling to men's apparel stores represents well-known quality lines of shirts, slacks, ties, and two lines of women's wear (for men's stores that have put in women's departments). He gets 6 percent commission but must pay all expenses. Such agents can make handsome earnings if they represent popular lines of merchandise.

Although distribution through manufacturers' agents is a bit more difficult to arrange than establishing relations with just one sales agent, usually the results are more satisfactory in the long run, because the manufacturer is not at the mercy of one man. If a manufacturers' agent decides to discontinue handling a line, the manufacturer is not faced with a complete loss of volume. New manufacturers' agents can be obtained, and considerably more flexibility of operations is realized. Frequently a firm can use manufacturers' agents in some regions and other channels in selected areas. Concerns often sell directly to dealers or industry in large metropolitan areas but use agents in sparsely settled regions. For the maker of a limited line of relatively low-priced products or items that are purchased infrequently, the manufacturers' agent can be a very attractive channel of distribution.

Suppose you wanted to distribute a new gift item for men through men's apparel stores. How would you actually locate manufacturers' agents to contact the dealers for you?

CHANNELS TO INDUSTRIAL USERS

Although many of the above-described wholesalers can sell either to retailers or industrial users, wholesaling to the industrial market is sufficiently important that a separate discussion of it will be helpful. There are a few wholesale institutions that deal almost exclusively in industrial products; the two types that will be discussed here are the industrial distributor and the mill supply house.

Industrial Distributors

Industrial distributors are really a cross between the full-service merchant wholesaler and a manufacturers' agent who carries inventories. Though they perform all the functions of a full-service wholesaler, they usually do not carry products of competing manufacturers but prefer to represent makers of related but noncompetitive goods. Often they will represent only one manufacturer who happens to produce a wide line of products. In many market areas the Caterpillar organization utilizes independent distributors who handle only Caterpillar products. These distributors sell, service, and finance their customers in addition to maintaining an inventory.

How can a manufacturer evaluate the abilities of a distributor?

These distributors can provide a most attractive channel for many industrial-goods manufacturers whose line of products is insufficient to sustain their own sales force in the field. The cost of using industrial distributors varies, depending largely on the unit price of the product and the market potential for it.

Sometimes the use of distributors is dictated by personnel, organizational, or financial considerations. Some relatively small industrial-goods producers are unable to hire top-notch salesmen for their organizations, but they can enlist the services of such talented men by using distributors. Usually a good distributor's success is based on a sound sales program executed by capable salesmen. At other times a manufacturer may lack financial resources to sustain, through good times and bad, a branch organization comparable with the one that established independent distributors offer him.

Mill Supply Houses

Mill supply houses are the industrial equivalent of the general-line, full-service merchant wholesaler. They carry an extremely large number of items, frequently from competing manufacturers, and they perform all the usual activities of the full-service wholesaler. They usually carry a wide line of such items as abrasives, brushes, small hand tools, and, in general, any item that is sold to a wide, horizontal industrial market.

In some industries, such as the oil industry, there are mill supply houses that supply a vertical market. In every oil field several supply houses carry a complete line of the usual supplies required for drilling and operating wells, such as casing, drilling compounds, pumps, compressors, motors, and other products incident to oil production. A manufacturer of a product going to one industry is therefore frequently able to locate wholesalers who specialize in servicing that particular industry alone. For example, a manufacturer of an item to be sold to garages and service stations used a network of automotive-parts-supply wholesalers.

In situations in which the customer wants quick delivery and is unable to predict his needs, the supplier must place his goods in supply stores prepared to make prompt delivery, or the product will not be present when the buyer is making his buying decision. The supplier, however, may employ psychological channels directly to the potential market. One manufacturer who had developed a new valve for mud pumps in oil drilling operations found it necessary to hire salesmen to sell the drilling contractors and oil companies on the advantages of the new valve. Nevertheless, he had to distribute the valve through oil field supply houses so that it would be available when it was needed.

RETAILER-OWNED WHOLESALING ESTABLISHMENTS

Although, strictly speaking, many marketing experts would not classify retailer-owned wholesaling institutions as legitimately a part of wholesaling, nevertheless they deserve to be discussed here. Actually the retailer is integrating backward toward the manufacturer and assuming many of the functions normally performed by independent wholesalers or manufacturers' wholesale outlets. When a food processor sells to the Safeway organization, he ships directly to the Safeway warehouse in each region, and at that point he ceases to control the merchandise. From that point onward, the retail organization takes over the distribution of the item and assumes the cost of doing so. Safeway spends about 4 percent of sales in performing wholesale functions for the manufacturer.

Many retailing organizations have wholesaling arrangements that almost parallel independently owned institutions in the services they perform. For example, Sears basically acts as a drop shipper in most of its transactions. Once connections are made with the "wholesale house" in Chicago, most orders are shipped directly from the manufacturer's plant to the retail store ordering the goods. The J. C. Penney Company has operated in a similar manner, but with its great expansion in recent years it has been establishing distribution centers—wholesale warehouses—from which it supplies its stores with a great deal of their needs.

Why build such warehouses rather than drop ship?

Retailer-owned wholesaling activities have grown considerably in recent years because, in general, they represent a lower-cost method of distribution, in which several activities have been eliminated. Where the independent wholesaler usually must sustain a rather expensive sales force in the field, a retailer-owned wholesale activity does not. Risk is greatly reduced because the wholesale activity is better able to judge just what goods will be demanded by its customers—the retail outlets. Practically the only costs incurred in the process are storage, handling, and delivery expenses, but these costs would have to be borne by someone anyway, and therefore they are not additions to the total cost of distributing the products.

Conclusion

Wholesaling activities are inescapable, inasmuch as goods must be moved from the producer to the vast multitude of retail and industrial concerns throughout the nation. The question is not whether but rather by whom wholesaling activities will be performed: the manufacturer, an independent enterprise, or the buyer. No matter who performs the activities, costs are incurred. Wholesaling costs can be reduced in only two ways: activities can be eliminated or they can be performed more efficiently.

For a few years during the depression of the 1930s it was thought that wholesaling was of declining importance. In recent years, however, it has become relatively more important in the distribution of goods. Although retail trade increased 21.9 percent between 1958 and 1963, wholesale trade went up 25.4 percent. One manufacturer of heavy industrial machines recently announced that he was discontinuing his direct-selling activities and resuming the use of a network of industrial distributors.

12 Retailing systems[1]

It takes a wise man to discover a wise man.
—LAERTIUS

Retail institutions are the main means through which the ultimate consumer obtains goods and services. Practically all manufacturers of consumer goods must use some form of retail distribution to get their products to the consumers.

[1] Much of this chapter is based on material in Richard H. Buskirk, *Principles of Marketing*, 3d ed. (New York: Holt, Rinehart and Winston, Inc., 1970), Chapter 13.

It must be stressed that *anyone selling to the ultimate consumer is performing the functions of a retailer, regardless of what he calls himself.* Many so-called discount houses claim to be wholesalers, but this is semantic nonsense, because by definition a retailer sells to people who buy a product to use it rather than to resell it. A wholesaler sells to those who purchase for the purpose of reselling the goods.

What difference does it make to whom the wholesaler sells?

WHAT THE RETAILER DOES

The retailer is the most expensive link in the chain of distribution; his costs alone vary between 20 and 50 percent of the price paid by the customer—a seemingly high cost that has disturbed many critics of business. Many people try to increase their standard of living by going around the retailer to "buy wholesale." Although this may be feasible sometimes, the retailer usually does certain things for his money. Those who evade the retailer often save no money by buying directly from a distributor.

Why is the retailer expensive?

First, the retailer is convenient; he creates both time and place utility. Most purchasers avoiding him travel greater distances and spend a lot of time doing so. The retailer sells merchandise at a convenient location and frequently delivers it free. For the thousands of small, insignificant items bought by the average family, convenient retail distribution is mandatory. Without it, such goods will not sell in adequate volume.

Why is convenience important?

Second, most retailers guarantee and service the goods they sell. There is always some risk involved in any purchase; no matter how reliable a manufacturer may be, mistakes are made and some materials are occasionally defective. When the customer buys an item, he really does not care about the product, only about the benefits he will get from it. Thus he wants to be certain he will get these benefits when he buys something. Retailers usually try to give their customers satisfaction. If merchandise is defective, they will replace it or have it fixed. This guarantee saves the buyer much of the inconvenience he would experience in negotiating directly with a wholesaler or manufacturer on defective items.

Third, the retailer frequently finances the buyer. Most department and other general merchandise stores offer open-book credit, which allows the customer to pay later.

What is happening to this credit function?

Fourth, retailers promote; their displays of merchandise stimulate sales, as there is a considerable amount of impulse buying of most products. The retailer usually has salesmen and does advertising and other promotional work for which he must be paid. Moreover, he lends whatever prestige he has to the goods he sells.

What does it mean to lend prestige?

Fifth, the retailer performs a storage function. He has goods available so that the customer can buy them as needed without waiting for delivery.

Sixth, retailers perform an intelligence function for the manufacturer, because they are in daily contact with the market. They are keenly aware of market trends and attitudes. Retailers can determine rather rapidly the reception of any given fashion introduced to the market. The automobile dealers were well aware of the small-car trend before Detroit seemed to notice it.

Friction usually occurs when the dealer tries to sell the consumer services that he does not want to buy. One of the reasons for avoiding the local retailer in buying appliances is that some people are unwilling to pay for the financing or convenience functions. For the man who has ample time and is buying a product in which the service risk is small, buying from a merchant who does not furnish these services may be an economically sound decision. Frequently small-town merchants overvalue the convenience function and overcharge, with the result that they drive trade to nearby larger towns.

What other reasons do people who live in small towns have for going to larger cities for shopping?

TYPES OF RETAIL OUTLETS

Each retailing institution is somewhat unique, but it is possible to classify them into certain meaningful categories that will clarify their operations.

Department Stores

A department store is a combination of many departments, each operated almost as a separate store under the direction of a person known as the *buyer*. Each *buyer* is responsible for the supervision of all personnel in the department. In essence, the *buyer* is running a store of his own under the guidance of top management.

The head of the department is called the *buyer* because buying is his main job; there is an old adage in retailing that "goods well bought are half-sold." The *buyer* knows that if he is diligent in his purchasing activities and buys merchandise that is desirable to his customers, selling problems are minimized. If he acquires goods that are less than desirable, he will be able to sell them only at a loss.

Department stores basically appeal to women and are strong in the sale of soft goods. Although they sell a significant volume of appliances and other hard-goods items, they are not famous for this trade. In fact, many department stores have eliminated hard-goods departments because of competition from the mass-merchandising appliance specialty outlets.

As a rough rule of thumb, most department stores operate on approximately 40 percent gross margin (an item that sells for $1 would cost the store 60¢), although furs have a higher markup and appliances a lower one.

Why do these markups differ?

Most department stores offer a wide variety of services such as credit, delivery, unlimited return privileges, and other fringe services which make their costs relatively high.

Department stores vary in the people to whom they appeal. Some department stores appeal to lower-income groups, others to the upper-income strata.

Currently, department stores face several problems. First, they are plagued by price competition from the so-called discount houses in lower-cost locations. Second, with their main quarters firmly anchored in downtown locations, many of which are becoming less desirable, they are encountering the tremendous problems of expanding into decentralized operations in the suburbs. Not only are serious personnel problems created by such expansions, but also operational and cost problems can critically affect profits.

Third, department stores, as well as the rest of the retail community, are having serious personnel problems. Although in past decades they have been attractive to the labor market, in recent years they have grown increasingly unattractive to highly talented persons, who are being enticed into other careers.

Finally, there has been a definite trend toward chain organizations in the department store field. Many individual stores have been purchased by chains such as Allied Stores, Federated Stores, or Marshall Fields.

Specialty Stores

Although the department stores need millions of dollars in sales volume each year to survive, many specialty stores make a satisfactory profit on an annual volume of $100,000. The margins of specialty stores vary tremendously—from the 25 percent of the independent automobile dealers to the 50 percent of the jewelry and furniture stores. In general, the slower the turnover, the higher will be the margin needed by the retailer. Although traditionally in the jewelry trade 50 percent has been the desired margin, certain promotional, high-turnover operators may be satisfied with less.

Why may certain operators be satisfied with less?

Typically, specialty stores offer somewhat less service than department stores. How many jewelry outlets offer open-book credit, free delivery service, and will readily take merchandise back if the buyer changes his mind?

The success of most specialty stores lies in their ability to appeal strongly to a specific group of customers. In its relatively narrow field, a good specialty store may carry a better selection of goods than can be found in many department stores.

How can a specialty store carry such a selection?

In practically every college town there are certain women's ready-to-wear stores that appeal only to the college coed, making no attempt whatsoever to carry goods that would be appealing to the older women in town. Similarly, there are specialty stores that appeal strictly to the townspeople and make no attempt to solicit trade from the campus community. Most specialty store owners realize that they cannot be all things to all people but must, because of their limited space and inventory, pick a definite market and buy for it.

It is a mistake to think that because specialty stores are small they cannot move substantial amounts of merchandise. A men's apparel store may sell more suits and other apparel than a men's department in a department store. The manufacturer must not assume that because a store is relatively small its volume is insignificant. The proprietor of one small ski shop in the Rocky Mountain region sells more skis and accessories than most department stores or general-line sporting goods stores—yet his total floor area is only 500 square feet. Similarly, a pro shop at a sizable golf course will usually sell more golfing equipment than the average sporting goods store.

Normally, specialty stores do not like to do much promotional work for a manufacturer. Instead, they prefer to sell merchandise for which the demand has already been established—they like proven winners. Indeed, competition between retailers for the exclusive distribution of particularly desirable brands is keen. In the men's apparel industry certain lines such as Levi, Pendleton, and Gant have such a strong demand that dealers vie with one another to get the right to sell these lines. Because of the tie-up between the manufacturers and retailers, it is sometimes difficult for a newcomer to break into the market.

Producers just entering the market are therefore often faced with the necessity of distributing their wares through marginal retailers, because most of the good, aggressive merchants already have affiliations. Because such new entrepreneurs are forced to take on marginal retailers, their resulting volume is usually disappointing. Frequently they are unable to improve the quality of their distribution; the better retailers refuse to handle their line because the poorer dealers have given it a bad name.

Why are dealers reluctant to take on new lines?

Specialty stores encounter several problems. First, they are unable to hire the type of people they need to build a self-sustaining organization. As a result, the owner frequently finds it difficult to get away from the day-to-day operations of the store.

Second, many are plagued with location and store modernization problems as a result of shifting trade patterns. They are reluctant to abandon old sites from which trade is slowly drifting, because they are afraid to plunge out into more expensive buildings or unproved locations, yet they know it is a matter of time before they must move.

Finally, many retailers are under strong price competition from price-featuring promotional outlets, usually located in larger cities, which are highly attractive to a large segment of the market.

One study of the plight of retail hardware dealers, whose gradual decline in earnings during the past decade has alarmed the industry, cited four major reasons for the present difficulties. First, hardware retailers have been slow in expanding to suburban locations; they have tended to stay with the old downtown locations. Second, scrambled merchandising in hardware lines has been widespread; drug stores, supermarkets, and garden supply outlets have been highly successful in selling lines of merchandise that have been normally sold through hardware stores. Third, the big mail-order houses and auto supply chains have greatly increased their activities in hardware lines. Fourth, hardware retailers have been slow to change their operating policies in such matters as store hours, credit, trading stamps, and promotional activities, so that they now find themselves out of alignment with the buying habits of their customers.

These findings about hardware dealers appear applicable to many other types of specialty stores that are having difficulty competing in today's changing markets.

Chain Stores

The category of chain stores overlaps all other classifications, inasmuch as chain operations can be found in department stores, specialty stores, supermarkets, and in practically every other type of retailing. They are predominant, however, in a few industries: groceries, drugs, variety goods, shoes, and budget-priced women's ready-to-wear.

The chain operation has a few characteristics of its own. First, one of the chain store's major economic differential advantages is its tremendous purchasing power, which is achieved through centralized buying. The store managers seldom have much authority to buy; instead, purchasing is done in central headquarters, and the goods are distributed throughout the system. The manager of a Lerner's store has no authority to buy any wearing apparel whatsoever; instead, it is purchased in New York by central buyers and shipped to him. Although chains such as Sears and Penney's do give their managers limited authority to buy merchandise, each of these organizations maintains central buying offices that closely control sales to these organizations.

It is a mistake to think that chain stores are willing to operate on a smaller margin than specialty stores. Many chains demand the same margins given to independent operations but attempt to feature lower prices by purchasing at lower prices. The manufacturer selling to chains must be prepared to cope with great pressure from the buyers for special price reductions, promotional allowances, and other devices that have the effect of lowering the price. Often these requests for price reductions are extremely tempting because the selling costs are relatively low.

Chain stores for the most part are interested only in fast-moving items. They are interested in selling merchandise, not storing it.

One factor that chain buyers carefully investigate is the supplier's ability to furnish the quantity and quality of materials desired. The large chains have had bitter experience in dealing with many small, new manufacturers who are unable to furnish adequate quantities of the goods at the times specified. In selling to chains one must therefore be prepared to prove his financial and physical ability to deliver as promised.

How would you prove your ability to deliver as promised?

Besides their tremendous buying advantages, chains have other advantages over the smaller independent operators. First, their total size allows them to hire staff specialists in such areas as advertising, store layout, window display, store location, warehousing, and control. While the independent operator must be a jack-of-all-trades, his chain competitors can call upon the experts in each of these areas. This specialization, of course, creates overhead problems for the chains that the independent escapes. Also, the independent can move faster and more flexibly than the chain organization—an important factor in many local situations.

Second, the chain organization has access to sources of money unavailable to the smaller operator. When an economic opportunity opens up, the chain store can jump in quickly with the needed capital, whereas the smaller merchant may not have the financial strength to take advantage of the opportunity. Also, owners of land and shopping centers give strong preference to chain operations, for they consider them better risks as tenants. They are not worried about the enforceability of leases against the chain store, but an independent may fold up operations in such a way that the landlord has no legal recourse. Chain stores have often been given highly attractive leases for prime space in exchange for signing up before construction of the shopping center begins. The promoter of the center then uses such signed leases as a basis for borrowing money from financial institutions for construction of the shopping center. The signature of some small merchant would be of no value whatsoever in securing such loans. Later, when the shopping center is completed, the smaller merchants frequently must pay rentals several times as large per square foot for space that is not as attractive as that allotted to the chain operator.

For what other reasons might a shopping-center promoter give concessions to a major chain for opening in his center?

Finally, chain operations benefit from their total national image. People know and recognize such names as Sears, Walgreens, Wards, and Safeway; units of the chain pick up a lot of business from transients and newcomers who are unaware of or uncertain about local merchants. Their national image and promotion helps all the units in the chain.

Why does the chain's national image help each unit?

Self-Service Outlets

Self-service has come to play an important role in recent years in the marketing of groceries, drugs, hardware, and many other types of goods. Because of the basic nature of a self-service operation, in which a customer walks into the store and is free to choose any product he wishes with a minimum of assistance by sales personnel, the manufacturer has the burden of preselling his merchandise, because the self-service outlet will do little other than display it. Also, manufacturers selling through self-service outlets find it necessary to devote considerable attention to packaging, not only because it is one of the most important sales promotional tools available to him, but also because it protects the merchandise from damage and theft.

Most self-service stores are volume-oriented, interested in handling only items that move fast with a minimum of effort. Because a large number of self-service outlets are also chain operations, many chain-store buying practices are also characteristic of self-service outlets.

Low operating costs are the backbone supporting the growth of self-service retailing. Some highly efficient supermarkets are able to operate on as little as 10 percent margin by eliminating all nonessential services, but this is rare; 20 percent is more typical. Operating costs of supermarkets have been rising as they have added services. One analyst of discount food operations published the data presented in Table 12-1, indicating that the small chain is able to operate more cheaply than its larger competitors—which is why small chains have been able to stay in business and grow.

Explain why such small chains can operate more cheaply than large ones!

Table 12-1 GROSS MARGINS, WAREHOUSE, TRANSPORTATION, AND SUPPLIES EXPENSE OF DISCOUNT FOOD STORE AND CONVENTIONAL SUPERMARKET OF LARGE CHAIN, AND VOLUNTARY CHAIN*

	Large Chain			Small Chain			Voluntary Chain		
	Disc.	Conv.	(Diff.)†	Disc.	Conv.	(Diff.)	Disc.	Conv.	(Diff.)
Grocery gross margin	17.3%‡	21.6%	(4.3)	12.2%	16.2%	(4.0)	14.5%	20.0%	(5.5)
Meat gross margin	21.1	25.6	(4.5)	17.6	22.6	(5.0)	15.8	23.3	(7.5)
Produce gross margin	31.7	33.8	(2.1)	27.5	32.8	(5.3)	24.9	29.5	(4.6)
Total gross margin	19.4	23.8	(4.4)	14.7	18.9	(4.2)	15.5	21.5	(6.0)
Warehouse and transportation expense	2.5	2.5		In Cost of Goods Sold			2.0*†	1.9*†	
Supplies expense	.3**	.3**		In Cost of Goods Sold			1.1	1.0	
Adjusted total gross margin	16.6%	21.0%	(4.4)	14.7%	18.9%	(4.2)	12.4%	18.6%	(6.2)

*For fiscal year most recently completed at time each company was studied.
†Number of percentage points that gross margin of discount food store is below that of conventional supermarket.
‡Grocery includes dairy, baked goods, nonfoods and frozen foods, except for frozen meat and fish which are included in meat.
**For large chain, supplies expense is for grocery department only; meat and produce supplies in cost of goods sold.
*†Warehouse and transportation expense for members of the voluntary chain assessed as a percentage of the cost of merchandise purchased plus a freight charge based on distance from the warehouse. Both stores studied were near warehouses of the voluntary. On a cost basis both experienced the same expense, 2.4 percent. The warehouse and transportation expense of the large chain's stores was an allocation on the basis of total sales of the total expenses incurred by the company.

SOURCE: Robert J. Minichiello, "The Real Challenge of Food Discounters." *Journal of Marketing*, April 1967, p. 38.

This is a classic illustration of the principle of increasing costs: costs do not go down continually with increases in size but rather hit an optimum low somewhere, depending on the industry, and then rise with growth. It is a wise executive who knows when to stop growing—or, better yet, how to manage growth to keep from increasing costs.

Supermarkets today are expanding rapidly into such lines of merchandise as clothing, prescriptions, appliances, records, toys, sporting goods, hardware, garden supplies, and nursery stock. Truly, they resemble an old-fashioned general store on a greatly expanded basis. Just where this trend will end or be altered is not certain.

Why is the supermarket able to sell this wide assortment of goods?

As an example of the vitality of retailing and its constant change, one executive of S&H Green Stamps said that supermarkets will be superseded within the next twenty years. Instead there will be large-scale warehouses offering direct delivery to homes. Such warehouses will be automated, with automatic order pickers operated by a computer. He envisioned orders being placed from the home on closed-circuit television tied into the warehouse. He maintained that shopping was a bore, something to be avoided.

Do you agree that shopping is a bore?

Convenience Stores

The rapid development of the so-called convenience food outlets has taken two forms. The first has been the establishment of chains of small stores, a few hundred square feet, carrying a highly limited line of high-turnover convenience goods, located in prime traffic locations, open twenty-four hours a day, seven days a week. The 7–11 Stores are but one example of this type of development; they have been highly successful to date. Naturally, they must charge a relatively high price, but they are able to get it because of their convenience.

Why have these convenience stores grown so rapidly?

The second type of outlet that seems to be developing quite rapidly is the gasoline-food store. One such chain in Atlanta, Ga., called Bread Basket, offers the motorist an assortment of 50 convenience grocery items delivered to him while he is getting gas, without his ever leaving the car. A fully stocked store contains $1500 of inventory and turns ten times a month. This development once again proves the marketing principle that wherever a large number of people pass, convenience-impulse goods can be sold.

Discount Houses

The so-called discount house deserves special mention because of its recent origin and the widespread interest in it shown by both manufacturers and consumers.

Actually, many different types of retailers call themselves discount houses. Some discounters are no more than mail-order outlets; the customer walks into a small shop, names the item he wants, and the retailer orders it from a distributor. Because the dealer incurs little cost in this operation, he is able to pass on a considerable saving to the customer.

The mass-merchandising specialty store, usually focusing on the sale of major appliances, frequently calls itself a discount house, but in reality it is nothing more than an aggressive specialty house that is more concerned with volume than with profit margin.

Then there are the discount houses that carry a wide line of products in inventory, such as appliances, soft goods, drugs, jewelry, sporting goods, furniture, and so on. They take several forms. Some stores are actually a group of separate specialty stores all brought together under one roof by a landlord-promoter.

Some of the nationally known discount houses, such as Woolco and K-Mart (Jupiter), closely resemble one-floor department stores. They are usually located outside the traditional downtown locations of department stores and keep hours more in alignment with consumer desires than their more traditional competitors do. For the most part, discount chains have restricted themselves to regional operations. On the West Coast such operators as Zody's, Fedco, and Akron are dominant, whereas in the midlands Target, Ayr-Way, and Gibson's hold forth. New York and its environs is the headquarters of the discount industry; 21 of the 53 largest discount firms are located in the New York metropolitan area.

Franchising

What is franchising? Basically, it is a license that entitles its holder to operate a particular type of business according to certain stated conditions and arrangements.

The franchise system of distribution is an arrangement by which a franchisor (manufacturer or supplier of goods or a service), who has developed a particular format for operating a business, grants franchisees (independent small businessmen) the right to operate such a business. Usually the use of trademarks, patents, and standard operating methods is included in the franchise agreement.

Although the franchisee remains an independent businessman, he does assume some specific responsibilities such as providing a minimum investment of funds for the franchise. For this investment he may receive a standard inventory or equipment package, managerial training, national promotional support, close initial supervision to get his enterprise underway, product or service know-how, and the use of the franchise trade names and trademarks. In exchange he usually agrees to pay a royalty or annual franchise fee, or to buy certain critical supplies from the franchisor at a price that allows him to take his profits from this source. For example, Dairy Queen franchisees must buy all their mixes and trademarked supplies from the parent company. From its franchised motor lodges, Howard Johnson's gets an initial fee plus $8.50 per room per month or 5 percent of gross sales, whichever is larger. National Biff Burger, a system of drive-in restaurants, wants no initial fee but asks 2 percent of gross sales. However, Chicken Delight makes its money from the sale of supplies and equipment, as does Midas Muffler.

The amount of capital required varies tremendously. McDonald's claims that up to $75,000 is needed for starting one of its units. Midas Muffler states that $18,000 to $25,000 is sufficient to get under way.

Franchising has proven both popular and successful in many lines of endeavor, because it offers some sound advantages to both parties and overcomes many weaknesses and problems encountered by the small, independent operator when he tries to go it alone.

The average small businessman, in attempting to develop a retail outlet similar to those offered by the typical franchising firm, is not competent to manage it properly, is underfinanced, is unable to buy advantageously, and does not have an already established national reputation upon which to lean. However, when he joins a good franchising operation he is provided with management training plus supervision and assistance. He is supported by a nationally recognized promotional program and trade name that has established a definite image of the products or services to be provided for his market. His problem concerning the design of building and equipment is almost eliminated, since this is standardized and provided. The parent concern provides quantity buying advantages where they would be helpful. Also, he finds it easier to finance his business, as potential lenders may have more confidence in the financing of franchise operations than they would have in the individual's ability to go it alone in the same type of business.

The franchising company also gains some definite advantages. First and definitely foremost, the system overcomes one of the biggest difficulties faced by the typical chain-store operations—that of management personnel. Chain stores have found it difficult to develop in their managers the devotion to the business that is needed for outstanding performance. No substitutes have been found to match the motivational powers of ownership. When a man owns his business he stops watching the clock—he works. So the franchisor has a distribution system comprised not of paid managers but rather of highly motivated independent businessmen. It makes a big difference.

Second, the franchising firm adds to its own capital that of its franchisees. The total capital commitment for the entire system would probably be beyond the capacity of the parent firm; hence, it is able to expand faster with the help of the dealer's investment and his accessability to local lenders.

Third, there are certain advantages in some communities to being a locally owned operation rather than a chain store. There is still resentment in some circles toward chain operations.

Finally, the parent company divorces itself from many bothersome and costly duties connected with running a retail business, such as local taxes, payroll, insurance costs, and licenses.

A word of warning: Franchising has become so popular that today, in many instances, it borders on being a confidence game. There are groups attempting to form franchise chains around ideas that are not economically sound. Other groups make promises of managerial support that they cannot deliver to the franchise holder, who has paid them a good deal of money for it. If an idea and its organization are not sound, franchising will not make it so. A shakeout of weak or marginal restaurant franchises may be in the offing, as they can hardly all prosper in the market areas they have overbuilt in their zeal to obtain national stature. A good deal of caution should be exercised in this industry during the next few years.

You have been approached by a group asking you to become a franchisee in their system. How would you go about evaluating the worth of their proposition?

Vending

A significant battle in the retailing revolution was won by the vending machine—the silent salesman with the built-in cash register that sold $3.2 billion of goods in 1963 in the United States. Although the vending machine as a marketing institution has been recognized widely only since the 1940s, actually it has been around for a long time. One study cites a book dated 215 B.C. entitled *Pneumaticka*, which describes an Egyptian coin-actuated device for peddling sacrificial water—insert five drachmas and you were saved, for the time being. Throughout the late 1800s and the early 1900s many vending devices were in operation, selling such things as paper and envelopes, post cards, stamps, tickets, liquid beverages, food, cigars, gum, perfume, and cigarettes.

Vending machines are not a low-cost means of distribution; their operating costs rank high at approximately 44 percent. The success of vending machines has rested instead upon their ability to sell goods in places and at times when other means of distribution could not be economically employed. A case could be made that a significant portion of vending-machine sales are additions to total retail sales, inasmuch as a great portion of that demand would have vanished if it had not been satisfied at that time.

There is no question but that vending-machine sales will continue to increase not only with population growth but through the development of new machines that make possible the sale of additional items.

What is the basic marketing principle upon which vending is based?

ECONOMICS OF RETAILING

Although this is not the place to delve into the details of retail operations, still it will be of great value to you to understand the economics of retailing, which vitally affect a great many aspects of your life.

Retailing Differential Advantages

There are five significant differential advantages a retailer can seek, and his success may be based on any one or a combination of them.

Location Many retailers are successful almost solely because they have a prime location. Location is a critically important differential advantage in the retailing of convenience goods. The sales of supermarkets, drugstores, hardware stores, service stations, and restaurants are significantly affected by their locations; they must have good ones in order to succeed.

In practically all lines of endeavor location can be a definite asset. Even the dealer of high-priced automobiles finds that a good location helps him considerably. In evaluating the success of some merchants, one can attribute their continuing prosperity only to their prime location.

Select a type of store and prepare a list of principles for selecting an excellent location for it.

In fact, location is so important to the ultimate success of most retail operations that one should seriously question opening a store in a marginal location. Experience indicates that it would be much wiser in most instances to wait until the right location becomes available, or else consider other trading areas in which to operate.

Often one finds it difficult to pay the price demanded by the owners of prime locations, but trying to save money by selecting a lower-cost location is usually false economy. This is not to say that there are no limits to the rent business can afford to pay, for certainly a merchant can afford to pay only a certain percentage of sales for rent and still make a profit.

Price   Some dealers attempt to gain a differential advantage over their competitors by featuring low prices. Though many retailers *attempt* to create the illusion of low prices, some merchants really do sell for prices lower than their competitors'. Several difficulties may be encountered in using this strategy. First, profits may be meager and the margin for error so slight that any miscalculations or unpredicted events result in a loss. Second, a price differential is easy to copy in the short run. Competitors can match low prices, if they so desire, in the short run. Price competition therefore can be vigorous. Third, price seems to have lost some of its market appeal in these relatively prosperous times; no doubt price would become a more important advantage if times were to become really difficult. Finally, price may not be an effective appeal in some relatively wealthy trading areas.

In what way do some retailers create the illusion that they have low prices when such is not the case?

Promotion   Some retailers are successful because they have been able to outpromote their competitors; their promotional campaigns are the largest single factor explaining their success. Promotional advantages are difficult for most competitors to copy. If a merchant gains a reputation for having prompt, courteous service, it is not easy for his competitors to match this advantage. Many small, intimate shops employ this technique effectively.

Advertising campaigns can also cause a merchant to stand out among his competitors. For example, the Akron Stores in the Los Angeles area have an advertising format (see Figure 12-1) that is most effective.
The problem in using a promotional strategy is that it takes time, money, and skill to be effective. Few promotional programs are successful overnight, and most of them cost lots of money.

Buying   Many retailers rely on their buying acumen in their race for the consumer's dollar. Through adroit buying they acquire merchandise that is highly desirable to their customers. Sometimes their success rests on one or a few highly salable lines. A Chevrolet dealer may be able to explain his success only by the fact that he is a Chevrolet dealer.

FIGURE 12-1: Unique Advertising Format of The Akron Stores

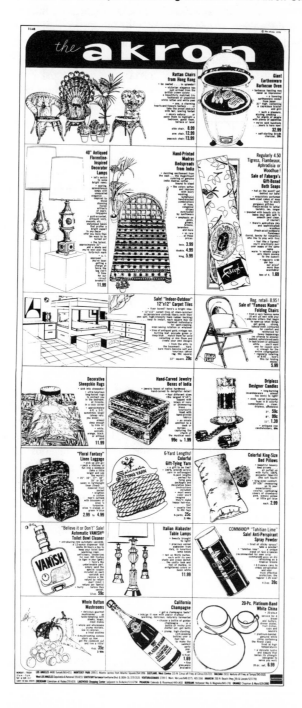

All merchants must employ a buying strategy to some extent. Nevertheless, some (such as drugstores) handle only standard items carried by all of their competitors, whereas others attempt to obtain distinctive merchandise not carried by competing stores. If one is an adroit buyer, it is difficult for the run-of-the-mill competitor to copy this advantage. All merchants are strongly advised to try to develop this advantage to the fullest extent possible within the conditions under which they operate.

What must a retailer do to become an excellent buyer?

Service If the customer wants service, his patronage goes to the dealer who serves him promptly and courteously, stands back of his goods, and in general treats him as if he were king. Service is an important element in most successful retail ventures; some merchants, though, make it their stock-in-trade.

RETAIL MERCHANDISING

Merchandising is a term used in retailing to refer to all activities connected with the goods that are sold: buying, displaying, promoting, pricing, and selling. Hence, it should be of interest to everyone to learn some of the fundamentals underlying merchandising activities.

Buying for a Market

Few retailers attempt to be all things to all people; they usually focus their merchandising efforts toward selling one segment of the market. Some women's apparel stores attempt to appeal to the wealthy, others to bargain-basement customers; some stores appeal to the young, others to the matrons. The retailer who attempts to please all segments of the market frequently is unable to please any. Most dealers find it highly advisable to focus their efforts on one market segment by carrying merchandise specifically designed for it.

Similarly, the entire physical environment of the store must be attuned to the segment of the market to which the dealer hopes to sell. The decor must be considerably different when selling to farmers than when selling to wealthy business executives. Even the location of the store should change, depending on the market solicited. It would be foolish to locate a high-priced store in a slum area. Even the type of personnel hired will vary considerably, depending on the clientele sought. Notice the difference between the women selling gowns in the French rooms of department stores and the clerks in the basement dress departments. Every action and attribute of a retail outlet must be in accord with the characteristics of the market segment being solicited.

Planning

Good retailers do not operate haphazardly; they plan minutely every article of merchandise they buy and stock. Indeed, much of the retailer's time is spent doing the paper work necessary to maintain stock control. The retailer must plan in such detail to be sure he has in stock at all times the proper sizes, colors, and models of the lines of merchandise he is carrying. The retailer who does not do so quickly learns that he is out of stock on many key items and overstocked on other articles not in demand. Soon his inventories become out of balance and he is left holding a large amount of unsalable merchandise without having the right items in stock to sell.

A good buyer knows exactly how much merchandise he is free to buy at any one time from the detailed merchandise budget he prepares of anticipated sales and the inventories needed to make these sales. He knows that if he buys and sells according to this plan, at the end of the year he will have his predetermined profit.

Moving Merchandise—Turnover

The smart buyer never lets merchandise stagnate in his store. All buyers make mistakes; they buy merchandise that was either overpriced or unappealing. When such mistakes are made, the sooner the buyer gets rid of the goods, the better off he will be. It is axiomatic in retailing circles that markdowns should be taken as early as possible on slow-moving merchandise—the sooner the better. First, if markdowns are taken early in the season rather than later there is a larger demand for the item and it is more likely to sell. It is easier to take a markdown on undesirable swimming suits in June than in August. Second, the longer the merchant waits to take his markdowns, the larger it will have to be. Third, the longer the merchandise stays around the store, the higher the likelihood that it will become soiled or damaged by handling. Finally, markdowns generate additional traffic in the store that will result in sales of other, more profitable, merchandise.

Naturally there are exceptions to this quick-markdown principle. Small merchants selling quality goods at relatively high prices find it inadvisable to hold many sales. If their clientele learns to anticipate these sales, it is difficult to obtain the full margin on regular inventory; the dealer can find himself selling almost everything at sale prices. Also, frequent sales can damage the quality image of certain stores. Regular customers become incensed at paying full price for some item only to see it marked down substantially a few weeks later. They feel cheated. Consequently, some top-quality retailers seldom have sales. Rather, they clear out their mistakes through other retail outlets. One women's apparel store in Tulsa obtains substantial quantities of merchandise from a widely known store in Dallas whose reputation will not allow it to clear out the goods in the Dallas area. Sometimes the tags are ripped out of such merchandise.

Display

Another fundamental tenet of merchandising is that goods must be well displayed to be sold. All merchants can relate stories of how a floor display at a certain location in their store will almost inevitably increase the sales of whatever article is placed there. One modern concept of the retail store is that it is nothing but a big display room. Some retailers actually pretend that their entire store is a show window. The trend is away from hiding merchandise behind counters and in cases. The general philosophy is to get the merchandise out where the customer can touch it and buy it. Careful planning of store layout and design is needed in building new outlets in order that display space is properly located and is most effective. Such things do not just happen; they require careful study.

Talk with a good retailer to determine his principles of display. What are they?

Atmosphere

In many retail situations it is important that the store have the right atmosphere for its intended clientele. Some stores fail to prosper because they are too cold and severe. Most customers prefer a warm, friendly atmosphere. Sometimes stores are too ornate or fancy for their customers. Retailers catering to a rural clientele frequently comment that many of their customers rebel if they try to make the store too plush or fancy. Creating the right atmosphere is an art that the merchant must carefully cultivate. Sometimes it is done with appropriate character pieces or decorations.

In most instances, people like to see a lot of merchandise. It has been proven time and again that mass displays sell more goods than meager ones. Some stores so crammed with goods that customers have difficulty getting around in them seem to attract more customers than outlets that are roomy. Merchandise attracts people. Also, people attract people. If a place seems empty, people are repelled. Let several women start crowding around a certain table and a rush may begin. If one stops to ponder these statements, he may see that they are logical when one considers the purpose of the shopper—to look at goods. The crowd is reassuring to the shopper who is uncertain of his judgment. How would you feel about walking into an unknown empty restaurant at dinnertime? You would conclude that there must be something wrong with it.

How do you create an atmosphere?

Dynamics of Retailing

No area in our economy is as dynamic and highly volatile as retailing. Indeed, if one were to list all the major changes that have taken place in our business community in the past fifty years, those in retailing would far predominate in number. Retailing in the 1970s bears little resemblance to that in the 1930s. Practically every institution has undergone revolutionary change. Gone are the old grocery stores, replaced by the modern supermarkets. Discount houses, drive-in merchandising—all are new. Investments are indeed risky in the retail field. Hence, most astute retail merchants demand quick paybacks, for one can seldom look farther down the road than one decade and be assured of the continued existence of any one retail institution.

What retail institutions exist today that did not exist in the 1950s?
What forces brought forth the rapid growth in the development of travel agencies?

The reasons for this dynamicism in retailing are not hard to fathom. First, the retailer is on the front line; retailing institutions are in direct, constant contact with the consuming markets and are the first to feel every nuance, every change, in the consumer's desires. While some manufacturers may not feel the impact of a market shift for some period of time, the retailer feels it the day it happens. This makes him most sensitive to consumer desires, and experience quickly teaches the successful retailer that he must alter his operations in compliance with the market's demands.

Second, entry into retailing is easy. It takes little money in many instances, and no formal training is required. Anyone with an idea can open up a store and test the validity of his thinking against the whims of the market, which results in continual testing of all retailing institutions. If there is any weakness or void in the existing market structure, some new entrepreneur will latch onto it quickly.

Third, changes are relatively easy to make in retailing. Whereas an oil manufacturer is captive to refining crude oil for his gasoline, most retailers are able to change operations relatively quickly, since they seldom own many fixed assets.

Current Problems in Retailing

Every segment of our economy has its problems; retailing is no exception. Some of these problems are of long standing, while others are of recent vintage. Some may have solutions, while others will continue to be intractable.

Chains versus Independents   One of the long-standing problems that has plagued retailing for more than four decades has been posed by the large and growing chain stores, which have all but eliminated the smaller, independent businessman from certain fields of endeavor. This problem continues unabated as size invades areas heretofore deemed to be the preserve of the small entrepreneur. For years restaurants were considered almost the sole preserve of the small businessman, but the last decade has seen the development of such large organizations as McDonald's, Howard Johnson's, and other franchise-type operations that are presently making it difficult for many independents. Moreover, the size and power of some retailers, such as Sears and Penney's, is such that they are nearly dominating their entire distribution systems. Manufacturers selling to them find themselves to be, for the most part, the weaker of the two partners.

Of what significance is the matter of who is stronger in the distributive network?

While some people might not consider this growth in importance of sizable institutions a problem, experience has indicated that when a few large organizations become powerful and dominate a sector of our economy, many unfavorable results can be expected.

Can you imagine some unfavorable results?

There is no answer to this problem. These firms are large because they have been delivering the goods in the manner desired by the market. They have been more successful than their competitors at giving the market what it wants, and certainly the economy would be injured if these large merchandising concerns were removed from the scene.

Occupancy Costs A combination of forces, such as rapidly increasing land values, increasing construction costs, and a shifting of retail trade to expensive suburban and regional shopping centers under the control of independent professional landlords, have all conspired to increase the occupancy costs to retailers. Rents are sky high. One small men's store located in Cinderella City, a large regional shopping center in Denver, pays $2000 or 5 percent of sales per month, whichever is greater, rent for 4000 square feet of space. Add to this cost situation the fact that choice locations are usually commanded by the large national chains, and it can be seen why the independent retailer has a difficult time making a profitable living in the modern shopping center. For the most part, such shopping centers are dominated by the national chains.

Why do the chains dominate shopping centers?

It is difficult for a small, independent retailer to obtain a choice location for his operation, yet location is one of the most vital factors affecting the success of his business.

Employees Employment in retailing has lost its attractiveness in the past two decades. At one time retailing was one of the better-paying fields for college trained individuals. Today young people do not find life in retailing too attractive. The late and long hours, combined with weekend merchandising, make life selling for IBM or Xerox seem idyllic. Consequently, retailers find it extremely difficult to hire the number and caliber of people they need.

Analyze the employee problem. What should retailers do to solve it?

Rising Costs Although rising costs are not a new problem or one unique to retailing, still they do pose some problems peculiar to retailing. All costs have been rapidly rising: labor, advertising, occupancy, supplies, transportation, and, of course, the goods themselves. While normally the retailer is protected against such cost increases by being able to increase the prices of his wares, lately he has been encountering difficulty in doing so, because the customers have not always accepted the price increases. Moreover, operating costs have been rising faster than merchandise costs in some areas, thereby forcing the merchant to take bigger margins. The men's wear manager in one large chain operation claimed that nothing in his department now carried less than 50 percent margin; the traditional margin had been 40 percent for decades. The increasing cost of operations forces the retailer to find less costly ways of operating, because experience shows that the system is unwilling to pay that much for the retailing function. History indicates that when retail institutions begin taking more than half the consumer's dollar, cheaper ways of doing the same things will be found.

Trends in Retailing

There are always several broad, overall trends at work that constantly change the retailing system. Outlined below are some of the more forceful trends affecting all retailing.

Self-Service   Self-service would have to head the list of major trends that have been affecting retailing during the past three decades. This simple method of selling by which customers locate the things they want in a store and take them to a central desk to pay for them eliminates much labor and cost. Self-service has been a blessing to the retailer in several ways. It alleviated the labor shortage, for without self-service it would be impossible to man the sales floors today without vastly increased costs. Self-service allowed the dealer to inventory and sell a great many more goods from his store than had been possible with the more conventional methods of selling. Moreover, self-service has proven to be a most effective method of promoting the sale of goods, for experience has proved that if the customer is allowed to wander around among a large assortment of goods he will buy far more than if he is waited upon by a clerk.

Why do people buy more goods if left alone to shop?
Why has the retail sales clerk been a vanishing breed?

Naturally, self-service is not an unblemished virtue, for with it additional problems have arisen; shoplifting has become a major concern, merchandise is easily damaged and soiled, and most of the promotional burden is placed upon display and product packaging. Self-service has taken over completely in such fields as groceries and it is just making itself felt in other areas, such as gas stations.

Why has self-service been delayed in the oil industry?

Mass Merchandising   The advent of mass markets, made possible by a large amount of discretionary purchasing power among a large number of people, created the need for mass-merchandising institutions. Small retail stores simply could not handle the tonnage of goods demanded by our affluent society. The system had to create huge outlets capable of moving large volumes of merchandise quickly and cheaply, hence the development of supermarkets, super discount stores, and other large-scale merchandising outlets. Large retail institutions were needed because the day had passed when we could satisfy our needs through the smaller merchandiser.

Relocation   Retailing is moving away from centralized downtown locations and locating where the people live—in suburban shopping centers. Although the movement has been under way for two decades, it shows no sign of abating. Most downtown areas are considered successful if they are merely holding their own. Many have been economically decimated and converted into financial and commercial centers.

Mixed or Scrambled Merchandising   The assortment of goods offered by most retail establishments has greatly broadened. J. C. Penney Company is a prime example of a concern that originally focused its attention on one line of wares—soft goods—but has extensively broadened its assortment to include appliances, sporting goods, hardware, and automotive supplies and repair with highly successful results. Grocery stores whose assortment was once confined to food now carry hardware, housewares, soft goods, drugs, garden supplies, and just about anything else that can be sold profitably.

Presold Merchandising Mass merchandising and self-service have been the major forces ushering in the era of presold merchandising, in which advertising presells the customer on the virtues of some product before he comes into the store to get it. In a great many instances the burden of selling goods to the consumer is now placed upon the manufacturer.

   This is not to imply that in-store buying decisions are not still significant factors in marketing, for they most certainly are. Presold merchandising exists in markets where brand preferences are significant.

Can presold merchandising play a role in selling a product that is bought largely by people who make the buying decision in the store?

Private Branding With the growth of large merchandising organizations, the need for handling the brands of nationally known manufacturers was lessened. The large merchandiser, such as Sears or Penney's, has no desire to spend money pushing the property of some other company. Instead, these organizations almost exclusively sell private brands—brands that they own and control. Some of these private brands are made in their own factories, while others are made for them by independent manufacturers. Sears' Kenmore washers are made by Whirlpool, but Sears owns its own paint factories.

Why would Whirlpool make washing machines for Sears?

The trend toward private brands has been strong and is growing rapidly. Many of the old principles relevant to private branding have had to be discarded as the mass merchandisers have continued to switch to their own brands. At one time private brands were considered to be inferior, low-priced entries in the market. Today many private brands have a quality image and have lost much of their cheap connotation. Many private brands have stronger consumer franchises today than many of the so-called national brands.

Conclusion

> Retailing, a dynamic, fast-moving field—once the stronghold of the small, independent businessman—has been increasingly dominated by the large chain operation featuring mass-merchandising techniques, private brands, and locations in rapidly expanding suburban shopping centers. Yet it remains one of the last vestiges of the free-enterprise system where a man with little money can go into business and succeed.
>
>   Retailing is hard work. The hours can be long, and the seven-day week is not unknown. But it has its rewards. There is money, of course, but there are other things, too. Most of the successful merchants actually love dealing in the goods they sell. It is a field that you should examine very carefully for a future career.

13 Pricing[1]

Fortune is like the market, where many times,
if you stay a little, the price will fall.
Sir Francis Bacon

Pricing is a measure of the marketing program. It reflects how well the marketing manager has done his job. If he has done it well, he will get his price; if not, he won't. Price is of concern to the public—fearful it will pay too much, trying to make its limited buying power go as far as possible.

Perhaps no business decision is as critical from both an economical and social standpoint as price. And yet less is known about how industry prices than is known about any other aspect of business.

[1] This chapter is based on materials in Richard H. Buskirk, *Principles of Marketing*, 3d ed. (New York: Holt, Rinehart and Winston, Inc., 1970), Chapters 17 and 18.

Price—The Most Important Determinant of Profit

Price is an important factor in determining both the sales volume and the profit of the enterprise. Profit equals sales revenue minus costs. Revenue equals price times volume, but volume also is affected by price (lower the price, sell more volume). Therefore, in determining revenue, price is not only half the equation but also a factor in the other half. Price also influences costs of production through its impact on sales volume.

If one wants to remove volume considerations from profit, he can visualize profit as being the difference between the price received for an article and its unit cost. The quickest path to higher profits is a price increase, if the demand for the product will not decline because of it. Consequently, when a firm's profits are unsatisfactory its executives first seriously look at price to judge whether or not it can be increased. In some cases in which a product's demand is sufficiently elastic, a price reduction may result in more profits, but most managers hesitate to cut price for they are uncertain of the outcome.

PRICE—THE REGULATOR

Price is a regulator: it regulates demand, the nature of one's customers, promotional activities, product characteristics, and competition.

If a price is set too low, more demand will be generated than can be supplied, and profits are foregone. If it is set too high, demand will be insufficient and profits will suffer.

So the firm cannot supply the demand—why is that bad?

Price determines one's customers. A tavern in a college town lowered its price of beer only to discover, to its dismay, that it had not attracted college students but rather some nearby skidrow bums. One of the tavern's competitors increased price with no appreciable change in volume; he realized a slight upgrading in clientele.

Price affects promotion. The higher the price, the more money available for promotional activities. When demand is affected more by promotion than price, then price is increased to allow for such promotion. Pricing decisions thus cannot be made independent of promotional strategies.

Price affects the qualities and attributes of the product. Everything costs money. Although it is not intimated here that price is always determined by cost, still, if a profit is to be made on an item, its price must be in excess of costs. A high price allows additional features and qualities to be put into the product. If the overall strategy is to penetrate the competitive, low-price market, however, the qualities and features of the product must be carefully controlled.

Price policies set the tone of competition in an industry. If a firm uses promotion as its basic volume-generating tool instead of price, competition will not be as cutthroat as if price were the major weapon.

What determines whether or not price is the major competitive weapon in an industry?

PRICE—THE ALLOCATOR

From society's viewpoint, price allocates resources—money, men, and material. Capital (resources) is attracted to industries where a relatively high price (profit) is being realized. Similarly, industries in which attractive prices cannot be maintained do not attract resources. This is society's way of encouraging and discouraging the production of the things it does or does not want. If society wants more of something, such as wonder drugs, it pays a relatively high price so that additional resources will be attracted into the industry to increase the total supply of the item.

If one prices his products too low, he will not attract sufficient resources to meet the resultant demand. Price thus directly affects one's attractiveness to the money market—and it is money that buys men and materials.

MEASURE OF MARKETING ACUMEN

Ability to obtain and sustain a relatively high price for a product indicates that the marketing plans behind the item are sound and well conceived. Price is often indicative of overall marketing effectiveness. IBM obtains a price substantially above that of many of its competitors, but nevertheless sells far more machines than any of them. This is fairly substantial proof that its overall marketing organization is far better than any of its competitors'. An ability to maintain prices and volumes in the face of relatively stiff competition certainly indicates an excellent marketing organization.

Properly priced goods facilitate all marketing activities. The marketing manager should realize that if his goods are priced too high, he will hinder all his other work. His promotional efforts will not be as effective as they would otherwise be, and he will find it more difficult to obtain the channels of distribution he desires. On the other hand, properly priced goods make the promotional program far more effective than it would otherwise be, and channels of distribution are usually more willing to handle items that represent good values.

AMOUNT OF FREEDOM IN PRICING

It should not be assumed that one is free to establish whatever prices he wants on his wares, for he is not. Price setting is encompassed by many restrictions, some of which should be welcomed because they may make the job easier. Often they establish certain bounds, and at other times they actually set the price.

Market Price

Sometimes the executive faces a fairly well-recognized market price for his product. A rancher has little control over the price he gets for his beef. He must sell it for the going market rate on the day he takes his steers to market. Although the existence of market prices is well recognized in most raw-materials and farm-products markets, actually effective market prices exist for many consumer and industrial goods.

Name some products for which there are market prices.

Price Leadership

Price leadership exists when all the firms in an industry follow the pricing practices of one dominant firm. When the leader increases or decreases prices, the others follow suit. Though price leadership is closely akin to market prices in its effect on the pricing decisions of the nonleading firms, it differs in its price-setting mechanism, ultimate price levels, and firm behavior.

Price leadership is usually found in situations where the products are of standard quality and are purchased on a price basis. Since the buyers do not care whose product they purchase, they buy from the firm with the lowest price; no firm can allow another to undersell it.

Price leadership is most frequently found in industries dominated by a few firms. The economic power of the large organizations is the force that keeps the smaller competitors in line. The executive in such situations realizes he is not free to establish independent prices; the price leader would quickly retaliate against any reductions below his established price, and it would be difficult to compete against the leader if prices were set above his list.

Role of Substitutes—Cross Elasticity

The price of Douglas fir plywood can go only so high before the contractors substitute lumber and other building materials for it. The price of copper increased to the point where aluminum was substituted in a great many applications; as a consequence, great downward pressures were placed on the price level of copper. As Detroit raised the price of American automobiles, low-priced foreign imports entered the market. As the price of beef increases, more pork and lamb are consumed. As the price of labor goes up, capital is substituted.

The marketing manager who does not recognize the limitations placed on his pricing by substitutes is only sowing the seeds of his eventual downfall. There have been many instances of industries that have priced themselves out of the market, not recognizing that with proper provocation the market will make substitutions despite inconveniences. Should the oil industry endeavor to increase gasoline prices too much, strong demands may be made for propelling motor vehicles by other fuels.

Governmental Control

In many areas of our economy the government establishes the price of a product or service. In the transportation, utility, and uranium mining industries, prices are determined by bureaucratic dictates rather than independent executive actions. The executive, however, still has considerable freedom to operate within these governmental orders. Frequently the establishment of special discriminatory rates is left to the judgment of the firm. An electric company may develop special rates to promote the use of electricity for home heating and cooling. Any changes in the rate structure must usually be obtained through overt actions of the manager, because the government seldom voluntarily alters rates. An executive operating under government controls still has considerable responsibility for establishing prices, even though the official rates may be set by the regulatory authority.

Monopoly

The manager has the maximum amount of autonomy over pricing when he has a monopoly on a market; however, he is still subject to the competition of substitutes. As a general rule, the more differentiated the product, the more freedom the manager will have in pricing. The closer an item is to its competitors, the less freedom the manager has.

ECONOMIC PRICE THEORY

An understanding of economic price theory helps one understand the marketplace. The following discussion will introduce some fundamental concepts.

Pure Competition

Economic price theory, for all practical purposes, began in the eighteenth century with the classical economists, who made several assumptions about the competitive environment and nature of the firms in the marketplace. They assumed the existence of many small buyers and many small sellers, none of whom was able to influence the market price of a commodity. They assumed the existence of a standardized product; all producers in an industry sold identical products—corn, wheat, wood, and other such standardized products. They assumed everyone had information concerning all relevant conditions in the marketplace. They assumed that everyone was rational and acted in his own long-run best interests. They also assumed that the businessman was trying to maximize profits.

Classical economists viewed the law of demand as shown in Figure 13-1, in which the quantity of a product demanded declined as its price increased—lower the price to increase volume. From these curves the economists derived what is known as marginal analysis.

Concept of the Margin

Throughout economic theory the term "marginal" is used to modify various nouns such as *revenue, costs, utility, firm, worker, efficiency of capital, operations,* or any other thing one wishes to describe as being marginal. Margin originally referred to a border or edge, but its meaning has been broadened in economics to designate what happens at the "edge" of the activity being described—the last unit brought into play. Thus:

Marginal revenue is the net addition to the total revenue of the firm from selling one more unit of a product.

Marginal costs are the net addition to total costs caused by making one more unit of a product.

Marginal utility is the satisfaction received by the consumer from using one more unit of a product. Marginal utility of the dollar is the utility provided by earning one more dollar.

Marginal efficiency of capital is the profit made from the last dollar invested.

Marginal operations are firms that are barely able to exist; they are either making little or no profit or are losing money slowly enough to remain in business for a short time.

A marginal firm is one making the least profit in the industry.

A marginal worker is one whose productivity barely covers his wages.

Marginal land is the least productive land in an area; it usually fails to make enough money to cover its costs.

The principle of diminishing marginal utility is a basic concept of economic theory. It refers to the observation that as one consumes or uses additional units of some product or service, the satisfaction derived from each additional unit diminishes. How is this principle at work in our system today?

What is the marginal cost of a kilowatt hour to the power company?

On the supply side, the supply curve might appear something like that curve *S* in Figure 13-1, where, as the price increases, more supply is made available by industry. The logic of this is apparent. At low prices only the firms with the lowest costs can profitably make the product. As the price increases, higher-cost firms are able to bring

FIGURE 13 -1: Demand and Supply Curves

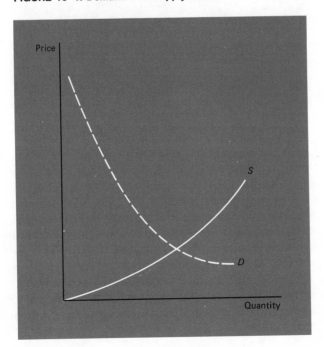

forth their products. Therefore, supply expands as price increases. For an entire industry, then, the price must be such that the supply and demand are equated. The price of a commodity will rise until supply satisfies the demand for it at that price. Of course, as price rises and supply expands, the demand is curtailed, so the two meet in some compromise, as shown in Figure 13-1. This is the view of the total industry, but not the viewpoint of the individual firm, for it sees a different picture.

In pure competition the entrepreneur sees an unlimited demand curve; he can sell all he can produce at the market price. Costs are his only worry, and his cost characteristics are unique to his firm. They depend entirely upon his technology. If he has no fixed costs and if his variable costs remain the same regardless of volume, then his unit cost curve will appear as depicted in line *A*, Figure 13-2. But if he has fixed costs, then his unit costs will drop with volume production (line *B*).

FIGURE 13 -2: Unit Cost Curve for Firm

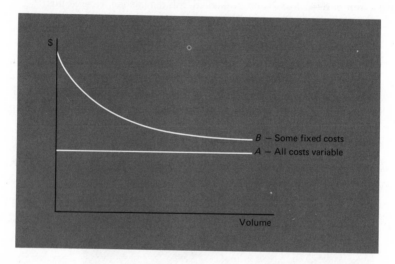

Imperfect Competition

Economists quickly recognized that in many situations competition was less than perfect. Some firms were becoming so big that their size affected the market on either the buying or the selling side. Product differentiation began to occur; where this differentiation was meaningful, the products were removed somewhat from competition and could command premium prices. Pricing under imperfect competition is represented by the situation shown in Figure 13-3, in which the entrepreneur prices at a point at which his marginal costs equal his marginal revenue. The various imperfections merely affect the shapes and locations of his cost and revenue curves.

As long as marginal revenues exceed marginal costs, the firm is making money by expanding production. When that point is reached, going beyond it would mean that marginal costs would exceed marginal revenues; therefore, the difference would be lost. Never mind now the fallacies of this theory, for we shall get to them presently.

This price-making mechanism is shown in Figure 13-3. Under conditions of pure competition the entrepreneur considers the market price to be his marginal revenue, for nothing he does can influence that price; he can sell everything he can produce without affecting price.

FIGURE 13 -3: Price Curves for an Individual Firm

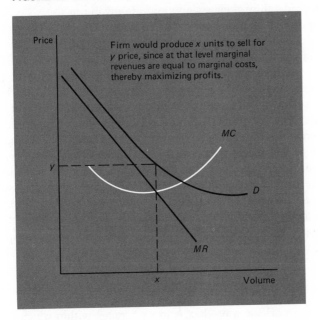

Monopoly

A *monopoly* is a situation in which one firm controls the entire supply of some product or service. A *monopsony* is a situation in which one firm is the only buyer for a product or service; it is a monopoly on the buying side. An *oligopoly* is a market in which relatively few sellers, all identifiable and known to one another, control the supply of a product, while an *oligopsony* is a situation in which a few firms control the buying of the product.

When competition is restricted on either the buying or the selling side of the market, behavior is altered. The monopolist seldom sees it to his advantage to lower price in order to expand the demand for his product.

Concept of Elasticity

The concept of elasticity refers to the impact upon the demand for a product caused by a change in its price. A product is said to have an inelastic demand if a price increase fails to stifle demand sufficiently to prevent total revenue from increasing. If total revenue declines with a price increase, then demand is said to be elastic. If total revenue increases with a price cut, demand is said to be elastic. If total revenue declines with a price cut, then demand is inelastic.

What are the characteristics of products with inelastic demand curves?

Criticisms of Economic Price Theory

The criticisms of economic theory must dwell upon the realism of the assumptions upon which their logic is based. If one accepts the assumptions of the economists, then their price theory is valid, because it is difficult to attack their logic. The problem is that practically all of their assumptions are invalid in today's economy. If one were to formulate a set of premises that were almost opposite from the truth, he could hardly do better. Reality in today's market sees: (1) the existence of huge firms on both sides of the marketplace, all of whom are able to influence the markets for their products; (2) products so highly differentiated that they enjoy substantially monopolistic positions in the market; (3) many monopolistic positions in the market, gained through advertising or locational advantages, that bestow effective control of certain markets upon certain firms; (4) imperfect information, in which few firms have adequate information on which to intelligently base prices; (5) emotional buying motives, in which people seldom buy things on the basis of the lowest long-run cost position; they not only lack information to do so, but also lack the intent; (6) firms that do not attempt to maximize profits in the short run but rather have numerous other objectives in their pricing. So what is the logic of economic price theory? A few concepts are valuable in modern price setting; one should master the concepts of marginal revenue, marginal costs, and price elasticity. And occasionally one can apply the theory to some situation.

THE PRICING PROCEDURE

The first step in pricing a product is to set a range within which the pricing decision must be made—a floor and a ceiling. In determining a pricing range for a line of earrings, a manager surveyed the market and found that few earrings were sold at prices above $10 a pair and that measurable volume began at $5. Though discount stores carried very cheap earrings for as low as 49 cents a pair, for his particular quality of product none sold for less than $1. He concluded that he should price his earrings to retail for somewhere between $5 and $1.

The manager in this instance surveyed the prices of *competitive* and *substitute* products, which are two important factors affecting the price range. Sometimes the price of a *complementary* product will influence the pricing range. A complementary product is one traditionally sold in conjunction with the product at hand.

Why are radios purchased with a new car so much more expensive than similar radios bought separately from an auto radio dealer?
Does a substitute product set the price floor or price ceiling for an item?
What sets the ceiling price on coal?

Usually the price floor is established by the firm's costs; it will not produce unless the price will at least recover full costs. This does not mean that costs establish prices;

it merely means that costs determine whether an enterprise will be undertaken and what its ultimate profits will be. Therefore, one's costs are a floor if the one set by the market is lower.

What should you do if the market is willing to pay you far in excess of your costs for a product?

Another yardstick for gauging the price a market may be willing to pay for an article is the amount of savings it will yield to its owner. If a new invention will save its buyer $10,000 a year, he should be willing to pay a substantial portion of these savings. The Hughes Tool Company is able to set an attractive price for its diamond rotary drilling bit because of the tremendous savings it creates in the total overall costs of oil drilling operations.

What share of the savings can you take from the buyer?

Finally, the reactions of middlemen and potential customers can serve as valuable yardsticks in establishing the pricing range. These opinions must be evaluated very carefully if the marketing manager is not to be misled.

How can the reactions of one's customers mislead him?

Establishing Basic Strategy

There are two fundamental, diametrically opposed pricing strategies: (1) skim-the-cream, and (2) penetration.

Skim-the-cream A skim-the-cream strategy calls for setting the price at the top of the range. Although this strategy of deliberately pricing high antagonizes many people, nevertheless it has several advantages.

First, a skim-the-cream price hedges against errors. It is easier to lower a high price than it is to raise one set too low by mistake. People begrudge price increases and welcome decreases; it is a wise manager who maneuvers himself into the position of having to lower price rather than to increase it in the event he makes a mistake.

Next, a manager is often wise in using a high price to limit the demand for a new product, because if it were priced lower he might not be able to supply the demand. Also, the firm probably needs the money provided by the high price, since costs are usually higher initially.

What costs are higher in the initial marketing of a product?

An initially high price also can have a favorable impact on the eventual market acceptance of the product, as it may establish a certain value in the consumer's mind that makes the sale easier when the price is lowered to a competitive position.

Finally, a skim-the-cream strategy should be used if an inverse demand curve exists; more is bought at a higher price.

In what circumstances can one expect to find an inverse demand curve?

The major disadvantage of the skim-the-cream strategy is that it attracts competitors, thereby inducing a chaotic competitive situation. Once a firm enters a market, exit is extremely painful and is accomplished only after much price competition. Before a firm with insufficient volume leaves a market, it prices below full costs in the hope that whatever it receives in excess of marginal costs will help minimize losses, while buying time in the hope that others will be driven out of the market first, thereby improving the market situation.

If entry into an industry is relatively easy, a skim-the-cream strategy can be disastrous to long-run success. Of course, many entrepreneurs have no intention of staying in a market for the long run—they are out for short-run profits.

A skim-the-cream price provides a springboard for a competitor; he brings out his "new and improved" version of the product at a price slightly under the skim-the-cream price.

Penetration Pricing   A penetration strategy sets the price at the bottom of the range to penetrate the market as rapidly as possible. The manager hopes that every potential user will at least try it; if he can get them to do that, his chances for success are good. A skim-the-cream price discourages trying a product. Of course, the ultimate in penetration pricing is free sampling—give it away.

One disadvantage of penetration pricing is that the organization can be deluged with orders. When one of the soap companies introduces a new brand, it expects a substantial volume immediately, which requires large investments in inventory just to fill up the pipelines to the market. Small concerns would not have the financial resources available to penetrate a market quickly.

What are the pipelines to the market?

Unquestionably, penetration pricing discourages the entry of competitors into a market, because the price is not high enough to make potential returns sufficiently attractive. If a product when handled properly has a steady, long-run demand, it is good judgment to price it so that competitors are discouraged from entering the industry.

PRICING BASE

It is all too easy to assume that the product unit is the pricing base ($20 per item), but this does not have to be so. Creative pricing often dictates otherwise. Hertz Rent-A-Car charges by days kept and miles traveled—a usage base. Usage bases make good sense because they offer the buyer an attractive proposition: he pays only for what he uses, not for idleness. Computer leasing companies have usage-pricing schedules.

Goodyear Tire and Rubber Company signed an agreement with Western Airlines to supply airplane tires, normally costing up to $250 each, based on the number of landings made by Western Airlines' planes. For a set fee per landing Goodyear supplies all of Western's tire needs, a creative pricing policy.

Could a usage base be developed for auto tires?

One pharmacy developed a pricing plan in which its customers paid a fixed fee of $3 per month per family, for which they were able to buy all drugs and sundries for cost plus 10 percent. Another pharmacy priced on a cost-plus-fixed-fee basis per prescription rather than on a percentage markup.

Creative pricing is the pricing equivalent of creative advertising or creative selling, and it can be just as effective, if not more so. It means using one's imagination to break away from traditional thinking to develop a new pricing system. It may be the designing of a different discount schedule or the development of an attractive way to pay for the goods. It may be the discovery of a different pricing base.

PRICE POLICIES

Price policies are separate and distinct from the product's price level; the same policies can exist for many different prices, and different policies can be established for the same price.

Purpose of Policies

Price policies have three basic purposes: (1) to ensure uniformity of pricing behavior, (2) to influence buying behavior, and (3) to meet legal requirements.

Uniformity of Decisions   Without clear-cut, stated policies it would be difficult for management to obtain much uniformity in pricing decisions. In a large company, price policies are necessary if all of the salesmen are to quote the same terms, allowances, and discounts. Even in small concerns, stated policies are of considerable value, because it is difficult for a person to remember just exactly what actions he took in certain instances. If policies have been established and one has scrupulously abided by them, he will know that he is treating every customer uniformly, an important factor in maintaining good will.

Influence and Control   Policies motivate buyers to do certain things. An attractive cash discount will stimulate early payment of invoices. Quantity discounts encourage larger orders. A seasonal discount can alter the timing of a purchase. Advertising allowances stimulate promotional activities by middlemen. Every policy motivates the buyer to do something. Competitive advantages can be gained by the institution of clever pricing policies.

Legal Restrictions   Pricing activities in American industry are regulated by both state and federal legislation. In order to ensure that one is not violating the law, certain policies must be formulated that are known to be legal. As long as pricing actions remain within such policies, management has some degree of assurance that it is abiding by the law.

POLICIES ON PRICE BEHAVIOR

Policies on price changes are helpful. The manager should have some guidance as to what he should do under the following circumstances.

Meeting Competition

Many managers maintain a policy of always meeting competition. If a competitor lowers price, the manager follows suit, having previously told his customers that he will do so. This policy has several advantages. First, it warns customers not to be stampeded into buying from another supplier; the company will meet any legitimately lower price quoted by the competition. This policy is a tremendous aid in cementing relations between buyer and seller; the buyer has some assurance that he is paying the lowest price for which the product can be bought. Second, the policy clearly notifies all competitors that price cutting will be met quickly and surely, which discourages them from cutting price.

Price Stability

Some firms adopt a policy of maintaining prices over a period of time. Once a price is set for a season, the firm may have the policy of adhering to it regardless of short-run fluctuations in costs or the market. Such a policy encourages buyers to carry larger inventories than otherwise. If the buyer believes that the price will drop, he buys hand-to-mouth, refusing to carry substantial inventories.

Why do businessmen seek price stability?

POLICIES ON DISCOUNTS

Each type of discount has a specific purpose. Each industry usually has its traditional discount policies, though usually a few "mavericks" see an advantage to altering these practices.

Cash Discounts

Probably the most commonly used discount is given to buyers who pay their bills within a stipulated period of time. The seller may grant terms of *3/10, net 30 days* (a 3 percent discount from the invoice price will be granted if it is paid within 10 days of date). The full amount is due at the end of 30 days. In essence, the manufacturer is willing to pay 3 percent if the buyer will allow him to use the due funds 20 days sooner. This is equivalent to 55.67 percent annual rate of interest.[2]

---

[2] $\frac{3\%}{97\%} \div \frac{20 \text{ days}}{360 \text{ days}} = 55.67\%$ annual rate of interest.

A buyer with money cannot afford to pass up cash discounts; if in some instance he can, the cash discount has been improperly set to perform its function.

A cash discount frequently lowers collection and bad-debt expenses. One television repairman relieved a critical accounts-receivable problem by giving a 5 percent discount if the customer paid cash at the time of the call.

Functional Discounts

Functional, or trade, discounts are used to effect different prices to different classes of customers. A manufacturer has to sell to wholesalers at a lower price than he sells to retailers. He might offer a functional discount of 40 percent off list to retailers and a discount of 40-15 percent to wholesale accounts. He might also give industrial firms a separate functional discount such as 40-5 percent. In addition, he might sell to an export agent to whom he gives a discount of 40-15-5 percent.[3]

Quantity Discounts

Quantity discounts are reductions in price granted for buying in certain quantities. There are two basic types of quantity discounts: noncumulative and cumulative. Each has its own function.

Noncumulative Quantity Discounts   A noncumulative quantity discount is a price reduction that depends on the size of the order. If a customer purchases one unit, the list price might be $1; however, if he purchases 100 units at a time, the firm might allow a 10 percent quantity discount.

Economically, quantity discounts are usually sound and advisable. Most of the costs incurred in taking and filling an order are fixed. It costs the same amount for a salesman to call on a customer and write an order for one unit as it does for him to write one for 100 units. The mailing, office-handling, and shipping room costs are about the same, regardless of the size of order. Relatively more profit is realized on larger orders than on smaller ones. In many concerns a large portion of small orders are actually unprofitable, because the costs of handling them exceed the gross profit realized. Some of these cost savings on quantity sales must be passed on to the buyer to motivate him to order in economical quantities.

Why are quantity discounts regulated by law?

Cumulative Quantity Discounts   A cumulative quantity discount is a reduction in the total price paid for goods purchased over a period of time. A firm may offer all customers a rebate of 5 percent if they purchase more than $10,000 worth of merchandise during the year, and to those buying more than $50,000 a rebate of 12 percent.

A cumulative discount does nothing to alter the average size of the order, because it makes no difference whatsoever what size orders the customers place with

[3] A $1 retail item selling for a 40-15-5 percent discount would cost $1 × .60 × .85 × .95 = 48¢.

the firm. It is simply the total volume of business placed with the company over a period of time that determines this discount. The major purpose of a cumulative discount is to obtain the entire business of an account. The cumulative discount discourages customers from dividing their volume among several different firms.

Under what circumstances is it nearly impossible to get the customer to give larger individual orders?

Seasonal Discounts

Seasonal discounts are reductions in price given for buying during a certain time of the year, usually the slack season. Fence erectors normally give a 5 percent discount for buying during the winter season. Seasonal discounts often are given to encourage buyers to stock up early in anticipation of the season. At other times they are given to transfer the storage function from the manufacturer to the buyer. H. J. Heinz Company usually puts an extremely attractive price on its catsup immediately after the packing season. The attractive discount persuades the consumer to buy a large volume, thereby alleviating storage problems for the manufacturer.

What advantages are gained by having dealers stock up early in a season?

POLICIES ON PRICE LEVEL

Odd or Even

Should a product's price be *even*—such as $3, $5, or $10—or *odd*, such as $2.98, $4.89, or $9.95? An even price is advised when it is preferable that the goods have a quality image. An odd price is advisable where the illusion of a bargain is wanted. For this reason odd prices are encountered widely in supermarkets and even prices in high-quality apparel stores.

Do these pricing policies work?

One-Price Policy

In comparison with those in many parts of the world, business transactions in the United States are unique in one respect. Legally and traditionally we are wedded to the one-price policy; that is, the seller establishes one price for his product and will sell it to all interested parties for that amount. In many foreign countries the seller does not have any one price in mind. Instead, he endeavors to obtain just as much above cost as he can. Although the one-price policy is fairly standard in our economy, certain intriguing islands of variable prices still exist. Most retail merchants stoutly maintain that they have a one-price policy, but the adroit bargainer is able to extract either a lower price or additional merchandise from the dealer who is tired of storing certain goods. Many manufacturers have discovered, to their chagrin, that in dealing with large buying organizations they are forced into a variable-price policy.

Although on the surface our system is well wedded to the one-price policy, *sub rosa* the variable-price policy is present, and one had better realize it if he wishes to remain competitive in the marketplace.

Price Discrimination

Many firms practice a policy of price discrimination within the law. Price discrimination is the charging of different prices for the same quality and quantity of product to different buyers. Electric utilities discriminate in their rates to customers, depending on the end use of the power being supplied.

Why do the power companies discriminate in price? In what way does the telephone company discriminate in price?

Price Lining

Price lining consists of grouping several products of varying costs and market attractiveness together and selling them all at the same price. Although this is most prevalent in retail stores, it is still practiced by some manufacturers. One shoe concern prices all its output at the same price, regardless of costs or relative market appeal. Most retailers group their offerings to sell in three or four price lines, such as suits to sell for $39.95, $49.95, $60, and $80.

There are several reasons for price lining. First, it is an administratively simple method for pricing many items in a product line. Executive time need not be utilized in setting separate prices. Instead, the company simply sets a price at which it knows it will come out all right in the long run if it sells all its volume at this rate.

Second, price lining reduces consumer confusion and frustration. Visualize the plight of a woman attempting to make up her mind whether she should buy a $29.95 dress or one priced at $28.74. She would be pondering whether or not the higher-priced garment was really worth the additional money. In her frustration a sale might be lost. Instead, the retailer prices both dresses at $28.98 and lets the customer choose the one she really wants; price lining in retail stores thus actually increases customer satisfaction and certainly decreases the amount of effort exerted in the process.

RENTAL POLICIES

One trend in distribution is the rapid growth of leasing. Renting is a pricing base with time inserted into the picture. In the usual sale the consumer pays a price as of an instant of time, but in renting he is paying the price over a span of time.

Objectives of Renting

From the buyer's point of view there can be several advantages to renting. First, renting converts fixed cost into a variable one. A firm that rents automobiles as it needs them, rather than maintaining its own fleet, has inserted flexibility into its costs. A garment maker can rent the necessary sewing machines for only the period of time he desires to be in business, thereby escaping fixed costs during times when he does not wish to be active. Second, renting reduces the capital investment required. Third, renting also allows one to buy the level of technology he desires. Instead of having to purchase the latest model on the market, a buyer can rent an older model for less. Fourth, renting may present tax advantages.

From the seller's point of view, rental policies—though troublesome and requiring considerable resources—can still be advantageous. A rental plan can facilitate sales. Office equipment dealers overcome buyer resistance by renting a machine to him and allowing him to apply the rental payments on its purchase price. Once the customer has used the product and sold himself on it, he frequently buys it.

Why does the customer often buy a rented product?

Many of the more famous rental policies, such as those of IBM and United Shoe Machinery Company, were instituted for other reasons. First, by renting the equipment the manufacturers maintained control of the servicing. Next, those companies maximized their revenues by renting; they were able to obtain relatively more money for their products over the given span of time than they could if they sold them. Finally, by renting the machines they maintained control over the supplies used for operating them. The exclusive rental policies of both concerns have been declared illegal. Both companies will now sell or rent, depending on the desires of the buyer.

Why do firms like to keep control over servicing?
Since IBM and Xerox will sell their equipment, why then do most of their customers still rent?

Problems Involved

From the seller's point of view the biggest problem involved in rental policies is that of financing. The financial burden of renting can be backbreaking to most concerns. Rental prices must be made high enough that the company can recover a disproportionately large amount in the first year or so of rental, because technological innovation reduces the machine's rentability in later years. The market risks involved in a rental policy are substantial; the machine can come back at any time.

Servicing costs can be substantial, because the renter has little incentive to take care of the machine.

POLICIES ON TERMS OF SALE

In negotiating a contract of sale, many terms must be decided in addition to price. Many adroit buyers have learned that it is far easier to extract price reductions from a seller by means of the terms of sale than argue with him on the price. The terms of sale are every bit as important in determining the final profitability of an order as are the discounts granted or the price established.

Transportation

Specific provision must be made designating the party paying the transportation charges. Usually firms adopt one of two policies: (1) f.o.b. factory, or (2) f.o.b. destination. In the last instance, it is the seller's responsibility to deliver the merchandise to the customer's dock. Most buyers treat transportation charges just as though they were part of the price of the goods. There is, nevertheless, more to transportation policies than just determining who will pay the freight bill. There are matters of risk and trouble.

Customers prefer goods delivered at a firm price to their docks. Most buyers do not like to be concerned with transportation allowances because they insert a degree of uncertainty into the transaction. F.o.b. destination puts the burden of shipping the order by the most economical route onto the seller. Much ill will results if a seller quotes terms f.o.b. factory and fails to ship by the most economical route. On the other hand, if transportation is a significant part of the delivered cost of an item, it is only fair that each buyer pay his own transportation costs. Under an f.o.b. destination pricing system, the total transportation costs of the firm are averaged over all customers so some buyers subsidize others.

Which buyers are subsidized with a destination pricing policy?

Some sellers agree to pay the freight on shipments over a certain amount, but ship f.o.b. mill on small orders. The economics of transportation force this policy, because most commercial carriers have a minimum charge regardless of the weight of the shipment. Problems are encountered in shipping heavy items of low unit value any distance. Transportation costs can become larger than the product's value.

Legally, it is highly advantageous to sell f.o.b. factory, because the goods belong to the buyer from that point forward, unless contractual stipulations specify otherwise. This may not sound like an important consideration, but it can amount to substantial savings in money and effort over a period of time. In any large operation a certain percentage of shipments will be damaged in transit. If they are the buyers' goods, then the buyers will have to fight the battles with the transportation firms over damages. If, for some reason, the goods incur some liability while in shipment, it falls upon the shoulders of their owner. Whenever risks exist over a long period of time, a certain percentage of them will be realized. The basic principle is to let the other fellow own the goods as long as possible so he has the risks. Bargaining power determines who will have his way.

Date of Payment—Delayed or Forward Dating

Considerable negotiating occurs for favorable dates of payment. In some industries it is common for the seller to give the buyer several months to pay. This practice usually exists in situations in which the manufacturer wants the retailer to carry substantial inventories. Some toy manufacturers bill their customers after the end of the Christmas selling season.

Other times sellers will use delayed dating as a means for breaking into important accounts. One shirt manufacturer offered to give a men's apparel dealer an extra 120 days if he would carry his line in a new store. However, a competitor did him one better and offered to put in a full stock on consignment; the shirts would be paid for as they were reordered, with the salesman maintaining the inventory in good shape. These offers were made because the sellers knew that the merchant would be pressed for cash in expanding his operations.

One capacitor supplier devised a delayed payment schedule for financing a large inventory for a customer by staggering payment throughout the year. If the customer bought $24,000 of capacitors on one order, $2000 would be due each month for the next 12 months.

PRICE FIXING

To better understand what makes otherwise honest businessmen take part in an illegal activity such as a price-fixing conspiracy, consider the case history of such a conspiracy involving the ready-mix concrete industry in a middle-sized city.

The ready-mix producers, discouraged by a continual drop in prices, agreed to "stabilize" prices through their local trade association. The principle of price fixing was opposed by most participants, and there was considerable debate on whether the "stabilized" prices were legal. The producers decided that they were not, but that they would rather go to jail than starve. A three-man enforcement committee was appointed to make sure that every producer was holding the price, but they were relatively powerless.

After little more than a year, the conspiracy gradually began to disintegrate, largely because of mutual mistrust. The producers began to accuse each other of price cutting, giving kickbacks, and using any and all means to steal jobs from each other. The largest producer finally announced that he was tired of doing business their way so he cut the price of his concrete. Prices once again began to tumble.

For several years the prices stayed unreasonably low, and business was tough for the small producer, who was barely covering expenses and was not paying overhead, to say nothing of making any profit. The trade association continued to function, but not as a price-fixing vehicle. However, the problem came full circle, and the members again talked about "stabilizing" prices as a solution to their difficulties.

Why will businessmen risk jail to participate in price-fixing conspiracies?
What was the basic cause of the ready-mix producers' low prices?

Though in many instances horizontal price fixing (an agreement among competitors at the same level of distribution) is in violation of the law, it is widely practiced. Price fixing among local retailers may be perfectly legal in the absence of state antitrust legislation as long as they are not in interstate commerce. It is not uncommon for gasoline stations, dry cleaners, barber shops, and appliance repair services to collude in setting price schedules. The Justice Department prosecuted car dealers for colluding on prices.

On the manufacturing level, price-fixing agreements are almost universally illegal, because most firms do business in interstate commerce. Nevertheless, price-fixing agreements are known to have existed, as proved in numerous court cases.

As a policy, price fixing is shortsighted; it almost inevitably leads to undesirable consequences. The businessman who allows himself to be trapped into thinking that a price-fixing arrangement between him and his competitors will solve his competitive ills is only deluding himself. One or more of several possible consequences can arise from price-fixing arrangements. First, there is the distinct possibility of discovery, legal suit, and severe penalty. This may, however, be the least of the businessman's worries. Far more important are the economic consequences of his actions.

When competitors fix a price, they do not fix it low but at a level that will allow the least efficient member to obtain his desired level of profits. Such an artificially high price almost inevitably attracts new entries into the industry and in the long run only complicates the competitive picture. Many gasoline service stations, through state or local associations, have established a schedule of "suggested" prices which in many areas is strictly followed by all dealers. The objective of this price list, of course, is to increase the profits of the service station. In the short run it can be successful. Such profits, however, almost inevitably cause the market area to be over-built with service stations. Entrepreneurs entering business are attracted not only by the high profits being earned but also by the prospect that price competition is nonexistent. Once the market area is overbuilt, the volume of stations reaches a point where profit is nonexistent. At this time, price wars usually erupt, as the marginal stations attempt to obtain sufficient volume to continue operations. Entry into an industry may be relatively easy, but exit is always painful and is effected only after the business-man has tried everything in his power to stay solvent. One of the first things he does is to cut prices in the hope that he can salvage something of his business. In the long run, therefore, price-fixing agreements tend to expand the capacity of an industry over what is economically justified, thereby making the competitive situation more difficult.

Conclusion

> Price is probably the single most important factor affecting profits. It is also one measure of the merit of the marketing program; a soundly conceived and executed marketing plan results in a profitable price. The resultant profits, or lack thereof, also determine the allocation of resources, as they are attracted to profitable endeavors.
>
> The manager is not always free to set prices on his wares; there can be many constraints on his pricing freedom.
>
> While economic theory has its limitations, the concepts of marginal revenue and marginal costs are of value.
>
> The price-setting procedure involves an investigation into such factors as competitive prices, the price of substitute products, the prices of complementary products, production costs, savings realized by using the product, and the reactions of middlemen and consumers.
>
> Not only can much imagination be used in the selection of the pricing base for an item, but creativity can be shown in the establishment of policies in terms of sale, discounts, and price behavior.
>
> Finally, the role of price in determining society's standard of living should not be overlooked.

14 Promotion[1]

*Advertising is 85 percent confusion
and 15 percent commission.*
FRED ALLEN

After the manager has developed his product, priced it, and established his distribution policies, he cannot just sit around to wait for orders to walk through the door. Sales do not occur automatically. They have to be promoted. Customers have to be told about the product, shown what it will do for them, and told where they can get it. Sales promotional efforts include such activities as personal selling, advertising, publicity, point-of-purchase displays, and special promotions such as contests, fairs and exhibitions, couponing, or sampling. We will not be concerned here with the details of executing an advertising campaign or a personal selling program; rather we will focus on the broad overall strategic uses of these tools.

[1] This chapter is based on material in Richard H. Buskirk, *Principles of Marketing,* 3d ed. (New York: Holt, Rinehart and Winston, Inc., 1970), Chapters 19, 20, and 21.

PURPOSE OF PROMOTIONAL ACTIVITIES

The goal of promotional activities is to shift a product's demand. Figure 14-1 shows that total demand is increased at every price, and the elasticity of demand is altered. Promotion should make demand more elastic to any decrease in price and more inelastic to a price increase.

FIGURE 14-1: Goal of Promotional Activities in Altering Demand Curve

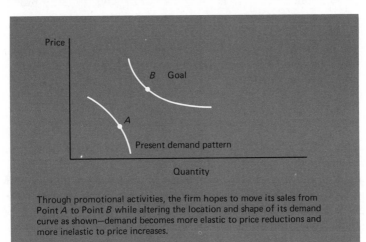

Through promotional activities, the firm hopes to move its sales from Point *A* to Point *B* while altering the location and shape of its demand curve as shown—demand becomes more elastic to price reductions and more inelastic to price increases.

This change in demand results from three things: information, demand stimulation, and values added.

Providing Information

Promotional material provides information about products available, their prices, where they can be purchased, and their characteristics. This information-giving function of promotion should not be underestimated, because it is probably its most important task. Visualize a world without advertising or personal selling. How would you know what products were available or where to buy them? You would spend a great deal of time going from store to store surveying goods. The economic costs of this search would be tremendous and the results disappointing. Promotion simplifies the search. "Let your fingers do the walking through the Yellow Pages."

In selling a new product, one of the major problems is informing potential customers that it is for sale at certain locations. If this is done adequately, some demand is usually forthcoming. However, getting information to millions of people is difficult. Contrary to the old adage that if you build a better mousetrap the world will come thundering to your door, the fact is that without promotion people will not know you have an improved mousetrap, much less the location of your door.

Stimulating Demand

Besides providing information, promotional activities can stimulate the demand for a product. Housewives may know that automatic dishwashers are for sale but be unconvinced of their merit. A well-formulated promotional campaign can educate them as to how an automatic dishwasher can make their lives easier. Some producers assume that buyers can easily comprehend the advantages of a product, but such is far from the truth. How would one know the advantages of a stereophonic record player over a regular one if he were not educated to its advantages by promotion?

A part of the educational process is the general upgrading of the consumer's standard of living. Promotional activities can stimulate the consumer to live better than he has in the past. The reader of *Better Homes & Gardens* is urged to improve her living standards when she looks at the luxurious ads and reads articles on how to improve her home.

In what ways and how does television improve one's standards of living?

Some products owe their success largely to clever promotional programs. International Mineral and Chemical Company introduced a standard chemical about two decades ago with much promotion. It was called monosodium glutamate (MSG) and was used in food preparation. Competitors have been frustrated over its success: "All they've got is their name!" But if you have a name, your product can be just like everyone else's if you promote it wisely. And Accent was soundly promoted.

Values Added by Promotion

Sales promotional activities can add value to a product by giving its buyer additional utilities. Promotion can create a public image that is in itself of considerable value to the buyer. It is doubtful that Cadillac would have its present-day prestige if it were not for the excellent advertising campaign behind it. Cadillac has nurtured the idea that owning a Cadillac is the ultimate success symbol and that a successful man owes it to himself to own one. Without this advertising campaign, the Cadillac owner would obtain less satisfaction from driving the car, because he would not be assured that everyone recognized it as the status symbol he wants to display. Without a doubt the Cadillac is worth far more to its owner because of advertising.

Why do many people prefer to own products that are well advertised?

DETERMINING PROMOTIONAL METHODS AND EXTENT OF USAGE

The first problem is to determine which promotional tools to use and to what extent. Seldom will two executives use precisely the same promotional methods. Several factors determine which methods will most efficiently promote sales; these are summarized in Figure 14-2.

FIGURE 14 -2: Factors Influencing Selection and Amount of Promotional Activity

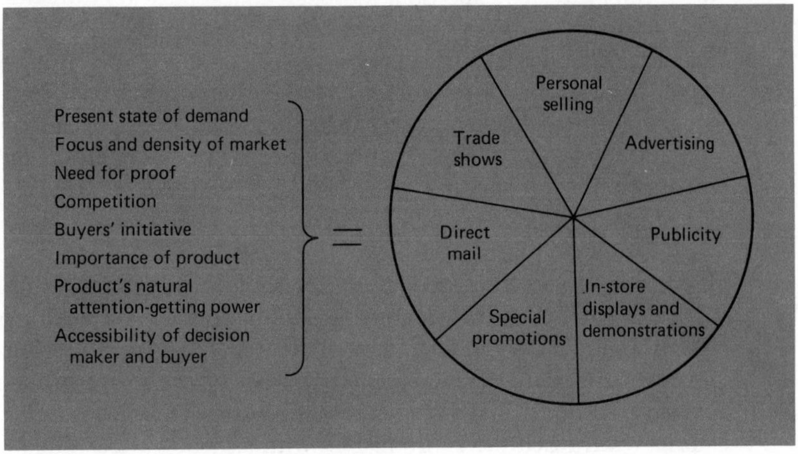

Present State of Demand

One key factor affecting the nature and extent of promotional activities is the state of the demand for an item. If the buyer recognizes that he has a need for the product and is well acquainted with various competing brands, the product is in the *competitive* stage. The primary demand for it already exists; the task of promotion is to switch the buyer's favor to the promoter's brand—selective demand. The housewife recognizes her need for a washing machine, so it is not necessary to sell her on the advantages of owning one. Instead, the promotional program is focused on why she should buy one brand rather than another.

On the other hand, if the buyer does not recognize his need for the product, he must be shown how it solves his problems, what it will do for him. This is called the *pioneering* stage of promotion, because the seller must pioneer the market if he is to be successful. In this stage promotional activities are aimed at creating *primary demand* rather than *selective demand*. In the early days of selling refrigerators, the producers faced the task of convincing the housewife that she ought to own a mechanical refrigerator rather than an icebox. If that job was done, the promoter received most of the resulting volume. There was little need to promote one brand against another, because the primary demand for the article was too scant to make such competitive promotion profitable. Selective demand cannot be created without an existing primary demand.

What products are now in the pioneering stage?

In primary-demand promotions the market must be educated to a product's usage and advantages. Heavy reliance is usually placed on publicity, personal selling, fairs and exhibitions, and other special promotions. Although advertising definitely plays an important role in pioneering promotions, frequently it lacks the ability to tell a complete story and do a thorough educational job.

Even in competitive promotions where pioneering is not a major factor, if the buyer does not recognize his need for the product, advertising may play a relatively minor role. Although several excellent encyclopedias have been published for years, the average person does not realize he needs one. Encyclopedia companies have therefore learned through long experience that the best way to sell their books is through personal selling.

Focus and Density of Market

If potential buyers for a product are concentrated geographically or industrially, promotion is facilitated. A manufacturer of drilling bits for oil field usage sells to a market that is well focused and concentrated in a few geographical regions. It is economically feasible for him to contact personally most of the major drilling contractors in the industry. Also, his advertising need not be extensive, because a few well-selected trade journals will reach the entire market with a modest expenditure.

What effect does the density and focus of a market have upon marketing costs?

On the other hand, chewing gum—which is sold through restaurants, variety, drug, and food stores—has such a widespread, unfocused market that it cannot be contacted personally; advertising must reach the masses, so mass-media advertising is used.

As a general principle, as markets become more clearly focused and restricted, personal selling becomes easier and more effective. Also, the efficiency of advertising is greatly enhanced when the potential market is easily identifiable and delineated.

Accessibility of Purchaser

The difficulties encountered in contacting the decision maker affect promotional methods used. A salesman might find it difficult to reach the president of a large corporation, but advertising in *Fortune, Time,* or *Business Week* might get through regularly. Direct mail, trade shows, catalogues, and publicity might have access to a buyer where a salesman might not.

On the other hand, often a salesman can reach a buyer when other media fail. Encyclopedia companies find it difficult to contact low-income families by advertising or direct mail, but their salesmen find it easy to gain an audience for their presentations.

Why are potential purchasers inaccessible? For what reasons do they make themselves accessible?

One of the big advantages of fairs and exhibitions is that prospective buyers make themselves accessible to the seller. The department store toy buyers in the nation congregate each March in New York City to attend the toy fair. A toy manufacturer at this market gains access to many thousands of large buyers at a relatively low cost.

Need for Proof

Sometimes a product's advantages must be proved beyond doubt before the buyer will act. If an important claim is made for an item, the seller must prove it.

If proof is critically important in a sale, personal selling, trade shows, and publicity all play dominant roles. Seldom can advertising and direct mail really give the concrete proof required by skeptical buyers. Automobile dealers know that a demonstration ride is their most powerful sales tool. Although millions may be spent on advertising to make persuasive claims about smooth rides, powerful pickup, and ease of handling, one ten-minute demonstration ride can make the difference in convincing the prospect.

On the other hand, if the buyer does not demand proof of claims before buying, advertising may play a substantial role. Consumers will believe many claims without demonstration; they will often accept at face value the statements made about most toothpastes, such as that they will prevent bad breath and decay. The proof required by the potential buyer frequently can be presented in advertising in a sufficiently effective way. However, if he is skeptical about an important claim, usually advertising will not persuade him. Only his actual use of the item will change his mind; this requires personal contact. Sometimes sampling can be used for proof.

If proof is required, how could a television ad supply it?
What techniques can be used to prove a point to a potential buyer?

Buyer's Initiative

The amount and type of promotion advisable for a product depends in part on the initiative potential buyers will take in acquiring it. Some buyers are willing to make an effort to acquire a desired item. An industrial purchasing agent wanting to buy a sizable quantity of fractional horsepower motors will take the initiative in contacting available suppliers to obtain the best price.

If the buyer will take the initiative, then catalogues, trade shows, and advertising can be effective. If buyers will not take the initiative, then the seller has to come to them. How many people voluntarily buy life insurance? Personal selling is necessary to sell it.

Buyers seldom take much initiative in procuring an item unless it is something they know they need. Even then, if a brand hopes to minimize its promotion it must either have a monopoly or be so distinctive that the market recognizes its superiority—conditions not frequently encountered. Buyers usually are extremely sluggish actors. Generally, competitive conditions relieve the buyer from having to make much effort in buying an item.

Why do monopolies, such as the electric power companies, advertise?
Why does the telephone company advertise in its Yellow Pages?

Product's Natural Attention-Getting Ability

Some products possess attention-getting power beyond normal expectancy. People are attracted to the car dealer's showroom, thus lessening the promotional task of selling autos. Home builders have discovered that people will travel many miles to visit a unique model home.

Importance of Product

The importance of the purchase to the buyer affects not only the amount of promotion required but also the methods utilized. This factor overlaps some of those previously discussed. Buyers take more initiative in buying goods that are important to them than in buying those that are not. The importance of the purchase also affects the purchaser's accessibility.

As a general rule, the more important a purchase is to a buyer, the more reliance he will place on personal contact with the seller. In making an important acquisition, seldom will a buyer rely solely on advertisements or catalogues. Instead, he wants a complete demonstration and personal service. If a purchase is trivial, however, the buyer may rely on advertisements. A man would not demand a demonstration when buying a pair of roller skates for his son, but he would if he were purchasing an automobile.

PERSONAL SELLING

The salesman, a much storied and misunderstood figure in both fact and fiction, is an important link in the chain of distribution. In many situations his adeptness is the difference between success or failure of the enterprise. In practically all situations, managers must use astute salesmanship at various levels to achieve their goals. The personal success of many people is based upon their abilities to sell both themselves and their products.

Salesmanship is simply another word for persuasion. The salesman is a persuader; he tries to persuade another person to do something. Personal selling is basic to all business; the businessman is continually trying to persuade someone to do something. He persuades investors to invest in his concern. He persuades his workers to work for him efficiently. He persuades his suppliers to give him what he wants on favorable terms. He persuades the market to buy his products.

Personal selling consists of contacting the prospective buyers of a product personally. It is by far the major promotional tool used in American industry. Many companies doing little or no advertising still maintain a large sales force, and firms spending millions on advertising may spend even more on personal selling. Procter & Gamble has more than 5000 salesmen to back up its multimillion-dollar advertising programs. Salesmen are the infantry who must go into the field to get the actual orders and service accounts.

ADVANTAGES OF PERSONAL SELLING

An activity of such magnitude as personal selling could not exist without forceful and cogent reasons. Few managers would spend money on personal selling if they were not thoroughly convinced that it was the best application of their funds. The advantages of personal selling are that it pinpoints prospects, gets their attention and interest, is able to meet specific objections, demonstrates the product to them, capitalizes on their social drives, closes the sale, and provides communication with the market—not to mention that the salesmen can do various nonselling work to boot.

Pinpointing Prospects

A salesman can seek out good prospects, whereas advertising and other promotional tools frequently are unable to separate likely from unlikely buyers. Advertising can be likened to a fisherman casting his bait into the water in the hope that some fish are in the area and will be interested. He is never quite sure whether any fish are interested in his bait and he never knows which fish will bite. On the other hand, the personal salesman can be likened to a hunter who stalks his prey with a rifle.

Economically, pinpointing prospects means much less waste of effort and expenditure in personal selling than in advertising. Although the cost per contact by a salesman is many times larger than that of advertising, the great portion of the contacts made by advertising may be with people who are not prospects. A salesman will call on real prospects.

Getting Attention and Interest

One must first get the attention and interest of a person before he can communicate with him. Although advertising employs many devices to gain the attention and interest of potential buyers, still research indicates that the percentage of success is small. Even the best ads in a magazine may be noticed by only 60 percent of the readers, while poorer ads have a readership of perhaps 5 percent.

But the salesman's physical presence plus a good approach almost guarantee the prospect's attention and interest. The salesman can tailor what he says to appeal to the most likely motives of that particular prospect.

Meeting Specific Objections

The salesman is able to tailor his presentation to fit the precise needs of the person on whom he is calling, and he is on the scene to meet the specific objections raised. The closer the seller can come to fitting his sales appeal to the situation of his buyers, the more likely he is to get an order.

Demonstrating the Product

A demonstration of the product or its use by the prospect is usually the most effective way to convince him of its merits. There are a great many "people from Missouri"—they must be shown.

Capitalizing on Social Drives

It is natural for men to want to help their friends; it is difficult to say no to someone you like. A good salesman cultivates a social relationship with buyers that provides him an inside track in the race for the business. In many instances competitive products are identical in quality and price; social relations, therefore, may be the only basis for giving business to one firm rather than another. Prospects do not always buy the best product offered. The social side of the human equation can cause other behavior. Perhaps, for example, the salesman for the "best product" may in some way alienate the prospective customer.

Closing the Sales

The salesman can push for an order and close the sale on the spot. It is difficult to move people to action by advertising. Although some advertisements attempt direct-action closes through the use of coupons and special offers, these are not nearly as effective as a salesman who can meet the objections that are delaying the prospect's purchase.

The actual order taking is often a relatively complicated procedure. The prospect may have to be measured, or other specifications may need to be obtained.

Providing Communication

A salesman provides a channel of communication between the seller and the market. He is continually calling on buyers and is usually bombarded by a multitude of suggestions, information, and attitudes that he can pass on to management.

Performing Nonselling Work

A sales force can perform other activities, such as gathering credit information, rendering repair service, adjusting complaints, and performing marketing research. Though these nonselling duties should not be overstressed, to avoid diverting attention from the primary objective of selling, the firm that maintains a sales force does have men in the field who are able to perform these services.

DISADVANTAGES OF PERSONAL SELLING

No promotional tool is without its limitations; selling is no exception.

Costs

The costs of selling are not small. As a rough guide, a manager should figure that to put a good salesman in the field and pay his expenses may cost between $10,000 and $20,000 a year at a minimum; costs can go as high as $50,000 a year. Therefore, unless a salesman can sell sufficient volume, his costs may be prohibitive.

If you can afford to pay 5 percent of sales for the performance of the selling function, how much does a salesman who is paid $15,000 a year and spends $5000 a year on expenses have to sell to pay his way?

Currently there is much concern over the rapidly rising costs of maintaining salesmen in the field. Some industrial concerns report costs per call of over $30 today, whereas a few years ago these same firms reported costs per call of $15–$18. Naturally, firms are taking steps to minimize selling costs; some such steps are the careful determination of economical call rates for various sizes and classifications of accounts, the substitution of telephone solicitation for personal contact, and the use of centralized showrooms to encourage the customer to come to the seller. However, these do not reverse the tide of costs, only stem them.

Shortage of Good Personnel

Good salesmen are scarce. Moreover, the field of selling is not attracting sufficient numbers of men of the necessary quality to staff the sales forces of America properly.

Why don't more good men go into selling?

Leading firms, however, continue to rely heavily on the development of outstanding sales forces as a basic keystone of their marketing strategy. They have excellent sales management organizations capable of locating and hiring men with good potential selling abilities, and then training them to be excellent salesmen. Such firms "grow their own." They know that salesmen are not born; they can be trained. The fruit of this endeavor is evidenced by the success of such firms as IBM, Texas Instruments, Dow Chemical, Armstrong Cork, and Avon; all have developed top-notch sales forces through excellent training programs.

FACTORS GOVERNING ROLE OF PERSONAL SELLING IN PROMOTIONAL STRATEGY

There are several principles to guide the manager in deciding to what extent personal selling should be employed in his promotional strategy. Though no one of the following factors is decisive in itself, the executive who takes all of them into consideration can, in most instances, determine the probable effectiveness of personal selling for his product. The decision to rely heavily on personal selling may be based solely on strategic considerations. While most cosmetics firms rely on advertising, Avon chose to use door-to-door saleswomen and leads the industry—a "hit 'em where they ain't" strategy.

Why can Avon use door-to-door selling?

The fewer the potential buyers of a product, the more likely it is that personal selling will be the main promotional tool used. This is one reason why personal selling is emphasized more heavily in industrial than in consumer-goods marketing.

The average size of order is an important factor in determining the economic feasibility of personal selling. It might be economically impossible for a salesman to sell a product averaging $5 per order, but it would be feasible if the average order were $500. The size of the average order is a function of the unit's price, the quantities purchased, and the number of items in the line.

While most lumber manufacturers rely on various agents to sell their output, large concerns offering a wide line of items to the lumber dealer can maintain effective sales forces, thereby gaining substantial advantages over their smaller competitors.

Weyerhaeuser keeps more than 300 salesmen in the field selling its entire line of lumber, plywood, doors, and home programs to the dealer. By so doing, it frequently obtains a premium price as well as selling more merchandise.

If a product must be demonstrated to convince the potential buyer of its merit, personal selling is almost mandatory. However, if the buyer will believe the producer's claims without a demonstration, advertising or other promotional tools may be effective.

Some products naturally create customer resistance. A buyer may purchase an inexpensive vacuum cleaner voluntarily, but personal selling may be needed to sell him a quality machine. How many persons voluntarily buy life insurance?

Quality is difficult to prove in many instances, particularly by advertising. An adept salesman can show the prospect why he needs quality and why he should pay for it. Many important qualities are completely hidden from the buyer and can best be brought to his attention by a salesman.

In many technical sales the sales engineer must exert unusual effort prior to the sales presentation in making up the proposal. Many products are tailor-made, and specifications must be developed, costs computed, and technical problems resolved before the sale can be consummated. Perhaps a machine tool salesman may have to redesign the entire layout of a plant. A fork-lift truck salesman may have to rework a prospect's material storage and handling procedures to show him how he can use the equipment. Advertising cannot accomplish these tasks; salesmen can.

Frequently the salesman's work has just begun when he receives the order. His new customer now requires a considerable amount of servicing. An IBM computer salesman has accounts with whom he works closely, making certain that they receive the services they need.

ADVERTISING

Of all the areas in marketing, advertising attracts far more attention and interest than any other. Unfortunately, too many people believe that marketing and advertising are one and the same thing, when in fact advertising is merely one tool that is handy to use in some circumstances. However, the glamor of advertising remains and will no doubt continue to blind many people.

Advertising is a paid form of nonpersonal presentation or promotion of ideas, goods, or services by an identified sponsor. The key factors identifying advertising are that it is paid for and that it has an identified sponsor. Propaganda may or may not be paid for, but in any event its sponsor is hidden. Publicity is not paid for but the sponsor is identifiable.

Advertising encompasses a wide range of media such as magazine, newspaper, and television ads, radio commercials, outdoor billboards, direct mail promotions, directories, catalogues, point-of-purchase displays, transportation display cards, handbills, sky writing, and display signs.

Objectives of Advertising

An advertising campaign should have one or more objectives. Only by comparing results with initial objectives can the effectiveness of the campaign be evaluated.

Brand Recognition and Acceptance Some advertising is conducted to obtain market recognition and acceptance of the brand name. The advertiser wants people to know that his brand is on the market, recognize it when they see it, and consider it acceptable or possibly prefer it. Actually, a case could be made that all advertising campaigns include this objective. Many of the campaigns behind industrial goods are largely for the purpose of obtaining brand recognition.

Trial Purchase Some advertising campaigns have the objective of getting people to try the product. The theory is that if the customer will try the product it will sell itself; thus a loyal customer will be gained. Many campaigns behind new food items have this primary objective; special deals or coupons are used to encourage people to try the new product.

Influence at Site of Buying Decision Some advertising campaigns are designed to place a message before the decision maker when the buying decision is being made, in the hope that it will influence the choice of brand. A motel owner attempts to place his advertising in front of a traveler at the time he makes his decision on where to stay. A television repairman tries to place his advertising where the owner of a set will see it when his set needs repair.

Addition of Values Many advertisers endeavor to add values to their brand. Through adroit advertising they hope to shape the consumer's image of the article in the desired fashion, both to achieve a higher price for the item and to make it more appealing to its market. In addition, by showing the prospect many uses that may not be readily apparent, advertising can increase the item's usage value.

Aid in Personal Selling Some advertising campaigns try to pave the way for the salesman, making his job easier and more effective. If a prospect recognizes the name of the company the salesman represents, he is far more likely to give the salesman an audience than if he has never heard of the firm.

Avon cosmetics advertises not only to create brand recognition and acceptance but also to help open doors for its direct-selling saleswomen. Salesmen selling to middlemen find that they are able to use their company's consumer advertising as a potent selling tool in convincing middlemen of the advisability of handling the line.

Building Distribution Firms with little or no distribution of their products frequently use advertising as a means of obtaining dealers and distributors. Alex Lewyt tells of the results of a double-page spread in *Life* used to introduce his firm's new vacuum cleaner. While the apparent purpose of the ad was to create consumer demand for the machine, this demand would have been somewhat difficult to fill because the cleaner had no distribution at that time. The underlying strategy was to get dealers and distributors to come to Lewyt asking for distributorships. He wanted them to come to him so he could avoid going to them, begging them to take on the line. The bargaining power of the two positions is completely different. He wanted to be in the position of selecting distributors rather than having to take what he could get. It worked!

Well-placed ads may trigger dealers to handle a product in anticipation of the consumer demand the dealer thinks the ad will create.

Selling Goods—Taking Orders   Some advertising asks for an order; it tries to make the sale then and there. A direct-mail letter may ask the recipient to send in an order for the product; a mail-order advertisement in a magazine may ask the reader to write for the item; a billboard asks the motorist to stop in to satisfy his needs; a point-of-purchase window display draws a buyer into a store to buy what is featured.

Many other ads ask the person for direct action: "Go to your nearest dealer tomorrow!" or "Buy now! Prices never so low!" Coupons may give the consumer a little shove toward a sale, or perhaps a special offer is made "good for a limited time only."

Retailers in particular seek direct action from their advertising; they feature specific goods that they want to sell. Sometimes the appeal is a special price, but it does not have to be. Special goods with unique features or timely articles may be featured.

Forming the Company Image—Institutional Advertising   Weyerhaeuser Company spends about $8 million a year on its "corporation advertising" in addition to amounts budgeted for selling specific products. The goal of this campaign is to develop the idea that the company is a responsible citizen of the business community.

Many large multiproduct corporations choose to advertise in general terms, trying to establish certain thoughts in the public's mind. General Electric wants to be thought of as a progressive firm. 3-M wants to be known as a firm based on research. Ford has ideas. United Air Lines flies in friendly skies. You are in good hands with Allstate. Such campaigns try to create certain strategically selected images of the advertiser in the public's mind; the programs can be highly successful if pursued with patience, skill, and sufficient money.

Increasing Product's Usage   Some advertising programs try to increase a brand's usage by increasing its frequency of use or frequency of replacement, by increasing the size of purchase, by increasing the number of uses for it, or by lengthening its buying season. It may be sound strategy, when demand for a product has leveled off in its existing markets, to try to expand sales by getting present users to use more. After all, it might be easier to get someone who is already sold on the product to buy or use another unit of it than it would be to try to sell a new user, someone who heretofore has refused to buy the brand. Coca-Cola has featured its 16-ounce bottle in an advertisement; it wants to sell more Coke per transaction. Firestone advertises four tires for the price of three; it wants to sell more tires.

Target Market   Sometimes a certain market is targeted for attention when management feels it is not getting its fair share of business from that market. More money is then funneled into that particular geographic area, demographic segment, or special interest group.

Education   An advertising program may be designed to educate the public. The American Cancer Society is trying to educate the public about the dangers of smoking. Such programs usually take considerable time and effort to achieve their goals.

Advertising Media

Each advertising medium has its own characteristics and limitations, which one must understand to design an effective campaign. Advertising media are the means by which advertising messages are delivered. If they are not chosen properly, the message either is not delivered to the intended person or is delivered in such a fashion that it is ineffective.

Newspapers   Newspapers are the largest advertising medium. They have extensive coverage; hardly a city or town is not served by a paper. In using newspapers, an advertiser can be highly selective about the markets to which he advertises; he can launch a campaign, for example, in a single city. Because newspapers are printed either daily or weekly, the advertiser can take advantage of local opportunities rather quickly; he can advertise in the paper on short notice. The costs per contact by newspaper are low.

Newspapers, nevertheless, have disadvantages. First, there is little selectivity within the area of circulation. Newspapers go to prince and pauper alike. Unless a product is purchased by a large cross section of the population, newspaper advertising may be expensive per contact with a potential customer. Second, the competition for the reader's attention in a newspaper is keen; an ad may easily be buried. Unless one advertises in sufficient size, such as by taking a full-page ad, the message may be lost in the shuffle. Third, the technology of newspaper printing limits what can be done in the way of color and reproductions of pictures. Fourth, the life of a newspaper is short, lasting only a few hours at best. The reader picks up the paper only once and skims it for a short time. If the ad is not seen on that perusal, it is lost forever.

Newspaper advertising is usually limited to situations where the company has something newsworthy to tell the market about a product for which demand has already been established. Newspapers are generally unsuited to the creation of primary demand or the enhancement of a product's image. Retailers use newspapers extensively because most of their promotions are newsworthy—featuring price—and newspapers cover their market in fine fashion.

Magazines   There are two basic types of magazines: (1) consumer and (2) trade. There is literally a magazine for almost every special interest group in the nation. There are magazines for those interested in gardening, radio, sports cars, homes, and such. Similarly, there are trade publications for just about every conceivable trade or occupation in the world. Magazines can therefore be highly effective in selling to certain interest groups or certain trades or occupations. A manufacturer of a skiing accessory has available to him several magazines aimed at his specific market. Though newspapers are selective on a geographical basis, magazines are often highly selective on a market-cleavage basis, such as occupations, race, and interests. The costs of magazines may be higher per contact than newspapers, but the cost per potential customer may be much less.

Magazines have an advantage over newspapers in that their life is considerably longer, depending on the frequency of publication. One advertiser in *Better Homes & Gardens* testified that he received inquiries from an ad long after it had appeared; indeed, advertisements in magazines often draw responses after more than a year. In addition, magazines are usually picked up more than once by the reader. Studies have shown, for instance, that *Reader's Digest* is picked up and read by the same person approximately 13 times. An advertisement placed in a magazine has multiple exposure, which lowers its per-contact costs. Many magazines are used by consumers almost as catalogues.

Some magazines have built up sufficient reputations among their readers that products advertised in them automatically gain a certain degree of acceptance. The *Parents Magazine* Seal of Approval is a definite sales aid among both middlemen and consumers.

Television   In two decades television has grown from nothing to the point where it challenges newspapers as the nation's leading advertising medium. The reasons for this growth are not difficult to understand. First, television can sell products creatively. Things can be done with this medium that are impossible with any other. On television a reasonably close facsimile to a personal sale can be made to the customer. The product can be demonstrated and shown in use. Television has all the sound of radio plus the additional advantages of sight. As a selling tool, television is unparalleled by any other advertising medium.

Television reaches an audience unequaled in the history of man. No other single advertising medium reaches as many people on such a continuous basis as does television. Studies have shown that the average person watches television 4 to 5 hours a day and that approximately 90 percent of the populace owns a television receiver. In this era of mass merchandising, television is the mass medium for reaching the mass market.

Television has geographical selectivity. Although it has no natural selectivity as a medium, the advertiser can achieve his own market selectivity by the type of program he chooses. If he wishes to solicit a high-income market, he can choose a spot that is predominantly watched by people of high incomes.

Although television's cost per contact may be relatively low, nevertheless the total amounts involved are substantial. It takes many thousands of dollars to make even a slight impression on the market. Companies have been known to spend a quarter of a million dollars on just one showing of a significant program.

Unfortunately, television messages are instantaneous. They have no lifespan as do messages in printed media. There are no bonus viewers over time, and the viewer of a television ad cannot go back to examine or study the message if he is interested.

Radio   Radio, like television and newspapers, has great geographical flexibility. It lacks the visual appeal of both television and printed media. Psychologists have clearly proved that the eye is a far better path to the brain than the ear is; people remember far more of what they see than of what they hear. Radio has tremendous advantages in flexibility of timing; a radio announcement can be made almost immediately to take advantage of such things as weather and current events.

One of the major disadvantages of both radio and television is the fact that once the message is given, it is gone forever. If the listener misses the message the first time through, that message is gone and another must be purchased to reach him. For this reason repetition and high frequency are far more important in time media than in space media.

Direct Mail   Direct mail has several advantages. First, unlike other media, a direct-mailing piece has less competition for the reader's attention. A magazine or newspaper ad may have to fight with hundreds of others for the reader's attention, but a person may receive only a few direct-mail pieces at any one time. Second, a much longer and more complete selling story can be told in direct mail than in other printed media. Third, through the judicious selection of mailing lists, direct mail can be sent only to potential customers, incurring little waste circulation. This lowers its relatively high cost per contact to a lower cost per contact with potential users.

Direct mail suffers considerably from the recipient's inertia. Unless the piece is well executed, it has a good chance of being thrown in the wastebasket unopened.

Management of direct-mail operations is a field unto itself. It requires continual testing of the variables that determine its effectiveness; these may be the type of postage, choice between letters or post cards, type of paper, offers, outside envelope imprints, number of enclosures, types of appeals, day of mailing, mailing lists, time of year, and length of letter. As an example, one Christmas card manufacturer who sells directly to department stores has discovered that, for some reason, mailing pieces that have metered postage rather than stamps pull better. He has tested it time and again with the same results, even though other firms have concluded exactly the opposite.

Make an evaluation of billboards, catalogues, skywriting, and directories as advertising media.

PRINCIPLES OF EFFECTIVE ADVERTISING

The principles of effective advertising could be summed up in one phrase, "Be in the right media, going to the right people, with the right message, at the right time."

The extent to which an advertising campaign does all this determines its effectiveness. Other factors, however, enter into the picture.

Importance of Claim

The most important factor determining the effectiveness of an advertisement is the importance of the claim it makes. Most ads make one or more claims about the product. If these claims are not important to the reader, the ad will be ineffective. If the reader buys automobile tires for reasons of safety and protection against blowouts, he will give little heed to an ad that talks mainly about low cost. Similarly ineffective is an ad that talks about quality when the buyer is interested in price.

Do you think for one moment that the Mazola Corn Oil headline, "How to lose weight while you eat more often" will not get the attention of a reader with weight problems who wants to do something about them? What about the executive who has been worrying about keeping his estate? Hasn't the Chemical Bank of New York hit the nail on the head with its headline, "A Man Works Hard to Get $650,000— He Wants the Bank That Works Hardest to Keep It in the Family." Industrial advertisers tend to use more forceful headlines featuring important claims than do consumer-goods sellers. Frequently industrial ads feature the dollar savings that will accrue to the user of the product.

A top executive for a leading advertising agency has written a book in which the extols the virtue of his USP principle. USP stands for Unique Selling Proposition. His agency maintains that each ad must make a unique proposition to the customers that will be sufficiently strong to pull them into the store to buy. The USP is the important claim. Moreover, the program emphasizes the importance of continually stressing the one important claim, driving it home time after time with repetition.

Believability

An ad must be believable. It matters little how important the claim if it is not stated in such a way that the reader believes it. There are many ways of building believability into ads. Some ads feature the results of laboratory or field tests to prove their claims, whereas others rely on testimonials from alleged users of the product. Often guarantees are made to increase believability. No matter what technique is used, however, care must be taken that nothing unbelievable is' included. If unusual claims are made, it becomes even more imperative that adequate proof be presented to back them up. In the industrial advertising case, histories of successful installations or users are frequently shown to gain credibility. Simple techniques such as the use of pictures or diagrams also increase believability.

Interestingly, the medium in which a given message is carried can enhance its believability. Certain magazines such as *Good Housekeeping, Better Homes & Gardens, Reader's Digest,* and *Parents* have proven that their readers are more apt to believe messages carried in them than the same messages carried in magazines of lesser stature.

Uniqueness

Finally, a unique ad is more likely to be effective than a run-of-the-mill ad. Uniqueness attracts attention. Without attention most ads cannot be effective, because they fail to get the necessary readership. It is a mistake, however, to depend entirely on uniqueness. Once attention is obtained, the claims must be important and believable.

Typically, advertisements whose major objectives are gaining brand recognition and acceptance rather than conviction or buying action tend to rely for attention on unique presentation. One night's review of television commercials will produce a good lesson in the various techniques used to gain attention and interest. Unusual colors or layouts are frequently used to gain uniqueness in print media.

Repetition

Repetition is one of the key concepts in advertising. It is usually better to have a long series of small ads than one extremely large ad. Repetition is a basic principle of memory. A person is much more likely to remember something he has heard repeatedly than something he has heard only once. Naturally, the more times an ad is run, the more likely it is that any person has seen one of the ads recently. Repetition and recency are usually closely related. Contrary to what one might think, readership of an ad does not usually fall off with repetition. There is some evidence that the ad is even better read when repeated. Certainly repetition lowers ad production costs.

Impression

If an ad makes an impression on a reader, it will be far more effective than one that fails to do so. Some ads either are so outstanding or have such strong emotional claims that the reader is permanently impressed with the message. Although numerous persons dislike many of the television commercials advertising headache remedies, the fact remains that such commercials do make a very lasting impression on the audience. As one executive claimed, "I really don't care whether or not the customers like our commercials; the important thing is that they notice and remember them." Though this philosophy is open to question, it still is prevalent in some circles.

CURRENT PROBLEMS

Because advertising is the segment of a firm's marketing program that is visible, it is the factor of American business most easily perceived by the public. Indeed, the public is bombarded thousands of times daily by messages to buy this or that. It is not surprising that any activity this predominant should come in for more than its share of criticism, and certainly advertising has—and with considerable justification!

Truth

Even the most devout marketing men must confess that too many advertising campaigns have left much to be desired in the way of truth. A quick perusal of the FTC's prosecutions of firms for misleading advertising discloses the nature and extent of such behavior in American business. Although this activity is lamentable, it is one of the prices paid for freedom.

While a few firms lie outright to their customers about either their prices or their products, many more mislead them by various cleverly worded messages specifically designed to deceive. There is no defense for this type of activity. Responsible businessmen concerned for the continued freedom of our system should do their utmost to see that such despicable practices are promptly unmasked and vigorously prosecuted. There is absolutely no excuse for deception in advertising. It is not only illegal, but shortsightedly stupid. Large, successful firms that have been in business a long while have found such policies not only repugnant but also unprofitable in the long run.

Power

Many critics of our business scene decry the power of advertising. Their criticisms lead one to believe that if he spends sufficient funds on advertising he can sell any product, no matter how shoddy. This is hogwash! Any experienced advertiser can readily attest to the relative weakness of advertising in the scheme of things. It has been proven a thousand times over that massive advertising campaigns cannot sell faulty products—or even good products that have faulty distribution or pricing policies. If advertising were as powerful as some people claim, the Edsel would be on the road today, for no car was ever backed by a larger, more massive advertising campaign— to no avail, for the product and its marketing policies were faulty.

Highly esteemed leaders in advertising refuse to accept a product for advertising unless all other aspects of its marketing are sound and the product is worthy. Advertising cannot work miracles. Even under the most favorable conditions a great deal of time and money are required to achieve even modest success.

True, there are a few fantastic success stories, in which a firm has introduced a unique product and on the basis of one large advertising campaign, had immediate, overnight success, but these are distinct and rare exceptions to the rule—exceptions that one cannot count on in his marketing program. Betting on the occurrence of miracles is a shortcut to the poorhouse.

Costs

One of the big current problems is the rapidly increasing cost of advertising, owing not only to inflation but also to the rapid rise in the importance of television in advertising campaigns. As audiences have grown in size and as television production costs have risen phenomenally, the costs of advertising on television are prohibitive for all but the largest firms.

One Chrysler dealer in the Los Angeles area was driven into bankruptcy by excessive advertising expenditures ($60,000 a month), which failed to bring in sufficient business for him to remain competitive with dealers who had slightly better locations and spent a lot less on advertising.

What impact did this firm's advertising expenditures have upon its ability to meet competition?

Many misconceptions exist about the impact of promotional expenditures on profits. Many executives look on them as just another expense to be minimized. However, a well-formulated promotional program, when it is effective, should result in more gross margin than it costs. One should thus not look on promotional expenditures and other expenses in the same light.

Take three advertising campaigns you have observed on television and hypothesize about the research findings upon which they are based.

PUBLICITY

The role of publicity should never be underestimated; in many circumstances it is far more effective than either personal selling or advertising. Indeed, the success of some products has been based solely upon some publicity break. The Hula-Hoop was an overnight success after it and Art Linkletter, one of its owners, were featured in *Life*. *Car Plate*, a product of S. C. Johnson Company, had immediate market success after an article about it appeared in *Reader's Digest*, as did Kent cigarettes. Promotional managers stumble over each other trying to get their products on the Johnny Carson Show or some other television show for a "free" plug. Automobile manufacturers vie with one another to get celebrities behind the wheels of their behemoths.

The whole idea behind publicity is to get the public to perceive the existence of your product within a very favorable context. The golf club manufacturers are convinced that if the public believes their products are being used by the leading pros, the image is bound to rub off on the duffer who would like to emulate the professional's game; "If Billy Casper uses Wilson clubs, I guess I should be using them, too!"

The borderline between publicity and advertising is a dubious one at best, for unquestionably publicity does cost money. Such things do not usually occur gratis. The difference between publicity and advertising is that in advertising one overtly purchases either time or space in some medium, whereas publicity costs are indirect, usually involving payment in some form to certain influential people.

PART

PRODUCTION SYSTEMS

HIDDEN from the view of the common man is the vast, complicated network of factories and laborers busily turning out the things—cars, furniture, clothes, washing machines, and hairpins—that we want. Many adroit marketers have fallen when the factories behind them failed to get out the goods as promised. Just as it is pointless to make something unless you can sell it, it is pointless to sell something unless you can make it and do so economically. Production . . . marketing . . . they go hand in hand, for they are the core of business. Most enterprises simply make something and sell it; that's where the action is. Other business activities are auxiliaries.

15 Creating the product

It would be simple to say that to create the product we need only do research, develop the result, and put it into production. But a great deal is involved in each of these phases, so let us examine them in more detail.

RESEARCH AND DEVELOPMENT

A distinctive earmark of our social and economic system in recent decades has been its dedication to research. While total U.S. research expenditures were but $100 million in 1928 and had grown to $5 billion by 1953, the next decade saw them explode to about $16 billion, or 3 percent of the Gross National Product. We spend this money willingly, because it has been proved times over that investment in research pays large dividends. Look around you! Practically everything you see is the result of research. The synthetic fibers you wear, the plastics of which so many things are made, the vehicles that carry people and cargo are only a few of its products. Without research you would still be living in an agrarian society, struggling to stay alive. You would be beset by diseases and afflictions, most of which have been successfully combated by research. Most problems that we face today, both technically and physically, can be alleviated or solved if we devote sufficient resources to research—although the price of much of this research is presently beyond our pocketbooks.

TYPES OF RESEARCH

Many different activities are conducted under the broad heading of research. In fact, much of what is called research in American industry is really developmental work, so business calls these activities research and development (or R&D) expenditures.

What is the difference between research and development work?

Pure Research

Pure research seeks truths or solutions to problems without an economic end result in mind. A chemist may become curious about the behavior of a certain element in some environment and study it, without having in mind any particular use for his work. Indeed, his results may have no practical use, but then again, who knows? Somewhere else perhaps some other researcher takes the results and combines them with some of his own for some useful finding. Such is the nature of pure research. It forms the basis for all other research.

Applied Research

Unlike pure research, applied research is carried on with an application in mind. Applied research seeks to solve some problem of practical or economic interest. Naturally, far more applied than pure research is done, for it is usually difficult to finance research not focused on some practical problem.

Product Research   Probably the bulk of research expenditures by industry are for product research, creating new products and improving old ones. Modern management realizes that product research is a continuing function, not a sporadic one to be turned on and off as needs become apparent. The business scene is strewn with firms that at one time had excellent, up-to-date products but chose to rest on their laurels rather than continually improve them. Chevrolet taught Henry Ford the painful lesson: he was forced to abandon his Model T and Model A designs, but only after losing his market position—one he never recovered.

Marketing Research   In the past two decades increasingly large amounts of money have been spent on seeking truths about the marketplace—possibly as much as $200 million a year, mostly by the large consumer-goods manufacturers such as Procter & Gamble, whose market research budget alone is about $6 million. The ability to afford such research gives large businesses a distinct advantage over the smaller concerns that must make marketing decisions without such guidance.

Marketing research tries to provide answers to such questions as:

How big is the market for the product?
What does the market want from the product?
What price should be asked?
How should it be distributed?
How should it be promoted?
How should it be packaged?
What brand names and trademarks are most appropriate?
How can the product be stored and transported to the market?
Who will use the product; who will make the buying decision; who will buy it?

Process Research   Somewhat akin to product research is the work done on improving manufacturing processes. Indeed, many of the most significant improvements in productivity have been made by improving the processes for making goods. Automatic welding machines have significantly lowered the cost of metal fabrication. The present work being done on automating manufacturing processes has delivered great results and promises more.

MANAGEMENT OF RESEARCH

Recognition that the management of research is a distinctly separate function is of relatively recent origin. Research efforts were once rather informal matters, usually under the jurisdiction of the engineering department. Today we recognize that research is a unique function requiring a separate organizational niche headed by an administratively oriented researcher. Frequently large companies establish research organizations separate from operations, much as the American Telephone & Telegraph system has established Bell Laboratories as its research arm. There are several reasons for this treatment of the research function.

First, research is a "people" business. It depends upon the creative talents of certain types of people. Researchers "work" twenty-four hours a day, seven days a week, for one cannot turn his creativity on at nine o'clock in the morning and off at five in the afternoon. The stereotype picture of the researcher spending long hours day and night in the laboratory is not completely fiction. Steinmetz, one of the geniuses originating General Electric, seldom worked in the laboratory furnished by the company; rather he had laboratory facilities in his home. He did not accept the usual regimentation imposed on the average operational employee.

We should hasten to point out that the days of the solitary scientist laboring alone in the confines of a confused laboratory are just about over. Today's research is a product of a team of men who work cooperatively in a carefully controlled environment in a most systematic way.

The personalities and problems of researchers tend to be unique. They are not always responsive to the usual incentives of money and promotion but rise rather to intellectual challenges. They must have a certain intellectual curiosity or fascination with the problem, or else they may not do much of a job on it.

Consequently, a special group of men, usually professional researchers themselves, have developed to administer these activities, for the nontechnical administrator is usually unable to gain the respect and control of scientists.

PROBLEMS IN RESEARCH

Problems in research largely fall into three categories: time, money, and personnel.

Time

Research takes time; good research takes lots of time. Action-oriented administrators, impatient for results, sometimes think that the only thing involved in speeding up a research project is to put more money in it. Such investment is frequently futile, for usually research projects are a matter of completing in sequence many smaller research projects on component problems before the big problem can be solved. Moreover, one cannot rush creativity. Truly innovative research seldom can be forced. The administrator who orders a subordinate to come up with an answer to a problem in a week or a month may be disappointed with the results. The time factor creates many frustrations among line executives who are used to performing on tight schedules. Their inability to schedule research to suit the convenience of the company bothers them considerably.

Money

Research can be frightfully expensive. Often only the largest corporations can afford the investments required to solve some problem. A small company could not have developed nylon, but Du Pont could back it with the millions necessary; a letter from Du Pont reproduced here tells the story (Figure 15-1).

The high cost of research forces small firms to rely upon the research efforts of the larger companies, which often sell the results of their research in the form of products. Moreover, new knowledge is disseminated rather quickly in industry in one way or another.

Men

One is tempted to consider all research people as equals, but such is simply not the case; like other professionals, there are good ones and bad. A Ph.D. in chemistry or physics does not guarantee that a man can do the quality of research desired of him. There is a great scarcity of the type of scientist that most businesses prize—the

FIGURE 15 -1.

E. I. DU PONT DE NEMOURS & COMPANY
INCORPORATED

WILMINGTON, DELAWARE 19898

PUBLIC RELATIONS DEPARTMENT

January 7, 1971

Dear Prof. Buskirk:

Information on the amount of time and money spent
to bring a synthetic fiber to commercial reality tends to
be rather vague, since the decision to assign research and
development costs is often a subjective one. We have on
several occasions released some "ball park" figures on the
amount of money we estimate we have spent on particular
products from initial research to commercialization. I am
sure these are reasonably accurate in terms of scale, but
we would have a very difficult time proving their accuracy
to plus or minus 5 per cent.

We estimate that some $27 million was spent on
research, development and plant construction before the
first commercial quantities of nylon were manufactured in
1939. By the time the first staple fiber of "Orlon" acrylic
was introduced to the market, Du Pont had invested more than
$60 million in this product. We have no reliable figure for
"Dacron" polyester, but it would be safe to assume that it
approximates the total for "Orlon".

The time span from initial research to commercialization varies with the product and is usually difficult to
establish absolutely. For nylon, for example, we could say
that the research effort which led to this first truly synthetic commercial fiber began in 1927, when Du Pont initiated
a fundamental research program which led to the development
of superpolymers. The polyamide molecule was synthesized in
the early thirties, but it took nearly five years to bring
it to commercial reality. Initial research on "Orlon" began
from a base built by the early fundamental program. Studies
commenced in 1941 on vinyl type compounds and in 1944 an
acrylic fiber was experimentally produced. We began commercial
production of "Orlon" in filament form in 1950 and in staple
in 1952.

I hope this information proves helpful. Please
feel free to call on us if you would like any additional
data.

Sincerely,

James P. Reynolds
Assistant Public Relations
Manager - Textile Fibers

JPR/ewt

man who does application-oriented research within the budgetary and time restraints of the company, yet is highly creative.

RISKS OF RESEARCH

The risks of research are great. One can spend millions of dollars seeking the answer to some problem, only to end in failure. Just doing research does not guarantee a payoff. The risks of failure are large, and unless a firm is able to bear them, it should devise some other way to solve its problems.

What alternatives to a research department are available to the management of a small company?

WHO DOES RESEARCH?

While the federal government supplies most of the money for the nation's research, such funds find their way into both public and private organizations by many diverse paths. The government allocates a great deal of money directly to its various agencies, such as the armed forces, the National Bureau of Standards, National Aeronautics and Space Administration (NASA), National Center for Atmospheric Research (NCAR), and its various administrative arms such as the Department of Agriculture. Most of this money is applied to the various problems faced by these organizations.

Other government funds are funneled into private institutions through government contracts, particularly defense and space contracts. Other money is granted to a relatively small group of large, research-oriented universities under a wide range of programs. Such funds are largely concentrated in work on the physical and biological sciences. Little money is devoted to social or economic research.

In business, about 60 percent of all research money is spent in five industries: aerospace, electrical equipment and communications, chemical, automobile and other transportation, and machinery. The large research-oriented firms may spend up to 10 percent of sales on research, while more typical firms spend less than one percent.

Among smaller concerns research is usually a secondary function performed by some operating executive on the side. Sometimes research is subcontracted to outside, independent research organizations, such as Stanford Research Institute, the Batelle Institute, or others less well known. Unfortunately, the cost of procuring the services of outside researchers may seem prohibitive to the managers of small companies, who are shocked to learn how much it costs to do even a little research. For this reason they frequently look to independent consultants, such as professors, retired executives, or individual experts who are for hire. It is difficult to hire such people for less than $25 an hour.

RESEARCH—AN INVESTMENT, NOT AN EXPENSE

Managerial attitudes toward research activities are frequently best exemplified by the treatment of costs. Many managements treat the money spent on research as an expense directly out-of-pocket, while others capitalize research expenditures on the balance sheet to be charged off against future income produced.

What are some of the problems that might be encountered in capitalizing research expenditures?

In theory, research expenditures are certainly an investment, inasmuch as one cannot anticipate revenue from them in the current fiscal period.

PRODUCTION PROCESSES AND PROBLEMS

For the past century our productive genius has been astounding, and the tremendous flow of goods yielded by relatively few man-hours of effort has lulled us into complacency about the production worker and the production manager. When you buy a car you see the salesman and the finance man at work, but the hundreds of productive workers are hidden from your view, and you may remain unaware of the genius and hard work that has gone into making your new vehicle.

Yet we should never forget that the key to wealth is productivity. Our success in the world is based upon our ability to produce huge quantities of goods that are in world-wide demand and to do so at acceptable costs. If our system ever loses its ability to produce goods at a reasonable cost, our way of life will be in jeopardy.

Have any other nations experienced such a drop in standard of living?

One might assume that the cost of producing some item would be about the same for all producers, depending upon the costs of the materials and the wage costs of the workers. Such is not the case. Plants have widely varying output cost characteristics, even though their raw-material and labor costs are identical. Production management is the difference. Some production managers are clever enough in devising ways of making things that their production costs are substantially lower than those of their competitors. Such lower production costs provide a real differential advantage to the firm in competing for the market; in most instances, long-run success is bestowed upon the low-cost producer, for he has the advantages of more money to spend or can charge lower prices than other sellers. The high-cost producer is always fighting from a distinctly disadvantageous position.

PLANT LOCATION

Low-cost production begins with a wise decision about where to locate the productive facilities. It makes a big difference! The success of many firms is based upon a locational advantage achieved by wise plant-location decisions. The cost variables connected with location are: transportation costs of inbound materials, transportation costs of products shipped to market, labor costs, utility costs and availability, taxes, land and building costs, and the quality of labor.

Freight In and Freight Out

Plant locations are oriented either toward sources of materials or the market. It all depends upon the nature of the product. When the production process requires heavy materials, causing transportation costs to be a significant factor in total costs, production tends to be located close to the point of origination of these materials, particularly if significant weight or bulk is removed from the materials in the production process. In making sheetrock, the production facilities must be located where the gypsum is mined, for to do otherwise requires shipping a great deal of water—a most expensive folly. Mined gypsum must be dehydrated immediately to minimize handling the water in it. Similarly, trees are processed into wood products close to the forests.

On the other hand, if the freight on materials is not large, manufacturers generally prefer to locate close to their markets in order to render better, faster service to customers. Wholesalers, dealers, and other manufacturers generally prefer to deal with nearby suppliers. In some cases manufacturers locate next door to their target customers. Many subcontractors to the aerospace firms literally locate at their gates in an effort to gain their business.

Why do buyers prefer to deal with nearby suppliers?

Utilities

Some utility companies are so desirous of expanding their economic bases that they grant manufacturers substantial concessions for locating in their operating areas. Utility costs vary significantly from region to region. Manufacturing operations that require large power, gas, or water commitments—and a great many do—pay careful attention not only to costs but also to availability. Many locations lack adequate supplies of such utilities.

Taxes

Tax burdens placed upon industry vary widely from state to state and city to city. Moreover, some governments in desperate need of building their economic bases entice manufacturers into their areas by granting them various tax moratoriums for a substantial period. Some southern states have been known to give tax relief to new plants for up to ten years.

What is the political and economic rationale for giving new businesses tax relief?

As will be shown later in the chapter on taxation, the tax burden of firms is not inconsequential at best; at worst, it is devastating.

Land and Building Costs

While the costs of land acquisition and building plants are not insignificant, particularly for new businesses, still when the cost differences are amortized over a period of twenty years they can be relatively small in comparison with other cost differentials. One may pay out in other costs many times the money he saves by buying cheap land. One manufacturer was enticed into locating a new plant in a remote southwestern town by the local banker's offer to give the company the land and build a plant on it, free. These cost savings were quickly dissipated by higher transportation costs, larger telephone bills, increased travel expenses, and other higher costs incurred because of the plant's remote location. A manager must be extremely careful to consider all of the cost factors when making a location decision. Today, given access to data on the cost factors involved, an operations researcher can use quantitative techniques to determine the location that will optimize costs—result in the lowest total costs.

PLANT LAYOUT

A plant can be likened to a machine—a big black box into which materials and man-hours are fed and out of which a product flows. And black boxes have varying degrees of efficiency, depending upon the arrangement of their innards. A great deal of engineering is involved in designing efficient plants. Sometimes the plants do not work out as designed, and there will always be mistakes made. Not too many years ago multistory plants were popular because they allowed the engineer to use the energy supplied by gravity to move goods from one floor to another. Things would start out at the top and gradually come out at the bottom. But those days are largely gone. Today's modern plant is usually on one floor and is so designed that everything flows inside it in long, straight lines. The whole idea of efficient plant layout is pushing materials in at one end of the plant, moving them through the structure in an orderly manner, performing various production processes on them at the appropriate time, and shipping them out of the other end of the factory with as little cross flowing as possible. Sometimes various subassembly lines must be accommodated and joined at various places in a plant, which tends to complicate matters somewhat. If some factor prevents a straight-line arrangement, other configurations are developed. Naturally, the plant layout depends upon the process used in manufacturing, as we shall see in a later section. Figure 15-2 illustrates various types of plant layouts.

TYPES OF PROCESSES

Production processes can be classified into five categories: custom, job lot, intermittent, repetitive, and continuous.

Custom Manufacturing

Although one might assume that custom manufacturing has largely disappeared in this era of mass production, there is still a considerable volume of it. Custom manufacturing refers to making a product to the buyer's specifications. A surprisingly large amount of custom manufacturing takes place in industrial goods. A custom order may entail only one unit or many, but after the order passes a certain size other processes may be more economically used, depending upon the circumstances.

As a general rule, custom manufacturing is extremely expensive, inasmuch as few of the basic principles of economic production can be brought into play. It

FIGURE 15 -2: Various Types of Plant Layouts

Circle:

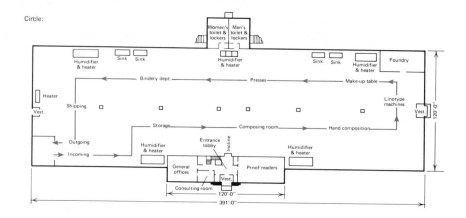

Snake:

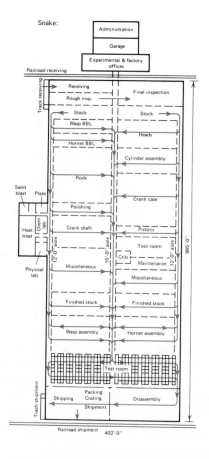

Straight:

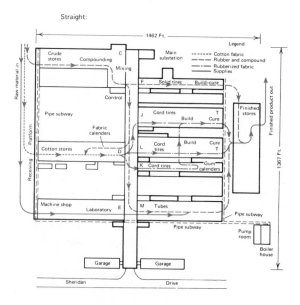

costs just as much to set up a machine to make a single part as it does to make a thousand. The production of only a few units of anything entails a greatly disproportionate amount of administrative time and overhead.

Job Lot

A great many small manufacturers are set up on a job lot basis, which refers to a process in which a certain number of items are produced at one time under one order, sometimes known as a job order. The economics of the job lot depend upon the size of the job. If there are enough units in the lot, the economies can be almost equivalent to those realized with repetitive or intermittent manufacturing. However, if the lot is small, then its characteristics will approach that of custom manufacturing.

In a job shop, management establishes procedures by which it can cost and schedule each job. Naturally, any manufacturing plant with a large number of job orders must make certain that they are processed on time and that the managerial costs to do so are carefully controlled. Production scheduling and cost control come to the fore as extremely critical skills in managing a job lot process.

Intermittent Production

Some manufacturers set up a production line intermittently to produce a certain number of units of an item for inventory and then shut it down in order to produce something else on it. Intermittent production is used when the production rate for a product vastly exceeds its sales rate—as when, for example, a plant can produce in one week enough product to supply the market for a year.

Production management in an intermittent manufacturing process is posed with the big problem of minimizing downtime—time between production runs when nothing is produced. Too much time spent tearing down a line and setting up for another production run renders the plant inefficient.

Why would sales forecasting be particularly important for a product made intermittently?

Continuous Production

The production manager, in his dream of Utopia, visualizes a production line that runs continuously twenty-four hours a day, 365 days a year. Probably the epitome of the continuous process is an oil refinery or chemical plant. The input materials go into the pipes on one end and the final product emerges from another end after all sorts of things are done; the processes never stop. Continuous processes are normally highly efficient, requiring few productive workers.

Repetitive Processes

The repetitive manufacturing plant closely approaches the continuous process. In an automobile plant, for example, various operations are performed on the product repetitively, day in and day out. The major difference between the continuous and the repetitive process is that in the latter, the operations are distinct and separate repetitive acts, whereas in a continuous process, such as oil refining, distinct repetitive acts cannot be identified.

PRODUCTION PLANNING AND SCHEDULING

Early production management recognized that one of the keys to efficient operations was the careful planning and scheduling of work—machine by machine, department by department—every day throughout the plant to make certain that downtime was minimized. An idle machine is a costly investment. Moreover, an idle machine may mean an idle worker waiting for something to do, which is even more costly. It is the job of the production planner to make an adequate amount of work available for all machines and all workers at all times. Many different techniques have been developed for planning and scheduling work, but they are really beyond the scope of this book. Suffice it to say that production planning and scheduling is one of the foundations of an efficient production operation.

MOTION AND TIME STUDY

A great deal of attention was given to motion and time study in the early days of scientific management, which was inaugurated late in the nineteenth century by Frederick Taylor and continued in the twentieth century by the Gilbreths. These people, with a few others, pioneered most of the concepts we now take for granted, but their ideas were startlingly new in their day. Their basic premises were rather simple. They maintained that time was money and that motion was time. They carefully analyzed all of the motions made by workers and classified them as shown in Table 15-1.

Table 15–1

CLASSIFICATION OF MOTIONS BY THE GILBRETHS

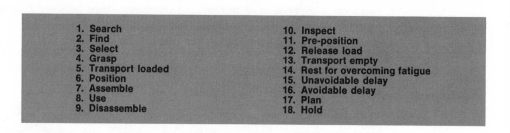

1. Search	10. Inspect
2. Find	11. Pre-position
3. Select	12. Release load
4. Grasp	13. Transport empty
5. Transport loaded	14. Rest for overcoming fatigue
6. Position	15. Unavoidable delay
7. Assemble	16. Avoidable delay
8. Use	17. Plan
9. Disassemble	18. Hold

Moreover, they measured the time it took the average worker to perform the various motions. Then they minutely wrote down every task in a production process, motion by motion, and prescribed exactly to each worker what his motion should be to accomplish the task most efficiently. The results of this approach were astounding. Wasted motion was reduced and productivity leaped upward. Great savings were realized by motion analysis and job studies.

Motion and time studies are focused on the smallest bit of human effort in the production process. Consequently, by minimizing the man-hours required for each identifiable segment of the work, they minimize the total number of man-hours for the production process. The concepts of job standardization, job studies, and job analyses are fundamental to all motion and time studies.

Concepts of Job Analysis and Job Standardization	Job analysis is the determination of the essential factors in a specific kind of work and the qualifications of a worker necessary for its performance. Job standardization consists of determining the one best way of performing a job under the conditions at hand.

PRINCIPLES OF EFFICIENT PRODUCTION

The following discussion presents a selected list of the basic principles that affect production costs.

Long Runs

Probably the best-known and most widely recognized principle of production is that costs tumble rapidly with the size of the order. Short runs are expensive; long runs are profitable.

Explain in economic terms why long production runs facilitate efficient production.

Simplification of Product

The production-oriented executive loves a simple product. He hates products with many variations and complexities. Every additional feature added to a product, every complexity, only adds miseries to his job. Henry Ford loved the Model T; Henry was a production-oriented executive. "They can have any color they want, so long as it's black." Henry did not want colors complicating his life. Simplification of the product and the production process yields great savings. Or, more accurately, complicating the product and the production process increases costs significantly.

What impact upon costs does the number of models in the line have for appliance manufacturers?

Division of Labor

Quite early in the Industrial Revolution we learned that division of labor paid great dividends. More precisely, job simplification yields efficiencies. The simpler management can make the job for the worker, the more efficient that worker will be.

What are some of the problems created by job simplification?

Bring the Work to the Worker

Experience indicates that it is cheaper to bring all materials and work to the worker than to have the worker go to the material. Workers are stationed at one point in a production process and the work brought to them.

Why does this principle save money?

The Learning Curve

The learning curve is associated with the concept of division of labor and the economies of long runs. We know that as workers perform a repetitive task they learn to do it quicker and better. In the defense industry it is fairly well recognized that on a task of moderate complexity one can anticipate what is known as an 80 percent learning curve; that is, if a worker takes x amount of time to perform 100 units of work, he will take $1.8x$ time to perform 200 units of that same work.

The learning curve is a basic characteristic of human behavior. What causes it?

Efficient production makes great use of the learning curve by seeing to it that the worker is not interrupted in his task, for interruptions set back the worker almost to the beginning of the learning curve.

Why? Apply this to your study habits!

Work Flow

Production management attempts to keep work flowing continuously in a plant. It detests having work stacked up. When feasible, the production manager does not want materials delivered until they can be put directly into production—no storage—and he wants the goods shipped out when they are completed.

What costs are incurred by work that has been stacked up?

Minimization of Downtime and Setup Costs

Downtime can be created by many different things. Perhaps raw materials or parts are not available. Perhaps machines have broken down. Perhaps labor is unwilling to work. Perhaps some station fails to complete its work on time. Perhaps the process is being shifted over to make something else. Whatever the reason, downtime is extremely expensive and must be minimized if profits are to be realized. During downtime most of the costs go right on while the plant is producing nothing of value, a circumstance that quickly leads to financial embarrassment.

Maintenance

Management has learned that regular, preventive maintenance pays dividends in its impact upon downtime. Production operations are extremely hard on equipment, and if the equipment is not properly maintained it will quickly become inoperative. Maintenance costs are usually small by comparison with costs incurred when machines fail.

Standard Parts

Every part a plant must carry in inventory costs money. If a plant is producing a number of different products, the more parts they have in common—standard parts—the cheaper production operations will be. Production engineers want all of the small parts—nuts, bolts, and other such items—standardized. This is really part of the simplification process.

Tolerances and Specifications

Costs rise rapidly as the production process is held to closer and closer tolerances and specifications. If the engineers have specified that a part is to be machined to an accuracy of ± 0.0001 inch, that part will cost more than the same part machined to ± 0.01 inch. A great deal of conflict arises between design engineers and production engineers over this matter of specifications. The production engineer wants specifications as loose as possible, whereas frequently the design engineer requires overly close tolerances in his desire for perfection. Such matters must be hammered out between the various departments. High-precision manufacturing is very expensive.

Design Engineering versus Production Engineering

Controversy frequently arises between the design engineer and the production engineer, for the product design coming from engineering is often impractical in some respect for production. The production engineer must take the design engineer's product and redesign portions of it so that it can be produced economically. The design engineer may specify materials, processes, or tolerances that are economically infeasible. Sometimes the design engineer will give the product a look for reasons of esthetics that the production man may have to overrule on the basis of practicality or costs. It is not at all unheard of for a design engineer to require things that are simply impossible to produce. Consequently, efficient production requires a good job of production engineering before a product is placed in production.

Housekeeping

Efficient production operations are usually neat and orderly. Production managers learned long ago that trash and debris lying around on the floor result in inefficiencies. Much time can be lost in a disorderly shop looking for proper tools and materials.

Automation

During the past decade or so, a great deal has been written on the automation of our production processes. It is true that, for the most part, our production machinery is being highly automated. Automation refers to substituting machines for workers. However, we have always done that. Modern automation means even more. In a fully automated plant, workers never operate directly on the product itself; rather, they simply monitor the machines in the production process; computers control them.

There are a great many very amazing automated machines. For example, not too many years ago welding took a great deal of labor. It took a man with a welding torch to do the job. Today there are automatic welding machines that automatically position the work and weld it in all of the spots required. Such machines are quite expensive—one available for the electronics industry was quoted at $750,000. In this same industry soldering machines are now available to take the place of workers who used to hand-solder the connections.

The basic forces underlying automation are compelling, and one can see no end in sight to its application to industry. The advent of the computer has made possible a great many things heretofore inconceivable. Today entire factories are controlled by computers; machines are directed to perform their various processes by means of punched tape or computer programs.

In order to automate a production process, what is necessary?
What are the social implications of automation?

While one could go on and on about the economics of automation, suffice it to say that it is almost impossible for a nonautomated plant to compete with an automated one for the business of mass markets. If an item can be produced in quantities sufficient to justify automation, the nonautomated plant will find it difficult to compete.

QUALITY CONTROL

Practically all production operations of any consequence today have separate quality control departments, responsible for ensuring that the quality of the product meets specifications. These departments have developed many sophisticated techniques, but these are beyond the scope of this course. However, several of the basic concepts are important to comprehend.

Good quality control management is far more than a matter of inspecting the final product, for if the product is defective at that point, little can be done to salvage it. If the product cannot be repaired economically, a substantial loss has been incurred; all of the materials used and the labor invested in it are wasted. Instead, sound quality control management dictates that the quality of the product be controlled at every step in the production process. "Catch the defect at its inception" is the watchword. If the product meets specifications at every step along the way, then the final inspection should be a formality. By this means the company avoids wasting money by working on defective products or items after they have become defective. In process industries, management monitors the process carefully to catch problems before the process goes out of control rather than afterwards. The entire emphasis in modern quality control is on controlling the production process rather than merely inspecting the product for defects.

A great many statistical techniques have been developed for sampling work rather than inspecting all of the units in a process. This saves a considerable amount of money. Obviously, if the product must be destroyed in order to be inspected, sampling is the only economical means by which it can be done.

MAKE-OR-BUY DECISIONS

Strictly speaking, a make-or-buy decision is not a part of the production process, but frequently it is computed by the production manager. Before instituting the production of a product or a part of a product, management usually wants to know whether it is more economical to make that item or buy it elsewhere. Usually management prefers to do the most economical thing, but not always. Sometimes companies will make something even though they could purchase it more cheaply.

When a plant is not being fully utilized, a company will prefer to keep as much work inhouse as possible to keep its work force intact. Or strategic considerations may dictate that a company make something rather than buy it. Make-or-buy decisions come down to a process of obtaining quotations from outside suppliers of the item and comparing the lowest bid with the computations of the production department on what it will take to make the product inhouse. A policy issue always arises as to whether or not management should use out-of-pocket costs or full costs in determining the cost of making an item inhouse.

What is the difference between out-of-pocket costs and full costs?

ADVENT OF MANAGEMENT SCIENCE

During the 1960s a separate business field developed in connection with production. A group of mathematically oriented scholars began applying various mathematical techniques such as linear programming, simulation, and model building to production problems. In most of the nation's universities traditional production management has taken a back seat to the newer, more sophisticated approaches, and the methods of management science have had many industrial applications. While the sophisticated mathematical techniques involved in management science are far beyond the scope of this discussion, still you should be aware of the existence of this field and the promise it holds for people of mathematical bent who wish to apply their talents to production problems.

Conclusion

Adept production management is most critical to the prosperity of the firm, for if the goods cannot be produced economically in the proper quantity and with the desired quality, then all else matters little; the firm will fail.

The product is sired in research, nurtured in development, and brought to maturity by the design and production engineers. The management of this process is a delicate one, for the creative process is difficult to stimulate and control.

The basic principles of efficient production are applicable to a wide range of productive enterprises—studying, housework, office chores, or whatever line of endeavor one may choose.

16 Materials management systems

Facts do not cease to exist because they are ignored.
ALDOUS HUXLEY

The *concept of materials management* concerns the purchasing, transportation, storage, and physical handling of all raw materials, fabricated parts, components, goods-in-process, and finished goods, which must be carefully controlled and managed at all times. The concept, a recent one, evolved from the general theory of logistics, which holds that three basic resources need managing—men, machines, and materials. Materials management developed organizationally by bringing under one executive all the functions concerned with materials: buying, handling, storing, transporting, and controlling them, physically and quantitatively.

Brought about in both large and small companies for economic, technological, and organizational reasons, the concept has served as a catalyst for such business actions as mergers, in which manufacturers have acquired their raw-material and component suppliers; the acquisition of retail or wholesale facilities for better distribution; or the use of private rather than public transportation systems.

Materials management concerns far more than the mere control of materials within the plant or corporate system. It begins with an interest in the sources of raw materials and continues with the semifinished goods from suppliers' production lines to the movement of the materials while they are taking form within the plant, ending as the finished goods move down through the entire distribution system until they reach their ultimate user. It is a total-cost concept—the total cost of the entire system for moving and managing materials.

Recent development of fast communications systems combined with high-speed, large-capacity electronic computers has greatly facilitated the application of the materials management concept to business situations.

OBJECTIVES OF MATERIALS MANAGEMENT

Materials management seeks several objectives:

definition and control of the entire materials system
reduction of costs
increase in proficiency of distribution system
materials considerations made part of major business decisions
materials management raised to profit center

System Definition and Control

The first objective of materials management is to define clearly the entire system it intends to manage. What is included within its scope of operation? To what extent is the firm concerned with the materials systems of its suppliers? Of its customers? The manager's scope of authority must first be established.

What factors determine the answers to these questions?

Next, the sticky matter of control must be decided. How much control over materials should be attempted as they move through other organizations such as suppliers and customers? Questions arise concerning whether or not the company should acquire its suppliers and/or its distributive organizations. It might make little sense to acquire a supplier of some minor raw material in plentiful supply, but it might be a shrewd move to control the supply of some critically scarce commodity.

Cost Reduction—Improved Efficiency

A great deal of money is involved in a firm's materials system. Not only does the system cost a great deal of money, but also substantial sums must be invested in inventory and equipment at all stages of the process from the mines and fields through the factories onto the dealers' shelves, thereby introducing considerable risk into the process.

The materials manager can justify his job only if he is able to reduce the total costs of the system while lowering the risks. Many opportunities for cost saving present themselves when the total materials system is under the control of one executive, who is able to eliminate costly duplication of efforts, bargain more effectively with the suppliers, and organize the entire system to optimize its operation.

Better Distribution

Prior to the advent of a unified materials system, most large organizations were plagued with the problem of managing inventory in their many warehouses. Often each was managed independently, and so distribution was spotty: some warehouses would be overstocked while others would be out of stock.

Modern materials management maintains tight control at all distribution points to ensure correct inventory balances throughout the system; communications systems combined with computers now make such centralized control feasible.

What are communications systems?

Participation in Top-Level Decision Making

Traditionally, the executives involved with materials played a small role in such top-level decisions as plant location, business acquisitions, location of distribution centers, inventory policy, and vertical integration policies. However, the materials management concept makes it rather obvious that the materials manager should play a critical role in such decisions.

Establishment as Cost Center

With all materials management unified under one command, it can be made a profit center. Its costs can be identified, isolated, and measured against the values it adds to the goods as they move through the system to determine its contribution to the firm's profits. The idea is to compare costs under the materials management system with what costs would be borne without such a system; the difference is profit.

THE MATERIALS MANAGEMENT SYSTEM

The sequence of events (see Figure 16-1) in an organized materials management system is fairly well established, although some deviation inevitably occurs as firms modify the system to suit their situations. A rigid, inflexible system would result in many inefficiencies and dissatisfactions; pragmatism is to be prized.

The process begins when top management decides that it wants to make something to sell. The engineering department creates a complete set of drawings and

FIGURE 16 -1: Sequence of Events in an Organized Materials Management System

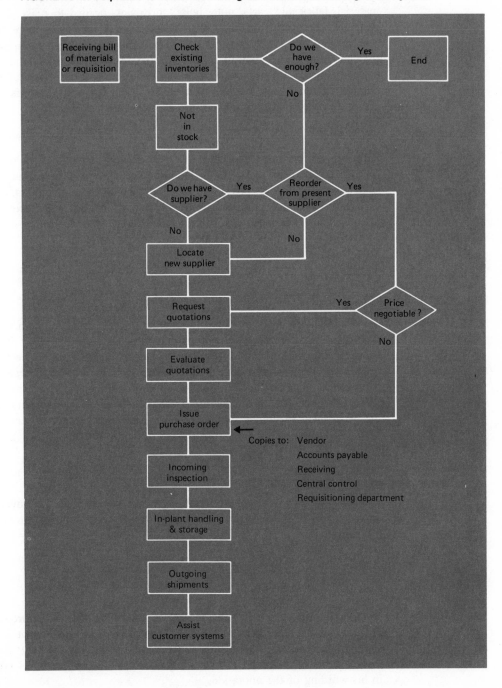

specifications from which a *bill of materials* is developed, listing every single item—raw material, fabricated parts, nuts, bolts, and paint—needed to make the product. Each item not already in inventory must be purchased; the job is large and complex for a product of any complexity. In making a ground communications set for the army, the contractor had to buy over 10,000 separate parts. Not only must the purchasing department seek out suitable suppliers of each item and negotiate contracts with them, but also it must make certain that each item meets specifications and is delivered on time in the right place and in the right quantity.

Check against Inventory

Before quotations are requested on an item a check is made of the existing inventory, for it may not need to be purchased. Engineers try to standardize specifications for as many small items as possible. Nuts, bolts, small motors, and standard components such as resistors and capacitors are usually carried in stock. Purchasing small quantities of such items is expensive, so it is avoided.

What makes the purchase of small quantities expensive? (Hint: There is more to it than quantity discounts!)

Location of Potential Suppliers

Sometimes there are hundreds of potential suppliers for an item, or perhaps there is only one and he is unknown. In any case, considerable effort is made to locate suppliers; purchasing history indicates that substantial savings can be realized by ferreting out previously unrecognized suppliers of an item. The lazy purchasing agent buys from the easy source, the one who is at his door, but he pays a price for his convenience. Many catalogues and directories are consulted in seeking out suppliers. A good purchasing department maintains files on potential sources of things it may need to buy.

Request for Quotation (RFQ)

While there is a great deal of telephoning of likely suppliers to identify those who can best provide what the buyer wants (be it price, quality, or delivery), most buyers eventually want a written quotation from the supplier. If the buyer is in a hurry, an order may be placed over the phone with a written confirmation or purchase order following.

Why do many companies prefer to issue purchase orders when buying something, rather than allowing the seller to write an order?

If there is little hurry and the market is apt to be shopped thoroughly, the buyer sends to all likely suppliers an RFQ that describes in detail what is desired. If the supplier is interested in the business, he will reply with a quotation, which may become a legal contract if accepted by the buyer, unless the supplier has taken precautions in his wording of the quotation.

Purchase Order

When a decision has been reached on a supplier, a purchase order (PO) is issued, which becomes a contract if accepted by the seller. Care must be taken that the goods are clearly described in the PO and that all terms are clearly specified.

Why is a PO issued? How many copies should be made? Who should receive a copy of each PO? Why?

Inbound Transportation

When transportation costs loom large in the delivered price of a purchased item, the buyer may institute actions to minimize such costs instead of leaving it up to the seller to arrange transportation. In some situations a clever traffic manager can save substantial sums by developing an unusual system for getting the goods from the supplier. One such executive located a private carrier that frequently had empty trucks traveling to his area from a city in which a significant supplier was located. He bought the available space well below the price asked by more conventional carriers.

Receipt of Goods

The arrival of the ordered goods is not a casual, routine event; it should be carefully controlled. When the carrier rolls up to the incoming dock the man in charge of the receiving room must do several things. First, he much check the goods or packages for any obvious damage, lest he impair the company's claim for damages against the carrier if it is later discovered that the goods were received in a damaged condition. Next, he must check the received goods against the *bill of lading* handed him by the driver, making sure that all the goods in the shipment are being delivered; if ten packages were shipped, then ten packages had better be delivered, or else the bill of lading must be corrected to show the actual number delivered and then signed by both the driver and the receiving room foreman.

Why is so much care required in checking shipments?

Incoming Inspection

Depending upon the nature of the goods received, several things can happen at this stage. If the goods are received in large cartons, then they may be opened and their contents checked for damage and for accuracy against the purchase order. Were the right goods received? Is the quantity correct? Perhaps the goods will be checked against the invoice, but more likely the seller's invoice will be compared with the PO. The firm does not want to pay for something it did not order or that was not received in usable condition.

Placed in Inventory

If the goods are satisfactory, then they will usually move into inventory unless they are immediately put into the production process. Care must be taken that goods are placed in the right location, for in large operations it is not at all uncommon to lose goods when some warehouseman fails to put them where they belong. Obviously, a system is required for keeping track of the location of all goods as well as protecting them from damage and theft.

Moving Materials Through Production

Considerable handling is usually required as goods are moved around a plant during the production process. Such in-plant movements should be coordinated with storage to minimize total costs.

Finished-Goods Inventory

The goods are completed; what should be done with them? Should they be shipped to distant warehouses? Should they be stored at the plant? Should they be shipped directly to the buyer?

Outbound Transportation

By what means should the goods be transported to storage or to the buyer? Answering this question involves considerable study, for it can be quite complex. There may be a number of good alternatives, so the *traffic manager*—the executive in the materials system in charge of selecting the mode of transportation for all goods—cannot rely on the traditional means of shipping as necessarily the best. New developments are making possible new ways of doing things every day. The Weyerhaeuser Company had shipped plywood in regular boxcars for years until an enterprising executive developed a better way: shipping it on flatcars with the bundles of plywood protected by plastic-coated blankets.

Why are flatcars superior to boxcars for shipping plywood?

Customers' Materials Systems

In a few cases a manufacturer's materials system extends into and through its customers' operations. One's competitive position is enhanced if his goods are handled efficiently all the way to the point at which they are consumed. Many customers who are in need of technical assistance in handling materials are unable to obtain it; the manufacturer who provides such help becomes a highly valued supplier.

PURCHASING

Four major activities comprise the bulk of most materials systems: purchasing, transportation, inventory control, and physical handling. We shall now examine some aspects of purchasing.

The Purchasing Agent

The executive in charge of purchasing activities is usually called the purchasing agent. His is a staff position of varying importance, depending upon the role of the purchasing function in the enterprise. In some large defense companies, in which hundreds of assistant purchasing managers must be hired to buy the many thousands of parts needed, the chief purchasing agent may be a vice-president.

What factors determine the importance of the purchasing function in a business?

Purchasing can be an attractive career for many men and women with some college training. The pay is relatively good and the job can be challenging. People who like to negotiate and deal with suppliers seem happy in the job.

While many people tend to think of the buying task as routine, any significant experience with it dispels such notions. First, there are great differences in the performance of purchasing agents; good ones save large amounts of money, all of which goes directly into profits. Second, life can be hectic, anything but routine, in a purchasing activity that is under pressure for performance. Locating better suppliers is much like detective work; dealing with them is more challenging than a chess game.

Make-or-Buy Decisions

For a number of items, management has the option either to make the goods or to buy them from outside suppliers. Such make-or-buy decisions are usually not too difficult, for they come down to determining how much it will cost the firm to make the item compared to what it will cost to buy it elsewhere. The implicit threat to make an item rather than buy it keeps some suppliers' prices in line.

There are several reasons why a firm might buy outside, even though it could make the article more cheaply itself. First, time pressures may make it impossible for the firm to tool up quickly enough to get the job done on schedule. Second, the plant may be running at capacity making things that contribute more to profit than the amounts to be saved by making the item. Third, the company may not know how to make it.

On the other hand, at times a firm will make something even though it knows quite well that it could buy the item cheaper elsewhere. Perhaps the plant is idle and looking for work; to keep the work force intact, all possible work is kept inhouse. Perhaps management wants to control the quality of workmanship and the delivery schedules.

The real key to make-or-buy decisions is an accurate estimate of the costs of producing the item, for experience indicates that many such computations are grossly low. Greater risks are involved in making a product than in buying it from a supplier.

What risks are borne by the supplier?

Price Determination

Price, or more accurately, "in use" cost is at the root of most buying decisions, so let us examine it.

What is meant by "in use" cost? Under what conditions do the price of a product and its "in use" cost differ considerably?

The price paid to a supplier depends on several factors: the quantity needed, how much the seller wants the business, the specifications required, the terms of sale, how much the buyer needs the item, the negotiating skills of the buyer in contrast to those of the seller, and various strategic considerations.

As a general rule, as the quantity needed increases, the price comes down; often it comes down rapidly with volume. The large buyer has power to command lower prices.

If the buyer will accept the standard specifications quoted by the seller, he will get a more attractice price than if he demands more stringent specifications. Quality costs money—sometimes a lot of money. The relaxation of some inconsequential specification may allow the seller to lower price significantly. Purchasing agents must question engineers carefully to make certain they are not specifying unnecessarily strict standards.

Sometimes the seller will lower price if the buyer pays cash or does not need quick delivery. The more demands placed on the seller, the higher the price. The buyer who is able to accommodate the seller can command a lower price. This is particularly true if the buyer can find a way to utilize the seller's idle capacity or downtime.

If the seller's plant is operating at full capacity and he has a big backlog of orders, the buyer can be assured that he will be quoted no bargains. Prices rise with backlogs. On the other hand, a hungry seller trims prices to the bone to keep his plant operating.

The buyer who must have an item and have it in a hurry usually pays a premium price for it. He has little bargaining power, unless the sellers themselves are in a weak position.

Certainly the negotiating skills of the buyer and seller come into the picture, for they can influence the price significantly. An adroit buyer can get a lower price in many instances than one who negotiates clumsily. Some sellers are better salesmen than others, and the results show up in the price they get.

How do buyers and sellers go about getting a better price for their firms?

Sometimes strategic considerations come into play. Some buyers will pay an attractive price to encourage some supplier; if the buyer faces a monopoly, he may go far out of his way to put another supplier into business so that he will have an alternate source of supply. Sometimes the buyer wants to keep a particularly convenient or accommodating supplier alive by paying him a higher price than would be necessary.

Types of Price Determination   There are three basic price situations: list or "on the shelf" prices, negotiated prices, and bidding.

List Prices.   Many times the seller has a product that he offers for a stipulated list price, take it or leave it. If you want to buy an IBM typewriter you pay IBM's list price or forget it.

Under what conditions will you find strict observance of list prices?

NEGOTIATED PRICES.   Many list prices are negotiable under certain circumstances; the quantities demanded dictate it, or the supplier is eager to sell. It never hurts to test the firmness of a list price, for nothing is lost by trying to negotiate a better deal.
Other times the buyer wants something that is not a standard product, but knows the supplier from whom it should be bought. Negotiations are undertaken to establish a price for it. Most jobs made to the buyer's specifications fall into this category.

BIDDING.   In most governmental buying the law requires that bids be solicited before a purchase can be made. Moreover, the law stipulates that the item must be bought from the lowest bidder, unless a sound reason for not doing so can be shown.

What reasons might there be for not buying from the lowest bidder? What are the problems connected with having to buy from the lowest bidder? How is the lowest-bidder provision circumvented by adroit buyers?

Bidding frequently is used by private industry in buying standard items for which there are several good suppliers. Fundamentally, bidding is nothing more than a negotiating tactic used by the buyer to force the sellers to quote their lowest possible price, for fear that they will not get the business if they try for a higher price. It does not always work out that way, for seasoned bidders have learned the dangers of being low too many times.

One business saying is that low bidders go broke. What is meant by that statement?

Centralized Purchasing

Large concerns have discovered many advantages to centralized buying, particularly from the negotiating viewpoint. One central buyer will negotiate a so-called *national* contract with a supplier, in which one price is agreed upon for all of the company's needs for all branches and plants in the country for the year, yet the goods are delivered in small orders to the units needing them.
While firms want to buy in as large a quantity as possible, they may not want delivery immediately. Perhaps the contract is for an entire year's supply, delivery of which is to be delayed as specified to coincide with the firm's needs. This minimizes the buyer's inventory problems and helps the seller schedule production.
However, such centralized buying proves to be burdensome in acquiring many small items at the local level, so usually the local manager has authority to buy certain types of things that cost less than some established amount, such as $500.

The Contract

Many purchases are made with a verbal contract; the buyer telephones the supplier to give an order for some standard item that has been ordered frequently in the past.

Perhaps a purchase order will be sent to the supplier to confirm the telephone order, perhaps not. But this describes routine buying done by the clerks in the purchasing office. Any significant purchase is more involved; usually a written contract is required for the protection of all parties. Many times the purchasing office has a standard contract that will apply to any transaction, or perhaps the seller insists on using a contract he has prepared.

Why is a written contract protection for all parties? What is meant by the word "protection" Why do parties prefer to use contracts that are prepared by their own organizations?

In significantly large sales, usually a contract prepared by the legal staff will be used. Some of these documents are awesome in size and complexity. Contracts for Department of Defense jobs run into hundreds of pages, each referring to standard clauses the government lawyers have previously prepared and published in standard government reference books. It literally takes days of intensive study to understand what is in such contracts, but study them one must, for the amount of money involved is so large and the possibilities for putting one's firm at a distinct disadvantage is so great that extreme caution is demanded in signing such documents.

Some Basic Concepts of Purchasing

Assured Supply   One waggish purchasing agent claimed that there were three basic principles of purchasing: Assured Supply, Assured Supply, and Assured Supply. He was referring to the fact that for each item requested by management, the purchasing agent must have the needed product in the right quantity, right quality, at the right place at the right time, lest the consequences of his failure to do so cause serious repercussions. The lack of one part may close the production plant completely with serious financial loss.

For this reason, purchasing agents will deal only with sources of supply that they know will perform according to contract. The observance of delivery schedules and the control of quality are mandatory. The undependable supplier will not be given much business, regardless of his prices.

Multiple Resources   The good purchasing agent does not like to have only one source of supply for an item. He will go out of his way to develop additional resources.

Why do purchasing executives avoid sole sources of supply if possible?

Value   Recent years have seen the development of the principles of *value analysis* and *value engineering* as aids to buying at lower cost. To execute these concepts, engineers are assigned to evaluate carefully an item to be purchased to estimate its costs of production (value analysis) as a guide for management in its negotiations with the supplier. If the price quoted is too far in excess of its estimated value, then other sources may be sought. Value engineering attempts to discover ways of reducing the item's production cost. Relaxing unnecessary specifications or simplifying its design may result in substantial savings.

Economic Order Quantity   It costs money to order something; paperwork, telephone calls, and purchasing agents' time are expensive. Frequent small orders become prohibitively costly, so why not always place large orders? Well, that is also expensive because of investment costs, storage, and inventory deterioration. Various formulas have been developed to help the buyer determine the proper quantity of an item to buy. It hinges largely on the item's rate of usage and its cost.

INVENTORY CONTROL

Inventory control accounts for, maintains or preserves, and manages the material assets of the firm, such as raw materials, semifinished goods, finished goods, and various supplies. While inventory control works in close coordination with purchasing, other functions such as production control, sales, and engineering are also involved.

The first objective of inventory control is to make certain that the goods, materials, or parts needed for production or resale are on hand in the proper quantity when needed. While accomplishing this main objective, the inventory control manager must still work toward a conflicting goal of having a minimum amount of money invested in inventory. Accounting for inventory, both items and dollar value, is accomplished by most sizable organizations through the use of computers; even smaller concerns are now computerizing their inventory control.

Some basic concepts of inventory control make its understanding relatively simple. Execution is another matter. First, when an item comes from the supplier it must be determined to be the item that was specified and in usable condition. Second, if it is to be stored, its location must be recorded. Third, the item should be protected from theft, deterioration, or spoilage and should be counted periodically by someone other than the person responsible for storage. Fourth, the correct item should be delivered to the production line or to the customer when it is ordered.

Unfortunately, many things happen to ruin this Utopian concept. Misidentifying the item, placing it in some remote area of the warehouse and not recording the location, or miscounting it at inventory time contribute to the dreaded comment on a material requisition, "No stock on hand."

STORAGE

Storage costs money—about six percent of the Gross National Product. Its importance should not be minimized, for everything is stored several times from its inception as raw material until it is finally consumed. (See Figure 16-2.) Goods are stored for a purpose: to await use, to await sale, for inspection, for grading and sorting, for repackaging, or for consolidation. However, business principles demand that storage be minimized, since it not only costs money but also creates risks one would prefer not to bear. And risks have a way of converting themselves into costs over the long run. So the basic concept of storage is not to let the goods stay in one place too long; keep them moving on to the next user as soon as possible.

FIGURE 16-2: Cycle of Physical Handling of Goods

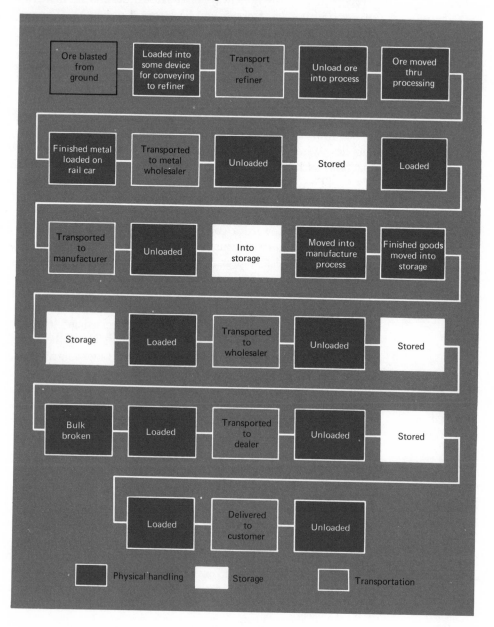

What risks are created by storage?

Why not minimize storage by buying in small, hand-to-mouth quantities?

Some Basic Concepts

Store Close to Use At one time the huge warehouse was in vogue; all things were stored in one place. Now studies indicate that costs are usually reduced if goods are stored close to their point of usage; it minimizes physical handling costs. In production operations, raw materials, parts, and supplies are stored right next to their point of usage.

What problems are posed by the maintenance of many smaller storage areas?

Protection Losses due to theft and damage are significant even when goods are protected from them while in storage; left unprotected, the losses mount disastrously. Security must be maintained.

Houskeeping The warehouseman must not only be able to locate everything in his care quickly, but also must take precautions that the oldest goods in stock are used first and not buried until the stock is depleted. Moreover, he or any other party should be able to ascertain quickly and accurately exactly how much of what item is in stock.

Placement of Stock In olden days the warehouseman placed the heavy goods nearest to the door to minimize the distance they would have to be carried; he tried to minimize the ton-miles the goods were carried. Today ton-miles are usually beside the point, because fork lift trucks make the matter of weight irrelevant. Now goods are stored in relationship to their call frequency. Goods for which there is a frequent call are placed nearby, while those items requested infrequently are placed in a far nook. This minimizes the time required for the fork lift to do its job.

PHYSICAL HANDLING

Goods are handled many times in their trips from the fields or mines into your home; they are continually being loaded into some type of vehicle and out of it into some storage area, only to be loaded out again onto some other vehicle. The cycle is repeated many times at a significant cost each time. See Figure 16-2 for a visualization of this process.

Ever empty a boxcar of something? Well, those innocent boxcars may not look large when you pass them on the road, but from the inside they look bigger than the whole world, if you are the man who has to unload one. But those days are nearly gone forever, we hope. Now physical handling is highly mechanized with fork lift trucks, conveyors, gravity unloading mechanisms, air suction devices, and the like. It simply costs too much to have a man pick up something; a machine must do the job.

Some Basic Concepts

Minimize Moving   Put the goods where they will be needed. Avoid handling goods unnecessarily by planning ahead about where they will be needed. One house contractor insisted that his suppliers unload right at the spot the material was to be used on the building. He did not want his $5-per-hour carpenters to carry a two-by-four an extra few feet; wood can become rather expensive when it is toted any distance at all by hand labor.

Use Equipment   Tool up for the job properly; it is cheaper in the long run. One manufacturer thought he could save some money by not installing a materials conveying system in his new plant; he thought he would rely on his old hand trucking methods for moving things within the plant. And he never understood why he could not get his costs in line with his competitors!

Unitize   The use of pallets and containers is well established for a a reason: they save money. Pack goods together in an adequately large container or unit so that enough of them can be hauled in one trip of the fork lift to keep the per-item costs low.

Delay Breaking Bulk   The old principle of shipping goods in large units as far as possible is still valid. Transportation and handling costs are minimized as long as goods are kept together in one large unit. But when that unit is broken open to start handling separate items, the costs soar. It costs as much to handle one tube of toothpaste as it does to handle a carton. Typically, we try to get the bulk delivered unbroken at least to the wholesaler; often it can be put into the dealer's hands before the bulk is broken.

Do Not Handle Goods Unless Required   Sometimes it is feasible to avoid handling the goods at all. A wholesaler who has a large sale to a dealer may be able to have them shipped directly to the customer rather than to his wholesale warehouse; this is called a drop shipment. Some retailers have customers pick up goods at a warehouse to avoid handling them through the store.

Maintain Access to Goods   Arrange the storage area so that equipment has direct access to all goods. It becomes expensive if other goods must be moved first before one can reach the articles that are wanted.

TRANSPORTATION

Transportation specialists can save the company far more than their salaries by cutting transportation costs. It is erroneous to assume that it does not matter how a product is shipped from Chicago to San Francisco because the costs will be the same. The confusing truth is that not only do costs vary between the types of carriers used, such as rail, truck, water, air, or parcel post, but they vary depending on the exact route chosen. In fact, the rate tariffs under which transportation companies operate are so complex and confusing that it takes an expert to know by which route costs will be minimized. One traffic manager of a plywood company discovered that it was cheaper to ship plywood from Portland to Chicago via San Francisco than directly to Chicago from Portland. A gypsum company found that it was cheaper to ship sheetrock from Los Angeles to Dallas by water through the Panama Canal to Houston and by rail to Dallas, than to ship directly from Los Angeles to Dallas by rail.

In addition, the mode of transportation is highly important to customer satisfaction. Often speed is essential; the customer wants the merchandise quickly. At other times the merchandise is of such a character that it would be damaged if shipped by certain methods.

Modes of Transportation and Their Evaluation

For many decades the railroads were the prime transporters of goods. Unfortunately, they abused the franchise they were given and failed to render the services demanded by the market. Though shippers and buyers wanted quick, fast service on less-than-carload lots (l.c.l.), the railroads continued to give very slow terminal-to-terminal service; frequently the shipper had to deliver the goods to the railroad and the buyer had to go to the depot to pick them up. The railroads are still the predominant means for moving large quantities of heavy merchandise. As long as the seller is shipping in carload quantities, rail is usually the cheapest method of inland transportation available. Railroads handle less-than-carload shipments, but the delivery time is exceedingly slow and the likelihood of damage or theft of merchandise is high.

When existing institutions fail to perform properly, new ones are developed to perform the desired tasks. Trucks were developed to handle the less-than-carload, full-service business that the railroads were not interested in servicing. Today most less-than-carload shipments move by truck, which is not only faster but also generally gives good service to both shipper and buyer. Trucking companies pick up the merchandise at the shipper's dock and deliver it to the buyer's dock. Traffic managers maintain that far less merchandise is damaged in shipping by truck than by rail, and that the motor carriers give faster service on damage claims. Is it any wonder that the trucking companies have grown rapidly while the railroads have languished? There is a real lesson to be learned in business from watching the competitive maneuvers of the railroads versus the truckers. Actually, it is not difficult to determine whether a company should be using the railroads or the trucks to ship its merchandise; the nature of the product, the quantities in which it is usually shipped, and the importance of quick delivery usually dictate the means of transportation.

Whenever possible, water routes are used for transporting goods because of their low cost, but too often the necessity for speed eliminates this carrier. Also, few manufacturers ship in sufficiently large quantities to employ ships economically.

Air freight is a fast-growing industry, despite its relatively high costs. It is used when fast delivery is imperative and the goods are not too bulky or heavy. Air freight's delivery speed sometimes allows buyers to carry a smaller inventory. Also, the increased speed of delivery has enabled some sellers to reduce or eliminate the number of branch warehouses maintained. At the height of the Hula Hoop craze its manufacturer was chartering planes to fly the much-demanded items to the large eastern markets. There is no question that this carrier will increase in importance in the future.

A large volume of small, light packages is sent via parcel post. Unfortunately, the many strict postal regulations regarding weight and size of package severely limit the usefulness of this service, and its costs are high.

Railway express is used by shippers desiring more flexibility in shipping requirements. There are no limitations on size, weight, or perishability on express shipments. Unfortunately, because railway express is a relatively expensive method of transportation, it is not used very often by manufacturers for their regular shipments. There is a serious gap in our transportation system between the point where the post office stops service and the point where economical truck shipments begin.

In a relatively free economy, when a demand for some product or service is going unsatisfied, some institution steps into the vacuum to serve that market. So it is with the small package shipments; buses in transporting passengers have a lot of unused baggage space that can carry small packages. The bus companies are now formalizing this service, called Bus Package Express (BPX), and it should prove quite popular for shipping small packages short distances. It is now only a $60-million-a-year business, but it has yet to be promoted and organized.

INNOVATION IN TRANSPORTATION

Because transportation charges loom large in the delivered cost of many products, numerous firms are constantly innovating new transportation procedures or methods that will either cut costs or give better service.

Piggyback Service

As railroads are the most economical means of transporting large quantities of goods over long distances, and trucks present many advantages in servicing short-haul business, it was only a matter of time before someone combined the two for greater efficiency. Loaded truck trailers are hauled at express speeds for great distances on rail flatcars and the goods distributed by truck from some major distribution point. By this means some shippers have reduced the handling of freight between carriers, obtained speedier delivery, and reduced the damage usually incurred in standard boxcars.

In any industry, no matter how stagnant it may be, there are always a few companies that innovate to meet competition. The railroads are no exception. The Denver and Rio Grande presented to its shippers the data shown in Table 16-1 to promote piggyback service. Observation quickly discloses that the Rio Grande has been successful in promoting piggyback, for long trains carrying truck trailers over the Continental Divide can be seen crawling up a mountain any time of the day or night. The whole idea is to develop plans to meet competition, and in transportation, meeting competition usually comes down to a matter of money.

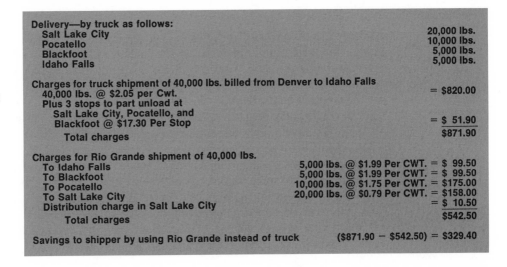

Table 16-1

A COMPARISON OF THE COSTS OF SHIPPING BY TRUCK VERSUS SHIPPING BY PIGGYBACK VIA THE RIO GRANDE TO THE SAME DESTINATIONS

Delivery—by truck as follows:	
Salt Lake City	20,000 lbs.
Pocatello	10,000 lbs.
Blackfoot	5,000 lbs.
Idaho Falls	5,000 lbs.

Charges for truck shipment of 40,000 lbs. billed from Denver to Idaho Falls
40,000 lbs. @ $2.05 per Cwt. = $820.00
Plus 3 stops to part unload at
Salt Lake City, Pocatello, and
Blackfoot @ $17.30 Per Stop = $ 51.90
Total charges $871.90

Charges for Rio Grande shipment of 40,000 lbs.
To Idaho Falls 5,000 lbs. @ $1.99 Per CWT. = $ 99.50
To Blackfoot 5,000 lbs. @ $1.99 Per CWT. = $ 99.50
To Pocatello 10,000 lbs. @ $1.75 Per CWT. = $175.00
To Salt Lake City 20,000 lbs. @ $0.79 Per CWT. = $158.00
Distribution charge in Salt Lake City = $ 10.50
Total charges $542.50

Savings to shipper by using Rio Grande instead of truck ($871.90 − $542.50) = $329.40

Another example of a competitive innovation to meet competition is the Santa Fe's development of its Super "C" service between Los Angeles and Chicago. It is an all-piggyback train that makes the run on a regular daily schedule in 40 hours. Comparative costs for the Super "C" service are presented in Table 16-2.

Table 16-2 FREIGHT CHARGES ON SELECTED COMMODITIES VIA RAIL BOXCAR, MOTOR CARRIER, AND AIR FREIGHT IN COMPARISON WITH SUPER "C" SERVICE CHICAGO TO LOS ANGELES (CHARGES BASED ON SHIPMENTS WEIGHING 35,000 LBS.)

	Super C		Rail (Boxcar)		Motor Carrier		Air Freight	
	Rate per 100 lbs.	Revenue	Rate per 100 lbs.	Revenue	Rate per 100 lbs.	Revenue	Rate per 100 lbs.**	Revenue
Machinery, NOIBN	$4.00	$1,400	$4.04	$1,414*	$4.11	$1,439	$15.75	$5,512
Magazines	4.00	1,400	2.68	1,072†	3.60	1,260	9.36	3,276
Batteries, electric storage	4.00	1,400	2.56	1,152‡	3.60	1,260	15.75	5,512
Prepared foods	4.00	1,400	2.92	1,022	4.61	1,614	15.75	5,512
Automobile parts	4.00	1,400	3.37	1,180	3.72	1,302	15.75	5,512

*At minimum weight of 40,000 lbs., rate of $3.74 per 100 pounds is applicable.
†As minimum weight of 40,000 lbs. to obtain lowest charges for a 35,000-lb. shipment.
‡As minimum weight of 45,000 lbs. to obtain lowest charges for a 35,000-lb. shipment.
*†When containerized, reductions of $0.35 to $1.00 per 100 lbs. applies depending on type container used.

Fishyback Service

Some shippers have used piggyback techniques in water shipments. By shipping loaded truck trailers aboard ship along the coastal and inland waterways, a considerable amount of effort is saved in loading and unloading the merchandise from the ship. In addition, loss from pilferage is greatly reduced.

Specialty Carriers

Transportation carriers have developed to deal with the transportation problems of certain industries. In southern Indiana the limestone industry sells a product of extremely great weight and bulk. Normally railroads were the only feasible means of transporting the stone. However, railroads gave slow service and could not deliver directly to the buyer. Truck companies evolved that transported only cut stone. They bought special trucks and developed special techniques for handling the stone.

Oil pipelines provide another example of the development of special transportation methods to meet certain problems peculiar to a product. Because of the tremendous importance of oil in our economy, means had to be developed to move huge quantities of it from the producing areas to the major consumption centers as cheaply, quickly, and safely as possible. The cost of moving oil by pipelines is less than half the cost incurred by rail. Before the building of the pipelines during World War II, most crude oil was shipped by coastal tanker to the eastern refineries, but wartime submarine warfare hindered deliveries.

Containerization

Traffic managers have discovered that if they unitize a group of packages going to one destination into one container, physical handling between carriers is greatly facilitated and losses are minimized. Modern materials handling machinery makes it much easier and cheaper to handle one large container than many small ones.

Though some effort is being made to standardize the size of shipping containers, not much progress has been made, because shippers have such diverse needs and requirements. However, a firm specializing in air freight has recently perfected a series of standard containers in several sizes to provide for consolidation of small shipments to the same destination. This development in containerization represents a potential savings of 14 percent to the shipper.

EFFECTING TRANSPORTATION ECONOMIES

There are several steps the manager can take to minimize the cost of transporting goods. First, his choice of carrier is of prime importance. Whenever possible, he should ship by water, because the costs are extremely low per ton-mile. Although general merchandise costs about $\frac{1}{2}$ cent per ton-mile if shipped by water, some oil firms report costs as low as $\frac{1}{25}$ cent per ton-mile. With modern ships and handling techniques it is now cheaper to ship oil from the Middle East to New York than it is to move oil to New York by pipeline. There is no question that, if speed is not essential, the use of the ocean or inland waterways is advisable.

Many manufacturers are rediscovering the inland waterways of the nation. Now that the St. Lawrence Seaway has opened, it is possible to ship from New York to Chicago by ocean vessel and gain access to the Mississippi, Ohio, and Missouri river systems by barge. The strategy is to move goods as close to the market as possible by water and then break down the bulk for shipping on more expensive carriers. Frequently it is possible to ship by water to public warehouses located in such seaports as New Orleans, Houston, Los Angeles, San Francisco, or Seattle, then break down the shipments for distribution by rail or truck from these points to nearby customers.

Second, there are several actions a shipper can take when using the railroads to avail himself of lower rates. Through the use of pool cars a seller may gain the advantages of carload rates if he is shipping less-than-carload lots of any one product or order. A pool car may contain the products of one firm destined for a number of buyers, or it may contain the goods of several companies to one or more buyers. The basic idea is that a group of shipments, each of which is less than a carload, are pooled together and shipped in one car to one destination, then broken down at that point for distribution to consignees. Whenever the use of a pool car can be arranged, a substantial saving is realized over an l.c.l. shipment. Goods should be shipped at carload rates as far as possible.

Frequently the services of a freight forwarder can be used to advantage. Freight forwarders take l.c.l. shipments of many shippers and consolidate them into carload lots to be shipped at the carload rates. Although the freight forwarder charges the shipper the l.c.l. rate and pays only carload rate, thus obtaining a margin on which to operate, the shipper does get quicker delivery of his merchandise than is usually true in normal l.c.l. shipments.

The manager should do everything in his power to facilitate the sale of carload quantities to buyers. If he is able to encourage carload sales through his pricing structure or terms, there is no question that the total delivered costs of the merchandise will be considerably lessened.

Package design affects transportation costs. Often firms are shipping a great deal of air in their packages. If they could reduce the bulk of their packing, their commodity rate might be considerably lessened, because they would be able to ship more units per car. Some firms have found that they can save substantially on shipping costs if they break their products down to minimize space. It often costs no more to assemble the product at the destination than at the factory. The executive should therefore do everything possible to make certain that he is not shipping empty space but filling every cubic foot of space in the carrier with matter.

The location of raw-materials processing can vitally affect total transportation costs of the finished product. The general strategy is to eliminate as much bulk as possible from a raw material as quickly as possible, so that one is not transporting useless weight. The closer to the fields a corn syrup manufacturer can process ears of corn into syrup, the less his total transportation costs will be, because he will not be shipping the bulk of cobs and waste material. To facilitate this economizing process, railroads allow certain products to be stopped in transit for processing and then proceed to their destination at a through rate. All the shipper must pay is a slight charge for the processing-in-transit privilege, which is much less than he would have to pay if two local rates were applied.

A firm analyzed the relative costs of making sheetrock at the mine site or in the market area in which it was to be sold. A brief analysis quickly proved there was no question that the gypsum had to be processed as close to the mine site as possible; otherwise, the shipper would be paying for the shipment of huge quantities of water to the market area. The mined gypsum had to be dehydrated before being made into sheetrock.

Finally, the actual location of a firm's plant influences the total transportation costs that its customers must bear. Theoretically, a manufacturer should seek to locate his factory to minimize the total ton-miles of merchandise shipped. In this modern era of operations research, mathematicians have undertaken to determine this statistically. By taking a sample of invoices over a previous period, they are able to determine the percentage of shipments of different market areas and the quantities shipped to each. Thus they can formulate some equations which, when solved, will tell the executive where he should locate his plant to minimize total transportation costs.

There are other considerations, however, besides quantities and distances to be traveled. Different sections of the country have different rate structures, which can significantly affect economies of shipping into certain areas. In general, the southern states have long complained that freight tariffs discriminate against the location of industry in the South. There is no question that a firm located closer to its market than its competitors may have a competitive advantage over them, unless that advantage is offset in other cost factors, such as labor.

There is nothing sacred about a transportation tariff; it is a price and can be negotiated just like any other price, if the bargainer has sufficient bargaining power. The Zale Corporation, a 397-unit chain of jewelry stores, cut its shipping costs 46 cents on every 100 pounds of freight shipped by rail from New York to its Dallas headquarters. Zale went to war with the railroads, and when the dust settled after the public hearings, it had a rate reduction. The arrangements were, "The new rate is in effect on shipments in excess of 30,000 pounds. We made an agreement that, in order to maintain our new low rate, we would ship from New York one freight car of at least 20,000 pounds—and then in 24 hours, ship another car with the same minimum weight."

Then Zale attacked its Houston-to-Dallas freight costs; through a complicated arrangement of piggyback shipments and the pooling of shipments with two other firms, significant savings were realized. "During 1967 we moved about 600,000 pounds of china from Houston to Dallas at 96 cents per hundred pounds. If all things were equal this year and we again moved 600,000 pounds of china on the route, we would reduce our cost by $2,580." And that is but one item—china—on one route. Multiply such amounts by all the goods purchased by a large company, and one can see that the adept traffic manager is well worth his salary.

In conclusion, the transportation industry is an immensely complex structure in which an extremely large number of variables go into the determination of the total transportation costs incurred by a firm. The wise firm either will hire a good traffic manager to minimize the transportation expenses and expedite the shipment of merchandise, or will obtain the services of a competent transportation consultant to set up and make routine its shipments to its major market areas. It is feasible for an outside consultant to determine which routes should be used for shipments of a certain size to certain areas. For example, Sears sends all its suppliers a looseleaf booklet that specifies exactly how each size of shipment shall be shipped to each of its retail outlets. One of the advantages of a small firm's selling to Sears is that Sears does its traffic management for it. One small company uses the Sears manual as a traffic guide for all shipments, because it makes sense that if a certain route is the cheapest way to send items to another Sears store in a given town, it is also the cheapest way to send things to a different store in the same town.

If great quantities of merchandise are being shipped by a company, it is wrong to assume that a traffic manager will be an expense. Usually he is able to save far more than his salary in filing for rebates on overcharges made by carriers and fighting for the proper rates for each shipment. The truth is that few carriers extend themselves to make certain that shippers are being charged the lowest rates possible and are shipping by the most economical routes. Clearly, the burden is on the shipper to protect himself at all times. There are firms that make a profit auditing the freight bills of other companies and taking a percentage of the overcharges they find in them. This is how prevalent overcharging is.

Conclusion

> While at one time the functions of purchasing, storage, inventory control, transportation, and physical handling were considered separate activities, now we see them as parts of an integrated materials management system whose purpose is to do a certain job for the lowest total cost.
>
> These business activities, while important to the ultimate success of the enterprise, have been neglected by many businessmen in favor of the more romantic fields of finance, marketing, and production.
>
> A great deal of highly technical information must now be mastered by people who wish to become specialists in materials management. Gone are the days when the sole requirement for a warehouse foreman was a strong back.

17 Personnel and labor relations

Labor was the first price, the original purchase money that was paid for all things. It was not by gold or silver, but by labor, that all wealth of the world was originally purchased; and its value, to those who possess it, is precisely equal to the quantity of labor which it can enable them to purchase or command.

ADAM SMITH

Few topics engender more emotion among businessmen and their employees than that of labor and its management. Some businessmen have folded their operations rather than negotiate terms of employment with their workers' union. Even more businessmen have fought long, expensive "wars" with labor, sometimes successfully, more commonly not. Even the most tolerant executive's emotional stability is taxed when discussing labor and its organizations.

And the picture on the other side is no better! Rare is the union leader who has many kind words for employers. More commonly, labor at best is suspicious of management's motives.

So in this setting, let us study labor and its management. Since most direct contact with labor in large organizations has been delegated to the personnel department, some discussion of it is necessary.

The field of personnel management has undergone great change in recent years. Whereas personnel management once was concerned largely with the mechanics of operating the personnel department of a firm, today personnel men are concerned with the much broader and deeper area of human behavior in organizations. The modern student of personnel management must be soundly based in the behavioral sciences and, in particular, the behavior of individuals in organizations and groups. Although personnel management has been given new dimensions by the inclusion of the behavioral sciences, still the individual interested in personnel management must focus his attentions on the demands of that job in the firm, so this discussion will follow the more traditional approach to the study of personnel management, focusing on the various activities connected with that job.

EMERGENCE OF PERSONNEL MANAGEMENT AND LABOR RELATIONS

While the personnel manager in many firms also performs labor relations work, the two functions are separate. Many of the nation's largest firms recognize this and separate the jobs. We will have a separate discussion of each function, although each has grown fairly much in parallel with the other and largely for the same reasons.

Personnel managers and labor negotiators were almost unheard of in nineteenth-century business firms; they are almost exclusively a creation of the twentieth-century. More particularly, they have come to fore with the rise in the growth of unionism and the tremendous amount of government regulation affecting personnel practices. The factors giving rise to professional personnel management are: growth in the number of employees, unionization, government regulations, and increased interest in employee welfare.

Growth in Number of Employees

The entrepreneur who hires 100 or so workers seldom feels a strong need for a personnel manager. As firms grow in size, the physical work involved in hiring people, keeping their records, and attending to various activities connected with their welfare becomes so burdensome that it cannot be performed by line executives or an office girl, so a staff man is hired—a personnel manager. Growth alone creates the need for such specialists.

About how many employees does a firm need before it should consider hiring a personnel manager?

Unionization

The advent of unionization, particularly after the passage of the Wagner Act in 1935, created not only an immediate need for labor negotiators, but also a department for administering all of the fringe benefit programs created for the benefit of the workers. Unionization has been a strong impetus for the creation of personnel departments.

Government Regulations

Today the personnel practices of all companies are so highly regulated by the various governments that a well-managed personnel department is almost mandatory if the firm is to abide by all of the laws. The law requires that firms maintain complete records on all of their workers.

Increased Interest in Employee Welfare

Modern management has become increasingly concerned with the welfare of its employees. Consequently, it has developed several programs—pension and retirement plans, insurance programs, recreational activities, and other such nonmonetary rewards. Such programs are complicated and require the attention of a professional executive trained in their administration.

FUNCTIONS OF A PERSONNEL MANAGER

While the precise job of a personnel manager will vary company by company, depending upon the situation in which he must operate, still there is a certain similarity and uniformity in the functions performed by personnel managers.

Job Studies

In a well-run company the personnel manager has carefully identified every job in the organization and has analyzed it to ascertain exactly what it entails. It is difficult to place too much emphasis upon job analysis, for upon it are based a great many other managerial techniques. For example, wages are frequently based on an analysis of the difficulty of the job and the skills necessary for its successful execution.

How would you go about making a job study? Study the job of the student!

From careful analysis of the job, a job description is developed, and from this description job specifications are formulated. An example of a job description is shown in Figure 17-1. The job specification describes the skills and attributes that must be possessed by the individual filling the job.

Recruiting

When a position is open, the job specification for it is used as the basis for recruiting applicants. The wise manager wants to look at a number of qualified applicants to increase his chances of hiring someone who will do an excellent job. In difficult times a great many applicants will present themselves voluntarily for jobs, but more commonly a search must be made to locate the right men. It is easy just to recruit bodies for a job, but it is another thing to recruit applicants who are all highly qualified for the position.

If you were looking for a salesman of rare chemicals, where would you recruit?
Should a firm advertise all job vacancies in the newspaper?

FIGURE 17-1: Example of Job Description

Bobbie Brooks, Inc.
REGIONAL SALES MANAGER

BASIC FUNCTION: The Regional Sales Manager is the field sales executive responsible for the sale of all of the Company's lines in a specified sales region. He reports to the General Sales Manager and is directly responsible for achieving sales objectives in his region. He directs the efforts of all salesmen in his region to assure budgeted performance.

REPORTS TO: General Sales Manager

SUPERVISES: Territory Salesmen and Office Staff

MAJOR DUTIES AND RESPONSIBILITIES

1. Develops marketing plans and programs for his region for submission to the General Sales Manager for approval.

2. Recommends, to the General Sales Manager, specific territorial assignments for the salesmen.

3. With the help of each salesman, develops a sales forecast and from it develops the overall regional sales forecasts and budgets and submits them to the Field Sales Manager for incorporation in the overall marketing forecasts and budgets.

4. Works with each salesman to develop a plan to be followed in working his territory. This plan should include a list of key potential accounts to be developed, as well as a pattern for covering his territory.

5. Appraises the performance of each salesman on a continuing basis and offers specific suggestions for improvement in salesman's performance.

6. Sees that each salesman is fully equipped with the sample line, swatch books and other sales aids before setting out to sell each line.

7. Periodically checks the salesmen's sample lines to be sure that all current garments are being carried and that all recalled items have been taken out of the sample line.

8. Makes sales calls with individual salesmen to demonstrate how to sell the company's products.

9. Personally works with the sales trainees in his region to assure that they are getting maximum training during their period of employment in his region.

10. Holds periodic sales meetings to disseminate information and to train the territory salesmen.

11. Stimulates the salesmen to submit ideas and success stories or new techniques on how to sell the company's lines and sees that this information is disseminated throughout the sales force.

12. Handles major accounts on a personal basis as assigned by the General Sales Manager.

13. Keeps the General Sales Manager fully informed of progress and any significant developments in the region.

14. Reviews sales performance reports and takes the necessary action to correct unsatisfactory results.

The Selection Process

Once applicants for a job have been obtained, a rather long and sometimes overly cumbersome selection procedure begins. The personnel manager is usually in charge of the selection process, but not always. Sometimes, particularly in the sales field, managers want not only to participate actively in the selection process but also to manage it, for they feel that the personnel manager is not the best qualified to recruit and select their specialists. Be that as it may, the personnel department is involved to some degree in most selection procedures.

Typically, the process begins by having the applicant fill out a brief application blank, which is used along with a short, preliminary interview, conducted by a clerk in the personnel office, to determine if he meets the basic specifications for the job. If he does, then he is generally given a much longer application blank, asking for detailed information about himself and his skills. Then the recruit has one or more lengthy interviews with the appropriate people in the company. Perhaps the first interview will be with the personnel manager, who, if he feels the man is qualified, will then pass him on to be interviewed by the operating men with whom and for whom he will work. For a job that carries any responsibility at all, the applicant will usually talk with several men in the department, perhaps several times. The more responsible the job, the more careful employers are about filling it.

Processing Papers

Once a decision has been made to hire a man, a substantial amount of paper must be processed to place him on the payroll; the personnel department handles such matters. A record is kept for every employee that contains his entire work history with the firm, including evaluation reports from superiors and various documents concerning his pay and promotions. The completeness and accuracy of these personnel records is especially important when the company becomes involved in some dispute with either the employee or a government agency concerning such things as unemployment compensation, workmen's compensation, and the like.

Training

The personnel department is usually in charge of all training activities within the company. These can be substantial, ranging from low-level indoctrination courses up to high-level executive training programs.

Testing

In conjunction with the normal selection process and with work improvement programs, considerable testing may be undertaken to determine both skills and knowledge. The personnel department has the responsibility for developing valid tests.

Work Studies

As mentioned in the chapter on production, manufacturers often must make detailed time and motion studies on various jobs to determine their complexity and to try to improve efficiency of operations. Usually the personnel departments are in charge of such studies.

Wage Studies

Most large organizations are concerned with the equity of their pay scales. They want to make certain that people are paid proportionately to the skills their jobs and responsibilities require. Consequently, they typically maintain a rather constant study of their wage policies and carefully administer periodic reviews of salaries and wage differentials within the company. Usually such studies are done by the personnel department.

Recreational and Welfare Programs

The paternalistic bent of most large corporations has been well documented. They furnish everything from bowling leagues and other sporting activities to flowers during times of illness. Such activities are usually handled through the personnel offices.

Labor Relations

A major responsibility of many personnel departments is labor relations, which entails essentially two different types of work. First, there is the critically important negotiation of contracts with the unions. Second, there is the matter of administering the contract once it is signed. Grievance committees must be formed and put to work. A continual flow of matters that arise under the contract must be handled. More will be said of labor relations later.

Personnel Policies and Practices

A company of any significance usually develops a body of personnel policies and practices by which it expects its employees to abide. The personnel department develops these personnel manuals and sees that they are disseminated throughout the organization.

Terminations

When a worker's employment with a firm is terminated, for whatever reason—resignation, discharge, or death—certain procedures must be followed. Usually a termination interview is given. The matter of severance pay and other benefits must also be settled.

What are the benefits to be gained from having an interview with a man leaving the company's employ?
What is the difference between layoffs and terminations?

Legal Conformity

Various laws administered by both the state and federal governments place restrictions on the personnel practices a company may follow. Many reports must be filed with the appropriate government agencies, and many times the government actually inspects operations to insure compliance with the law. Contacts with these agencies are usually in the hands of the personnel department.

LABOR RELATIONS

Since the passage of the Wagner Act in 1935, relations with labor and particularly with unions have become an increasingly important and highly sensitive area in management. At one time the top management of most firms felt that they could deal directly with labor themselves, but experience proved this to be a serious mistake. The average top executive is not competent to negotiate with union leaders on an equal basis, for they are experienced hands at it and he is a novice. Instead, professional labor negotiators have developed to perform this function for industry. But first, let's understand something of unions, their growth, and their functions.

The Concept of Unions

The concept of unions is not a new one. There have been forms of unions since the beginning of commercial enterprise. Indeed, the trade guilds of the Middle Ages were nothing more than unions. People of similar bent have always joined together to gain advantages through size and to restrict competition among them.

Why have members of the same trade usually tried to restrict competition among various members of the trade?

Trade unionism, as we know it in the United States, had its beginning in the nineteenth century. The first leader to gain national recognition was Samuel Gompers with his Workers of the World. Such facts, however, are much less important than the concept. To appreciate the factors that gave rise to unionism you must project yourself back into the factory of 1880 or 1890 and visualize all of the things that were happening to you, the conditions around you, and your pay scale. You must visualize the standard of living that you were able to bring home and contrast it to that of your boss. You must understand that your boss was far more than your boss; almost your very life was dependent upon his favor. He could discharge you for any reason or with no reason. What he said was law, and if you didn't like it you could look elsewhere for your paycheck. Your wages were held down by the fact that there were hundreds of other workers begging your boss to let them have your job, so what bargaining power did you have?

Clearly, the individual worker of that time felt himself to be a helpless pawn, thrust into vicious competition with all of his fellow workers for the benefit of his employer. Such feelings encouraged him to get together with his fellow employees in order to gain more bargaining power. The concept of the union is that while any one or a few workers have little bargaining power with an employer, the total work force has great bargaining power and is able to negotiate more successfully with the employer. The union is a device by which workers gain bargaining power with their employer. In recent years employers have banded together in employers' councils to bargain as an industry with the unions, because in many cases the pendulum has swung the other way; the union is so much bigger and more powerful than the individual employer that the employer has little bargaining power. So the employers in an industry get together and bargain on an industrywide basis.

Growth of Unions

Until the passage of the Wagner Act in 1935, the growth of unionism was severely hampered by the law. Employers and the courts were able to combat with varying degrees of success attempts to unionize their plants on the basis that unions were a conspiracy in violation of the law or that unions were an attempt to monopolize in violation of the Sherman Act.

Monopolize what?

The history of unionization is a rather violent one, with strikes, riots, lockouts, suits, and countersuits. Employers were just as determined to keep their bargaining rights, powers, and prerogatives as labor was to obtain them. But the advent of the Great Depression, with its large-scale unemployment and general hard times for labor, gave the working man special reason to doubt the wisdom of his employers; labor was then able to gain sufficient political power to get favorable statutes enacted. Labor wanted a law that gave it several rights. First, labor wanted the right to organize a union if it so desired. Second, it wanted the union's right to bargain with the employer and be recognized as a union of his workers. Third, it wanted to prevent employers from penalizing workers who were active in union affairs or were responsible for unionizing the company. Fourth, the unions wanted to make several practices illegal—declare them to be unfair labor practices.

Why were each of these rights so highly desired by union leaders?
Can a company be organized strictly from the outside?
If you were a pre-Wagner Act employer, free from present-day legal restraints, what could you do to thwart unionism in your plant?
If you are the manager of a nonunionized company and you want it to stay that way, how do you accomplish it?
If you are a union leader looking for a company to unionize, what do you look for in a company to determine whether or not it is ripe for unionization?

Functions of Unions

Unions can serve several functions other than that of strictly acting as the workers' bargaining agent in determining salaries and working conditions. In some industries, the unions act as a hiring hall. In most cities of any size, if you want to hire five carpenters, you will call the carpenters' union hiring hall or the construction trade's hiring hall to make your needs known; they will send out five union carpenters. If you are a ship owner with some cargo to unload, you will call the union hiring hall for the labor. If you are in the garment trade and need to hire seamstresses, you will call the hiring hall of the International Garment Workers of America for your supply.

What happens if the carpenters who are sent out prove to be submarginal—no good?
What conditions give rise to the hiring-hall function of the union? Why do the unions want to operate hiring halls?

Pension-Fund Management   One goal of most unions has been the development of pension funds to sustain their members after retirement. Many contracts contain provisions in which employers and employees put money into pension funds, such funds being administered by the union, management, or sometimes by a combination of the two.

Some young people find it difficult to understand the powerful emotional drives behind pension-fund negotiations, but that is largely because they fail to appreciate the average worker's deep fear of being left destitute in his old age. Social Security is inadequate to maintain the living standards he desires.

Welfare Programs   Many unions maintain substantial welfare programs for their members and their families, which include unemployment benefits in case of layoff, accident and health insurance, and other such services. Actually, the early unions were formed largely as mutual welfare associations; the workers took care of each other in times of trouble.

Seniority Systems   Unions, from their inception, have been most concerned about the seniority of their members, and for good reasons. In a great many instances, employers would fire a worker past his prime in favor of a younger man who was able to turn out more production for a lower wage. In olden days a man past 40 had good reason to worry about the security of his job. Most unions are extremely adamant on the issue of seniority—the older worker has rights to his job. The slogan, "Last hired, first fired," has been the union's basic policy.

What is the union's logic supporting the layoff of the younger men first? Whom does management want to lay off first?

Work Rules   A great deal of negotiation between company and union concerns work rules, for pay rates mean little if the amount of work to be performed for the unit of pay is not carefully defined. Unions have been most sensitive to attempts on the part of management to speed up production lines or otherwise obtain more work from the employee.

Social   In many instances, unions serve a social function in the lives of the workers and their families. Numerous social events such as picnics, dances, and bowling leagues help weld the worker and his family to the union and his fellow workers.

Identity   Some students of unionization have claimed that a commonly overlooked function of unions was to give the worker an identity; he was someone, not just another card in the time-clock rack. The union became his reference group, an important force in his life. This explains in part the fierce loyalty frequently encountered among union members. For a long time management was puzzled by the workers' behavior, as loyalties to the union and their co-workers far exceeded their loyalty to the company or its management.

The matter of company loyalty has been a most sensitive topic to most managers, who
seem to expect more than they get. What loyalty does an employee owe his employer?
Why do employees become disloyal? What is disloyalty?

Negotiating Issues

The general public is sometimes puzzled by what seems to be an inordinate amount
of time taken up in labor negotiations. Negotiating teams work many weeks, if not
months, in pounding out a contract. Yet the press reports only that they settled for
a wage increase of so many cents per hour. Buried in those headlines are many more
issues.

Wages   Make no mistake about it: the major, primary negotiating issue in the vast
majority of instances is money—how much the workers are going to be paid for a
unit of work. While, as a general rule, production workers have negotiated for hourly
wage rates, presently there is pressure by several of the nation's leading unions for
a guaranteed annual wage.

As a rule, unions have been very reluctant to accept piece-rate wage payments. Why?
Why do unions want a guaranteed annual wage? Why are the employers reluctant to
give it? What impact would a guaranteed annual wage have upon a firm's hiring policies
and production planning?

As a general principle, unions base their wage demands on increases in the cost of
living and upon increases in the productivity of labor.

If you were a union negotiator, how would you prove that your members should get
higher wages because they had been more productive? What kinds of statistics would
you use?

Working Conditions   In the early days of unionization, working conditions were almost as important as wages in the demands of the workers, for unquestionably
many of their places of employment were dangerous pestholes. Most of the safety
precautions that we now take for granted were nonexistent. Workers were killed and
maimed daily on the job because of such dangerous conditions. And keep in mind
that not too many years ago, if a worker was disabled, his family suffered almost
unimaginable hardships, for there was no Social Security or other financial crutch to
sustain them. The workers wanted clean, safe places to work. This right seems so
unquestionable to us now that one must wonder why employers of that time opposed it.

Why did they?

Security   A man who depends for his livelihood, and his family's, upon wages paid
him by an employer has a gnawing fear of the consequences if he were to be laid
off or fired, particularly if the unemployment was not a result of his own misdoing.

Workers have always sought protection from the whimsy of capricious managers, who play favorites among workers or who systematically lay off older employees in favor of younger ones who are willing to work cheaper.

Why were young men willing to work for less than older men?

Quite early in their history, unions were most concerned with seniority and job protection. They insisted that men be given seniority according to their years of employment with the company and that they could not lose their jobs except for just cause. Moreover, the just causes were spelled out clearly in the labor contract.

What are the just causes normally recognized in a labor contract that justify the discharge of an employee?

Fringe Benefits   In addition to monetary wages, unions have long sought to gain nonmonetary fringe benefits, such as insurance plans, pension plans, health services, and other such benefits. While the employee tends to regard fringe benefits as nonmonetary rewards, the employer sees them as a dollar cost just like wages, for they all cost him money. The cost of fringe benefits today is not inconsequential.

Work Standards and Rates   The establishment of wage rates would have little meaning if the amount of work to be done for the wages was left undetermined. Unions have been rather adamant in establishing modest work standards. Management is often incensed over what it feels to be relatively low levels of productivity.

If you are the union negotiator, what basis do you use to decide what will be a fair rate of work for your members? Why is this basis generally unacceptable to employers?

Not only is quantity of work established in the contract, but quality of work must also be considered, for if the workers do not do a workmanlike job on the product, it is worse than no work at all. The employer and the union must agree on what will be an acceptable quality of work, for if a worker does not meet the contractual standards he is subject to dismissal.

Union Membership   Particularly in the early days of unionism, employers and union leaders argued vehemently over the relationships of the employer, union, and the workers. Unions wanted a *closed shop,* meaning that the employer could only hire men who already were members of the union. If the potential employee did not belong to the union, he could not be hired; he had to join the union before employment. Moreover, unions wanted the employer to deduct union dues from the employee's wages and give them to the union—act as the union's collection agency. Employers were noticeably unenthusiastic about performing this *"check off"* function. In a *union shop,* the employer can hire a nonunion worker, but the worker must join the union after employment.

In an *open shop* the worker can belong to the union or not, as he prefers. The employer will in no way force the man to join the union. Employers traditionally preferred the open shop and many state legislatures gave legal voice to their desires by passing so-called right-to-work laws. These laws usually stated that a man would not be forced to join a union if he did not wish to do so.

Upon what grounds do union leaders object to an open shop? (Hint: Union leaders call nonunion workers in such open shops "freeloaders.")

Jurisdiction   Often an employer has to negotiate with many unions, each of which governs one type of work. There is the plumbers' union, the carpenters' union, the Teamsters' Union, and so on—all of which seems relatively simple. But suppose there is an automatic garbage disposal unit to be installed. Who does it, the electrician or the plumber? Can the plumber hook it up electrically? To the outsider, these jurisdictional disputes are purely trivial, petty, senseless, and downright infuriating; to the union, they are extremely sensitive issues.

Why do the unions jealously protect the work over which they have jurisdiction? Why do they really care who hooks up that garbage disposal unit?

Where employers deal with a multitude of trade unions, the matter of jurisdiction over types of work must be settled by contractual negotiation. These jurisdictional disputes were one of the big weaknesses of the trade-union form of organization. The advent of the industrial union, in which all of the workers in a plant or an industry are organized within one union, greatly diminished such jurisdictional disputes.

Injustices—Grievance Procedures   Workers have always wanted a system by which they could obtain redress for injustices on the job. Consequently, labor contracts establish procedures and organizations by which workers and union management can file grievances against the employer for some alleged violation of the terms of the contract. These grievance procedures can become quite involved, leading all the way up to arbitration if they cannot be settled at lower levels. Many labor contracts provide that disputes arising under the contract be settled by a process of arbitration, rather than through the costly, time-consuming process of resorting to the court system. What usually happens in arbitration is that labor selects an arbitrator, the employer selects an arbitrator, these two arbitrators select a third arbitrator, and the three hear the dispute much as a court would, only with greatly relaxed rules of evidence and procedure. The arbitrators then try to arrive at a fair and equitable decision on the matter. Most contracts provide that the decision of the arbitration board is binding on both parties.

Can an employer file a grievance against a worker or the union?

Mediation is a different matter. A mediator is a third party, neither union nor management, who acts as a labor expert trying to bring both sides together in agreement.

His thoughts are not binding on either party; he is just an advisor. The U.S. Department of Labor frequently furnishes a mediator in labor disputes in the hope of settling them sooner.

Union Organization

The Knights of Labor, founded in 1869, achieved a membership in excess of 700,000 by 1886, but was rendered ineffective by serious discord among its members. Some factions had revolutionary goals, wanting the government to take over the ownership and management of most significant economic institutions. Other factions were more interested in improving their own economic well-being and remained unimpressed with the government's ability to manage anything properly.

In 1881 a few craft unions formed the Federation of Organized Trades and Labor Unions; these merged with the dissident Knights of Labor groups in 1886 to form the American Federation of Labor under the direction of Samuel Gompers.

Gompers had a concept of organizing all of the workers of the world into one, huge union, but his ideals gave way to the more classical idea of unionism, in which each separate trade or craft organized its own union. There were unions representing the carpenters, plumbers, electricians, hod carriers, bricklayers, and so forth. Most of these independent unions were united at the top level of management under the banner of the American Federation of Labor (A.F. of L.). It was not at all unusual for a contractor to have to deal with ten or twenty unions on a job, which gave him great difficulties. The jurisdictional disputes between these various trade unions were notorious and infuriating, as each union vied with the other for greater power and more jurisdiction over the work. Much of this interunion bickering over the work was at the expense of the employer, who really did not care who did the work as long as someone did.

Beginning in the early 1930s, a different concept of unions was brought forth under the title, "Congress of Industrial Organizations" (CIO), in which unions were formed to organize entire companies or industries rather than trades, thereby simplifying things for both labor and management. From labor's point of view, the resulting union theoretically would be stronger, and from management's point of view it would be dealing with just one union rather than twenty.

For years the A.F. of L. fought the CIO in various organizing battles, but the top leadership joined forces in 1955 to form the AFL-CIO. To look at the basic structure of unions from the grassroots level, let us examine a small company that has expanded—the hypothetical Farm Implements Company.

It was started as a small manufacturer of farm equipment twenty years ago by two enterprising young men who hired ten workers with whom they worked closely and shared many pains and joys. As their business prospered, they hired more workers. As the enterprise enlarged the two managers grew more remote from their workers and more insensitive to their needs. They no longer knew them personally and had ceased working directly with them. There was some general dissatisfaction among the work force over a number of things, and a few of the men decided that they should unionize, though they didn't know how to go about it. One man, having had some experience with unions, called the auto worker's union in Detroit and said that he would like to talk with an organizer. The organizer from union headquarters arranged to meet with the group, and he outlined for them the legal procedures necessary to unionize the company and form what is known as a "local."

In similar situations certain legal formalities are prescribed. An election must be held among all of the firm's workers to determine if the majority wants to organize a union. Sometimes they must vote to select which union they want to represent them, if more than one union is trying to organize the plant.

The chain of command is this: the individual worker belongs to the local chapter, which usually has a number, such as Local 307. The local chapter belongs to a particular union, such as the United Automobile Workers, which in turn belongs to the overall national group, the AFL-CIO. So there are three levels of union organization: the local chapter, the parent organization, and the national organization. Each has its own management hierarchy. The local has its officers, the parent union has its officers and, of course, the national organization has its official structure.

Why have local unions felt it necessary to become members of larger, national organizations?

Union politics have been quite volatile, as various union leaders have formed alliances with one another and discarded them for varying reasons. It would serve little purpose at this point to try to outline in detail the present alignments, for by the time the book was published they would probably be outdated. This knowledge is something one has to acquire at the time he is involved with it.

In theory, union organization is completely democratic, in that the members elect their officers. The evidence indicates that in practice such democracy is not always realized.

But let us return to the Farm Implements Company and its labor problems. After the necessary legal work was completed, the National Labor Relations Board supervised an election as described above: all of the company's production workers voted on whether or not they wanted a union to represent them in negotiations with management, and, if so, which union (if more than one was trying to organize the company's work force).

The result was a disappointing setback for management, who had been confident of defeating the organizers. The workers voted to join the United Auto Workers of America. A local was formed, and another management learned of unions.

Union Problems

Like any institution, unions have their problems, of which a few are governmental relationships, internal management, growth, automation, pensions, and worker discipline.

Governmental Relationships   History clearly tells the unions that their existence depends upon a favorable legislative environment. Without protective statutes, labor is well aware that its position would be extremely precarious. For this reason, unions zealously guard the gains they have won and are continually pushing for additional protections. Since governmental relationships are extremely important to their well-being, unions are quite active in politics.

Internal Management   Again, like every institution, the unions also have management problems. Unions, in their own right, are big businesses handling millions of dollars annually, and they are run by professional staff people much as any corporate business. They have all the managerial problems of a large corporation.

Growth   Union membership grew rapidly in the 1930s and 1940s, but has plateaued in recent years. Many unions have actually lost members, and this worries them. The industries and companies that were ripe for organization were unionized quite early in the game. As the union movement continued to grow, unionizing became increasingly difficult, because the remaining nonunion companies were consciously trying to maintain good relations with their workers. Today the union movement is looking worriedly around for new fields to conquer. They have gazed longingly at the huge white-collar work force and made sporadic attempts to unionize them, but these attempts have largely met failure.

Why have unions been unsuccessful in organizing salesmen and office workers?
Would engineers in large aerospace firms be likely targets for unionization?

Automation   In a very real sense, the members of many unions face a loss of their jobs; they are being automated out of work. You do not need a welder to operate an automatic welding machine. You do not need a machinist to push the buttons on a computer that runs an automated turret lathe. The fork lift truck replaced a great many strong men. What happens to members of the construction trade on the day that houses are built in factories rather than on the building site? Perhaps this is the biggest problem facing most unions: what to do about automation. Although they want to protect the jobs of their workers from the impact of automation, most union leaders are realistic enough to know that while they will be able to delay automation for a few years, ultimately it must become a reality; they can only buy a little time.

As a union leader, what would you try to do to lessen the impact of
automation on your members?

Pensions   The advent of significant pension programs administered by the union has created a problem in the management of those funds. After some years of experience, it now appears that some union funds have been badly mismanaged—the money could have been put to work for a much higher wage. It is ironic that although union leaders are able to get top dollar wages for their members, they have not been able to get top dollar for the employment of their money.

Worker Discipline Unseen by the average individual is the great amount of work involved in seeing that workers abide by the terms of the labor contract. A responsible labor union leader expects the employer to live up to the terms of the contract, and he also expects his union members to live up to their end of the bargain. A *wildcat strike,* one unauthorized by the union, is a headache to union leadership, for it destroys their power to bargain with the employer. Why should an employer sit down to negotiation with a union leader who cannot control his membership? Of what value is a contract that is not observed by all parties?

MANAGEMENT AND LABOR LOOK AT EACH OTHER

The feelings of both labor and management vary widely, industry by industry and company by company, depending upon their previous conflicts with one another. In some situations, management and labor have had such a protracted struggle over many issues that bitter hostility exists on both sides. A few famous labor battles have lasted for years—a union fighting a management adamant in its opposition to unionization; but such attitudes are a rarity these days. In some situations the union and management are cordial, but again, these situations are rare.

In the more typical case, management resists tenaciously what it considers to be increasing encroachment by the union upon its managerial prerogatives. Originally management believed that it was its prerogative to tell workers what work they should perform, how much work they should do, and the conditions under which it would be done. Management has greatly resented the union's limitations upon these rights. It tends to regard union leaders as considering only the welfare of their members, to the detriment of the company. In general, management regards labor as being anti-management in stubbornly opposing many of management's plans for innovation and improvement in worker productivity. Managers resent being unable to discipline workers as they see the need; they resent the union's seemingly tolerant and lax attitudes toward workers. Particularly frustrating to management is the inability of some union leaders to control completely the behavior of their members, as evidenced by wildcat strikes and other behavior not sanctioned by the labor contract.

Labor's Viewpoint

Some union leaders have had such prolonged bitter experiences in dealing with management that their attitudes are quite hardened. The ardent union leader tends to regard management as being solely interested in profiting at the expense of labor. He tends to see the prosperity of management and the well-being of the company in relationship to his members, and he wants a larger cut of the pie. He is convinced that management would love to get rid of the union and would go to great lengths to do so, that management is constantly trying to get more work out of labor for the same pay, that management really does not care about the welfare of its workers, and that all of the gains hard-won by labor in the past four decades would be swept away quickly if management could only find legal ways to do so. In short, the union man is suspicious of almost everything management wants to do; he tends to interpret almost every action as being in some devious way antilabor.

Occasionally situations exist in which management and unions have a healthy relationship with each other and each accurately perceives the role of the other in the system.

What are the relative roles of union and management in the business situation?

ABOUT STRIKES

Strikes deserve special discussion, for they are most significant economic happenings. The casual reader of the newspaper or the man in the street seldom gives much thought to labor strikes unless they inconvenience him in some way—his garbage is left on the curb or he is unable to find a taxi. But the economic consequences of a strike to both the company and the worker can be most serious; real hardships develop in a prolonged strike. In the case of a strike against a major company, even the economy is affected. The 1970 General Motors strike was felt widely in lower total payrolls in twenty-four states. Automobile economists estimated the cost of the strike to be $50 million each day.

Why should a strike at General Motors have such a widespread impact?

Rather typically, the man in the street reacts by wondering, "Why in the world are they striking? They will never get back the money they are losing by being out of work!" And in some instances that is correct; the workers suffer irrecoverable losses, but so do the employers. Then why strike? Seems like economic insanity! In a manner of speaking, perhaps it is, but one has to understand the basics of negotiation to understand strikes.

Negotiation is a mockery if both parties are not free to walk out—or, to put it in reverse, one has little bargaining power if he is forced to make an agreement. The strike is labor's ultimate weapon if logical and verbal persuasion fails; labor's real threat in negotiations is its power to withhold its services. If labor is forced to work, then the employer has little need to bargain realistically. Conversely, employers feel that they must be free to "lock out" workers if the situation seems to dictate it.

Why do employers sometimes "lock out" their workers? What advantage is gained if the firm prevents workers from working if they are willing to do so?

Real philosophical problems arise when the workers are engaged in activities considered vital to the public interest. Should policemen strike? How about public school teachers? Garbage collectors? If such workers are not allowed to strike, then how do they enforce their wage demands?

What would happen if the Teamsters closed down the entire trucking industry by strike?

Existing federal legislation (Taft-Hartley) gives the President power to call an 80-day cooling off period, thereby delaying a strike for awhile, when he feels that it is in the nation's best interest to do so. Most presidents have been extremely reluctant to use this power. In a few instances the government has moved in with federal or state troops to do critical work, as was the case in the Postal Workers strike in 1970. Labor reacts strongly to such government intrusions into the bargaining process.

What is the purpose of the 80-day delay?
Why is labor so opposed to government intervention in labor disputes?

So far we have not yet developed any method or technique to replace the strike as a bargaining tool, but we badly need one!

Have any suggestions?

Wildcat Strikes

"Did you hear? They fired Old Joe down in plating; claimed he was drinking on the job! Let's hit the bricks, boys!" Such is the stuff that wildcat strikes are made of! A wildcat strike is an unauthorized walkout of unionized workers; a group of workers feels it has been given reason to strike regardless of the union's position. The facts may have been that (1) drinking on the job was in violation of the union's contract and was agreed upon as a valid reason for dismissal, and (2) Old Joe was drinking on the job. But his fellow workers may have other feelings about the matter and take things into their own hands.

Union leaders, while not approving of wildcat strikes, must handle the situation carefully, lest they alienate their membership. A wildcat strike is usually a violation of the union contract; some employers have tried to place penalty provisions in contracts to make the union responsible for financial damages caused by unauthorized walkouts, but they have had little success in doing so.

Conclusion

The importance of personnel and labor relations has grown immensely during the past forty years, as enterprises have grown in size and society has become increasingly interested in the welfare of the workers.

The personnel department performs several important functions: recruiting and selection of employees, training, wage studies, time and motion studies, labor relations, work records, and termination procedures.

Unionization deserves separate study because of its unique aspects and its critically important impact on business operations. Unions and the workers' attitudes toward them can only be understood when we study them in historical perspective, taking account of the workers' problems in the early part of the twentieth century.

PART

6

FINANCE

MONEY makes the mare go. At least that is the old saying. Many businessmen will testify to its validity. Good ideas, sound productive systems, and excellent marketing organizations have been severely hampered—or worse—for lack of funds. It takes money to finance operations, buy goods, make things. Money is invested in goods every inch of the way from the fields or mines into your home. Somebody has his money tied up not only in the products but in the organizations, factories, and distributive efforts continually. And it all costs money. Money is a commodity that is bought and sold, and its price is interest. Pay too much for funds and your costs are too high. Refuse to pay enough and you won't get any money.

And where does one find money? That is the art of the financier—locating money with which to operate. Learn to tap the money market adroitly and you will always be in demand.

18 Money systems

Since money is an important factor common to all institutions and processes in our system, you should understand it thoroughly. One way or another it will be a continual problem to you the rest of your life. You will either have too much or not enough of it—both are problems.

THE FUNCTIONS OF MONEY

From primitive times man has sought convenient ways to exchange the things he made for the things he needed. He sought some method of measuring the value of what he produced. Men who produced more than they immediately needed wanted to save their excess production for future use. Through a slow process of trial and error, a money system was fashioned that performed the three basic functions of money: a medium of exchange, a standard of value, and a store of value.

Money—The Medium of Exchange

An adequate supply of money is mandatory to lubricate the economy. If the money supply is inadequate, transactions are severely hampered for lack of it. During certain traumatic times in our history the money supply failed this purpose. In the early 1930s actions by the banking community shrank the money supply drastically in the face of an urgent need for it, thereby contributing to an economic panic, which ultimately forced the banks to close for a time in 1933. Again in the early 1970s the government deliberately limited the expansion of the money supply in an attempt to control inflation, thereby greatly hampering transactions in certain fields, such as home building, for money simply was not available to finance such activities.

Money—The Store of Value

If money is to perform its function successfully, it must act as an effective store of value. You work hard for your money. No money system is very attractive if it allows the value of what you earned to evaporate over time through no fault of your own. The value of money can diminish over time either through inflation or by governmental edict or confiscation. People's confidence in a money supply will quickly evaporate, once they suspect that it fails to serve as a good store of value. One reason why most of the world's rich people keep their wealth in either Swiss francs or American dollars is that over the last 40 years only these two currencies have been a reasonable store of value. All other currencies have been badly debased, including the once-exalted British pound, which has been devalued from $4.80 per pound to $2.40.

Money—The Standard of Value

After days of diligent work you complete a fine wooden chest-of-drawers with which you intend to obtain some food. How much is that chest worth? How can you communicate your idea of its value to a potential buyer? You might barter for the food you need, but that poses serious problems.

Barter

Barter is defined as the direct exchange of one product or service for another product or service; no money is involved. Although it was widely used in primitive times and is still used to a limited extent today where money is scarce, it is a most cumbersome way of making an exchange. Long ago we discovered that we were wasting considerable time and effort seeking to make trades—time much better spent making more goods.

What are the limitations of the barter system?

Clearly, some standard of value is required so that you can measure and communicate to others the value of your produce. Call it dollars, pounds, francs, marks, rubles, yen, pesos, spengoolies, or what have you, an economy must have some monetary unit to serve as a standard of value, a common denominator in terms of which all things of value can be rated.

HISTORICAL DEVELOPMENT OF MONEY

Money has traversed four identifiable stages. First came the commodity money stage, then the development of specie money, largely gold or silver. Slowly evolving from the gold standard was paper money, which in modern times has formed the backbone of most money systems. In recent years, demand deposits and credit systems have come to fore in lieu of paper.

Commodity Money

The barter system was gradually replaced by commodity money. Values were established for staple commodities, such as salt, tea, or grain, that could be measured or counted and that had widespread acceptance among the populace because of their intrinsic value. Such commodities served the purpose of money, but they were extremely cumbersome to handle as well as difficult to store over long periods.

Concept of Value

> The old Greek philosophers saw that an item had two values: value in use and value in exchange. Millions of words written on the theory of value by economists since that time have added to this basic idea. If a good has more value to you in use than in exchange, you will keep it, and vice versa. The value of something in exchange is what it will buy in the market—more precisely, the utilities to you of what it will bring. Value is a most personal concept; values are determined in the mind and are unique to the individual. What is of value to one person may be valueless to another.

Specie—Metal Money

As a substitute for commodities, we turned to the use of metals, for these had a much-needed permanence, particularly gold and silver. A standard of value could be assigned to them, they could be stored for future use, and they could be divided into convenient portions to form different values.

The Gold Standard   Rather early in the history of Western civilization gold became a widely recognized metal money common to all economic systems. Most money systems were on gold standards; that is, the monetary unit of the realm was pegged at being worth a certain weight of gold. The U.S. dollar was pegged at $35 per ounce.[1]

---

[1] This price for gold was made largely academic in August, 1971, when the U.S. ceased selling gold for that price to foreign banks, thus the value of the dollar was cut loose from gold and allowed to "float"—find its own relationship to other currencies. Great pressure is now (December, 1971) being exerted on the U.S. by other nations to raise the price of gold, perhaps to $38.00 per oz.

By this means the currencies of all nations were linked together through a common standard. This situation still generally prevails in international trade, but things have become immensely more complex—and the complexities are far beyond the scope of our present discussion.

Bimetallic Standard   When the big silver mines of the West began pouring out tons of that metal, the U.S. went on a bimetallic standard—both gold and silver. The dollar was defined in terms of weight of either gold or silver. Only in recent years has the Treasury Department pulled the peg on silver prices and allowed the commodity to find its own price in a free market.

What was the result of freeing the price of silver? Why was it done?

The use of silver as specie did accomplish something other than making millionaires out of silver mine owners. It vastly increased the supply of metal available for money at a time when it was needed to fuel economic growth.

Gold and silver had three distinct disadvantages as servants of a growing and prospering nation. First, they were too scarce to serve adequately as an economic lubricator. Second, as inflation required larger and larger sums with which to do business, they became too inconvenient to carry around. The bulk of metals required to finance large business transactions posed serious transportation problems. Finally, the problems of protecting gold and silver physically from theft were not inconsequential.

Why are men of means in other nations so concerned with gold and the valuation of foreign currencies?

Paper Money

For more than two centuries people tenaciously resisted paper money. The Continental Congress issued a form of paper money to finance operations during the Revolutionary War, but people had little confidence in the ability of the government to redeem it, and it sold at tremendous discounts, thereby proving its poor quality as money.

During the Civil War greenbacks were issued but again people resisted them tenaciously, for they were highly suspicious of paper money, such was the strong faith in gold. People still did not have sufficient faith and confidence in the government that they were willing to accept the greenbacks as equivalent to gold. And for good reason, for if you were on the wrong side of the Civil War and accepted Confederate money in payment, just what did you have at the end of the war? Paper money is no better than the government that issues it.

Slowly the American people came to believe that the federal government was here to stay, and they grew more willing to accept its paper as money. But in the meantime, many banks were free to issue paper money. Such money was nothing more than a promissory note, in which the bank agreed to pay the bearer a certain number of dollars in specie upon presentation of that note at the bank. Naturally, the value of such bank money was no better than the people's confidence in the bank that issued it. There were a great many frauds by banks of less than top stature.

Nonetheless, the tradition of banks' issuing money carries over to the present, for technically the federal government does not issue the money supply you commonly use. Most of the dollars in your pockets are Federal Reserve Notes issued by the Federal Reserve Banking System, not by the federal government. Through appropriate federal legislation these Federal Reserve Notes are given all the legal stature of currency issued by the government. Nevertheless, the fact remains that our money system is created entirely by the private banking system as regulated by the semipublic Federal Reserve Banking System.

Why doesn't the U.S. government issue money directly?

At one time the federal government issued United States Notes and also silver certificates. Not very long ago practically all of the $1 bills in circulation were silver certificates, each being a note promising that a bank would give the bearer of that note one silver dollar upon demand. The paper simply was a symbol to stand for a silver dollar. Similarly, before the United States went off the gold standard in 1933, the federal government issued gold certificates that the bearer could exchange at a bank for a twenty dollar gold piece. These forms of money have all but vanished today except from the realm of the coin collectors, as their rarity has raised their market value far beyond their face value.

Today the average man unquestioningly accepts the paper money in circulation, unmindful of the long history of trials and tribulations that made it feasible.

Demand Deposits

While currency is used for a wide variety of small transactions, in dollar volume most money payments in our system are made by checks drawn on demand deposits. Eighty percent of our total money supply at the beginning of 1972 was in the form of demand deposits.

A demand deposit is a deposit of money—either currency, coin, or checks drawn on other demand deposits—that you have given to a bank to be held in account for you and upon which you may write checks. A check is simply a written order to your bank to pay from your demand deposit a specified sum of money to the party presenting the check.

The demand deposit is unlike the time deposit or savings account, against which you do not have the right to draw checks and from which technically you may not be able to withdraw your money upon demand.

Credit

The United States is now on the threshold of forming a new money system—credit. It is entirely feasible that someday there will be no paper or metal currency in circulation, but rather all transactions will be handled on a credit basis through the use of a vast computer network. To buy something, you will present your credit identification card to the seller; he will put it in a machine that will immediately transfer the amount of purchase from your account to his without your having to write a check or pay him money.

The credit money system is technically feasible now, but it fails to meet security requirements. The opportunities to counterfeit, embezzle, and cheat are so large that the system will remain unworkable until a foolproof method is developed to prevent criminals from beating the game.

The Concept of Money

Neither paper money nor demand deposits have any real value as commodities. Intrinsically, a $100 bill is just a piece of paper with some ink on it; its only intrinsic value is as a piece of paper, and that value has been diminished by the ink. Then why is it valuable? Deposits are merely book entries. What then makes these instruments—checks or paper money—acceptable at face value in payment of all debts?

The $100 bill is worth $100 because of the power of the federal government to make it so. By law, the $100 bill is legal tender that must be accepted in payment of all debts, public and private, and is acceptable at face value for payment of all taxes. By law, one knows that the $100 bill is good for a $100 credit against his tax bill. He knows that if he owes a man $100, the creditor must accept the $100 bill in payment of that debt, and if he refuses to do so he cannot enforce his claim in court, for the courts most assuredly will recognize the $100 bill as payment in full of the debt. The fact is that the $100 bill is worth $100 because the law says it is and because the government is sufficiently powerful to make that pledge stick.

The true value of the $100 bill is another matter, a matter determined by the price levels in the economy. The real source of money's value is neither its commodity content nor what people think stands behind it. Money is like anything else; it derives its value from its usefulness. Its usefulness is its ability to command goods and services, a command it permits its holder to be constantly ready to exercise. How much money is needed depends upon the total volume of transactions in the economy at any time and the amount of money individuals and businesses want to keep on hand to take care of unexpected or future transactions.

REQUIREMENTS OF A GOOD MONEY SYSTEM

Just what is a good money system? Obviously one must develop one if he wishes to have a sound and healthy economy. But what constitutes such a system?

Stability

A good money system must have a stable value. Since 1933, the U.S. has tried to peg the value of the dollar by relating it to a fixed amount of gold. The government stipulated that it would buy or sell gold for $35 an ounce. (U.S. citizens cannot legally own gold.) In August, 1971, the government suspended gold sales to protect its gold supply, which for a number of years had been dwindling to a dangerously low level because of an unfavorable balance of payments.[2]

Despite pressures on the value of the dollar and occasional calls upon the U.S. to increase the price of gold (devalue the dollar) the government steadfastly

[2] In May of 1971 a group of speculators in Europe decided that they would rather have their money in German marks than in U.S. dollars, so they began selling dollars for marks, causing consternation in the world's money markets. The basic cause of their disillusionment with the dollar was our continuing inflation and unfavorable balance of payments which has flooded foreign banks with dollars.

maintained the price of gold at $35 an ounce as a matter of international financial policy. Since much of the world's trade was done in dollars and the world's financial institutions were big owners of dollars, it was necessary to give that world currency as much stability as possible. People are reluctant to do business in a currency whose value is unstable. When the government stopped selling gold for $35 an ounce in August, 1971, it pulled the peg on the value of the dollar in foreign markets.

Stability also refers to price levels, for money and prices are inseparably married to each other. While the dollar may be pegged to gold in the international markets, that is of little consequence to the American citizen, for he cannot legally own gold. He is concerned with the amount of goods and services he can buy with his dollars, and that has been declining with inflation. A good money system requires a stable price level, for if inflation is rampant, the value of money drops rapidly, thereby voiding money's function as a store of value.

Moreover, it was our inflation that was the strong force which caused our unfavorable balance of trade. As U.S. prices rose relative to the prices of goods produced by other nations, more foreign goods were bought and fewer U.S goods were sold, here and abroad. Hence, in reality, inflation had been devaluing the dollar for years; the government just officially recognized the fact in 1971.

Legal Backing

A good money system must have the backing of a government that is able to enforce its laws and whose continued existence is a widely accepted fact. It is difficult to have a good money system when the government that issues it is in jeopardy.

Protection—Security

Criminals are attracted to money as bears to honey. Wherever there is money, there will be a considerable endeavor to obtain it by criminal shortcuts. Historically, counterfeiting has been the most direct route. Unless a government has the ability to protect its money supply from counterfeiters, that money system will fail. Consequently, counterfeiting is regarded by most governments as a most serious offense against the state.

Is credit money?

Exchangeability

A good money system must facilitate exchanges. It must be convenient to use. The American system has created checking accounts in preference to currency for reasons of convenience.

THE BANKING SYSTEM

While we do not have a government bank per se, still our private banking system has many aspects of a quasi-public utility, for it is not only heavily regulated by both the state and federal governments but also it is supported by them in many ways. The institution created to accomplish this regulation and support is known as the Federal Reserve System, the central bank to which all significant commercial banks belong.

Banks

Banks are the focal point of economic activity. Few transactions in our system do not flow through the banking system in one way or another. More and more, the banks have become the chief instrument in determining the money supply.

While early banks were largely custodians of gold, charging customers for storing it, today's banks perform a wide range of financial services for their customers. They provide checking accounts, thereby creating a money mechanism more convenient to use than currency; they establish savings accounts on which interest is paid; they lend money, act as trustees, perform escrow services, buy and sell foreign exchange, maintain safety deposit vaults for the physical protection of assets, and offer many other small financial services needed by the public. Indeed, the role of the bank in today's business world is so critical that the businessman prizes his banking connections. The firm that has excellent banking connections has a tremendous advantage over competitors in that it can raise needed money quicker and more cheaply.

Early banking in the United States was a rather frightening experience; it was replete with bank failures, runs on banks, money panics, and outright fraud. Not without reason were our grandparents and their forebears highly suspicious of banks; it was not at all uncommon to find people who refused to trust their wealth to a banker, preferring to bury it in the ground somewhere. Such was people's confidence in our early banks.

Theoretically, a banking system should be able to expand or contract the money supply according to the demands of business. The ability of the commercial banks, through the lending process, to expand or contract the money supply should provide the funds needed for financing business activity. Early commercial banks, however, while they could expand credit money somewhat, could not add much to the amount of available money, inasmuch as their depositors had a legal right to withdraw all of their money in the form of currency or coin at any time: thus these banks were forced to provide for ordinary withdrawals by retaining a large part of their deposits as a cash reserve.

What role did transportation and communications play in determining a bank's cash reserves?

These cash reserves usually consisted of currency and coin and deposits in other nearby banks. However, if there was a general demand by depositors for their money at a time when deposits created by loans were high, the currency available might not cover the withdrawal demands. Any unusual demand by depositors forced the banks to seek ways of converting these assets into currency. An attempt by one bank to obtain currency by withdrawing its reserve cash from another bank usually resulted in a shortage of currency throughout the entire system, for the other bank was probably experiencing similar withdrawals, as panic may have been widespread. A bank facing unusual withdrawals and finding itself unable to convert its assets into currency was forced to close. Many banks that were closed could have converted their assets into currency if allowed sufficient time, but insistent demands of depositors had not allowed them that time.

What happens when a bank is forced to convert long-term assets into cash on short notice?
Why do banks invest largely in government bonds?

A widespread closing of banks invariably brought on a depression. These high demands for withdrawals were called money panics or runs on the bank. One that occurred in 1907 set into motion a congressional study of our money system. The investigating commission found that almost all sound, stable money systems that could expand or contract to meet the needs of the economy had some form of central bank, which had the power to issue a currency that depositors had to accept. Consequently, in 1913 Congress created the Federal Reserve System to remedy the deficiencies in our previous banking system.

Federal Reserve System

The Federal Reserve Act, which created the Federal Reserve System, established twelve regional Federal Reserve banks, the capital stock of which is owned by the member banks in each district. However, the member banks do not control the Federal Reserve System; control is vested in the Board of Governors. The Federal Reserve is operated in the public interest and its authority can be changed by act of Congress. The law requires that all national banks be members of the Federal Reserve System; state banks may join if they desire.

Why are banks' investments in real estate limited to 10 percent of their deposits?
Why can a bank lend to any one party only 10 percent of its capitalization? Of what significance is this to a borrower?

The operating policies of each Federal Reserve bank are established by its board of directors, of whom six are elected by member banks and three are appointed by the Board of Governors. In order to give more segments of the economy a voice, the number of bankers on each board is limited to three; the other six members are expected to bring to each board a wide range of experience and opinion. The seven men who comprise the Board of Governors are appointed by the President and confirmed by the Senate. Political pressures on these men are relieved by making their terms of appointment 14 years, with the terms staggered. No two members of the Board may be from the same Federal Reserve District.

The Federal Reserve System and the Government The federal government uses the services of the Federal Reserve banks as private citizens use the services of their commercial banks.

The Director of Internal Revenue deposits all tax monies with the Federal Reserve banks. Other governmental agencies, such as the Postal Service, also have deposit accounts. All checks drawn on the Treasury of the United States are payable at any Federal Reserve bank. Hence, the Federal Reserve banks handle the bank accounts of the federal government.

The federal government is a big borrower of money, so the Treasury must sell its various promises-to-pay in the money market. These promises or evidences of debt have different names, depending upon the length of time the money is to be borrowed. One obligation, called a Treasury Bill, is usually payable in 91 days. Another, the Certificate of Indebtedness, is payable in one year or less. A Treasury Note is payable in five years or less, while the Treasury Bond is usually payable in more than five years. The series of Savings Bonds sold primarily to small investors also is part of the Treasury's borrowing program. When the Treasury borrows money or repays it, the Federal Reserve banks take care of the clerical work. So the Federal Reserve banks are the mechanism by which the federal government taps the money market and repays it.

The Providing of Currency and Coin   One of the most important functions of the Federal Reserve banks is to provide its members with currency and coin. When a member bank finds it needs additional currency to supply its customers, it orders such cash to be sent from its reserve account in its Federal Reserve bank. When a member bank accumulates more currency than it needs, it deposits it with its Federal Reserve bank. Note that the currency notes in your billfold are Federal Reserve Notes; that is, they are obligations of the regional Federal Reserve bank designated on the paper. The Treasury Department's Bureau of Engraving and Printing is only the printer of the currency; the Federal Reserve Banks are the issuers.

Collection of Checks   About ten billion checks are written annually to pay for goods and services. Remember that a check is a written order to a bank to pay a sum of money to the bearer. Those receiving checks want payment as quickly as possible, for any delay postpones the time when they can use the funds. When a check is received in the immediate area of the bank on which it is drawn, the process in presenting for payment is simple. If Dudley Doowright gives you a check for $100 ordering his bank, Hooterville National, to pay you the funds, you can take that document to Hooterville National and, after proper identification, they will pay you $100 in currency if you so demand. Not very many checks are cashed in such a manner.

More typically, you will take Dudley's check to your bank, the First National Bank of Hooterville, and deposit it in your account, so you now have $100 more in your checking account; no currency exchange takes place. Then, through the local clearing house, the First National Bank of Hooterville presents Dudley's check to the Hooterville National. Since both banks have accounts with each other, the First National's account at Hooterville National is increased $100 and Hooterville National deducts $100 from Dudley's account. Each community with more than one bank maintains a local clearing house through which all local transactions are cleared. If you maintained your account also at Hooterville National, the accounting would be even simpler; the bank would simply put the money in your account and take it out of Dudley's—a simple bookkeeping transaction.

But suppose you don't live in Hooterville; you don't even live in the same state. Banks receiving checks drawn on other banks outside their trade area find it costly and inconvenient to send these checks directly to the banks on which they are drawn, so various systems for collecting out-of-town checks have been developed. Usually the Federal Reserve banks act as the collectors for intercommunity transactions.

The Federal Reserve banks receive millions of checks daily. Figure 18-1 shows the journey of a typical out-of-town check through the Federal Reserve System. If you examine the endorsements on the back of any check that was sent out of town, you can see the route through the Federal Reserve System the check has taken.

If the out-of-town check is between two banks in the same Federal Reserve district, then the one Federal Reserve bank can handle the bookkeeping transaction by itself. But if the check is between two banks in two different Federal Reserve districts, then two Federal Reserve banks are involved.

Regulation of Money Supply   The Federal Reserve Act provides that each member bank must have a certain percentage of its total deposits on deposit in its Federal Reserve bank. These deposits with the Federal Reserve banks are known as member banks' reserve accounts. They are used by the member bank in the same manner as an individual or business firm uses his deposit at the commercial bank, but with a difference. The law requires that the reserve account must average a certain required percentage of the member bank's total deposits. Presently that percentage is established at 17 percent for checking accounts and 5 percent for savings accounts.

Why do commercial banks prize and promote savings accounts in preference to checking accounts?

Commercial banks expand the money supply by making loans. But when a loan is made, bank deposits are increased, thereby requiring an increase in the amount of reserve held in the Federal Reserve. Therefore, the amount of excess reserves in the Federal Reserve banks puts a limitation on the ability of the commercial banks to expand the money supply by making loans. If a member bank is short of reserves, it can increase its reserve balance by borrowing from the Federal Reserve bank, for which it is charged interest. The percentage it is charged is known as the discount rate. Or the bank can sell, or rediscount, some of its assets to the "Fed."

The Federal Reserve System can increase or decrease the amount of reserves available to banks by changing, within broad limits, the percentage of deposits required as reserves. It also can regulate the amount of money available by selling or buying securities in the money market, or by raising or lowering the rediscount rate.

FIGURE 18-1: Journey of a Typical Out-of-Town Check Through the Federal Reserve System

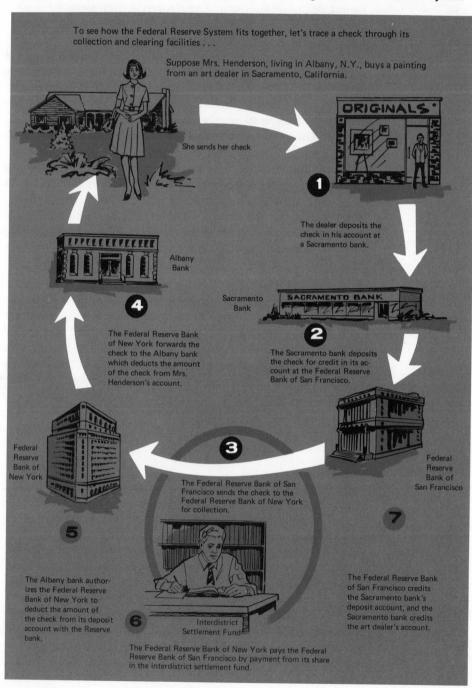

To see how the Federal Reserve System fits together, let's trace a check through its collection and clearing facilities . . .

Suppose Mrs. Henderson, living in Albany, N.Y., buys a painting from an art dealer in Sacramento, California.

She sends her check

1

The dealer deposits the check in his account at a Sacramento bank.

Albany Bank

Sacramento Bank

4

The Federal Reserve Bank of New York forwards the check to the Albany bank which deducts the amount of the check from Mrs. Henderson's account.

2

The Sacramento bank deposits the check for credit in its account at the Federal Reserve Bank of San Francisco.

Federal Reserve Bank of New York

3

The Federal Reserve Bank of San Francisco sends the check to the Federal Reserve Bank of New York for collection.

Federal Reserve Bank of San Francisco

7

5

The Albany bank authorizes the Federal Reserve Bank of New York to deduct the amount of the check from its deposit account with the Reserve bank.

6

Interdistrict Settlement Fund

The Federal Reserve Bank of New York pays the Federal Reserve Bank of San Francisco by payment from its share in the interdistrict settlement fund.

The Federal Reserve Bank of San Francisco credits the Sacramento bank's deposit account, and the Sacramento bank credits the art dealer's account.

If the Federal Reserve bank goes into the open market and buys bonds from its member banks, how does this increase the supply of money? How does the Federal Reserve System's selling bonds to commercial banks restrict the supply of money?

Figure 18-2 illustrates the controls used by the Federal Reserve System to regulate the supply of money in our economy. It operates in the money market by either buying or selling government bonds. If the Federal Reserve System buys bonds, then it must pay for them by check, thus increasing the reserve accounts of the banks from whom the bonds were purchased. If the Federal Reserve sells bonds, they must be paid for by check on the accounts of the commercial banks buying them, thus reducing their reserve accounts at the reserve bank. This increase or decrease in the reserve accounts affects the commercial bank's ability to loan money, thus changing the supply of money.

FIGURE 18-2: Controls Used by the Federal Reserve System to Regulate Money Supply

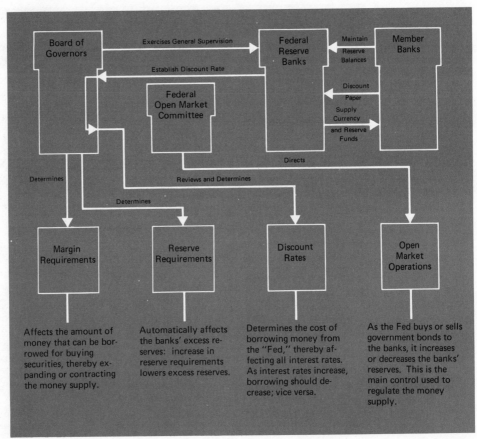

Why does the federal government leave the determination of its money supply in the hands of private parties—the commercial banks? Why not determine it by administrative edict?

GOVERNMENT CONTROL OVER THE MONEY SUPPLY

Figure 18-3 shows the impact of various factors on bank reserves, which in turn determine money supply. Anything that increases the member banks' reserves also increases the money supply; conversely, anything that decreases reserves in turn decreases the money supply. Note that ten factors under the control of the Treasury affect bank reserves.

What happens to the money supply when governmental expenditures are increased? What happens when governmental expenditures are curtailed? Assume taxes remain constant!

FIGURE 18-3: Impact of Various Factors on Bank Reserves

	Federal Reserve Banks		
	Assets	Liabilities	
		Member Bank Reserves	Other
Public Operations			
Increase in currency holdings		−	+
Decrease in currency holdings		+	−
Treasury and Foreign Operations			
Increase in Treasury deposits in F. R. Banks		−	+
Decrease in Treasury deposits in F. R. Banks		+	−
Gold purchases (inflow)	+	+	
Gold sales (outflow)	−	−	
Increase in Treasury currency outstanding	+	+	
Decrease in Treasury currency outstanding	−	−	
Increase in Treasury cash holdings	−	−	
Decrease in Treasury cash holdings	+	+	
Increase in foreign and other deposits in F. R. Banks		−	+
Decrease in foreign and other deposits in F. R. Banks		+	−
Federal Reserve Operations			
Purchase of securities	+	+	
Sales of securities	−	−	
Loans to member banks	+	+	
Repayment of loans to member banks	−	−	
Increase in Federal Reserve float	+	+	
Decrease in Federal Reserve float	−	−	
Increase in other assets	+	+	
Decrease in other assets	−	−	
Increase in other liabilities		−	+
Decrease in other liabilities		+	−
Increase in capital accounts		−	+
Decrease in capital accounts		+	−
Increase in reserve requirements		−*	
Decrease in reserve requirements		+*	

*Effect on excess reserves. Total reserves are unchanged.
Note: To the extent reserve changes are in the form of vault cash, Federal Reserve accounts are not affected.

THE MONEY MARKET

Figure 18-4 illustrates the various factors and institutions on both the supply and demand side of the money market.

FIGURE 18-4: The Money Market

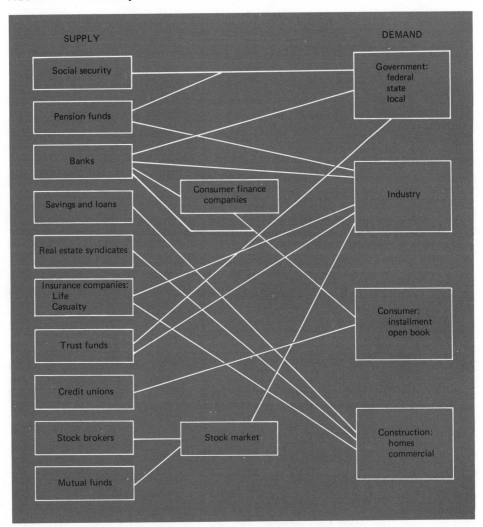

The money market is little different from any other market, in that there are people who want money and people who will supply it at a price—the interest rate. Interest is the price paid for money. It fluctuates as the balance between supply and demand varies. When demand exceeds supply, the interest rate rises, not only to ration available funds among the people most able to afford them, but also to stimulate additional savings in order to expand the supply of money.

When the supply of money exceeds demand, interest rates drop, in the hope of not only stimulating more demand for the money but also to discourage saving. The interest rate, then, is the factor that balances the demand for funds with the supply of them.

Why do interest rates rise during prosperity and drop during recessions?

The Demand Side of the Money Market

It can be seen from Figure 18-4 that the big users of money are the governments, industry, and the consumer. The governments borrow heavily in the money markets to finance fiscal operations—deficit financing. We have built most of our social capital—roads, schools, and other civic improvements—by borrowing money in the money market, using either U.S. Government Bonds or various municipal bonds as instruments of debt.

Concept of Deficit Financing

Beginning in the 1930s, the concept of deficit financing for governments became popular. Deficit financing simply means that the government spends more money than it takes in from taxes, so that it must go to the money market to borrow the difference. By spending more than it takes in, the government is putting the difference it borrows into circulation, thereby increasing the supply of money. Deficit financing is inflationary.

A fiscal surplus is the opposite of deficit financing, in that the government is taking in more money from the economy in the form of taxes than it is spending (putting back into the economy), thus curtailing the money supply: the effect is deflationary. In theory, a balanced budget is neutral.

Why was deficit financing popularized in the 1930s?

Industry borrows money heavily to use not only in financing plants and equipment but also as working capital for inventory and accounts receivable. It obtains money from the money market largely by selling common stock or bonds, or by borrowing from the banks. Lately industry has also tapped insurance companies and pension funds for money.

The consumer taps the money market for durable-goods purchases such as automobiles, homes, and other items purchased on installments.

Segmentation of the Money Market

The money market is not one large, homogeneous pool of money into which investors throw their savings and into which all users reach and grab. Most institutions on the supply side channel their money into highly specific end uses. The U.S. Government obtains its monies largely by borrowing from the commercial banks and from a few auxiliary sources, such as Social Security and some consumer savings bond sales. Industry obtains its funds from the stock and bond markets, commercial banks, insurance companies, and pension funds. Savings and loans channel most of their money directly into the consumer home-building markets. Insurance companies place their savings largely in two sectors: commercial and residential construction, and industry; they also hold a goodly amount of government debt. Pension funds place most of their money in the stock and bond markets, thereby financing industry. Credit unions finance consumer-goods purchases. Ironically, the so-called "consumer finance company" is really a middleman in the money market, for it borrows its money wholesale from commercial banks and retails it to consumers to purchase durable goods.

Intimate knowledge of potential sources of money in the money market is essential to any businessman, particularly corporate financial officers. Many little nooks and crannies of relatively untapped funds await the clever financier.

Trace the flow of your various savings through the money market to their probable end use.

THE PRICE OF MONEY

As indicated earlier, the interest rate is the price paid for money. A great deal of economic theory is connected with interest rates and their impact upon the economy. In 1970, savers enjoyed an almost unprecedentedly high interest rate, of which the users of money were all too painfully aware (Table 18-1). The reasons for this high interest rate are rather easy to understand. Naturally, one could say that interest rates are high because the demand for funds exceeds the supply of them, but one can pinpoint present-day problems more closely. The current high interest rate is a result of a combination of three forces: (1) unprecedentedly high, sustained spending by the federal government to finance the war and domestic programs, leading it to tap the money market for huge sums; (2) unparalleled demands for funds by industry to construct

Table 18-1
RANGE OF INTEREST RATES FOR VARIOUS TYPES OF DEBT

Long-term bonds	Easy-Money Low (1967)	Tight-Money High (1969–70)	JUNE 1971
U. S. Treasury	4.37%	7.21%	5.96%
Top-grade corporate	5.00%	8.60%	7.42%
Prime state and local (tax-exempt)	3.25%	6.95%	5.00%
Short-term rates			
Treasury three-month bills	3.386%	8.096%	4.213%
Treasury six-month bills	3.692%	8.101%	4.243%
Short-term notes of big corporations	4.63%	9.08%	5.38%
Short-term notes of finance companies	4.38%	8.19%	5.25%
Federal Reserve discount rate	4.00%	6.00%	5.00%
Banks' prime rate (business loans)	5.50%	8.50%	6.00%
Stock-exchange call loans	5.50%	8.50%	6.00%
Banks' loans to each other	3.35%	10.05%	4.27%
Mortgage loans			
FHA-insured loans, legal ceiling	6.00%	8.50%	7.50%
Conventional loans	6.40%	8.55%	8.30%

SOURCE: Federal Reserve Board, Moody's Investors Service, Federal Housing Administration.

new plants and equipment; and (3) a fairly steady increase in home building, absorbing even more money. The combination three-way punch quickly depleted available money supplies. Someone had to be squeezed out of the money market if supply was to meet demand, so interest rates leaped, forcing many companies to curtail their expansion plans and making it expensive for many municipalities to borrow. Many state and local governments had to forego spending plans because the interest rate had increased above their statutory limits. Many would-be homeowners were driven from the market by $8\frac{1}{2}$ to 9 percent interest rates. Thus, one could see the interest rate at work to curtail the demand for funds, bringing it into alignment with the available supply. Also, such high interest rates brought forth additional savings, for any wise investor could see the virtue of lending money at 10 percent interest; now was the time to get money placed for the long haul. Investors, starved by twenty years of receiving 3 to 4 percent on their money, relished the thought of locking in 10 percent for the next twenty-year period.

Explain the differences among the various rates of interest.

Economic Importance of Interest Rates

The interest rate determines who shall get money and who shall not. Those people or institutions whose enterprises cannot earn at least as much as the interest rate must delay their plans. If they do not stay out of the money market, they will be paying more for their funds than those funds will earn in their ventures.

In predicting the future course of interest rates, one must focus his attention upon what will happen to the demand side of the money market, for the supply side is rather stable, inasmuch as most savings are planned or forced. Your Social Security, pension fund, and insurance savings are planned for you; you save a certain amount every period regardless, for you are contractually saving money. It matters not what the interest rate does; these savings remain stable year in and year out. The interest rate will come down in the future only when demand slacks off. Either the government must quit tapping the money market so heavily, or industry will have to back out.

Concept of Marginal Efficiency of Capital

One of the basic concepts of business is that one must employ his capital for a higher return than he pays for the use of the money. When one pays 10 percent per year interest on funds, those funds must earn in excess of 10 percent, or else the venture is economically unsound. The profit earned by incremental funds invested in some enterprise is called the marginal efficiency of capital. It is the return earned on the last increment of investment. A high interest rate drives out enterprises with a low marginal efficiency of capital. A low interest rate allows many low-profit concerns to continue operation.

What relationship exists between corporate profits and the demand for money by corporations?

THE CROSS OF GOLD

Economic cynics have characterized our economy as nailed to a cross of gold. They refer to the gold-flow problem in international trade. We have been trying to free ourselves from it since we went off the gold standard domestically in 1933, but the international market will not allow us to do so. Although, rationally, gold is no different from any other commodity, in that it has a certain value to certain people for certain end uses, emotionally it is much more than that; to many people around the world, gold has almost sacred connotations. Mention the word gold and men's imaginations burn. Although many elements are far more valuable than gold, gold holds some special niche in greedy hearts that impels them to many rash acts. So we must deal in gold to satisfy the gold bugs of the world, who will have no other commodity in exchange for their goods. Of course, gold is utter economic nonsense, but so are many other things. Perhaps someday in the enlightened future we will be able to rid ourselves of the gold bug.

MONEY—THE NAME OF THE GAME

Many businessmen maintain that money is the name of the game. Those who have it, have all the powers it bestows; those who don't, spend most of their waking hours trying to correct the situation.

Certainly, money seems to be the focus of most economic efforts, though certain cavalier entrepreneurs may hold the philosophy voiced by the fictional Cash McCall: "Money itself is not important. It's just how we keep score."

There is considerable truth to Cash's statement, for throughout society we seem to look to money in determining who won or lost the game. Companies that are wealthy are regarded as successes, those whose bank accounts are low are considered failures—regardless of the intrinsic merits of their products.

Conclusion

> Economic endeavors rely on an ample supply of money—sound money. There is no such thing as a sound economic system without a sound money supply. When money turns sour, all else soon follows. A good money system provides a stable store of value, a rapid means for effecting exchanges, and safeguards against its destruction by the elements or dishonesty.
>
> The money mechanism in our society is focused in our banking system, which has the power to create and destroy money. Because of the critical role of the banks in our economy, we have regulated them closely and have put them under the control of the Federal Reserve System, which through various devices has the power to expand or contract the money supply as public policy dictates.
>
> The money market is comprised of the funds supplied by all the people and institutions who have saved money and all the people and institutions who want to use those savings in their own endeavors. We have devised a wide range of institutions to facilitate the movement of these savings into the hands of those who are willing to hire their use.
>
> Our system is now in the process of substituting a credit money system for a paper one. When a few technical difficulties are solved, paper money will become a historical curiosity.

19 Corporate finance

When you see a situation you cannot understand, look for the financial interest.
TOM L. JOHNSON

Money is the lubricator that makes things go. Without it, raw materials cannot be bought, labor cannot work on them, and the end product cannot be distributed—for money makes all these things possible. In the corporate enterprise the financing function usually rests in the hands of the controller,[1] although usually top management and the board of directors are also involved.

[1] He is sometimes called the treasurer, comptroller, or vice president of finance. The treasurer is sometimes a separate officer of the corporation, since the law requires it to have an official treasurer—who may or may not have much to do with the financial accounting function.

Why are the financing and accounting functions usually the responsibility of the same man? Need they be?

Unwise or inadequate financing can drive a firm into bankruptcy just as easily as a poor product, inept marketing, or high production costs. If one pays too much for his funds, his profits are jeopardized. If unwise sources of funds are used, the company may be financially embarrassed when the time for repayment comes around.

Adequate financing, or even redundant financing, can provide an important differential advantage to the firm in the marketplace. Manufacturers' programs for financing middlemen's inventories are increasingly influencing their buying decisions. In the computer industry, leasing has become such an important weapon that the manufacturer who cannot finance attractive leasing plans is almost uncompetitive.

In fact, some large, well-financed organizations literally buy their market positions. Investments in automated plants, adequate inventory, and huge advertising campaigns all require tremendous amounts of money that are unavailable to the small firm. The importance of finance should not be underestimated, for a great many worthy ventures have failed to become realities because the entrepreneur was unable to obtain financing.

FINANCIAL STRUCTURE AND FINANCIAL INSTRUMENTS

To the beginner, capital structure and the various financial instruments involved seem quite complicated, but in fact the subject is quite simple. There are only two basic types of financing for an enterprise: equity or debt. The principles governing their use are relatively few.

Equity

Equity is the money invested and earnings retained in a corporation by its stockholders, the people who ostensibly own it. Let's take a hypothetical company—Ideas, Inc.—and follow its financial planning from inception through several years of operation.

First, Ideas' incorporators, in their Articles of Incorporation, filed for an authorized one million shares of common stock with a par value of $1 per share. Though par value has little meaning for the man on the street or the buyer of stock on the stock market, it does have some legal significance. For example, the company must receive at least $1 for every share that it issues, either in money or in value received. Had the incorporators specified that the common stock had no par value (no-par stock), the company could issue it for whatever price it desired. The company could have sold its $1 par value stock for more than $1. (In accounting courses you will learn how this particular transaction is handled technically; there is no need for going into it at this time.)

What, other than money, can be used to pay for a company's securities?
What is the difference between authorized stock and issued stock?

The incorporators could have created several classes of common stock, such as Class A and Class B. This is usually done when the incorporators wish to give different types of investors different rights in the corporation. Sometimes one class of stock will be called voting common, whereas the other will be nonvoting. Sometimes one class of stock will have different rights in the event of liquidation or different rights to dividends. Sometimes one class of stock must be paid a certain amount of dividends before the other class may receive anything.

Some classes of stock that are given preference to dividends are called "preferred stocks"; these will be dealt with in a later section.

From the corporation's point of view, the important thing about common stock—or equity—is that *it never has to be repaid at any future date.* It is permanent, long-term capital. Moreover, the company does not have to pay dividends on the common stock unless its board of directors feels it should do so. There is no liability for the company ever to pay the common stockholder a penny. Consequently, equity presents no demands upon the corporation for capital outgo. This is most significant, for in theory it indicates when equity should be used.

Equity should be used to finance long-term, permanent investments. Equity forms the financial base for all other types of financing. Financiers refer to a "thin equity" corporation in describing one whose equity is small in relation to its debt.

Getting back to Ideas, Inc., and its one million shares of authorized stock, the directors decided that the corporation needed only $500,000 to begin operation, so they issued 500,000 shares to be sold to the public at $1 per share; 500,000 shares were left unissued. They can be sold at any time in the future by authorization of the board of directors as long as the company receives at least $1 per share in value for them. If Ideas, Inc., for some reason sees fit to repurchase part of the 500,000 shares issued, the repurchased shares become treasury stock.

What might be the difference between unissued stock and treasury stock?

If Ideas' directors find it necessary at some future date to sell more stock than the amount authorized, they will have to meet the legal provisions of the state of incorporation, which usually requires getting stockholder approval for the change in capital structure. This may be easy or difficult to do, depending upon who the stock owners are and how they react to the proposed change in capital structure.

Sometimes this expansion of authorized and issued capital stock can lead to what is known as "watering" the stock. This tactic is used by unscrupulous managements to gyp their minority stockholders. In watering stock, the management sells to one group of stockholders stock valued at $1 per share, and then subsequently sells a great deal more stock at perhaps a penny a share. A $10,000 investment at a penny a share controls the same voting rights as a $1-million investment at $1 per share. Such watering dilutes the equity of the original stockholders. The wise investor makes certain that legal provisions in the Articles of Incorporation protect him from such maneuvers.

The key to a stockholder's rights lies in the company's articles of incorporation and bylaws. These documents prescribe what management can and cannot do and what procedures it must follow to do certain things. The corporation law in the company's state of incorporation also may impose restraints, but such protection should not be counted on too heavily.

Sources of Equity   The sources of equity are many and varied. If the corporation has much promise or has been prospering, it can obtain equity funds by floating a stock issue through the traditional security underwriting system. Here, an underwriter[2] goes through the necessary legal formalities to distribute the stock through the brokerage system to interested investors throughout the nation. Unfortunately, this source of equity money is not always available. When the stock market is depressed, investors are reluctant to buy any common stock, old or new. The years 1969-70 were poor ones for selling new stock.

Lesser-known firms must look elsewhere for equity money. In very small enterprises one's own capital or that of his family usually provides the needed equity. In other situations, the entrepreneur may be able to find private parties interested in equity investments; such money is called *venture capital.*

Why would a wealthy man prefer to invest his money privately in the equity of a small corporation rather than buy stock on the New York Stock Exchange? By what means can a private investor protect himself in a small corporation?

Retained earnings form a great portion of the equity base of most large corporations today. Over the years, most companies have paid out only a small portion of their earnings as dividends; they have retained 60 to 70 percent of earnings for capital expansion. This is shown on the balance sheets as "earned surplus"—part of the corporation's equity base.

It is not unknown for small companies, unable to sell stock through an underwriter, to sell common stock by a direct public offering. This occurs mainly when the amount needed is relatively modest (under $250,000) and the proposed enterprise has some local appeal. Frequently such distributions are restricted to the residents of one state to avoid SEC regulation.

Debt

The other major source of money with which to finance operations is debt—money borrowed from other parties, such as banks, insurance companies, private investors, or the government. Debt is evidenced by instruments known as notes or bonds.

The board of directors of Ideas, Inc., decided that the corporation needed an additional $100,000 with which to finance a warehouse. Since the payback period on the warehouse was less than twenty years, the board decided to issue one hundred $1000 bonds and sell them to the public through an underwriter. After the legal technicalities had been fulfilled, the sale was made; the company agreed that in consideration

---

[2] Underwriting is usually performed by institutions referred to as stock brokerages. Many legal technicalities must be met in selling a stock issue to the public.

of being loaned $100,000 for twenty years, it would pay each bond holder 10 percent interest per year, semiannually ($50 every six months). Moreover, the company agreed to put $5000 each year into a sinking fund from which it would call (buy back) the bonds if it desired. The bonds were callable only after five years, and the bond holder had to be paid a call premium of two points—he would be paid $1020 for each bond called, plus accrued interest.

What is a payback period? How would you go about figuring one? Suppose you drive a car that gets 10 miles per gallon of fuel, and fuel costs $.40 a gallon. What is the payback period for a car costing $2500 that gets 30 miles per gallon, if you drive 25,000 miles per year?

Ideas' bonds were called *debenture bonds,* inasmuch as they were general credit obligations of the company. This means that in case of default (if the company cannot pay the interest on the principal) the bond holders have only the legal position of any other creditor. The company could have issued *mortgage bonds,* pledging certain specified property as security for the debt. In this case, if the company defaulted, the bond holders would have a preferred legal position; they could seize the pledged property to satisfy their claims. In this case the company could have mortgaged the warehouse. Perhaps they should have.

As a general rule, which are higher-grade bonds: debentures or mortgage bonds? Why? Why do companies almost universally make their bonds callable?

The flotation of a bond issue is a rather lengthy and cumbersome process, entailing a great many things that are beyond the scope of this discussion. Whenever possible, companies prefer to borrow money directly from a bank or insurance company, for it is much easier, usually cheaper, and saves the cost of selling the bond issue. However, banks rarely make a loan for longer than a few years. It would be nearly impossible to obtain a twenty-year loan from a bank unless it was secured by a real estate mortgage. Even then the banker would not be overly eager to make such a long-range commitment. Banks prefer to loan money on a one-year cycle, though they will make term loans for up to five years if the circumstances warrant it. Longer-term direct loans must usually be obtained from insurance companies or pension funds—institutions that are able to make longer-term commitments.

Why are banks reluctant to make long-term commitments? Why can insurance companies make twenty-year loans to industry?

Dangers of Debt   The key characteristics of debt and its dangers to the businessman—dangers that have been ignored all too frequently in recent years—are that the debt must be serviced (the interest must be paid) and the principal of the debt must be repaid on time, or else the company may be thrown into bankruptcy. For some odd reason, some businessmen have remained unimpressed by the fact that debt can force them into bankruptcy. Equity never can! No company has gone into bankruptcy because it could not pay dividends on its common stock, but the courts are currently littered with firms that cannot pay their debts. Debt is what gets one into financial hot water, whether he be an individual or a large corporation. Naturally, when one borrows money he always thinks he will have the money to repay the debt in the future, but Dame Fortune frequently deals unexpected cards. Since debt presents such grave dangers to the survival of a company, then one could ask why anybody borrows money. The answer is: he wants to gain leverage and keep control.

Concept of Leverage

> Leverage refers to the financial manipulation that enables the owners of a company to enhance their return on equity by borrowing funds for one rate of interest and using the money to earn a higher rate of return, keeping the difference for themselves. It is called making money by using other people's money.

Let's take two identical, hypothetical companies, each having a $1 million capital structure, though one has borrowed half its investment while the other has only equity. Both earn $200,000 profit.

	Company A	Company B
Profit	$200,000	$200,000
Equity	1,000,000	500,000
Debt		500,000
Interest (10%)		− 50,000
Left for equity	$200,000	$150,000
Rate of return on equity	$\frac{200,000}{1,000,000} = 20\%$	$\frac{150,000}{500,000} = 30\%$

By using a great amount of leverage, management can earn a handsome rate of return on small equity, and this temptation has been the largest propellant of debt in recent years. Through leverage a man can get into business on a shoestring and make a fortune on it—or go broke. The concept of leverage is fine if one can earn more on the borrowed money than it costs, but woe to the man who fails to do so, for there is also such a thing as negative leverage—that is, borrowing money at 10 percent to find that it can earn only 5 percent. The difference comes out of the stockholders' equity, so leverage can be a two-edged sword.

As the interest rate climbed to record highs, it became increasingly difficult for companies to earn enough to pay the interest and debt over the long haul. And there you have the bind in which a great many companies found themselves during 1970. They had borrowed money at a high rate of interest, only to have the recession pull their profits down below the level of the interest. Since the interest had to be paid, it represented a serious cash drain on a company at a time when it could least afford it. This caused what is known as a liquidity crisis, a crisis which quickly spread throughout the industry, for when a few firms find themselves short of cash, they sharply curtail their cash outflow—payments—to other companies, thereby creating a liquidity problem in those firms. Any significant shortage of cash in the industrial system quickly makes itself felt throughout the system. A liquidity crisis simply means that companies do not have the cash to pay their bills. The Penn Central bankruptcy is a case in point, for the company had billions of dollars in assets, but did not have the cash to pay its bills. You cannot very well send a mile of railroad track to a creditor.

Dilution of Control   Many firms, particularly closely held companies or companies in which a few people hold a significant share of the ownership, prefer to obtain money for expansion by the use of debt rather than by selling equity, because the owners do not wish to dilute their share of the ownership. When one sells stock, he may find that the new stockholders want a voice in management. Sometimes the book value of a company is so high that stockholders do not wish to relinquish their proportional claim on it by being forced to sell stock at a price less than book value.

Why would a company have to sell common stock for a price less than book value? (Think in terms of what people buy when they buy common stock. Are they buying book value or are they buying earnings?) Under what circumstances would one buy book value?

Hybrids

Earlier we said there are only two sources of corporate funds: debt and equity. One might ask, "How about preferred stock, convertible bonds, or income bonds?" Preferred stocks or convertible bonds are simply hybrids put together by an imaginative finance man to attract money. They are combinations of debt and equity.

Preferred Stock   Preferred stock is a modified form of equity in which dividends usually must be paid if earned, but the principal amount need never be repaid; it is a permanent investment—hence, equity. Usually preferred stock is callable, which makes it somewhat like bonds.

Why would a company want to make its preferred stock callable?

Preferred stock usually has no voting rights unless dividends are missed. A preferred stock on which dividends are accumulated (that is, the company owes the dividends to the preferred stockholders and cannot pay out common-stock dividends until all dividends-in-arrears are paid off) is called *cumulative preferred*. Issues that do not provide for ultimate payment of missed dividends are called *noncumulative preferreds*.

Depending upon the features incorporated in them by the board of directors, preferred stocks vary in the following ways: when dividends must be paid; what happens to missed dividend payments; voting rights; rights in liquidation; callability and call premiums; and the extent of participation in the earnings of the company.

While the typical preferred stock is paid a fixed rate of return similar to that paid bondholders, if management feels that it is necessary to let the preferred stockholder participate in the prosperity of the company, it will make the preferred stock a participating preferred. The old Bon Ami Company had a 4 percent, cumulative, fully participating after common stock had been paid $2 per share, preferred stock. For years the preferred stockholders received their regular $4 per share dividends and also received an additional $4 per share on the participating feature along with the common stockholders. Sometimes limits are placed on the extent to which the preferred stockholders are allowed to participate.

What determines the features management builds into a preferred stock issue?

Preferred stock is usually issued to minority investors who wish to make certain that the board of directors pays them regular dividends; they gain this assurance by the provisions that preferred stock dividends cumulate if they are not paid and that the owners of the preferred stock acquire the right to vote in case preferred stock dividends are missed. A great deal of pressure is placed on management to pay such dividends if at all possible. Unfortunately, preferred stock has become rather impractical under today's tax laws, for the federal government treats dividends paid on preferred stock as dividends not deductible as an expense to the corporation. Yet, if the corporation issued bonds to the same investor and paid him interest in the same amount, the interest would be fully deductible. Hence, any company paying out money as preferred dividends instead of interest is losing 48 percent of that amount to the government as income taxes. For this reason, preferred stock as a financing instrument is not presently in favor. It is now used mostly in mergers in which the owner of a company being acquired by a large firm demands preferred stock for his common stock because he is fearful of not receiving dividends after the merger is consummated.

Convertible Bonds   The convertible bond was developed to attract funds from investors who wanted all the safeguards of a bond but who also wanted the advantages of common stock—to participate in the profits of the company. A convertible bond has all the features of a debenture bond, plus the feature of being convertible into the common stock of the company at some specified rate for some specified period in the future. The terms of conversion vary widely, but once they are fixed the price of the bond will vary on the upside with the price of the common stock. On the downward side, the bond is valued on the basis of its interest rate and intrinsic risk.

   Companies have used convertible bonds in the past decade largely for two reasons: they helped sell the security and did so at a lower interest rate. The potential dilution of stockholders' equity was usually not given too much consideration.

Income Bonds   Income bonds are usually the result of a bankruptcy. They are bonds on which the interest need not be paid unless it is earned. Sometimes the interest accumulates, sometimes not.

Why would the bankruptcy courts create such a security as an income bond?

In conclusion, one should never forget that the person who has money is in the driver's seat. If you want him to give you his money, you must provide him with the instruments he desires—the instruments that meet his particular needs at that time. The financial community is continually developing financial instruments that are attractive to the investor.

Characteristics of the Industry

The determination of how much debt and how much equity should be used in the capital structure of a company lies largely in the characteristics of the company and the industry in which it operates, although admittedly managerial philosophies play a significant role.

Stability and Reliability of Income Flow   Traditionally, the stability and reliability of future income flow have been the most important factors in determining the amount of debt advisable in a company. If a firm operates in an economic environment in which it is assured of a steady, adequate income flow over a long period, it is able to use large amounts of debt in its capital structure. Such is the case of the utilities—telephone, power, and gas companies; a utility knows that income will be available with which to service and pay off its debt when it comes due. It is not fearful of the future. On the other hand, a company in a highly unstable industry, such as women's clothing, should have no debt whatsoever in its permanent capital structure. Any borrowing such a company does should be for only a few months duration to finance seasonal inventories or accounts receivable.

One of the major factors underlying the difficulties of many firms in the early 1970s was that their managements believed their income flow during the 1960s would continue on for twenty years, when in fact such was not to be the case. Management tends to be optimistic; it is doubtful that one could manage a company properly if he were not optimistic about its future. Reality, however, has a way of sneaking up on unwise optimists, making them pay dearly for their lack of caution.

Rate of Earnings in Industry   Industries vary widely in profitability. Some industries are notoriously poor profit makers—meat packing and department stores are but two examples. Other industries have a record of returning high profits on investment. Management should not use debt in the capital structure if the expected rate of earnings is less than the rate of interest that must be paid for the money. Low-profit industries must be financed by equity.

It has been difficult to understand why the management of public utilities would borrow money at 10 percent interest when their rate of earnings on capital employed was regulated in most states at a level of 6 or 7 percent. When the interest rate climbed above the level the state regulatory commissions allowed them to earn on investments, business theory dictated that they should sell equity, yet they did not do so, thereby subjecting their stockholders to negative leverage. Then these managements use the argument that the interest rate is high as a lever to pry rate increases from their governing bodies, a most interesting game.

COST OF CAPITAL

Few things in the world are free, and money is certainly not one of them. Money costs money. Money is one of the costs of doing business—in some instances a most significant cost. In the consumer finance business, the cost of borrowing the funds they lend is a significant part of the total cost of operation. In financing large enterprises, the difference of one percentage point can amount to several million dollars profit. Hence, the price one pays for the money he uses can be an extremely important determinant of his profit. One must learn when money is too expensive and refrain from using it. Webb & Knapp, the huge New York real estate firm, went bankrupt because its founding "genius," Bill Zeckendorf, paid far too much for the money he borrowed in the latter days of the enterprise when the properties the company owned were barely earning 6 percent.

Zeckendorf was quoted as saying, "It's better to be alive at 18 percent than dead at 6 percent!" What did he mean? Was he right?
How does one measure the costs of capital?

Costs of Debt

It might seem that the cost of debt would be its interest, but in most instances that is only part of the picture. Borrowing can be far more costly than just the interest one pays for the money. Often banks require that the borrower maintain compensating balances, which have the effect of raising the interest rate on the effective money the borrower can use. (A compensating balance means that the borrower must keep a certain minimum amount in the bank—he cannot draw out all of the money he borrows.) Bankers use this device as a means of forcing each borrower to provide the reserves necessary to sustain the amount he borrows. If the reserve ratio is 20 percent and the borrower requests $1 million, the bank may stipulate that he keep $200,000 of that money on deposit at all times; the borrower is furnishing the reserves to back his own loan, thus raising the cost of available funds to him.

How much is the rate increased in this instance?

One small men's apparel firm learned about the true costs of borrowing the hard way. It borrowed $70,000 from its banker in order to finance the inventory of a new store it was opening in a nearby large community. The face interest rate on the note was $8\frac{1}{2}$ percent—not bad, considering the market at the time—but that was only the beginning. For the first time, the firm also had to have a physical audit made annually of its operations by a certified public accountant. This cost an additional $6000. Moreover, no stock could be bought or sold and no assets transferred without the bank's approval. Other restrictions, such as not borrowing additional funds elsewhere and maintaining certain balance-sheet ratios, were included in the provisions. Hence, the restrictions the lender places upon the loan can add significantly to the cost of borrowing funds. In some complex situations, the lender requires that the borrower hire additional people just to keep track of field inventories or payments on accounts receivable. These additional costs are all costs of borrowing, inasmuch as the company would not incur them if the funds had not been borrowed.

Costs of Equity

Even the experts debate the true cost of equity. The traditional school insists that equity costs the proportionate share of assets and earnings existing stockholders give up to the new stockholders. This presents many problems in valuation, for the value of claims on earnings is an open question. Using this approach to the cost of equity, it is impossible to place a finite dollar figure on it, other than to say that in issuing a certain amount of new equity one is giving up a certain share of the business. If the directors of Ideas, Inc., issued the last 500,000 shares of their stock, then it could be said that the new equity cost the stockholders 50 percent of the business—that is, half the claim on earnings and assets, whatever they are worth.

A more realistic school of thought maintains that the cost of equity is only the amount of dividends one pays on it—that if one never pays any dividends, then equity costs nothing. Suppose a firm is paying $4 a year per share dividends on its common stock and intends to continue doing so. If it sells 100,000 additional shares of stock, the cost to the firm will be $400,000 a year. This view would seem to be a far more pragmatic and realistic way of looking at the cost of equity. It results in an interesting proposition that the cost of equity is what management wants to make it. Of course, the matter of control of a corporation may or may not be part of the cost of equity, depending upon the situation.

DETERMINING CAPITAL NEEDS

Professional management no longer waits until the company obviously needs operating capital before it inaugurates plans for getting it. Well-managed enterprises plan their capital needs well in advance.

Operations are budgeted at least one year and frequently three to five years ahead. The cash-flow budget is the instrument most used for planning the short-run cash needs of an enterprise. The small men's apparel store that borrowed $70,000 from its banker was required to formulate a three-year cash-flow budget showing how the money would be repaid from earnings over those three years. Table 19-1 is an example of a cash-flow budget.

Of all the documents for the management of modern enterprises, probably no one instrument is as important as the cash budget. It shows management exactly what it can expect in cash income and outgo and what the difference will be. When cash outflow exceeds cash income, the difference must be financed from some source.

PRINCIPLES OF CORPORATE FINANCE

There are certain simple principles of corporate finance with which you should now become familiar. The principle of leverage, explained previously, needs no further discussion here, though it is at least as important as any of the other principles we shall now discuss.

Table 19–1 **CASH-FLOW BUDGET FOR MEN'S APPAREL STORE**

	Jan.	Feb.	March	April	May	June	July	August	Sept.	Oct.	Nov.	Dec.
Planned Inventory:												
at retail (4 mo. sales)	34,700	35,300	35,800	34,700	36,200	44,100	52,000	60,200	71,600	63,100	55,300	48,700
at cost B.O.M.*	20,800	21,200	21,500	20,800	21,720	26,640	31,200	36,120	42,960	37,860	33,180	29,220
Purchases at retail	9,100	8,200	8,400	10,500	17,300	15,800	16,600	21,900	8,800	8,000	10,000	10,000
at cost	5,460	4,920	5,040	6,300	10,380	9,480	9,960	13,140	5,280	4,800	6,000	6,000
Sales Forecast	8,500	7,700	9,500	9,000	9,100	8,200	8,400	10,500	17,300	15,800	16,600	21,900
Cash Balance B.O.M.*	3,300											
Cash Received—Sales**	3,400	3,080	3,800	3,600	3,640	3,280	3,360	4,200	6,920	6,320	6,640	8,760
accts. receivable	9,600	4,080	3,696	4,560	4,320	4,368	3,936	4,032	5,040	8,304	7,584	7,968
2 months	1,824	2,280	969	877	1,083	1,026	1,037	935	958	1,197	1,972	1,801
Total Cash Available	18,124	9,440	8,465	9,037	9,043	8,674	8,333	9,168	12,918	15,821	16,196	18,529
Cumulative Cash	18,124	27,564	36,029	45,066	54,109	62,783	71,116	80,284	93,202	109,023	125,219	143,748
Less Cash Paid Out:												
accts. payable (goods)	6,000	5,460	4,920	5,040	6,300	10,380	9,480	9,960	13,140	5,280	4,800	6,000
operating expenses (25%)	2,125	1,925	2,375	2,250	2,275	2,050	2,100	2,625	4,325	3,950	4,150	5,475
equipment investment			1,000					3,000				
Total Cash Paid out	8,125	7,385	8,295	7,290	8,575	12,430	11,580	15,585	17,467	9,230	8,950	11,475
Cumulative Cash Paid out	8,125	15,510	23,805	31,095	39,670	52,100	63,680	79,265	96,732	105,962	114,912	126,387
Cash Balance	9,999	12,054	12,224	13,971	14,439	10,683	7,436	1,019	(3,530)	3,061	10,307	17,361

*Beginning of month.

**Experience in this store indicates that 40 percent of sales are for cash. Moreover, 80 percent of accounts receivable are paid the following month; 19 percent paid the second month following; 1 percent never paid at all.

Manager plans a 40 percent margin (goods cost 60 percent of retail price) and plans operating expenses of 25 percent of sales. In actual practice the operating expenses would be itemized more specifically. He plans to buy $1000 of office equipment in March and a $3000 truck in August. He plans to have four months sales in inventory, a turnover of three times a year.

Long-Term Needs

Long-term capital needs should be financed preferably by equity, or if not, then by long-term bonds. Long-term capital requirements should never be financed through the use of short-term debt. To do so creates the possibility of being forced to liquidate one's investments to repay the short-term note when it comes due. A great many managements found themselves in this predicament in 1970 when short-term debt undertaken two or three years earlier became due and they were unable to find funds with which to refinance it.

Under normal business conditions one can usually count on being able to refinance a short-term obligation when due by borrowing money elsewhere, or even by renewing the obligation with the individual to whom it is due. But not always—for if the enterprise gets into difficulties or if business conditions turn downward, refinancing becomes difficult at best. Thus, conservative financing dictates that one should obtain long-term money to finance long-term needs.

Short-Term Requirements

Short-term money needs are usually for the financing of inventory or accounts receivable. In line with the previous principle, these short-term requirements can be financed by short-term borrowing, usually from banks. A sound inventory loan usually is for no longer than a year. The bank wants to see the loan cleaned up when the inventory is liquidated. The permanent base inventory or accounts receivable should be financed by long-run capital; only seasonal expansions of inventories or receivables are financed with short-term loans.

Adequate Working Capital

Net working capital is defined as the difference between current assets and current liabilities. The firm without adequate working capital finds itself in aggravating binds, for it is unable to do the things it needs to do for profitable operations. Once working capital is impaired, suppliers are reluctant to grant credit, banks are reluctant to loan money, and one's activities are restricted. When a company loses money, the entire loss is taken out, almost directly, of working capital. Hence, adverse developments jeopardize working capital first. The first thing that usually happens is that the company does not have sufficient cash on hand to pay its current liabilities. This is the first indication of trouble in the enterprise. Progressively, it is unable to buy the things it needs with which to operate, and finally it is unable to meet its payroll. When that happens, bankruptcy is usually around the corner.

Full Employment of Money

In theory, the perfect financial manager maintains a cash balance of zero, inasmuch as by so doing he has all of the firm's money fully employed. Under normal circumstances cash does not earn one penny if it is not put to use in some fashion.

Under what circumstances might cash earn money?

A company is said to have redundant capital when its cash is far in excess of that needed to finance operations; it has idle cash. Even though good management would have such cash invested in highly marketable securities, such as high-grade government or corporate bonds or high-grade stock, still in theory such cash is wasted, for the company's stockholders do not need to pay management for investing their money in securities. They could have done that for themselves. The stockholders have given the corporation their money to earn with it a greater return than such securities provide. A corporation with large amounts of redundant capital becomes little more than a mutual fund—suggesting that its management may lack the imagination necessary to employ such funds.

What are some of the evils of a large, long-run excess capital condition?
What are the virtues?

Source and Application of Funds

One of the most useful accounting documents available to the financial analyst is the "Source and Application of Funds" statement. It shows where the company has been using its money and the sources from which it was obtained. Such a statement can be constructed from the balance sheets of any corporation. An example is shown in Table 19-2. In a nutshell, the source and application of funds statement shows what has been going on in the enterprise.

Table 19–2

ARA SERVICES, INC. SOURCE AND APPLICATION OF FUNDS, 1969–1970

	October 3, 1969 (in 000's $)	October 2, 1970 (in 000's $)	Source (where $ came from)	Application (where $ went)
Current Assets:				
Cash	16,828	17,489		661
Securities	5,312	6,102		790
Receivables	36,888	51,092		14,204
Inventory	31,752	36,530		4,778
Prepayments	4,433	4,745		312
Total Current	95,213	115,958		20,745
Investments in Subsidiaries	7,942	8,776		834
Other Investments	8,188	8,531		343
Net Property	105,635	112,053		6,418
Investment in Land	30,151	33,475		3,324
Deferred Charges	7,536	6,914	622	
Total Assets	254,665	285,707		31,042
Current Liabilities:				
Notes Payable—Bank	1,136	7,070	5,934	
Long-Term Debt Due	7,537	7,099		438
Accounts Payable	33,494	35,312	1,818	
Accrued Expenses	17,079	17,384	305	
Fed. Income Taxes Due	3,696	4,552	856	
Total Current Liabilities	62,942	71,417	8,475	
Deferred Income Taxes	8,370	9,707	1,337	
Long-Term Debt	69,387	71,839	2,452	
Stockholders' Investment				
Preferred Stock	7,939	6,541		1,398
Common Stock	4,325	4,403	78	
Capital Surplus	27,637	33,989	6,352	
Retained Earnings	74,605	87,954	13,349	
Treasury Stock	(540)	(143)	397	
Total Net Worth	113,966	132,744	18,778	
Total Liabilities and Net Worth	254,665	285,707	31,042	

INTERPRETATION: While one could go down the list item by item to see where the money went and where it came from, the big picture could be stated as follows: ARA Services, Inc., applied $31 million to growth in assets; $20 million to current assets, of which $14 million went into receivables and about $5 million into inventory. About $10 million was invested in various things. The money came largely from earnings as represented by the growth of $18 million in equity; the remainder came from an increase in liabilities—$5.9 million in notes payable at the bank.

Return on Investment (ROI)

The criterion by which the financial man makes most investment decisions is the rate of return on invested capital, which is determined by dividing profit from an investment by the amount of money invested:

$$\frac{\text{profit}}{\text{investment}} = \text{ROI}$$

Some large firms use a modification of this concept in evaluating the efficiency of various divisions, measuring performance by the rate of return on capital employed in a division's operation.

Unquestionably, the rate of return on investment realized by various companies is the common denominator by which members of the financial community compare them. ROI is the common yardstick used to measure efficiency and productivity of an enterprise.

Capital Turnover

Capital turnover is measured by dividing a company's sales volume by its invested capital. Some analysts use the total assets of the enterprise as the equivalent of investment, while others use only equity; the proper denominator to use depends entirely upon the purpose for which the ratio is being computed. The capital-turnover ratio indicates how much investment is needed to produce $1 of sales volume. Some industries, such as utilities and railroads, have a capital turnover of less than one, meaning that they require relatively large investments for every dollar of sales volume they obtain each year. Other industries, such as the grocery business, obtain a capital turnover of 12 to 15 times a year, which means that every dollar invested in the industry brings in $12–$15 sales volume. As a general principle of business, a high-capital-turnover business is a far more attractive investment than a low-capital-turnover one. The capital-turnover ratio is one half of the ROI formula—the other half being the profit margin.

$$\text{ROI} = \frac{\text{Profit}}{\text{Investment}} = \underbrace{\frac{\text{Profit}}{\text{Sales}}}_{\substack{\textit{Profit} \\ \textit{margin}}} \times \underbrace{\frac{\text{Sales}}{\text{Investment}}}_{\substack{\textit{Capital} \\ \textit{turnover}}}$$

Hence, multiplying a company's capital turnover by its profit margin, one obtains its rate of return on investment (ROI).

$$\underset{40\%}{\frac{\$10,000}{\$25,000}} \underset{=}{=} \underset{10\%}{\frac{\$10,000}{\$100,000}} \underset{\times}{\times} \underset{4}{\frac{\$100,000}{\$25,000}}$$

Another way of looking at a firm's capital turnover is in terms of its conversion cycle of operations. Earlier we spoke of the time it takes a company to convert its fixed assets into cash. The capital-turnover ratio is no more than the mathematical expression of this conversion cycle; a firm with a rapid conversion cycle would have a high capital-turnover ratio and vice versa.

HOW A FINANCIAL MANAGER EARNS HIS PAY

Unquestionably, in various ways the clever financial manager earns his salary many times over. The larger the sums involved, the more he can save by adroit financial management.

Cash Management

Most healthy, growing businesses are short of cash, but nevertheless there are times in their operational cycles when they have excess cash. A clever financial manager sees to it that every dollar of excess cash is invested in short-term government securities or other prime short-term investments. Over a period of a year, if the financial manager can keep an average of $1 million invested at 6 percent, he more than earns his salary.

The interest on $1 million at 6 percent for just one day is $166—seemingly a small sum, but it adds up to $60,000 for the year, which makes a difference in the company's profit performance. Clearly, all funds not immediately needed for operations should be invested somewhere for a reasonable rate of interest. One precaution, however, is never to invest such funds in securities that cannot be sold immediately without loss.

Controlled Investment

More than a few companies have run into trouble by not carefully controlling their investments in various enterprises. Someone must control the amount of money invested in various activities and make certain that it does not run rampant, thereby rendering an otherwise sound enterprise relatively unprofitable. It is the financial manager's responsibility to control such investments.

Cost of Capital

Money is no different from other products. Some money costs more than other money. The adroit financial manager who is able to secure funds one percent cheaper saves his employer a great deal of money over the term of the debt. The comptroller of one consumer finance company was able to borrow $100 million for his concern from a large pension fund at an interest rate 1.2 percent lower than the price offered by the next lowest bidder, a large insurance company. That financial manager saved his firm $1,200,000 a year, simply by knowing where to buy the money.

More than anything else, a money manager must have exceptional knowledge of the money market's nooks and crannies, where money lies waiting to be called into higher productivity. You must remember that the money market is not a perfect one in which all suppliers have knowledge of all users. There are investors just waiting to hear an attractive proposition from a borrower. The clever finance man learns where he can get money other than from the usual bank channels.

FINANCIAL PROBLEMS

If pressed, one could devise a long list of various financial problems worthy of discussion; we will mention here only a few of today's more important ones.

Growth

In the past two decades, the financing of growth has been a significant problem to American enterprise. A great number of companies have been trying to grow faster than their profits would allow. Historically, the basic principle has been that a company should grow on its profits, meaning that the growth of a firm should be financed out of retained earnings. This was, and is, the soundest way to finance growth. But in many instances retained earnings were not being generated fast enough to satisfy growth-minded executives. Faster means of financing growth were sought. Some companies went the merger route; others borrowed money, both long- and short-term, with which to finance expansion. Some floated new stock issues. Whatever the means, the funding of growth beyond that permitted by retained earnings has been a prime problem of financial management. History indicates that those firms that financed their growth by equity or very long-term borrowing have usually fared better than those who took the shortcuts via the merger and acquisition routes. The firms that got into financial difficulty most quickly were those who attempted to finance growth with short-term borrowing.

Venture Capital

One of the problems plaguing our free-enterprise system today is the dire shortage of venture capital—money to finance new enterprises. Historically, new enterprises have been risky investments. The chance of losing everything is large. New ventures are attractive to investors who are willing to gamble; when they succeed, the return is extremely lucrative. Investing in new enterprises is a gambler's game. Unfortunately, tax laws and other barriers have greatly restricted venture capital, for the gains are fully taxable and the deductions for losses are often limited. Unless the investor has some way of writing off all the losses on such an investment, the gamble is not too attractive. This is not to say that taxes are the only barrier to the flow of venture capital, for unquestionably there are many others.

Why does a new business have a difficult time attracting venture capital?

The venture-capital problem is complicated by the psychology of many entrepreneurs, who refuse to allow venture capital sufficient return to reward it for the risks involved. Normally, venture capital wants equity, not debt. The risks of losing one's investment in a new enterprise are just about the same, regardless of whether one has an equity or a debt position, but if the enterprise succeeds, the returns on equity vastly exceed those given to debt.

Why is the risk of losing one's money in a new enterprise about the same whether he takes debt or common stock? When would debt be advisable?

Moreover, the promoter of a new enterprise is frequently reluctant to give venture capital its demanded equity; he wants to keep the enterprise for himself. In many instances the entrepreneur views the money man as a leech, a parasite undeserving of a share of the business. He refuses to understand that money is a factor of production just as much as a machine; if one does not have the money, he cannot produce, just as he cannot produce without the machine.

Dividend Payout

Historically, America's large corporations have felt an obligation to maintain an adequate dividend policy, paying out a portion of their profits each year as dividends to their stockholders. The percentage of profits paid out varies from year to year, depending upon earnings of the company, but the more responsible firms have tried to maintain a level dividend in order to allow their stockholders to plan on income, for a great many investors—widows, retired people, and trust accounts—are counting on dividends as part of their income. As the interest rate increases and as it becomes increasingly difficult for firms to borrow funds with which to finance operations, the pressures to retain earnings are vastly increased. And so financial management must weigh its responsibility to the stockholders to maintain dividends against its responsibility to the company to retaining sufficient money with which to operate.

Interest Rates

Certainly the high interest rates of recent years have greatly complicated the financing of business operations. Money has been in short supply, thus being restricted to firms with well-established contacts in the money market. During such periods the new firm and the marginal enterprise have most trying times. The young man just entering the business world should take careful note of what happens during periods of money shortages and resolve not to allow himself to get caught in some future "money crunch."

Conclusion

Money propels the enterprise; without it, nothing happens. Although the procurement of funds is a critically important skill for the financial officer, it is equally important for him to know how to structure those funds in the organization. The management of debt and equity becomes critical in the long-run success of the endeavor. Debt has a bad habit of coming due and, of course, it constantly requires its interest. Miscalculations about one's ability to service and pay off debts result in many unpleasant things, among which bankruptcy may be one. Equity has its problems, but they are not as pressing. Control of the enterprise is the biggest problem facing the management that seeks equity money.

The management of cash is the most urgent task of the financial executive. If he can manage to have the cash available with which to pay debts as they arise, he has done his biggest job.

The skillful financial man has an intimate knowledge of the money market; he knows where he can get money at the most reasonable price. Consequently, he can earn his wages many times over by savings in interest costs.

20 Investments

Never follow the crowd.
BERNARD M. BARUCH

Follow the crowd!
MY BROKER

Few topics in business generate as much attention and interest as the subject of investments. Every person who has had even modest economic success is faced with the problem of what to do with his savings—how best to invest them. It is no fun to work hard to make money, only to lose it in some investment. So it seems appropriate to examine this subject carefully.

YOUR UNIQUE POSITION

An excellent investment for someone else may not be at all appropriate for you. You must design a program for your own specific needs and goals, refusing to allow people who are unfamiliar with your situation to influence your investment decisions unduly. Of particular repugnance is the insurance salesman or investment broker who blindly recommends a certain policy or stock to you without knowing your complete investment plan, for the likelihood that it fits into your program is remote. For this reason, people with wealth rely upon their professional investment advisor in much the same way as they do their doctor, lawyer, or CPA.

THE PROBLEM OF MANAGING RISK

The essential ingredient common to all investments is the element of risk. One must throughly understand the theory of risk and risk-bearing if he is to be a successful investor or businessman. Risk is the probability of loss of one's investment. Fortunately, risk is often a two-edged sword: investments involving considerable risk of loss also offer large chances for gain. Sometimes investments in which the risk of loss is great offer only a slight chance for gain. Such would be a most stupid investment. If the risk of loss is great, the chances for gain must be commensurately large, or else one should forget about the investment. The management of risk is an essential part of the management of all investment programs. But there are several kinds of risk: financial risk, purchasing-power risk, interest-rate risk, political risk, and income risk.

Financial Risk

Financial risk is the chance that one will lose all or part of his money in an investment. There is a certain element of financial risk in all investments, even U.S. government bonds. Suppose you buy stock in General Motors for $80 a share and must sell it for some reason or another at a later date for $60 a share; you have suffered a loss of $20 a share that must be ascribed to financial risk. Suppose you invest $10,000 in a gasoline station that goes bankrupt! Creditors seize everything! You lose the entire $10,000—financial risk at work.

Amount of Financial Risk One Can Assume   In investment circles, the widow with her two kids is the classic case; she is unable to assume much financial risk at all. If she loses her money in an unwise financial investment, she is unable to earn money to replace it. Her investment program must entail a minimum of financial risk. A retired couple living on earnings from their investments should not accept much financial risk, for if they lose their money, their standard of living may be jeopardized for the rest of their lives.

On the other hand, some young man in a highly lucrative professional position or some young executive making handsome earnings may feel completely free to accept substantial risks. Suppose a man of great wealth invests $100,000 in a business and loses it all. So what? He's not really hurt, inasmuch as he still has more than ample funds on which to live and operate. The acid question is whether or not the individual can afford to lose his money. If the answer is no, then financial risk must be minimized in the investment program. If, on the other hand, the individual's standard of living would not be jeopardized by losing a certain sum, then substantial financial risk may be acceptable.

Why take financial risks?

Coping with Financial Risk Parties who are unable to accept any significant amount of financial risk usually invest in U.S. government bonds, high-grade corporate bonds, and perhaps the highest-grade blue chip common stocks, although there is legitimate dispute over the wisdom of buying common stocks by someone unable to accept much financial risk.

Why do banks, insurance companies, and trust funds invest largely in high-grade government bonds?

Most advisors would agree that the least financial risk is usually provided by U.S. government bonds, because as long as the federal government is stable, one will receive the face value of the bond when it comes due. But this does not mean that one can always get all of his money back before that time. If the bond market is depressed, he will be unable to sell the bond for its face value—but that is the result of interest-rate risk, which we covered later.

While investments in small, closely held corporations, highly speculative common stocks, the commodity exchanges, and real estate are commonly considered to hold substantial financial risk, actually the risk is determined by the particulars in the situation; the enterprise, its management, its market, and the price paid for the investment. The financial risks are always large when one pays too much for something. Some small companies entail less risk than some of the blue chip corporations. If one knows what he is doing, speculating in commodities may be less hazardous than buying some corporate bonds. It all depends on the situation.

One of the most difficult problems facing the investor in managing financial risk is to realize that what, at one time, was a gilt-edged investment can rapidly deteriorate into a large financial risk. At one time railroad bonds were generally considered a safe investment, but today one is lucky to get any money back at all from some of the bankrupt railroads. The financial risk of any investment can change abruptly; hence, you must continually reappraise your investments. You can never put something in your safety deposit box and forget about it.

Income Risk

Income risk is akin to financial risk, but slightly different. While one's principal in an investment may not be jeopardized, sometimes the income is. In theory, if the income from an investment declines, the value of that investment declines, thereby creating financial risk, but such is not always the case with nonmarketable securities or other investments whose value is not being constantly appraised by a market mechanism. Suppose you invested $25,000 in a Dairy Queen operation that returned the $10,000-a-year profit you anticipated, but competitive conditions reduced that income to $8000 a year after a few years. While you could probably get your principal back if you sold the business, escaping financial loss, still you would have lost some of the income upon which you had based the investment.

Admittedly, loss of income can cause financial loss, but one only has the financial loss when he wants to take it. One may be willing to go on with the reduced income because it is still more than any other available investment would provide.

Acceptable Amount of Income Risk   Certain types of investors must have a minimum of income risk. Consider again the widow and her two children. As long as her income is maintained at the desired level, she really does not care too much about the principal value of her investments. If she has her money in high-grade utility preferred stocks yielding $8000 a year, and this is enough income for her needs, the current market value of those stocks is not of great concern to her. The retired couple, as another example, are most interested in income stability; they need that income to sustain their standard of living.

On the other hand, a young man with an independent source of income may not need the income from his investments to live on, so he frequently disdains income-yielding investments in preference to investments that will grow rapidly in value.

Coping with Income Risk   The investor who must have a stable income level from his investments seeks fixed-income securities, such as high-grade bonds and preferred stocks. Sometimes investment in good apartment houses is attractive to such investors. The dividend policies of some blue chip companies, such as American Telephone & Telegraph (AT&T), are so stable that their common stock meets the requirements of investors seeking a dependable income source.

Purchasing-Power Risk

Purchasing-power risk is a different creature; it is the risk of loss of one's purchasing power because of inflation. Financial risk is concerned only with the dollars invested—the investor wants to get back at least the number of dollars that he put in. The investor concerned with purchasing-power risk wants to regain from his investment the same standard of living he put in.

In recent decades, purchasing-power risk has loomed as the biggest single problem in most investors' minds. The rapid inflation from World War II to the present has frightened the average investor away from fixed-principal investments. Investors saw all too clearly what an investment of $1000 made in 1940 was worth in goods thirty years later. In 1940, $1000 was a substantial sum. It represented the annual income for some workers; it would buy a new car. In 1970 it was only a month's income to a large segment of American society and would not buy even a good used car. Inflation had confiscated about three-quarters of the purchasing power of the money invested in 1940.

Investors Subject to Purchasing-Power Risk   Not all investors are concerned with purchasing-power risk. Many institutions—banks, insurance companies, and others whose liabilities are fixed in terms of dollars rather than purchasing power—have no need to fear it. It is the private investor, particularly the smaller one who is saving to provide himself a standard of living at a later date, who is most concerned with purchasing-power risk. The young man should be far more concerned with purchasing-power risk than the 80-year-old retiree; the older man may be subject to only a few more years of inflation while the younger man has to deal with it for possibly half a century.

Coping with Purchasing-Power Risk   Anyone who invests his money in fixed-principal securities such as bonds, savings accounts, insurance policies, or mortgages is subject to the full force of the purchasing-power risk. If he places $1000 in a fixed-obligation investment, he will get back his $1000 regardless of the price level at the time. Investors desiring to mitigate the purchasing-power risk avoid such fixed-price obligations in favor of common stocks, real estate, commodities, and investments in small businesses.

Indeed, one can ascribe the tremendous bull market in securities during the 1950s and 1960s largely to investors' fear of inflation. A widely held theory is that investments in common stock provide a hedge against the inflation risk. While there are some serious flaws in the logic underlying this theory, the fact remains that a great many people believe it. This was sufficient reason to cause them to boost the prices of certain stocks beyond all reasonable levels. The fear of inflation has been so strong that it has encouraged some investors to pay 30, 40, or 50 times earnings for the common stock of some companies that they believe have a bright future. But to hedge successfully against inflation, it is not enough to invest blindly in common stocks; you still must be highly selective in your purchases, for not all common stocks will increase in value with inflation.

What types of stocks might be the most attractive investments for a person desiring a hedge against inflation?

Many investors have been putting their money in real estate on the theory that real estate prices have always led any general inflation. This has more validity than the common-stock theory, but it poses serious management problems, for not all real estate will appreciate in value.

Some investors, as an inflation hedge, endeavor to place their money in closely held corporations that present attractive possibilities for future growth. The theory is that the profits of some small companies will vary directly with inflation.

Interest-Rate Risk

The interest-rate risk is limited to those marketable fixed obligations and investments bearing a rate of interest, such as bonds and preferred stocks. Suppose you pay $1000 for a 6 percent bond; as long as the market rate of interest remains at 6 percent, you can sell your bond in the market for about $1000, thereby getting your money back. But suppose the market interest rate increases to 10 percent for the type of bond you purchased. Your bond pays $60 interest each year until it matures, at which time you get your $1000 back. But if you want your money back before maturity, you will have to sell it in the bond market. The people buying in the bond market at the time you want to sell will demand the market rate of interest—suppose it is 10 percent at the time. They will only be willing to pay you $600 [$60 interest divided by 10 percent ($60/0.10 = $600)] plus a portion of the $400 additional that would be realized by holding the bond to maturity ($1000 - $600), which is apportioned over the remaining life of the bond with the amount properly discounted by the rate of interest.[1] Because of the increase in interest rate, you have suffered a loss of about $370 if you must sell that bond. True, you do not suffer the loss of principal if you hold the bond to maturity, but you have suffered a loss nonetheless, for you are getting only a 6 percent yield on your money while other investors are enjoying a 10 percent yield on theirs.

Table 20–1

INCREASE OF BOND PRICES BECAUSE OF AN INTEREST-RATE DECREASE

Bonds of $1,000 Face Value	1970 Low Price	1/15/71 Price	Yield to Maturity at Recent Price
U.S. Treasury Bonds			
3% bonds of 1995	$596	$712	5.05%
Industrial Bonds			
General Electric 3½% bonds of 1976	$760	$868	6.44%
Sears, Roebuck 4¾% bonds of 1983	$680	$809	7.06%
Standard Oil (N.J.) 6% bonds of 1997	$765	$899	6.83%
U.S. Steel 4% bonds of 1983	$660	$699	7.80%
Railroad Bonds			
Atchison, Topeka & Santa Fe 4% bonds of 1995	$510	$575	7.95%
Southern Railway 5% bonds of 1994	$600	$650	8.45%
Utility Bonds			
American Tel. & Tel. 2⅝% bonds of 1986	$511	$570	7.29%
Consolidated Natural Gas 4¾% bonds of 1990	$611	$695	7.80%
Pacific Gas & Electric 5% bonds of 1989	$651	$775	7.22%
Tax-Exempt Bonds			
New Jersey 6% bonds of 1989	$940	$1060	5.50%
Indiana Toll Road 3½% bonds of 1994	$590	$720	5.70%
Nassau County, N.Y., 6.70% bonds of 1990	$1000	$1128	5.60%

During the short period of time covered by this table, the prime interest rate dropped from 8 percent to 6 percent. Note how the prices of the bonds increased as a result. Which of the bonds would have been the best speculation? Why?

Coping with the Interest-Rate Risk   People minimize the interest-rate risk by maintaining sufficient liquidity to avoid being forced to sell bonds at a loss. Second, they lessen the interest-rate risk by buying bonds that will mature in the near future. One can always hold a bond to maturity, and the borrower will pay the holder its face amount; consequently, the interest-rate risk is felt most severely on bonds maturing in the distant future. This phenomenon of time is one of the reasons for the popularity

---

[1] This is a complicated mathematical equation that is used in financial circles, but is not necessary here. Suffice it to say that the bond buyer would be willing to pay about $630 for the bond.

of treasury bills and other short-term government obligations. One is not subject to much interest-rate risk by investing in ninety-day treasury bills, he can always wait ninety days and get all of his money back.

Political Risk

Political risk is the chance of losing money because of some decision of a governmental authority. It is an underestimated and overlooked risk, for every investment in the world contains some element of it. It is most obvious when one invests in foreign nations with unstable governments. How much did the owners of Russian czarist bonds get back on their investments when the communists took over? What happened to bond holders in Cuban enterprises when Castro took over? Many American oil companies are presently learning about the dangers of political risk as their investments in foreign oil fields are confiscated by hostile governments.

While one can avoid such obvious risks by not investing money in any nation that lacks a stable government, other political risks are not so obvious.

One independent oil distributor purchased a particularly choice corner location on which to build a service station, paying a rather handsome price for that parcel of real estate. The city zoning commission destroyed his investment by refusing to grant him the zoning he needed for his project, thereby forcing him to suffer a substantial loss in reselling the location for a purpose of lesser value.

How could he have avoided the loss?

All political bodies are continually making decisions that affect the value of properties and businesses. A highway is relocated; some businesses are hurt, others are enhanced. An airport operator negotiated a favorable lease with a city council that encouraged him to make certain improvements in the city-owned airport, only to have a later city council repudiate the agreement—a political risk.

Investors who have recently lost money in the aerospace and defense industries have been victims of political risk. The federal government simply changed its mind about where it wished to spend its money. A few years ago, the investors in American Telephone and Telegraph were badly hurt when an FCC investigation of long-distance rates had the effect of depressing the price of AT&T's common stock.

Coping with Political Risk   There is no pat solution to handling political risk. One must simply use good judgment in appraising the political risks inherent in a given situation. One seems to minimize political risks by avoiding unstable governments or situations where the government changes hands and philosophies rather rapidly. The investor seeks a stable, consistent position from the government, whatever it may be; he detests changing governmental postures because it is difficult to anticipate them.

THE LIQUIDITY PROBLEM

Table 20-2 shows the spectrum of liquidity from cash-in-hand to investments in bankrupt corporations. Liquidity refers to one's ability to convert his investments into cash quickly without suffering a loss because of the need to sell. When one must sell something, he must often accept a lower price for his impatience. The only perfect liquidity is cash-in-hand; all others suffer to some degree from nonliquidity. Even demand deposits in a commercial bank are not always liquid. Have you tried cashing a check in a large city on Saturday night if no one knows you? A check is not always the same as cash. The savings account is another step removed from the demand deposit, for one cannot draw a check against it, but must wait until the institution is open to draw the money out. But these are merely minor degrees of nonliquidity; demand deposits and savings accounts are almost the same as cash to the average man. Even investments in common stock that is listed on major exchanges are considered fairly liquid, for one can obtain his money from such investments within a week without losing appreciably because of the need to liquidate.

Table 20–2
RELATIVE
LIQUIDITY
OF VARIOUS
INVESTMENTS

Highly liquid:	**Cash in bank**
	Savings and loan accounts
	Credit unions
Liquid:	**Cash value in life insurance**
	Common and preferred stocks listed on exchanges
	Federal government bonds
	Listed bonds
	Mutual bonds
Relatively liquid:	**Over-the-counter stocks**
	Municipal bonds
Highly unliquid:	**Mortgages**
	Commercial real estate
	Apartment houses
	Land
	Stock in closely held corporations
	Securities in default

But when one moves into areas such as real estate, over-the-counter securities, or closely held corporations, he is getting into investments that can be highly nonliquid.

Take real estate as an example! A widely recognized weakness of real estate investments is its high degree of nonliquidity. If one must pull his money out of a real estate investment in a short time, he may take a tremendous financial beating. Indeed, to liquidate such investments at anything resembling market value may take several months, if not years. Most land speculators recognize that investments in land will take five to ten years to liquidate profitably.

Unforeseen circumstances requiring cash that one does not have on hand but must pull from investments are the culprits creating the liquidity problem. If one could foresee with complete accuracy his cash needs in the future, there should be no liquidity problem, for he could provide for the needed money. A secondary complicating factor is that sometimes one makes investments that he believes to be liquid, only to have circumstances make them unliquid at a later date. One may buy highly marketable bonds in a good company, only to have that firm later go into bankruptcy, making those bonds highly unsalable at any price, even though in the end the bond holder may survive the bankruptcy with most of his money.

THE MANAGEMENT PROBLEM

All investment programs require two things other than money: knowledge and time. First, one must have knowledge of the investment media he selects. He must become an expert in them. The investment market is no place for amateurs with faulty knowledge of what they are doing. At best, investments in common stock or real estate are exceedingly complicated matters. For this reason, many professional investors specialize in a single area, fully realizing that it is impossible to master all of them.

Second, the management of an investment program takes time. Unless a person is willing and able to devote a certain amount of time to his investments, he should leave them in the hands of others. There is no known investment that can be bought blindly, placed in a safety deposit box, and then forgotten. One can even lose money heavily in government bonds if the interest rate climbs. Smart investors foresaw the increase in interest rates and sold off their bonds without incurring substantial losses, but they had to stay on top of their investments—and this requires time.

Some investments take far more time to manage than others. An individual investing in small, closely held corporations may spend a great deal of his time managing the enterprises. A man investing in land or real estate who does not employ a professional real estate manager will spend a great deal of time—perhaps all of his time—just managing his investments.

Lack of time and knowledge are the basic reasons many investors hire professional managers to invest their money for them. Most wise apartment-house investors turn the management of their properties over to real estate management firms. Most big investors in securities retain the services of a professional investment advisor to manage their portfolios. In a large portfolio, decisions must be made when the positions of stocks weaken, additional funds are made available for investment, and new opportunities are presented. Table 20-3 presents the portfolio of one professionally managed

Table 20-3
PORTFOLIO OF PROFESSIONALLY MANAGED ACCOUNT

ACCOUNT OF: Mr. J. Q. Investor PORTFOLIO AS OF: January 1, 1971 For	Cost	Market Value
Fund A – For Liquidity		
Treasury Bills	$300,000	$309,550
Fund B – For Income		
150 Municipal Bonds	$110,000	$135,000
Fund C – For Growth		
1000 Shares Disney	$55,000	$140,000
Fund D – For Speculation		
100 Corporate Bonds	$84,000	$91,000
1000 Shares Weyerhaeuser Common Stock	$340,000	$550,000
Fund E – Real Estate	$300,000	$300,000*

Why are corporate bonds considered speculative? Why aren't the municipal bonds also speculative? Why all the money in treasury bills? Does this explain the basic strategy of the account at the time? Why haven't they taken their Disney profits? What is the thinking underlying the Weyerhaeuser stock?

*No market value has been established

account. This document was given to the investor to summarize the manager's position and attitudes during the first quarter of 1971. The investor receives one of these documents at the beginning of each quarter, summarizing the major premises underlying the decisions and the strategies that will be following during the coming quarter.

INVESTMENT MEDIA

The wise investor seldom keeps any more money in his checking account than he needs for meeting current bills. Instead, he keeps excess cash in a savings account earning daily interest, which can amount to some money. If you are able to keep $1000 invested in a savings account at 5 percent you will have $50 at the end of the year to show for your trouble; this may not sound like much, but it beats nothing. The art of keeping one's money earning more money all the time pays handsomely over a period of time; it is known as compound interest, and investors believe in it.

The power of compound interest is demonstrated by the figures in Table 20–4, which show the results of compounding $10,000 at various interest rates for

Table 20–4
INTEREST COMPOUNDED ANNUALLY ON $10,000

Year	Percentage					
	5	10	15	20	25	30
1	$10,500	$11,000	$11,500	$12,000	$12,500	$13,000
2	11,025	12,100	13,225	14,400	15,625	16,900
3	11,576	13,310	15,208	17,280	19,531	21,970
4	12,155	14,641	17,490	20,736	24,414	28,561
5	12,762	16,105	20,113	24,883	30,517	37,129
6	13,401	17,715	23,130	29,859	38,146	48,268
7	14,071	19,487	26,600	35,831	47,683	62,748
8	14,775	21,435	30,590	42,998	59,604	81,573
9	15,513	23,579	35,178	51,597	74,505	106,045
10	16,289	25,937	40,455	61,917	93,132	137,858
11	17,103	28,531	46,523	74,300	116,415	179,216
12	17,959	31,384	53,502	89,161	145,519	232,980
13	18,856	34,522	61,527	106,993	181,899	302,875
14	19,799	37,974	70,757	128,391	227,373	393,737
15	20,789	41,772	81,370	154,070	284,217	511,858
16	21,829	45,949	93,576	184,884	355,271	665,416
17	22,920	50,544	107,612	221,861	444,089	865,041
18	24,066	55,599	123,754	266,233	555,111	1,124,554
19	25,270	61,159	142,317	319,480	693,889	1,461,920
20	26,533	67,274	163,665	383,376	867,362	1,900,496
21	27,859	74,002	188,215	460,051	1,084,202	2,470,645
22	29,253	81,402	216,447	552,061	1,355,253	3,211,839
23	30,715	89,543	248,914	662,473	1,694,066	4,176,390
24	32,251	98,497	286,251	794,968	2,117,583	5,428,008
25	33,864	108,347	329,189	953,962	2,646,978	7,056,410
26	35,557	119,181	378,567	1,144,754	3,308,723	9,173,333
27	37,335	131,099	435,353	1,373,705	4,135,903	11,925,333
28	39,201	144,209	500,656	1,648,446	5,169,879	15,502,933
29	41,161	158,630	575,754	1,978,135	6,462,349	20,153,813
30	43,219	174,494	622,117	2,373,763	8,077,936	26,199,957
31	45,380	191,943	761,435	2,848,515	10,097,420	34,059,944
32	47,649	211,137	875,650	3,418,218	12,621,775	44,277,927
33	50,032	232,251	1,006,998	4,101,862	15,777,219	57,561,305
34	52,533	255,476	1,158,048	4,922,235	19,721,524	74,829,696
35	$55,160	$281,024	$1,331,755	$5,906,682	$24,651,904	$97,278,605

various periods of time. The great impact of the interest rate on the resultant sum demonstrates why investors push hard to increase the yield on their investments.

Until you have an adequate reserve in a savings account to support your needs, you have no business at all making other investments. It is rather frightening to hear of people who have nothing in a savings account investing their first $1000 of savings in the stock market. One should only begin thinking about other investment media after he has built up an adequate savings account. Adequacy depends entirely upon individual circumstances, but it is difficult to see how anything less than $3000 to $5000 can be adequate with today's level of living. One could build a strong case, if he had a generous standard of living, that he should keep at least $10,000 in a savings account. So you can see that there are a great many people in America whose entire savings programs should be built around savings accounts. They have no business considering bonds, common stocks, or other investments.

Bonds

Certain investors should buy bonds—a fixed-income obligation. The borrower promises to pay a stipulated rate of interest on the bond (the coupon or face rate), usually semiannually, and promises to pay the face amount of the bond at maturity. People needing an assured, regular income use bonds. The advantage of bonds over savings accounts is the higher yield; in 1971, for example, while savings accounts were paying about $5\frac{1}{2}$ percent, high-grade bonds yielded from 6 to 8 percent. For a person living on his investments, this is a significant difference. A retired person with a $200,000 savings account would receive interest of $11,000 a year at $5\frac{1}{2}$ percent, but if he were to buy 8 percent bonds he would get $16,000 per year—providing him a significantly different standard of living. If the bond account were managed carefully, the additional financial risks would be slight. It would be difficult to distinguish the difference between the financial risks of a federally insured savings account and a U.S. government bond.

The bond market is divided into four categories today: U.S. government, municipal, corporate, and corporate convertible bonds.

U.S. Government Bonds   Bonds of the federal government present a minimum financial risk, and their yields usually represent the base from which all other bond yields are figured. Although traded on the over-the-counter market, federal bonds are still fairly marketable, because one can sell them rather easily if he so desires; however, they are subject to the interest-rate risk discussed earlier. Interest on federal bonds is fully taxable.

Municipal Bonds   The obligations of various cities and states are so numerous that it is almost impossible to classify them—there are school bonds, water bonds, sewer bonds, street bonds, general improvement bonds, highway bonds, and bonds used to finance about every other type of government activity imaginable. Their outstanding feature is that their interest is exempt from federal income taxes. Moreover, the states exempt from their income taxes interest earned on obligations of governments within that state.

Municipal bonds have been a haven for investors in high tax brackets. Because of their freedom from income tax, their yield is usually less than that of federal bonds. In 1970, municipal bonds were yielding about 6 percent; investors were willing to take the lower yield on such obligations because it was tax-free money. A man in the 50 percent tax bracket is actually receiving an effective yield of 12 percent if he is paid 6 percent interest tax-free. Institutions paying a 48 percent income tax find the true yield on municipal bonds attractive.

What is the effective yield of a 7 percent municipal bond to a man in the 30 percent federal income tax bracket and a 5 percent state income tax bracket?

Municipal bonds vary greatly in their financial risks; some of them are very shaky enterprises. One has to be an expert to separate the wheat from the chaff in the municipal bond market, for one can lose his money in it.

One unseen drawback to buying municipal bonds is that they can be rather unliquid. Few institutions make markets in municipal bonds, so unless one is prepared to hold the bond to maturity, the may find that he has to suffer a bit in price if he has to sell it.

One financial expert maintains that it is very difficult to have much of a market in a bond issue of less than $30 million; most municipal offerings are usually well below this amount.

Why is the size of the bond issue a determinant in making the market for it?

Perhaps the "average" municipal bond buyer would be best advised to buy one of the closed end municipal bond mutual funds put together monthly by a few large brokers. The costs seem reasonable in relation to the advantages offered—liquidity, management, diversification.

Corporate Bonds   The quality of corporate bonds varies widely; some are regarded almost as highly as federal government bonds, while others are worthless pieces of paper. Much money has been lost by people buying what they thought were high-grade corporate bonds, only to have the situation sour on them later.

The interest on corporate bonds is fully taxable. They are particularly subject to the interest-rate and purchasing-power risks as well as all of the other risks of any investment. The attraction of corporate bonds is their higher yield. The choice between corporate and municipal bonds depends upon the tax position of the investor and is a matter for mathematical calculation.

Convertible Corporate Bonds   The convertible bond is a regular corporate bond subject to all the risks and problems presented by any corporate bond, but it contains a feature that allows its owner to hedge the purchasing-power risk; he has the privilege of converting his bond into shares of the company's common stock at a stipulated price during the life of the bond. Therefore, convertible bonds have speculative values. If the price of the company's common stock climbs above the conversion price, the price of the bond will reflect the excess—and perhaps more if investors feel the stock's price will continue to rise. The advantage to the investor is that the bond pays interest, thereby assuring him of a regular income, but still provides a speculative protection hedge against inflation.

When should the owner of a convertible bond convert it into stock?
(Be careful; this question is a trap!)

Why not simply buy the company's stock? For two reasons: (1) if the price of the stock drops, little loss is suffered on the bonds unless the company's financial position has deteriorated, so he has protection on the downside; and (2) the dividends on the stock are not apt to be as much as the interest and they are far less predictable.

Summary

For two decades, during the fifties and sixties, bonds were highly unpopular with investors because of their high purchasing-power risk; inflation made them unattractive investments for the average man. However, the high interest rates of the early 1970s and the relatively poor performance of the stock market has once again brought the bond market into consideration by a great number of highly sophisticated investors. This is merely an example of how the fashions of investment media shift as times and conditions change.

STOCKS

Stocks are classified into two categories: common and preferred.

Preferred Stocks

Preferred stocks are a cross between a bond and a common stock—they pay a fixed dividend but need not pay it if it is not earned. The principal need not be repaid, as is true of bonds, so the only way the investor can liquidate the investment is to sell the stock to another investor.

A participating preferred stock shares in the company's earnings to a stipulated extend, while the dividend of a nonparticipating preferred stock is limited to a fixed face amount.

A preferred stock can be almost anything, depending upon its provisions. Some preferred stocks have more advantages than common stock, while others offer almost the protection of a bond.

Common Stocks

We shall first discuss publicly held stocks, both those traded on recognized exchanges such as the New York Stock Exchange and the American Exchange, and those traded in the over-the-counter (OTC) market. Next we will discuss the common stock of closed corporations. Then we will talk about investing in common stocks by buying shares of mutual funds.

The theory underlying the purchase of common stocks is that one can share in the profits of company if the firm prospers. The investor in common stocks hopes for a large return on his investment; he is not content with receiving interest on his money—he wants more. It is impossible to predict what his return on investment will be, for it depends entirely upon the stock and the price at which it was purchased. Unquestionably, many people have made fortunes by investing in the common stocks of the right companies. But just as unquestionably, many people have lost fortunes by investing in the wrong ones. The financial risks involved in buying the common stock of any company are great. Investors attempt to reduce the financial risks by acquiring only those stocks listed on the New York Stock Exchange, or even more conservatively, only those stocks known as "blue chips." But one can also lose money investing in blue chips, as any experienced investor can attest. Similarly, one should not discount the risks associated with a stock simply because it is listed on an exchange, for in fact many over-the-counter stocks are far better investments than many of those listed on an exchange. The listing of a stock guarantees very little about its merits.

Publicly Held Issues   Any common stock that is publicly held must conform to various reporting regulations set forth by the Securities and Exchange Act and the Securities and Exchange Commission (SEC). Information about companies with publicly held stock is available in practically every library in the nation; *Moody's, Standard & Poor's,* and *Fitch's* services are the leading sources for such data.

The virtue of investing in publicly held rather than closely held securities is twofold. First, it is easier to obtain information on the financial well-being of publicly held companies. They must publish annual reports and make other information available. Second, it is easier to liquidate investments in publicly held companies. This is particularly true of companies listed on an exchange. The stock listed on one of the exchanges has a market price established for it and thereby becomes more readily marketable. Frequently one is unable to sell his stock in a closely held company for any money at all, no matter how little. Even if such stock is marketable, one seldom knows its value because no market price has been established for it.

Consequently, to insure the marketability of their positions, many professional investors refuse to buy the stock of any company not listed on one of the major exchanges. They want to be able to liquidate their positions quickly and surely with a minimum of loss.

Then why do people buy over-the-counter securities? The answer is high yield. The yield obtained on many over-the-counter securities is quite handsome. Because of the lack of liquidity, people are unwilling to pay as much for an unlisted security as a listed one; hence, one is more apt to find bargains, if he knows what he is doing. Moreover, many small growth companies must start out as over-the-counter securities because they are too small to qualify for listing. People who are playing the growth game and want to get in on the ground floor are forced to deal in the over-the-counter market, but this game is a risky one.

Some brokers maintain markets in some over-the-counter issues in which they have positions, and they obtain the difference between the bid and asked prices for

Table 20–5

QUOTES ON OVER-THE-COUNTER STOCKS IN WHICH DEAN WITTER & COMPANY MAKE A MARKET

DEAN WITTER & CO.
INCORPORATED

DEAN WITTER O–T–C PRIMARY MARKETS
Approximately 11 a.m., April 16, 1971

When dealing with clients in any of the securities listed below, the Account Executive must disclose that Dean Witter & Co. is a market maker.

TRANSACTION SERVICES BULLETIN

Code	Company	Wire	Quote
AAX@	Alexander & Baldwin	WB	69 1/2 – 70 1/2
ALH	Allergan Pharm	UL	33 – 33 1/2
	Amer Exp Spec Fund	UL	9 3/4 – 10 1/8
AMM	Amer Micro-Systems	WB	56 – 56 1/2
ADI@	Anadite	AB	2 1/2 – 2 3/4
AJA	Anderson Jacobson	WB	8 1/8 – 8 1/2
AMA	Applied Magnetics	AB	19 1/8 – 19 5/8
ARM	A J Armstrong	UL	8 7/8 – 9 3/8
ASI	ASI Communications	UL	3 3/4 – 4 1/8
BAD	Bandag, Inc	UL	48 3/4 – 49 1/2
BTO	Bank of Tokyo	WB	36 3/4 – 37 1/2
BAM@	BankAmer Corp	UL	68 – 68 3/8
BYI	BankAmer Realty SBI	UL	27 7/8 – 28 3/8
BRV	BankAmer Realty 6¾/90	UL	30 – 33
	BankAmer Realty Units	UL	1220 – 1240
BNA@	Bankers Natl Life	UL	22 3/4 – 23 1/4
	Bass Financial	UL	12 1/2 – 14
BEK	Bekins Co.	AB	17 – 17 1/2
BZO	Bernz-O-Matic	UL	12 1/4 – 12 5/8
BLU	Blue Chip Stamps	UL	18 1/4 – 18 5/8
BHM	Bohemia Lumber	WB	26 1/8 – 26 7/8
BRU	Breuner	AB	18 1/2 – 18 7/8
	Cabot, Cabot & Forbes Units	UL	224 – 228
	Cabot, Cabot & Forbes Bonds	UL	109 – 112
	Cabot, Cabot & Forbes Com	UL	23 – 24 1/2
CPU	Cal Pac Utils	WB	19 1/8 – 19 5/8
CFW	Cal Water Svc	WB	27 3/4 – 28 1/4
CWS@	Calif Western Life	WB	19 1/4 – 19 3/4
CAI@	Cap Intl Airways	UL	5 1/8 – 5 1/2
CHP	Champion Prod	UL	21 1/8 – 21 5/8
CMD	Chanco Medical Ind	AB	12 1/4 – 12 3/4
	Citinatl Dev Tr Com	AB	21 3/4 – 22 3/4
	Citinatl Dev Tr Units	AB	27 – 28
	Citinatl Dev Tr Wts	AB	5 1/4 – 5 3/4
CTY	City Natl Corp	AB	26 1/2 – 27
CSI	Cit & So Rlty Inv Tr Com	UL	27 5/8 – 28 1/8
CSD	Cit & So Rlty Inv Tr Units	UL	33 3/4 – 34 1/2
CUI	Cit & So Rlty Inv Tr Wts	UL	6 1/4 – 6 1/2
CLV	Clevepak	UL	23 3/4 – 24 1/4
	Clevetrust Rlty Units	UL	25 3/4 – 26 1/4
	Clevetrust Rlty Com	UL	20 – 20 3/8
	Clevetrust Rlty Wts	UL	5 3/4 – 6
COK	Coca-Cola Bottling LA	AB	42 5/8 – 43 1/8
CWL	Coldwell Banker	AB	31 – 31 1/2
CPE	Colonial Penn Group	UL	41 1/4 – 41 3/4
CTS	Colwell Mtg Com	UL	27 – 27 3/4
CTT	Colwell Mtg Wts	UL	9 5/8 – 10 1/8
	Colwell Mtg Units	UL	36 – 37
CFS	Columbus S & L	WB	17 7/8 – 18 3/8
CPS	Com'ity Psychiatric Ctrs	WB	15 7/8 – 16 3/8
CCC	Continental Capital	WB	11 – 11 1/2
	Contl III Wts	UL	14 – 14 1/2
DTE	Data Tech Corp	WB	7 3/8 – 7 3/4
DEL	Del Monte Prop	WB	17 – 17 1/2
DOL	Dollar General	UL	34 1/4 – 34 3/4
EHR	E H Research	WB	9 1/4 – 10 1/4
ERL	Early Calif Ind	AB	4 3/8 – 4 5/8
EEX	Educators & Executives	UL	29 7/8 – 30 3/8
ELP@	El Paso Elec	UL	15 3/8 – 15 3/4
FMY	Family Life A	WB	23 3/4 – 24 1/4
FCV@	Fidelity Corp (Va)	UL	11 1/4 – 11 1/2
	Fidelity Corp Deb 5½/88	UL	82 – 84
FAF	First Amer Financial	AB	19 3/4 – 20 1/2
FDU	First Denver Mtge Units	UL	24 – 24 1/2
FCA	FNB San Jose	AB	24 1/8 – 24 5/8
FSC	First Security Corp	WB	41 1/8 – 41 5/8
FLI@	Franklin Life	UL	19 3/8 – 19 5/8
GEO	Genovese Drug Stores	UL	9 5/8 – 9 7/8
GWS	Golden West Financial	WB	16 3/8 – 16 7/8
GRT@	GRT Corp	WB	3 5/8 – 3 7/8
GUR	Gulf Mtge & Rlty Com	UL	20 3/8 – 20 3/4
GUU	Gulf Mtge & Rlty Units	UL	26 5/8 – 27
GUW	Gulf Mtge & Rlty Wts	UL	6 1/4 – 6 1/2
HLH	Hallcraft Homes	UL	37 – 37 1/2
HMI@	Hamilton Internatl	UL	4 7/8 – 5 1/8
HAT	Hathaway Instrument	AB	5 3/8 – 5 3/4
HXC	Hexcel Corp	WB	17 – 17 1/2
HIB	Hibernia Bk	WB	45 – 46
HLB	Hillen Brand Ind	UL	43 – 43 1/2
HRZ@	Horizon Corp	UL	38 1/4 – 38 3/4
HBR	Howard Bros Disc	UL	12 3/4 – 13 1/4
HYT@	Hyatt Corp	UL	28 1/4 – 28 3/4
HYA	Hyatt International	UL	13 3/4 – 13 7/8
HYS@	Hyster Corp	WB	40 – 40 3/4
IMT@	Informatics	UL	11 3/4 – 12 1/8
IDA	Interdata, Inc	UL	10 3/4 – 11 1/8
INT	Intermountain Co	UL	10 1/2 – 11
IAL	Intrnatl Aluminum	WB	23 1/2 – 24 1/2
IPG	Interpublic	UL	NA
IRW	Irwin, Richard D., Inc	UL	22 1/4 – 22 3/4
	Itel Corp Wts '78	UL	16 1/2 – 17 1/4
	Itel Corp Wts '79 (Old)	UL	9 3/4 – 10 1/2
JUR	Jurgensens	AB	5 – 5 3/4
KAS@	Kaiser Steel Common	UL	33 1/4 – 33 3/4
KAR@	Kaiser Steel $1.46 Pfd	WB	19 1/2 – 20 1/2
KEA@	Kearney & Trecker	UL	15 – 15 3/8
KLW@	Kellwood Co	UL	41 1/4 – 42
KLY	Kelly Services	UL	32 5/8 – 33 1/8
KNU	Knudsen Corp	AB	37 3/4 – 38 3/4
LNC@	Lance Inc	UL	38 1/2 – 39
LWR	Lawry's Foods	AB	26 – 27
LEI	Leisure Group	UL	13 1/2 – 14
LEV	Levi Strauss	UL	57 7/8 – 57 3/4
LBH	Liberty Homes	UL	19 1/2 – 20
LIV	Life Investors Iowa	UL	23 1/2 – 24
LIN@	Lin Broadcasting	UL	12 1/8 – 12 3/8
LOI	Logicon Inc	AB	6 7/8 – 7 3/8
	Lucky Breweries	UL	6 – 6 3/4
MBL	Mfgs Bank Los Angeles	AB	15 1/2 – 16
MAU	Maui Land	UL	12 3/4 – 13 1/4
MEQ	Mission Equities	AB	19 7/8 – 20 1/4
MVY	Miss Valley Str Stl	UL	12 1/2 – 13
MOR	Morlan Pacific	WB	15 3/8 – 15 7/8
MGG	Mtge Trust Amer SBI	UL	25 – 25 3/8
MGU	Mtge Trust Amer Units	UL	32 3/4 – 33 1/4
MGW	Mtge Trust Amer Wts	UL	7 7/8 – 8 1/8
NBR	Natl Com Bk Rutherford	UL	32 3/4 – 33 3/4
NME@	Natl Med Enterprises	UL	39 1/8 – 39 5/8
NWA@	Nationwide Cl. A	UL	11 3/8 – 12
	NoWest Mut Life Units	UL	239 – 242
	NoWest Mut Life Com	UL	24 3/4 – 25 1/4
	NoWest Mut Life Bonds	UL	116 – 119
NWG@	No West Natl Gas	WB	10 – 10 1/4
NWP	Northwestern Pub Svc	UL	22 1/8 – 22 5/8
ORB	Orbanco	WB	13 3/4 – 14 1/2
PAB@	Pabst Brewing	UL	52 1/8 – 52 5/8
PLU	Pacific Lumber	WB	33 3/4 – 34 3/4
PPN	Pacific Plantronics	WB	26 1/4 – 26 3/4
PSC	Pacific Scientific	AB	7 1/2 – 8
	Pacific Sci Cv Deb 6½/89	AB	65 – 70
PUS	Pacific Utd Serv	UL	13 – 73 3/8
PAL	Palo Alto S & L	WB	30 1/8 – 30 5/8
PAY	Payless Drug No'west	WB	19 3/4 – 20 3/4
PYN@	Pay'n Save Corp	WB	21 – 21 1/2
PIH	Pinehurst Corp Com	AB	7 3/4 – 8 1/4
PIU	Pinehurst Corp Units	AB	19 1/2 – 20 1/4
PIY	Pinehurst Corp Wts	AB	4 1/4 – 4 3/4
PNU	PNB Mtge Realty Units	UL	28 3/4 – 29 1/4
PNS	PNB Mtge Realty Com	UL	22 1/8 – 22 1/2
PNW	PNB Mtge Realty Wts	UL	6 1/2 – 6 3/4
POP	Pope & Talbot Inc	UL	29 1/2 – 30 1/4
RAH	Rahall Communication	UL	12 3/4 – 13 1/4
REC@	Recognition Equip	UL	20 3/4 – 21 1/4
RSS	Ross Medical Corp	WB	12 1/4 – 13 1/4
SAC	Santa Anita Consol	AB	52 1/4 – 53 1/4
SAT	Santa Monica Bank	AB	10 3/4 – 11 1/2
	Schlage Lock	WB	52 – 54
SPA@	Security Pac Natl Bk	UL	37 7/8 – 38 1/4
SVU@	Seven-Up Company	UL	60 1/8 – 60 5/8
SHA@	Shakespeare Co	UL	12 1/4 – 12 5/8
SLX	Siliconix Inc	UL	14 5/8 – 15 1/8
SKA	Skaggs Payless Drugs	WB	25 1/8 – 25 1/2
SLO	Sloan Tech Corp	AB	6 – 7
SWT	So Calif Water	AB	15 1/2 – 16
SWG@	Southwest Gas Corp	UL	16 3/8 – 16 3/4
SDU	SSI Computer 6¾/89	UL	65 – 66
SUM	Standum Inc	AB	32 – 33
SPI	Sumitomo Bank	WB	42 1/2 – 43 1/2
	Superior Ind Intl	AB	16 – 16 1/2
	Super Mold	WB	5 3/4 – 6 1/2
	Technivest	UL	8 5/8 – 9
TCM	Telecomm Inc	UL	16 1/4 – 16 3/4
TPW	Thermal Power	WB	14 1/2 – 15 1/4
TOW	Towle Mfg	UL	16 1/2 – 17
TPI@	Trancontl Gas Pipeline	UL	18 3/4 – 19
TWI	Twin Disc Inc	UL	27 – 28
UBC	Untd Bk Colorado	UL	20 – 20 3/8
USB	U S Bancorp	WB	33 1/8 – 33 7/8
USS	U S Natl Bk San Diego	AB	29 – 30
UTC	Unitek Corp	AB	20 – 20 3/4
ULF@	Untd Life & Acc	UL	16 1/4 – 16 3/4
WNG@	Wash Nat Gas	WB	16 – 16 3/8
WEF	Weisfield's Inc	WB	12 – 12 3/4
WFM	Wells Fargo Mtge Com	UL	19 1/8 – 19 1/2
WFW	Wells Fargo Mtge Wts	UL	4 – 4 1/4
	Wells Fargo Mtge Units	UL	23 5/8 – 25 1/8
WPD	West Coast Prod	WB	9 3/4 – 10
WCA	Western Cas & Surety	UL	62 1/2 – 63
WGE@	Western Gear	WB	8 5/8 – 9
	Yosemite Park	WB	
ZIO	Zions Utah Bancorp	UL	15 1/8 – 15 5/8

@ Denotes stocks eligible for Margin under Fed regulations.

Wire Code for Market Maker: UL – NY / AB – SO.DIV / WB – NO.DIV

making such markets. Table 20-5 shows some quotes on OTC stocks in which Dean Witter & Company make a market. The bid price is what the broker says he will pay for the stock and the ask price is that amount for which he will sell it.

As a general rule, investing in over-the-counter securities should be left to professionals who know what they are doing. A great many questionable practices occur in this market, and it has not been unknown for people to be swindled in it.

Closely Held Corporation Stock   The closely held corporation has been discussed previously as a business organization. Investments in such corporations are indeed hazardous; in essence, the investor owns part of the business and has all of the risks entailed in running it. Since such stock lacks marketability, may not pay any dividends, and has no market value, then why buy it? Simply because, if the situation is right and one knows how to protect himself, the rate of return can be exceedingly lucrative for shrewd investors on the local scene who know what they are doing.

Investments in closely held corporations present problems of ethics and legal protection as well as management. One must make certain that he has legal protection in such investments and that he is not joining with a scoundrel who will swindle him. Moreover, he must be prepared to participate to some degree in the management of the enterprise. The subject of protecting oneself when investing in such corporations is a book unto itself; suffice it to say here that the business scene in every community is littered with bitter investors who have been squeezed out of their minority positions in some prospering, closely held enterprise at considerable loss to themselves. When large sums of money are at stake, greed seems to transform friends into adversaries.

In theory, why would investing in small, closely held concerns be more profitable than buying listed securities?

FIGURE 20–1: The Workings of a Mutual Fund

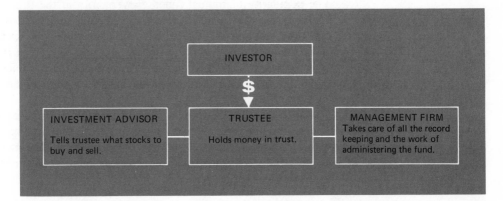

Mutual Funds   Mutual funds were created to meet an obvious need in the market for an investment media by which unsophisticated investors could put money into common stocks but not have to manage them. Mutual funds testify to the need for managing common stock investments. The irony is that the very success of mutual funds has hindered their ability to manage the money entrusted to them. Figure 20-1 diagrams the workings of a mutual fund.

Large accumulations of common stock become unmanageable. For a portfolio of stocks to be manageable, one must be able to liquidate positions quickly without loss, which the large mutual funds are unable to do. Their positions in some stocks are so large that it is impossible to liquidate them on the market without badly depressing the price of the securities. One reason mutual funds fared so badly in their bear market of 1969 was that on the downside they found themselves unable to bail out of bad situations without losing much money for they were, in essence, selling against themselves. One mutual fund manager confided that he owned so much IBM stock that he could not get rid of his position if he sold every share of IBM stock that was sold on the New York Stock Exchange for an entire month.

Mutual funds are for the amateur investor—the man who knows little or nothing about common stock investments. Anyone with investment expertise will avoid them, for they are expensive. The yields on mutual funds have not been particularly attractive. The investor pays for hiring the management of the fund; the managerial fees run about $\frac{1}{2}$ of 1 percent per year of the total value of the fund managed. If the dividend income from the portfolio is 4 percent (the average has been around that level), that means management costs are 12 percent of income—a significant reduction.

In theory, what would a fund management have to do to justify the fund's existence?

There is literally a mutual fund for every conceivable type of investment strategy. If one wants dividend income, he can buy a fund that specializes in that. If he prefers great growth potential, he can find a fund playing that game.

The popularity of mutual funds grew rapidly in the two decades following World War II because of people's vastly broadening interest in purchasing stocks. For the first time, millions of workers had sufficient savings to set them looking for an investment medium superior to the savings account. The stock market has always been a rather romantic institution to the average man, for it conjures up visions of the Golconda—get rich quick. And they were sold by aggressive salesmen.

OPEN-END VERSUS CLOSED-END FUNDS. The open-end fund, the more common and popular type, has no limit on how many shares it sells. It will keep on selling additional shares for their net asset value at the time of purchase as long as there are buyers. Such funds also redeem their shares for net asset value at the time of redemption, minus a small service charge.

How can an open-end mutual fund afford to buy back its shares?

The closed-end fund is very similar to a regular corporation in that only a limited number of shares in the fund will be sold; once the fund has sold them, it sells no more. Moreover, it does not redeem these shares; the investor must sell them on the open market. Table 20-6 is a list of such closed-end funds and the prices for which they were selling. Note that they sold for less than their net asset value.

Table 20–6
PROFILE OF
PERFORMANCE
OF CLOSED-END
MUTUAL FUNDS

1970 Price Range	Distributions 1970		Company	1-1-71 Price	Recent Premium or Discount	Net Asset Value
	Capital Gains	Invest- ment Income				
16¾-11⅛	$0.72	$1.24	Adams Express	14¼	−1.8%	$14.51
49½-27¾	0.00	0.70	American South African	42⅛	33.1	31.46
32¼-25⅝	1.50	2.50	Carriers & General Corp.	30	−19.2	37.13
22½-13	1.23	1.45	Central Securities	14¼	36.1	11.02
13⅜- 7	0.76	0.97	Dominick Fund	8⅞	−17.4	10.75
21¼-13⅜	0.70	1.10	Eurofund International	17¾	−9.8	19.67
28⅜-16	1.26	1.73	General American Investors	21¾	−6.5	23.26
19¼-11¼	0.96	1.43	International Holdings	13⅞	−15.9	16.49
12½- 7½	1.387	1.487	Japan Fund	8¾	9.4	8.00
21¼-13⅝	1.02	1.325	The Lehman Corp.	16⅜	10.4	14.83
26¾-14⅛	1.54	1.99	Madison Fund	16¾	16.0	14.44
26⅞-16	0.36	1.64	National Aviation	20	−12.4	22.84
20⅜-13¼	0.725	1.10	Niagara Share Corp.	15⅝	6.7	14.65
22¾-14⅝	0.68	1.53	Petroleum Corp of America	20	−6.0	21.27
28⅝-18½	0.19	0.67†	Standard Shares	21¼	−22.7	27.38
7 - 4¾	0.06	0.255	Surveyor Fund	5⅛	−8.7	5.62
33⅞-21¼	1.82	2.71	Tri-Continental	28¼	−6.2	30.11
12⅛- 8	0.25	1.175	United Corp.	9⅛	−18.0	11.14
35 -22	2.98	3.84	U.S. & Foreign Securities	33	−3.9	34.34

Why do these shares sell for less than their net asset value?
Why would anyone want to buy closed-end mutual funds?

PROBLEMS IN THE SELECTION OF FUNDS. It is a serious mistake to believe that all mutual funds are the same, for they vary widely in several characteristics.

  1. Performance First, their performance varies widely, as shown in Table 20-7, so selecting the mutual fund that one should buy can be just as complicated, if not more so, then selecting a stock to buy. A mutual fund that is highly successful one year may be a loser the next because of the vagaries of chance; its stocks may

Table 20–7
PERFORMANCE
OF SELECTED
MUTUAL FUNDS

Name of Fund	Net Asset Value Per Share, 1961 Price	Net Asset Value Per Share, 1971 Price	Total Dollars Received in Dividends and Capital Gains, 1961–1971
Bullock Fund	$14.07	$15.19	$10.56
Dreyfus Fund	8.54	12.53	5.74
First Investors Fund	10.51	10.15	6.32
Massachusetts Investors Fund	14.60	14.54	10.69
Value Line Fund	7.29	7.12	7.96
Wellington Fund	15.17	12.07	9.09

have a very fortuitous year and then encounter disaster. Many mutual fund managers are successful for a short period largely because of luck. Someone has to guess correctly.

2. Overhead   It costs money to manage a mutual fund, some more than others. Some funds are relatively so inefficient that their shareholders are paying far too much for having their money managed.

3. Sales Costs   Mutual funds are marketed in several ways. Some are sold directly to the public by a hard-hitting sales force—an expensive distributive system which has to be paid for. Guess who pays the bill? It runs about 8 percent of the investment. Many of these direct-selling funds have a "front end load," which means that the buyer's money pays the salesman's commission before any of the money that he gives the fund starts buying mutual fund shares.

It is strongly recommended that you do not deal with such concerns, but rather buy "no load" funds, which pay no sales commissions. Of course, not many salesmen have been known to push such wares, for understandable reasons. You must contact the "no load" funds directly yourself. They are advertised in financial journals.

Real Estate

Real estate should play some part in each investor's program. One of the first building blocks in a man's estate should be his home. It is just as much an investment as apartments, land, commercial structures, and office buildings. In the long run, diligent, knowledgeable investors have had quite good results in real estate. Fortunes have been made as real estate values have constantly increased over the years.

The basis for the increasing values in real estate lies in our increasing population. People must have somewhere to live and land to stand on. Moreover, increased population brings on an increased need for commercial and industrial property. This increased demand increases the price of real estate, for its supply is fixed. There is only so much land in the world, and little of it is usable immediately. Hence, the real estate man is operating in a market in which the demand side is rapidly expanding and the supply side is diminishing. As available, usable land is taken up by existing people, the land remaining for sale diminishes. This two-way squeeze greatly raises land values.

Let us make it clear from the beginning that investing in real estate is a field in its own right. Normally, people who place their money in real estate concentrate on that market entirely, leaving the stock market to less industrious individuals. Unquestionably, it takes more effort to invest in real estate than to buy common stocks. One must have more knowledge and more management know-how.

The attractions of real estate to the investor are several. First, one is able to obtain a great deal of leverage on his money; one can usually borrow 80 to 100 percent of the value of the real estate. In some exceptional real estate deals the owner has been able to borrow more than 100 percent of the cost of the property. The idea is to let the investment pay itself off over a period of time. This works out nicely if one's forecasts of income from the property are accurate. Second, there is the favorable demand picture in real estate. Third, real estate has tremendous income tax advantages, not enjoyed by investors in other media, centering around what is known as "cash flow," resulting from the rapid depreciation allowed plus the ability to exchange real estate for other real estate without being taxed on the gain. Fourth, the tangible nature of real estate appeals to many men. Stocks have been known to become worthless pieces of paper, but if one owns land, at least he can always grow something on it.

Home   One's home should be considered an investment, for it is just as easy to lose or make money on it as it is in the stock market. Too many people, failing to realize the investment aspects of their home, buy it in much the same way as they buy a car or television set. Large sums of money are involved, despite the illusion created by a low down payment. The home's value will appreciate if it has been purchased with wisdom.

The pitfalls awaiting the unwary home buyer are so many that it is difficult to delve into all of them here. Entire books are available on the subject, and the diligent home buyer would be wise to read one of them. But a few key thoughts might be appropriate at this point.

LOCATION.   The most important factor determining the marketability and long-range value of a property is its location. One wag once said there were three important factors in real estate: location, location, and location. It *is* that important. Buy a home in the wrong location and you will not only suffer a loss when you sell it, but also you will have difficulty doing so. A properly located home moves fast at a fair price. The right location appreciates substantially in value with the years.

What constitutes a good location for a home? What are the factors one should avoid when selecting locations?

True, location costs money, but so do good stocks and other good investments. Location does not cost money; it makes money. It simply increases the amount one must invest to play the game.

Location is even more critical in making other types of real estate investments. Truly, the key to successful investing in real estate lies in selecting the right location.

BUY RIGHT.   As with any other investment, one cannot profit on a real estate deal if he pays too much. The problem of investing in a home is that emotions come into play far more strongly than in other investments. If your wife falls in love with a particularly cute bungalow, she may be willing to pay far too much for it, simply because of her emotions. If you pay too much, do not expect the next buyer to bail you out of your mistake. The bigger-fool theory does not always work.

What is the bigger-fool theory?

Real estate prices are highly negotiable. You must realize that as a buyer you have the upper hand and can make attractive purchases if your timing is right and if the owner wants to sell. Keep in mind that someday you may want to sell and be under similar pressures.

This brings up a key factor in dealing in real estate: have patience. Never be in a hurry to buy or sell a property. If you must act fast, you will pay a price for your haste. The man who comes to town and must buy a house within a few days must accept whatever is on the market and does not have much time to dicker with the owner. The man who must sell his property within a short period must take whatever is offered by the first buyer who comes along. Once a buyer or seller detects that the other party is impatient, all bargaining position is lost.

APPEARANCE. Eye appeal is most important in selling a house. Good landscaping, good painting, and tasteful decorating vastly enhance the marketability of any property. Avoid run-down property unless you are prepared to make additional investments to repair it.

MARKETABILITY. Try to think like the person to whom you eventually want to sell the property. Avoid properties that appeal to some unique aspect in your makeup or needs, for the next buyer will not appreciate or value those characteristics. Pity the person who designs an oddball house to fit his whims; if he tries to sell it, he will usually take a beating. The average home owner will sell his home at some time in the not-too-distant future, so he should buy with an eye to its marketability. One man with five sons built a house with only two bedrooms—one was a large dormitory with an open bath in which to barrack the boys. Yes, he decided to move to another town. Yes, he took a large loss on his house, for there were very few families with five boys who wanted his house.

FINANCING.   It has been said truthfully many times that people do not buy houses, they buy financing. If you are able to present a financial plan to the buyer that enables him to buy your house for a low down payment, your property's marketability and value are vastly enhanced. High down payments remove most people from the market.

Apartments

The attraction of apartment houses is that with a growing population, the need for housing units is rapidly expanding; therefore, the demand side of the market is attractive. Moreover, apartments have considerable leverage: one can borrow anywhere from 70 to 100 percent of their value, depending upon the circumstances, and 90 percent loans are not uncommon in this activity.

But apartments also have their disadvantages. One can lose his money rather rapidly if occupancy rates are below the break-even point. The overhead and carrying charges against an apartment house are often such that a high occupancy rate is necessary just to break even. If the complex suffers significant vacancies for any length of time, the financial picture can become rather dismal.

What determines an apartment's vacancy rate? How can one minimize vacancies?

Typically, apartments get into trouble because of either a poor location or a poor design. However, one professional investor in apartment houses claims that success rests upon three factors. First, the apartment must be managed by a professional real estate management firm; this service costs about 6 percent of rentals. Second, the apartment complex must have a minimum of 32 units. (Of course, there is nothing sacred about the number 32; this is an estimate of the threshold for economies of size.) Third, the apartments must be purchased at a realistic price. It is difficult to profit from the investment if one pays too much in the beginning.

In this one narrow field of investment there are many different games one can play. Some investors concentrate on building new apartment complexes with all the latest features; others concentrate on finding old apartment houses for sale at an attractive price and fix them up. Some rent to students while others seek the single working person. Some say, "Never rent to men," while others say, "Never rent to women." Operating philosophies have a wide scope.

Commercial Property

Some investors have found it lucrative to invest in shopping centers, retail stores, warehouses, and other such commercial structures. The risks entailed in these ventures may be large; if the tenant is not financially responsible, one may find himself with a vacant, relatively unrentable structure on his hands. For this reason most professional investors in commercial properties will only lease to large, nationally recognized tenants such as the national chain stores. Firestone Tire & Rubber Company has a program for getting its specially designed retail tire outlets built by private money; they will give the investor a guaranteed return on his money that is most attractive, clear of all expenses. Such leases are known as "net-net" leases, meaning that the tenant pays all costs including property taxes and insurance. The investor is simply given a payment for the use of his funds.

Why do large, financially responsible companies want to lease such properties at a seemingly high rate of interest from private investors?

Land

Raw land is highly speculative. Normally, investors in land are very wealthy parties who have huge sums of money to invest and are willing to wait for the land to appreciate in value, which may take from five to fifteen years. Land speculation is a most hazardous undertaking; to engage in it profitably, one must buy large tracts of land at low prices and then wait for its value to rise as the population moves closer to it. This is no game for the typical small investor. The highly advertised land speculations in which a man is asked to buy a lot or two in the middle of the Arizona desert or the high Sierras are usually little more than confidence games and are shunned by knowledgeable investors.

Land development is even more expensive. One large development in Southern California—Rancho Bernardo—disclosed the following costs: Land—$6.5 million; two golf courses—$1.9 million; hotel and restaurant—$5.5 million; clubhouse—$350,000; adult community center—$750,000; two swim and tennis clubs—$700,000; model homes—$2 million; industrial park improvements—$3.5 million; roads, water, sewer, electric systems—$4 million; 3,200 living units—$96 million.

Real Estate Syndicates and Trusts

The small to moderate-size investor is frequently blocked from participating in investments in such things as large apartment houses, large shopping centers, tracts of land, and industrial locations because of the huge sums of money that are required. Even $100,000 does not buy much of an apartment house. So our system has responded by creating some unique institutions to solve this problem—the real estate syndicate, real estate trust, and the limited partnership. Basically, they have the same principle, differing only in legal formalities. But the formalities are important, so they should not be ignored by the investor, even though we cannot discuss them here.

The basic principle is that a group of similarly minded investors band together under some legal organization to pool their money to invest in a proposed real estate enterprise. Some provision for managing the investment is made, and that costs some money, and the profits are split up among the investors. So many different arrangements are being sold, that any summary of them is fruitless. Let it be known, however, that one must be careful in entering into such arrangements.

Insurance

Although insurance has investment characteristics, it is of such importance and complexity that we shall treat it in a separate chapter.

INVESTMENT ADVICE

In line with the principle that everyone's investment problems are unique and his program must be tailored to fit his own requirements, it is impossible to give any definitive investment program for one to follow. Instead, a few generalities that seem to be rather good advice will be passed on here.

Liquidity

Experience indicates that a great deal of misery results when people place too much of their money in relatively unliquid investments. When investing in relatively nonliquid ventures, one must keep sufficient liquidity in reserve that he can never be pressured to liquidate his investment at a loss. Moreover, he must make certain that he is being sufficiently rewarded for forfeiting his liquidity when investing in such ventures. There is great virtue in investments that one can easily convert into cash with little loss.

The Long View

The true investor has a longer view of his investments than the in-and-out speculator. Investments in long-run growth situations require foresight and patience. The investor who is impatient to get rich quick overnight seldom succeeds. It takes time for certain investments to mature, and people who are always chasing the quick buck seldom get in on the really big killings. How many investors who bought Xerox and IBM early in their growth bailed out after these stocks had a short rise, taking a quick profit, rather than holding on for the long pull that has been extremely profitable? Indeed, a modest investor placing his money in IBM stock during the forties is an extremely wealthy man today. Most of the true investors in the stock market take the long view and ignore the short-term swings. They put their money in what seems to them to be a pregnant growth situation and then allow that opportunity to mature, thereby reaping their financial harvest.

Rate of Return

Greed has been the downfall of more than one investor. One must not expect too much of his money; it can only work so hard. Usually the higher the rate of return, the greater the financial risk. The investor who continually invests *all* of his money in high-risk ventures will sooner or later be destroyed; inevitably one of these ventures will wipe him out, if he has *all* of his money so placed. It is either a very foolish man who places all of his money in high-risk investments, or an exceedingly capable one, but he is still gambling—gambling upon his judgment.

Knowledge

While it has been emphasized time and again that knowledge is essential to successful investing, one cannot repeat it too often. One must learn the rules of the game he wishes to play if he hopes to win. It takes time and effort to study and become proficient in the technique of investing in any of the investment media discussed. If you are not willing to pay the price of learning and acquiring the necessary knowledge, then stay out of the game! Put your money in a savings account for other people to play with who do know the game.

Other People

While painful experience is probably necessary to teach anyone the truth about other people, still candor demands that we mention this aspect of human nature here. Human nature being what it is, character and honesty seem to degenerate when exposed to your money. It is difficult to believe what other people tell you about investments they are selling; they frequently lie. There are those who will tell you that worthless, barren, desert land will make you a millionaire and that chinchilla farming is the way to riches overnight. And then there are those who tell you that with a little work and investment in vending machines or a franchise that you will be on the road to wealth. There are countless ways that people have of enticing you to invest in their propositions, and when you tire of hearing the old, worn ones they always have some new pitches to throw your way. Extreme caution is the watchword in all of these instances. There are many hidden pitfalls and traps awaiting the unwary.

Whenever in doubt, just remember this: if the deal is so good, why is the man beseeching you to invest your few dollars in it? Why isn't he keeping it for himself? And why is he finding it so difficult to get money if the proposition is so attractive? Good investments do not need to be huckstered like snake oil. There are always professional investors eager to place their money in sound investments. When a man promises to make you rich overnight, you have reason to question his honesty, for why in the world does anyone else want to make *you* wealthy? What he is trying to do is make *himself* wealthy with your money.

Unfortunately there is no definitive method by which one can protect himself from making bad investments; in the end it all depends upon using your own sound judgment based upon a knowledge of the realities of the world in which you live.

Conclusion

> By now you should have gotten the message. If you were expecting advice on how to invest your paltry savings so that you would soon be wealthy, you should now realize the difficulties facing you. Get-rich-quick schemes for investing are highly suspicious at best, fraudulent at worst. There are no easy ways to riches. Investing is hard work. It takes time and knowledge and, above all, considerable sound judgment.
>
> There are a great many avenues one can travel in seeking investment goals; the choice depends largely upon one's personality and needs. Each person's situation is unique, so his investment program must be tailored to meet those unique needs.
>
> There is no answer to the investment dilemma: "Where can I best invest my money?" Any decision one makes has its risks. And it is most important to realize and contemplate those risks—financial, interest-rate, political, purchasing-power, and income. Moreover, the problems of liquidity and management must be successfully resolved if the program is to succeed. Good luck! It takes a bit of that also.

21 The securities markets

Everything is worth what its purchaser will pay for it.
PUBLILIUS SYRUS

Remember Ideas, Inc., that was formed a few chapters back? Well, all this time it has been growing and prospering through your adept management. Now its growth is being hampered by lack of capital. You need more money—a lot more money—to build a new plant in order to capitalize upon the market opportunity available. But your banker refuses to lend you any more money—he claims it is not the bank's function to provide you with equity capital on which to grow. He says that you need to sell stock: $4.5 million is what your planners say will be needed within the next year. The time has come for you to go public. Moreover, you find that the thought of going public is not particularly repugnant, because you have been worried for some time about the value of the stock that you own.

You know the company is worth a lot of money; its book value is now $3 a share, but you know that you could not sell for that if forced to do so. Going public would rectify that problem, because a market would be created for Ideas' common stock.

Your affluence acquired over the past few years has allowed you to purchase various securities for your own account, using the services of a moderate-sized broker, Bull & Bear, affectionately known in the trade as BB. BB is also an investment banker: a firm that specializes in raising money to start or expand businesses. When an especially large block of stock or bonds of a corporation are to be sold, several investment banking firms may work together; such groups are called *syndicates*. Investment bankers actually buy the security issue from the company and resell it, hopefully at a higher price—a process which is called *underwriting*. As president of a prospering young growth company, Mr. Bull has become a personal acquaintance of yours, so you take your problem to him. After a series of meetings, during which BB's analysts carefully scrutinize Idea's financial performance and appraise its future prospects, BB indicates an interest in underwriting a common stock issue of 1,000,000 shares at $5 a share, netting you the $4.5 million new capital you need: underwriting costs were $500,000.

BB is a marketing institution. Its business is selling securities, receiving a commission for its efforts. This commission is negotiable and varies widely, depending upon the difficulties involved and the bargaining powers of the parties. For some highly speculative issues, the commissions may run as high as 20 percent of the sales, in which case Ideas, Inc., would be paid only $4 million for the $5 million stock issue; BB would keep $1 million for its troubles. In the present case BB feels that a 10 percent commission is adequate, so Ideas would be paid $4.5 million for its stock.

But let's talk about Bull & Bear for a minute. . . .

Concepts of the Stock Brokerage House

The institution normally referred to as a stockbroker really is a combination of several things. The typical New York stock brokerage house wears eight different hats—performs eight different functions, some of which create severe conflicts of interest. First, most brokerages are also investment bankers who perform the *underwriting function;* they do all of the work connected with creating and bringing forth and selling new issues of securities. Second, they perform the *brokerage function,* in which they act in behalf of buyers and sellers of existing securities to facilitate transactions between them. Third, they perform a *banking function* for their customers buying on the margin, for they procure and lend funds, for which they charge interest rates. Fifth, they provide an *investment advisory service,* giving advice to anyone who cares to listen to it. Sixth, they perform a *research function,* admittedly in conjunction with advising, as they attempt to discover important information about companies. Seventh, they also act as *investors* themselves by placing their own money in various situations. Eighth, they provide a *dealer function* when they carry an inventory of various securities for the purpose of selling them at a profit.

So the so-called stockbroker is really eight different things. He has acquired these different hats in his desire to provide his customers with a full-service securities store. The typical broker wants to be able to furnish the customer anything he wants to buy, just like any other good merchant. This is the motive that has led the broker into these widely varied activities.

While the typical stock brokerage is the backbone institution in the securities business, there are advisory services such as Standard & Poor's and Moody's, plus many others, that endeavor to provide much pertinent information with which investors may better evaluate companies. And then there are the official stock exchanges: the New York Stock Exchange, the American Stock Exchange, and several regional exchanges, of which more will be said later. There is also the Securities and Exchange Commission, a governmental agency which endeavors to regulate the entire affair. Finally, there are many diverse institutions, such as put and call dealers, mutual funds, investment advisory services.

But let's get back to Ideas' new public financing.

The management of Ideas, Inc., agrees in principle with BB's proposal, and the requisite legal papers are drawn up by which Ideas agrees to allow BB to form an underwriting syndicate to buy and distribute Ideas' new issue of common stock. BB agrees to do all the legal work necessary to register the issue with the SEC and assemble all of the data needed to produce the required prospectus.

The prospectus demanded by the SEC is a most important document, for in it the company must disclose all relevant and pertinent information concerning it and its plans; any relevant omissions may be punished severely. It is unfortunate that most investors do not take the time to read the prospectus of a security before they buy it, for if they did so, they might have second thoughts about the wisdom of the purchase.

Go to a stockbroker and obtain a prospectus of some stock issue. After reading it, give your evaluation of the securities. Would you buy if you had the money?

After all of the legal requirements for distribution have been met and the issue has been properly registered with the SEC, the syndicate can go ahead with the stock sale. It is important to understand that the SEC never gives an evaluation of the merits of any stock issue. The SEC's approval merely means that the company has met the legal requirements for the stock sale.

A date is set on which the syndicate will commence selling the Ideas stock issue. BB formed a syndicate because it would be difficult for it to sell $5 million of Ideas stock to its own customers, and it is most important that all of the stock be sold in a relatively short time.

Why is it important that the stock sale be completed quickly?

The distributive facilities of a large investment banking network are required. If you look at the prospectus of most stock offerings, you will note that many significant investment bankers are members of the syndicate. Each has agreed to buy a certain portion of Ideas' stock issue, thus guaranteeing Ideas, Inc., that it will get its money. If any syndicate member fails to sell his share, he will keep it to sell later. If the issue looks particularly attractive, some syndicate members may take a position in the security for their own portfolio.

It is this cooperative effort among all of the nation's investment bankers to distribute quickly any new security issue that makes possible new equity financing for most substantial corporations. The system works rather well in normal times, but becomes rather sticky when the stock market is depressed.

PROCEDURE FOR BUYING AND SELLING EXISTING SECURITIES

There are two basic systems for buying or selling existing securities: (1) through recognized exchanges, or (2) over the counter. Each of these will be examined.

Listed Securities

Now that Ideas, Inc., has gone public, you would like to have its securities listed on an exchange. But to do so requires that the company meet additional standards, for not every company is eligible for listing. The eligibility terms for the American and New York Stock Exchanges are given in Figure 21-1. You can note the differences. In general, companies listed on the New York Stock Exchange must be larger, have a longer history of successful operations, and must have a wider distribution base—more shares of stock outstanding in more hands.

FIGURE 21–1: Listing Requirements for the New York and American Stock Exchanges

	New York	American
Number of publicly held shares	Minimum of 800,000 out of 1,000,000 shares outstanding	Minimum of 300,000
Number of round-lot shareholders	Minimum of 1800 out of 2000	Minimum of 600 out of 900
Total market value of publicly held shares	$14 million	$2 million
Net tangible assets	$14 million	$3 million
Earning power	$2.5 million before taxes for most recent year; $2 million in each of two previous years	$500,000 before taxes

Why don't the stock exchanges want to list the securities of a company when significant blocks of it are held in the hands of a few individuals?
Of what function is a broad distribution base for a security?

Ideas, Inc., does not qualify for listing, but its management sees what it must do in the next few years to qualify and sets its sights on doing so, for it believes the virtues of being listed are significant.

What are the virtues to a company of being listed on the New York Stock Exchange?

Having looked at the dealings of BB with a corporation wanting to sell stock, let us now look at the broker's dealings with a potential buyer of that stock. To do so you must change hats—do a bit of pretending.

You have just won $10,000 in a contest for students showing the most promise in business; you feel it fitting to invest your newly acquired wealth in some stock. After much diligent study, you decide to invest in Growth, Inc. (listed on the NYSE), which appears to you to have a bright future and is reasonably priced in relationship to its future prospects. You go to an office of a large brokerage company to open an account, for you have not previously done so. The receptionist refers you to a young man a few years out of college who manages the accounts of many people such as yourself—an account executive. Practically all of your contacts with the brokerage will be with your account executive, mostly over the telephone. The relationship between you and your account man is such that you must have full confidence in his ability. If you do not have such feelings, then by all means pick another man to handle your money. It is your choice as to who will manage your funds—remember, it's your money. If you want to buy or sell something, call him; if he has something he wants to sell you, or if he feels it wise for you to divest yourself of some holding, he will call you to make his recommendations. He is a very important person in your financial life. If he is good, he may make you some money; if he is bad, he will lose your money.

You and your new account executive will talk at length while he gathers information needed to open your account and learns of your investment objectives and philosophies. If he is to do a good job for you, he must become familiar with your investment goals and financial situation, for he cannot make intelligent recommendations without such knowledge.

He asks whether you want a regular cash account or a margin account; you are not interested in borrowing money, so you stay away from margin accounts.

Margin Account

There are two basic types of accounts in a brokerage house: cash accounts and margin accounts. The cash account is simply one with which you buy or sell securities and pay, or get paid, cash for them. You borrow nothing. The margin account, on the other hand, is one in which you borrow money—possibly up to 30 percent of the value of that security—and leave that security in the hands of the broker as collateral for the loan. You pay interest on the money you borrow. Suppose you purchased on margin 1000 shares of Ideas, Inc., selling at $5 a share—a round lot whose total value is $5000. You would have to pay only $3500 (70 percent) for it, inasmuch as the broker could obtain a brokerage loan of $1500 for you. The purpose of buying on the margin is to allow one to buy more stock than he has money, thereby giving him more leverage on his existing money supply. Buying on the margin is inflationary; therefore, the margin requirements are regulated by the government. In highly inflationary times of the 1950s, the margin requirement was 80 percent—you could borrow 20 percent—but the margin was decreased to 70 percent in the 1970s bear market in order to stimulate interest in buying stocks.

Your account executive strongly recommends that you buy 100 shares of High Flyer, a company in which he is currently interested, but you are adamant that you want to buy Growth, Inc. So you give him an order to buy 100 shares of Growth, Inc. *at market*. At market means that you order him to pay whatever has to be paid to buy the stock; the broker is legally obligated as your agent to do the best he can for you. You could have given a *limit order* to buy at a stipulated price, say $44, in which case your order would not be filled unless the broker could find someone willing to sell for $44 a share or less. Or you could have placed a *GTC order* (good

FIGURE 21-2: System for Buying Stocks

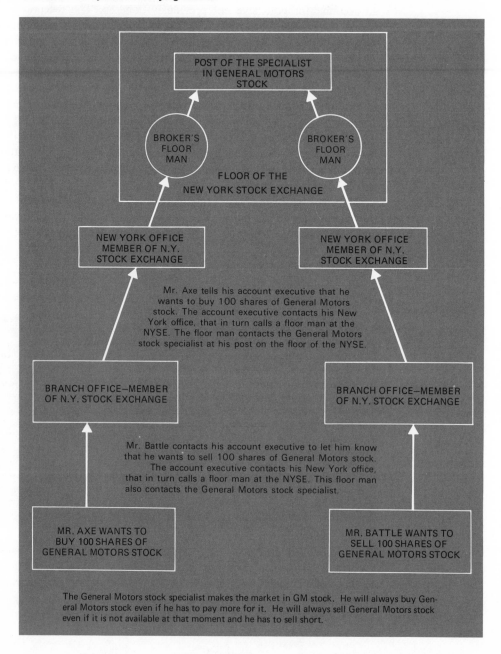

POST OF THE SPECIALIST
IN GENERAL MOTORS
STOCK

BROKER'S
FLOOR
MAN

BROKER'S
FLOOR
MAN

FLOOR OF THE
NEW YORK STOCK EXCHANGE

NEW YORK OFFICE
MEMBER OF N.Y.
STOCK EXCHANGE

NEW YORK OFFICE
MEMBER OF N.Y.
STOCK EXCHANGE

Mr. Axe tells his account executive that he
wants to buy 100 shares of General Motors
stock. The account executive contacts his New
York office, that in turn calls a floor man at the
NYSE. The floor man contacts the General Motors
stock specialist at his post on the floor of the NYSE.

BRANCH OFFICE—MEMBER
OF N.Y. STOCK EXCHANGE

BRANCH OFFICE—MEMBER
OF N.Y. STOCK EXCHANGE

Mr. Battle contacts his account executive to let him know
that he wants to sell 100 shares of General Motors stock.
The account executive contacts his New York office,
that in turn calls a floor man at the NYSE. This floor man
also contacts the General Motors stock specialist.

MR. AXE WANTS TO
BUY 100 SHARES OF
GENERAL MOTORS STOCK

MR. BATTLE WANTS TO
SELL 100 SHARES OF
GENERAL MOTORS STOCK

The General Motors stock specialist makes the market in GM stock. He will always buy General Motors stock even if he has to pay more for it. He will always sell General Motors stock even if it is not available at that moment and he has to sell short.

till cancelled) for some price, say $40, which would be held by the broker to be exercised if the price of the stock dropped to that level.

He pushes a little device on his desk and learns that the last transaction for Growth, Inc., was for $44\frac{1}{2}$, which means that you will have to pay about $44.50 per share. He writes up the order and sends it to New York. Within a few minutes, confirmation will come back that the transaction has been completed. In the meantime, the order is processed as shown in Figure 21-2, all of which happens in a surprisingly short time in this electronic age.

After buying Growth, Inc., stock at $44\frac{1}{2}$, you give the broker a *stop order* to sell it at $40; if the price drops to 40, your stock will be sold. Such orders are sometimes called *stop-loss orders,* for that is their purpose—to limit losses.

Why place a stop-loss order on a stock? In what other situation would one care to use a stop-loss order?

You continue to chat with your account man for a few minutes, then a young girl hands him the confirmation of your order. You have bought 100 shares of Growth, Inc. at $44\frac{3}{8}$. It was down an eighth of a point from the last transaction. Your total bill including taxes and commissions is shown in Table 21-1.

Table 21-1

Stock purchase—100 shares @ 44⅜	$4437.50
Broker's commission	41.19
New York State Sales Tax	5.00
TOTAL COST OF STOCK	$4483.69

You still have $5516.31 left from your original $10,000, so your account executive recommends a particularly attractive over-the-counter stock for you to buy: Ideas, Inc.—a small, local company that has been growing rapidly and has shown excellent management. He says the stock was issued a few weeks ago at $5 a share, but is now selling over the counter for $6.50 and may hit $15 by the end of the year, when its 1972 earnings are made public. Management currently predicts earnings of $2 a share, and he feels that it should sell for a P/E (price/earnings) ratio—a multiple—of ten, which would make Ideas' price rise to $20 a share.

Inasmuch as this money means a lot to you and you do not want to lose it, you decide to delay making a decision on Ideas, Inc., until after you have had an opportunity to look at their products and meet some of their people. You tell the account executive that you will call him in a few days after investigating the company. After doing so, you call your broker and tell him to buy 500 shares at no more than $6.50 per share. This time the order is handled in a different fashion, for Ideas, Inc., is not listed, so the exchange cannot be used.

First, the account executive checks to see if his own firm has a position in the stock and will sell for $6.50 a share. Management tells him that although it does have a position in Ideas, Inc., it wants $7 a share. The account executive contacts Bull & Bear, who are known to make a market in the stock. He asks them for a quotation; they reply that they are asking $6.40 and bidding $5.75—they will sell for $6.40 a share and buy for $5.75. Upon notification of this, your account executive calls to tell you that you have bought 500 shares at $6.40 a share. Had you been able to buy the shares from your own brokerage house, you would not have had to pay any commission whatsoever on the transaction, but since they are purchased from someone else, then a commission is due.

At any time in the future if, for any reason, you decide to sell these securities, all you have to do is tell your account executive to do so. If you have left the stock certificates in his care, you need do nothing other than telephone him. But if you have had them sent to you, then you will have to sign the stock certificates and send them to him.

In general, if these investments are made for a long-term investment, you should have the stock certificates sent to you for safekeeping. But if you are trading in a security—buying and selling for short-term profit—it is far more convenient for the broker to keep the securities. Traders usually deal in margin accounts, in which it is mandatory that physical possession of the stock be kept in "the street's" name, in which case you are sent no stock certificates.

Short Selling

You work for a new chain of franchised fast food restaurants in the exalted position of counter clerk. Fast Foods, Ltd., is typical of the many such operations that have proliferated during the past decade, grown rapidly, and gone public—sold stock to the public. From your position in the company you have concluded that the future of this company is most certain—it has to collapse. Aside from your contributions to the chaos, management does not seem to know what it is doing.

You see that its stock is currently selling for a high of $35 a share, 32 times earnings. You cannot see how that can continue. So you decide to make some money on your judgment.

You call your account executive and tell him to sell 100 shares of Fast Food short. This will require that you open a margin account and put up some money to cover possible losses on the transaction should the price of Fast Food go up rather than down. You do so. He sells 100 shares of Fast Food for $34 a share; you are credited with $3400 minus commissions. The broker borrows the stock certificates for Fast Food from someone who owns 100 shares and is willing to loan them to you. You must return those 100 shares to cover your "short." But you have time—time during which you hope the price of Fast Food goes down.

You were right. The market soon senses that Fast Food's future is doubtful, and the price drops daily. At $25 per share, you decide to cover; you are happy with your profits. So you order your account executive to buy 100 shares of Fast Food—cover your short. He puts in the order and you buy for $23; the price is dropping fast. So you have sold 100 shares for a total of $3500 and bought it for $2300; you have a profit of $1200 minus two commissions and taxes. That is short selling. You sell first at a high price and then buy later for a lower one.

Why didn't you stay short and let the price go on down?

The advice of most professionals to the average man about short selling is . . . don't! If you are wrong, your losses can be huge; if you are right, your gains are limited by the price of the stock.

THE COMMODITY EXCHANGES

A completely different, separate system exists for buying and selling commodities known as the commodity exchanges. These are located largely in Chicago and New York, although there are some minor exchanges elsewhere.

Trading in commodities should be left to the professionals who believe that they know what they are doing. It is not something for the average man on the street, for one can lose money quickly in the commodity market. Buying and selling commodities is a highly speculative endeavor for the trader, for one is able to do it on a very small margin. It takes only $500 to finance a corn contract. That is, one needs to put up only 5 percent in cash for the value of the contract; he can borrow the other 95 percent. This sounds marvelous until one stops to think that if the price drops only 5 percent, he has lost 100 percent of his investment. If the price drops more than that, he must put up more money.

Markets are made in practically all standard commodities, such as corn, wheat, potatoes, soybeans, plywood, silver, cotton, tobacco, pork bellies, oats, rye, barley, sugar, cocoa beans, cow hides, and many others in which there is an interest in having a market made.

Why do people want markets made in commodities?

There are legitimate business purposes for creating markets in these commodities. Many firms must buy, inventory, and resell commodities. Pillsbury must buy wheat and corn with which to manufacture its products. It must carry inventories in these commodities. It buys the grains in the cash markets at all times, but it has no desire to speculate in the price behavior of these commodities. These markets allow the grain merchants to transfer their risks of loss due to price drops onto the shoulders of the speculator.

What dangers do such price variations present to firms that use the grains?

Prices are highly volatile, because supply conditions are so greatly affected by such various factors as weather, blight, and the vagaries of demand. One year the price of wheat skyrocketed when the Russians came into the wheat market to buy heavily, because their own crop failed.

FINANCIAL REPORTING

Information is the lifeblood of the securities system; without it, chaos reigns. Since the need for data—accurate, pertinent, and prompt data—is critical to intelligent investment decisions, a great number of institutions are devoted to obtaining and selling it. Any financial publication such as *The Wall Street Journal, Barron's, Forbes,* and *Dun's Review* carries advertisements of the many firms endeavoring to sell their data to the information-hungry investor. Such information is usually processed to a significant degree to provide a more meaningful analysis. This is not the place to delve into the intricacies of the mathematical manipulations performed by the various technical people in the market, for that is a field unto itself. Suffice it to say that there is no shortage of this type of information: the problems are those of its accuracy and timeliness.

Newspaper Financial Reporting

The financial pages of *The Wall Street Journal* or your morning newspaper are the first primary source of data investors use to learn of their fortunes, or misfortunes. You should learn to read the statistical sections. Figure 21-3 illustrates how to interpret the mass of numbers.

Sources of Information

Sources of information can be classified into two categories: published and private.

Published Information   The basic document from which most public information is obtained is the company's corporate report, which is normally made available annually. It contains a great deal of pertinent information about the company. These corporate reports are on file with the SEC and are usually available from the company. Many universities maintain relatively complete files of corporate reports.

It is an exceedingly poor library that does not have complete sets of either *Moody's* manuals or *Standard & Poor's* services. The better libraries will have both and possibly *Value Line* and *Fitch's* services also. The economic justification for these institutions is that they digest and put together in a far more convenient form the information from thousands of companies.

A great deal of published information is available in trade publications, such as *The Wall Street Journal, Barron's,* and *Forbes.* Even the business and financial sections of local newspapers contain much information about the current economic well-being of corporations. Practically every financial news article gives information that affects the value of a company in one way or another.

Stock brokerage houses publish a plethora of information about industries and companies. The large ones, such as Merrill, Lynch, Pierce, Fenner, and Smith, are particularly prolific in their publication of such data.

Private Information   There are a number of privately published, syndicated services which the investor may purchase. These vary widely in quality; some are less than worthless while others have a seemingly excellent track record.

And then, of course, there is always the insidious inside information one obtains from company officials, or people who know company officials, or people who know people who know company officials. It is impossible to predict the accuracy and validity of inside information. Some of it is good. Most of it is bad. Separating out the good from the bad is next to impossible, so the investor is left with the dilemma of deciding whether or not he should act on it.

FIGURE 21-3: How to Read the Financial Page

1. The abbreviated name of the company issuing the stock is given—in this case, Aetna Life Insurance Company. It is common stock unless

2. "pf" follows the name—indicating a "preferred stock."

3. Columns showing the "highest" and "lowest" prices paid for a stock on the Exchange during the year—in this case $46.00 and $38.50.

4. Numbers following names show the rate of annual dividend—for this stock, $1.40. The amount is an estimation based on the last quarterly or semiannual payments. Letters following the dividend numbers indicate other information about the dividend. For instance,

5. The "b" indicates that in addition to the annual dividend rate shown ($0.75 for this stock) a stock dividend was paid. Other symbols used are explained in the table appearing in each newspaper.

6. This column shows the number of shares reported traded for the day, expressed in hundreds—for this stock 19,200. This number does not include stocks bought and sold in odd-lot quantities—that is, quantities less than 100 shares for most stocks. The "z" means the actual number of shares traded—for Allied Stores, 100 shares.

7. The opening price is given in this column; for American Hess the first trade was at $66.125 per share.

8. The highest price paid for this stock during the trading session was $47.00—the lowest was $46.625 per share.

9. The closing or last price in this stock was $25.00 per share—$0.12 $\frac{1}{2}$ more than the closing for the previous day as indicated by the "$+\frac{1}{8}$."

1971 High	Low		Sales (In 100s)	Open	High	Low	Close	Net Chg.
		—A—						
18-1/4	14-1/4	AbacusF .50g	24	17-1/2	17-1/2	17-1/2	17-1/2	......
85-3/8	69	AbbtLb 1.10	154	68-5/8	69-7/8	68-1/2	69-1/2+	1/2
60	45-1/4	ACF Ind 2.40	19	57-5/8	57-5/8	57-3/8	57-3/8—	1/4
47-1/2	13-1/2	AcmeClev .80	2	14-1/2	14-1/2	14-1/2	14-1/2+	1/8
53-1/4	42-1/2	Acme Mkt 2b	32	49-3/4	50-1/2	49-1/2	49-7/8—	1/4
14-3/4	13-1/2	AdmsEx .66g	29	13-5/8	13-7/8	13-5/8	13-7/8+	1/4
19-5/8	13-5/8	Ad Millis .20	68	15-1/8	15-3/8	14-7/8	16-3/8+	3/8
43-3/4	23-7/8	Address .30g	282	40-1/2	42	40	41-5/8+	7/8
19-1/8	8	Admiral	377	18	19-3/8	18	19-1/8+	7/8
62-1/2	47-5/8	AetnaLife 1.60	236	56-3/4	58	56-3/4	57-1/8+	3/8
61-1/2	39-1/4	AetnaLf pf2	1	49-3/4	49-3/4	49-3/4	49-3/4+	1/4
12-1/4	8-1/2	Aguirre Co	40	9-1/8	9-1/4	8-1/2	8-1/2—	1/4
52-7/8	40	Alleon Inc	43	48	48-1/2	48	48-1/2+	1/2
57-3/4	44-7/8	Air Prod .20b	130	55	55-7/8	55	55-5/8+	5/8
153-1/2	123	Aird pf	18	143-3/4	145-3/4	143-3/4	145-3/4+	1-3/4
26-1/2	20-5/8	AirRed .10g	282	24-3/8	24-7/8	24-1/4	24-3/4+	1/2
5-3/8	3-7/8	AJ Industries	74	4-1/4	4-3/8	4-1/4	4-1/4—	1/8
46-3/4	34-1/4	Akzona 1a	143	42-3/4	44	42-1/2	42-1/2—	1/2
17-7/8	16	Ala Gas 1.10	x3	16-1/2	16-1/2	16-1/2	16-1/2+	1/4
38-1/4	30	Alaska Inters	68	22-1/2	23-1/8	22-3/8	22-3/8+	1/4
46	38-1/2	AlbertoC .32	48	39-3/4	39-7/8	39-1/2	39-7/8+	1/2
15-1/4	12-1/4	Albertns .36	13	12-3/8	12-1/2	12-1/4	12-1/2+	1/8
24-3/4	21-3/4	Alcan Alum 1	140	23-3/8	23-3/8	23-1/8	23-3/8+	1/4
24-1/4	17-1/2	AlcoStand .30	27	20-5/8	21-1/2	20-5/8	21-1/4+	5/8
31	22-3/8	Alexndrs .30r	86	29-3/4	30	29-3/8	29-3/8—	3/8
17-1/2	12-1/2	AllAmLf .24g	41	16-3/8	16-1/2	16-1/8	16-1/4—	1/8
18-1/2	11-1/4	Alleg Ch	178	15-1/2	15-5/8	14-5/8	15-1/8—	5/8
32-1/2	26-7/8	AllegLtd 1.40	11	28	28-1/2	27-7/8	28-1/4	......
45-3/4	37-1/2	AllegLtd	8	41-1/2	41-1/2	41	41	— 1/4
25-1/8	20-7/8	AllegPw 1.36	136	21-1/8	21-1/4	21	21	......
32-1/4	23-3/8	Allied Ch 1.20	281	32	32-5/8	32	32-5/8+	5/8
36-3/4	26-1/4	Alld Main .40	3	35-3/4	36	35-3/4	36	+ 1/2
28-7/8	23	AlldMil .75b	7	25-3/8	25-3/8	25-1/8	25-1/8—	1/4
21-3/8	16	Allied Pd	67	20	20	19-1/2	19-5/8—	1/8
37-1/2	26-5/8	AlliedStr 1.40	17	38-5/8	37	36-1/2	37	+ 1/2
60	52	AlliedStr	z100	55	55	55	55	......
10	6-1/2	Allied Super	641	7-1/2	7-5/8	7	7-1/4—	3/8
19-3/4	15-1/4	Allis-Ch .10g	90	17-1/2	17-5/8	17-1/4	17-1/4—	1/4
27-1/2	20-1/2	AllrgtAut .60	3	26-1/4	26-1/4	25-3/4	25-3/4—	1/4
19-3/4	17	Alpha P Cem	6	18-1/8	18-1/4	18-1/8	18-1/8—	1/4
69	66-1/4	Alcoa 1.80	192	68-1/2	70	68-1/2	70	+1
38-3/4	25-5/8	AmalSug 1.60	2	30-1/2	30-5/8	30-1/2	30-5/8—	1/8
16-1/8	11-1/2	AMBAC .50	19	14-7/8	15	14-5/8	14-5/8—	1/4
25-1/8	22-1/4	Amm Es 1.20	29	22-1/4	22-3/8	22-1/4	22-3/8+	1/8
44-3/4	39-1/4	Am Es pf2.60	17	40-1/2	40-1/2	40	40-1/2—	1/2
68-3/8	43-1/4	AmHess .07g	109	66-1/8	66-7/8	66	66-3/4+	5/8
150-1/2	96-1/4	AmeH pf3.50	1	145	146-1/4	145	145-5/8+	5/8
66-1/2	53-1/2	AAirFiltr .80	13	62-3/4	63-3/8	62-5/8	63	+ 5/8
31-5/8	21-7/8	Am Airln .80	148	34-3/8	34-1/2	34	34	— 3/8
24-1/2	16	ABaker .10g	27	24-1/4	24-1/4	24-1/4	23-5/8—	3/8
49-3/4	43-1/2	A Brnds 2.20	142	47	47	46-5/8	47	......
48	25	AmBdcst 1.20	508	44-1/2	47	44-1/4	43-1/2—1	1/8
45-7/8	39-5/8	Am Can 2.20	183	39-1/4	39-1/4	38-5/8	38-5/8—	5/8
29-1/2	25-1/8	A Can pf1.75	3	26-7/8	26-7/8	26-7/8	26-7/8+	1/8
10-3/4	7-1/2	Am Cement	54	8-7/8	9	8-3/4	8-7/8+	1/8
39-1/8	25-1/4	A Chain 1.60	18	28-3/8	28-3/4	28-3/4	28-3/8	......
23-1/2	21-7/8	ACrySug 1.40	11	24-7/8	25	25	25	+ 1/8
37-7/8	32	ACyand 1.25	207	35-5/8	35-56*	35-1/8	35-1/8—	1/2
23-3/4	17-1/2	Am Distill 1	4	20-3/4	20-3/4	20-1/2	20-1/2—	1/2
45-7/8	25-3/4	A Dist Tel .10g	73	43-3/4	43-3/8	43-3/8	43-1/2+	1/2
10-5/8	7-5/8	Am DualVest	46	10-1/4	10-3/8	10-1/8	10-1/8	......
14-3/8	13	ADuVt pf.84a	3	13-3/8	13-3/8	13-3/8	13-3/8+	1/8
32-3/4	28	AmElPw 1.70	480	28-3/8	28-3/8	28	28-3/8+	1/4
14-3/8	10-1/2	Am Exp Ind	237	12-1/8	12-5/8	12	12-1/2+	1/2
62	31	Am Exp pf	z240	38-3/4	38-3/4	37-3/4	38-3/4+	3/4
28	24-7/8	AGnBFd .76g	15	26-1/4	26-1/4	25-3/4	25-7/8—	1/8
23-1/4	16	A Genins .50	320	23-7/8	23-1/2	22-7/8	23-1/2+	3/8
34-1/8	27-3/8	A Gnin Pf1.80	38	33-7/8	33-7/8	32-7/8	33-1/8+	1/4
14-1/2	8-7/8	Am Hoist .40	44	13-7/8	13-7/8	13-1/4	13-1/2+	1/4
71-5/8	70	A Home 1.70	80	78	78-5/8	77-7/8	78-5/8+	1/2
118-3/4	104-3/4	A Home pf 2	21	116-3/4	116-3/4	116-3/4	116-3/4+	1/4
38-7/8	31-5/8	Am Hosp .26	256	34-3/8	34-1/2	33-3/4	34	— 3/8
19-7/8	13	Aminvst .25g	62	19	19	18-3/4	19	+ 1/4
38	23-5/8	A Medical .12	245	35-1/4	35-1/2	34-1/2	35	— 1/2
37-3/8	32	A MtlCix 1.40	105	35-3/4	36-1/2	35-3/4	36-1/2+	3/8
9	5-7/8	Am Motors	942	6-3/4	7-1/8	6-5/8	6-7/8+	1/4
43-1/8	36-1/8	ANatGas 2.20	147	37-7/8	38	37-5/8	37-5/8+	1/8
66-1/4	41-1/2	A ResDv .04g	205	62-3/4	62-3/4	61-1/2	61-3/4—	3/8

Finally, but certainly not least important, is observation. One should never sell short the validity of his own observations about companies, methods of operation, and products. If you see a company that particularly impresses you with its operation or product, more careful investigation is certainly called for to see if it has investment possibilities. Similarly, if one observes a situation that seems to be poorly managed, he might consider acting on that observation.

How would you profit if you found evidence that led you to believe the price of a stock would soon drop significantly?
Why do some insiders deliberately lie about the future prospects of their company?

CRITICISMS OF PRESENT SECURITIES SYSTEM

Few systems are perfect; the securities system is no exception. Certainly it has many faults—but in recounting them never lose sight of the fact that it has worked well and has proved to be far better than other securities systems. It is a most complex network of institutions that operate amazingly well with a minimum of legal difficulty. The entire system operates upon the validity of a man's word. In the securities business, a man had better live up to his word or he will not be in it for long, for one cannot handle a large volume of transactions by creating legally binding agreements on paper each time he wants to buy or sell something. The entire system exists on trust and faith and this gives rise to a few problems, which are policed largely within the system.

Paperwork

Much has been written of the breakdown in the paperwork system within the securities industry. Certainly the system has lagged behind the automation age.

The paperwork snarl was largely the result of a tremendous increase in the volume being handled by institutions that had not appreciated the importance of automating their systems.

In the scheme of things this is really a minor problem, for it can be solved if sufficient resources are applied to it, and unquestionably they will be. It simply takes a little time for any system such as this to computerize.

Manipulation Potentials

While the Securities and Exchange Commission and the various exchanges work as diligently as possible to prevent manipulations of the market, and such manipulations are illegal and punishable by fines and jail sentences, still, wherever there are large sums of money there will be people plotting to get it.

Unquestionably, some manipulation of market prices still exists; how extensive it is, no one knows.

Inside Information

While criticism was being leveled at the validity of inside information, one should not conclude that there are not people who do possess valid inside information and who are able to act upon it to their profit. The law defines insiders quite clearly as those who work for a company in certain positions, such as directors or officers. The stock transactions of these legally defined insiders are watched carefully, and there are laws regulating what they can and cannot do. But this does not mean that these people are not able to find other means for profiting from their inside information. Make no mistake about it, there are people in companies who have advance information on events that will definitely affect the price of the company's stock one way or another. They have this information far enough in advance to be able to act upon it profitably.

From a practical standpoint, there is really no way that one can stop an insider from profiting by his knowledge, for he can find a way to do so if he is determined.

Sales Motivations

The entire system is fundamentally marketing-oriented—it is designed to sell securities. Inasmuch as its role is that of a salesman, the investor must realize that the securities system has a vested interest in his buying common stocks, for that is where the system makes its profits. The account executives are paid a percentage of the gross commissions they generate, so they have a tremendous incentive to encourage you to buy and sell securities when it may not be to your interest to do so. This is a very real weakness in the present system.

Speculation

The entire system encourages speculation. Experience clearly shows that profits are made when the market is rising rather rapidly. Fortunes are made in bull markets, for few people have the foresight or courage to make them in a bear market. The broker loves the trader who buys and sells with rapid turnover, speculating for his profit. The system encourages this in many ways by the information it gives out and by its willingness to finance the trader.

Effect on the Economy

The price behavior of the stock market has a profound psychological impact on people's attitudes toward the economic well-being of the entire system—an impact far out of key with reality. During the 1970 bear market, no economic analysis could possibly indicate that the economy was doing anything other than taking a little breathing spell from rapid growth. In reality, our economy was healthy and sound, but that was not good enough for the speculator. In his speculative fervor, he had bid the prices of many stocks up to ridiculous highs; when the companies did not match the performance expected of them, he drove the prices down. This downward readjustment is called a bear market, and many people interpret it as a recession. There is no truth in this interpretation, but the fact that a great many people lost large amounts of paper profits certainly affected the real economy in a real way by altering consumption plans. A paper millionaire spends a lot more money than a paper pauper, even though the actual cash in his pocket may be the same.

And so one can criticize the present securities system for its excessive psychological impact upon the general economy. What happens on the New York Stock Exchange should not really matter to the real world. Whether or not General Motors sells for $100 or $50 a share does not in the slightest bit alter that company and the reality of its operations. The company remains the same at $50 as it was at $100 a share. But people do not see it that way. Prices on the stock market are affected by many things other than the economic well-being of the economy or the company.

Why do economic observers criticize speculation?

Conclusion

We have created a complex network of institutions that could be roughly called a securities distribution system. It is quite unique and has a set of rules of its own by which it must operate. Anyone wishing to use this system should take care to learn all of its rules, they are most complex.

The focal point of the system is the so-called stock brokerage house, which performs a great many functions. It is supported by numerous other institutions that perform special tasks.

You should remember at all times that the purpose of this system is to sell securities, not make you money. You must do that for yourself.

There are many attractive career opportunities in this field for the bright young person who is interested in securities.

22 Insurance systems

Whoever controls the volume of money in any
country is absolute master of all industry and commerce.
JAMES GARFIELD

The insurance industry represents one of the biggest economic activities in our system. With more than $197 billion in assets, it is a most significant economic force and one worthy of considerable study, for you will have a great many dealings with insurance in your lifetime—automobile, fire, health, and life insurance. An industry of such size must have something to offer, but to understand it you must first understand its economic justification.

THE THEORY OF INSURANCE

Insurance exists because there are risks involved in living and in doing business; if there were no risks, there would be no need for insurance, because its function is to accept certain risks individuals or business firms want to transfer onto its shoulders. Insurance involves risks and risk-bearing.

Life contains many risks. A man may die prematurely, leaving his family in a difficult financial bind. One's home may burn down, incurring a large financial loss. You may wreck your automobile or damage someone else's, thereby incurring liability for damages. A thief may steal your property. A visitor may be injured on your property and sue you for damages. A severe windstorm may damage your house. A fire may destroy a business, an employee may embezzle money from it, or a customer may be damaged by a product it produces. These are but a few of the risks entailed in living. If a man were sufficiently wealthy, then these risks might not overly concern him; he would have enough money that such losses would not jeopardize his well-being. But that is not true of the average man on the street nor the average businessman, for if his house or store burns down or his automobile is destroyed, the loss creates financial hardships. If a large judgment is levied against him as a result of a liability suit, he may be bankrupted. Hence, if one is not able to bear the consequences of risks, he endeavors to transfer them onto the shoulders of someone who can—and that is where insurance comes into the picture, for the insurance industry is willing to accept many risks in return for the payment of a premium.

What kinds of risks are uninsurable?

The theory of insurance is that by taking premiums from a large number of people wishing to transfer the same risk, a company can accumulate a fund from which the people can be paid for any loss against which they are insured. For insurance to be workable, a large number of people must have the same kind of risk and wish to transfer it, and the chance of the event's happening must be sufficiently low that the premium is reasonable.

If the likelihood of an event's happening is certainty, why is the transfer of that risk by insurance impractical?
If the likelihood of an event's happening is one chance in 100, and the insurance company wants 20 percent of the premium as payment for its services, what would the premium be if one took out an insurance policy with a face value of $10,000 against the happening of that event?
Why is earthquake or flood insurance extremely difficult to buy?

While the same fundamental theory is common to all types of insurance, each type has many unique aspects that are important to its users.

LIFE INSURANCE

While life insurance can be used to achieve a large number of goals, basically they can all be put into one of two categories: (1) to transfer the financial risks entailed should the insured have an untimely death; or (2) to provide a sum of money at some future date.

Let's examine some of the financial pressures that may be created when someone dies. Money is needed:

for final expenses
for estate taxes
for family living costs until a new source of adequate income is obtained
in a business to pay the man's heirs for his share of the business
to pay off debts, particularly home mortgages or business obligations
to compensate a business for the loss of the man—so-called key man insurance

Life insurance can provide future funds to:

retire upon
pay for children's education
provide a fund from which money can be borrowed
give dependents gifts safe from estate and income taxes

But these are the end results; let's first understand the basics.

Types of Life Insurance

Strictly speaking, there is only one type of true life insurance—*term insurance.* All other forms combine term insurance with some kind of savings program. Traditionally, the industry has featured four major types of policies, with many minor variations, designed for special markets.

Term Insurance   Term insurance furnishes more pure protection for the money than any other type of policy. Table 22-1 shows the amounts of insurance that can be

Table 22-1

AMOUNT OF INSURANCE THAT CAN BE PURCHASED BY A 25-YEAR-OLD MAN FOR $1000 PER YEAR

Type of Policy	Face Value of Policy
Term	
5-year renewable term	$217,391.00
15-year term	208,333.00
20-year term	198,807.00
Term age 65	124,378.00
Whole Life	
Ordinary	$66,979.00
Life paid up at 65	60,422.00
10-year-pay life	24,348.00
20-year-pay life	41,271.00
30-year-pay life	52,882.00
Endowments	
At age 65	$50,050.00
10-year endowment	10,515.00
15-year endowment	16,507.00
20-year endowment	22,928.00
30-year endowment	36,643.00

SOURCE: Rate Book, Teacher's Insurance and Annuity Association.

bought by a 25-year-old man for $1000 per year. When one has no need for the savings aspect of life insurance, then a term policy is his best buy. It provides protection for any specified number of years in return for a premium that may be paid monthly, quarterly, annually, or lump sum.

Suppose you and your wife feel it wise for her not to return to work until your recently born son is old enough to go to school. Should you die during the next five years, she would be forced into the labor market and presented with the problem of finding good care for her preschooler. Since you feel she would need $10,000 a year on which to maintain her standard of living, you buy a $50,000, five-year term policy for a premium of $230 per year (age 25).[1] If you are removed from this world at any time during the next five years, your widow will receive, tax free, $50,000 on which to live. Of course, you could reduce your premium with a policy whose face value declined $10,000 each year—*a declining term policy*. Declining term policies are widely used for providing credit and mortgage insurance in which the face value of the policy declines along with a declining balance of debt.

The Rate-Making Process

Suppose an insurance company sells each of 100,000 men, age 25, a $1000 term policy. What will the premium be?

Mortality tables indicate that out of every 1000 men, age 25, 1.35 will die during the next year.

MORTALITY TABLE

Age	Deaths 1000	Age	Deaths 1000	Age	Deaths 1000	Age	Deaths 1000
<1	22.39	18	1.15	35	2.09	52	8.89
1	1.35	19	1.21	36	2.27	53	9.71
2	.87	20	1.27	37	2.45	54	10.59
3	.66	21	1.33	38	2.65	55	11.56
4	.57	22	1.37	39	2.86	56	12.58
5	.60	23	1.37	40	3.10	57	13.65
6	.49	24	1.36	41	3.36	58	14.75
7	.40	25	1.35	42	3.66	59	15.90
8	.33	26	1.34	43	4.00	60	17.12
9	.29	27	1.34	44	4.37	61	18.44
10	.28	28	1.38	45	4.78	62	19.94
11	.30	29	1.44	46	5.23	63	21.66
12	.37	30	1.50	47	5.72	64	23.58
13	.47	31	1.58	48	6.26	65	25.62
14	.61	32	1.68	49	6.84	66	27.79
15	.77	33	1.76	50	7.47	67	30.16
16	.93	34	1.93	51	8.14	68	32.76
17	1.06						

The company can expect 135 deaths among its 100,000 new policyholders, requiring it to pay out $135,000 to the named beneficiaries. Therefore, it must charge that amount plus its overhead costs and profit. So the premium is calculated at $1.35 plus loading costs per $1,000 of coverage.

[1] At the termination of a term insurance contract, if you want to renew it, the premium is increased. At age thirty, if you want to continue your $50,000 coverage, it will cost you $247.50 per year.

Compare this theoretical rate with the actual rates shown in Table 22-3.

Whole Life Insurance   Whereas term insurance is for a relatively short, specified length of time, whole life covers the insured for his lifetime in return for the payment of a premium that remains the same each year (level premium) despite the increasing risk as the years roll on. Whole life is further divided into two categories: *ordinary life,* on which one pays premiums each year for the entire life of the policy; or *limited-payment policy,* in which the premium is paid only for the specified number of years, usually 10, 15, or 20 years, but the face of the policy remains in effect for one's "whole life." Naturally, the premium for whole life is much greater than it is for term insurance. The difference is savings that are placed into a *reserve.* This reserve, which is invested in securities and mortgages to earn money, is then used for several things.

First, in the later years of the policy, should the insured live that long, when the payments necessary for the *term* portion, or pure protection, of the policy exceed the premium then being paid, the difference is taken from the reserves. In other words, the insured has saved enough in his early years by paying more than what was required for protection alone that he does not have to pay the full cost of the protection in his later years.

Second, the reserve forms the basis for the policy's *cash value,* which approximates the reserve. This cash value can be withdrawn as cash if the policy is canceled, or 95 percent of it can be borrowed at 5 percent interest if so desired.

Why should you pay interest to borrow your own money?
What are the advantages of borrowing against the cash value
rather than cashing in the policy?

Third, the reserve provides money for buying *"paid-up"* insurance if the insured so chooses. Paid-up insurance refers to a policy whose lower face amount will remain in force for the rest of the insured's life without another cent's being paid as premium.

What is the advantage of paid-up insurance?

Fourth, premium payments for *extended* insurance are made from the reserve. Extended insurance is the time one can have full face-value coverage without paying any more premiums.

Fifth, the costs of many secondary features are paid from the reserve. Ordinarily, policies have a *disability waiver premium* clause, which provides that no premiums need to be paid should the insured become disabled for more than 31 days.

Insurance companies have developed so many special features to meet the needs of certain market segments that they cannot all be covered here. Suffice it to say that each feature costs money over and above the payment one makes for the pure-protection portion of his whole life policy.

In a very real sense, a whole life policy is but a term policy combined with a savings program that finances whatever benefits are to be provided above payment of death benefits.

Table 22-2

EXAMPLE OF THE FEATURES OF A WHOLE LIFE INSURANCE POLICY

An Equitable Special   AGE **12**

THE ADJUSTABLE WHOLE LIFE POLICY—MALE

Low Cost Lifetime Protection Plus Guaranteed Flexibility

FACE AMOUNT . . . . $25,000   **ANNUAL PREMIUM** $304.25

ILLUSTRATIONS

(Based on the January 1, 1964 Dividend Scale)

INSURANCE AMOUNTS

DIVIDENDS USED TO BUY PAID-UP ADDITIONAL INSURANCE

		Total Insurance—Face Amt. Plus Additions*	PAID UP INSURANCE AVAILABLE IF PREMIUMS DISCONTINUED		
			Guaranteed	Dividend Additions*	Total*
End of Year	5	$25,700.00	$ 2,500.00	$ 700.00	$ 3,200.00
	10	$27,075.00	$ 6,200.00	$ 2,075.00	$ 8,275.00
	20	$30,850.00	$11,600.00	$ 5,850.00	$17,450.00
Age	60	$45,350.00	$20,900.00	$20,350.00	$41,250.00
	65	$48,600.00	$21,800.00	$23,600.00	$45,400.00

If premiums are paid for 29 years (to age 41) total paid up insurance available, including additions, will equal the full face amount.*

CASH VALUES

		Guaranteed Cash Value	Cash Value of Dividend Additions*	Total Cash Value*†	Total Premiums
End of Year	5	$ 725.00	$ 200.00	$ 925.00	$ 1,521.25
	10	$ 2,000.00	$ 650.00	$ 2,650.00	$ 3,042.50
	20	$ 4,625.00	$ 2,325.00	$ 7,135.00	$ 6,085.00
Age	60	$14,350.00	$13,975.00	$28,899.00	$14,604.00
	65	$16,125.00	$17,450.00	$34,200.00	$16,125.25

LIFE INCOME

The policy may be used to provide a life income from the cash value. For example, at Age 65, this policy could provide:

From guaranteed cash value . . . . $ 81.25
From cash value of dividend additions*† . . . . . $ 91.00
Total income $172.25 per month,

payable for 240 months, whether you live or die—a return of $41,340.00—and then $172.25 per month continues to you for as long as you live.

OTHER DIVIDEND OPTIONS

IF DIVIDENDS TAKEN IN CASH*				IF DIVIDENDS APPLIED TO PREMIUMS* 20-Year Summary	
Year	Dividend	Year	Dividend		
2	$39.75	10	$ 95.25	Average Annual Dividend . .	$ 93.50
3	$46.50	15	$124.00	Aver. Ann. Net Outlay . . .	$210.75
5	$60.25	20	$146.50	Aver. Ann. Net Return	
				if surrendered†	$ 29.75

Dividends may also be left to accumulate at interest. For income tax purposes, interest allowed on dividend accumulations is includible in gross income in the year credited.

ADJUSTABLE FEATURES

The policy grants the privilege of changing at age 55 to a Limited Payment Life Policy or an Endowment Policy, with increased premiums and increased cash values. If neither option is elected, the policy automatically continues under the original plan as illustrated above.

ADDITIONAL BENEFITS

		Annual Premium
Disability premium waiver		$ 4.75
Accidental death benefit		$18.75
Option to purchase additional insurance (option amount $10,000.00) .		$ 9.30

---

* Dividends and figures derived therefrom are based on the January 1, 1964 dividend scale and are not to be construed as guarantees or even estimates of dividends to be paid in the future. Dividends will depend upon claim experience, interest and other earnings, and expenses of the Society in the future. The Society's dividend scale may be changed in any year.
† Includes termination dividend, if any, based on the January 1, 1964 dividend scale.

SOURCE: The Equitable Life Assurance Society of America.

Table 22-3   1971 RATE TABLES FOR TERM, WHOLE LIFE, AND ENDOWMENT POLICIES

Term Insurance

Term policies are ideal for providing a large amount of level protection for a limited time at lowest premium outlay. Term insurance is temporary insurance that offers protection for the period you select—5, 10, 15 or 20 years—or to a certain age, such as 60, 65 or 70. The face value of the Term policy will be paid to your beneficiary if you die during the Term period. If you live until the end of the term, you will have had the protection at very modest yearly cost and the policy will then expire.

Term policies allow you to convert the full amount of insurance to an Ordinary Life, Limited Payment Life or Endowment policy without medical re-examination at any time while the insurance is in force (see page 2).

The 5-Year Renewable Term policy may be renewed for successive 5 year periods without medical re-examination by paying premiums based upon your attained age at the beginning of each renewal period. The policy may be continued by renewal until age 70. The rates in the table below apply to renewals through age 55. For figures at ages after 55 please write.

Premiums Per $1,000 of Insurance; Minimum Policy Issued, $5,000
(Disability Waiver of Premium Included—see page 3)

Age Nearest Birthday	5-Year Renewable Term		10-Year Term		15-Year Term		20-Year Term		Term To Age 65		Term To Age 68		Term To Age 70	
	Annual	Monthly	Annual	Monthly	Annual	Monthly	Annual	Monthly	Annual	Monthly	Annual	Monthly	Annual	Monthly

[Dense numeric rate rows for ages 20–60 appear here.]

Cash Dividend Illustrations*—For a $25,000 20-Year Term Policy

	Age 25	Age 35	Age 45
	(Age At Issue)		
First annual premium	$125.75	$193.75	$377.00
Dividend at end of first year	53.00	66.25	102.00
First-year net payment	$ 72.75	$127.50	$275.00

* Based on 1965 dividend scale for $25,000 policy (see page 1). Dividends not guaranteed.

13

Whole Life Insurance

This type of insurance gives lifetime protection—for the "whole of life." You may select a policy under which premiums are payable as long as you live (Ordinary Life) or one of several plans where premiums are limited to a specific period of years (20-Payment Life, Life Paid-up at Age 65, etc.). The insurance money is paid to your beneficiary at your death, whether this is before or after the premium payment period ends.

Ordinary Life is the lowest-premium form of permanent, level insurance. Premiums for Limited Payment Life are larger than for Ordinary Life because you are buying the same lifetime protection with only a limited number of premiums. The longer the payment period, the smaller the premiums.

All Whole Life plans have a savings element in their Cash Surrender Values. You can stop paying premiums at any time and take your cash value in one sum or as income; or you can use the cash value to continue a reduced amount of paid-up insurance for life (see page 1).

Premiums Per $1,000 of Insurance; Minimum Policy Issued, $2,000
(Disability Waiver of Premium Included—see page 3)

Age Nearest Birthday	Ordinary Life		Life Paid-Up at 65		18-Pay Life		20-Pay Life		30-Pay Life	
	Annual	Monthly	Annual	Monthly	Annual	Monthly	Annual	Monthly	Annual	Monthly

[Dense numeric rate rows for ages 20–60 appear here.]

Cash Dividend Illustrations*—For a $10,000 Ordinary Life Policy

	Age 25	Age 35	Age 45
	(Age At Issue)		
First annual premium	$149.30	$201.90	$289.80
Dividend at end of first year	23.40	29.90	41.50
First-year net payment	$125.90	$172.00	$248.30

* Based on 1965 dividend scale for $10,000 policy (see page 1). Dividends not guaranteed.

15

Endowment Insurance

Endowment policies combine a systematic savings program with life insurance protection. The face amount is paid to you on the future maturity date that you choose when you begin the policy. If you die before that date the insurance is paid immediately to your beneficiary. If you live to the maturity date, you can take the money in one sum or as a regular monthly income. Or you can leave it with TIAA, receiving guaranteed interest earnings until you want to withdraw it. The same choices are available to your beneficiary if you die before the maturity date.

For a given amount of protection, Endowment policy cash values accumulate more rapidly than under lower-premium forms of insurance. Endowment insurance is useful in saving towards specific goals such as the children's education or your own retirement. At the same time it guarantees completion of the savings program, because your beneficiary receives the face amount if you die.

Premiums Per $1,000 of Insurance; Minimum Policy Issued, $2,000
(Disability Waiver of Premium Included—see page 3)

Age Nearest Birthday	Endowment at Age 65		15-Year Endowment		18-Year Endowment		20-Year Endowment		30-Year Endowment	
	Annual	Monthly	Annual	Monthly	Annual	Monthly	Annual	Monthly	Annual	Monthly

[Dense numeric rate rows for ages 20–60 appear here.]

Cash Dividend Illustrations*—For a $10,000 Endowment at 65 Policy

	Age 25	Age 35	Age 45
	(Age At Issue)		
First annual premium	$199.90	$292.20	$483.60
Dividend at end of first year	18.40	22.50	30.50
First-year net payment	$181.40	$269.70	$453.10

* Based on 1965 dividend scale for $10,000 policy. Dividends not guaranteed.

16

SOURCE: Teacher's Insurance and Annuity Association.

DIVIDENDS   Do not let the magic word dividends fool you . . . insurance dividends are not income. The company is returning some of your money—you paid too much! For safety, insurance companies have used extremely conservative mortality figures—deaths are usually fewer than they anticipate in their rates. So they return to you the unused portion of that part of your premium that went to pay for death benefits. The details of a whole life policy are presented in Table 22-2.

Notice the flexibility provided by a simple ordinary life policy when options are included. One can convert it into whatever he needs at a later date.

Rate tables for term, whole life, and endowment policies are provided in Table 22-3. Note how sharply the rates rise with the institution of various savings programs.

Endowment Policies   An endowment policy pays off its face value in cash at the end of its term regardless of the continued good health of the insured. Meanwhile, it would have paid the beneficiary in full had the insured died during that term. However, once the policy has endowed (paid off), all death benefits cease. The policy no longer exists.

The principle underlying the endowment policy is rather simple. The premiums are increased sufficiently to accumulate a cash value at the end of the policy's lifetime equal to its face amount. You get back your reserve.

Endowment policies are used to provide funds at some future date when it is expected they will be needed. A father might buy a $20,000, 20-year endowment policy on his newborn infant to provide funds for the child's college education. A man might buy an endowment-at-age-65 policy to provide for his retirement.

Role of Life Insurance in Your Estate

Let's take a look at an insurance plan for Bill, a young man, age 25, married, with two children ages 1 and 3. He owns a $25,000 home with a $23,000 mortgage against it, and makes $10,000 a year. His wife, age 24, is not gainfully employed. They now have savings of $4000, but owe $2000 on a car and some appliances. A State Farm Mutual representative[2] drew up the plan shown in Table 22-4 for Bill. Note how each of Bill's risks has been provided for.

> Traditionally, the insurance industry has been divided into two categories: *life* and *all other*. The all other has been called *casualty,* but that disguises a wide range of vastly different types of insurance. So we shall ignore this artificial cleavage and discuss each type of insurance separately.

[2] Buzz Jackson, Corona Del Mar, California.

Table 22-4
INSURANCE PROGRAM DRAWN UP ESPECIALLY FOR BILL

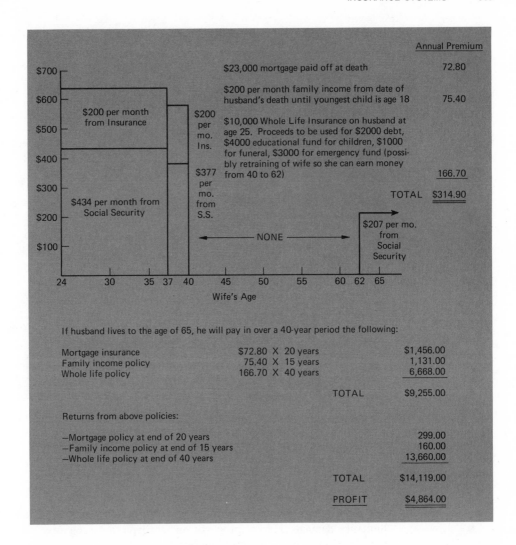

If husband lives to the age of 65, he will pay in over a 40-year period the following:

Mortgage insurance	$72.80 X 20 years	$1,456.00
Family income policy	75.40 X 15 years	1,131.00
Whole life policy	166.70 X 40 years	6,668.00
	TOTAL	$9,255.00

Returns from above policies:

—Mortgage policy at end of 20 years	299.00
—Family income policy at end of 15 years	160.00
—Whole life policy at end of 40 years	13,660.00
TOTAL	$14,119.00
PROFIT	$4,864.00

FIRE INSURANCE

In earlier times fire was a most dreaded risk; once started, it almost certainly resulted in the total loss of the structure and could wipe out an entire community. So the concept of fire insurance evolved rather early. It was usually a mutual association of people who agreed to chip in equally to cover the loss of any one member. Many times, a private fire department would also be involved in the hope of minimizing fire losses.

If an insured home or business structure is damaged or destroyed by fire, the fire insurance company in its contract (policy) with the insured agrees to do several things. A claim might arise from events other than fire, depending on the type of policy purchased.

A typical homeowner's policy coverage is shown in Table 22-5.

Table 22-5

COVERAGES OF STATE FARM HOMEOWNER'S POLICY

Property Covered:
Dwelling
Dwelling extensions—other structures on property
Unscheduled personal property—furniture, appliances, etc.
Additional Living Expenses—pays up to two weeks rent if you can't remain in your home

Covered Against:
Fire
Water damage
Debris removal
Theft
Fire department service charge
Credit card and depositor's forgery losses
Lightning
Windstorm and hail damage
Explosion
Aircraft crashing into property
Vehicles crashing into property
Smoke damage
Vandalism or malicious mischief
Falling objects
Weight of snow and ice
Collapse of buildings
Explosion of hot water systems
Freezing of plumbing, heating, and air conditioning system
Glass breakage

Personal liability for bodily injury and property damage
Medical payments to others

Why has the fire insurance industry gone to the broad *homeowners* policy rather than just insuring against fires? (Hint: Exactly what is the risk of fire in a home today? What would be the true premium to cover that risk alone?)

Additional Concepts

Co-Insurance Clause   Fire seldom destroys the entire value of the property; modern fire departments combined with good construction technology have done much to limit fire damage. Hence, property owners have a strong urge to underinsure—take out a $25,000 policy on a building worth say $50–75,000. Insurance companies frown on this, so they usually include in the policy a co-insurance clause, which provides that the property must be insured for at least 80 percent of its actual value or else the property owner must bear his proportional share of any loss.

Extended Coverage   The risk of fire is only one of a group of similar catastrophic events; damage from windstorms, tornados, hurricanes, hail, explosions, riots, vandalism, auto and aircraft crashes can be just as serious and perhaps more likely. Extended coverage protects one from such losses.

Although extended coverages have been incorporated into the homeowners policies, there are still a great many fire policies written with extended coverage, particularly on business properties.

Why not include flood and earthquake damage coverage in the homeowner's policy?

Business Interruption Coverage   While a policy might compensate a businessman for the loss of his property due to fire or other disasters, he would still suffer loss of income because his business would not be able to operate while the damage was being repaired. Business interruption coverage pays the businessman the profits he loses while his operation is shut down by any of the events insured against.

Advice

Buy your coverage from a company or agent that gives you good service, that will pay off claims fairly and quickly, and that is big enough to be financially sound. It is pointless to save a few dollars by buying a cheap policy with a marginal company only to be unable to collect when the need arises.

Small mutual companies present an additional risk, in that policyholders may be held legally liable for the firm's debts if it gets into financial difficulty.

Keep a careful record of your property and its value, lest you have trouble documenting your claim if it is destroyed.

Read your policies! It is an education. Give all your business to one agent; be important to him and you will get better treatment and service.

AUTOMOBILE INSURANCE

The likelihood that you will sustain some loss because of your automobile is quite high; the amounts can range from a few dollars to over $100,000. The problem of protecting the injured from loss by a financially irresponsible individual has become so serious that most states require all car owners either to carry a certain minimum amount of liability coverage or to show financial responsibility. It is much easier and better to carry the insurance.

Liability Coverage

Liability insurance protects the car's owner or operator from loss due to damage done to other people and/or their property. There are two types of liability insurance: *bodily injury,* which protects against claims arising from death or injury to other persons; and *property damage,* which protects against claims for damages done to other people's property by you or your car.

No driver or car owner should be without these coverages, for he can be held responsible even though he was not involved in the accident. Suppose you loan your car to a friend; you are responsible for his damages. You hire a salesman who has a wreck in his car while working for you; you may be responsible.

Do not settle for minimum coverages ($5000—one individual, $10,000—one accident); it costs only a little more to get coverage sufficient to fully protect one's assets. The more one has to lose, the more insurance he needs. Even a man of modest means should carry $100,000–300,000 coverage—it's the big judgments that ruin you, not the little ones.

Medical payments coverage is available to buyers of liability insurance. It pays the medical costs up to the stated limited for the driver and the car's occupants, regardless of fault or liability in the accident. It is a wise purchase.

Collision and Comprehensive Coverage

Collision Whereas the various forms of liability insurance protect one from the claims of others, these coverages protect one's own investment. *Collision* pays for the damage to your car resulting from a collision with something else regardless of fault. While one can buy full-coverage collision, which will pay for all damages up to the market value of the car (if the car is totaled, you get only its current market value), such coverage is not only too expensive, but unnecessary. You can afford small losses, not big ones.

So the industry offers two other types of collision coverage that are more practical: *the deductible policy* and *the 80 percent coverage*. With $50 deductible coverage, the company pays all but $50 of the repair bill. Damages under $50 are borne by the owner. The larger the deductible amount, the less the policy costs. The 80 percent policy requires that the owner pay 20 percent of the repair bill.

Comprehensive coverage protects one against loss from forces other than collision. It covers such risks as fire, theft, wind damage, vandalism, and glass breakage and damage—about half of all comprehensive claims are for glass replacement.

Uninsured motorist's coverage is a bit different in that it takes the place of the other person's insurance company in case you are damaged by someone who is uninsured. Your insurance pays you whatever valid claims you have against the other party. It is low-cost, personal protection.

Emergency road service pays tow-in costs should your car become disabled on the road.

Advice

Deal with a reputable company that promptly handles claims with no contesting of valid ones, one that has nationwide, intensive distribution; no telling where you may need an agent of the company.

Do not buy insurance that you do not need. It is a waste of money to buy collision or comprehensive coverage on an old car.

HEALTH AND ACCIDENT INSURANCE

The last two decades have seen a phenomenal growth in the sale of health and accident insurance, which is designed to help the insured defray the medical costs and the loss of income resulting from illness or accidents.

It is difficult to summarize such plans, for they vary widely in their coverages. Some policies provide almost 100 percent protection—pay all costs. Naturally, these are rather expensive. Other policies, called *major medical insurance*, cover only large losses, leaving the smaller bills to be paid by the insured; these policies are much less expensive.

The growth in popularity of health insurance is due largely to skyrocketing medical costs, which have turned most serious illnesses or accidents into major financial catastrophies. Table 22-6 gives the details of one group plan.

The future of this type of insurance is in question, as the government continues to move toward socialized medicine. Some sort of government-financed health insurance seems to be in the offing.

Table 22–6
BLUE CROSS–
BLUE SHIELD
MEDICAL PLAN:
GROUP PLAN
FOR CALIFORNIA
STATE COLLEGES

Benefits	BASIC PLAN
Hospital room and board	Pays up to a 3 or more bed ward rate for up to first 70 days of hospitalization
Hospital services	Provides full payment during the first 70 days of hospitalization
Surgical	Provides payment in full
Anesthetist	Provides payment in full
Additional accident benefit	Provides up to $100 per calendar year for dependents requiring nonsurgical services for accidental injury
Hospital diagnostic X-ray and laboratory	Provides full payment when hospitalized primarily for the treatment of an illness or injury
Outpatient diagnostic X-ray and laboratory	Provides up to a maximum payment of $150 per person per calendar year for illness. No maximum for accidents
Doctor's hospital calls (all members)	Provides full payment during first 70 days of hospitalization for routine calls. Includes payment for approved consultations
Doctor's office calls (Employee and annuitant only—no coverage for family members)	Provides full payment for accident / Provides full payment for illness — A $25 deductible per person per calendar year applies for illness ONLY
Doctor's home calls (Employee and annuitant only—no coverage for family members)	Provides full payment for accident / Provides full payment for illness
Maternity	Provides payment up to $75 to the hospital; $100 to the physician (employee or annuitant) / Provides payment up to $75 to the hospital; $75 to the physician (family member) / These benefits are provided after 9 months of membership
Ambulance	Provides payment up to $50 each accident or sickness (does not apply to maternity cases)

Premium Cost Before Employer Contribution	
Employee only	$25.22
Employee and one dependent	44.90
Employee and two or more Dependents	52.35

DISABILITY INCOME INSURANCE

Suppose the breadwinner for some reason becomes disabled—unable to work—for a significant length of time. Had he died, his life insurance would have met his family's financial needs, but instead his income is cut off while costs rise—a formula for severe hardship.

Regular income is the key to a family's solvency. Disability income insurance provides such income. It is a much overlooked policy which should be given wider publicity.

VARIOUS BUSINESS COVERAGES

Businesses are exposed to several risks to which the average individual is not. When one is in business, a great many unfortunate things can happen to customers, employees, and the public. People trip on faulty steps or rugs, things fall on people, products hurt people. All sorts of bad things happen that can give rise to court suits for damages against a firm.

Public liability   policies protect against a wide range of risks in which other people are hurt on company property or by company activities.

Product liability   policies protect against claims from people hurt by defects in one's product.

Fidelity and surety bonds   Employees have been known to steal or embezzle; *fidelity bonds* insure against such thefts. Contractors have been known not to fulfill their obligations under a contract; *surety bonds* guarantee against loss from such failures.

Robbery and Burglary Insurance   Theft by either robbery or burglary can be covered.

Marine Insurance

No, it does not protect you from marines; it is protection from loss while goods are in transit. *Ocean marine insurance* covers goods while at sea, while *inland marine insurance* protects against the hazards of shipping by rail, truck, barge, or what have you. The *personal property floaters* sold to individuals, covering one's personal property wherever it may be against all loss, are a form of inland marine insurance.

Workmen's Compensation

Inevitably, some workers are injured while working—some slightly, others seriously. By state law, employers must protect their employees from losses due to such accidents. Some states enforce a state-operated workmen's compensation insurance program, levying a charge for it against the company. Other states require that firms carry such policies with private insurance companies.

SOCIAL SECURITY

The popular term *Social Security* covers several different types of insurance that are paid for by deductions from paychecks matched by equal payments by the employer. Social Security provides payments:

to surviving widows and children
to retired people
to disabled workers
for health care in old age

The Social Security rates are constantly being changed. Therefore, it would not be practical to list them all here. A local Social Security office can give you all the facts you need at any time.

Conclusion

Insurance is a huge industry—huge because the risks entailed in living and doing business are huge. Insurance is a widely varied industry, because risks are widely varied. Insurance is something with which you will have continual dealings throughout your life, so you had better learn something of its nature, lest you leave yourself exposed to risks you cannot bear.

Again, each person's unique needs require insurance programs designed specifically for him. Beware the salesman trying to sell you a "patent medicine"—an insurance policy that he just happens to be selling to everyone. The chances that it meets your needs are remote.

The areas of automobile and fire insurance require considerable study, for they offer the buyer a wide variety of policies of varying coverages.

The rapidly growing field of medical insurance is so complex and varied that it almost defies generalization. Its nature is such that one could question whether it is legitimately called insurance. It now resembles more of a joint sharing of certain costs.

Finally, one should not be unaware of the career opportunities the insurance industry offers young people. Money can be made in insurance. And it is not a bad life.

PART

CONTROLLING OPERATIONS

IT'S not romantic! There's not much fun in it! It can mean a lot of labor on dull details—figures and the like. It's hard to work up much enthusiasm for controlling operations; perhaps that's one of the problems. But control, nonetheless, is the key to profits. All sorts of operators who have been able to go out and sell the wheels off their wagon—many of them production whizzes too—have ridden to the business boneyard with enterprises that lacked control. Management had been unable to keep expenses in line with sales volume, and so profits could not be realized.

      The manager who fails to control his operations will not long be a manager. The survivor will be one who appreciates control and learns it.

23 Control systems

It is better to learn late than never.
PUBLILIUS SYRUS

The business firm is a total operating system, all parts of which must operate correctly if it is to achieve its objectives. Sales, production, and finance must operate properly and in harmony for the firm to prosper. An automobile engine is an analogous system; although removal of a small spring from the carburetor may appear minor, it will still prevent the entire system from running properly. The driver controls the engine's speed with the accelerator and ignition switch; gauges on the dashboard monitor the performance of cooling and electrical subsystems and indicate when they are not operating correctly so proper action can be taken. Similarly, management must develop ways of controlling the various operating parts of the firm so that it performs as desired.

Management requires a few more gauges on its dashboard, for it must control a system that contains more variables than the automobile. Business' main gauges are its accounting statements, budgets, production standards, sales quotas, cost analyses, and various internal reporting systems. If January sales volume fails to meet the sales budget, management is immediately informed that the system is experiencing some difficulty. It can then appraise the situation to determine what, if anything, should be done.

What might be some of the reasons that caused sales volume to fall short of the budget?

Management must conscientiously design properly responsive and efficient control systems. Poor control mechanisms may indicate that the firm is functioning properly when it is not, or they may sound warnings when no danger exists. A good control system responds accurately. Moreover, it must not cost too much. It makes little sense to institute a control over some activity when the cost of the control exceeds the losses of activity malfunction.

Control procedures are designed to signal variances from expected operations. These variances, or apparent changes in the way things are being done, will act as red flags, signaling managers to investigate the circumstances and take whatever action is necessary to restore proper operation.

A good control procedure entails four steps. First, standards must be established for the activity to be controlled. Second, accurate and current records must be maintained, continually comparing the activity being controlled with the standards established for it. Third, when a significant difference appears between actual performance and the standard, investigation must be made to determine the reasons for the variance. Finally, corrective action should be taken to restore performance to the desired standards.

Standards are established for many activities that affect the firm's performance, such as

Sales by product, territory, salesman, time period, and type of customer.
Costs by product, department, time period, distribution channel, customer, or unit of work.
Units of work output per worker, department, or time period.
Profits by product, division, time period, territory, or market.

All of these activities can have an allowable or reasonable number established as a standard for them, from which variance either above or below may signal good or bad performance.

A control system will identify jobs that are being done too well in addition to those being done poorly. A desired level of quality is established for a product. Reducing the number of defects to a level approaching zero may be feasible if additional man-hours are devoted to each product, yet the price of the product might thereby be driven so high that few people could afford it. Car manufacturers, in order to hold prices down, find it necessary to accept levels of quality that result in some defects due to workmanship or defective parts.

HOW DO WE CONTROL?

Management has many control mechanisms to insure fulfillment of its objectives. Some are very subtle and automatic, others very obvious and deliberate, in their setup and operation.

Certain automatic control mechanisms exist in almost every organization, although most are qualitative in nature rather than quantitative. A qualitative control is not measured in numbers or amounts but rather guides (controls) nonnumerical organizational behavior along desired lines; for example, what should a store manager do with a 12-year-old boy caught shoplifting? Company policy controls his actions. Policies form automatic control systems, as do supervision, job descriptions, wages, and organizational structures.

Policies

Policies are premade decisions. Any deviation from them should arise through appeal to superiors. Exceptions to policies should be reviewed by their makers, rather than being handled routinely by those who administer them. Therefore, policies establish standard decisions, deviations from which will be brought to the attention of management so violations can be controlled. A great deal of organizational behavior at all levels is controlled by policy.

Supervision

Supervision insures that tasks by employees are done as expected. While a supervisor cannot observe an employee all the time, he can provide a considerable amount of guidance that helps the employee perform his job in accordance with management's expectations. A supervisor of an assembly operation cannot guarantee that all items will be assembled properly, yet his mere presence in the assembly department provides more control over the employee's work than could be achieved without him.

Job Descriptions and Specifications

Job descriptions are another subtle method of control, since they specify the task to be performed and describe the type of individual needed to perform it. They assist in insuring that the employee knows exactly what his job entails and what he should do, and that he is able to do it.

Organizational Structure

Organization provides numerous subtle controls, as it gives assignments to particular positions and divides up the work in ways deemed best by management, thereby controlling who does what.

Wages

Wages not only control the firm's cost of doing business but also affect the quality and amount of work that may be done. Excellence can be motivated by wage policy. Salesmen are continually urged to greater sales by incentive compensation plans such as straight commissions. Eli Lilly Company, a large drug manufacturer, has incentive pay plans in many of its critical departments to control the excellence of its workers' performance. Visualize the tragedy should the wrong label be placed on a bottle, or the wrong bottles in a shipment. As long as a man works error free, his wages rise each period with an ever-increasing bonus. But should he make an error, his bonus reverts to zero and he starts the process again. A man with a large bonus becomes rather careful about what he does—just exactly as management intends him to do.

How can wage policy control an accountant's performance? a secretary's?

Budgets

Budgets are quantitative plans for the firm's operation in a coming period of time, usually a quarter or a year. The sales budget tells the sales department how much it is expected to sell and what must be produced to sell it. Each budgetary unit projects what money it will need to operate at the planned level of activity—wages, supplies, equipment—and it should then stay within those limits, thereby insuring management's control over the sales/cost ratio.

Budgetary behavior can be most vexing and rather complex, but it is quite critical to a potential manager's career that he master it.

Budgeting frees management from examining all expenditures for all departments throughout the year; it limits their concern to those cases in which budgetary limits are exceeded. All levels of supervision affected by a budget must take part in forming it and then must accept the responsibility of making that budget work by keeping expenses within the limits.

Benefits of Budgeting An important goal in operating a business is to continually maintain the desired relationship between expenditures and income. The objective of a business is to buy revenues at a reasonable cost, and the budget clearly shows what this cost should be. If an executive forecasts sales of $5 million for the coming period, he can establish how much his firm can afford to pay for that revenue. If the company wants a profit of 10 percent on sales, then $4.5 million can be paid to buy the $5 million in revenue. Part of the $4.5 million will go to the production and administrative departments, according to their requirements, and another portion will be available to operate the sales department. Thus the sales executive has a definite sum to use in selling the merchandise. In this way, the budget restricts the sales manager from spending more than his share of the available funds. Hence, the budget helps to prevent expenses from getting out of control and keeps them in proper alignment with sales.

Coordinating Mechanism Budgeting is the best way to plan, control, and coordinate the activities of the segments of a large enterprise. It is axiomatic that production must be coordinated with sales; it is folly to produce more or less merchandise than can be sold. A budget serves quite well as a coordinating tool. With the sales budget, the production manager can closely plan his output so that the necessary goods will be available when required. But until the sales department tells the production manager its anticipated needs, he has no way of knowing how much to produce.

Budgeting also allows the financial executive to plan for coming financial burdens. Without some established forecast of what the organization will be selling and what it will be spending for materials, labor, and marketing expenses, the financial executive has no way of knowing how much money will be required during periods of the conversion cycle. The sales budget allows the controller to judge how much money the firm will require to finance accounts receivable, inventory, and various overhead expenses. The production budget allows him to predict the expenditures for purchases of raw materials and labor. Without an accurate budget, the firm would be forced to carry more money than is necessary for efficient operation. If excess capital were not carried, the company frequently might be required to undertake emergency financing.

Standard of Performance The budget serves not only as a plan of action but also as a goal or standard of performance for the various departments. Once the budget is established, the departments can begin organizing to realize that performance. If the budget has been based on a sound analysis of potential markets and competition, it will encourage the organization to realize its full potentiality. Otherwise, the men may not know what they could or should be achieving.

Evaluation Tool Once established, a goal always becomes a tool for postperformance evaluation. If the organization meets its goals, management has some assurance that the performance can be considered successful. Since a manager usually establishes his own budgets, if he is unable to meet his budgetary requirements he is usually viewed with suspicion: he must be either a poor budgetary officer or a bad manager.

Quotas

Quotas resemble budgets in that they establish a projected level of achievement for a specific period for an operating unit. Quotas usually do not relate to expenses as do budget systems, but rather to sales and production output. Quotas project an expected level of performance against which actual performance is later compared. A sales quota may be set for a man, territory, or division. The manager then carefully compares actual performance with the quota. Units not achieving their quotas may have some explanations to make as to why they failed to perform as expected.

Quotas, like budgets, have the advantage of being a control mechanism that permits management by exception, since managerial concern will arise only when the performance of an individual or unit of the firm raises a red flag by not reaching or significantly passing a quota.

Accounting System

While accounting is discussed in a separate chapter, it still deserves mention here because it is the main quantitative control system used by all firms and has a great many legal control aspects. Creditors, stockholders, the Internal Revenue Service, and the Securities and Exchange Commission are but a few of the outside parties who have a legal right to accurate quantitative data concerning the firm's performance.

Most of the data flowing into other control systems are originated by the accounting system, which should be able to give sales and expenses by products, territory, division, or man. Budgets are usually formulated by referring to past accounting records.

Work Evaluation and Review

Sound managerial principles dictate that the work record of each employee be periodically evaluated and reviewed with him in person. His progress and deficiencies should be brought to his attention at this time. Often salaries are reviewed and revised in conjunction with the work review. The knowledge that one's work will be reviewed carefully at frequent intervals acts as a control over one's behavior.

Do employees object to such work evaluations?

Reporting Systems

Reports are a vital part of management's information and control system. They may be quantitative reports of sales, production, costs, or some other aspect of operations that can be measured, or they may be qualitative reports, such as an evaluation of a competitor's new product or the progress the research laboratory is making on a certain project.

Management reviews all or part of these reports for unusual statements or variances from expected performance. Operating reports from production departments may reveal an absentee problem or employee turnover problem in one department that would require action by management. William H. Moore, appointed president of the Penn Central Railroad during its reorganization in 1970, implemented a daily report system that summarized every exception to normal operating procedures for the railroad during the previous day. As president he reviewed this summary of individual department reports and personally investigated the action taken to remedy each exception.

But reports cost money in the time of those who prepare them and those who are supposed to read them! Useless reports have plagued organizations that do not continually evaluate them for usefulness. If a report does not serve a purpose that justifies its costs, or is not read by management, then it should be discontinued.

What is a useless report? How does one come about? How can management prevent such reports from continuing?

Inspection

Inspection is often the best method for identifying variations from standards. Production quality is usually controlled by an inspection of the finished product. It may be an inspection of all products made or a random inspection of a few products, relying on statistical techniques to judge the overall quality of the assembly process for all units. Obviously, all television tubes cannot be inspected for the number of hours that they will operate, for all tubes would be used and there would be none left to sell. A visual inspection of every tube for cracks in the glass could be undertaken easily. But testing for tube life must be done by sampling—say one out of every hundred tubes is pulled out at random for testing.

What determines the percentage of tubes tested?

Computer

The computer is but a mechanical-electronic device for storing and manipulating numbers; still, it must be considered a control mechanism, for it allows the institution of much more complicated reporting systems than were possible a decade ago. More-over, a good computer system allows management to receive complicated reports quickly, whereas to process the same data by old-fashioned hand methods would take months.

The connection of long-distance communication systems with the computer allows data to be fed into it daily from distant operating plants and warehouses, so that management can keep tighter control over remote operations.

WHAT IS A GOOD CONTROL SYSTEM?

Good control mechanisms have a number of things in common. First, the system should detect variances promptly. Deviations from desired performance usually are expensive; if they are not detected quickly, losses can mount rapidly.

Second, the system should be simple to administer. A system that is too complicated is relatively costly, and its intended reader may ignore or slight it because of the effort or expertise that it may require.

Third, its costs must be in proportion to its benefits. It is folly to institute controls that cost more than they can save. Would you care to institute a reporting system on the number of paper clips used each day? No, few people would—but there are numerous other reports that make just as little sense.

Fourth, the control mechanism should be difficult to circumvent or avoid. If inspections are used as a method of control, it should be difficult to avoid them. Budgets become rather meaningless if executives can easily juggle funds between accounts or otherwise ignore the budget's limitations.

Fifth, a control system must fit in with the firm's total operating system. Its sophistication and degree of control must be consistent with the company's objectives. A management wanting to sell an extremely high-quality product should design control mechanisms that can insure achievement of these objectives at the lowest possible cost. A firm less conscientious about image and product quality may find less elaborate control mechanisms more attractive.

Finally, the output of a control system should go to the executives who need the data and are able to act upon it. The "need to know" principle applies, partly for security and partly for economy; those people, and only those people, who need to know the information are given access to it.

Conclusion

All studies have indicated that a major reason underlying business failures has been management's failure to control operations properly—its failure to keep costs in proper ratio to sales. Accounting systems of failed businesses often have been almost nonexistent if not quite faulty. Other controls were absent.

On the other hand, one of the earmarks of the large professionally managed corporations is their dependence upon a wide range of control procedures and mechanisms to insure that operations are going as desired and as planned.

A problem arises because the basic nature of control conflicts with the natural desires of the creative, aggressive executive, who is most apt to disdain such dull, detailed tasks as being little more than red tape, paperwork. The man who rises in modern corporate organizations most likely has been able to develop a workable compromise between his dislike for control work and the need for it.

24 Accounting systems

In every enterprise consider where you would come out.
PUBLILIUS SYRUS

Most games have their scorekeepers; business is no exception. Accounting serves as scorekeeper by providing a record of company activities expressed in dollars. While a firm's score ... its effectiveness, success, as an enterprise ... may be measured by evaluating such intangibles as the degree to which management is able to stimulate creativity among its employees, or the extent to which it is able to develop useful products for society, or the employment it provides for the community, it is not easy to judge the quality of a firm's management by such evaluations. The activities of an enterprise can be more easily, more accurately expressed quantitatively as dollars received from various activities and dollars spent on various things. The accounting department tallies all expenses, sales, changes in ownership, and property bought or sold in a company; it is the firm's scorekeeper. Accountants record all transactions and note their affect on the financial condition of the firm. They are charged with analyzing and interpreting these transactions, thereby evaluating the firm's performance.

You will be introduced here to the need for accounting information, the procedures by which accounting records are prepared, the two major scoreboards—the balance sheet and the profit and loss statement (income statement)—and some of the basic methods for analyzing financial statements.

WHY ACCOUNT?

The management of an enterprise must know both its financial past and present. It should be able to identify what its sales and expenses have been for specific periods of time, and it should be able to identify what it owes to whom at any time. Moreover, it needs to know what property it owns and what goods it has for sale. Such information enables management to control the firm's operations. Knowledge of current indebtedness and the present values of properties is essential in planning future expenditures or judging the firm's ability to acquire new facilities or undertake new enterprises.

Financial records assist management in identifying problems that the firm is facing. Who has owed us money too long? Accounts receivable records will pinpoint those customers who have been negligent in paying. Are we spending too much on advertising? An analysis of advertising expenditures in relationship to sales revenues may help supply the answer. Should we raise prices? A look at the gross margin combined with an analysis of the costs of production may provide insights to help answer the question. The accounting department can provide data that will assist in solving just about any internal problem facing management.

Accounting records reflect the contribution of specific people or programs to the firm's total performance. Is Salesman Sam doing his part, selling what he should? Is the overseas sales program profitable? Is the finishing department efficient? Are the costs of making the widget too high? Accounting records may be compiled in such a way as to throw light on the answers to such questions.

What data would you want for judging the effectiveness of a sales training program?

The company's owners or investors are constantly questioning its financial performance, particularly its profitability. Creditors want to know its ability to pay its bills. Banks want to know its financial condition before extending a note or making a new loan. The governments are most interested in making certain they collect taxes due them—income taxes, social security taxes, taxes that have been withheld from employees, excise taxes, property taxes, sales taxes, and unemployment taxes.

Groups outside of the firm find its accounting information helpful in dealing with the enterprise. Labor unions use a company's financial reports as a basis for supporting wage demands for their workers. Financial experts use a firm's annual reports as a basis for their analysis of its investment potential.

The need for accounting information and control is made even more acute by the *revenue lag* experienced by most companies. The typical firm must spend money in advance of receiving it back in sales volume—sales lag expenses. If careful accounting is not instituted, management may find itself in the embarrassing position of spending more money than it will later take in.

HOW WE ACCOUNT

The basic unit of all accounting is the transaction. Each transaction—the company buys or sells something—must be recorded. In each transaction two things always happen—the company gains something and loses something. Plus and minus! It sells a product; plus is money or an account receivable, minus is the product (inventory). It borrows money from the bank; plus is its cash account; minus is a bit more complicated, for it represents an increase in notes payable, a liability. Think a minute and you will realize that increase of liabilities represents a loss (minus) to the company's financial status. The company pays a bill; minus is cash, plus is a decrease in accounts payable. A worker is paid his salary; plus is the value of goods in process, minus is cash. Things can become far more complicated in actual accounting, but essentially it records the two things that happen in each transaction. If you will carefully examine any transaction with which you have been connected, you will find that two things happen to you.

Identify the two things that happen to you in each of the following cases: you buy a car on credit; you make a payment on the car; you borrow $50 from a friend; you give a friend $10 as a gift.

The effect of all transactions upon the firm can be viewed by a survey of the things of value it owns and the amounts it owes. Its assets are the things it owns. Its liabilities are the amounts it owes. The difference between the value of a firm's assets and its liabilities is called the owner's equity or proprietorship.

A highly simplified discussion of a college student's financial condition can be used to illustrate changes in his assets, liabilities, and proprietorship. If Rick Joseph earns $10 and retains it in cash, his financial condition can be represented by the following:

RICK JOSEPH
August 31, 1971

Cash	$10	Proprietorship	$10

Rick buys a ballpoint pen for $1, reducing his cash by $1 and adding a $1 ballpoint pen to his personal properties.

RICK JOSEPH
September 10, 1971

Cash	$ 9	Proprietorship	$10
Pen	1		
	$10		$10

Borrowing $50 on a student loan again results in two things for Rick: he increases his cash by $50 and his liabilities by $50. His financial position now is reflected by the following statement:

RICK JOSEPH
September 15, 1971

Cash	$59	Loan	$50
Pen	1	Proprietorship	10
	$60		$60

Consider the following transactions for Rick and identify the two things that happen to his financial structure each time. Prepare a summary of his financial condition after these transactions.

1. Purchase college textbooks for $50 at the college bookstore.
2. Purchase $10 textbook on a credit account at the college bookstore.
3. Inherit $100.
4. Pay bookstore account of $10 on October 15, 1971.

Rick's financial condition after the transactions above is represented as follows:

RICK JOSEPH
October 15, 1971

Cash	$99	Loan	$ 50
Pen	1	Proprietorship	$110
Books	60		
	$160		$160

Accounting for Rick's transactions has permitted us to examine his assets, liabilities, and proprietorship (owner's equity) at various points in time, which leads us to a detailed discussion of the basic accounting statements, the balance sheet, and the profit and loss statement (income statement). The summaries of Rick Joseph's financial condition are simplified balance sheets, a concept which will now be explained more thoroughly.

RECORDING TRANSACTIONS

Recording the two effects of each transaction requires that *accounts* be established, for there must be someplace where they can be recorded. Two accounts are affected by each transaction. Here are some examples of various accounts, placed into their usual categories:

Assets	Liabilities	Profit and Loss	Net Worth or Equity
Cash Accounts Receivable Notes Receivable Inventory Plant Land Equipment Investments	Accounts Payable Notes Payable Wages Payable Taxes Payable	Sales Expenses such as: Advertising Postage Salaries Travel Cost of Product Supplies Interest	Proprietorship Capital Stock Surplus

To review the firm's financial condition at any point in time, one must summarize the balances in all such accounts. Accounts are summarized in the balance sheet if they represent items of value currently owned, amounts of money owed to others, or funds contributed or claimed by the owners. All accounts relating to sales and expenses are summarized in the income statement, and the resulting profit or loss is transferred to the balance sheet as a change in equity. A profit increases equity, a loss decreases it. A balance sheet is a snapshot of the firm's financial condition as of any *point in time;* the income statement is a moving picture showing what has happened during a *period of time.*

Accounts are summarized at varying intervals, but most commonly at the end of each three months (quarterly reports) and a year (the annual report). The increased use of the computer has allowed some concerns to obtain daily or weekly summaries of their financial position. Moreover, they can recall from the computer's memory just the accounts desired.

What advantages and disadvantages are there to such frequent reporting?

THE BALANCE SHEET

All accounts that affect assets, liabilities, or owner's equity are summarized in the balance sheet, which provides a momentary financial picture of the firm. It represents the firm's assets, debts, and owner's capital on the date of the balance sheet. It does not show what has happened to the firm over a period of time, but merely represents its financial condition at one point in time. The December 31, 1970, balance sheet and the December 31, 1971, balance sheet of a firm do provide information to analyze what has happened to the balance-sheet accounts during the year 1971; this was done in the sources and application of funds statement we examined in a previous chapter.

The balance sheet is prepared in two columns. The column totals are equal to each other. One column includes all assets; the second column summarizes liabilities and stockholders' or owner's equity (proprietorship). All monies either borrowed or contributed by the owners are represented in total by corresponding items of value owned by the firm—assets. This is formally identified as the accounting equation, represented as follows:

$$\text{Assets} = \text{Liabilities} + \text{Owner's Equity}$$

The hypothetical balance sheet presented in Figure 24-1 will serve as an example for the following discussion of assets, liabilities, and stockholders' equity.

Assets are any item of value owned by the business enterprise. They may be tangibles, such as a building, or intangibles, such as the right to control a product's patent. Items that have a value to the firm are represented in the balance sheet as assets. Typically, they are classified as current, fixed, investment, and intangible assets. *Current assets* are cash and all assets that will be converted into cash in the near future, usually within a year, such as accounts receivable, inventories, and prepaid expenses. While an inventory balance will be present at all times and may not seem to be of short-term nature, probably the current inventory will be sold and new items will be in the inventory on the balance sheet prepared next year. Since some of the accounts due from customers, accounts receivable, cannot be collected a reasonable allowance for bad debts is used to reduce total accounts receivable.

Why would a firm with an excellent credit department still have bad debts? How does the nature of the industry affect the amount of bad debts realized by a company? How can one minimize bad debts?

Prepaid expenses would be exemplified by an insurance premium paid in advance for three years. The unused part of the premium at the end of the year is recorded, because the firm has the right to this amount of protection for the next two years.

Fixed assets are such items as buildings, land, store fixtures, or equipment—property that management anticipates will be in its possession longer than one year. Such items tend to decrease in value with time as they are used up or wear out. We reflect this in the balance sheet by reducing the value of the asset when it was acquired by an amount identified as accumulated depreciation, which is the amount the asset has decreased in value since it was acquired. Automobile owners recognize that while a car may cost $3000 new, at the end of a year it is probably worth only about $2000, and at the end of the second year perhaps only $1500. A balance sheet for this automobile at the end of the second year would be:

Automobile Asset Value after Two Years	
Automobile: cost	$3000
Less accumulated depreciation	1500
Net asset value	$1500

What if the car later becomes a "classic" and increases in value to $5000. How would that be treated by an accountant?

The $1500 accumulated depreciation would have been recorded as an expense of the business in the income statements ($1000 in the first year, $500 in the second year).

Investment accounts include money a firm invests in other ventures. Ownership of stock in other corporations is shown on the balance sheet under this heading at its cost.

What if the market price goes up significantly? Drops significantly? The valuation principle, "cost or market whichever is lower," is frequently used by accountants. Why?

Intangible assets are such items as patent rights, research, and goodwill. The true value of owning a patent may be represented in the balance sheet as long as that patent right exists for the corporation under government patent laws.

Why capitalize research expenditures? Why not charge them off as a current expense?

Goodwill is the value that has been set on a firm's name or brand names. In theory, goodwill is the amount of money a firm would sell for in excess of its net assets (total assets minus liabilities) or equity. Since we usually defer to the all-seeing wisdom of the market, when that market seemingly places a higher value on assets than is shown by a balance sheet, then we must assume that other values were present that were not being reflected. If the seemingly high price cannot be specifically attributed to some tangible asset that has been undervalued (such as land that is carried on the books at $100,000 but is actually worth $1,000,000), then we assume the buyer is paying the extra money to buy the firm's goodwill.

Liabilities are amounts of money that the firm owes to other individuals or organizations. Some are termed current liabilities, since they are due within a year. Accounts payable to suppliers, wages payable to employees, interest payable to bond holders, and notes payable due within a year would be included in this category. Long-term liabilities, long-term notes payable and bonds, are not due within the next year.

Stockholders' equity includes money contributed directly to the firm by its owner, partners, or stockholders. The proceeds from any stock sold by the corporation will be recorded in this section. Also recorded here is the amount of profit earned by the firm. Net profits after taxes are recorded on the balance sheet as retained earnings or earned surplus. If the firm incurs losses, they are subtracted from earned surplus or retained earnings.

INCOME STATEMENT

The income statement summarizes the firm's transactions relating to sales revenue and expenses of operations. Expenses are generally grouped by their nature: cost of production, sales costs, or expenses of administering the firm. The income statement provides a picture of the firm's operation over a specified time period. Figure 24-2 represents a hypothetical income statement for the BGR Corporation.

Net sales of the firm are the total gross sales less any amounts of goods returned or any discounts granted to customers to reduce stated sales prices. *Cost of goods sold* is then subtracted from net sales to obtain gross profit on sales. Cost of goods sold in a manufacturing firm includes the total cost of raw materials used in production during the accounting period, direct factory labor, and all factory overhead such as rent, lights, heat, property taxes, and equipment depreciation expenses. The cost of goods sold for a nonmanufacturing firm such as a retail store would include the firm's purchase price of all goods sold during the period. A service firm may find that it does not have a direct cost of goods sold and therefore may not include such a section in its income statement. *Expenses* are generally recorded as being applicable to sales, such as sales salaries and advertising, or general administration. Administration expenses may include executive salaries, office salaries, postage, and general overhead costs of administering the firm. Subtracting these expenses from gross profit yields net profit before taxes. Usually firms deduct the income taxes paid on profits to arrive at a figure for net profit after taxes.

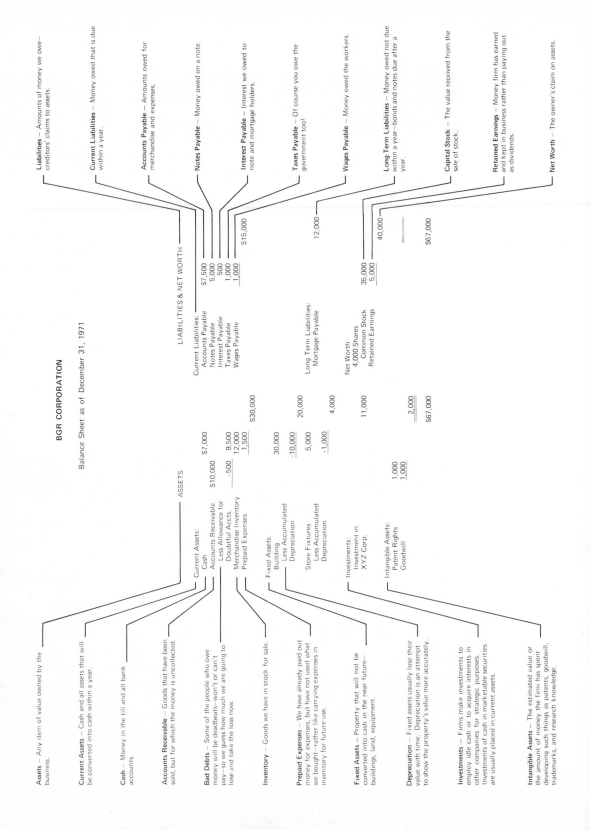

FIGURE 24-1: Balance Sheet for BGR Corporation

FIGURE 24 -2: Income Statement for BGR Corporation

BGR CORPORATION

Income Statement for the Period of December 31, 1970 to December 31, 1971

Gross Sales		$75,000
Less Returns and Allowances		5,000
Net Sales		70,000
Less Cost of Goods Sold:		
Beginning Inventory	$9,500	
Purchases	25,500	
Goods Available for Sale	$35,000	
Ending Inventory	12,000	
Cost of Goods Sold		23,000
Gross Margin		$47,000
Less Expenses:		
Administrative Expenses	20,000	
Marketing Expenses	20,000	
Financial Expenses	1,000	
Total Expenses		41,000
Net Profit before Taxes		$6,000
Federal Income Taxes		1,320
Net Profit after Taxes		$4,680

Gross Sales. This is what we thought we had sold—it moved out the door.

Returns and Allowances. But some goods came back through that door—they didn't stay sold.

Net Sales. Now here's where things really begin. We sold this much.

Less Cost of Goods Sold
First, let's find out what the goods actually cost that stayed sold.

Beginning Inventory. This is what we had on hand at the beginning of the period.

Purchases. We bought this much goods during the period.

Goods Available for Sale. So we had available in our place of business at various times during the period this much that could have been sold.

Ending Inventory. But this much didn't sell; we still have it.

Cost of Goods Sold. So we sold this much—simple logic.

Gross Margin. Subtracting the cost of goods sold from Net Sales gives us our gross margin. Some people call it gross profit, but that is misleading for it is in no way profit.

Expenses. Now let's subtract all our expenses. We have grouped them into three simple categories. In actual practice they are detailed out; e.g., postage, travel.

Administrative Expenses. Under this heading come a great many overhead items such as rent, postage, salaries of administrative personnel, administrative travel and entertainment, supplies, depreciation on office equipment, property taxes, etc.

Marketing Expenses. Such expenses as salesmen's earnings, travel costs, entertainment of customers, advertising, etc. would be included here.

Finance Expenses. Interest, accounting costs, and bank charges would be included here.

Net Profit before Taxes. Depending upon your theory of profits, here is your profit on operations.

Income Taxes. The federal government takes 22 percent of the first $25,000 profit, 48 percent of all over that amount—unless this corporation had filed the proper papers to be considered a Sub Chapter S corporation, in which case there would be no corporate tax. We assume that this company is located in a state that has no corporate income taxes.

Net Profit after Taxes. For people who consider taxes a cost of doing business, this is the true profit from operations.

ACCOUNTING SYSTEMS

To the accountant, what we have been discussing is but the basics, the ABC'S. His real challenge is developing a control system, an accounting system that gets everything done that needs doing. All sorts of documents must be created and recorded. Checks must be written to pay bills, to pay employees, to pay the government. Money is received on accounts receivable that must be recorded and put into the bank. Things are bought and sold. People throughout the organization are handling money and shuffling paper. And, if all is not put together into a meaningful system that can be continually monitored and audited, experience clearly indicates that a great deal of dishonesty is encouraged, not to mention the confusion and breakdown in operations.

A large publishing house had been having a great deal of trouble with its accounting systems for handling customer orders. The wrong books in the wrong amounts were being sent to the wrong customers, if they were sent at all. Customers were outraged, and so were the salesmen who had sold the orders. The company's accountants simply had not devised a foolproof system for processing orders—a most critical subsystem of the entire control system. Figure 24-3 illustrates one subsystem

FIGURE 24-3: A System for Using a Combination Sales Order-Shipper-Invoice

Procedure for Use of Combination Sales Order — Shipper — Invoice

Sales Department	Production Control Department	Shipping Department	Accounting Department
Customer order			
Combination sales order set	Balance of order set held until released to production	Order set held until shipment is made	Billing completes invoice copies
Mail acknowledgement copy to customer (9)	Production planning and scheduling file (2)	Packing list included with shipment to customer (3)	Mail one or more invoice copies to customer (5)
Mail copy of order to salesman (10)		Shipper (4)	Mail copy of invoice to salesman (6)
Open order file (1)	File is cleared as orders are shipped	Shipper (8)	Accounting copy used to post to accounts receivable (7)
File is cleared as orders are shipped			

Typed on order set by sales department:
1. Date order is written
2. Customer's name and address
3. Shipment destination
4. Customer's purchase order number
5. Quantity and description of items ordered
6. Selling price

Typed on order set by shipping department:
1. Date shipped
2. Quantities shipped
3. How shipped—freight, express, etc.

Typed on order set by accounting department:
1. Amount of billing
2. Sales tax, freight, etc.

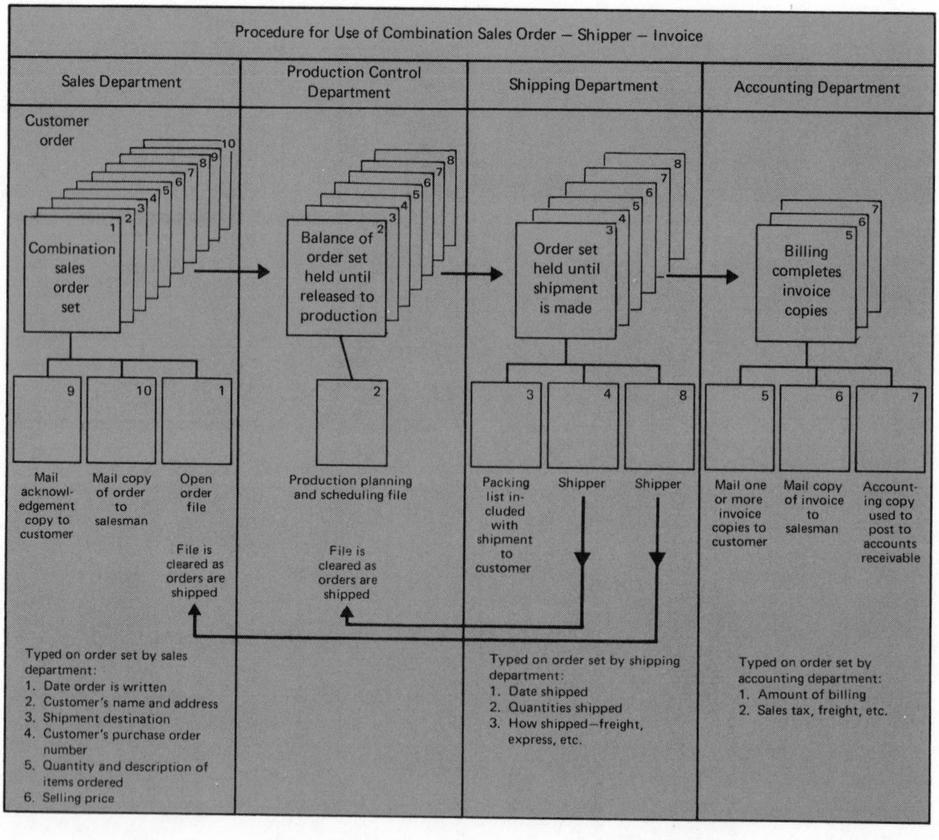

devised to handle an incoming order. But let us hasten to point out that each firm must devise such subsystems to fit the particular characteristics of its business.

The recent experience of many Wall Street brokerage houses with their accounting and control systems is a most forceful illustration of what can happen when the accountant cannot—or is not allowed to—develop a system that can do the job. The basic problem was that systems adequate to handle the paperwork load at one level of operations proved totally inadequate to handle a vastly increased volume of business—a common experience, one that most firms go through as they grow in size. After all, when a business is just getting started, its books can be kept on the back of an envelope. As the number of transactions increases, and they grow more complex, simple bookkeeping systems will no longer do the job; a more comprehensive system is required.

FINANCIAL ANALYSIS

While the balance sheet and income statement provide pictures of the financial condition of the firm and of its operation over a specified period, one must look deeper to determine how good or bad the firm's financial performance has been. By reading these statements one can identify how money was spent by the firm, but more detailed analysis is required to establish whether or not it should have been spent in such a manner. One major interpretive tool for analyzing balance sheets is the statement of sources and application of funds, discussed in a previous chapter. Another important tool is *ratio analysis.*

A ratio is a comparison of two numbers. There are six people in a room, four men and two women. The ratio of men to women is 4 to 2 or, reducing it, 2 to 1. For convenience we further reduce the ratio by dividing the first number by the second: $2/1 = 2$. So we would say the ratio of men to women is 2.

When ratios are used for economic analysis, it is most helpful if they can be compared with some meaningful yardsticks outside the organization being analyzed. Suppose that the ratio of workers to foremen in a company is 8. Is that good or bad? There is no way of telling, unless we have some outside yardsticks by which to measure—and even then we must be careful. Suppose that the average ratio in that company's industry for workers to foremen was 12. Now what? We know that the subject firm's management is hiring proportionately more supervision for its workers than the average firm in the industry. But so what? That might be good or bad, depending upon the results. If administrative costs or factory overhead were too high, this fact would help explain it. But if such supervision paid off in lower labor costs—if the workers were more than proportionately productive—then management's strategy paid off. The moral of the story is that one must be exceedingly careful in jumping to conclusions about ratios. They can be very misleading. What looks bad can be good, and vice versa. For this reason, ratio analysis has fallen somewhat from favor among the more sophisticated analysts. But you still need to be aware of it, for in business people will be using ratios almost daily to tell you something about a company.

While ten basic ratios will meet the needs for most occasions, you should not be at all hesitant to develop whatever ratios you feel have some meaning for you. Ratios need not have textbook sanction to be useful. We can classify these ten ratios into four categories: profit ratios, current-position ratios, capital-structure ratios, and capital-turnover ratios.

Profit Ratios

Three ratios are widely used to measure a firm's relative profitability: profit to sales, profit to net worth, and profit on total capital.

Profit-to-Sales Ratio   By dividing the firm's profits by its sales volume (profit/sales), we get the profit-to-sales ratio, which is usually stated as a percentage. All ratios can be stated as percentages if the division is carried out. The BGR Corporation's profit-to-sales ratio was

$$\frac{\$6,000}{\$70,000} = 0.0857, \text{ or } 8.57 \text{ percent.}$$

Another way of saying it is that BGR Corporation made a profit of about 8.5 cents out of every sales dollar.

Profit on Net Worth   By dividing net profit by net worth, we see the rate of return the owners of the business are getting on their investment:

$$\frac{\text{profit}}{\text{net worth}} = \text{return on investment}$$

The BGR Corporation earned 15 percent:

$$\frac{\$6,000}{\$40,000} = .15$$

Return on Total Capital   Economically, a more meaningful ratio is computed by dividing profits by total assets, thereby determining what the assets in the business are earning. BGR earned 8.95 percent profit on its assets:

$$\frac{\$6,000}{\$67,000} = .0895$$

Summary   All these profit ratios can be compared with similar ratios of competing firms and with the industry to judge how efficiently, how profitably, the firm is in comparison with other companies. If the enterprise is not earning at least 10 percent on invested capital, there is good cause to wonder about the wisdom of the investment. Similarly, if the assets are not earning 5 or 6 percent, then the money had best be put to other use, for it could be placed in the bank and do as well with far less risk and no work.

Current-Position Ratios

These following ratios assist in evaluating the working-capital position of the company.

Current Ratio   The ratio of current assets to current liabilities is referred to as the current ratio. The traditional 2-to-1 ratio is probably one of the best-recognized standards in the business world. It supposedly measures the firm's ability to pay its bills. With twice as many current assets as current liabilities, a company should not have too much difficulty paying its debts, or so it is thought.

When might a firm have a current ratio of 3 and still be unable to pay its current debts?

The BGR Corporation has a current ratio of

$$\frac{\$30,000}{\$15,000} = 2$$

Acid-Test Ratio   This ratio, a more rigorous refinement of the current ratio, compares current liquid assets to current liabilities. It measures the ability of the firm to pay all short-term obligations immediately, rather than as they may come due during the next year.

$$\text{Acid-test ratio} = \frac{\text{current liquid assets}}{\text{current liabilities}}$$

Current liquid assets are those items that can be converted into cash very readily. They typically would include cash, marketable securities, and accounts receivable, since the latter can be sold to outside agencies readily and thereby turned into cash. This ratio's standard is about 1:1, which would indicate that the firm can meet all of its current obligations with the cash it can generate immediately. Again this ratio may vary between firms and industries. The acid-test ratio for the BGR Corporation is

$$\frac{\$16,500}{\$15,000} = \frac{110}{100} = 1.1$$

Accounts-Receivable-to-Sales Ratio   By dividing accounts receivable by the average daily sales, we obtain some estimate of the collection period for the receivables. BGR has about 50 days' sales as receivables:

$$\frac{\$9,000}{\$70,000/365} = 49.5$$

As is true with all ratios, comparison of a firm's performance over time can be most enlightening. The fact that BGR has 50 days' sales in receivables is by itself not too significant, unless management definitely desired some other level of receivables. But suppose this ratio for earlier years had been 35 days' sales as receivables. Now management would have something to investigate for here would be a strong indication that credit collections were lagging. Action would be indicated. It is amazing how fast collections can slow down if credit management becomes negligent, or if for one reason or another one's customers are out of work.

Inventory Businessmen long ago learned the importance of keeping their inventories under control, in proper ratio to sales volume. By dividing inventory at cost by average daily cost of goods sold, we can estimate how many days' sales are being carried in inventory. BGR is carrying about 190 days' sales in inventory:

$$\frac{\$12,000}{\$23,000/365} = 190 \text{ days sales}$$

Sometimes we approach this same aspect of a company's operations in a slightly different manner by calculating what is known as the inventory turnover, which is:

$$\frac{\text{cost of goods sold}}{\text{average inventory at cost}}$$

BGR's inventory turnover is

$$\frac{\$23,000}{\dfrac{\$9,500 + \$12,000}{2}} = \frac{\$23,000}{\$10,750} = 2.14 \text{ times}$$

Capital-Structure Ratios

Investors are usually interested in certain ratios that reflect the nature of a firm's capital structure. The two main ratios are *fixed assets to net worth* and *total debt to net worth.*

Fixed Assets to Net Worth This ratio, usually expressed as a percentage, is obtained by dividing the firm's fixed assets by its net worth. If the percentage is more than 100 percent, people begin to worry that equity is insufficient. Business theory indicates that the fixed assets of a firm should be financed by equity. BGR's ratio is 60 percent:

$$\frac{\$24,000}{\$40,000} = 0.60$$

Total Debt to Net Worth   People begin to worry when a company's assets are owned more by the creditors than by its owners, which would be the case if this ratio were more than 1. BGR's ratio is

$$\frac{\$27,000}{\$40,000} = 0.67$$

Capital-Turnover Ratios

Business analysts, concerned with the efficiency with which a management uses the capital at its disposal, have devised some ways to measure it.

Sales to Net Worth   How many times does the business turn over its equity in sales? Divide sales by net worth for the answer. BGR's ratio is

$$\frac{\$70,000}{\$40,000} = 1.75$$

Sales to Total Assets   A better measure of the true efficiency in using the capital assets of a business is obtained by dividing sales by total assets. BGR's ratio is

$$\frac{\$70,000}{\$67,000} = 1.04$$

The Rate-of-Return-on-Investment Formula

By putting together some of the above ratios, we can devise a formula for summarizing the business equation:

$$\frac{\text{rate of return on}}{\text{invested capital}} = \text{profit margin} \times \text{capital turnover}$$

$$\frac{\text{profit}}{\text{investment}} = \frac{\text{profit}}{\text{sales}} \times \frac{\text{sales}}{\text{investment}}$$

Multiply a firm's profit margin by its capital turnover and you will have its rate of return on capital. And that presents the two basic avenues to a good rate of return on a business enterprise: a high profit margin or a high turnover. It would be nice if you could get both, but competition seldom allows it. BGR's profit margin was 8.57 percent and its capital turnover was 1.75 percent, making its rate of return on investment 15 percent (8.57 × 1.75)—exactly what was previously computed.

A FINAL VIEW OF ACCOUNTING

Accounting strives to provide a financial picture of the business firm by keeping careful record of all transactions and periodically reporting their effect on the financial condition of the firm. This picture of the firm may not provide a completely adequate basis for judging the merit or effectiveness of a management. Accounting records and financial statements do have limitations and may pose difficulties for those who do not look beyond them.

The value of assets in the balance sheet is expressed as the original price paid for them less accumulated depreciation. The amount given in the balance sheet may be quite erroneous in representing the true *current* value of the assets.

Intangible costs are not reflected in financial statements. Such factors as the social cost of a firm's polluting rivers or air cannot be expressed in the firm's income statement. Similarly, firms that may successfully eliminate water or air pollution will show only the direct cost of pollution controls in their income statement without balancing them against any "social profit" that may exist because of such controls. There is a degree of "social profit" that is not reflected in the income statements of firms that keep numerous members of our society employed, and thus reduce the unemployment insurance expenditures and welfare expenditures. In general, many expenses and values of assets are difficult to identify or express in dollars.

Pronouncing judgment on the merit of an enterprise and the effectiveness of its management may require significant amounts of information that cannot be obtained from typical accounting statements. The accounting function is necessary, useful, and generally provides answers to significant questions about the performance of the firm. Questions whose answers are not available in accounting statements should not remain unanswered, but additional sources of information should be consulted to fully satisfy the one attempting to evaluate the business organization.

25 Management information systems (M.I.S.)

Tell me quick and tell me true.
ANON.

"How many units of Model 77 do we have in stock in the Miami warehouse?"

"What were our traveling expenses last month for the southeastern region?"

"What's our sales potential in the Seattle sales territory and how much of it is the salesman realizing?"

"What's it costing us to operate that number 2 warehouse?"

These are but a few of the types of questions asked daily of the executives of almost any firm. Usually the answers are not available, so the business continues to operate as best it can without them. But in recent years matters have become immensely more complex for the management of any substantial enterprise. More products to make, store, and sell; more people involved in the processes; more money at stake; and, to top it off, the competition is much keener than before. Answers, quick answers, must be forthcoming to certain critical questions that people keep asking, such as "How much product do we have and where is it?" and "What does it cost us to do this or that?"

In the past, management was frequently forced to operate without such information; at best, accounting could provide quarterly financial information, usually a few months late. A few able managements were able to get monthly data within a reasonable time, but these were rare exceptions. Decisions simply had to be made without good information.

The bottleneck in the information flow was the costly and time-consuming hand labor required for processing data. Business lore is replete with little men in green eyeshades perched atop stools grinding out needed numerical data. The costs of this information system limited it to the traditional mandatory accounting records and a few extremely critical supporting records such as inventory control. And then came the computer!

THE COMPUTER

In the 1930s, IBM developed a system by which information could be placed on punched cards and stored for retrieval and printout by its tabulator. It was a most significant breakthrough, for it provided the springboard for the advanced computer technology we enjoy today. IBM's fantastic success bears witness to the need for such services. Big business was desperate for a solution to its information problem because the paperwork burden was growing beyond its control and threatened to cause serious problems—much as it did to the Wall Street brokers in 1970. A firm simply cannot grow beyond a certain level of volume without an information system that can handle the load. In line with the principle that demand creates its own supply, the computer evolved.

Let us understand clearly right now what a computer is and is not. Fundamentally, a computer is a big, fantastically fast, adding machine that can be directed (programmed) to do desired things with numbers and can remember what it is told to do and what the numbers are. So a computer system contains the following elements:

Input	The means by which we get numbers and directions into the computer.
Storage Bank	The mechanism that contains stored information and sets of directions.
Data Processing	The electronic network that processes (adds) the numbers as directed after they are pulled from the data storage bank.
Output	The mechanism that prints the desired results as directed.

Why do we say nothing of the computer's ability to subtract, multiply, divide, and do extremely complicated mathematical computations, but say only that it is a fast adding machine?

But how do we tell a computer what to do? Well, we have to talk to the beast, using a language that it understands. Computers have been set up to understand all sorts of languages, but the two used most frequently in business are Fortran and Cobol.

Don't worry about learning these languages here. Computer technology and computer languages are changing so fast that there is little purpose in learning one until you have need for it. Suffice it to say that millions of college students have learned to use computers without undue difficulty. And probably the time will come when you will want to learn to use a computer, for they have become most practical tools even for small jobs. Any serious student of business should now consider the computer in the same light as a typewriter . . . just another piece of useful hardware that one should have in his tool kit.

Unless you are a computer technician you need not know the computer's inner workings; just think of it as a black box and learn to talk with it.

TALKING WITH A COMPUTER

You should learn how to talk to a computer and how it talks back to you. There are four ways by which you can communicate with the contraption: punched card, console machine (a typewriter), optical scanner, and tape (either punched paper or magnetic).

Punched Cards

The oldest method for putting data into a computer is the now familiar 80-column punched card. Though still in use, its popularity has waned and it is now almost obsolete. It remains useful especially when the same card must serve two functions; the punched-card payroll check, for example, is not only a check but also the input to the system for the information on that check. However, this function is being taken over by the optical scanners.

The punched card has several disadvantages. First, it requires key punching, which is a separate, time-consuming operation subject to error. Second, the information on one card is limited by the 80-column capacity, thereby requiring that several cards be punched if more information is needed for a specific operation—an additional key-punching burden. Third, it is relatively slow in comparison to some other input methods. Fourth, in large numbers the cards are bulky, creating a storage problem.

Console Machine

The use of consoles is rapidly expanding, as they have come down in price. A console is a relatively simple machine, often a typewriter, connected to a computer and allowing direct access to it. A credit manager might have the firm's credit records in a computer storage bank subject to retrieval by consoles. The sales department requests approval of Sadie Betz's purchase of a $150 dress; the manager punches in Sadie's name, or perhaps her credit number if the machine is so programmed, and back comes a reply giving Sadie's credit record—what she owes and her past payment record. Or perhaps the computer will just say that Sadie is a good credit risk, make the sale.

The future may well see a console on the desk of every executive of any significance in a company. The sales manager wants to know the sales of Widgets in Walla Walla, so he pushes the right buttons and back comes the information. The treasurer wants to know what accounts payable have to be paid this week ... the button, the answer. The engineer wants to know the square root of π ... the button, the answer. The slide rule will take its place alongside high button shoes and trolley cars.

Optical Scanners

Certain applications call for the use of optical scanners that can read letters and numbers from documents. Banks use them for reading the bank and account numbers from the bottom of checks; the numbers are printed in special forms that the machine recognizes and transforms into electrical charges. National Cash Register's information system for retail stores uses optical tapes that are created by the cash registers. Go to a K Mart discount house and watch the checkout procedure. A complete transaction and inventory system is tied into the cash register; each item has a number, and as it is sold, that number is punched into the register along with the dollar figure, thereby giving the company its inventory control system.

Why do retailers want a close inventory control system?

Tapes

Information can be put on rolls of paper or plastic tape either by punching or magnetic means and fed into the computer. Tapes are popular when large amounts of data are to be stored and speed is desired.

Outputs

The computer has five major ways of telling you what you asked for: punched cards, tapes, printers, consoles, and neon tube display.

The computer will punch out its answer onto the 80-column card, a method preferred when the whole system is on a punched-card basis and the answers are to be stored and reused by the computer at a later date.

Similarly, the computer will put its reply on tapes, either paper or magnetic. Again, this is used when the system is set up on tapes, but there is no automatic printout; the tapes must then be put through a printer for visual communication.

The high-speed printer is the major output mechanism found in most computer systems. It is a very fast typewriting device capable of printing many lines of type a minute; the computer tells it what to type and where to type it.

Console output is closely akin to the printer. The same console machine that queried the computer provides the means by which it answers. The computer takes over control of the typing mechanism to give the requested information.

The neon tube is another matter. It is used on computers that are devoted largely to mathematical computations; the answer appears in neon lights. There are other tube displays, stockbrokers use a tube-display device in asking about information on a stock. They punch the stock's symbol, and a great deal of current information about it is flashed on the screen.

INFORMATION SYSTEMS

In the early days of the computer, businessmen spoke of data processing, for that was the way they thought; the computer was just a means for processing data, a great deal more data, faster, a great deal faster, than was possible previously. Now things could be done that would have been folly earlier. Timely reports could be made on a great many aspects of the operation. It was possible to get daily or weekly reports on operations with year-to-date summaries compared against budgets or other control standards.

At first, data processing was a rather spotty activity. It was only natural that accounting data would be the first to be computerized; payroll applications were a favorite, for they were so burdensome, but accounts receivable and payables were close to follow, for they too took a great deal of manpower. Inventory control has been a problem since the Phoenicians first started peddling dry goods around the Mediterranean. Too much inventory or not enough of it has brought many a firm to its financial knees, so inventory control was quickly computerized. But then we began to take a broader view of data processing, seeing it as part of a total information system encompassing both internal data and external information. And so the field of management information systems was born—a field that is still an infant. What is it? Look at Figure 25-1 for a visual explanation!

Both internal and external information are inputs of MIS, representing a distinct improvement over previous data systems, which were largely focused around the accounting system. Presently, several syndicated services will provide computer-digested market information for the firm. One such concern, World Data Bank, sells a service that furnishes detailed information concerning the people and economy of each country of the world. A firm's computer can be tied into the World Data Bank's computer for direct access to the information. Aggressive marketing organizations usually maintain rather detailed files on their customers; one cannot really know too much about them. Now marketing managers can avail themselves of such information whenever the need arises.

What information would you want to know about your customers?

THE PROGRAMMER

The computer is a dumb beast, it must be told to do everything it does. It does precisely what it is told to do, and if it is told to do the wrong things, the wrong things are done. If bad data are given to the creature, bad information is given back.

The responsibility for giving the computer the correct directions lies with the programmer, who knows how to make the machine do what is desired. But the responsibility for good data lies elsewhere, for the programmer has little or nothing

FIGURE 25 -1: A Management Information System

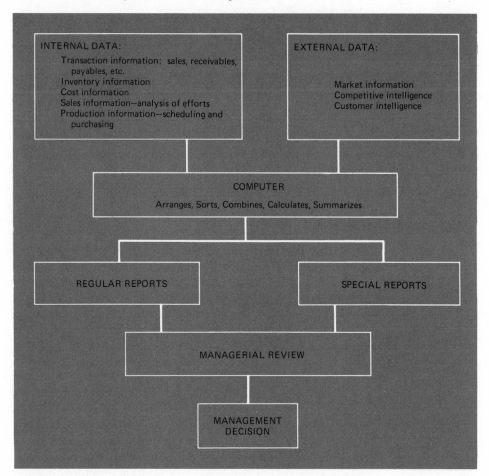

to do with data collection. Instead, the operating and staff people in the organization responsible for collecting and assembling the data must take full responsibility for its correctness. This point needs emphasis, for often when a computer operation results in incorrect output, a great deal of blame is misplaced on the programmer.

While he is technically responsible for giving the computer directions—a program—he can do so only if given a great deal of help by the operating people in the company. He cannot develop a good inventory program without the assistance of the people who will be using the information. Often the programmer errs not in ignorance, but through misinformation—he was given incomplete or erroneous instructions as to what management wanted. Clearly, close liaison must be maintained between the programmer and the management people who will be using the programs.

This stress is placed on the importance of the programmer's talents for good reason. As organizations have rushed to computerize their organizations, their experience has not been one of unblemished success. Numerous executives can testify to near disasters in their computer programs, many of which can be traced to faulty programming and incompetent programmers. Many firms have abandoned their own computer operations in favor of time-sharing arrangements. One advantage of the time-sharing computer company is that it can afford to avail itself of top-notch talent able to program its client's operations correctly. The average operational executive has so little knowledge of computers that he is unable to evaluate accurately the qualifications of the people who apply to him for work as programmers.

How do you tell a good programmer from a bad one?

**The Concept of
Time Sharing**

Time sharing is the joint use of one computer by several organizations. Sometimes the machine is owned by one firm that bought it for its own use and then discovered it had excess capacity that could be sold to other concerns. But a new institution has evolved—the time-sharing company, organized for the purpose of buying a computer, assembling the people to run it, and selling time to those organizations that feel it wise not to own a computer themselves.

The feasibility of time sharing rests on three factors: (1) today's computers are so fast and so large that they have excess capacity for all but the very largest users, (2) the high cost of a computer operation forces a high utilization of the computer's capacity, and (3) top-notch computer talents are scarce and generally unavailable to small concerns as employees.

The problem arises because numerous people have learned how to make a computer operate and can devise rather simple programs, but few can master the complex programs required by most businesses of any scale.

THE INDIVIDUAL IN THE INFORMATION SYSTEM

We have been describing an information system as a network, but what does the network connect, and what flows through its various branches? The information network connects people—people who know certain things and need to know other things. Every person in the organization is a part of the information system; he feeds data to it and in turn is given information he needs to do his job.

Let's look at Sam Salesman out in Broken Bow, Wyoming. What role does he play? As a matter of fact, Sam feeds the system a great deal of critical information; a great many things begin with Sam. First, he takes orders for goods and writes them up on an order form, thereby creating probably the single most important document in the information system—the sales ticket. From this document, sales data are collected by products, customers, territory, and time periods. This document must be accurate or all sorts of bad things happen; customers get mad, management gets mad, owners get mad, and men get fired. And then there are Sam's expense and call reports, which feed more information to the system; they tell what Sam has been doing and how he has spent the company's money. The expense reports eventually show up in the profit and loss statement, but are used first for other things.

Of what use is a salesman's expense report to management?

A call report is a record of each call Sam made on a prospective customer or an existing account and what transpired during that call.

What type of information should Sam report to his manager on the call report?

Sam needs information too! He wants to know how he is doing in comparison with what he is supposed to be doing—how his performance compares against the budget. He wants to know where the business is in his territory—he needs leads. He wants to know what the company is doing in new products, new sales methods—what is happening back at the home office. He wants to know what the competition is doing. So management must arrange to get such information to Sam. Appropriate computer printouts may be sent to him, giving his sales as compared to budget; possibly he will be shown how he is doing in comparison with the other salesmen. But most of the information the system sends to Sam does not come from the computer. Most of it comes from other communication media that were used long before anyone even thought of a computer.

INFORMATION COMMUNICATION MEDIA

In the excitement over computer printouts and the wealth of information they provide, one is apt to lose sight of the various old workhorses that for years have been carrying information to people who need it. Exciting things have been happening to them also, for the engineer has made possible some rather astounding developments.

Telephone Transmission of Printed Matter

A branch plant manager needs certain documents for a contract job. Not too many years ago, they would have had to travel by mail—air mail, special delivery. If the documents were really important, someone might put them aboard a plane and have them picked up at the other end. Now we have instruments that can transmit facsimiles over the telephone almost immediately for low cost. In most modern information systems we use the telephone lines for a great many things. Various branch offices can tie into a central computer via telephone to transmit data to it and receive printouts from it. One small men's store has a computerized accounting and inventory system on a time-sharing basis; it calls in its data daily to the computer; in a matter of two minutes, the job is completed.

Wide Area Telephone Service (WATS)

It has long been recognized that not only is the mail a slow and time-consuming communication medium, but it is also quite inefficient. Most business discussions involve numerous questions and answers. Letters can be semantic booby traps, as the reader can read things into words that were not meant to be. The tone of a letter is such a delicate matter; the businessman in his haste frequently leaves the wrong impression on paper, whereas over the phone he can be more assured that the other party really understands what is said.

Where clear, quick communications have been desired, the telephone has long been a favorite instrument, but an expensive one. Telephone bills mount rapidly with any significant amount of long-distance calling.

Now the telephone companies offer the WATS service for lower long-distance tolls. For a flat rate, usually around $1800 per month, a firm can have one line on which it can direct-dial anywhere in the United States without additional charge. It does not take a very large business to justify a WATS line, just one whose business is spread over the nation. Moreover, sales departments are learning how to use the telephone to take the place of expensive personal visits to established accounts.

High-Speed Copying Machines

Xerox did far more than provide Wall Street with a favorite growth stock; it made possible the rapid distribution of copies of memos, reports, and other documents throughout the organization. A customer wants to see his account records; run a copy off for him. An article appears in a trade journal that seems pertinent to the job of some subordinate; make a copy and send it to him. Information can now be copied cheaply and quickly for transmission to units in the system that need it.

Personal Contact, Memos, Letters, and Reports

In our romance with modern technology and the hardware it creates, let us not lose sight of some old-fashioned devices for communicating information throughout the system. When the boss's secretary tells a young junior executive that he should come to work on time, some needed information has been communicated. Perhaps a memo or letter would have had the same result.

When might a letter be more advisable than a telephone call? (Ignore costs.)

Reports seem to be one of the hallmarks of business operations. It seems as if we are always preparing a report, giving a report, or reading one. The time and effort expended on reports are beyond comprehension; sometimes a report is even useful.

Why the urge among executives to have a report prepared on some problem?

Memos are almost a standing joke in some organizations. It would seem that there must be hundreds of little men sitting around small cubicles passing as offices straining their brains to think up some memo to have distributed throughout the organization. But they have their purposes.

So what is wrong with writing memos? How can you judge whether or not memos in an organization are excessive? How do you cure compulsive memo writers?

PROBLEMS IN MANAGEMENT INFORMATION SYSTEMS

Information systems are not without problems. We will examine four of the more apparent ones: too much information, costs, undue delays, and lack of interpretation.

How Much Information?

Ironically, just as operations in the past often were hindered by too little information, there are instances in which today's operations are being inundated with too much information for efficient management. When a man receives information, even information he does not need, it takes some of his time to scan it to determine what should be done with it. It even takes time to wad it up for the circular file. If the information does appear to the receiver to be useful, he must then make disposition of it after reading it sufficiently to decide what needs to be done.

Some executives spend hours each day just wading through all the stuff sent to them by various well-meaning co-workers—a report on this, an article on that, a memo on this, and a letter on that. The stuff inefficiency is made of! Before sending that casual information to the man, think! Can the man really benefit by it? Does he need it? Or are you just trying to impress him with your own skills?

What do some executives do to protect themselves from needless communications?

The need-to-know principle must be applied in the information system for more than one reason. Not only does it minimize the amount of information going to each person in the system, but it keeps restricted data from falling into the wrong hands. If the man does not need to know the information to do his job, then spare him the trouble and the firm the risk.

Costs

Information costs money. The more information, the more money! Unless the information is worth its costs, let it remain undiscovered or undisseminated. Having that computer sitting there tempts many men to put it to work turning out reports and doing things. That would not be so bad if it stopped there, but it does not; those reports evoke further efforts.

The information system must be tested against a cost criterion: are the data worth their price?

Delays

Much information is of value only if it is timely; if it is late, it is relatively worthless. One might think that the computer guarantees promptness, but in too many circumstances experience indicates otherwise. More than a few executives have reported that they received critical data faster under older information systems.

Lack of Interpretation

Raw data is of little use to most operating executives; they have neither the time nor talent to digest the essence from it. When and where indicated, information should be passed on to the person in a form that can be best comprehended by him. Many times he does not really want to see the raw data; he just wants to know what it means. Give him an interpretation!

EXTERNAL INPUTS—COMPETITIVE INTELLIGENCE

Most discussions of information systems focus on the commonly recognized internal inputs such as sales and cost data plus inventory and production information, for these do form the backbone of such systems; the business cannot be run without such data. However, the systems approach to the information problem has brought forward the importance of external inputs such as competitive intelligence and market data. We have spoken previously of market information but have ignored competitive intelligence, a fast-growing field that has yielded some interesting results.

Some large concerns have created a staff position, usually somewhere in the marketing or research organizations, whose sole duty it is to create and maintain complete files on each competitor—an industrial intelligence operation. Not only is an amazing amount of information available on most publicly owned companies, but even more can be collected with a little effort. Trade journals are carefully combed for all articles on competitors. All press releases, publications, price lists, and catalogs of each competitor are filed. Credit reports are obtained on each company and its key officers. Salesmen report anything pertaining to competitive activities that they hear. Everything is accumulated in one central file, where it can be studied when need be.

What information would you want to know about your competitor?
What ethical considerations are involved in an intelligence operation?

Sometimes secrecy and trade secrets can be involved. Manufacturers have been known to buy competitors' products and study them carefully, either to copy certain desirable features or to learn costs. Men have been planted inside plants to learn trade secrets; more commonly, men have been hired away from companies for their knowledge of company secrets. But these tend to be the exceptions; most intelligence operations center on publicly available information.

Conclusion

The administration of an enterprise of any substance requires a great deal of timely pertinent information on which to base decisions. The modern concept of a management information system evolved as the computer came into widespread use. The computer allowed management to process, store, and disseminate a great deal more information than was previously possible. Moreover, rapid communication with a central computer from remote locations now allows close monitoring of branch operations.

But in our fascination with computer hardware, let us not forget the critical role of the software—the programs—and the men who develop them—the programmers. The computer is useless without proper programming.

Also, you must not assume that the information system is solely dependent on the computer, for there are other important means we use to get information to the men who need it. Telephone transmissions, memos, letters, reports, and copying machines all play an important role.

26 Governmental control

Free trade, one of the greatest blessings which a government can confer on a people, is in almost every country unpopular.

MACAULAY

Normally one would expect a chapter on governmental control of the business system to dwell largely on the multitude of laws—federal, state, and local—that minutely regulate what businesses can and cannot do. Most of the laws pertaining to the government's control of the economy are presented in the appendix on legislation (Appendix A), where you can refer to them whenever you deem it advisable, but this discussion will focus on the theory of governmental regulation—why it exists, what is regulated, how it is regulated, and the problems arising therefrom.

One of the problems in studying governmental regulation by discussing the laws is that one's education can be outmoded by an act of Congress or a decision of the Supreme Court. What is true one year may be nullified the next. Therefore, any definitive understanding of the statutes governing business operations must, of necessity, be completely current. The laws are so technical that it takes considerable study in depth to understand them. Generalizations about the law are dangerous. One needs legal counsel when dealing in these areas; still, an understanding of the law and its areas of regulation can warn the businessman of potential trouble.

EVOLUTION OF GOVERNMENTAL CONTROL

Ever hear a businessman wistfully lament the passing of the good old days, when business was free to do as it wished, when the government did not interfere? Well, he is living in the world of mythology, for such times never existed. Even in the days of so-called *laissez faire,* governments closely regulated economic activities, because they recognized that their continued political power depended upon the economic well-being and strength of the realm. Historically, governments have always regulated who could go into business, in what business they could engage, and have always claimed a share of the revenue.

The real question has never been whether or not a government should regulate business, for that is a naive question; governments will always regulate. Rather, the question is how the government can regulate best without stifling the productivity, creativity, and freedom of its people.

The American Experience

In the beginning, because of stifling experiences with the British crown, colonists were extremely reluctant to submit their economic activities to the regulation of any governmental authority. Their experiences with the governments of the Continent had been disillusioning and disheartening; thus they wanted no part of them. Consequently, early American business was burdened with few regulations. Our development of governmental control could be termed one of growth by perceived need. The regulation of American business has been a step-by-step process, in which the government took away certain privileges of the businessman when it was seen that he could not handle them to the satisfaction of the legislatures, public, and fellow businessmen. It must be pointed out that a great deal of the regulation of business has been demanded by the businessmen themselves.

TYPES OF LEGISLATION

Legislation can be grouped into five categories: special interest, revenue, health and welfare, economic system, and financial system.

Special-Interest Legislation

A great deal of the legislation governing business affairs has been created at the behest of special interest groups for the purpose of advancing or protecting their own interests. In this category would fall most of the tariff acts, some of the taxation laws, and many of the regulatory commissions. While some of this special-interest legislation serves the general public, unfortunately much of it does not. The oil depletion allowance is a commonly used whipping boy in this category, but others too numerous to mention litter the legislative landscape.

Revenue-Raising Legislation

Some legislation is aimed at raising revenues for the governments. This includes not only direct taxation laws but also many registration and licensing laws. Indeed, it is difficult to find a taxing authority that does not have licensing and report-making legislation on the books. Every business must procure numerous licenses, and must file a great many reports with practically every governmental authority having jurisdiction over it.

Of increasing concern to many businessmen is their role as tax collector for the government. Every businessman is required to withhold taxes from the wages of his employees and forward them to the government; he is required to collect taxes from his customers and forward them to the government; his failure to do so is severely penalized by the law.

Why has the government made businessmen its tax collectors?
Why don't businessmen relish this role?

Health-and-Welfare Legislation

A broad spectrum of laws govern business activities affecting the health and welfare of the people. Companies doing business in food, drug, cosmetics, automobiles, medical devices, and other such industries are all heavily regulated. The recently enacted truth-in-lending bills fall into this category; consumer protection has been receiving greatly increased attention in recent years.

Economic-System Legislation

The government has propagated among businessmen a certain philosophy of business operation that it deems advantageous. The so-called anti-trust acts (the Sherman and Clayton Acts), express the philosophy that our economy prospers best when businessmen are prohibited from monopolizing, conspiring together, or acting in collusion with each other. A great deal of activity by the Justice Department is aimed at preserving the competitive atmosphere of our business system.

The federal government is also fully committed to maintaining the economic wellbeing of the nation. President Nixon's strong, economic actions of August, 1971 were proof of the administration's great concern for our continued prosperity.

Financial Legislation

Recognizing that the backbone of an economic system is its money and banking subsystem, a great deal of legislation is aimed at protecting and perfecting the economy's financial system. The Federal Reserve Act and various securities acts are all aimed at this area.

AREAS CONTROLLED

We have been looking at legislation from the government's standpoint. Now let us examine it from the point of view of the businessman. He tends to look at it in terms of which of his decisions are regulated.

Business Engaged In

The government regulates the businesses in which one is allowed to engage. A great many businesses are forbidden. One has no legal right to manufacture atomic weapons or certain drugs and must obtain government approval to enter into many other businesses, such as the distilling of alcohol or the manufacture of ethical drugs. The procurment of licenses is common, even for the most mundane businesses. In fact, a few governmental officials have insisted on making fools of themselves by prosecuting children for operating unlicensed Kool-Aid stands.

Product

The nature and characteristics of one's product may be highly regulated. A pharmaceutical manufacturer cannot produce an internal drug without first obtaining approval from the Food and Drug Administration. Even the automobile industry is being told what characteristics its products must have. It would be difficult to find a product not affected in some way by legislation. Clothes must meet the Wool Labelings Act. Food must meet the Pure Foods Law. Many industries have commercial standards to which they must adhere. A $\frac{3}{4}$-inch sheet of AD interior plywood must have so many layers, can contain only a certain number of knotholes of a certain specified size, and must be bonded by certain types of adhesives. Plywood must meet fairly rigid standards. Much of this product legislation is hidden from public view.

Pricing

The government gives considerable attention to the pricing practices of business. While the federal government endeavors to prohibit price discrimination by the Clayton Act and its Robinson-Patman amendment, the states are more concerned with protecting retailers from price cutting by enacting fair-trade laws and unfair-practices acts. So you can see that the federal and state governments are often acting at cross purposes with one another. Some states go so far as to fix prices, largely under the guise of health and welfare. The state of Oklahoma fixes prices of haircuts and dry cleaning under such camouflage. California attempts to fix the minimum price of haircuts.

The August, 1971, 90-day wage and price freeze by the federal government is indicative of the ultimate power government has over prices. When economic or political conditions require it, governments will institute rigorous price control.

Why do businessmen frequently seek legislation to protect themselves from price cutting?

Business Methods

The businessman's methods of operation are brought under legislative scrutiny in numerous ways. The Internal Revenue Service dictates his accounting methods. The

Federal Trade Commission tells him what are unfair business practices. Yes, the government delineates what are fair means of competition. The Federal Trade Commission Act of 1914 established the Federal Trade Commission and empowered it to regulate unfair business practices, the definition of which has largely been left up to the Federal Trade Commission as modified by the federal courts. A furrier cannot give a mink-dyed pussycat some exotic name, but rather is told exactly what he can call this beast's contribution to feminine ego. The truth-in-lending laws tell the businessman exactly how he must bill his customers and precisely what he must tell them. In some states his days of operation are regulated by so-called "blue laws," which prohibit Sunday openings.

Merger and Growth

A great deal of governmental attention is directed to the growth of American enterprises. Most large companies must now clear any merger or acquisition of other firms with the Justice Department before proceeding. Numerous companies have been forced to divest themselves of certain acquisitions when they proceeded without such approval and when the acquisitions were later considered by the Justice Department to be possibly damaging to competition.

Why is the federal government so greatly interested in controlling the acquisition and merger policies of American business firms?

Promotion

The Federal Trade Commission regulates misleading advertising and other deceptive selling practices. Door-to-door salesmen of stainless steel cookware were ordered to cease and desist from intimating to customers that aluminum cookware was responsible for cancer. The salesmen of one company were ordered to cease and desist throwing sand in competitors' machines while unobserved by customers. Cigarette companies were ordered to cease advertising on television January 2, 1971. Retailers are strictly regulated as to the signs that they may display in most cities. Billboard advertising is regulated by both federal and state governments. Door-to-door salesmen are severely regulated by local municipal ordinances—the so-called Green River ordinances.

Labor

A great body of legislation at all governmental levels regulates labor and labor practices. Such legislation can be classified into three categories: wage legislation, working-conditions legislation, and bargaining-power legislation.

Wages Not only has the federal government established minimum wages that must be paid to all workers falling in certain categories (there are very few exceptions), but they have also dictated that time-and-a-half must be paid for overtime and double-time must be paid in other instances.

Many critics of minimum wage legislation claim it is responsible for unemployment among unskilled workers. Explain their reasoning.
What is your evaluation of the wisdom of minimum wage legislation?

Working Conditions Working conditions were notoriously bad in the early days of the Industrial Revolution. Consequently, legislation was enacted quite early to bring some modicum of safety and health into the factories. For the most part, factories and offices have very pleasant environments today, but there are still some critical areas remaining, such as certain marginal mines that present hazards to workers.

Unionism and Bargaining Legislation regulates the activities of unions and of companies bargaining with them. The federal government created the National Labor Relations Board to administer this body of law. The Taft-Hartley Act is the current federal legislation affecting this matter.

Market

The government regulates many markets, some rigorously, others not so rigorously. Bear in mind that the governments themselves are big markets for the products of business, and when doing business with a government you must play by its rules and regulations, which may be extremely complex and burdensome. The boiler plate[1] in a government defense contract is awesome to behold.

Markets for farm products are closely regulated by the Department of Agriculture. Markets for housing are strongly affected by governmental policies on interest rates and the Federal Housing Administration's (FHA) rules.

METHODS OF CONTROL

The various governments use seven basic methods for regulating and influencing business activity: licensing, taxing, inspection, judicial prosecution (both civil and criminal), moral suasion—better known as "jaw boning," economic pressure through withholding governmental purchases and favors, and administrative control.

Licensing

Almost every business must procure several licenses before commencing operations. Every employer must obtain an employer's identification number from the Internal Revenue Service and the state's employment agency. Manufacturers frequently must have licenses for manufacturing various prescribed products. Retailers must obtain business licenses and sales-tax licenses from both their city and state governments. The walls of any retailer bear silent testimony to the licensing burden placed upon the typical businessman.

While in theory licensing serves as a means of communications whereby the government knows who is doing business, in actual practice many small communities use it to raise revenue, setting cigarette-licensing or vending-machine licensing fees substantially in excess of the costs of clerical handling of the licensing procedure. So one can see that licensing and taxing overlap. Also, licensing serves as a means of governing competition and determining the character of the business community.

---

[1] "Boiler plate" is legal slang for the unbelievable multitude of clauses and covenants contained in such contracts.

Taxing

As has been said many times, the power to tax is the power to destroy. The government, by its taxing regulations, directly affects business operations. When the government wishes something discontinued, it can tax it out of existence. When it wishes to encourage something, it can alter the tax laws so as to encourage it.

A prime example was the manipulation of the investment credit provisions in the Internal Revenue Code. When the government wished to stimulate the purchase of equipment by businesses, it gave a 7 percent income tax credit for monies so invested. But when the government wished to put the damper on economic activity, it quickly removed the investment credit provisions, for they had been most effective. Then the economy boomed so the government discontinued the investment credit. In late 1971, the government reinstituted it to help stimulate a sagging economy. At that time, the Federal government also repealed the 7 percent excise tax on automobiles to bolster demand in that slackening industry while temporarily placing a flat 10 percent tax on all imports as an effort to restrict import buying, thus improving our unfavorable balance of trade with other nations.

So the tax laws are certainly used for purposes other than raising revenue. They shape the basic forms of business. Indeed, a clever framer of tax laws could achieve any result he set out to reach, simply by changing provisions in the law.

What would happen if the tax laws were amended to disallow contributions and interest as legitimate deductions and business expenses?

Inspection

When the government is really adamant about enforcing laws, it uses inspectors. Government inspectors are located in meat processing plants to enforce the governmentally controlled grading system. Government inspectors are found in practically all defense plants to insure that the contractor meets the governmental specifications in the contract. Building inspectors enforce the building codes.

If the government suspects any business firm of violating its laws, it will obtain a court order and come into the place of business for a physical inspection of records and operations. The Labor Department is free to inspect working conditions and the nature of one's employees at any time.

Judicial Proceedings

Whenever a law has been violated, the government may take the alleged misdoer to court on either a civil or a criminal charge. This occurs at all levels of government. A municipality may haul some retailer into court for a violation of its zoning code, or the state government may prosecute for a violation of the Workmen's Compensation Act, or the federal government may file a civil anti-trust suit.

A civil suit is one in which a business firm may be fined or may be told to do or not to do something, but in any event no one is going to go to jail. There are no criminal charges. A criminal charge means that those accused may, if proved guilty, go to jail in addition to being fined.

Moral Suasion

The governments are continually trying to persuade businesses to do something or other by talking to them. Far more of this goes on than can ever be known. It happens from the lowest level clear to the top. President Kennedy forced the steel industry to rescind a price increase by threatening governmental retaliation. A great many disputes are settled on the local level simply by the local officials' talking things out with the businessmen.

Economic Pressures

As a large customer, a government can affect business behavior by boycotting firms that are out of step with government thinking. Political favors are bestowed upon businessmen whose behavior pleases the governing powers.

Administrative Control

Many industries are almost completely regulated by administrative branches of the government. The airlines must obtain approval of all schedules and are told exactly where they may fly and what prices they may charge for doing so by the CAB (Civil Aeronautics Board). The same is true of the railroads, regulated by the ICC (Interstate Commerce Commission). State and local governments regulate the power, gas, water, and telephone utilities in each state.

PROBLEMS POSED BY GOVERNMENTAL REGULATION

Most of the problems posed by governmental control of business could be listed under the heading of "not killing the goose." Under that category can be placed several types of problems.

In all of these criticisms, bear in mind that they are made in relationship to our national goal of increasing the productivity and well-being of our people. A problem is considered to be anything that stands in the way of our system's achieving that goal.

Mistakes on a Grand Scale

Traditionally, decisions made by the government that affect the economic system have been severely criticized on the basis that when some bureaucrat or politician in Washington makes an error, everyone in the nation may be affected. Prime illustrations might be some of the key decisions in the Viet Nam war, certain Defense Department procurement policies such as the F-111 contract, the agricultural program of the past four decades—the political landscape is littered with thousands of other mistakes that have affected a broad spectrum of our society. When central planning makes a mistake, everyone suffers.

The practical economist sees great virtue in hedging this risk by having many thousands of small businessmen making many diverse decisions. True, some of these businessmen make bad decisions, but their area of damage is severely restricted—the whole nation does not suffer for their follies. When Henry Ford III brought forth his infamous Edsel, everyone did not pay for his folly. When decisions are made, a certain percentage of them will be in error. There is no escaping it. Hence, the conservative standpoint is to create a situation in which the errors of one man affect as few people as possible.

One of the major problems posed by governmental regulation is to establish a system that minimizes the possibility of making grand-scale mistakes. We try to set up ways to isolate the area of damage when we are wrong and to protect ourselves from the whims and follies of any one man.

Costs

A glance at your father's tax bill will readily disclose the price paid for increasing governmental regulation. Governmental regulation does cost money. Every time an additional law is passed, more people must be hired to administrate it, and the program must be funded—up go taxes! The problem is: just how much government can we afford?

Maintenance of Initiative

One of the attributes we have greatly prized in the American system is that of personal initiative. People who demonstrated initiative and courage to get out and do things were highly regarded and usually well rewarded. Government regulation tends to stifle initiative. Many times, in order to do something different or initiate something new, one must run counter to governmental controls, and to get such controls changed is frequently quite difficult and always most frustrating. Woe to the man who attempts to institute a new order of things in a government. Bureaucracy has stripped the initiative of more than one daring soul. We have yet to solve this problem. The weight of bureaucracy is stifling our initiative and we do not know what to do about it.

Creativity

Closely akin to initiative, but still distinctly separate, is the matter of creativity. Traditionally we have prized creativity in individuals and have sought to facilitate it in every way possible. We have recognized that our truly great breakthroughs in technology, art, and the humanities have come from people we describe as creative. Creativity is certainly one of the vital essences of our system, one which must not be lost. But government regulation seldom allows for creativity.

Increased Lead Time for Projects

The imposition of governmental controls on any social or economic activity automatically increases the time required for inaugurating that activity. The lead time necessary before beginning a program may now amount to years because of the time it takes to gain governmental approval. It takes several days to gain approval for a simple home remodeling project. A firm cannot sell securities until it has passed through all the red tape of registering with the Securities and Exchange Commission (SEC), which takes months.

These increased lead times are something the businessman has had to learn to live with and anticipate in his planning, frustrating as it may be.

Competition

The affect of governmental control on competition is not clear-cut. Many of the federal governments' efforts, particularly its anti-trust activities, are aimed at preserving and honing the competitive edge among business firms. The activities of a great many other agencies at all levels of government generally tend to stifle competition. Even local building codes and licensing procedures greatly restrict the competition among tradespeople. Zoning affects competition among retailers. If competitors get too vicious with one another, the FTC may step in to make them mend their ways. The government does not allow competition among the airlines and other transportation agencies.

Therefore, with the exception of the anti-trust efforts of the Justice Department, by and large most governmental control efforts have the net result of reducing competition in our system.

God Complex

The old saying that power corrupts and absolute power corrupts absolutely has been thoroughly validated by experience. One of the big dangers of governmental control is that the controllers tend to develop "god complexes," believing that what they do is best for everyone concerned and that they can do no wrong. This leads to a great many things, few of which are good. About the only antidote we have found is to keep rotating the control rapidly enough to prevent "god complexes" from growing too large.

Goals

Ironically, one of the major problems of governmental control is that the various arms of the government are not agreed upon their goals—they frequently work at cross purposes. The federal government may wish to speed traffic via interstate highways, while various local governments attempt to get the traffic routed through towns to protect vested business interests. The Labor Department may wish to increase the minimum wage while the Commerce Department opposes it. The Department of Agriculture may want a certain agricultural program while others branches of the government operate programs in opposition to it. For example, while we want to keep the cost of living down, we would like the farmer to get more for his goods. Those two goals are mutually exclusive.

There is no solution to this dilemma, for in any complex system such as ours the government must serve many masters, and each master presents his own demands. All of these conflicting aims of government simply must be resolved in conferences, from which compromises are reached that perhaps few people really like.

FUTURE COURSE OF EVENTS

The history of governmental control is quite clear. It has been increasing, in the past few years, at what seems to be a geometric rate. Moreover, as the federal government takes over more and more power, such control is becoming centralized in Washington. But do not be misled, for control at all levels has increased vastly.

Government Corporations

More government corporations, of types such as the Atomic Energy Commission, the new Postal Service, and the Tennessee Valley Authority, are on the horizon. Politicians apparently are beginning to see some virtues in divesting themselves of direct bureaucratic, civil-service-type control over some types of governmental functions.

Better Administrators

There seems to be recognition of a crying need for better administrators in government. The past few administrations have tried desperately to attract into civil service the caliber of individual that is so badly needed. While the success of these efforts has been modest, the situation is still a vast improvement over the old political pork barrel days, in which governmental administrators were not selected on the basis of their capabilities. Given the proper stimulus, more headway can be expected in making governmental administration attractive to talented individuals. The pay is now more than competitive with most similar positions in business, except at the very top.

What other trends in governmental control do you foresee?

Conclusion

> Governmental control over business activities has existed since the beginning of time. Our problem is not one of deciding whether or not to control, but rather how to do it wisely, retaining the virtues inherent in our system that have made us so productive: initiative, creativity, freedom of enterprise, and motivation.
>
> Government is big business, the biggest in the world. And it has all the managerial problems of any other business. It needs good administration, wise policies, and efficiency. The basic cause of big, continually growing government is our increasing population. And government seems to grow disproportionately large with increases in the populace.
>
> Furthermore, once the system gives over control to the government, it is almost impossible to reverse the process. The activity becomes a vested interest of numerous people both in and out of government who protect it. It is not the government, per se, that keeps outdated functions operating, but the pressure groups that have become used to the services rendered. Everybody wants to close up many of our overly numerous military bases, but let the Defense Department try to close down one in particular, and the people in nearby communities start yelling to their congressmen who in turn yell at the Pentagon. They always want somebody else's ox gored.

27 Taxation

Taxation under every form presents but a choice of evils.
RICARDO

Shortly after the world was created, people first complained about taxes. They have been complaining, to little avail, ever since that time, for taxes keep rising. But this chapter will not bemoan taxes, for they are one of the realities of any system.

Taxes are the price you pay for governmental services; it's that simple. The more services the government provides for you, the more taxes it must charge. There is no escape from this reality. Few things in this world are free, and certainly not governments.

This discussion will consider the intelligent imposition of taxation and the dilemmas and problems posed by it. As remarked earlier, the power to tax is the power to destroy. Unquestionably, activities and institutions can be killed off quickly by the imposition of unwise tax policies.

It is important for you to understand that the wise imposition and collection of taxes is of utmost importance to the continued well-being of our economic system. Far too many people do not understand the economics of taxation.

TAX BURDEN OF BUSINESS FIRMS

Theoretically, business itself bears no tax burden, but rather passes all taxes on to the consumer. Some taxes, such as state sales taxes, are merely collected by business from the customer on whom they are imposed, with the firm acting as the tax-collecting agency of the government. While other taxes are directly imposed on business, it in turn includes them as part of the price of its products, thereby passing them on to the consumer in the form of higher prices.

Can the consumer pass on taxes to anyone? Make an analysis of the final imposition of taxation upon society.

Table 27-1 lists the various taxes a retail men's store must pay in the state of California. Discouraging, isn't it? The paperwork routine behind these taxes is frightening. Continual reports must be filed on every tax by each firm.

Table 27-1

TOTAL ANNUAL TAXES PAID BY MEN'S APPAREL STORE FULLERTON, CALIFORNIA, 1971

Facts: Sales, $300,000; Payroll, $50,000; Property value, $100,000; Inventory value, $75,000; Telephone, $1000; Two automobiles using 2400 gallons of gasoline and two sets of tires. Sub Chapter S corporation.	
City license	$73.50
Payroll taxes	2,669.00
Property taxes	2,590.30
Inventory tax	1,838.90
Excise and sales tax on purchases	690.00
State corporation income tax	210.00
State franchise tax	100.00
TOTAL	$8,171.00
Sales taxes collected from customers	$15,000
Forwarded to State	14,285
Income Tax on Owner's Salary	$4,950

General Motors paid a total tax bill of $2,537,000,000 in 1969—$10\frac{1}{2}$ per cent of its revenue.

The true costs of administering the tax work of a business are not inconsequential. The director of General Motors' tax section, in a letter to one of the authors of this book, stated that he had fifty men in the central office alone who were employed on tax work; moreover, each division maintains a separate staff to attend to its tax matters. He said, "Overall, the total administrative burden of tax compliance is clearly substantial."

Why have the governments made the business firms their tax collectors?

IMPACT UPON BUSINESS BEHAVIOR

Though businesses do in fact pass on their taxes to the consumer, this does not mean that tax laws do not significantly affect their economic behavior, for they most certainly do. Most business decisions today are affected one way or another by tax considerations. Lease-or-buy decisions are strongly tainted by tax considerations. Investments in various enterprises are greatly affected by tax positions. Business firms would stop doing a great many things if it were not for the tax laws. It makes a big difference to a decision maker whether he is spending a 52 percent dollar or a 100 percent dollar; with a 48 percent corporate income tax on income over $25,000, the decision maker considers that every dollar he spends is actually costing his firm only 52 cents.

THEORY OF TAXATION

Yes, there is a theory of taxation, widely violated as it may be. Cynics maintain that the major theory of taxation is summarized by the old adage, "Pluck the duck where it squawks the least!" Today's duck, however, has so few feathers remaining that we are now looking for places where we can slice off some flesh without killing the poor bird.

But let us look at some of the theories underlying sound taxation.

Basis for Taxation

There are four fundamental bases upon which taxes may be levied, depending upon the whim of the legislature: benefit, ability to pay, administrative convenience, and regulation-motivation.

Benefit Theory   One of the earliest theories of taxation was that a tax should be imposed upon the people who benefit from the governmental activities paid for by the tax. The prime example is the levying of gasoline taxes by both the federal and state governments. These taxes are normally earmarked for road construction. Hence, the motorist—through his gas-tax money—is paying for the benefits he receives from roads. In theory, this is the soundest type of tax, for the moral logic is inescapable that one should pay for the things he receives. People are used to this line of thinking, and there is little rebellion against taxes formulated on this basis.

Is the cigarette tax a benefit-levied form of taxation?
Name other benefit-based taxes of which you are aware.

Unfortunately, there are several obstacles to widespread use of benefit-based taxes. First, many of the people who benefit most from a governmental activity are least able to pay for it. It would be difficult to expect welfare recipients to support the welfare programs.

Are postage stamps a type of benefit tax?
How might benefit-based taxes be expanded?

Real estate taxes were imposed largely on the benefit theory, the idea being that property owners benefit from the governmental protection of their property.

The problem of continuing to rely upon real estate taxes for government revenues has been that the levels have grown to such heights that today's real estate taxes amount almost to confiscation of property. Also, the imposition of high property taxes discourages the purchase of individual residences by placing too much of the tax burden upon the family man who owns his own home. Nonproperty-owning transients are left to enjoy the benefits of society with a proportionately lower tax burden.

Ability to Pay

Beginning with the imposition of income taxes in 1913, federal and state governments have relied upon another tax base to raise most of their revenue.

The theory underlying the income tax is that money is obtained from the people who can afford to pay it, in line with the theory that one should "pluck the duck where it squawks the least." In theory, a millionaire will squawk less about losing 50 percent of his income than a poor man will about being taxed $1000. Also, the "soak the rich" philosophy has great appeal to the masses, because few people get worked up over the plight of the well-to-do.

While this theory held some validity in the early days of the income tax, when only the wealthy paid any significant amount of taxes, the present level of taxation makes the "soak the rich" philosophy infeasible, for if the federal government were to confiscate every dollar earned by people making more than $20,000 a year it would fall far short of financing its operations. Clearly, if the governments are to continue to spend at their present levels, everyone must be substantially taxed. The poor man must share part of the tax burden because of the mathematics involved.

The state sales taxes are also fundamentally based on the ability to pay, the theory being that if you can afford to buy an article you can afford to pay taxes on it. Some states exempt food and other such necessities from taxation on the theory that one should not tax absolute necessities. The sales tax has been popular because it hits those who do not own property as well as those who do. If you consume, you pay taxes; hence, the sales tax is a very broad-based tax.

Many critics argue that it is a regressive tax in that it taxes large families and the poor proportionately more than the wealthy. This is true; it does do that.

How can one avoid the regressive features of the sales tax?

Originally the property tax was also thought to abide by the ability-to-pay principle; it was assumed that property owners were among the more wealthy and thus could afford to pay the taxes. This is not always true today. Retired people and widows may own property but lack the income with which to pay high taxes. Mere ownership of property no longer guarantees an income, as it did in the days of an agrarian society. The shift from an agrarian society to an industrial one is one of the developments underlying the shift in tax emphasis.

Tariffs are another tax based largely on the ability to pay, under the theory that if one can afford to import goods he can afford to pay some money for it. Admittedly, tariffs also have some regulatory aspects. The flat across-the-board 10 percent tariff proposed in August, 1971, was intended to regulate the ratio of our exports to imports, thus remedying our unfavorable balance of trade which had been causing us a great deal of trouble with foreign bankers and speculators.

What is the rationale for estate and gift taxes?
For excise taxes on telephones, cigarettes, and tires?

Regulatory and Motivational Taxation

Many taxes are levied in order to regulate activities or to motivate various segments of society to do what the government wants them to do. Tariffs are frequently designed to limit the import or export of goods. Whiskey taxes were designed to limit the consumption of that stimulant.

On what basis were cigarette taxes levied?

Many features of the income tax were designed to regulate certain aspects of behavior and to motivate business firms to do certain things. The investment credit provisions of the income tax were designed to stimulate investments in productive goods. The allowing of deductions for contributions is designed to stimulate gifts to various charities. Chain-store taxes levied by state governments were an unsuccessful attempt to limit their growth. Taxes on gambling devices were aimed at regulating and eliminating those machines. The federal tax on gambling and gamblers is designed to eradicate that element from society.

The principle of using taxation to regulate an unwanted activity has a very spotty history, which, for the most part, has been rather dismal. History teaches us that when tariffs become too high, smuggling becomes rampant. Gambling taxes have not stopped gambling, nor have whiskey taxes stopped drinking. Sometimes the cost of administering these regulatory taxes exceeds the revenues received from them, casting doubt on the efficiency of this method of taxation.

The history of taxing for motivational purposes, however, is considerably different, for we have had many experiences, both favorable and unfavorable, in which certain taxes have motivated people to do or not do certain things.

Administrative Convenience

Some taxes are difficult to defend on any basis other than administrative convenience—they are cheap and easy to collect. One of the reasons for the tenacity of the property tax is that it is easy to administer and collect, and the taxpayer cannot evade it, for his property can be seized.

Sales taxes have been particularly popular because of their ease in collection, since it is relatively easy to police retail firms for this purpose.

One of the unfortunate aspects of the income tax is the difficulty posed in assessing the tax and sometimes in collecting it. The withholding feature of the income tax law was introduced to facilitate collection, for it is doubtful if our present high level of income taxes would be tolerated if people had to pay taxes in a lump sum.

One of the difficulties cities encounter in levying occupational and income taxes on suburbanites who live outside the city but work inside it is that of administering and collecting the taxes. It is too easy for many people to evade them.

What is a Good Tax?

In theory, a good tax is one that can be fairly and equitably assessed and easily collected at low cost. It cannot be passed on by the person paying it and has no undesirable economic or social consequences. It should not be levied at such a level that it amounts to confiscation of property.

One famous economist, Henry George, advocated a single tax in which all of the governments would combine and levy a single tax on every individual in the system. There would be just one tax law and one base for taxation. His theory has much to recommend it, but unfortunately, no one has ever figured out how to administer a single tax in any equitable manner.

EFFECT OF TAXATION

There are grave dangers in taxation. The worst is that governments may confiscate so large a portion of the gross national product that people lose their incentives. History is rich in cultures that were destroyed when their governments became too expensive for the people to afford them. History clearly shows that rulers' greed is insatiable. Once a tax is levied, it stays and grows larger. Ridding a system of so-called temporary taxes proves most difficult, as politicians are reluctant to give up control of any money.

Therefore, the first critical question that taxing authorities face is just how many feathers can be plucked from the duck before the poor beast expires. There is considerable debate in this country whether or not that level has been reached. Statistics indicate that the United States ranks relatively low in the per capita taxation of its citizens, taking in total about 29.1 percent of the gross national product for all levels of governments. The Scandinavian countries lead the taxation rate, confiscating upwards of 40 percent of their productivity for governmental purposes. Table 27-2 presents the relative tax burden of various cultures in the world.

Table 27-2
TAXES PEOPLE PAY— IN U.S. AND OTHER NATIONS IN CENTS OF EACH GNP DOLLAR

	Direct Taxes (on incomes, corporate profits, estates, gifts)	Indirect Taxes (sales and property taxes, excises)	Social Security Taxes	Total Tax Burden
Sweden	20.2¢	13.9¢	8.2¢	42.3¢
Norway	13.8¢	15.2¢	9.2¢	38.2¢
Netherlands	13.2¢	11.2¢	13.4¢	37.8¢
France	6.5¢	15.9¢	14.5¢	36.9¢
Austria	12.0¢	16.5¢	8.2¢	36.8¢
West Germany	10.4¢	13.7¢	10.6¢	34.7¢
Denmark	16.3¢	16.5¢	1.9¢	34.7¢
Britain	13.1¢	16.2¢	5.1¢	34.4¢
Belgium	10.2¢	13.3¢	9.5¢	33.0¢
Canada	12.7¢	15.1¢	3.4¢	31.2¢
Italy	6.8¢	12.6¢	11.1¢	30.5¢
UNITED STATES	15.5¢	9.1¢	5.3¢	29.9¢
Japan	7.9¢	7.5¢	3.5¢	19.0¢

SOURCE: Organization for Economic Cooperation and Development.

Table 27-3 shows the sources and application of the federal government's budget dollar. Note the reliance on income taxes! Note also that 8¢ of every dollar goes to pay for money previously borrowed—not an insignificant amount.

Table 27-3
SOURCES AND APPLICATION OF FEDERAL FUNDS

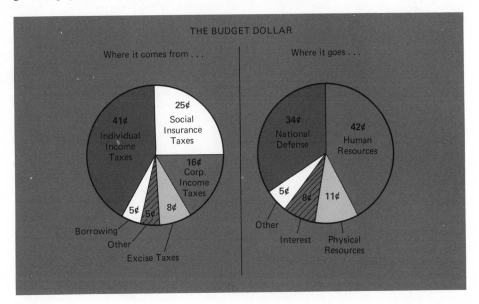

THE BUDGET DOLLAR

Where it comes from . . .

- 25¢ Social Insurance Taxes
- 41¢ Individual Income Taxes
- 16¢ Corp. Income Taxes
- 5¢ Borrowing
- 5¢ Other
- 8¢ Excise Taxes

Where it goes . . .

- 34¢ National Defense
- 42¢ Human Resources
- 5¢ Other
- 8¢ Interest
- 11¢ Physical Resources

The data in Table 27-4 indicate the varying tax burden among the states. There is a most significant difference in one's tax burden, depending upon which state he resides in.

What accounts for such differences?

Taxation affects the national character and the development of our system in many ways. Unquestionably, taxation is a most powerful force that shapes our system's future. Let's examine some of the major stakes, keeping in mind that multitudes of minor ones are always involved in any taxation proposal.

Incentive

Probably the facet of our national character that we wish most to maintain is our incentive to work, produce, and be innovative. These characteristics are so valuable that if they are significantly lessened because of some tax program, our system will be jeopardized.

Yet this is precisely what many taxes have done. The income tax has become so large a burden to many people that it has greatly lessened their incentive to make more money—to be productive. As a rule of thumb, a frightening change of attitude occurs when a government keeps more of a man's paycheck than is given to him—when the government takes more than 50 percent. Questions are asked about the purpose of working so hard, if the government is going to be the major benefactor of one's efforts. Numerous economic projects have not been undertaken because of various

Table 27–4
STATE AND LOCAL TAX BURDENS, PER PERSON, 1969

State	Total Taxes	Property Taxes	Sales, Income, Other Taxes	State	Total Taxes	Property Taxes	Sales, Income, Other Taxes
N. Y.	$576	$211	$364	S. D.	$353	$204	$149
Calif.	$540	$249	$291	Mont.	$351	$194	$157
Hawaii	$480	$ 87	$393	Kans.	$346	$179	$167
Nev.	$466	$165	$302	Pa.	$340	$106	$233
Mass.	$453	$225	$228	N. D.	$338	$163	$175
Wis.	$439	$193	$246	Ind.	$334	$165	$169
Mich.	$428	$165	$263	Fla.	$330	$114	$216
D. C.	$428	$151	$277	Idaho	$328	$117	$211
Wyo.	$414	$196	$218	Utah	$327	$130	$197
Md.	$411	$145	$265	N. M.	$324	$ 77	$247
Wash.	$410	$135	$275	Va.	$314	$ 83	$231
Minn.	$406	$156	$250	Me.	$308	$149	$159
N.J.	$406	$227	$179	Ohio	$306	$146	$159
Conn.	$392	$210	$182	Mo.	$301	$122	$179
Alaska	$390	$104	$287	N. H.	$299	$185	$114
Iowa	$389	$177	$211	La.	$298	$ 60	$238
Oreg.	$387	$181	$206	Okla.	$287	$ 89	$198
Ariz.	$387	$155	$232	Ky.	$278	$ 64	$213
Colo.	$386	$171	$215	Texas	$276	$118	$157
Vt.	$384	$151	$233	Ga.	$270	$ 82	$188
				W. Va.	$263	$ 64	$199
U.S. Average	$380	$152	$228	N. C.	$259	$ 68	$191
				Tenn.	$252	$ 68	$184
R. I.	$379	$157	$222	Miss.	$242	$ 60	$182
Ill.	$373	$173	$200	S. C.	$225	$ 49	$176
Del.	$372	$ 77	$295	Ala.	$224	$ 36	$188
Nebr.	$362	$201	$161	Ark.	$221	$ 58	$162

Note: Figures are for the year ended June 30, 1969. Property and other taxes, in some cases, do not add up exactly to total taxes because of rounding of figures.
SOURCE: U.S. Census Bureau.

technicalities in the tax laws that confiscate a large portion of any earnings on such ventures while limiting the amount of losses one can take. Unquestionably, incentives have been greatly diminished by our taxation program. We must learn how to tax without destroying any more incentives, for we are approaching a danger line. Some people have found the tax burden so prohibitive that they have relinquished their U.S. citizenship and moved to Switzerland.

Growth

Our economy has been greatly concerned with growth, for if the system is to provide an increasing standard of living for an increasing number of people, it must grow faster than the population. Economic growth requires investments in new enterprises, and we have seen how taxation reduces incentives for such expansion. Our taxation programs seem to be significantly stifling the growth of our economy.

First, it is extremely difficult under the present tax laws for small businesses to retain sufficient money from their profits with which to finance growth, and yet they find it exceedingly difficult to obtain capital in the money market. When the governments insists upon skimming off cash ticketed for investment, then growth is stifled. Some economic systems solve this problem by not taxing money reinvested in productive enterprises, waiting to tax the money later as it is taken out of investments and consumed—a change in philosophy from taxing income to taxing consumption.

What are the advantages and disadvantages of levying taxes on consumptive behavior rather than on income-producing behavior?

Subsidies

Most taxation laws, in one way or another, subsidize some economic activities and penalize others. The present federal income tax laws greatly subsidize the oil, timber, real estate, medical, money-lending, and charity industries plus H&R Block Company and a horde of CPA's and tax lawyers. They penalize the working man, whose total income is subject to withholding, while, as a general rule, the small businessman and farmer have distinct advantages.

Perhaps this will persuade the wage earner that he ought to be in business for himself, so in a backhanded way the income tax does provide some incentive to become an entrepreneur.

Other tax laws provide other tax-derived subsidies. Every tariff subsidizes the industry it protects. The exclusion of certain types of institutions from payment of property and income taxes certainly subsidizes them. The research activities of educational institutions are heavily subsidized to the detriment of private, tax-paying research organizations. So, in a very direct fashion, tax laws shape the direction of our system.

In what manner does government taxation subsidize airlines?
Why do we subsidize such institutions?

Evasion

It is an unfortunate corollary of taxation that it creates evasion. Once a significant tax is imposed upon any activity or thing, people immediately begin to figure out ways to either avoid that tax or evade it. Tax avoidance is legal; it is legally conducting one's affairs in order to avoid incurring the tax. Tax evasion is illegal; it is behavior in violation of the law.

In many countries of the world tax rates are such that tax evasion is rampant because tax assessors are amenable to bribes. Of course, any widespread evasion of taxes eventually brings down the entire tax system, for other people see the injustices and react accordingly.

One of the unique aspects of American taxation has been the success of our self-appraisal system of income taxation—it has worked marvelously well. In most countries of the world it would be a total failure. Remember that under our system of federal income tax you figure out your tax and submit it on the proper documents to the government for verification. They question it only when they detect something askew.

Why is the self-appraisal feature so necessary to our income tax laws?

The unfortunate thing about evasion is that it destroys the national character and the people's moral fiber. Some critics of the income tax have complained that it has made us a nation of liars. There is no way of validating this claim, but certainly it implies that many people do not play square with the Internal Revenue Service.

FUTURE OF TAXATION

Clearly, our system has some serious soul-searching ahead in deciding tax policy. The governments are hard pressed to find new sources of tax revenue; they are understandably reluctant to raise the existing high taxes even higher, yet people's demands for services constantly mount. Something has to give; it's either more taxes or fewer services.

Evaluate the cries for better use of existing tax money.

Moreover, our tax system is far too complicated for efficiency and contains too many discriminatory provisions. It would seem quite likely that a substantial tax reform movement might be successful at some future time.

Why have the perennial attempts at tax reform in the past had only modest results?

There is some evidence that in the future we may have a single tax-collecting authority for all levels of government. The Internal Revenue Service, or some counterpart created for the purpose, will collect all taxes and parcel out the money to the various levying agencies.

Evaluate the wisdom of a single tax-collecting authority.
What forces will bring it into existence?

As for the total amount of taxation, no matter how conservative one might be it would be foolish to expect taxes to go down. Total taxes will continue to rise as governments grow bigger.

Should total taxation be limited by constitutional amendment?
At what level would you place it?

It is quite likely that the governments will use their tax powers more frequently for economic motivation. The success of the investment credit provision of the federal income tax impressed many people with the power of taxation to cause certain desired behavior.

Conclusion

There will be no conclusion to taxation!

Appendix A
Laws Pertaining to Business Operations

AGRICULTURAL MARKETING AGREEMENT ACT (1937): authorized the Secretary of Agriculture to enter into marketing agreements with processors, producers, and others as a method for enhancing farm income; such agreements would be held lawful and not in violation of anti-trust laws.

ANTI-MERGER ACT OF 1950: prohibits the acquisition of stock or assets where such would substantially lessen competition, or tend to create a monopoly. All types of mergers are banned—vertical, horizontal, and conglomerate—provided it can be shown that the effect *may be* a substantial lessening of competition or a tendency to create a monopoly.

ATOMIC ENERGY ACT OF 1946: established a commission of five people with the power to engage in research and development activities on nuclear processes; the production of atomic energy; the utilization of fissionable materials for medical, agricultural, and industrial purposes whether in its own facilities or by contract with private individuals or firms; also to produce atomic weapons under direction of the President; provides for compulsory licensing of patents that are affected with a public interest.

CIVIL AERONAUTICS ACT OF 1938: provides for a five-man administrative agency (CAB) to prescribe economic regulations and safety rules for the air transportation industry; to require any report deemed necessary from any carrier; and to set rates.

CLAYTON ACT (1914): prohibits price discrimination in the sale of commodities of like grade and quality when the effect is to injure or prevent competition; prohibits the corporate ownership of stock in competing corporations; prohibits interlocking directorates in large banks and competing corporations. Provides for triple damages for private suits won against wrongdoers.

CIVIL RIGHTS ACT OF 1964: law concerning discrimination in business and other fields because of race, sex, or religion.

EMPLOYMENT ACT OF 1946: confers upon the federal government the obligation to use all its powers to promote: (1) high and expanding levels of output, (2) reasonably full employment, (3) price stability within the limits necessary to bring about high-level employment, (4) strengthening of the system of free and competitive enterprise. Provides also for a council of three Economic Advisors, and requires the President to transmit to Congress at the beginning of each regular session an economic report describing prevailing economic conditions and providing a program and recommendations as the President may deem necessary or desirable.

EQUAL PAY ACT (1963): law stating that women must receive the same pay as men for doing the same job under like conditions.

EXPORT TRADE ACT: see Webb-Pomerene Act.

FAIR EMPLOYMENT PRACTICES CODES: state laws with the same objectives as the Civil Rights Act of 1964.

FAIR LABOR STANDARDS ACT: federal law concerning wages and hours of workers in private industries whose products enter *interstate* commerce.

FAIR TRADE LAWS: state laws allowing manufacturers to establish and enforce retail prices (resale price maintenance).

FEDERAL COMMUNICATIONS ACT OF 1934: provides for creation of FCC, an independent regulatory agency of seven members with powers of regulation over (1) all interstate and foreign common-carrier operations of domestic companies by wire and radio; (2) nonbroadcast radio facilities (safety and special); (3) broadcast stations, radio, TV, to provide for orderly development and operation; to insure service at reasonable charge; to promote safety via improved communications systems; and to strengthen the national defense. Requires licensing of all transmitters and operators. Requires equal time for politicians. FCC has authority to supervise charges and practices of common carriers (telegraph and telephone).

FEDERAL POWER ACT OF 1935: (newer name for Federal Water Power Act of 1920): provides for a federal power commission of five members to control water-power resources subject to federal jurisdiction for the benefit of all people and to regulate interstate electric and natural gas utilities so their rates, service, and financing will be in the public interest.

FEDERAL SECURITIES ACT (1933): law demanding full disclosure of facts and figures by any company issuing a new security. (See *Securities Act of 1933* for complete definition)

FEDERAL TRADE COMMISSION ACT (1914): provides for establishing the FTC and declares unfair methods of competition to be illegal.

FISHERY COOPERATIVE MARKETING ACT OF 1934: provides that persons engaged in the fishery industry as fishermen, catching, collecting, or cultivating aquatic products, or as planters of aquatic products on public or private beds, may act together in associations, and so on. (Same as *Agricultural Marketing Agreement Act.*)

FLAMMABLE FABRICS ACT OF 1953: law administered by FTC that prohibits the manufacture for sale, the sale, the importation, or the transportation for sale of any wearing apparel that "is so highly flammable as to be dangerous when worn by individuals."

FOOD, DRUG, AND COSMETIC ACT OF 1938: administered by the FDA, it prohibits adulteration and misbranding of food, drugs, devices, and cosmetics and the movement of such in interstate commerce.

FUR PRODUCTS LABELING ACT OF 1951: administered by FTC, this law requires manufacturers and distributors in interstate commerce of furs to attach labels showing the name of the animal that produced the fur, country of origin, area of hide used, and state of color (whether bleached or dyed). Purpose is to protect consumers against misbranding, false advertising, and false invoicing.

FULL EMPLOYMENT ACT (1946): charges the federal government with the responsibility of maintaining the economic health of the nation. (See also *Employment Act of 1946.)*

GRAIN FUTURES ACT (1922): law designed to prevent manipulative and misleading practices on the organized commodity exchanges; amended in 1936 and renamed "Commodity Exchange Act."

INTERSTATE COMMERCE ACT (1887): established the ICC (eleven members) with jurisdiction over all forms of interstate public transportation except air carriers, pipelines for gas and water, and certain motor and water carriers operating in metropolitan areas. The ICC regulates rates for railroads, oil pipelines, express service, motor carriers operating interstate and foreign; water carriers in coastwise and intercoastal commerce and inland waters of the U.S., freight forwarding companies, and certain private car lines.

INVESTMENT ADVISERS ACT OF 1940: requires all investment trust companies to register with the SEC and prescribes rules for their conduct. Individual advisers are also required to register with the SEC, and prohibitions are placed on the use of any scheme, device, or practice to defraud or mislead a client. SEC is empowered to enforce this law.

INVESTMENT COMPANY ACT (1940): law regulating investment companies that requires them to register with the SEC and provides rules for their conduct. Prohibits use of any scheme, device, or practice to defraud or mislead a client.

LABOR-MANAGEMENT REPORTING AND DISCLOSURE ACT (1959): federal law requiring unions to file annual financial statements and to hold down racketeering.

LABOR MANAGEMENT RELATIONS ACT [Taft-Hartley] (1947): federal law regarding labor; prohibits unfair practices, outlaws closed shop.

LANHAM ACT OF 1946: repealed prior trademark laws; provides for the legal right to register any mark that has become distinctive, not merely those that show origin or ownership; provides for the registration of "service marks, certification marks, and collective marks."

MANPOWER DEVELOPMENT AND TRAINING ACT (1962): provides for retraining or occupational training for unemployed.

McCARRAN ACT (1945): partially exempts insurance companies from the federal anti-trust laws, to the extent that such businesses are not regulated by state law.

McGUIRE ACT (1952): pertains to fair trade; makes it permissible for manufacturers selling in interstate commerce to use the nonsigner clause within a given state in accordance with the legislation of the state. Also authorizes fixing a minimum or stipulated (actual) resale price. On the basis of this act, a manufacturer is able to require all retailers in a "fair trading" state to observe the minimum or actual prices that are fixed in a written contract made with one retailer in that state.

MILLER-TYDINGS ACT (1937): legalizes resale price-maintenance contracts in interstate commerce. Provides a loophole in the Sherman Act so that fair-trading firms cannot be prosecuted for price fixing.

NATIONAL BANKRUPTCY ACT (1898): specifies protection for both creditors and debtors in insolvency proceedings.

NATIONAL INDUSTRIAL RECOVERY ACT [NIRA] (1933): provided that while the nation was in a state of national emergency (the Great Depression of the thirties), businesses would be exempt from the anti-trust laws. The main idea seemed to be that big business needed permission to fix prices and curb production because of extreme price competition from smaller companies. The law did not work very well and was declared unconstitutional by the Supreme Court in 1935.

NATIONAL LABOR RELATIONS ACT OF 1935 [Wagner Act]: law to help workers organize into unions and to protect them from employer interference; stipulates "unfair practices" on the part of the employer and declares them illegal. Set up the National Labor Relations Board, which plays a critical role in labor-management relations.

NATIONAL WOOL ACT OF 1954: declares congressional policy to be the encouragement of wool production in the interest of national security and the general welfare and provides for payment of incentive prices to wool growers.

NATURAL GAS ACT OF 1938: authorizes the FPC to control the rates of companies engaged in transporting natural gas in interstate commerce; authority is limited to transportation and sale.

PACKERS AND STOCKYARDS ACT OF 1921: provides patrons of the public stockyards with open competitive markets free from collusion and unfair trade practices by those in livestock marketing or by the meat packing industries.

PATENT ACT OF 1952: provides that patents will be granted to "whoever invents or discovers any new and useful process, machine, manufacture, or composition of matter, or any new and useful improvement thereof." It provides that patentability shall be determined on "the differences between the subject matter sought to be patented and prior art." If the differences are substantial, a patent will be issued. However, if the differences would have been obvious at the time of the claimed invention to a person having ordinary skill in the art, a patent will not be granted.

PUBLIC UTILITY ACT OF 1935: sought to control the abuses existing in the electric and gas utilities as a consequence of the holding-company form of organization. Gives the FPC authority to regulate mergers, the issuance and acquisition of securities, and interstate rates and service at the operating company level. Supervision over the holding-company level is vested in the SEC.

REED-BULLWINKLE ACT (1948): amendment to the Interstate Commerce Act; provides that agreements on rates made by railroads, truck lines, and inland waterway carriers subject to the jurisdiction of the ICC, if approved by and filed with the Commission, shall be relieved from the operation of the anti-trust laws.

REVENUE ACT OF 1916: prohibits importing or selling imported articles at a price substantially less than the market price of the articles in their country of origin plus freight, duty, and other expenses incident to their importation into the U.S., provided that such acts are done with an intent to injure an industry or the establishment of an industry in the U.S. Penalties similar to those of Sherman Act.

ROBINSON-PATMAN ACT (1936): aims to provide small and big buyers with a comparable purchasing price, so that competition in the resale market can begin on a fair basis. Makes price discrimination between purchasers illegal.

RURAL ELECTRIFICATION ACT OF 1936: authorizes making federal loans to farm cooperatives for the construction and operation of generating plants, transmission lines, and distribution systems. Rural electric cooperatives can borrow 100 percent of their investment capital from the federal government at 2 percent interest for 35 years.

SECURITIES ACT OF 1933: requires full disclosure of all material facts with respect to the issuance of new securities before they are publicly offered for sale. Places the burden on the seller to disclose pertinent information in hopes that the light of publicity will deter misconduct and assist the investor in making an informed investment decision.

SECURITIES EXCHANGE ACT OF 1934: aims to eliminate fraud, manipulation, and other abuses in trading securities, both on the organized exchanges and over-the-counter; to make available publicly information about condition of corporations whose securities are listed on any national securities exchange; to regulate the use of the nation's credit in securities trading.

SHERMAN ACT (1890): aims to protect trade and commerce against unlawful restraints and monopolies; to prevent monopoly and preserve and maintain the institutions of free entry and price competition.

SHIPPING ACT OF 1916: provides that every common carrier by water in foreign commerce, in interstate commerce on the high seas, or on the Great Lakes, as well as any persons engaged in forwarding or furnishing wharfage, dock warehouse, or other terminal facilities in connection with a common carrier by water, shall immediately file a copy of all agreements with any other carrier or person subject to the act with respect to rates, fares, charges, and other cooperative arrangements. Provides for a regulatory commission to supervise common carriers by water, called Federal Maritime Board.

SMALL BUSINESS INVESTMENT ACT OF 1958: administered by the SBA, it establishes a program for providing equity capital and long-term capital through privately owned and operated small business investment companies and state and local development companies; makes loans to such investment companies.

SOCIAL SECURITY ACT OF 1935: federal law providing for nationwide retirement program and protection for workers' survivors.

TAFT-HARTLEY LAW: See *Labor Management Relations Act.*

TARIFF ACT OF 1930: stipulates that an import duty shall be placed on goods entering the United States equal to the net amount of any bounty or subsidy that is granted in the country of production or export by government or by any person, partnership, association, cartel, or corporation.

TRANSPORTATION ACT OF 1940: an amendment to the ICA, it establishes a "national transportation policy"—one of developing, coordinating, and preserving a national transportation system while keeping in mind the interests of the shippers.

WHEELER-LEA (amendment to the FTC Act, 1938): prohibits unfair or deceptive acts or practices in interstate commerce. Makes the consumer of equal concern before the law with the merchant or manufacturer injured by the unfair methods of a dishonest competitor.

WOOL PRODUCTS LABELING ACT OF 1939: provides that all products made with wool, except carpets and the like, must disclose on a label attached to the merchandise the kind and percentage of each fiber contained in the product.

TRANSPORTATION ACT OF 1958: authorizes the Commission to approve federal guarantee of certain loans to railroads; stipulates that a proceeding involving competition between carriers of different modes of transportation, in determining whether a rate is lower than a reasonable minimum, shall consider the facts and circumstances attending the movement of the traffic by the carrier to which the rate is applicable. Rates of a carrier shall not be held up to a particular level to protect the traffic of any other mode of transportation.

WALSH-HEALEY ACT (1936): law requiring employers who deal with the government to treat and compensate their laborers according to prescribed governmental regulations.

WEBB-POMERENE ACT (Export Trade Act): provides that nothing contained in the Sherman Act shall be construed as declaring to be illegal an association entered into for the sole purpose of engaging in export trade, provided such association, agreement, and act is not in restraint of trade within the U.S., and is not in restraint of the export trade of any domestic competitor of such association.

Appendix B
Encyclopedia of Business Terms

ABSENTEE MANAGEMENT: condition existing when owners or other top executives of an enterprise are not physically present at the scene of operations, but make key managerial decisions in absentia.

ACCOMMODATION PARTY (INDORSER): one who has signed a note without receiving value therefor, and for the purpose of lending his credit to some other person.

ACCOUNTS RECEIVABLE: money due from customers carried as "open book" accounts. Carried in the current-assets section of the firm's balance sheet.

ACCUMULATION BONDS: bonds on which all interest is received at maturity; difference between face value and discounted purchase price is the amount of interest.

ACID-TEST RATIO: method of judging firm's ability to meet current debt quickly.

Formula is:

$$\frac{\text{total cash + receivables}}{\text{current liabilities}}$$

One common standard is 1:1.

ADMINISTERED PRICES: prices set by executive judgment (in contrast to "market prices," which are determined by market competition). While market conditions are taken into consideration in setting administered prices, other factors also play a role, such as strategy, company policy, government intervention, and costs.

ADMINISTRATIVE LAW: regulations issued by government administrative agencies that have the effect of law.

AD VALOREM DUTIES: customs tax on goods, based on percent of their invoiced value.

ADVERTISING: paid form of nonpersonal presentation or promotion of ideas, goods, or services by an identified sponsor. Key factors in identifying advertising are that it is paid for and has an identifiable sponsor. Propaganda may be paid for, but its sponsor is hidden. Publicity has an identifiable sponsor, but is not paid for.

ADVERTISING AGENCY: specialized institution that aids businesses in all phases of advertising. Usually works for a 15 percent commission of the total billings paid by the media in which the advertisements are placed. Client pays for other direct costs on a cost-plus basis.

ADVERTISING MEDIA: various publications, devices, and structures that carry messages to the public (newspapers, radio, TV, billboards, direct mail, and so on).

AFTER-ACQUIRED CLAUSE: restriction on mortgage bonds, requiring that property acquired after sale of the original bonds must also be added to the property originally pledged under the mortgage.

AGENCY SHOP: labor situation in which worker must pay dues to union, but need not join it, if union negotiates for him. Legal only in some states.

AMALGAMATION: combination; consolidation of two or more companies resulting in *one new* company.

ANTI-TRUST LAWS: federal and state legislation that outlaws monopolies, attempts to monopolize, or conspiracies in restraint of trade. The Sherman Act (1890) and the Clayton Act (1914) are the backbone of federal anti-trust legislation.

APPRENTICESHIP SYSTEM: training program whereby a novice is attached to a craftsman for a specific period to learn trade; largely obsolete now except for building trades.

ARBITRATION: method of settling disputes, both contractual and noncontractual, between parties by impartial outsiders; designed to circumvent slow, expensive, and unsophisticated judicial system.

Compulsory: parties required to submit to arbitration; decision of arbitrator is legally binding on disputing parties.

Voluntary: parties agree to submit dispute to arbitrator, whose decision is morally binding.

ARRAY: a list of all figures in a statistical universe arranged in numerical order. The numbers 7, 3, 9, 2 would be arranged 2, 3, 7, 9 or 9, 7, 3, 2.

ARTICLES OF PARTNERSHIP: written contractual agreement between parties defining in detail the important features of the partnership arrangement so that future controversy is minimized.

AUCTION COMPANY: an institution that provides a place where products are bought and sold, using an auction method (the highest bidder is the buyer) for determining the transfer price.

AUTOMATION: the operation or control of a mechanical process by automatic means. Human hands do not work on the product. Rather all work is done by machines, with men controlling the machines either from remote stations or by computer programs that in turn tell the machines what to do.

BABY BONDS: bonds with face value of less than $500.

BAILEE: party who receives goods for specific purpose (not sale) and returns them eventually to owner in like or better condition; examples are pawnbrokers, freighters, repairmen, and parking lot operators.

BAILMENT: temporary physical transfer of personal property between two parties for a specific purpose and length of time; ownership does not change.

BALANCE OF TRADE: the value difference between the exports and imports of a country.

BALANCE SHEET: an accounting statement showing the financial condition of a company at a point in time; presents assets, liabilities, and net worth.

BANK ACCEPTANCES: bank drafts endorsed by the bank on which drawn.

BANK DRAFT: check written by a bank that draws funds from a larger (correspondent) bank; often used in distant transactions to assure negotiability.

BANKRUPTCY: financial state of affairs where liabilities exceed assets.

Voluntary: declaration of insolvency by debtor for protection from creditors.

Involuntary: declaration of insolvency by federal court forced by legal action of creditors.

Act of: acts of bankruptcy by a person shall consist of his having (1) conveyed, transferred, concealed, removed, or permitted to be concealed or removed any part of his property with intent to hinder, delay, or defraud his creditors; or (2) transferred, while insolvent, any portion of his property to one or more of his creditors with intent to show preference; or (3) suffered or permitted, while insolvent, any creditor to obtain a lien upon any of his property through legal proceedings; or (4) made a general assignment for the benefit of his creditors; or (5) while insolvent or unable to pay his debts as they matured, he procured, permitted, or suffered the appointment of a receiver or trustee to take charge of his property; or (6) admitted in writing his inability to pay his debts and his willingness to be adjudged a bankrupt.

BARTER ARRANGEMENTS: agreement to exchange goods or services directly without using money as a medium of exchange.

BEAR: investor or speculator who expects stock prices to drop.

BEAR MARKET: market in which prices are generally declining.

BEHAVIORAL SCIENCE: field that studies human behavior; psychology, sociology, anthropology, and economics.

BENEFICIARY: person designated to receive money or property of trusts, wills, insurance policies, and so on.

BETTER BUSINESS BUREAU: institution created and supported by local businesses to protect consumers from unethical business practices.

BIG BOARD: The New York Stock Exchange.

BILL OF EXCHANGE: draft form used largely in international trade.

BILL OF LADING: written document, a receipt, given by a transportation company showing the names of the shipper and the party to get the goods itemizing the goods shipped.

BLACKLIST: document that conveys between two parties information about a third party that is likely to prevent them from entering into business relations with that third party.

BLUE SKY LAWS: laws regulating security sales to eliminate fraud.

BLUE CHIP: common stock in a company that has a reputation for quality and wide acceptance of its products or services, and for its ability to produce income and pay dividends in good times and bad. Such stocks are relatively high priced, thereby offering low yields.

BOARD OF DIRECTORS: group elected by stockholders of a corporation who are responsible for directing affairs of the business.

BONDS: Long-term, interest-bearing promissory notes issued by a corporation.

Accumulation: sold at discount; interest paid at maturity (such as Series E Savings Bonds).

Baby: less than $500 face value.

Bearer: has no owner named on it; the bearer of the bond is the owner.

Callable or redeemable: may be redeemed at the option of the issuer.

Collateral trust: has stocks and bonds as security.

Convertible: may be converted into stock on specific terms at option of purchaser.

Coupon: bears no evidence of owner; interest paid to bearer upon presentation of coupon.

Debenture: pledges the credit of the corporation only, with no special collateral.

Fully registered: shows name of owner on face; interest checks are mailed to him.

Income: interest paid only when company earns it.

Mortgage: bonds with property pledged as collateral.

Registered: Bond registered in name of owner.

Serial: bond series in which bonds mature in different years.

Sinking fund: seller deposits a certain percentage of the total amount of the issue annually for repayment.

Subordinated: claim of bond holder is subordinated to claims of other creditors.

BOYCOTT: to abstain from dealings with a company or individual.

Primary: act of union members who refuse to do business with a company involved in dispute with them.

Secondary: the boycotting of parties not directly involved in the dispute.

BRANCH DEPARTMENT STORE: additional facility of original store, often located in a suburb.

BROADSIDES: advertising sheets intended for hand distribution.

BROKER: individual or institution not maintaining constant relations with either the buyer or the seller, but acting in behalf of either, depending on the situation. Does not take title to goods or possession of them. The only service rendered is that of negotiation for exchange of title. Found most frequently in the real estate and securities business.

BROKERAGE: firm that buys and sells for others and charges a commission for its services.

BUDGETING: estimating and planning income and expenditures for given period of time for various activities of the firm.

BULL: investor or speculator who expects the price of stocks to rise.

BULL MARKET: market in which prices are generally rising.

BUSINESS GAMES: program of presenting participants with simulated business situations in order to train them in decision making.

BUYING COMMITTEE: group within a retail company that determines the acceptability for purchase of products presented by wholesalers or manufacturers.

BYLAWS: rules and regulations under which a board of directors operates a corporation.

CALL PRICE: stipulated price at which bond or preferred stock may be redeemed by issuer.

CALL OPTION: agreement in which the seller agrees to sell to the buyer a named stock for a given price within a stipulated period of time in exchange for a premium paid by the buyer. It is the buyer's right to "call" the stock at any time within the period if he so desires. It is a method used by sophisticated "bulls" to speculate that a price of a stock is going to rise significantly within that period of time.

CAPITAL: the wealth (money, property, or both) owned or employed in business by an individual, firm, corporation, etc.

Goods: material assets.

Funds: cash assets.

CAPITAL GAIN OR CAPITAL LOSS: profit or loss from the sale of a capital asset. A short-term capital gain (6 months or less) is taxed at the reporting individual's full income tax rate. A long-term capital gain (more than 6 months) is taxed at a maximum of 35 percent, depending on the reporting individual's tax bracket. Up to $1000 of net capital loss (that is, when you sell securities at a lower price than you paid for them) is deductible from the individual's taxable income during the year reported. If the capital loss is more than $1000, as much as $1000 annually is deductible in each of the next five years. The amount of capital loss that may be deducted is reduced by the amount of any capital gain.

CAPITALISM: a word coined in the early days of the industrial revolution to represent a social-economic system in which all surplus revenue, in excess of true costs, goes to the owners of the capital. Usually the ideas of free enterprise, private property, and freedom to contract are included with this concept of capitalism, but they are separate concepts. Pure capitalism probably exists nowhere in the world today. All governments now recognize some form of socialism, differing only in form and extent.

CAR CARDS: display advertising commonly used on buses, trains, and taxis.

CASH DISCOUNT: amount that may be deducted from invoice for payment within stipulated time period.

2/10 net 30 = 2 percent discount if paid in ten days; total amount due in thirty days.

8/10 EOM = 8 percent discount if paid ten days after the end of the month.

CASH FLOW: figure derived by computing net income and expenses not requiring outlay of funds minus income that did not generate cash; usually a considerably higher figure than net income. *Also:* (1) method of forecasting financial condition by computing cash needs for income and expenses (usually monthly); (2) sometimes called "cash budget," which is the document reflecting cash flow.

CAVEAT EMPTOR: Latin way of saying, "Let the buyer beware."

CENTRALIZED MANAGEMENT: concentration of decision making at one location, usually the home office.

CHAIN STORE: two or more stores in the same general kind of business operated by the same firm.

CHAIN OF DISCOUNTS: series of reductions applied to original invoice; offered by seller to buyer. Example: $1,000, 40-10-5% = $1000 × 0.60 × 0.90 × 0.95 = $513.

CHAIN-STORE TAX LAWS: special tax levies that progressively increase with the number of stores a chain owns.

CHANNELS OF DISTRIBUTION: systems of economic institutions through which a producer of goods delivers them into the hands of the users.

CHARACTER LOAN: money granted to borrower solely on basis of his signature and promise to repay.

CHATTEL MORTGAGE: mortgage under which personal property is pledged as security for a debt. Most common example is encountered in buying a car on installment credit. The car is pledged as security on the note; the lender has a chattel mortgage on the vehicle.

CHECK: negotiable instrument signed by depositor directing bank to pay specified amount of money to designated party (payee).

Certified: guaranteed collectible funds; bank sets aside depositor's funds for payment of check when presented by payee, thereby guaranteeing payment.

Cashier's: check purchased by party drawn on the bank's funds.

CHECKOFF: collection of union dues by employer via payroll deduction.

C.L. and L.C.L. (carload lots and less-than-carload lots): quantity designations used in railway freight shipping rates (l.c.l. rates are often 15 to 30 percent higher).

CLOSE CORPORATION: a corporation in which ownership is usually limited to a few stockholders; stock is not for sale publicly.

CLOSED DOOR DISCOUNT HOUSE: retail stores that sell only to membership-card purchasers, who have the privilege of shopping there for ostensibly lower-priced goods.

CLU (Chartered Life Underwriter): insurance salesman who has taken a training program and passed an examination prescribed by the American College of Life Underwriters.

COINSURANCE CLAUSE: requirement that policy owner must purchase insurance coverage of a stipulated percent (usually 80 percent) of the total value of the property.

COLLUSION: an agreement between two parties prejudicial to another party; conspiracy.

COLLUSIVE BIDDING: illegal practice of supposedly competing firms that agree to submit identical bids or agree to which will be low bidder before submitting.

COMMERCIAL BANK: a financial institution offering a full line of services such as checking accounts, savings accounts, loans on a wide range of activities, trust and escrow services, and serving as a government depository.

COMMERCIAL DRAFTS: a type of promissory note created by the creditor and accepted by the debtor.

COMMERCIAL PAPER: an unsecured promissory note sold in the open market by corporations having a prime credit rating. Such paper usually has a short maturity and carries a low interest rate.

COMMISSION MERCHANTS: agent middlemen with direct, physical control over goods consigned to them, and sold on a percentage commission; most commonly found in the distribution of agricultural products.

COMMODITY: raw materials; any standardized product whose price is determined in a competitive market.

COMMODITY MARKET: an established, regulated open market, such as the Chicago Board of Trade, in which commodities are openly bought and sold, thereby establishing market prices.

COMMON STOCK: shares that represent a residual ownership interest in a corporation. Both common and preferred stock have ownership rights, but the preferred normally has prior claim on dividends and, in the event of liquidation, assets. Both common and preferred stockholders claims are junior to claims of bondholders or other creditors of the company. Common stockholders assume the greater risk, but have the voting power and generally exercise the greater control and may gain the greater reward in the form of dividends and capital appreciation. Common stock and capital stock are terms often used interchangeably when the company has no preferred stock.

COMPUTER: ultra high-speed adding machine that can store information and process it as directed.

CONDITIONAL BILL OF SALE: document provided to buyer of movable property in lieu of title, which is retained by seller until paid in full.

CONDITIONAL SALES: a sales contract in which the title to the property does not pass to the buyer until the conditions of the contract are met (usually payment for the goods in full). Considered to be superior to taking a chattel mortgage on a time payment sale because the legal procedure for repossession of goods is easier. Court issues a Writ of Replevin in case of a defaulted conditional sales contract, but the holder of a defaulted chattel mortgage must foreclose.

CONGLOMERATE: a firm resulting from the merging of dissimilar businesses.

CONSIGNMENT: act of entrusting goods to dealer for the purpose of resale, but retaining title on goods until sold. The dealer pays only when and if the goods are sold.

CONTRACT: an agreement between two or more parties that they each will do certain things. For a contract to be legally enforceable, it must have the following essential elements: offer, acceptance, consideration, competent parties, and legal objective.

CONVENIENCE GOODS: goods that the consumer wants to buy with a minimum of effort; usually relatively low-priced items that are purchased frequently.

CONVERTIBLE: a bond, debenture or preferred share that may be exchanged by the owner for common stock or another security, usually of the same company, in accordance with the terms of the issue.

COOPERATIVE (co-op): Business institution owned and patronized solely by its members.

Producer: institution engaged in marketing products of its members.

Buying: unit engaged in buying for its members.

Consumer: user-owned retail outlets.

CORPORATE IMAGE: the impression the public has of a firm.

CORPORATION: a form of organization wherein ownership is vested in shares of stock. Chief Justice John Marshall's classic definition (1819) reads:

> A corporation is an artificial being, invisible, intangible, and existing only in contemplation of law. Being the mere creature of law, it possesses only those properties which the charter of its creation confers upon it, either expressly, or as incidental to its very existence. These are such as are supposed best calculated to effect the object for which it was created. Among the most important are immortality, and, if the expression may be allowed, individuality; properties, by which a perpetual succession of many persons are considered as the same, and may act as a single individual. They enable a corporation to manage its own affairs, and to hold property without the perplexing intricacies, the hazardous and endless necessity, of perpetual

conveyances for the purpose of transmitting it from hand to hand. It is chiefly for the purpose of clothing bodies of men, in succession, with these qualities and capacities, that corporations were invested, and are in use. By these means, a perpetual succession of individuals are capable of acting for the promotion of the particular object, like one immortal being. [*Dartmouth College* v. *Woodward,* 4 Wheaton (U.S.) 518 (1819).]

Close or closely held: corporation whose stock is held by few people and generally not for sale to the general public.

Domestic: referred to as such only in state where it was organized.

Foreign: referred to as such in any state other than the one where it was organized.

Private: stock not for sale publicly.

Profit-seeking: intent on making money for shareholders.

Publicly held: stock owned by the general public.

Non profit: never pays dividends, but may make profit.

Governmental: organized by federal, state, or city.

Alien: company organized in country other than U.S.

COST OF GOODS SOLD: purchase price of merchandise sold by a retailer; the cost of raw materials, purchased parts, and labor in making a product; that which is deducted from net sales to determine gross margin (gross profit).

CO-SIGNER (or co-maker): a party who signs a note on the face in addition to the maker, and is equally liable for payment.

COUPON BOND: security having dated coupons attached that must be detached and presented to collect interest.

C.P.A. (Certified Public Accountant): accountant who meets standards established by state law. Such laws usually require passing an examination, certain education, and experience.

C.P.C.U. (Chartered Property and Casualty Underwriter): salesman who has passed a training program and examination prepared by his professional association.

CREDIT UNIONS: cooperatives that handle savings and loans for their members, restricted to a homogeneous industrial group.

CREDITOR AGREEMENT: voluntary arrangement for liquidating debts of a party in dire financial condition.

Extension agreement: decision signed by *all* creditors allowing additional time for debt satisfaction.

Composition settlement: decision of creditors to accept an amount less than that due.

CREDITORS: individuals or firms to which money is owed.

General: class of claimants who are paid from funds remaining after preferred and secured creditors have been satisfied; they have no preferred status or security for their claims.

Preferred: class of claims that must be paid first, by order of court in bankruptcy cases, including: taxes, wages, court costs, secured creditors.

CRITICAL-PATH METHOD (CPM): a visual means of analyzing a project to determine its completion time and the identification of time-critical steps in its completion.

CROSS ELASTICITY OF DEMAND: the change in demand for one product when the price of another product changes; for example, the price of Fords goes up, so the sales of VW's increase.

CUMULATIVE VOTING: a method of voting for corporate directors enabling the shareholder to multiply the number of his shares by the number of directorships being voted on and cast the total for one director or a selected group of directors. In ordinary voting, a 10-share holder has 10 votes for each position open on the board of directors. In cumulative voting, if three directorships were open, the stockholder would have 30 votes (10 × 3), all of which could be voted for one man. Cumulative voting is required under the corporate laws of some states and permitted in many others.

CURRENT ASSETS: cash or property that can be converted to cash in a short period of time; usually accounts receivable; inventory, and short-term notes receivable.

DEBT CAPITAL: funds or assets acquired by borrowing.

DECENTRALIZED MANAGEMENT: managerial system in which decision making is done at lowest levels feasible in an organization.

DELEGATION OF AUTHORITY: bestowing upon one's subordinate the power to carry out a responsibility or decision.

DELIVERED PRICE: price quotes by seller that include all costs of putting goods on buyer's dock.

DEMAND DEPOSIT: money placed with financial institution that must be returned upon demand by its owner; checking account is the most common form.

DEPARTMENTALIZATION: subdivision of personnel and functions of organization into groups for management purposes.

DIRECT MAIL: advertising sent via mail to potential customers.

DISCOUNT: an amount that the seller allows the buyer to deduct from his bill under stipulated conditions.

> *Cash:* amount allowed for payment of bill within a stipulated period of time; e.g., 3/10, N 30.
>
> *Functional:* discount used to effect different prices to different classes of customers; often called trade discount.
>
> *Quantity:* reductions in the unit price granted for buying in certain volume. Noncumulative: depends on the size of the individual order from buyer. Cumulative: reduction in total price paid for goods purchased over a period of time.
>
> *Seasonal:* reductions in price given for buying during a certain time of the year, usually a slack season.
>
> *Price-level discounts:* method of varying prices by using standard price list supplemented by discount notices to the trade.

DISCOUNT HOUSE: a retail outlet selling goods at prices that it claims are lower than those charged for the same goods in more traditional stores.

DISCOUNTING: a loan upon an evidence of debt, where the compensation for the use of the money until the maturity of the debt is deducted from the principal and retained by the lender at the time of making the loan.

DISSOLUTION: legal termination of corporation, which entails liquidating liabilities and distributing the remaining assets to the company's stockholders.

DIVIDEND: a payment made to the stockholders of a corporation.

> *Bond:* payment made with a bond.
>
> *Cash:* payment in cash.
>
> *Extra:* a dividend paid in either stock or cash in addition to the regular or usual dividend the corporation has been paying.
>
> *Property:* payment made in assets other than cash—inventory, marketable securities of other companies, fixed assets, etc.
>
> *Stock:* payment of dividend in stock without changing stockholder's equity.

DOLLAR COST AVERAGING: a system of buying securities at regular intervals with a fixed amount of dollars invested over a considerable period of time, regardless of the prevailing prices of the securities. Under this method, the investor acquires not 10 shares of XYZ every month or every six months, but $50 worth of XYZ. Over the long term, if the price trend of a stock is upward, and periodic investments are maintained in good times and bad, dollar cost averaging may be a rewarding investment technique.

DORMANT (Sleeping) PARTNER: part-owner who is publicly unknown and who does not actively participate in the business.

DOW THEORY: a market analysis theory based upon the performance of the Dow-Jones Industrial and Rail Stock Price Averages. The theory says that the market is in a basic upward trend if one of these averages advances above a previous noted high level, accompanied or followed by a similar advance in the other. When the averages both dip below previous noted low levels, this is regarded as confirmation of a basic downward trend. The theory does not attempt to predict how long either trend will continue, although it is widely misinterpreted as a method of forecasting future action. Whatever the merits of the theory, it is sometimes a strong factor in the market because many people either believe in it or believe that a great many others do.

EDP (Electronic Data Processing): processing of information with a computer.

ELASTICITY OF DEMAND: change in demand caused by change in causative force, such as:

> *Price:* change in price of the article.
>
> *Income:* change in income of market.
>
> *Promotional:* change in advertising efforts.

ENTREPRENEUR: individual who owns and operates his own business.

EQUITY: total assets *minus* total liabilities *equals* equity or net worth.

EQUITY CAPITAL: funds invested in a business by its owners.

EXCISE TAX: duty levied on manufacture, sale, or consumption of goods, such as those on alcohol, tobacco, and gasoline.

EXPORT CONTROL: governmental restriction of sales abroad, particularly strategic military goods.

EXPORTER: one who sells and/or ships goods to customers in other countries.

FACTOR: financial institution that buys accounts receivable directly and bills customers directly, in contrast to a bank that only lends on accounts receivable.

FEDERAL RESERVE SYSTEM: banking system consisting of the following elements: (1) board of governors—appointed by the President, (2) Federal Reserve banks—owned by member banks, (3) Federal Open Market Committee—to create liquidity, (4) Federal Advisory Council, (5) member banks.

FEDERAL TRADE COMMISSION: group that enforces various laws, including: Robinson-Patman, Federal Trade Commission Act, Wheeler Lea Act, Clayton Act, Sherman Act, Wool Products Labeling Act, Fur Products Labeling Act, Textile Fiber Products Identification Act, and Flammable Fabrics Act.

FEEDBACK: relaying information at one point in a system back to a previous point in the system for the purpose of correcting the system's behavior.

FIDELITY BOND: type of insurance indemnifying employer for any losses incurred because of dishonesty of employee covered by bond.

FIELD WAREHOUSING: storage method wherein warehousing is done at buyer's premises; a bonded custodian is installed who dispenses goods when they are paid for. Often used as collateral for bank loans.

FISHYBACK: transportation of freight-laden truck trailers by ship.

FIXED ASSETS: property with relatively long life, such as land, buildings, and equipment.

FIXED CAPITAL: money invested in fixed assets.

FLOW CHART: diagram of logical step-by-step process or system.

F.O.B. (free on board): freight term used to denote point at which buyer takes ownership of goods and starts paying the freight.

FOREIGN EXCHANGE: money transactions in international trade.

FRANCHISE: a contract between two parties. In modern usage, it is a license that entitles its holder to operate a particular type of business according to certain stated conditions and arrangements.

FREEDOM OF CONTRACT: concept that one may enter into any agreement he chooses.

FRINGE BENEFITS: items of value offered in addition to salary, such as life insurance, medical insurance, pension plans, profit sharing, club membership, company cars, and paid vacations.

FUNCTIONALIZATION: organizing according to type of activity—production, sales, finance, personnel, engineering, and so on.

FUTURES CONTRACT: agreement to deliver a given quantity of some commodity at a date in the future.

GOLD STANDARD: monetary system based on gold of specified weight and purity as the definition of the nation's monetary unit; e.g., the U.S. dollar is defined as 12.631 grains of fine gold, or $\frac{1}{35}$ ounce.

GREEN RIVER ORDINANCE: local laws restricting door-to-door salesmen (in municipalities).

GROSS MARGIN: net sales minus cost of goods sold; sometimes known as gross profit.

GROSS NATIONAL PRODUCT: estimated dollar figure representing the value of all goods and services produced in the U.S. compiled by the Department of Commerce (and others) quarterly, annually, or monthly.

GUARANTEED ANNUAL WAGE: concept of assuring hourly employees a certain annual income regardless of business conditions.

HAND-TO-MOUTH BUYING: purchasing only quantities that are immediately required; maintenance of minimum inventory.

HEDGING: to offset or minimize a risk by taking some other action.

HOLDER IN DUE COURSE: a person holding a negotiable instrument under the following conditions: (1) it is complete and regular on its face, (2) he became the holder of it before it was overdue, and without notice that it had been previously dishonored, if such was the fact, (3) he took it in good faith and for value, (4) at the time it was negotiated to him he had no notice of any infirmity in the instrument or defect in the title of the person negotiating it.

HOLDING COMPANY: a corporation that owns a controlling interest in another company or all of its shares. The accounts of a wholly-owned subsidiary may be consolidated with those of the parent company.

HORIZONTAL COMBINATION: companies engaged in exactly the same business activity who get together in some manner either legally via merger or illegally via collusion.

IMPORTER: one who buys goods from foreign markets.

IMPULSE GOODS: goods purchased without prior planning on the buyer's part. The sight of the products in the store triggers the purchase.

INDENTURE: legal document creating a trustee for bond issues and stipulating his duties.

INDEX NUMBER: quantitative statistical device for measuring change in a group of related items over a certain time period.

INDORSEMENTS: signature and/or qualifications on a negotiable instrument. There are five kinds:

Special: specifies to whom payable, such as, "pay to Hall."

In blank: specifies no indorsee; "Pay to order of Brown" indorsed "Brown" would be in blank.

Restrictive: notifies all subsequent indorsees that they acquire no greater rights than those conveyed to the first restrictive indorsee, such as "Pay to First National Bank for collection (deposit) only."

Qualified: constitutes the indorser a mere assignor of the instrument. "Pay to Fox without recourse. Brown."

Conditional: by its terms it qualifies the conditional indorsee's rights against to conditional indorser. "Bates, with recourse after all security has been exhausted."

INDUSTRIAL DISTRIBUTORS: wholesalers operating in industrial equipment fields.

INJUNCTION: court order to do or not to do certain things.

INNOVISTIC COMPETITION: business rivalry based on innovation of new products and processes.

INSOLVENCY: condition existing when assets are insufficient to cover debts.

INSURANCE: transfer of a risk, by a person who does not wish to bear it, to someone else—an insurance company. For the payment of a premium the insurance company will pay the agreed-upon sum to the insured (the party having the risk) if the event being insured against happens—if the risk becomes a reality. *Life:* insurance against the risk of loss of life.

Property: falls into two general classifications: (1) to indemnify the insured in the event of a loss or damage to his own property; (2) to pay damages for which the insured is legally liable, the consequence of negligent acts that result in injuries to third parties. Major groupings are: marine, fire, casualty.

INTERSTATE COMMERCE COMMISSION: federal agency created to regulate surface transportation.

INVENTORY CONTROL: process of balancing incoming and outgoing stock to assure that adequate supplies are on hand with which to do business.

INVESTMENT BANKING COMPANY: firm engaged in marketing securities for issuing corporation.

INVOICE: itemized list of goods sent by seller to buyer. Usually gives prices, terms of sale, shipping dates, or any other information relevant to the sale.

JOB ANALYSIS: detailed study of the duties and actions required by a specific employment position.

JOB DESCRIPTION: detailed information portraying tasks involved in a specific job or position. Gives precise instructions as to what the person holding the job should do.

JOB SPECIFICATION: statement of qualifications necessary for employment in a certain position.

JOBBER: wholesale merchant.

JOINT COST: cost of basic raw material from which several products are made. The individual cost thereof is largely indeterminate. For example, the cost of a sirloin steak in contrast to the cost of an ox tail; the cost of the steer is a joint cost.

JOINT VENTURES: generally short-lived partnership with each partner sharing in cost and rewards of project. Common in research and investment banking.

JOURNAL: accounting record book in which transactions are recorded in chronological order.

LABOR TURNOVER: replacements in working force made necessary by workers leaving employment of company. Formula:

$$\frac{\text{number of terminations}}{\text{average number of employees}}$$

LAISSEZ FAIRE: (Fr.) "Leave it alone." Commonly used to signify noninterference by government in business.

LAYOFF: temporary nonemployment of worker, usually due to lack of available work.

The man has not been fired; he will have his job back again, if he wants it, when there is work for him to do.

LEDGER: an accounting book that contains all the various accounts used by the company—cash, accounts receivable, accounts payable, property,—and so on.

LEGAL ENTITY: a being or unit recognized by law, such as a person or a corporation, legally regarded as an artificial individual.

LETTER OF CREDIT: a bank's written guarantee of funds available for drafts written on it.

LIFE INSURANCE: a contract in which the insurance company agrees to pay the insured's beneficiary the agreed-upon sum in case of the insured's death during the life of the policy.

Credit insurance: term policy on life of a debtor in the amount of his debt, which will pay off the debt in event of his death. The creditor is the named beneficiary.

Endowment: face value of policy is paid to policy's owner at the end of a stipulated time period. Death benefits are paid if insured dies during period of policy's life.

Group insurance: usually written on group of employees of some organization. Rates are usually lower for the type of policy taken than any one person in that group could have bought individually. Sometimes employers contribute to premiums. The policy can take any form.

Key man: insurance on important men in a company payable to the company to compensate for the loss should they die.

Limited-payment life: premium is paid for a limited number of years but death benefits remain in force for life of insured.

Term: pays death benefits only during specified time of policy. No cash benefits. Cheapest form of pure protection.

Whole or ordinary life: a policy that combines the death benefits of term insurance with a savings program that creates cash values that can be used in many ways.

LINE OF CREDIT: short-term financing granted by bank up to a predetermined limit; firm borrows as needed up to the limit of credit.

LIQUIDITY: cash, or ease of converting to cash.

LISTED SECURITY: stock or bond approved for trading by stock exchange.

LLOYDS OF LONDON: an association of insurance underwriters willing to insure against all types of hazards.

LOCKOUT: refusal of employer to permit employees to work or enter premises.

LOGISTICS: operations concerned with the procurement, movement, and disposition of supplies and equipment. Originally used largely in the military, it is now being used in materials management systems.

MAIL-ORDER HOUSE: retail firm that conducts business by mail or by phone and generally offers its goods and services for sale from a catalogue or other printed materials.

MAINTENANCE-OF-MEMBERSHIP AGREEMENT: union arrangement stipulating that an employee-member must remain a union member for the duration of the contract as a requirement for continued employment.

MAKER: person who signs a note or check.

MANUFACTURERS' AGENT: an agent who generally operates on an extended contractual basis; often sells within an exclusive territory; handles noncompeting but related lines of goods; and possesses limited authority with regard to prices and terms of sale.

MARGIN: a practice of buying securities but using them as security for a loan to help pay for those same securities. In 1971, the margin requirement to buy stocks as set by the Federal Reserve Board of Governors was 70 percent: the buyer must pay 70 percent of the security price in cash. (Also called "margin account" or "trading on the margin.")

MARGIN CALL: a broker's demand upon a customer to put up money or securities to cover a margin purchase or when the customer's equity in a margin account declines below a minimum standard set by the Exchange or by the firm.

MARGINAL COST: actual additional out-of-pocket cost of producing one more unit.

MARGINAL EFFICIENCY OF CAPITAL: return obtained from investing one additional capital unit in a productive capacity.

MARGINAL PRODUCTIVITY: additional value produced by the last worker hired; in theory, that value should just equal his wages in order for the firm to maximize profit. The concept can also be applied to the last unit of any productive factor put into service, such as machines or plants.

MARGINAL REVENUE: the amount of increase in total revenue that results from the sale of one additional unit of production.

MARKDOWN: reduction in price (usually in connection with retail pricing).

MARKET ANALYSIS: a subdivision of marketing research that involves the measurement of the extent of a market and the determination of its characteristics.

MARKET POTENTIAL: a calculation of maximum possible sales opportunities for all sellers of a good or service during a stated period.

MARKET SEGMENTATION: dividing the market for a product into segments according to demographic, personality, or life styles of the people in each segment and then devising marketing plans for each segment to be solicited.

MARKETING: the performance of business activities that direct the flow of goods and services from producer to consumer or user; the delivery of a standard of living; the generation of revenue for a firm.

MARKETING MANAGEMENT: the planning, direction, and control of the entire marketing activity of a firm or division of a firm, including the formulation of marketing objectives, policies, programs, and strategy, and commonly embracing product development, organizing and staffing to carry out plans, supervising marketing operations, and controlling marketing performance.

MARKETING RESEARCH: the systematic gathering, recording, and analyzing of data about problems relating to the marketing of goods and services. Such research may be undertaken by impartial agencies or by business firms or their agents for the solution to their marketing problems.

MARKUP: amount added by merchant to the cost of a product to determine its retail price; usually expressed as a percentage of the *retail* price, not the cost base. A product costs the dealer $60; he prices it at $100. His markup on cost is 67 percent; his markup on retail is 40 percent.

MASSACHUSETTS TRUST: form of ownership wherein trustees accept funds from investors, who are issued trust shares. The trustees invest those funds, and distribute profits to investors. Most mutual funds use this form of organization.

MATERIALS CONTROL: inventory procedure used to keep management informed of quantities and location of all supplies, raw materials, and other goods in inventory.

MEDIATION: action by third party to effect an agreement, compromise, or reconcilliation between disputing parties.

MERCHANDISE MANAGER: executive in retail store who supervises activities of buyers, or department managers.

MERCHANT: a business unit that buys, takes title to, and resells merchandise.

MERCHANT WHOLESALER: wholesaler who takes title to goods he buys for resale to institutions that intend to either resell the goods as they are or process them in some way for resale.

MERGER: legal combination of two or more organizations into one, with the dominant one usually absorbing the smaller units.

MICROMOTION STUDY: time-study method employing movie camera focused on a worker and a clock simultaneously; the film is later analyzed by a trained engineer.

MIDDLEMAN: a business concern that specializes in performing operations or rendering services directly involved in the purchase and/or sale of goods in the process of their flow from producer to consumer. Middlemen are of two types: merchant and agent.

MINIATURIZATION: significant reduction in physical size of some functional product; e.g., integrated circuits are a miniaturization of printed circuits.

MINORITY SHAREHOLDER: technically, the owner of less than 50 percent of the common stock of a corporation. Actually, in most cases involving large corporations one can gain control with less than 50 percent ownership.

MIP: Monthly Investment Plan established by the New York Stock Exchange. A pay-as-you-go method of buying New York Stock Exchange listed shares on a regular payment plan for as little as $40 a month, or $40 every three months. Under MIP the investor buys stock by the dollars' worth. If the price advances, he gets fewer shares; if it declines, he gets more shares. He may discontinue purchases at any time without penalty. The only charge for purchases and sales is the usual commission for buying and selling, plus the regular odd lot dealer differential. The commission ranges from 6 percent on small transactions to slightly below 1½ percent on larger transactions.

MONETARY STANDARDS: the coinage or currency basis of a country.

MONOPOLISTIC COMPETITION: many sellers competing for share of market with differentiated products.

MONOPOLY: complete control of some factor by one party; usually applied to control over a product or a market.

MORTALITY TABLE: listing of statistics of ten million people from birth to age 99 showing death rate per thousand for each age group. It is used to compute life insurance premiums. The table is properly called the *Commissioners Standard Ordinary Mortality Table.*

MULTINATIONAL BUSINESS: firm that has a home base in one country and extensive foreign operations.

MUTUAL COMPANIES: firms owned by users of their particular service, such as life insurance or savings banks.

MUTUAL FUND: investment company that sells shares to investors and uses this money to buy securities in other companies. The owner of a mutual-fund share owns a portion of a large portfolio of securities.

NATIONAL LABOR RELATIONS BOARD (NLRB): group of five men, created by National Labor Relations Act, to administer that law.

NEGOTIABLE INSTRUMENT: form of business paper that can be transferred among parties as a money substitute, such as drafts, checks, and notes.

NEPOTISM: patronage or favoritism shown on the basis of family relationship.

NETWORK: in broadcasting, a group of transmitting stations linked together so the same program is carried by all; in management science, a visualization of a system showing inputs, transformations, and outputs.

NIELSEN RATINGS: research on the total audience for a single radio or TV program, plus the number of sets tuned in at the time of the commercial. A meter attached to the set records on tape when the set is on and every time a program is changed.

NONPRICE COMPETITION: vying for markets by means other than price, such as advertising, product differentiation, service, or convenience.

NO-PAR STOCK: common stock without a stated value.

NOTICE OF DISHONOR: notification to drawer and each endorser of a negotiable instrument that it is not being paid.

NUMERICAL CONTROL: automation of machine tools by coded tapes.

ODD LOT: any amount of stock less than the established 100-share unit used in trading on the stock exchanges; an additional charge of $\frac{1}{4}$ to $\frac{3}{4}$ of a point per share is made. An odd-lot sale may be delayed until other shares are offered to make an even unit.

ODD LOT BROKER: stock dealer who specializes in handling orders for less than 100 shares. He buys round lots of 100 shares and sells them off in smaller quantities.

OLIGOPOLY: a few firms, producing a standardized product, each of which has the ability to influence price.

ON-THE-JOB TRAINING: a program of teaching the employee while he is working.

OPERATIONS RESEARCH: the use of model building and applied math in the study of man-machine combinations: it has been paraphrased as "quantitative common sense" or the "application of science to decision making."

OPTIMUM: the best result or greatest degree of success obtained or obtainable under specific conditions.

ORDER BILL OF LADING: receipt from freight company to shipper which, when accompanied by draft, is presented to buyer's bank. Buyer pays draft, is given the order bill of lading, and can then claim the goods.

OVER-THE-COUNTER: securities that are not listed on recognized exchanges, such as the NYSE or AMSE, but for which limited markets are made by individual brokers.

PAR VALUE: stated value of share of common stock that the company must obtain in original sale; has no necessary relationship to true market value of the security.

PARTNERSHIP: an association of two or more persons as co-owners to carry on a business for profit. *Limited:* composed of one or more limited partners and one or more general partners. The liability of the limited partner is limited to his contribution to the capital of the partnership. A limited partnership may not be organized unless its organization is authorized by the statutes of the state. To organize a limited partnership, the parties must sign, swear to, and file with the designated official, a certificate that complies with the requirements of the statute. (Based on Uniform Limited Partnership Act.)

PATENT: government grant to an inventor giving exclusive right to an invention or process for 18 years.

PAYEE: person in whose favor a note or check is drawn; the party to whom the money is paid.

PAYROLL TAXES: various state and federal levies against wages, such as unemployment insurance, workmen's compensation, and social security (FOAS); does not include income taxes.

PERT: acronym for "Program Evaluation and Review Technique." It was first used to plan and control development of Polaris missile program. Procedure enables management to determine the development steps whose completion on time is critical to the overall program's completion on schedule. This approach uses judgmental estimates of the completion time for each step, enabling the analyst to make forecasts of total program completion time and to control deviations from planned performance.

PIGGYBACK FREIGHT: shipping loaded truck trailer by rail aboard flatcars.

PORTABLE PENSION: benefits that can be transferred by a worker to a new place of employment.

PORTFOLIO: total securities held by an investor.

PREFERENTIAL SHOP: union-management agreement to give union members special consideration in hiring and layoffs.

PREFERRED STOCK: a corporate security that has preference over common stock in receiving dividends and as to assets. Its dividend is usually stated as fixed percentage of par value or as a stipulated sum each year, but the company has no legal liability to pay it if the company has not earned the money to pay it.

Cumulative: if the dividend is skipped, it accumulates as a backlog that must be paid before common stockholders receive dividends.

Noncumulative: if the dividend is missed, it is gone forever.

Participating: can enjoy additional earnings after the common stockholders are paid a stated amount.

Nonparticipating: cannot receive any dividends other than the fixed amount offered.

Voting: has voting privileges.

PREMIUM: payment on insurance policy by purchaser. *Bond premium:* amount by which the price exceeds the bond's face value.

PRICE: the sum of money (or equivalent) for which something is bought or sold. While tradition held that it was the amount paid by the buyer, the government now leans to the view that it is the amount received by the seller at his plant—the price paid by the buyer minus transportation costs.

PRICE DISCRIMINATION: charging different prices for the same (or similar) products in the same quantities to different buyers at the same level of distribution.

PRICE LEADER: a firm whose pricing behavior is followed by other companies in the same industry; a product whose price has been reduced to attract people into a store to buy other things. If the price is below cost, then it is called a "loss leader."

PRICE LINE: a series of predetermined levels at which merchandise is to be sold, such as $1.95–$3.95–$5.95, with no goods offered for sale at any other level. Designed to simplify pricing for the dealer and buying for the customer.

PRIVATE BRAND: brand owned by merchant or agent, as distinguished from those owned by manufacturers or producers.

PROBABILITY: the likelihood that a particular event will occur.

PRODUCT DIFFERENTIATION: a marketing strategy that depends upon the creation and promotion of product differences. The differences may be real or imagined.

PRODUCT LINE: a group of products that are closely related because they either satisfy a class of need, are used together, are sold to the same customer groups, are marketed through the same type of outlets, or fall within given price ranges.

PRODUCT MIX: the composite of products offered for sale by a firm or a business unit.

PRODUCTION CONTROL: procedure for coordinating all elements of a production process to achieve the efficiency and coordination necessary for good return.

PRODUCTS LIABILITY INSURANCE: policy designed to protect the holder from claims made by the public for real or fancied injuries received while using the insured's facilities or products.

PROGRAMMER: person who instructs a computer how to handle given data.

PROMISSORY NOTE: written negotiable instrument in which the maker promises to pay to the named party a definite sum on a definite date.

PROPERTY: belongings, possessions.

Personal: movable belongings.

Real: land, buildings, immovables.

Intangible: stocks, bonds, money, accounts.

PROSPECTUS: condensed version of registration (for stock sales) information given to prospective purchasers of new security issues.

PROTECTIVE TARIFF: tax levied on imported goods to increase the price to a level at which domestic producers can compete with them.

PROXY: written authorization for another person to exercise your vote.

PUBLIC UTILITY: regulated private industry; an approved monopoly, usually a service such as electric power or telephone.

PUBLIC WAREHOUSE: independent storage company's facility. It is a business that rents storage space.

PUBLICITY: nonpersonal stimulation of demand for a product, service, or business unit by the planting of commercially significant news about it in a printed or broadcast medium that is not paid for by a sponsor.

PURCHASE ORDER: formal specification sheet issued by the buyer to the supplier to secure goods or services.

PURCHASE REQUISITION: notification to purchasing department of need to buy specific items.

RACK JOBBER: a wholesaling business unit that markets specialized lines of merchandise to certain types of retail stores and provides the special services of selective brand and item merchandising and the arrangement, maintenance, and stocking of display racks.

RECESSION: decline in business activity.

RECIPROCAL BUYING: purchasing from one's customers.

REDISCOUNT RATE: interest rate charged bank by Federal Reserve Bank for discounting eligible paper.

REFEREE: representative appointed by a judge to handle details of a bankruptcy case.

REFUNDING: practice of issuing new bonds to acquire cash to retire previous security issue. Sometimes referred to as "rolling over" a bond issue.

REGISTRATION STATEMENT: detailed, extensive financial and operating data sheet filed with S.E.C. by a company wishing to issue securities. Prospectus is a condensed form of this statement.

RESALE PRICE MAINTENANCE: control by a supplier of the selling prices of his branded goods at subsequent stages of distribution by means of contractual agreement under fair trade laws or other devices.

RESIDENT BUYING OFFICE: purchasing facility in buying centers maintained and staffed by distant retailers for purpose of convenient buying.

RETAILING: selling to the ultimate consumer.

REVENUE TARIFF: tax intended to generate cash for government.

RIGHT OF EMINENT DOMAIN: power of government to seize private property by paying a fair price, often determined by a court.

RIGHT-TO-WORK LAWS: state laws protecting the right of workers to continue employment without union membership.

RIGHTS: certain privileges to buy stock. When a company wants to raise more funds by issuing additional securities, it may give its stockholders the opportunity, ahead of others, to buy these new securities in proportion to the number of shares each stockholder owns: this privilege is called a right. Because this additional stock is usually offered to stockholders below the current market price, rights ordinarily have a market value of their own and are actively traded. In most cases these rights must be exercised within a relatively short period of time. Failure to exercise or sell them may result in an actual loss to the holder.

ROUND LOTS: one-hundred-share units of stock.

SALES BUDGET: the part of the marketing budget that is concerned with planned dollar sales and planned costs of personal selling during a specified future period.

SALES FINANCE COMPANY: firm that purchases installment contracts from dealers (such as GMAC, CCC, CIT).

SALES MANAGEMENT: planning, direction, and control of the personal selling activities of a business unit, including recruiting, selecting, training, equipping, assigning, routing, supervising, paying, and motivating as these tasks apply to the personal sales force.

SALES PROMOTION: in a specific sense, those marketing activities other than personal selling, advertising, and publicity that stimulate consumer purchasing and dealer effectiveness, such as displays, shows and exhibitions, demonstrations, and various nonrecurrent selling efforts not in the ordinary routine. In retailing, it includes all methods of stimulating customer purchasing, including personal selling, advertising, and publicity.

SALES QUOTA: a projected volume of sales assigned to a marketing unit for use in the management of sales efforts. It applies to a specified period and may be expressed in dollars or in physical units.

SAVINGS AND LOAN ASSOCIATIONS: mutual companies (88 percent) or stock (12 percent) for purpose of accepting deposits and lending funds (usually for building homes).

SCHEDULING: creating timetables to govern work, processes, arrival of purchased goods, or the delivery of finished goods.

SCRAMBLED MERCHANDISING: the carrying of a wide line of unrelated merchandise by a retailer.

SEALED BIDS: secret written offers to supply a needed item at a specific price.

S.E.C.: the Securities and Exchange Commission, established by Congress to monitor stock market practices and corporation affairs for the protection of the investor. The S.E.C. administers the Securities Act of 1933, the Securities Exchange Act of 1934, the Trust Indenture Act, the Investment Company Act, the Investment Advisers Act, and the Public Utility Holding Company Act.

SECRET PARTNER: one who is active in the affairs of the partnership but who is unknown to the general public.

SENIORITY: priority or status obtained as a result of length of service.

SERVICE INDUSTRY: economic segment of society that produces help, aid, or performance of work or duties for another; e.g., doctors, lawyers, dry cleaners, golf pros.

SERVICE RETAILER: sells help, not goods—such outlets as dry cleaners, barbershops, bowling alleys, TV repairmen.

SERVOMECHANISM: electronic control system using low-energy signal to activate and control hydraulic, pneumatic, or other types of control mechanisms.

SEVERANCE PAY: amount given over and above wages that are due at termination of employment.

SEVERANCE TAX: state tax levied on timber cut, minerals mined, or oil pumped.

SHOPPING GOODS: consumer goods that the customer in the process of selection and purchase characteristically compares on such bases as suitability, quality, price, and style. Examples: millinery, furniture, shoes, automobiles, and major appliances.

SHORT SALE: sale for future delivery of something not owned. An individual who believes that a stock will decline and sells shares of this stock although he does not own any has made what is commonly called a short sale. For example; you may instruct your broker to sell short 200 shares of XYZ. Your broker will borrow the stock so that he can deliver the 200 shares to the buyer. The money value of the shares borrowed is deposited by your broker with the lender. Sooner or later you must cover your short sale by buying the same amount of stock you borrowed for return to the lender. If you are able to buy XYZ at a lower price than you sold it, your profit is the difference between the two prices (not counting commissions and taxes). But if you have to pay more for the stock than the price you received, that is the amount of your loss. Federal regulations and Stock Exchange regulations govern and limit the conditions under which a short sale may be made on a national securities exchange.

SIGHT DRAFT: a written order issued by the drawer to the drawee to pay to a third party (the payee) a sum of money either on sight or on demand.

SILENT PARTNER: a partner who plays no active role even though he may be known to the public as a partner.

SINGLE-LINE STORE: small independent outlet that carries only one type of goods, such as drug, food, hardware, millinery.

SOLDIERING ON THE JOB: deliberate slowdown of work pace by laborers to impede production.

SOLE PROPRIETORSHIP: a business firm owned by only one person and operated for his profit.

SPECIALIST: a member of the Exchange who assumes two major responsibilities: First, to maintain an orderly market, insofar as practicable, in the stock in which he is registered as a specialist. The specialist must be prepared to buy or sell for his own account, to a reasonable extent, when there is a temporary disparity between supply and demand. Second, the specialist acts as a broker's broker. When a commission broker on the Exchange floor receives a limit order to buy, for say, an $80 stock then selling at $90, he cannot wait at that particular post where the stock is traded until the price reaches the specified level; thus, he will leave the order with the specialist, who will try to execute it in the market if and when the stock declines to that specified price. At all times the specialist must put his customers' interests above his own. There are nearly 400 specialists on the New York Stock Exchange alone.

SPECIALTY GOODS: consumer goods having unique characteristics and/or brand identification for which a significant group of buyers are habitually willing to make a special purchasing effort, such as fancy foods, hi-fi and stereo components, sporting equipment, cameras, men's suits.

SPECIALTY STORE: retail outlet carrying a large selection in limited merchandise lines; sometimes departmentalized.

SPECIALTY WHOLESALER: middleman who deals in a limited line of goods.

SPECULATIVE PURCHASING: buying in larger than normal quantities in anticipation of a price rise.

SPECULATOR: a man who believes he knows the outcome of a future event and acts on it today.

SPIN-OFF: reorganization process of a corporation whereby stock of a division or subsidiary is transferred to shareholders of parent company without exchange; may eliminate incompatible businesses and reduce corporate taxes.

SPONSOR SYSTEM: personnel training program whereby older employee teaches newly hired worker the details of the job.

STATISTICAL INFERENCE: the process by which the statistician makes assertions about the underlying parameters of some population of interest based on sample data.

STATUS: individual's rank in the total social system (or subsystem) as perceived by other members of the system. The status of an individual is partially determined by the status of the social group (class) to which he belongs but also partially by his personal characteristics. Personal characteristics that affect the status of an individual include (1) his rank within the social class and (2) special contributions to society.

STEWARD: a union representative selected from the employee membership.

STOCK RIGHT: legal right of a stockholder to buy additional shares within a stipulated time and at a designated price.

STOCK SPLIT: a division of the outstanding shares of a corporation into a larger number of shares. A 2-for-1 split by a company with 2 million shares outstanding would result in 4 million shares outstanding. A holder of 100 shares before the 2-for-1 split would have 200 shares after the stock split, although his proportionate equity in the company would remain the same, since 100 parts of 2 million are equivalent to 200 parts of 4 million. Ordinarily splits must be voted by directors and approved by shareholders.

STOCK TURNOVER RATIO: the number of times during a given period in which a business sells its entire stock inventory.

STOP ORDER: an order to buy or sell a stock at a specific price. As soon as the price of the stock reaches or sells through this price it becomes a market order and is executed. A stop order may be used to limit a possible loss to a certain amount. Since it becomes a market order when the stop price is reached, there is no certainty that it will be executed at exactly that price. Stop orders are often disallowed by the Stock Exchange when their execution might result in a serious unchecked decline or rise in a security.

STOP PAYMENT: command to a bank to refuse to honor a check written on an account.

STRIKE: refusal of employees to report to work until management agrees to meet certain of their demands.

Jurisdictional: strike between competing unions to force employer recognition of one or the other.

Sitdown: employees appear, but refuse to work or leave the premises.

Wildcat or outlaw: strike without consent of union or in violation of a contract.

SUBSIDY: financial assistance or its equivalent paid to a business by the government to induce, assist, or otherwise stimulate the business to help make an uneconomic operation profitable.

SUPERETTE: small self-service retail grocery outlet.

SURETY BOND: insurance to protect against loss incurred by nonperformance of contract or by dishonesty.

SYNERGISM: the interaction of factors in an activity so as to yield aggregate effects that are beyond the limits anticipated from simply combining individual effects; the creation of additional values through the interaction of two economic institutions working in combination.

SYSTEM: the systems concept of business sees society as one huge system comprised of millions of subsystems of which the business firm is but one small subsystem competing in a slightly larger system, its industry.

SYSTEMS ANALYSIS: the selection of elements, relationships, and procedures to achieve a specific purpose.

SYSTEMS SIMULATION: a set of techniques for modeling the mechanism and output of some process or man-machine combination by testing the system on paper or in a computer. This permits experimentation at a much lower cost and in much less time and risk than would otherwise be possible.

TARIFF: a schedule or system of duties levied by the federal government on importation of goods; also, transportation rates.

TENANCY IN COMMON: ownership of real property in which each owner has title to an undivided share of the property. If one owner dies, his interest passes to his heir, not to the surviving owner or owners of the estate.

TERM LOAN: credit in the form of a loan ranging from one to ten years.

TIME DRAFT: a bill of exchange constituting a written order to pay a third party a certain amount of money on a designated future date as shown on the instrument.

TIME SERIES: a set of observations over time.

Cyclical fluctuations: variations caused by the business cycle.

Irregular variations: caused by unpredictable factors.

Seasonal variations: month-by-month change due to the variations in buying activity during the year.

Secular trends: long-term factors (such as population).

TRADE BARRIER: legal device to restrict flow of goods such as tariffs, import quotas, embargoes, exchange controls, and travel restrictions.

TRADE DISCOUNT: reduction in price granted to each distribution level; sometimes called "functional discount."

TRADEMARK: a brand or part of a brand that is given legal protection because it is capable of exclusive appropriation; because it is used in a manner sufficiently fanciful, distinctive, and arbitrary; because it is affixed to the product when sold; or because it otherwise satisfies the requirements set up by law.

TRADE-OFF: term used in value theory to denote the amount of some objective a decision maker is willing to give up to achieve a given level of some other desired outcome, when both levels cannot be obtained simultaneously.

TRADING AREA: a district whose size is determined by boundaries within which it is economical in terms of volume and cost for a marketing unit or group to sell and/or deliver.

TRAFFIC MANAGEMENT: planning, selection, and direction of all means and methods of transportation involved in the movement of goods in the marketing process.

TRANSFER AGENT: party who records changes in ownership of stock.

TREASURY STOCK: stock repurchased by a company after it was issued. While held by the company it has no vote and receives no dividends. It may be held in the company's treasury indefinitely, reissued to the public, or retired.

TRUST: a combination of businesses operated under trust agreements by trustees for the benefit of the members; an organization for holding the property of one person for the benefit of another.

TRUST COMPANY: firm that manages, for individuals or other firms, estates and financial holdings that are placed in trust with it.

TRUSTEE: person in whom property is vested in trust for another.

ULTRA VIRES ACT: an act of a corporation that is beyond the powers conferred upon the corporation.

UNEMPLOYMENT BENEFITS: money paid to certain qualified persons who are involuntarily out of work.

Supplementary: payments from employers to eligible laid-off workers to augment federal and state unemployment benefits.

UNFAIR LABOR PRACTICES: illegal behavior and actions by either labor or management.

UNFAIR PRACTICES ACTS: state laws to establish minimum resale prices—usually cost plus 6 percent unless goods are in distress. Such laws are generally not enforced.

UNIFORM CODES: a movement by the American Bar Association to standardize legislation among the 50 states concerning civil law. They presently cover: Partnership, Sales, Commercial Code, Negotiable Instruments.

USURY: taking more interest than the law allows upon a loan or for forbearance of a debt. Illegal interest; interest in excess of the rate allowed by law.

UNEMPLOYMENT: number of people who are able and willing to take work but are unable to find it.

Frictional: unemployment caused by such things as people being between jobs or not knowing of jobs that are open.

Structural: unemployment caused by a change in the basic structure of society, industry, or technology.

Seasonal: unemployment caused by people's being unable to work owing to seasonal conditions, such as in the agricultural and construction industries.

Appendix C
Statistical Methods

Although the term statistics has a number of definitions, it basically relates to meaningful numbers; therefore meaningful numbers are statistics. The number fifty in itself is not a statistic because it does not have a distinct meaning other than that it is an integer composed of the digits five and zero. The following statement uses the term fifty so that it suddenly becomes a statistic because it has specific meaning attached to it: "The sales office of the Chicago Elevator Company sold fifty elevators last month." This use of the number fifty makes it a statistic because it is presented in such a manner that it has distinct meaning to anyone who happens to be interested in the sales level of the Chicago Elevator Company. Business finds many meaningful numbers (statistics) that are helpful in making decisions and solving problems.

Some of the statistics used by firms to make decisions may relate to factors *within* the firm such as the number of employees, production rates, profit rates, employee turnover rates, and other statistics or meaningful numbers. Other factors *outside* the firm may be of interest to management such as various demographic characteristics of the population. An example of this would be the number of males or teenagers within a specific geographic area or amounts of snowfall in specific areas (especially if you manufacture snowplows). A businessman contemplates marketing a new line of automatic garage door openers. He might like to know several statistics: How many garage door openers were sold last year? How many garage doors will be installed this year?

Statistics may not be of any assistance to a problem solver until he is able to analyze such numbers so that they have more meaning for him. A list of the ages of 100 employees does little more than provide a page filled with numbers. These ages should be grouped into a small number of age ranges, represented by an appropriate average of the numbers, or summarized in some other way. While statistics are meaningful numbers they can be used to derive other more meaningful numbers. Thus statistical analysis is a simplifying process by which information is condensed and made easier to understand and use.

WHERE DO WE FIND STATISTICS?

Business statistics are derived from either internal or external sources. *Internal* sources of information are those that exist within the organization. For a business firm, production rates and sales statistics are considered internal data. For the American Red Cross, the number of packages delivered to soldiers or the number of disasters serviced would be internal data. Any organization has internal statistics that may be used as needed.

External sources of information are those that are outside of the organization. Business firms may seek information about the general population or the economy of certain regions from either private or governmental sources. External data can be gathered from either primary or secondary sources. The *primary* source gathers statistics and publishes them. A *secondary* source of data publishes statistics another organization has gathered. When the United States Department of Labor gathers statistics on unemployment rates and publishes them, this is a primary source of statistics on unemployment. If you see such unemployment figures in the newspaper, you have a choice of:

1. Using the statistics published in the newspaper as a secondary source.
2. Contacting the Department of Labor for the same statistics as a primary source.

It may seem unnecessary to follow the second choice when you already have the figures in the newspaper, but the newspaper may have a typographical error of which you are not aware. Printing errors are a disadvantage when using secondary sources as the chance of errors increases whenever information is republished. It is also possible that the newspaper only published a part of the unemployment statistics gathered by the Department of Labor. Some of the omitted statistics may have seemed unimportant to the newspaper but may contain exactly the detailed data that you need. Almost without exception secondary sources of information condense the primary data bringing out only the salient factors. Secondary sources tend to be easy to find and are usually inexpensive to acquire and use. Since any good secondary source will indicate *where* it acquired the information, secondary sources are frequently used as means to locate valuable primary sources. Good researchers always try to get the primary sources.

METHODS OF GATHERING STATISTICS

Internal and external information can be gathered by alternative methods. If you were gathering information regarding the ages of professors on your campus you might contact all professors to determine their age and then begin to analyze an impressive list of meaningful numbers. Secondly you might consult only a small number of the faculty and trust that it is representative. In the first case you conducted a *census*, while in the second you used a *sample* technique.

Census vs. Sample

Use of a census indicates that the data gatherer is contacting or examining all elements that are under study. It may mean testing *all* tires for defects in a tire factory, road-testing *all* cars in an auto factory, testing *all* college students on their political awareness or questioning *all* holders of driver's licenses on their style preferences in automobiles. Use of a sample technique calls for examining or contacting a selected few elements for study. In each of the above investigations of tires, cars, students and drivers a sample could have been used, and the researcher would then test *some* tires, test *some* cars, test *some* students or question *some* drivers. A sample could be used to estimate how good all tires produced by a tire manufacturer are, based on a close inspection of a few tires. If 1 percent of the sample of tires had serious defects we would conclude that about 1 percent of *all* tires produced had serious defects. A tire producer must decide whether the 1 percent level of defects is acceptable or unacceptable and take any necessary action in his plant to reduce defects in the future.

The United States completes a full census of the population every ten years. The 1970 census was revolutionary in that it attempted to reduce the time element by contacting over 200 million people through the use of mail questionnaires rather than by the previous method of personal interviews. All citizens were instructed to complete and mail their census questionnaire by midnight of April 1, 1970. In spite of this simplified method it was months before any substantive information could be drawn from the 1970 United States Census. Recording, analyzing and checking this information for 200 million people was a massive undertaking, even with the aid of computers. In January of 1971, eight months after the census, many questions were unanswered that will be eventually solved when the census data of April 1970 is completely analyzed.

Difficulties of a Census

If the size of the group being studied is very large, a census may take too long to complete and be too costly. Contacting all eligible voters in the states of California, Illinois, and Florida might be desirable when predicting political attitudes, but it would be time consuming and costly. The study would be completed long after the election for which it was being done.

Sometimes a census is impossible. Testing all tires to determine the number of miles they will last before a blow-out occurs would not be recommended for a tire producer as he would then know a great deal about the quality of his tires but would have none left to sell. He should test a small sample of his tires, assuming them to be representative of those tires he is producing.

A census may also be undesirable if all subjects to be interviewed are not easily accessible. A census of all marijuana users would be impossible.

Selecting a Sample

Samples are selected on either a probability or nonprobability basis. In a probability sample the likelihood that any element in the group studied will be included in the sample is known and equal. If 1000 things are being studied by examining a sample of 100 elements (note that a census would examine all 1000 items), each item could be assigned a number, and 100 such numbers could then be drawn from a hat to determine the sample group. It should be obvious that each element has one chance in ten of being drawn for the sample. Sometimes this is called a *random sample*.

This same sample may be selected on a nonprobability basis by selecting the first 100 elements, the last 100 elements, every tenth item beginning with number 1, or any similar method. In these cases each element does not have a known or equal probability of being included in the sample. Item number 100 must be included in the first and third sample methods, but can't possibly be included in the second since it is not one of the last 100 elements. Item 123 has no chance of being included in any of these samples. The probability sample let elements 100 and 123 have equal and known chances of being included, (1 in 10), but the suggested nonprobability samples gave item 123 no chances of selection and item 100 a perfect chance in the first and third methods yet no chance in the second sample selection process. While a nonprobability sample may bias the elements included, it can give good results in a study and has advantages for the data gatherer since it is selected systematically and may be quite convenient for the researcher to use.

There are many reasons for and justifications for the use of either of these two techniques of selecting samples. A detailed course in statistics will provide you with a background in the specifics of selecting samples on a probability or nonprobability basis.

STATISTICAL ANALYSIS

Having assembled a quantity of detailed information from a sample or census, it must be analyzed and made more meaningful. One method is to provide a picture of the data by grouping it into categories that enable you to prepare charts or graphs of the information. Another approach is to summarize it with some standard quantitative measures such as averages or measures of variation.

Charts and Graphs

Data is frequently summarized and represented in graphic form by preparing a line-chart, bar-chart, pie-chart, or pictograph. Examples of these charts are presented in Figure 1. Figure 2 contains a graph with suggestions for preparing good charts and graphs.

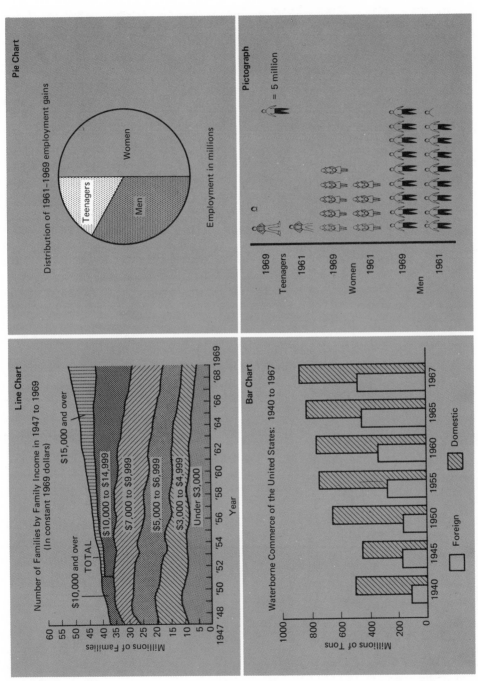

FIGURE 1: Examples of Graphic Presentation of Data.

FIGURE 2: Vacancy Trends in Rental and Homeowner Housing: 1956 to 1969

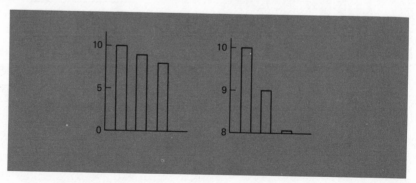

SOURCE: Federal Housing Administration.

Characteristics of a Good Chart

1. Clear and complete title. Shows time period of data if relevant.
2. Clear and complete labels of horizontal and vertical axes.
3. Clear labels of lines plotted, bars or symbols.
4. Source or sources of information in the diagram indicated in notes at the bottom of the figure.
5. Scale on the vertical axis starts with 0 avoiding distortion in the chart caused by a shortened vertical scale.

   Consider the following bar charts that plot the *same* data:

Chart B shows a more radical change by the size of its bars since its scale starts at 8 rather than 0.

STATISTICAL METHODS

At this stage of your business career it will be helpful for you to learn about a few of the more basic statistical techniques that are widely used in business. More sophisticated statistical methodology will be given to you in separate courses in the later stages of your studies.

Raw Data

First, the businessman encounters what is called *raw data,* information just as he finds it wherever that may be. For illustrative purposes, we shall process the test scores from a hypothetical class. The raw data would be the scores as they appear on the exam papers. The professor first processes them by entering them in the book:

Axe	8	Ham	9	Olson	10
Bull	9	Inn	7	Penny	6
Coy	7	Joy	8	Quick	7
Doll	8	Kute	7	Rope	9
Eager	9	Lam	7	Sully	8
Fox	10	Moon	8	Toll	8
Golly	6	Nilly	5	Upson	5

But in this alphabetical form the test scores would still be considered raw data as we have done nothing to them statistically. The first statistical step would be to array them.

Array

An array arranges all scores in order from high to low:

10	8	7
10	8	7
9	8	7
9	8	6
9	8	6
9	7	5
8	7	5

From the array we can begin statistical processing.

Range

The range refers to the high and low number of a statistical series. In this case the range is 5 to 10 as shown above in the array.

Number (N)

In all statistical calculations, the number of items in the statistical universe is referred to as "N". In this case N equals 21.

Summation (ΣX)

Very early in most statistical calculations, it is necessary to add the scores. This is referred to symbolically as summation $X(\Sigma X)$ which in this case is 161.

Note

> It is most important for you to pay careful attention as to the exact size of all statistical symbols for each has its own meaning. For example, summation with a large X (ΣX) indicates a summation of raw data whereas summation with a small x (Σx) refers to an entirely different summation, one which we will discuss presently.

Measures of Central Tendency

Mode (Mo.) The mode of a statistical array is the most frequently occurring number which in this case is 8. You will notice that the mode in this case is the same as the median; however, this does not necessarily have to be for in other instances it may differ.

Median (Md.) This is a relatively easy task to determine as the median is the score in the middle of the range—in this case it is 8. In this instance it is the 11th item out of 21 scores. Had there been only 20 scores, then we would have split the differences between the 10th and 11th scores in the array.

Arithmetic Mean ($\overline{X}$) The arithmetic mean, more popularly referred to as the arithmetic average, or just plain average, is obtained by dividing the summation (ΣX) by N as shown below:

$$\overline{X} = \frac{\Sigma X}{N} = \frac{161}{21} = 7.66$$

The reason we call this statistical measure the mean rather than the average is that both the median and mode are also forms of averages so using the word average leaves one in doubt as to exactly what statistical method has been used.

Statisticians prefer the arithmetic mean to the mode and median for it is used extensively in more sophisticated mathematical processing of the data whereas the mode and median have no further mathematical applications.

All of these calculations are called *measures of central tendency,* for they have been developed to facilitate communicating something of the nature of the raw data from which they have been computed. They are a form of shorthand which results in a better understanding of the whole body of data. It would be most cumbersome to have to reply to a student asking about the test scores by giving him the entire array. Rather the professor could say, "They ranged from five to ten with a mean of 7.66 and a mode and median of 8." Now the student who scored 10 knows exactly where he stands in relationship to the class. See Figure 3 for illustration of these measures.

Measures of Dispersion

So far we have discussed statistical symbols which describe the central tendency of the raw data, but know little of the distribution of the data around the mean. You might be told that the mean score on one test was 75 and on another it was 80, but the characteristics of the distribution of scores on those two tests may be startlingly

FIGURE 3: Processing the Raw Data to Determine the Measures of Central Tendency.

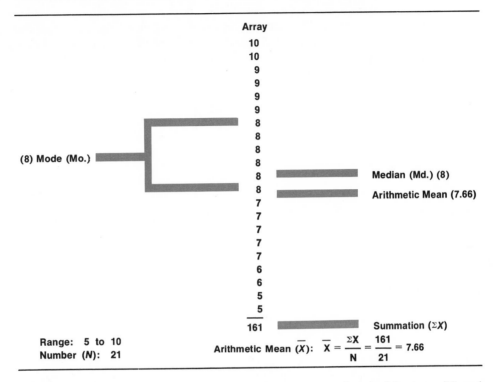

different. Perhaps all of the scores on the first test were bunched between 70 and 80 whereas the scores on the second test were spread rather evenly between 60 and 100. So when given a measure of central tendency alone one knows nothing of the distribution of the data around that central tendency.

The simplest measures of dispersion around the central tendency are Quartiles, Deciles and Percentiles.

Quartile A quartile is, as its name suggests, 25% of the data. The lowest quartile would be the bottom 25% of the scores, the third quartile would be those scores between the lowest quartile and the median which, you will recall, represents the 50/50 dividing point of the data. The top quartile is the highest 25% of the scores and the second quartile would be those scores from the median to the top quartile.

Deciles Deciles are simply blocks of data which use the same approach as quartiles, but break the universe into segments of 10%.

Percentiles Percentiles take the same approach to a more refined degree. A percentile is 1% of the scores. For example, a person ranking in the 5th percentile of his graduating class would be one below whom 95% of the students rank and above whom 4% of the students rank.

Standard Deviation (SD or σ)   For many mathematical reasons, statisticians strongly prefer to calculate the standard deviation to ascertain the dispersion of data around the mean. The standard deviation is calculated by taking the difference between each score and the arithmetic mean, squaring it, summating it, dividing by N, and taking the square root of the result as shown by the formula below:

$$SD = \sqrt{\frac{\Sigma x^2}{N}}$$

Since computing x^2 is extremely laborious, mathematicians have evolved a shortcut:

$$\Sigma x^2 = \Sigma X^2 - \Sigma XX$$

The calculation of this formula is shown below:

ΣX	ΣX^2
10	100
10	100
9	81
9	81
9	81
9	81
8	64
8	64
8	64
8	64
8	64
8	64
7	49
7	49
7	49
7	49
7	49
6	36
6	36
5	25
5	25
161 = ΣX	1275 = ΣX^2 $\overline{X} = 7.66$

$$SD = \sqrt{\frac{\Sigma x^2}{N}}$$

$$= \sqrt{\frac{\Sigma X^2 - \Sigma XX}{N}}$$

$$= \sqrt{\frac{1275 - 161\,(7.66)}{21}}$$

$$= \sqrt{\frac{41.74}{21}}$$

$$= \sqrt{1.98}   = \text{Standard Deviation} = 1.40$$

Now it can be said of the test scores that the arithmetic mean is 7.66 with a standard deviation of 1.4. You say, "So what! What's 1.4 ?" This gets us into a rather deep bit of statistical theory which you will study later in your academic career, but which we will expose you to only briefly at this point. The 1.4 is a measure used in reference to data contained in the so-called *bell curve*.

A great deal of statistical theory and practice is based upon the assumption (surprisingly valid in most cases) that data is distributed around the mean in the bell curve as shown in Figure 4.

FIGURE 4: Bell Curve.

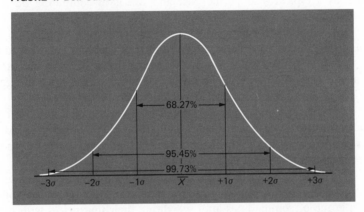

It seems to be a basic law of nature that phenomena are grouped roughly around the mean in such a fashion with extreme scores tailing off drastically as shown. Admittedly, there are instances in which one encounters data that differs significantly in its distribution around the mean and in which more sophisticated statistical techniques must be used.

The standard deviation relates the percentage of scores that will be found within the range. For example, in our case 68% of the scores will lie within the mean plus or minus one standard deviation or:

7.7 plus or minus 1.4 or between 5.3 and 9.1

Technically, 95% of all scores will lie within plus or minus two standard deviations of the mean. Thus, when one knows the mean and the standard deviation of a body of data, he can determine where the bulk of the observations lie.

The computer has greatly simplified the processing of large amounts of raw data.

PRICE INDEXES

Another statistical technique frequently used in the field of business involves the calculation of price indexes. A price index is a calculated value derived by comparing one current price with another comparable price that occurred in the past. It shows the current price as a percent of the previous price. An index number 110 means that the current price is 110 percent of the previous price, or there has been a 10 percent price increase since the previous period.

If the price of a dozen eggs was forty cents in 1960 and a comparable price for a dozen eggs in 1970 was fifty cents, a clear view of the price change is provided by calculating an index number for egg prices. In doing this we compare the price of fifty cents for the last year with forty cents for the first year through a division operation:

$$\frac{.50}{.40} \times 100 = 125.0$$

The first year is the *base year*, meaning that all prices of eggs studied would be compared to that year. When finding index numbers one must select a base point such as a typical year in the past and use it in computing *all* index numbers for that series.

Note that the above division operation was multiplied by 100 merely to move the decimal point two places to the right thus enabling you to read the index number as 125.0. If you consider the mathematical operation, you find it is possible to say that the price of eggs in 1970 was 125 percent of the price of eggs in 1960 or that prices of eggs have increased 25 percent since 1960.

This egg index number would be more useful if you had computed the price index for eggs in each year between 1960 and 1970. This list of index numbers would let you observe the *rate* at which prices were increasing *yearly* by observing the percentage increases as we did in the first case.

The above price index for eggs is a simple price index as it considers only the price for one commodity. A more typical index considers the total price effect of a group of commodities after weighting their unit prices with the quantity of each used. A food index may be desired to see the total effect of price changes for selected food items on a family's budget. Rather than studying only eggs, the following food items may seem important to review: bread, steak, tomato soup, potatoes, and eggs. The index for these items would be found by summing their prices currently and comparing this to the price for these items in a base year. The index would be useless unless the prices for the items were affected by the quantities of these goods used in a day, a week, a month or some similar period. Consuming one dozen eggs would hardly be comparable to consuming one loaf of bread or one pound of potatoes. It would be more realistic to consider one dozen eggs, four loaves of bread, and five pounds of potatoes, hence we have quantities of these products to use as weights in summing the prices to compute an overall price index. Presented below are the commodities, their unit prices and the quantities that could be used as weights in finding their price index.

COMMODITY	UNIT PRICE	QUANTITY CONSUMED (WEIGHT)	PRICE OF QUANTITY CONSUMED
Bread	25¢ per loaf	4 loaves	$1.00
Steak	$1.00 per pound	2 pounds	2.00
Tomato Soup	20¢ per can	1 can	.20
Potatoes	10¢ per pound	5 pounds	.50
Eggs	50¢ per dozen	1 dozen	.50
			$4.20

Suppose the above prices are for a specific week in 1971 and we wish to compare prices paid today with those of the year 1960. In this case we have decided on 1960 as our base period. Assume that the price for the above goods in the same quantities cost $3.15 in 1960. The price index for these food items should be:

$$\frac{\$4.20}{\$3.15} \times 100 = 133.3$$

The food price index calculated could be expanded to include prices of all goods purchased by a family by including such items as gasoline, insurance premiums, rent, movie tickets, and so on. Including all items purchased by the normal family would yield an index number that could be compared to the family's income to see whether its income was increasing as rapidly as were the prices it pays.

A very common index number is the *Consumer Price Index*. This number is derived by continually comparing the total price for a list of commodities that are consumed by the typical urban wage earner with the price for these identical goods in an established base year. It is calculated monthly by the United States Bureau of Labor Statistics, which checks current prices for the list of goods and services studied in this index. If the base year for the consumer price index is 1957–1959 and the current price index is 148, we can observe that general prices have increased 48 percent since the 1957–1959 period. Figure 5 shows movements of the general price level over recent years as measured by the consumer price index. These index numbers use an average of 1957–1959 prices for the subject commodities as their base.

FIGURE 5: Consumer Price Indexes, Commodities and Services.

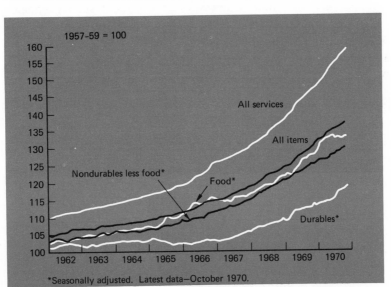

SOURCE: Bureau of Labor Statistics.

The consumer price index may oversimplify analysis of price movements for the following reasons:

1. The weights used are assigned for the typical urban wage earner and are not necessarily correct for *all* who use the index.
2. The general CPI includes many goods and service prices so that it may not be detailed enough to show movements in specific prices.
3. The goods and services included are not necessarily consumed by everybody who uses the index but are a Bureau of Labor Statistics list of typical commodities and services.

While the CPI has some shortcomings, it does provide a very understandable picture of the overall price performance of the goods included in it within our economy on a monthly basis.

Name index

A

Accent, 204
ADT, 124
AFL–CIO, 276
Akron, 173
Alcoa, 61
Allied Stores, 164
American Federation of Labor, 276
American Law Institute, 21
American Management Association, 97
American Marketing Association, 97
American Motors, 138
American Stock Exchange, 334, 349
American Telephone, 79, 227
A & P, 149
Atomic Energy Commission, 424
Avis, 78
Avon, 211
Ayr-Way, 170

B

Barron's, 356
Baruch, Bernard M., 55
Batelle Institute, 230
Bell Laboratories, 227
Better Business Bureau, 446
Better Homes & Gardens, 204, 216
Blue Cross-Blue Shield, 373
Bread Basket, 169

Brown, Ray E., 99
Buick, 38
Bureau of Labor Statistics, 484
Bus Package Express (BPX), 258
Business Horizons, 97
Business Week, 97, 115, 206
Buskirk, Richard H., 88, 112

C

Cadillac, 36, 42, 132, 204
California Management Review, 97
Calvin, John, 15
Car Plate, 221
Caterpillar, 158
Chevrolet, 138, 173
Chicken Delight, 170
Clorox, 130
Colgate, 38
Congress of Industrial Organizations, 276
Continental, 40
Crest, 38

D

Dairy Queen, 170
Dean Witter & Co., Inc., 1, 336
DeBeers Consolidated, 61
Denver & Rio Grande Railway, 258
Department of Agriculture, 230

Department of Commerce, 423
Department of Justice, 418
Department of Labor, 420
Disraeli, 44
Dow Chemical Company, 120
Du Pont, 120, 228

E

Einstein, Albert, 225
Eli Lilly Company, 382

F

Fedco, 170
Federal Housing Administration, 419
Federal Open Market Committee, 297
Federal Trade Commission, 219, 418, 423
Federated Stores, 164
Federation of Organized Trades and Labor
    Unions, 276
Firestone Tire and Rubber Company, 343
Fitch's, 335, 356
Food and Drug Administration, 417
Forbes, 97, 356
Ford, Henry III, 422
Ford Motor Company, 25, 136
Fortune, 115, 206
Fowlkes, J. K., 125

Subject index

Interest Income   Debit =   15 —
Unearned Income   Credit =   15 —

b) Office Supplies   100 —
      Office Exp.   100 =

c) Office Supp.
      Office Exp.   100 =

D) Subscr. (unearned)   6,000 —
      Subscr. (Income)   6,000 =

Interest Expense   80 —
      Interest Payable   80 =

1 A   7 E   14
2 E   8 R   15
3 A   9 A
4 E   10 R
5 XL   11 E
6 E   12 A
           13